THAILAND, MALAYSIA AND SINGAPORE 2001

Other titles in this series include:

Independent Traveller's Europe 2001
The Inter-Railer's and Eurailer's Guide

Independent Traveller's USA 2001
The Budget Travel Guide

Independent Traveller's Australia 2001
The Budget Travel Guide

Independent Traveller's New Zealand 2001
The Budget Travel Guide

THAILAND, MALAYSIA AND SINGAPORE 2001

THE BUDGET TRAVEL GUIDE

Sean Sheehan
and Pat Levy

Published by Thomas Cook Publishing
A division of Thomas Cook Holdings Ltd
PO Box 227
Thorpe Wood
Peterborough PE3 6PU
United Kingdom

Telephone: 01733 503571
E-mail: books@thomascook.com

ISBN 1 841570 94 X

Publisher: Donald Greig
Commissioning Editor: Deborah Parker
Project Editor: Edith Summerhayes
Map Editor: Bernard Horton
Text design: Tina West

Cover design: Pumpkin House
Copy-editor: Jane Egginton
Proofreader: Merle Read
Maps prepared by: RJS Associates

Text typeset in Book Antiqua and Gill Sans using QuarkXPress
Layout and imagesetting: Z2 Repro, Thetford
Printed in Spain by GraphyCems, Navarra

Help improve this guide

This guide will be updated each year. The information given in it may change during the lifetime of this edition and we would welcome reports and comments from our readers. Similarly we want to make this guide as practical and useful as possible and are grateful for any comments, criticisms and suggestions for improving future editions.

A free copy of this guide will be sent to all readers whose information or ideas are incorporated in the next edition. Please send all contributions to the Editor, *Independent Traveller's Thailand, Malaysia and Singapore*, Thomas Cook Publishing, at: PO Box 227, Thorpe Wood, Peterborough, PE3 6PU, UK, or e-mail: books@thomascook.com

Written and researched by:
Sean Sheehan
and Pat Levy

Transport information:
Peter Bass, Assistant Editor, *Thomas Cook Overseas Timetable*

The Authors

Sean Sheehan was born and brought up in London and worked as an English teacher before visiting Thailand and Malaysia in 1986. Since then he has made many return trips and lived in the region for over six years. Sean now has his home in Ireland.

Pat Levy worked and studied in Singapore for many years and spent much of her time travelling around the region. Pat now lives in London but the lure of south-east Asia often draws her back and she is a still a regular visitor.

Acknowledgements

Patricia Levy and **Sean Sheehan** would like to sincerely thank the following people who gave their time to help in the research work for this book.

Thailand

Sutat Praesurin in Udon Thani
Yupaporn Chaisatit and **Nares Puangthonthip** in Khorat
Surachai Yomchinda in Ban Phe
Dumrongsak Nokbunjong, Kanokros Wongvakin, Natchanok Chundasuta, Panita Leongnarktongdee, Paveenatat Boonnop, Surapan Somthai, Srima Chaturansomboon, Israporn Posayanond and **Thurdsak Suksasilp** in Bangkok
Lieutenant Colonel Terry Beaton in Nam Tok
Vorapong Muchaotai, Sawatdiwatana Chaikuna and **Surachai Leosawasthiphong** in Chiang Mai
Duncan Jamieson in Chiang Saen
John Stall, David Good, Frederic Simmen, Naruemoi Thierkarochanakul and **Chompunute Hoontrakul** on Ko Samui
Petcharat Atiset in Phuket
Pierre-Andre Pelletier in Pattaya
Sreerat Sripinyo in Ko Chang

Malaysia

Ann Victor and **Daulat M. Jethwani** in Kuala Lumpur
Angela Lin Sam and **Sabrina Wong** at the Sarawak Tourist Board
Manfred Kurz, Doris Ong and **Layla Leeza Bolek** in Kuching
Calixtus James Laudi in Lahad Datu
Alice Yap and **Noreadah Othman** at the Sabah Tourism Promotions Corporation
Farizal Jaafar, Koh Teck Guan, Annie Chung, Faizul Hassan and **C L Chang** in Kota Kinabalu

UK

Razally Hussin at Tourism Malaysia in London.
Last, but not least, **Deborah Parker** and **Edith Summerhayes** at *Thomas Cook Publishing* and **Stephen York**, ex-*Thomas Cook*, without whose support and hard work this guide would never have appeared.

Photographs and Illustrations

Thomas Cook Publishing would like to thank Spectrum Colour Library for supplying the photographs, with the exception of those otherwise credited below (and to whom the copyright belongs).

Opposite p. 64 Northern tribes children; elephant round-up in eastern Thailand
Opposite p. 65 Mekong River at the Golden Triangle; Damneon Saduak floating market
Opposite p. 96 Grand Palace, Bangkok
Opposite p. 97 Bangkok traffic; inset: *tuk-tuk* on Sukhumvit Road, Bangkok
Opposite p. 160 Summer Palace Temple at Bang Pa-In; gold-leaf Buddha (ffotograff/Mary Andrews); saffron-robed Buddhist monks
Opposite p. 161 Woman working in rice paddy field; River Kwai bridge
Opposite p. 192 Phuket beach; view of Phi Phi Le island
Opposite p. 193 Kuala Lumpur railway station; bullock cart in Malaysia
Opposite p. 256 Petronas Towers, Kuala Lumpur (Tourism Malaysia)
Opposite p. 257 Fishing village, Penang; inset: orchid
Opposite p. 288 Goddess of Mercy Temple, Georgetown, Penang
Opposite p. 289 Cameron Highlands tea estate
Opposite p. 352 Mount Kinabalu, Sabah; climbing Mount Kinabalu (Tourism Malaysia)
Opposite p. 353 Danum Valley canopy walkway; orang-utan; traditional Malay house (all Tourism Malaysia)
Opposite p. 384 Singapore skyline at dusk
Opposite p. 385 Traditional Chinese actor, Singapore

Cover photos of Ko Phi Phi, Thailand, and Wat Enalong Temple, Phuket, supplied by ffotograff.

Thanks are also due to the **Thomas Cook Archives** for supplying the historical illustrations.

Contents

General Information

Routes & Cities

Contents

SINGAPORE
P. 414

Reference Section

Special Features

Introduction

'To live in one land, is captivitie
To runne all countries, a wild roguery'

John Donne's third *Elegie*

A journey to Thailand, Malaysia and Singapore – three countries in south-east Asia joined by railway and road – is a traveller's version of the pick and mix system that operates for some types of goodies in supermarkets. The basic procedures are undemanding and easy to learn, and the enjoyment comes from considering the choices and selecting what appeals to you as an interesting combination. This is just what Thailand, Malaysia and Singapore offer to the traveller – easy accessibility, undemanding procedures, plenty of choices and the freedom to tailor-make an itinerary without paying out good money for fancy wrapping and presentation.

It really is as simple as this, and there is absolutely no need to incur the extra cost of having your holiday organised and planned by a tour company. Visas are not required for European and North American citizens, and a host of international airlines are competing vigorously for passengers so that the cost of the long-haul flight is kept within reason. Accommodation is equally easy to arrange and all it takes is a fax or e-mail to secure a reservation for your first couple of nights. After that, you can either make it up as you go along or have planned every night's accommodation in advance. As for meals – a trip to south-east Asia could change your life as far as food is concerned. British and American cities may seem increasingly cosmopolitan in their range of international restaurants and fusion menus, but this will all seem rather banal after experiencing the incredible diversity of authentic tastes on offer in the orient.

To cap it all, a trip to south-east Asia is not prohibitively expensive. The airfare is going to be the largest compulsory expenditure because once you have arrived there are options to suit all budgets, and they all offer better value for money now than ever before. The cost of meals can account for a sizeable proportion of a travel budget, but in south-east Asia this can easily be kept to a minimum without having to eat food that tastes cheap even when it isn't. A delicious lunch in Bangkok or Kuala Lumpur can cost not much more than the price of a bar of chocolate and a bottle of mineral water back home, while the bill for a three-course meal in an elegant restaurant will amount on average to about one-third of what you might expect to pay in any half-posh establishment in Europe or North America.

Similarly with accommodation, a clean room in a hotel with a bathroom, air-conditioning and a telephone will cost between £10 and £15/$16 and $25 in Thailand or Malaysia, and a lot less for a room in a guesthouse with a fan (perfectly adequate in the tropics, where air-conditioning is not as essential as many think). A stylish room in a luxury five-star hotel can cost the equivalent of a mid-range hotel back home, and the level of pampering will be in a class of its own. Singapore is an exception in the money department and your budget will largely determine the length of stay there.

So, to get back to the pick and mix, where do you go and what are the choices to be considered?

SIAM

Thailand, called Siam until 1939, stretches from the Golden Triangle in the far north, where it is enveloped by Myanmar (Burma), Laos and Vietnam, to a southern border with Malaysia. Thai islands are found off the west coast and along the east coast, which stretches to a border with Cambodia.

MALAYSIA AND BORNEO

Peninsular Malaysia, called Malaya under the British, is the land mass that stretches from Thailand in the north to a narrow causeway in the south that can be crossed in half an hour on foot to reach Singapore. Part of the huge island of Borneo, separated by sea from peninsular Malaysia, is also part of Malaysia and consists of the two states of Sarawak and Sabah.

SINGAPORE

The island of Singapore is a mere 42 kilometres long and 23 wide, and it is situated just above 10 kilometres north of the equator. For two years in the 1960s it was part of the Federation of Malaysia but in 1965 was booted out in the wake of Malay fears of Chinese domination. It is now an independent republic.

The promise of sun and sand is easy to satisfy in the tropical heat of south-east Asia and the coastal beaches and islands of Thailand and Malaysia. Popular Thai islands like Ko Samui and Phuket have highly developed beach resorts and plenty of bars and discos for an active nightlife. Lesser-known but equally alluring islands, like Ko Samet, Ko Chang and Ko Lanta, welcome visitors who wish to laze and sunbathe on their white-sand beaches but without the hype. Move south to Malaysia and the entire east coast is one long sandy beach stretching for 200 kilometres and including the beautiful island of Tioman, which first came to fame when it was chosen for idyllic scenes in the film *South Pacific*. There are also the tranquil Perhentian islands off the north-east coast and Pulau Pangkor's tropical beaches on the west coast.

When it comes to activity and adventure holidays, the traveller is spoilt for choice. The largest mountain in south-east Asia, Mount Kinabalu, is in the state of Sabah on the island of Borneo (part of which belongs to Malaysia), and every year thousands of people from the age of eight upwards make it to the summit at 4101 metres, half the height of Everest. It involves sleeping a night on the side of the mountain and a dawn start next morning to reach the top for the sunrise. Back at sea level, watersports have been developed to a fine art in areas of Thailand and Sabah and there is nowhere better to learn scuba diving. Opportunities for snorkelling, enriched by a polychromatic marine life, occur so often along the coasts and islands of Thailand and Malaysia that it is worth finding luggage space for your own gear. The most fulfilling activity holidays are likely to be ones that combine the adventure with elements of trekking and opportunities to observe the astonishing wildlife of the region.

There are unique trekking possibilities, the best of which are only now starting to come into their own, although northern Thailand has a well-developed tradition of hill walks that combine water-rafting and elephant rides with overnight sojourns in the villages of ethnic hill tribe people. Not so well known are the options for trekking in the jungles of Borneo in the Malaysian state of Sarawak. These start with one- and two-day trips that can be extended for up to ten-day real-life adventures involving climbing hills, crossing rivers on fallen timbers, sleeping in longhouses of the indigenous tribes, and crossing into Indonesian territory when the jungle shrugs off borders that cannot be regulated deep in the steamy jungle.

Shorter treks and boat rides often feature in trips undertaken to observe the compelling natural wildlife of the region. The proboscis monkey, unique to Borneo, is not difficult to find and orang-utans can be seen at survival school in a rehabilitation centre. Pitcher plants, usually spotted while climbing the lower regions of Mount Kinabalu, are common in Bako National Park in Sarawak, while neighbouring Sabah is home to the world's largest flower, the rafflesia. The tropical forests of Malaysia – even Singapore has a very small but highly significant area of primary rainforest – are rich in wildlife, and visitors can hope to see gibbons, orang-utans, monkeys and an increasing succession of colourful birdlife that culminates in the spectacular hornbills. Taman Negara, Malaysia's greatest natural asset, is a national park in the heart of the country where visitors can trek through primary rainforest, sleep in the jungle, and experience the painless thrill of having some blood taken by a harmless leech.

When it comes to the cultural landscape, every bit as diverse and appealing as the natural world, it is difficult not to start with the Thai people, whose ancient cultural forms, imbued with the spirit of Buddhism, are a constant source of fascination. Malaysia and Singapore are multicultural societies where Malays, Chinese and Indians, not to mention the rich ethnic groupings of Borneo, live together without sacrificing their cultural traditions. All three countries covered in this guide are deeply traditional and yet they embrace aspects of the contemporary world with a bewildering adaptability. E-mails are easier to send than in Europe, the work of post-modern architects runs riot in city skylines, while inside a temple in Bangkok rests a carved sculpture of the British footballer David Beckham, placed there by a devout Buddhist soccer fan with the blessing of the senior monk.

The various traditional cultures help account for the rich array of arts and crafts that make shopping so inescapably a part of a visit to south-east Asia. Fabrics, clothes and cultural artefacts are a constant shopper's temptation in Bangkok and Chiang Mai, while computer software, music CDs, brand-name watches and designer clothes, both pirated and original, throng the street markets of Bangkok, Kuala Lumpur and Penang. Singapore itself can be imagined as one giant shopping mall devoted to planet-wide consumerism, and a wide range of products can be bought for less than back home.

This gives only a taste of what awaits the visitor who travels through Thailand, Malaysia and Singpore. Every day will be different because the history of these lands has produced complex, evolving societies where tradition and modernity rub shoulders, and where the traveller is welcomed one moment and healthily ignored the next as people go about their daily lives. There is nowhere else like it in the world. Start picking and mixing.

Sean Sheehan and Pat Levy

PRICES

Current costs are indicated throughout the book by a rating system. This gives an instant idea of the level of budgeting required for accommodation, food and places of interest. All prices are subject to variation, due mainly to unpredictable fluctuations in currency exchange rates.

Accommodation

Based on the average cost of a double room, prices are listed in Thai baht (**B**), Malaysian ringitt (**RM**), or the Singapore dollar (**S$**).

$	under 350**B** under **RM**40 under **S$**40
$$	350–600**B** **RM**40–80 **S$**40–150
$$$	600–1500**B** **RM**80–130 **S$**150–300
$$$$	1500–2000**B** **RM**130–270 **S$**300–370
$$$$$	over 2000**B** over **RM**270 over **S$**370

HOW TO USE THIS BOOK

This guide covers the very best of what Thailand, Malaysia and Singapore have to offer the traveller. It is written by two authors who between them have spent over 15 years living and working in south-east Asia and travelling extensively by train, bus, boat and air throughout Thailand, Malaysia and Singapore. The chapters are route based and vary in approach to suit the appeal and attractions of each particular route.

Each route chapter gives detailed information on transport, accommodation, eating, tourist offices and places of interest along the way. Large cities like Bangkok, Kuala Lumpur and Singapore have their own chapters covering the same essential information for the visitor.

The Thailand routes start in Bangkok and radiate out to the north, west, east and south of Thailand. The last southern route, Ko Samui to Hat Yai, arrives at the Malaysian border and covers cross-border travel. The routes in Malaysia start in Kuala Lumpur and cover the west and east coasts before moving across the sea to east Malaysia and the states of Sarawak and Sabah in Borneo. Sometimes a train suggests itself as the best mode of travel. At other times it will be a bus, boat or plane ride or a combination of these.

KEY TO ICONS

RAIL	Rail
	Bus
	Car
	Ferry Services
i	Information
	Accommodation
	Food

Food

Based on the average cost of a meal for two people, excluding drinks.

$	under 200**B** under **RM**15 under **S$**10
$$	200–400**B** **RM**15–40 **S$**11–30
$$$	400–700**B** **RM**40–80 **S$**31–60
$$$$	700–1200**B** **RM**80–120 **S$**61–100
$$$$$	over 1200**B** over **RM**120 over **S$**100

Other costs

Based on admission for one person to a museum or place of interest.

$	under 30**B** under **RM**5 under **S$**3
$$	30–60**B** **RM**6–15 **S$**3–10
$$$	over 60**B** over **RM**15 over **S$**10

Public Transport Details
Mode of travel, journey time and frequency of service are provided for each route. ▶

Bangkok – Ayuttaya
OTT TABLES 7060/7076

Transport	Frequency	Journey Time
Train	Daily, frequent	1½hrs
Bus	Daily, frequent	1hr
Boat	Daily	All day cruise

Bangkok – Bang Pa-In
OTT TABLES 7060/7076

Transport	Frequency	Journey Time
Train	Daily	9hrs
Bus	Daily, frequent	1½-2hrs
Boat	Sunday only	1hr

Bang Pa-In – Ayutthaya
OTT TABLES 7060/7076

Transport	Frequency	Journey Time
Train	Daily	15mins
Bus	Daily	30-50mins

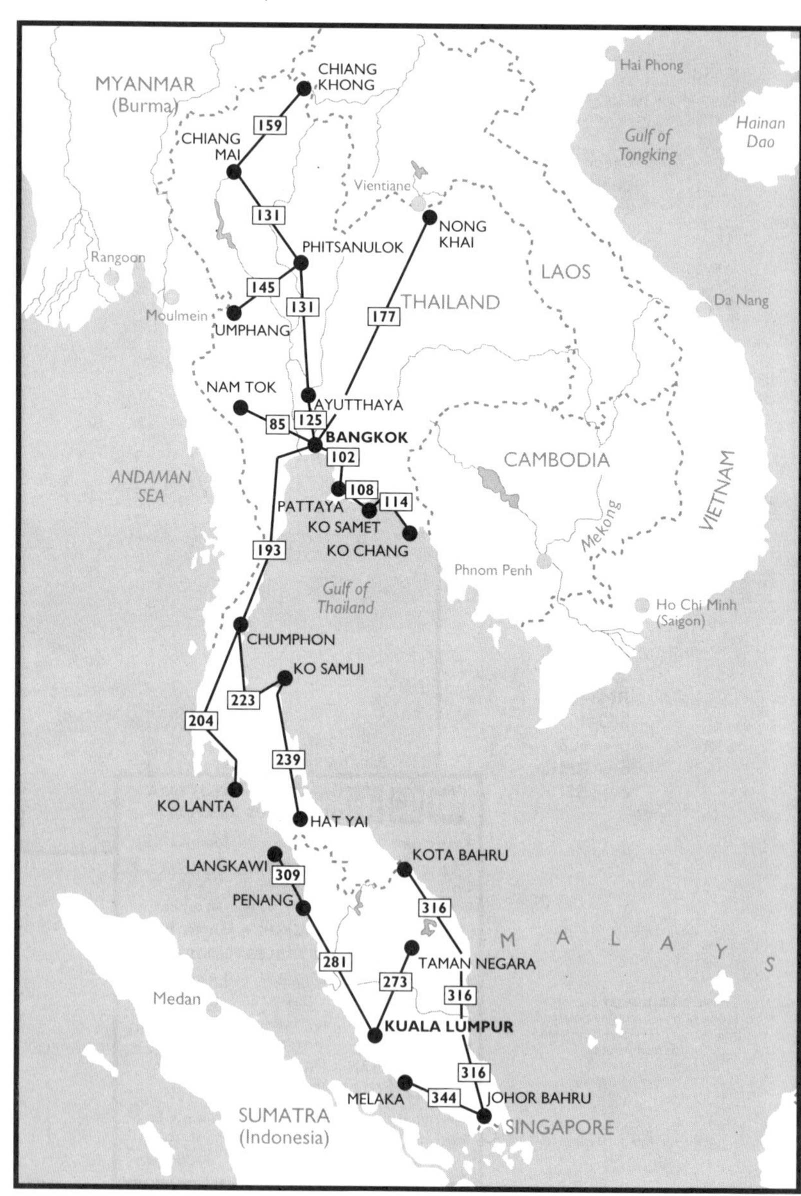
MYANMAR
(Burma)
CHIANG
KHONG
159
CHIANG
MAI
131
Vientiane
NONG
KHAI
PHITSANULOK
Rangoon
145
131
Moulmein
UMPHANG
177
THAILAND
LAOS
Hai Phong
Gulf of
Tongking
Hainan
Dao
Da Nang
NAM TOK
85
125
AYUTTHAYA
BANGKOK
102
108
114
PATTAYA
KO SAMET
KO CHANG
ANDAMAN
SEA
193
CAMBODIA
Mekong
VIETNAM
Phnom Penh
Gulf of
Thailand
Ho Chi Minh
(Saigon)
CHUMPHON
KO SAMUI
223
204
239
KO LANTA
HAT YAI
LANGKAWI
309
PENANG
KOTA BAHRU
316
M A L A Y S
281
273
TAMAN NEGARA
316
Medan
KUALA LUMPUR
316
MELAKA
344
JOHOR BAHRU
SUMATRA
(Indonesia)
SINGAPORE

ROUTE MAP

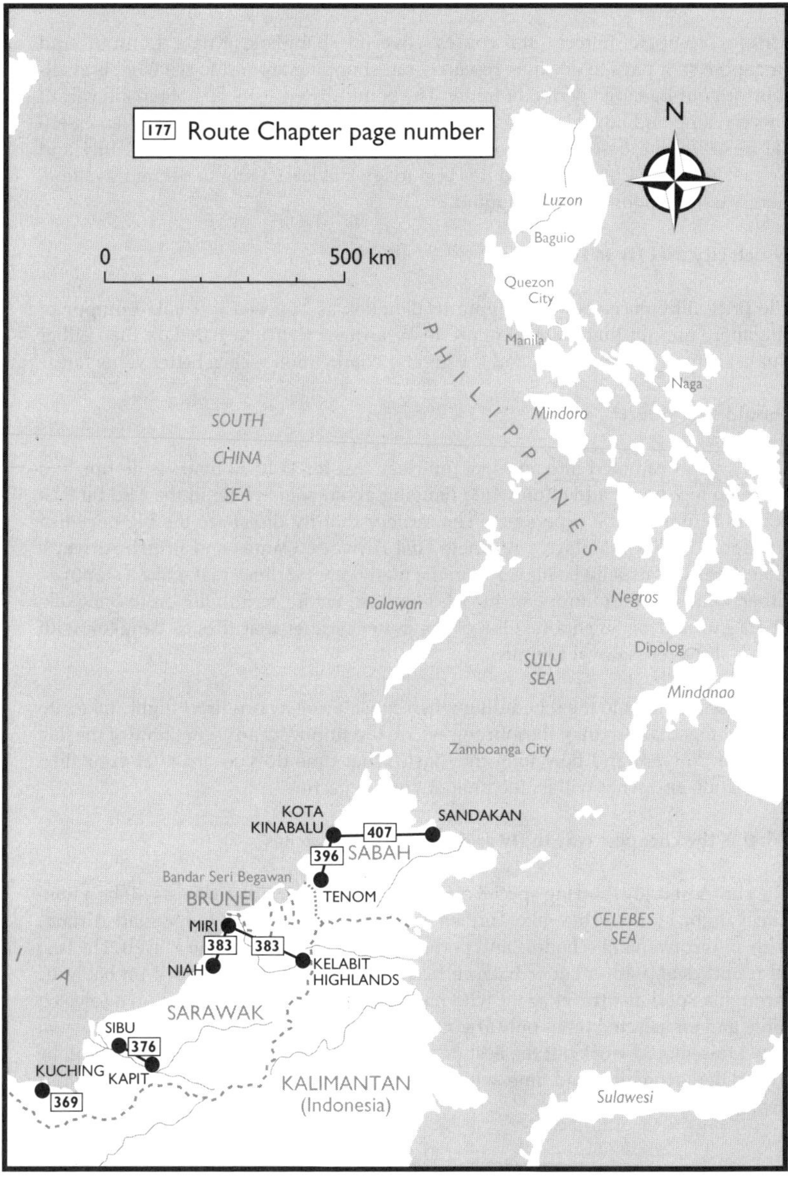

177 Route Chapter page number
N
0
500 km
Luzon
Baguio
Quezon City
Manila
PHILIPPINES
Naga
Mindoro
SOUTH CHINA SEA
Palawan
Negros
Dipolog
SULU SEA
Mindanao
Zamboanga City
KOTA KINABALU
407
SANDAKAN
396
SABAH
Bandar Seri Begawan
TENOM
BRUNEI
MIRI
383
383
NIAH
KELABIT HIGHLANDS
CELEBES SEA
SARAWAK
SIBU
376
KAPIT
KUCHING
369
KALIMANTAN (Indonesia)
Sulawesi

Airlines compete fiercely for routes covering Bangkok, Kuala Lumpur and Singapore so it pays to do some research and shopping around to see what is available for your intended period of travel. The better-priced seats do not remain vacant for very long and advance booking - weeks if not months ahead – is often essential to secure the best possible deal. Demand for seats is highest during July and August and over Christmas, and it is best to book at least a month before travelling. Here are some points to bear in mind.

Which city do I fly to first?

The price differences between flying to Bangkok as opposed to Kuala Lumpur or Singapore are not huge but there are more airlines flying to Bangkok than either Kuala Lumpur or Singapore, and the greater competition means better value fares.

Should I fly direct?

Ideally, yes. Crammed into an economy-class seat for 11 to 13 hours is no fun, and having a few hours added on while hanging about somewhere in the Middle East does not improve the experience. The airlines that fly direct are the big ones like Singapore Airlines, Malaysia Airlines, Thai Airways, Qantas and British Airways. Their fares will usually be higher than the many other airlines that make a stopover, either somewhere in Europe or the Middle East, before continuing on to Bangkok, Kuala Lumpur or Singapore. One of the better airlines that flies to Bangkok with such a stopover is Royal Emirates.

Pay close attention to the scheduling when considering a non-direct flight. Take into account the total length of the journey, where the stopovers are, what time of the day or night they are and how long they last. What time do you arrive at your final destination and what will be the time of your departure?

What is the cheapest way to fly and what are the catches?

The cheapest flight, barring special offers by one of the major airlines, will be a non-direct flight by an airline like Turkish Airlines, Air Lanka or Indonesian Airlines with an inconvenient schedule and perhaps with a change of plane as well. The best all-round deal, with a better balance between cost and comfort, will probably be through a specialist travel agent who has negotiated a good discount on a selected route and for selected times only. If you have some flexibility over when exactly you travel this should work out the best deal. The catch on many of these flights will be a fixed departure date and time, with a charge incurred if you decide to extend your stay.

MALAYSIA AIRLINES

The best reason for flying with Malaysia Airlines (MAS), apart from their generally very competitive fares, is the fact that without an international ticket from them it is not possible to purchase the Discover Malaysia Air Pass (see page 30). The same restriction does not apply to Bangkok Airlines and their internal travel pass ticket (see page 27).

FLYING FROM THE UK

Unless you are a student or under 26 expect to pay around £500 and upwards for a direct flight to Bangkok from London. A reputable company like Royal Emirates flying to Bangkok with one stopover along the way will charge around £400. Fares that are significantly less than £400 should be looked at carefully to determine where the saving is being made. Return direct flights to Kuala Lumpur and Singapore start at around £550, dropping to below £400 on the cheaper airlines with stopovers.

MAJOR AIRLINES IN THE UK

British Airways
tel: (0345) 222-111

Eva Airways
tel: (020) 7380-8300

Kuwait Airways
tel: (020) 7412-0007

Malaysia Airlines
tel: (020) 7373-2314

Qantas
tel: (0345) 747-767

Royal Emirates
tel: (020) 7808-0033

Thai Airways
tel: (0870) 606-0911

Students and travellers under 26 should start by getting a quote from STA Travel, tel: (020) 7361-6262, http:www.statravel.co.uk, and UsitCampus, tel: (0870) 240-1010, http://usitcampus.co.uk. Their fares will not always be the cheapest but they should be able to offer a discounted fare on a major airline with good in-flight service and flexibility about changing the date of return.

Travel agents worth a telephone call when researching fares are Trailfinders, tel: (020) 7938-3366 and tel: (0161) 839-6969; Travelbag, tel: (020) 7287-5556, http://www.travelbag.com; and Bridge the World, tel: (020) 7911-0900. Online enquiries can be made at http://flynow.com and online bookings at http://www.buzzaway.com. The weekend travel sections of newspapers like *The Guardian* and *The Independent* are a good source of information for travel agents and discounted fares. Some companies, like Travel Mood, tel: (08705) 001-002, offer flight and accommodation packages that are worth considering

FLYING FROM THE USA

It is less expensive to fly from the west coast than the east coast. At peak times expect to pay somewhere in the region of US$1000 for a flight to Bangkok from a west coast city and up to US$200 more from the east coast. There is not much difference between the cost of flights to

REACHING THAILAND, MALAYSIA AND SINGAPORE

MAJOR AIRLINES IN THE USA

Air Canada
tel: 1-800-776-3000

Air France
tel: 1-800-237-2747

Cathay Pacific
tel: 1-800-233-2742

Delta
tel: 1-800-241-4141

Malaysia Airlines
tel: 1-800-552-9264

Singapore Airways
tel: 1-800-742-3333

Thai Airlines
tel: 1-800-426-5204

United Airlines
tel: 1-800-538-2929

Kuala Lumpur as opposed to Singapore. Prices are around US$850 from the west coast and up to US$200 more from the east coast.

Newspapers like *the New York Times* and the *San Francisco Examiner* have hefty weekend travel sections that carry all the contact numbers you need to start checking out fares. A good source of low fares, which can be as little as US$500 from the west coast during low season, is Ticket Planet, 59 Grant Avenue, 3rd Floor, San Francisco, CA 94108. Tel: (415) 288-9999, ext.110, toll free tel: 1-800-799-8888, fax: (415) 288-9839, e-mail: nick@ticketplanet.com, http://www.ticket-planet.com.

Train

This is the most comfortable and enjoyable way of travelling between Thailand, Malaysia and Singapore, but it is not the fastest. Between the State Railway of Thailand (SRT) and the privatised Keretapi Tanah Melayu (KTM) of Malaysia it is possible to travel by train between Bangkok and Singapore, via Kuala Lumpur and Butterworth. Bookings should be made as far in advance as possible. This is essential at peak holiday periods like the middle of April in Thailand and around the Chinese New Year in all three countries.

From Thailand to Malaysia and Singapore

Padang Besar is the border crossing for trains between Thailand and Malaysia. Passengers get off the train with their luggage and clear immigration and customs before reboarding. At Butterworth there is a change of train for Kuala Lumpur and onward travel to Singapore. The immigration procedures for entry into Singapore are conducted on board the train and on arrival at Singapore.

From Singapore or Malaysia to Thailand

Immigration formalities from Singapore are handled at the station in Singapore. At Butterworth there is a change of train for onward travel to Thailand, with the train stopping at the border station of Padang Besar for immigration procedures.

Bangkok–Butterworth–Bangkok: Train Times

OTT TABLES 7013/7055

Station	Train IE/35 ↓		Train IE/36 ↑	
Bangkok	departs	1320	arrives	1100
Hat Yai		0655		1850
Padang Besar		0850		1725
Butterworth	arrives	1255	departs	1410

Butterworth–Kuala Lumpur–Singapore: Train Times

OTT TABLE 7005

Station	Train ER/1 ↓		Train ER/2 ↑	
Butterworth	departs	0800	arrives	2215
Ipoh		1104		1838
Kuala Lumpur		1455		1455
Johor Bahru		2010		0900
Singapore	arrives	2130	departs	0800

Travelling Between Thailand, Malaysia and Singapore

Other Trains There is also the daily EL/7 service that departs Hat Yai at 1545 and crosses the border at Padang Besar before travelling on to Alor Setar at 2000 and reaching Kuala Lumpur the next morning at 0530 (stopping at Taiping and Ipoh but not Butterworth). The daily train EL/8 does the route in reverse, departing Kuala Lumpur at 2100 and reaching Hat Yai the next morning at 0950 (OTT tables 7005 and 7013).

Thailand Train Fares The train fare from Bangkok to Padang Besar is 767B for 1st class and 360B for 2nd. Supplementary charges include 40B for an express train, 60B for a rapid train and between 250B and 350B for air-conditioning. Sleeping berths cost from 100B (from 220B with air-conditioning) for a 2nd class upper berth in a rapid train and up to 520B per person for a 1st class double cabin.

Malaysia and Singapore Train Fares The train fare from Padang Besar to Butterworth is RM25 in 1st class and RM11 in 2nd class. Fares on express trains from Butterworth to Kuala Lumpur are RM67 in 1st class, RM34 in 2nd class and RM19 in 3rd class. Butterworth to Singapore fares are RM127 in 1st class, RM60 in 2nd and RM34 in 3rd class. Lower/upper berths in 1st class are RM70/RM50 and in 2nd class are RM14/RM11.50.

Information and Bookings

KTM are well organised and efficient but their train schedules are subject to change, so times and fares should always be checked in advance. For up-to-date information and bookings, tel: (03) 2273-8000, (03) 2275-7350 and (03) 2275-7358, e-mail: passenger@ktmb.com.my, http://www.ktmb.com.my. You can make online reservations 60 days before the date of travel and pay for the tickets on arrival either in Malaysia or Singapore. There is no online payment facility.

Advance bookings on SRT trains can be made online at http://www.royalexclusive.com. For a small fee tickets can be booked in advance and delivered free of charge to your hotel in Bangkok or, by paying a supplement, delivered by courier service to your home address. For train enquires, telephone SRT in Bangkok on (02) 223-3762, 224-7788, 225-0300 ext. 5200, fax: (02) 225-6068.

Tickets can be booked in advance at the central train station in Bangkok, at most railway stations in larger cities and from travel agents in Bangkok who will add a surcharge of around 100B. Tickets can also be booked in advance in Kuala Lumpur and other large cities as well as from the train station in Singapore.

TRAIN AND BUS/TAXI

There is another train route from Bangkok that doesn't actually cross the border with Malaysia but stops within a mile of it at Sungai Kolok (Rantau Panjang on the Malaysian side), south-west of Hat Yai (OTT table 7055). The crossing point is 1 kilometre away at Golok Bridge and there are motorbikes and *trishaws* (motorised tricycles) waiting at the station to take you there. On the other side of Golok Bridge, in Malaysia, it is another 1 kilometre to Rantau Panjang – again transport waits to take passengers there. From here buses and taxis go to Kota Bahru and other Malaysian destinations. Sungai Kolok is a grotty town but fortunately train schedules mean there is no need to spend a night there.

From Thailand The Rapid 171 train departs from Bangkok at 1225 and stops at Hat Yai the next morning before departing at 0630 for Sungai Kolok. It arrives at Sungai Kolok at 1000, giving plenty of time to make the crossing on foot and travel on to Kota Bahru the same day. The same arrangement works with the Express 37 train that departs Bangkok at 1445, stops at Hat Yai before departing at 0725 and reaches Sungai Kolok at 1055.

From Malaysia You need to cross the border at Golok Bridge in the morning in order to catch the Rapid 172 train that departs Sungai Kolok at 1100. This train goes on to Hat Yai and departs at 1445 before steaming up north to arrive at Bangkok at 0835 the next morning. The same arrangement works for the Express 38 train that departs from Sungai Golok at 1405, leaving Hat Yai at 1740, and getting into Bangkok at 1035 the next morning.

BUS

Buses travel on a daily basis between Thailand and Malaysia, between Malaysia and Singapore and even between Thailand and Singapore.

Thailand – Malaysia – Thailand Although there is also a road border crossing at Padang Besar (where the cross-border trains stop), most buses between Thailand and the west coast of Malaysia cross the border at Bukit Kayu Hitam, on the main North-South Highway between the two countries. Buses run regularly in both directions between Hat Yai and Georgetown (Penang), taking about 4 hrs, and travel between Hat Yai and Kuala Lumpur in around 12 hrs.

It is also possible to travel between Hat Yai and Alor Setar on Malaysia's north-west coast. This involves taking a bus from Hat Yai to the border post at Bukit Kayu Hitam, walking across the border and handling the immigration and customs formalities before catching a bus on the other side to Alor Setar. The same journey can be done from Malaysia by taking a bus to the border crossing from Alor Setar.

A less common way of using a bus to cross between Thailand and Malaysia is via the border crossing at Sungai Golok (Rantau Panjang on the Malaysian side). This is covered in the previous section and involves taking a 90-minute bus journey from the border to Kota Bahru.

MALAYSIA – SINGAPORE – MALAYSIA The Causeway that links Johor Bahru in southern Malaysia with Singapore handles bus transport, with the train line running alongside, between the two countries. Bus number 170 runs every 15 minutes during the day between Johor Bahru (from just before the Causeway) and Singapore. Passengers jump off with their luggage to go through immigration before reboarding the same bus (or the next one that comes along) that waits just beyond the passport control offices.

There is also an express bus that runs between Johor Bahru's bus station, six kilometres outside town and Singapore. If you are travelling from Singapore just to Johor Bahru this is still the fastest bus, but do not rejoin it after getting off for passport control. Just walk into town, or you will be whisked away to the bus station outside town.

Long-distance buses travel daily between Singapore and Kuala Lumpur, Melaka, Ipoh and Butterworth on the west side of Malaysia and to Mersing, Kuantan and Kota Bahru on the east coast. It is worth noting that you can save a significant amount of money by taking the express bus from Singapore to Johor Bahru's bus station and catching a bus from there to another destination in Malaysia. As well as being cheaper, there is a wider choice of bus routes and times, which means you shouldn't have to wait long for a connection.

THAILAND – SINGAPORE – THAILAND The buses used for long-distance travel between Thailand, Malaysia and Singapore are modern and comfortable with air-con, a toilet and television. Nevertheless, you would have to be a masochist to stay on one all the way from Bangkok to Singapore, even though a daily service does run between the two cities. It would make more sense to combine bus and train for such a long journey.

AIR

There are any number of flight connections between the three countries. Thai Airways connect Bangkok with Kuala Lumpur (14 flights a week), Penang (daily) and Singapore (49 flights a week). From Kuala Lumpur, Malaysia Airlines flies up to seven times daily to Bangkok, twice a week to Chiang Mai and three times a week to Hat Yai. There is a shuttle bus service, operated by Malaysia Airlines and Singapore Airlines, between Kuala Lumpur and Singapore that costs S$129 from Singapore or RM222 from Kuala Lumpur. Singapore Airlines also flies regularly between Singapore and Bangkok. If you are planning to fly to Sarawak from Singapore, you can save money by taking Malaysia Airlines' shuttle bus to the airport at Johor Bahru and flying from there.

As well as the three national airlines, there are three smaller airlines that operate flights between the countries. Bangkok Airways have a daily flight between Singapore and Ko Samui in both directions. Angel Air, based at Bangkok international airport, tel: (02) 535-6287, fax: (02) 535-6289, and Singapore international airport, tel: (065) 541-3210, fax: (065) 541-3161, operate flights between Chiang Rai and Singapore and between Bangkok and Singapore. Silk Air, the regional wing of Singapore Airlines, tel: (065) 223-8888, fax: (065) 221-2221, http://www.silkair.net, fly between Singapore and Hat Yai, Langkawi and Phuket.

THAILAND

TRAIN

Thailand's rail network covers most of the routes in this guide and travelling by train is the most enjoyable and safest way of getting around the country, if not always the quickest. It is also very affordable. Travelling by night, of course, saves the cost of a night's accommodation.

There are three classes of train travel, but 3rd class travel is not recommended except for the short journey between Bangkok, Kanchanaburi and Nam Tok. Seats in 2nd class travel are comfortable and perfectly adequate for long journeys, though for night journeys a berth is highly recommended. Seats convert into a bed, clean linen is provided and there is a curtain to ensure privacy. Some 2nd class trains have air-con sleepers but are hardly worth the extra money because at night the train's fans are sufficient. First class comes in the form of private cabins for one or two people. All fares can and should be booked as far in advance as possible (up to 60 days), and at Hualamphong station in Bangkok there is a special advance booking office (see page 22 for advance bookings from abroad).

Meals are available in 1st and 2nd class trains. On long or overnight journeys staff will take orders for evening meals and breakfast and bring them to your seat. Meals are overpriced at between 90B and 200B, so it's well worth bringing your own food.

Examples of 2nd class fares from Bangkok are 281B to Chiang Mai, 64B to Kanchanaburi and 345B to Hat Yai. There is a 40B/60B/80B surcharge for rapid/express/special express trains. A sleeper in a 2nd class sleeper ranges from 100B/150B for an upper/lower berth to 250B/320B for an upper/lower berth with air-con in a special express train.

Bangkok's central Hualamphong station is well geared up for travellers and a condensed timetable with schedules for all the main routes should be available. All train stations have a left luggage facility, but always confirm their operating hours because they do vary.

TRAIN PASS

A rail pass, only purchasable at Bangkok's Hualamphong station, offers 20 days of unlimited, 2nd class travel for 1100B. The pass includes the small surcharge for rapid and express trains but not sleeping berths or extra charges for air-con. A pass for 1st class travel is 2000B which includes all supplementary charges. It's debatable how economical or convenient a rail pass is. To make it pay you need to cover over 2000 kilometres and advance seat reservations still need to be made for popular long-distance routes like Bangkok to Chiang Mai.

BUS

Government buses connect with every town in Thailand. They run reliable long-distance routes using modern, comfortable vehicles and charge very reasonable fares. Government buses on long distance routes are air-conditioned (to the point of requiring something warmer than a T-shirt) and seats are allocated by ticket number. Local government buses are orange. They are not air-conditioned, but wonderfully cheap.

For popular routes the system is in competition with a range of private bus companies that tend to charge more for their vehicles – both modern coaches and minibuses. Private buses can be OK but passengers are at the mercy of a private company that may cut corners by using inferior drivers and vehicles. Some of the companies operating from Khao San Road in Bangkok have been known to offer some very bad deals for travellers. When there is a choice the government bus service is usually a more comfortable and safer ride.

Tickets are normally bought on the bus, but larger bus stations have ticket offices and advance booking is possible, and recommended, for popular routes.

AIR There is an extensive domestic air service, managed primarily by Thai Airways and supplemented by Bangkok Airways and Angel Airways. Nearly all the routes in this guide are covered by an air link, except for east Thailand and the Pattaya – Ko Samui and Ko Samet – Ko Chang routes. A journey by air can save a lot of time and avoids the hassle of sometimes having to return to Bangkok. It only takes two hours to fly to Phuket from Chiang Mai, but this journey will take up two days by train and bus.

AIR PASS

Thai Airways issue an air pass that covers any four domestic flights for US$199. All four routes must be fixed in advance. The date of the first route must be strictly adhered to but the other three can be open-dated. There is a penalty charge of US$25 if any of the routes are changed. To make the Pass cost effective you need to be planning a fair degree of travel around the country as a whole, and be in a position to utilise some of the longer trips like the Chiang Mai to Phuket flight which normally costs 4500B one way. Unlike the Malaysian air pass, you do not need to use Thai Airways for your international flight but the Pass must be purchased from the agent who issues your international ticket.

ROAD No one would want to drive a hired car around traffic-congested Bangkok but in other parts of the country it is a viable means of transport, and an excellent way to get off the beaten track and visit some out-of-the-way places. The far north of the country is especially suitable for driving because there is little traffic and fewer crazy drivers.

On popular islands like Ko Samui and Phuket and tourist destinations like Chiang Mai it is easy to rent a jeep or motorbike. It is common to be asked for your passport as a deposit for a motorbike. This should be strenuously resisted as in the event of a dispute you would have very little bargaining power. Offer your international driving licence instead. When hiring a car, which normally involves leaving a cash deposit, be very careful about checking your liability in the event of an accident. People will glibly assure you that insurance is included, but check exactly what that means and ask to see it in writing.

To hire a Honda or Toyota saloon car will cost from around 2000B a day, including insurance, from a reputable company like Avis. On Ko Samui a jeep can be hired for 800B a day and a motorbike without insurance for between 150B and 200B per day. When buying petrol, currently about 15B a litre, stick to the modern petrol stations with electric pumps. The antiquated hand-operated systems that simply run a tube into a petrol barrel may look quaint but the fuel will cost between 50% and 700% more.

RULES OF THE ROAD IN THAILAND

Driving is on the left. Bear in mind that bigger vehicles expect to have the right of way and will drive accordingly. There are national speed limits – 60 km an hour in built-up areas and 80 to 90km on the highways – though like most rules of the road in Thailand they are subject to liberal interpretation. Police checks and speed traps are not unknown and military road checks pop up when you least expect them. Foreign drivers are required to have a valid international driver's licence, obtainable through motoring organisations back home for a small fee.

TAXIS AND *SONGTHAEWS*

Taxis are metered in Bangkok but not in the rest of the country. This means that it is essential to establish the fare before departure, and it is a good idea to ask staff in your hotel or guesthouse about the standard price for a particular journey. Fares are usually very reasonable but the temptation to rip off an unknowing foreigner is often too difficult for drivers to resist. You should expect to pay a little over the local rate.

In parts of southern and eastern Thailand shared taxis are common and usually congregate at fixed places around town. Motorbike taxis can be found in cities like Bangkok and remote rural areas.

A *songthaew* is a pickup truck with two benches (*songthaew* literally means 'two rows') which can be hailed anywhere along its route. The fare is paid at the end of the journey and passengers can get

TUK-TUKS

A *tuk-tuk* is a motorised, three-wheeled taxi vehicle that takes its name from the sound of its engine. As with any form of non-metered taxi it helps to have a rough idea of the local rate before departure. Drivers in tourist areas will sometimes try to charge an exorbitant fee but friendly discourse should bring it down to an acceptable level.

off anywhere by ringing the bell that is usually installed in the seating area. The routes for *songthaews* are flexible and a fare can always be negotiated for a special journey. As with taxis it helps enormously to know what the fare should be to avoid being cheated. In rural areas the *songthaew* operates as a local bus.

MALAYSIA

TRAIN As in Thailand, trains provide the most enjoyable and comfortable way of getting around the country. Although there are only two main lines they cover most of the main west coast route in this guide as well as accessing Kota Bahru on the east coast. The main railway line runs between Singapore and Butterworth via Kuala Lumpur and Ipoh and the second line branches off at Gemas and heads north-east to Kota Bahru.

The train company Keretapi Tanah Melayu (KTM) is well run. You can travel from Kuala Lumpur to Butterworth in a 2nd class express train for RM34, for example. From Singapore to Wakat Bahru (the station for Kota Bahru on the east coast) the fare is RM51. On night trains the cost of an upper/lower berth in 2nd class is RM11.50/14 and RM50/70 in 1st class. Advance bookings can be made in Malaysia at any of the main stations or at Singapore railway station, and online bookings can be made up to 60 days before the date of travel and paid for when the tickets are collected (page 22).

MALAYSIAN TRAIN PASS

A 30-day rail pass costs US$120 while a 10-day pass is US$55. The pass, obtainable from the station in Singapore or from the stations in Kuala Lumpur, Johor Bahru, Butterworth, Penang, Padang Besar and Wakaf Bahru, does not include berth charges on express night trains. As with the Thai rail pass you need to cover a lot of ground to make it cost effective.

BUS Getting around Malaysia by bus is every bit as easy as it is in Thailand and equally affordable. Government buses cover countless local routes as well as long-distance travel between all large towns, and tickets for long journeys can be booked in advance. The public buses are in competition with a host of private companies but the private firms are on the whole safer and more reliable than some of their Thai equivalents.

AIR Malaysia Airlines handles all domestic routes within Malaysia. In Sarawak and Sabah a plane is sometimes the only way to travel. Bario in the Kelabit Highlands, for example, can only be reached by plane. A short flight to Gunung Mulu National Park from Miri saves a whole day on buses and boats, and doesn't cost much more. Because air travel is the only quick way to get about in Sarawak and Sabah fares are heavily subsidised and are well worth considering. Malaysia Airlines are very helpful when it comes to making changes to tickets; any of their offices can amend a ticket for no charge.

Malaysian Air Pass

Malaysia Airlines' Discover Malaysia Pass costs US$99 for up to five flights within *either* peninsular Malaysia *or* within Sarawak *or* within Sabah. An air pass covering the whole of Malaysia is US$199. Both passes can only be purchased by passengers holding an international ticket with Malaysia Airlines. This includes flights between Thailand and Malaysia but *not* between Singapore and Malaysia.

Another catch is that the pass for the whole of Malaysia can only be used once for a flight between peninsular Malaysia and Sarawak and Sabah. Changing your route after purchasing the Pass is possible at US$25 per change, but altering the time of any of the five routes doesn't cost anything. The Pass can be purchased from Malaysia Airlines abroad or in Malaysia within 14 days of arrival.

Road

Car rental is more common than in Thailand. A selection of familiar companies have their cluster of desks at airports, and most four and five-star hotels can arrange car hire. Expect to pay at least RM150 per day for a standard saloon car, although cheaper rates are available through some local companies, and especially if the car is rented for longer than just a few days. Drivers are expected to have an international driving licence and be over 23 years of age. Driving in Kuala Lumpur is not as hair-raising as in Bangkok but a car is not a great advantage because the road system is complicated. Outside the capital driving is usually a breeze and most Malaysians drive with care. Driving is on the left. Using the horn when overtaking is common.

Taxi

City Taxis: Taxis are mostly metered in Kuala Lumpur but not elsewhere. This means establishing the fare before setting off on a journey. As with Thailand, try to establish the going rate from a third party and then act as if you are an old hand.

Long Distance Taxis: Shared taxis for long-distance travel is more widespread in Malaysia than in Thailand. Most towns have an area where taxis wait to fill their vehicles with passengers. If you turn up early in the morning you should have no trouble finding a taxi waiting to take off on a regular route. Over-charging is relatively uncommon. Fares are fixed on the basis of one charge for the whole taxi which is then divided by four when full. The taxi can be chartered by one, two or three people as long as they cough up the full charge.

SINGAPORE

Singapore is justly famed for its public transport system. There is no other city in south-east Asia where it is so easy to get around. The modern Mass Rapid Transit (MRT) subway system is comfortable and quick, and using it is simplicity itself. There are machines in every station that issue rechargable, single-trip tickets, or stored value tickets that can be used for any journey.

The public bus system is comfortable and reliable. An increasing number of buses have a fixed fare and do not issue change, so you need to have the right money. The stored value card can be used on both the MRT and on buses equipped to read the card. Explorer tickets are also available for three days of unlimited bus travel.

Taxis are plentiful in Singapore and all are metered, with a 50% surcharge between midnight and 0600 and a variable surcharge on all trips into the Central Business District (CBD) during rush hour.

Car rental is readily available but of limited value. There is a surcharge for entry into the CBD during rush hour, little free parking and severe policing to boot. Cars rented in Singapore are not normally insured for travel in Malaysia and, given the difference in cost, it makes sense to travel over to Johor Bahru and hire a car there.

WHEN TO GO

THAILAND Thailand can be visited any time of the year but there are seasonal variations to bear in mind. The cool season – November to February – is the most pleasant time but also the busiest in terms of visitor numbers. During these months international travel to Thailand is at its peak and a flight needs to be booked as far in advance as possible. The demand for sleepers on the train from Bangkok to Chiang Mai and the route south to Ko Samui and on to Malaysia dramatically increases, and the price of accommodation in popular tourist destinations like Phuket and Ko Samui is at its highest.

The impact of the hot season – March to May – is most keenly felt in the north-east when temperatures approaching 40°C are not unknown. The rainy season, roughly May or June to October, is not severe enough to prevent travel. Even though a lot of rain falls in the south you can still expect an average of five hours of sunshine each day. During this time the amount of rainfall in any one week is purely down to luck.

MALAYSIA Expect a temperature somewhere between 25° and 30°C most of the time in most of Malaysia. The amount of rainfall is more variable and affects a visit to the east coast between November and February when the north-east monsoon makes itself felt. It is not going to rain non-stop for days on end, and an hour or two of rain is invariably followed by a period of sunshine. But heavy rainfall and high winds mean that boat transport to the Perenthian Islands becomes uncertain, and as a result nearly all the accommodation closes for a few months. Many resorts along the east coast also close down during these months.

SINGAPORE There are no significant changes in the climate and the temperature is somewhere between 25° and 30°C every day of the year. Singapore is virtually on the equator and so the sun rises and falls at roughly the same time every day of the year.

PASSPORTS AND VISAS

IS YOUR PASSPORT VALID FOR THE NEXT SIX MONTHS?

To enter Thailand or Malaysia your passport must be valid for six months from the time of arrival.

THAILAND Most nationalities can enter Thailand without a visa for 30 days. Your passport will be stamped for the 30 days and there is nothing to pay. Your visit can be extended for up to ten days on payment of 500B at an immigration office. It is also possible to hop over to Malaysia and return the same day in order to get a stamp for another 30-day visit. A 60-day tourist visa is also available for US$15 but this should be obtained in advance from the Thai embassy or consulate in your home country.

MALAYSIA Most nationalities are automatically granted a 30-day or 60-day visa upon arrival in Malaysia. Extensions for up to three months can usually be obtained through an immigration office. The states of Sarawak and Sabah have their own immigration control and most nationalities are granted a 30-day visa upon arrival.

SINGAPORE Most nationalities do not require a visa and visitors are normally granted a 14-day or 30-day permit upon arrival. Extensions for up to 14 days are easily obtainable at the immigration office.

EMBASSIES ABROAD

Thai embassies abroad

UK: 29 Queen's Gate, London SW7 5JB; tel: (020) 7589-0173
USA: 1024 Wisconsin Ave NW, Washington DC 20007; tel: (202) 944-3600
Malaysia: 206 Jalan Ampang, Kuala Lumpur; tel: (03) 248-8333
Singapore: 370 Orchard Rd, Singapore; tel: 737-2644

Malaysian embassies abroad

UK: 45 Belgrave Square, London SW1X 8QT; tel: (020) 7235-8033
USA: 2401 Massachusetts Ave NW, Washington DC; tel: (202) 328-2700
Singapore: 02-06, 268 Orchard Rd; tel: 235-0111
Thailand: 35 South Sathorn Rd, Bangkok; tel: (02) 248-8350

Singaporean embassies abroad

UK: 9 Wilton Crescent, London SW1X 8RW; tel: (020) 7245-6583
USA: 3501 International Place, NW Washington DC, 2008; tel: (202) 537-3100
Malaysia: 209 Jalan Tun Razak, Kuala Lumpur; tel: (03) 261-6277
Thailand: 129 Sathon Tai Rd; tel: (02) 286-2111

WHAT TO PACK

The single best piece of advice is to bring as little as possible. Apart from special medicines, vital documents and money there is nothing really essential that you need to take. Spare clothes should be kept to an absolute minimum but bring one warm garment if you are planning to climb Mt Kinabalu in Malaysia or to head into northern Thailand during the cool season. Tampons are readily available in Malaysia and Singapore but they are not so common in Thailand outside of Bangkok.

Some items that could be brought with you are just as easily obtained in Thailand, Malaysia or Singapore and will often be cheaper. These include sunglasses, sun lotion, a small torch and a lighter for lighting mosquito coils if staying in beach huts, and maybe ear plugs for noisy neighbours and overnight journeys. If swimming and snorkelling is on your agenda it may be worth bringing your own gear, although again this kind of equipment is easy to purchase in Kuala Lumpur or Bangkok. Suitcases are a nuisance if a lot of travelling is planned and a backpack or travelpack makes a lot more sense.

ACCOMMODATION

Between them, Thailand, Malaysia and Singapore offer every kind of accommodation, from the ultimate in luxurious five-star hotels with spoil-yourself-rotten 'hotel within a hotel' floors and comfortable mid-range hotels right down to rooms with a fan and a mattress for a couple of dollars. Singapore is not in the same category as Thailand or Malaysia when it comes to budget accommodation and the extra cost of staying in Singapore should be taken into account.

The room rate is usually just that – the rate for the room – though sometimes it is possible to obtain a cheaper rate for single occupancy. It is not usually a problem for young children to share a room without having to pay any extra. Outside of expensive hotels, it is normal practice to be shown a room before paying any money and with budget accommodation this should be done as a matter of course.

It makes sense to have accommodation for your first couple of nights booked in advance, and with all but budget places it should be possible to arrange this by fax or e-mail from your home country. There are a few websites (page 35) where hotels can be booked online. Although these sites invariably exclude budget accommodation, they very often offer attractively discounted rates that make the hotels they feature surprisingly affordable.

THAILAND Thailand has a bountiful supply of accommodation options to suit most people's preferences and wallets, but at peak times, especially between December and February, it wouldn't be wise to turn up at Ko Samui or Phuket without something booked in advance. The cheapest accommodation in Thailand is usually in a guesthouse, hostel or beach bungalow with shared bathroom facilities. Such places tend not to take advance bookings over the phone, and at peak periods it is a matter of arriving early in the morning with money in your hand.

Apart from the cost, there are advantages of staying in inexpensive accommodation. Good budget places offer the chance to meet fellow travellers and exchange travelling tips. Most are geared to travellers' needs, providing safety boxes, notice boards

ACCOMMODATION ONLINE

A good place to start is http://travel.excite.com which has accommodation links for all three countries. Reservations can be made online and there is information about travel advice, literature and maps.

THAILAND

http://www.thailandhotels.net/ Offers online booking for a range of over 200 hotels in Thailand.

http://www.phuket.com Compiled by locals, the site enables reservations to be made for 70 hotels in Phuket.

http://www.samuibeach.com Offers discounts on a range of accommodation in Ko Samui.

MALAYSIA

http://www.tourism.gov.my The Malaysian government tourist site, with information on hotels throughout Malaysia.

http://www.sarawak.tourism.com Under construction at time of writing.

SINGAPORE

http:///www.singaporehotels.net Reservations can be made for hotels in Singapore from US$70 and upwards.

AIRPORTS

http://www3.sympatico.ca/donna.mcsherry/asia.htm Detailed information and advice by travellers on their favourite places to sleep at Bangkok, Kuala Lumpur and Singapore airports.

with travel news, and often a travel desk for arranging onward travel and tours. These places usually have an affordable café or restaurant on the premises.

Mid-range hotels cover upmarket guesthouses where rooms have a fan or air-con and their own bathroom, as well as a range of hotels that offer rooms of varying quality, sometimes with a choice of air-con or fan, usually with attached bathrooms. Luxury hotels abound in Bangkok and other major tourist destinations, and they always cost a lot less than their counterparts in the West. The rack rates are impressively expensive but many can be booked online with substantial discounts.

MALAYSIA Malaysia has a range of accommodation options fairly similar to Thailand, and most towns have places to suit a variety of budgets. Backpacker-friendly budget places are not as common or as well organised as their Thai counterparts, but more English is spoken around Malaysia and it is easier to sort out travel arrangements and other matters. The kind of guesthouses that in Thailand would rarely have staff with a smattering of English are relatively uncommon in Malaysia and most places can be telephoned to establish rates and availability of rooms. Malaysia excels in good value mid-range hotels, like those belonging to the Seri Malaysia chain that offer clean and comfortable rooms, but without the extras of more expensive hotels. Kuala Lumpur and Penang have their fair share of luxury hotels, and other large towns or tourist areas will usually have one or two above-average hotels.

Singapore Singapore is more expensive than Thailand or Malaysia and the cost of accommodation reflects this. There are budget travellers' areas around Beach Road and elsewhere, and mid-range places are growing in number even though it is the plush international-style hotels that make an emphatic visual statement in Singapore. As with Thailand and Malaysia these hotels are very pricey if you ask for their room rates at reception but substantial discounts are often available when booked through a travel agent from home or online.

FOOD AND DRINK

The food and drink of Thailand, Malaysia and Singapore are reason enough to confirm that flight reservation and take off for south-east Asia immediately. Unless you have an acutely sensitive stomach or very strict food taboos, there are some wonderful food experiences in store for you. New arrivals to Thailand and Malaysia are inclined to worry too much about hygiene in informal restaurants and hawker stalls.

Remember that the food has usually been cooked to order and at temperatures that will kill any bacteria. As long as you avoid tap water there is not too much to worry about. Some of the best food in these countries is not going to be found in expensive Western-style restaurants and sooner rather than later you should head for a night market and order food from a stall being patronised by other customers.

Thailand Fresh ingredients, seafood, coconut milk, lemon grass, galangal, ginger, coriander, tamarind, basil, lime juice, chillies and fish sauce are just some of the characteristic features of Thai cuisine. Thai food can be very hot but if you stay too long in tourist ghettos – of the five-star kind as well as budget beach huts – you may not notice how the kitchen tones down the cooking to suit Western palates. When a long-distance bus pulls in for a pit stop at a roadside restaurant, you will notice with nose-running alarm just how hot a plate of Thai food can be. Knives are rarely used to eat a meal – bite-sized portions of everything make them unnecessary – and a fork and spoon or chopsticks are the standard cutlery.

Thai food can be very basic, but it can also be very luxurious. Royal Thai cuisine, served up in expensive restaurants, is delicately seasoned with lemon grass, galangal, whole fresh peppercorns, coconut, holy basil and kaffir lime leaves. A typical popular dish all over Thailand is Tom Yam soup, a fiery soup based on fish sauce with kaffir lime, lemon grass and galangal flavouring which often contains prawns.

EATING THAI STYLE

A Thai meal ideally consists of a selection of small dishes shared by a small group. Rice is ladled on to each individual plate, with all the other dishes arranged on the table. To achieve a sense of balance between sweet and sour, hot and cool, fried and steamed, start by ordering one or two appetisers and one plate of salad. Order rice, soup, one curry and one main dish. All of this should arrive together, with perhaps a very short interval between the appetisers and the rest. Dessert is always ordered separately after the meal. A good book of Thai recipes for when you get home is *The Taste of Thailand*, Vatcharin Bhumichitr, published by Pavilion in the UK.

MALAYSIA AND SINGAPORE

Both countries have a multi-cultural food scene, including Western food. The least expensive way to enjoy good local food is to visit a hawker centre or food centre. Chinese and Malay food monopolise these places but there is always at least one Indian Muslim stall, and fresh fruit drinks are usually available from more than one outlet. There is always a common seating area and the food ordered from one or more stalls is brought to your table.

Chinese Regional Cuisines: Stir-fried **Cantonese** dishes, originally from the province of Guangdong, are common in Chinese restaurants and food stalls in both Malaysia and Singapore. A version of Cantonese cuisine popular in the West, they are characterised by very fresh bite-sized pieces of food fried very quickly and then coated in often quite sweet sauces. In both Singapore and Malaysia this tends to be much more chilli influenced than it would be in Hong Kong.

A traditional Cantonese lunch is made up of a number of *dim sum* – literally 'little heart'. These small snacks are wheeled around on a trolley for customers to choose what they like from a whole variety of different kinds. *Pau* are steamed rice dumplings which arrive in cane steamers. The filling may be sweet, such as red bean paste, or savoury. Other items might include deep-fried pastry cases filled with prawn or crab, or even deep-fried chicken claws served with mustard.

Szechuan cooking is very popular in both countries. Its style is said to have evolved because chilli is a preservative which also disguises the taste of food, and Szechuan province is a long haul from the sea. Again, bite-sized pieces are stir-fried but this time they are presented without the sauce and are strongly flavoured with chilli. With some, huge pieces of dried chilli are served beside the meat or seafood. Sesame oil and garlic are other strong flavours often used. Often a dish will be made up of contrasting textures – such as soft, fast-cooked meat, crispy dried chillies and crunchy cashew nuts.

Beijing Style Cooking is the cuisine of the emperors and can be quite expensive. Beijing cooks like to think of their style as the haute cuisine of the genre. Whereas other cuisines are based on rice this is based on wheat. Typical of Beijing food are noodles, steamed buns or the pancakes used in the famous Beijing dish Peking duck. Here the duck is highly roasted until crispy and rolled in pancakes with plum sauce.

Teochew is less popular although there are some places dedicated to the style in Singapore. The cuisine comes from a southern China region called Swatow. Food is cooked longer and in its own juices rather than in fat.

There is a long tradition of **vegetarian** cooking among the Chinese and lots of Chinese people often eat only vegetables on certain days of the lunar calendar. It is associated with Buddhism, and there are often vegetarian restaurants in or near Buddhist temples. One style of vegetarian cooking which is very tasty and a good introduction to Chinese vegetarian food is *yong tau fu* which originates from Hainan. Stalls have rows of vegetables, deep fried and steamed tofu, beancurd skin, green vegetables like water convolvulus or pak choi and huge vats of soup.

Customers collect a pile of vegetables and take them to the stall owner who cuts them up and dips them for a few seconds in one of the vats of soup. Noodles are also dipped and the resulting lightly cooked melange is served up with some of the soup. Rows of condiments can be added to heighten the taste and soups can be plain or thick. Strict vegetarians should take care at *yong tau fu* stalls as some of the vegetables are stuffed with fishcake and not tofu.

MOCK MEAT

Some vegetarian restaurants are dedicated to making their customers feel like they are eating meat when they aren't, creating fake meat dishes which are often very convincing. Tofu in its various states can be twisted and strangled into the texture of meat or sinew and beancurd skin becomes chicken skin or the ingredients for vegetarian Peking duck. Wooden stakes take the form of chicken bones and gluten balls imitate other meats.

Singaporean Chinese Cuisine: Singaporean Chinese cooking has evolved its own special style, which is seafood-based and includes such classic dishes as pepper crab. Part of the fun of eating this dish is getting to the crabmeat in the first place, using what looks like a set of woodworking tools. Don't dress up to eat pepper crab and keep a wary eye out for pieces of flying shell. Drunken prawns is a bloodthirsty dish where live prawns are dipped into a glass of brandy. The creature drowns on the brandy but sucks it into whatever it has instead of lungs as it dies. The head of the prawn, flavoured with the brandy, is regarded as a delicacy.

STEAMBOAT

Another Singaporean favourite is steamboat. Each table is given a metal contraption with charcoal inside an inner section (or now more often a little gas burner) and bubbling stock in the outer part. Diners collect raw pieces of food from a buffet, which is dipped in the stock and cooked. As the meal progresses the soup becomes more and more tasty until it is the last thing to be eaten. Some competitively priced steamboat restaurants have warning notices about fines for leftover food.

Malay Cuisine: There are very few Malay restaurants in either country. Malay food is basically home cooking and very few people open restaurants dedicated entirely to this cuisine. It is most often seen in hawker centres and food courts with *nasi padang* or *nasi kampur* written above the stall. It consists of a vast range of meat, fish and vegetable dishes, often deep-fried or cooked in thick curry gravy. Customers pick their dishes and add them to a plate of rice. In some areas this is *nasi lemak*, rice cooked in coconut milk with a much richer more glutinous texture. The sauces are dominated by lemon grass, chilli, and garlic and thickened with a kind of nut. Often fish or meat dishes are wrapped on pandan or banana leaves and cooked slowly.

Fusion Dishes: What has happened to Singaporean palates over the years is that the Chinese have grown to love Malay style chilli flavoured food while the Malays have come to appreciate the quick stir fry. The fusion of these two cooking styles has resulted in the stalls most often found in hawker centres in Singapore. Noodles are Chinese in origin but *mee goreng* (fried noodles) has a Malay name and is strongly flavoured with Malay ingredients. Other fusion dishes include *tahu goreng* (deep-fried tofu). Chinese in origin, it is served with spicy peanut sauce and chopped raw vegetables, which is Malay in style. *Mee rebus* (noodles served with coconut sauce and other toppings) is again a mixture of the two cuisines. Another popular dish in Singapore which draws in the region's third cooking style – Indian – is *roti John* (French bread dipped in egg and minced meat with chillies and fried).

Indian Food: For many people not used to the fiery nature of Malay food stalls, Indian food will come as a godsend while they are travelling, although it is very far from the rather watered down versions common in Western countries. Singapore and Malaysia have three basic Indian cooking styles. Most common all over Singapore and Malaysia are *daun pisang* coffee shops – very inexpensive fan-cooled places where men in dhotis wander around dishing up curries and sauces onto banana leaves instead of plates alongside pappadoms and unusual chutneys. Customers eat with the right hand (or you can ask for cutlery) and after the meal the leaf is folded over, hiding any leftovers.

Many banana leaf places are strictly vegetarian but others serve up meat and fish curries which are hotter than most westerners are used to. As well as the banana leaf curry these places also often serve wonderful breakfast dishes such as *masala dosa*, rice flour pancakes served with spicy mashed potato filling and coconut sauce. Some places such as the vegetarian Woodlands in Singapore have about 15 different breads which are served up with small pots of curry.

A small proportion of the Indian communities in the region are Muslim. Known locally as Chettiars or Chittys, their style of cooking is very spicy. These places often have hot plates full of curry dishes as well as griddles to cook thick leavened dough pancakes, called *roti prata* in Singapore or *roti canai* in Malaysia. Variations on this pancake include stuffing it with chicken (*roti ayam*), beef (*roti dagang*), egg (*roti telor*) or vegetables (*roti sayur*). In Singapore the stuffed version is called *murtabak*. Often common in these restaurants is an Indian version of chicken rice, cooked in a huge vat in a mildly flavoured cinnamon and cardamom sauce.

North Indian food is the one most likely to be familiar to westerners and is usually served up in air-conditioned restaurants, although there are some north Indian hawker stalls. The cooking is characterised by thick nutty sauces, yoghurt side dishes called raita and flat leavened breads cooked in a tandoor.

Nyonya cuisine: Nyonya cuisine is currently flavour of the month in Singapore and Malaysia. It is basically Malay style food with some Chinese influence. Meat dishes are served up in sauces flavoured with lemon grass and lots of coconut (in the Melaka version) and chilli (in the Penang version). The most common Nyonya dish, found in every hawker centre, is *laksa*, a noodle based dish with prawns, other seafood and vegetables served in a rich coconut sauce and topped with boiled egg. In Penang *laksa* has less coconut and the fish stock is stronger, making a rather sourer soup.

DESSERTS AND SWEETS

These are not a big part of life in Malaysia and Singapore and when they are found they are barely recognisable to western eyes as dessert. In Chinese cuisine dessert is often tapioca or red beans while Malay desserts might be very sticky cakes made with rice flour and flavoured with equally un-dessert like ingredients. Sweetcorn features in many dessert dishes in both cuisines. Common all over is the hideous looking dessert called *ais kacang*, which is a mountain of shaved ice covered in syrupy, brightly coloured sauces and topped with sweetcorn, red beans, pandan jellies or black beans and condensed milk.

DRINKS

There are a few drinks that might be unfamiliar to westerners. Chinese tea is found everywhere in Chinese restaurants and takes many different forms. The basic tea ingredient is often flavoured with other things such as jasmine.

Herbal teas are sold in shops dedicated to the drink from strange shaped pots containing the ready-made brew. They also often sell soybean milk, as do most drinks stalls in hawker centres. In addition these places sell fresh juices such as guava or water apple juice – both are worth a taste. Chrysanthemum tea is sold everywhere.

Stalls which crush sugar cane and sell the very sweet, olive green juice are less common than they once were. In Malaysia you can also get fresh young coconuts.The stall owner will hack off the top so you can drink the delicious milk and then scoop out the jelly. Traditional coffee shops – rather than expensive designer coffee bars – sell thick black coffee, often with an inch of undissolved white condensed sweetened milk at the bottom. Tea arrives in a similar state, although you can ask for these drinks without milk. Indian Muslim places 'stretch' their tea and coffee by pouring it from a great height from one pot to another until it is ready to drink, looking very pale and milky and covered in froth.

SAFETY

All three countries are generally very safe for travellers and there are no areas that are even remotely dangerous. Sensible precautions should always be taken against thieves – fellow travellers in some cases – and in crowded tourist areas you should always be aware of pickpockets. You can carry a doorstop in your luggage to help make you feel safe at night in budget places where the door lock seems inadequate.

A growing risk, and one that is hard to control, is the danger of your credit card details being copied and used for illegal purchases. This can happen in a five-star hotel (recently, an assistant manager of a well-known international hotel chain was arrested for participating in such a fraud), a mid-range hotel or any shop where you use your card. Try not to let the card go out of your sight.

The Latest Safety Information

For up-to-the-minute travel safety advice and information on Thailand, Malaysia and Singapore contact the website of the UK Foreign and Commonwealth Office's travel section: http://www.fco.gov.uk/travel/.

Thailand Travellers on their own, especially women, should take extra care if arriving at Bangkok airport or Hualamphong station late at night. Don't use unofficial taxis. In 2000 there was another case of a visitor being robbed at gunpoint, and shot when he resisted, in an unofficial taxi taken at the airport in the early hours of the morning.

Take particular care over your luggage on buses and trains, especially on the popular runs between Bangkok and Chiang Mai and Bangkok and Ko Samui. Train staff will often show you a warning printed in

SAFETY TIPS

Carry photocopies of your passport and your air ticket separately from the documents themselves. Details of traveller cheques should always be kept in a different place from the cheques themselves. Keep a record of contact numbers to telephone in the event of losing your traveller cheques or bank cards, and the contact number for your health insurance policy. Budget travellers may benefit from their own small but sturdy padlock to supplement those used to lock the doors of beach huts and chalets. A small padlock for rucksacks and backpacks is a good idea.

English about the risk of accepting drinks or food from strangers, which is based on cases of passengers being drugged and waking to find all their valuables stolen. Thailand has its share of touts and scams but use common sense and a polite but firm refusal and they should not be too troublesome.

MALAYSIA Generally Malaysia is a very safe country. Sensible precautions should still be taken, especially at night, and there have been isolated cases of handbags being snatched at Batu Ferringi in Penang. On the east coast peninsula of Malaysia the influence of Islamic fundamentalism has, in the last few years, begun to make itself felt in an unpleasant way. Western women unaccompanied by a man are likely to be deemed as loose and treated with a lack of respect.

DRUGS AND THE DEATH PENALTY

Malaysia and Singapore both have mandatory death penalties for what would be considered fairly small quantities in the West. Even more alarming is that judges do not make the distinction between soft drugs like marijuana and hard drugs like heroin and cocaine. In Thailand it is illegal to use any kind of drugs and the fact that the police seem to be inconsistent in the application of the law only adds to the risk. There is no shortage of westerners languishing in Bangkok prisons for drug offences and there are heavy fines – you won't be let out of jail until the fine is paid in cash – for the possession of small amounts of marijuana and other soft narcotics.

SINGAPORE Singapore is probably the safest country in the world and the chances of being mugged or the victim of a crime are very low indeed.

HEALTH AND MEDICINE

It is highly recommended that you organise health insurance in your home country before you leave. A good policy will cover theft of money and belongings, and provide full cover in the event of illness or an accident. If you are planning to engage in activities like scuba diving or even trekking it is worth clarifying whether they are included in your policy. Similarly, check where you stand in the event of an accident involving a hired motorbike or other vehicle. Remember that in order to make a claim for the theft of belongings you will need some documentation to show you have reported the matter to the police, usually within 24 hours.

Visit your doctor well before departure to discuss what inoculations you might need. You should be protected against hepatitis A, polio and typhoid. There is a risk of developing malaria in parts of Thailand and Malaysia, although if you stick to tourist areas the danger is slight. Border areas in Thailand that are close to Myanmar (Burma), Laos and Cambodia have a higher risk. If planning to travel in these areas you should discuss with your doctor the pros and cons of taking an anti-malaria prescription drug.

HEALTH INFORMATION ONLINE

Two useful websites for current information and advice on health matters affecting travel in south-east Asia are: http://www.masta.org and http://www.tmb.ie.

Mosquitoes can spread dengue fever and Japanese B encephalitis as well as malaria, and precautions should be taken to avoid being bitten. There are various mosquito repellents on the market. Hotels in mosquito-prone areas often provide nets, although you may want to bring your own.

Small cuts can become infected quite quickly and it pays to reduce the risk by wearing plastic shoes while swimming. The most common health problem encountered by travellers is a bout of diarrhoea brought about by poor hygiene on the part of someone handling your food. So much food is stir-fried using fresh ingredients that the risk of catching something from a food stall or restaurant is not as great as you might think. If you are vegetarian the risk is very low indeed. Tap water should never be drunk, and although in good hotels there should not be a problem using tap water to brush your teeth many people prefer to use bottled water for everything.

Diarrhoea is best treated by drinking plenty of fluids and taking it easy for a couple of days. Medicines like Imodium are readily available in pharmacies, and while they only relieve the symptoms they may be useful if a journey or some other activity is unavoidable. If symptoms continue for more than 48 hours consult a doctor.

Sunburn is always a danger if precautions are not taken. Use sun lotion, avoid being exposed to the sun for long periods during the hottest part of the day, and wear sunglasses and some form of headwear. Prickly heat is a common ailment but can usually be dealt with by using prickly heat powder, which is available throughout all three countries.

Aids is a real risk, especially in Thailand, and no chances should be taken. Under Singapore's Immigration Act, amended in 1998, foreigners suffering from Aids or infected with HIV are classified as prohibited immigrants.

Talking about the kinds of illnesses that could happen to you while visiting Thailand and Malaysia (it's tempting to say that all germs and viruses have been officially banned from ultra-clean Singapore) can sound alarming and off-putting. In reality, the chances are that you will come home feeling healthier than ever before.

Sunshine, fresh fruit every day and fresh ingredients in meals are a tonic in themselves and the most likely mishap is a stomach disorder that lasts one or two days at most. Equally reassuring is the fact that all three countries have excellent hospitals and medical services.

MEDICAL KIT

Unless you have a specific problem there are no essential medicines that need to be brought with you. In all three countries there is usually no problem finding a pharmacy that can supply any of the items in this list over the counter without a prescription. If, however, you like to be prepared and especially if you are planning to travel in out-of-the-way places, such as hillwalking in northern Thailand or trekking in the jungle in Sarawak, then the following might be useful:

Aspirin, paracetamol or other mild painkiller for general ailments

Antihistamine for known allergies and for the relief of itching caused by insect stings or bites

Antiseptic for general cuts

Band-aids for small cuts and scraped skin on the feet from wearing new sandals

Imodium or Lomotil for treating the symptoms of diarrhoea and perhaps a rehydration salt mixture as well

Insect repellent

Sun lotion and something for chapped lips

Travel sickness tablets

MONEY AND BANKS

There is no black market in the exchange of Thai, Malaysian or Singaporean currencies. At the time of writing exchange rates were stable for all three currencies but the turmoil in the currency markets over the Thai baht in mid 1998, which spread to the Malaysian ringitt, means there is no guarantee of future stability. Current exchange rates are posted in banks and money exchange offices in all three countries, as well as appearing daily in the national newspapers. It is worth keeping an eye on them because rates tend to change a little on a daily basis and you may as well catch a good day to exchange your money.

There are exchange offices at the international airports of all three countries so there is no need to bring foreign currency with you unless you are arriving at a very unsociable hour. Traveller cheques are the safest way to carry money and exchange rates are often marginally better for traveller cheques than for cash. Try to bring mostly large denomination traveller cheques to save on the commission charge for each individual cheque, as well as a couple of smaller ones for last-minute cash needs. Bringing some pounds sterling or US dollars in cash is also useful for small exchanges, emergencies and in out-of-the-way places where there may not be official exchange facilities. Money can be changed at banks and money exchange offices. Try to avoid using hotels because their rates are always the poorest.

Check with your bank or credit agency before you leave home about using your card to obtain cash advances from a bank machine in Thailand, Malaysia or Singapore. If you think you may be using your cash for some large purchases you may want to have your credit allowance raised for this purpose. The more expensive hotels in all three countries expect guests to settle their bills with a credit card, and will ask for details when you are checking in. Guests without a credit card are almost regarded with suspicion and a cash payment upfront may be requested.

THAILAND The currency is the baht (B) and coins come in 1B, 5B and 10B. Banknotes come in 10B, 50B, 100B, 500B and 1000B, and increase in size as their value goes up. The Thai currency took a beating in the money markets after mid-1998, and exchange rates have still not returned to their former levels. At the time of writing the pound sterling was worth between 55B and 60B, and the US dollar between 36B and 40B.

SENDING MONEY WORLDWIDE

MoneyGram is a quick international money transfer service, offered by a number of Thomas Cook offices. It operates in Thailand and Singapore but, inexplicably, not yet in Malaysia. Money can be sent or received using a credit card or with cash.

UK tel: 008-008-971-8971

USA tel: 1-800-543-4080

Thailand tel: 001-800-12-066-0542

Singapore tel: 800-1100-560.

Travel Basics

If planning to cross into Laos or Cambodia from Thailand it helps to have some US dollars with you in cash.

Malaysia The currency is the ringitt (RM) and coins come in RM1, RM5, RM10 and RM20. Banknotes come in RM2, RM5, RM10, RM20, RM50, RM100, RM500 and RM1000. At the time of writing the pound sterling was worth approximately RM5.5 and the US dollar was worth RM3.5.

Singapore The currency is the Singapore dollar (S$) and coins come in 1c, 5c, 20c, 50c and S$1. Banknotes come in S$2, S$5, S$10, S$100, S$500 and S$1000. At the time of writing one pound sterling was worth S$2.5 and the US dollar was worth S$1.6. The Singapore dollar is easily the most stable of the three currencies and the one least likely to experience volatile shifts in value.

Tipping Tipping is not normal in Thailand or Malaysia and even more unusual in Singapore. Top hotels and expensive restaurants will add local tax and a service charge onto the bill and unless there is some special reason there is no obligation to tip on top of this. Taxi drivers do not expect a tip though rounding up the fare is not uncommon, especially in Thailand where a few baht does not amount to a lot of money.

Bargaining

Bargaining is commonplace in Thailand and Malaysia, and not just in obvious places like markets and street stalls. As a general rule anything that doesn't carry a marked price may be open to negotiation. In Thailand, apart from shopping, the most likely situation where bargaining is necessary is when taking a taxi. This is also true, though to a lesser extent, in Malaysia. In both countries, it is sometimes worth bargaining for a hotel room. Instead of straightforward bargaining, suggest a reason for a discount (staying more than one night? arriving late?) and then make an offer. This can work even in more expensive hotels when business is slow.

RECOMMENDED READING

As well as offering an insight into the region, the following books are all worth reading in their own right. It is a good idea to try and get hold of them before you leave. Bookshops are not common in Thailand, Malaysia or Singapore and when you do find one the price of their books will astonish you. Taxes push up book prices and a cynic might think the governments are happy not to encourage reading.

General *Southeast Asia*, Mary Somers Heidues, is a concise history of the region and its current dilemmas and conflicts. *Lords of the Rim*, Sterling

Seagrave, is a populist account of the economic power of the Chinese in south-east Asia and elsewhere.

THAILAND *The Railway Man*, Eric Lomax, and *The Bridge on the River Kwai*, Pierre Boulle, are two books for any trip west of Bangkok to Kanchanaburi and the Kwai River. Both are available on audiotape from Chivers Press, http://www.chivers.co.uk.

Arts and Crafts of Thailand, Warren and Tettoni, and *The Grand Palace Bangkok*, Naengnoi Suksri, are two richly coloured illustrated books published by Thames and Hudson.

A Siamese Tragedy, Walden Bello, Shea Cunningham and Li Kheng Poh, is the story of how Thailand's love affair with international capitalists turned sour in 1997-98 and the influence of the IMF.

MALAYSIA *The Malay Dilemma*, Mahathir Mohamad. It is easier to pick up this book in Kuala Lumpur than at home. Written in 1970 by Malaysia's Prime Minister before he was a name to reckon with, it continues to offer a remarkable insight into how many still regard the country's Malay-Chinese matrix.

The Malay Archipelago, Alfred Russell Wallace, republished by Oxford. This is the book for anyone with an interest in nature to take to Sarawak and Sabah.

For a more modern adventure try *Into the Heart of Borneo*, Redmond O'Hanlon, also available on audiotape. See page 395 for other books on wildlife in Borneo.

SINGAPORE In Joseph Conrad's *Lord Jim*, Singapore is the novel's 'great Eastern port'. It also features in Conrad's *The Shadow Line*, which has period descriptions of the area around St Andrew's Cathedral and the Padang.

King Rat by former POW James Clavell is set in Singapore's POW camp under the Japanese.

Paul Theroux was a teacher in Singapore and his *Saint Jack* is set in the city. He also wrote an essay on Singapore in *Sunrise with Seamonsters*. Philip Jeyaratnam is an interesting Singaporean writer.

Look for *Raffles Place* and *Abraham's Promise* in Singapore bookshops. *Lee Kuan Yew*, T J S George, is still the best account of Lee's rise to power and how he kept it. *Rogue Trader* is Nick Leeson's personal account of his fall from grace.

USEFUL READING

Referred to throughout this guide as the **OTT,** the *Thomas Cook Overseas Timetable* is published every two months, price £9.50 per issue. Indispensable for independent travellers using public transport in Thailand, Malaysia and Singapore, it contains timetables for all the main rail and bus services, plus details of local and suburban services. It is available from UK branches of Thomas Cook or by mail order, phoning (01733) 503571 in the UK. In North America, contact Forsyth Travel Library Inc., Westchester 1, 44 South Broadway, New York 10604; tel: (800) 367 7984 (toll-free). A special edition of the *Overseas Timetable* is available from bookshops and from the outlets given above - the *Thomas Cook Overseas Timetable Independent Traveller's Edition* - which includes bus, rail and ferry timetables, plus additional information useful for travellers. Please note that the OTT table numbers very occasionally change - but services may easily be located by checking the index at the front of the *Overseas Timetable.*

GENERAL

Bot	main hall in Buddhist temple (Thai)
Chedi	see *stupa* (Thai)
Dada	drugs (Mal)
Farang	a European (Thai)
Gunung	mountain (Mal)
Isaan	north-east Thailand
Jalan	road (Mal)
Kampung	village (Mal)
Ko/koh	island (Thai)
Kota	city, fort (Mal)
KTM	Malaysian Railways System
Kuala	river mouth (Mal)
Lorong	lane, narrow street (Mal)
MAS	Malaysia Airlines
Masjid	mosque (Mal)
Mat mee	technique of tie-dying silk or cotton before weaving (Thai)
MRT	Singapore railway system (Mass Rapid Transit)
Noi	little (Thai)
Nyonya/Nonya	*Peranakan* (see below) women and cooking style (Mal, Sin)
Padang	central grassed square of a town (Mal)
Pantai	beach (Mal)
Peranakan	culture resulting from intermarriage of Chinese immigrants in Singapore, Penang and Melaka with Malays (Mal)
PIE	Pan-Island Express, Singapore's main highway
Prang	temple tower (Thai)
Pulau	island (Mal)
Samlor	*taxi tricycle*
Sampan	small boat (Mal)
Shophouses	domestic houses with the ground floor given over to a shop
Soi	lane, side street (Thai)
Songthaew	taxi: pick-up truck with two benches (Thai)
Stupa	monument housing a Buddha or holy relic, also *chedi*
Sungai	river (Mal)
Thanon	road, shown on road signs, abbreviated to Th. (Thai)
Trishaw	three-wheeled bicycle taxi (Thai)
Trok	alley (Thai)
Tuk-tuk	three-wheeled motorised taxi (Thai)

Viharn	temple assembly hall, home of the main Buddha image (Thai)
Wat	temple monastery (Thai)
Wisma	shopping centre, office building (Mal, Sin)
Yai	big (Thai)

FOOD GLOSSARY

Birds' nest	Chinese medicinal swiftlet nest soup
Biryani	North Indian spiced rice with meat or vegetables
Cendol	Malay dessert of ice shavings, red beans, coloured syrups, jelly and coconut milk
Chapat	Indian flat, thin wholewheat bread cooked on a griddle
Chicken rice	casserole of chicken, rice and vegetables, originally Chinese
Dim sum	various small Chinese dishes served for breakfast and lunch
Fish head curry	a fish head floating in curry, in Singaporean Indian restaurants
Gaeng	Thai for curry
Galangal	aromatic root of an Asian plant of the ginger family, used in Thai cuisine
Garoupa	white fish popular in south-east Asia
Halal	food prepared according to Muslim custom
Idli	Indian steamed rice cakes
Ikan	Malay for fish
Laksa	spicy soup of noodles, prawns, bean curd and vegetables
Mee rebus	yellow noodle, potato and hard-boiled egg soup, popular Malay dish
Meekong	Thai whisky
Murtabak	Indian Muslim pancake bread filled with meat and/or vegetables
Nasi goreng	Malay for fried rice
Nasi lemak	rice boiled in coconut milk, a Malay dish
Roti	thin, flaky Indian bread
Roti canai	roti bread, sometimes made with eggs, often served for break fast with small bowl of curry in Indian and Muslim restaurants
Tahu goreng	fried soya bean and bean sprouts in peanut sauce, Malaysian and Singaporean vegetarian dish

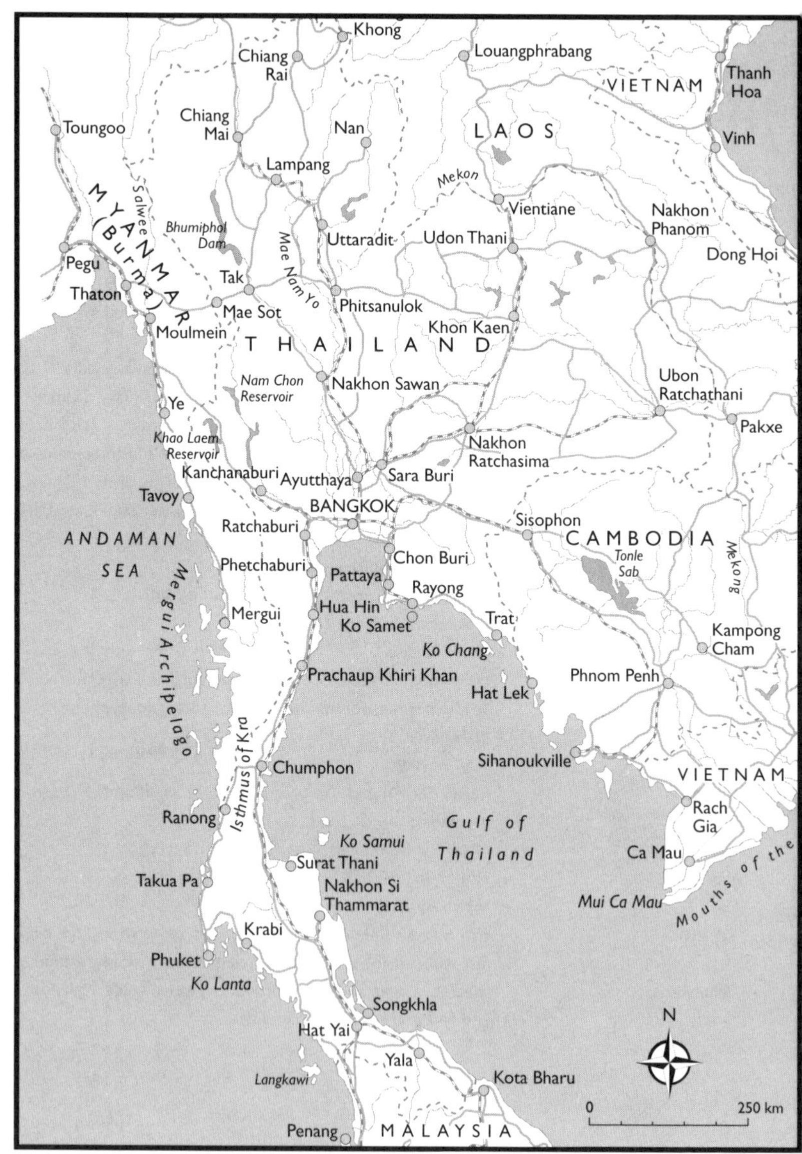

THAILAND MAP

Thailand is a destination to conjure with. Two recent Hollywood films have only increased its deserved popularity with visitors. *The Beach,* starring Leonardo DiCaprio, explores the country's backpacking phenomenon and the search for an exotic paradise. *The King and I,* starring Jodie Foster, shows shining gold temples and a playful but contemplative royal court in the land of Siam – as Thailand was called until 1939. Both movies depict distinctive aspects of modern Thailand that most visitors soon recognise, but no film can capture the surprises waiting to be encountered and enjoyed whilst travelling around the country.

In the south and east of Thailand are idyllic islands splashed with beachside bungalows and affordable restaurants looking out to sea against a backdrop of palm trees and banana plants. Beautiful islands like Ko Samet and Ko Chang are off the coast that stretches from Bangkok east to Cambodia, while directly to the south the land mass of Thailand narrows to a thin strip of territory squeezed between the Andaman Sea and the Gulf of Thailand. The waters here are filled with famed resort islands like Ko Samui and Phuket, superb coral reefs and small, relatively unknown islands that welcome visitors.

The north of Thailand has a very different kind of appeal. Comfortable towns like Chiang Mai and Chiang Rai serve as rest and recreation centres as well as filtering the streams of curious visitors who come to explore the rich local cultures on treks and elephant rides into the countryside. A short way north lies the border with Myanmar (Burma) and Laos, where it is very safe to travel despite the proximity of the infamous Golden Triangle. Far fewer tourists make it to the north-east of Thailand, which is equally rich in culture and benefits from a lack of commercialism.

At the heart of Thailand is vibrant Bangkok, a world city that embraces modernity and tradition in such a way that bewilders and astonishes visitors, whether arriving for the first or tenth time. The capital city is another experience, another part of a complex country that opens its arms to visitors with a smile.

Bangkok

Like many Asian capitals Bangkok is a beguiling mixture of the non-Western and the ultra modern, where urban chaos sits amid shimmering skyscrapers. But no other city accomplishes this balancing act with such abandon. The neurotic noise of *tuk-tuks*, the sheer number of bodies, poverty rubbing shoulders with gold-leaf Buddhas and depressing sex shows make the city in a class of its own. You know you are fully experiencing Bangkok when one day you think you could live here and the next you want to leave instantly.

There are three major cultural buildings, the Grand Palace, Wat Po and the National Museum, which first-time visitors feel obliged to see, but once these have been visited the real sightseeing begins. Find time for a trip on the Chao Phraya River which, apart from being a hassle-free way of travelling through the city, opens up a fresh vista rich in history and culture.

Shopping and eating can easily monopolise time, but there are so many options, from shopping malls to street merchants and the amazing weekend market, and fine dining to pavement stalls, that allow you to see a cross-section of Bangkok's social and cultural richness.

ARRIVAL AND DEPARTURE

Bangkok's Don Muan international airport is 25 km north of the city. Tel: (02) 535-1254 or (02) 535-1386 for arrival and departure information.

Taxis should be booked at one of the taxi counters. You have a choice of a flat-rate or a metered fare in a licensed taxi. Expect to pay around 250B. Ignore any touts; a traveller was robbed and knifed using an unlicensed taxi in 2000.

The airport has an information office, exchange counters, left-luggage facilities, a post office, an e-mail café and various places to eat. The cheapest place to eat is the Food Centre half way along the walkway between the domestic and international terminals. A coupon system operates and the menus are not in English. At the international terminal end of the walkway there is a 24-hr convenience store.

AIRPORT BUS

The airport bus runs daily 0430–0030, tel: (02) 995-1254, and is far more comfortable and convenient than the public bus. Four routes depart at regular intervals from directly outside the arrivals hall. Leaflets explain the routes and the major hotels passed on the way. The airport bus stops at the domestic terminal after first dropping off or collecting passengers at the international terminal. The fare is 70B.

Route AB1 goes to the bottom of Silom Rd before returning to the airport, passing Amari Watergate, Grand Hyatt Erawan, Regent, World Trade Centre, Oriental and Shangri La.

Route AB2 passes Victory Monument, Democracy Monument and Banglamphu (for Khao San Rd).

Route AB3 runs up and down Sukhumvit Rd and accesses the Eastern Bus Terminal.

Route AB4 goes to Ploenchit Rd, Siam Square and Hualamphong railway station.

To catch a bus to the airport you need to hail one from a bus stop on the route. This can be daunting when buses are speeding along and you're burdened down with luggage, so choose a bus stop which gives a clear view of approaching traffic. Buses tend not to stop unless it is clear you are flagging them down.

TRAIN Trains arrive in Bangkok at the centrally located Hualamphong station, tel: (02) 220-4334, (02) 223-7010. It has a range of facilities, including a left-luggage office on platform 12, an advance booking office near platform 3, an information counter and a tourist office, tel: (02) 613-6725, on the walkway above the main concourse. Up here there is also a café and a place for sending e-mails.

For transport to/from the station, a useful bus that shuttles between Siam Square (for a Skytrain connection) and the railway station is No 73, sometimes with air-conditioning and sometimes not. Come out of the station and cross the busy junction and take the one-way road heading east, to your left, and the bus stop is outside the 7-11 store. Another useful bus is the No 53 which goes to Khao San Rd; the stop is reached by taking the station exit near the KFC. Bus No 75 connects the railway station with Charoen Krung Rd in the Silom Rd area.

A sure way of reaching the station from town is to take a skytrain to Chit Lom and catch the 73 bus to the station from opposite the World Trade Centre building.

BUS There are several long-distance bus stations in Bangkok. If arriving from or departing for Malaysia or southern Thailand you use the **Southern Terminal** in Thonburi, tel: (02) 435-1199 or (02) 435-1200. The easiest way to reach this station is by bus No 7 (see page 61).

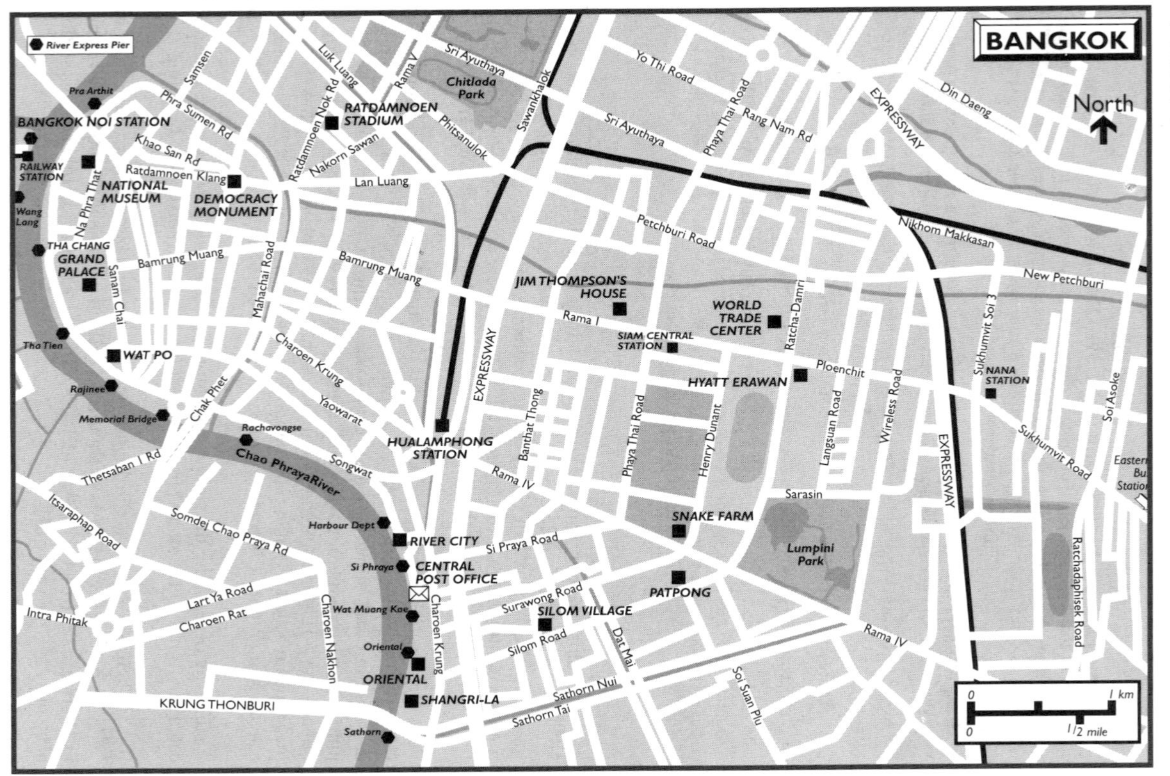
BANGKOK
North
0
1 km
0
1/2 mile
River Express Pier
Pra Arthit
BANGKOK NOI STATION
RAILWAY STATION
Wang Lang
Samsen
Phra Sumen Rd
Khao San Rd
Ratdamnoen Klang
NATIONAL MUSEUM
Na Phra That
DEMOCRACY MONUMENT
THA CHANG
GRAND PALACE
Sanam Chai
Bamrung Muang
Mahachai Road
Tha Tien
WAT PO
Rajinee
Memorial Bridge
Chak Phet
Luk Luang
Ratdamnoen Nok Rd
RATDAMNOEN STADIUM
Nakorn Sawan
Rama V
Sri Ayuthaya
Chitlada Park
Phitsanulok
Sawankhalok
Lan Luang
Bamrung Muang
Charoen Krung
Yaowarat
Rachavongse
Chao PhrayaRiver
Songwat
HUALAMPHONG STATION
EXPRESSWAY
Banthat Thong
Rama IV
Thetsaban 1 Rd
Itsaraphap Road
Somdej Chao Praya Rd
Harbour Dept
RIVER CITY
Si Phraya
CENTRAL POST OFFICE
Si Praya Road
Lart Ya Road
Charoen Rat
Intra Phitak
Charoen Nakhon
Wat Muang Kae
Charoen Krung
Oriental
ORIENTAL
SHANGRI-LA
KRUNG THONBURI
Sathorn
Sathorn Nui
Sathorn Tai
Surawong Road
SILOM VILLAGE
Silom Road
Dat Mai
Soi Suan Plu
Yo Thi Road
Sri Ayuthaya
Phaya Thai Road
Rang Nam Rd
EXPRESSWAY
Din Daeng
Petchburi Road
Nikhom Makkasan
New Petchburi
JIM THOMPSON'S HOUSE
Rama I
SIAM CENTRAL STATION
WORLD TRADE CENTER
Ratcha-Damri
HYATT ERAWAN
Ploenchit
Phaya Thai Road
Henry Dunant
Langsuan Road
Wireless Road
EXPRESSWAY
Sukhumvit Soi 3
NANA STATION
Soi Asoke
Sukhumvit Road
Eastern Bus Station
Sarasin
SNAKE FARM
Lumpini Park
PATPONG
Rama IV
Ratchadaphisek Road

THE HELPFUL TOUT: PART ONE

At the railway station you are likely to be approached by obvious taxi touts but also watch out for the well-dressed solicitous 'official' who carries a large name badge with a photograph and the words 'tourist information'. Don't be surprised if you find yourself being led out of the station to one of the travel agent shops across the road where attempts are made to press you into buying a tour.

The **Northern Terminal**, at Mo Chit, tel: (02) 936-2841 or (02) 279-4484 (Skytrain: Mo Chit), services buses to and from the north and the north-east. The **Eastern Terminal**, at the eastern end of Sukhumvit Rd, tel: (02) 391-2504 (Skytrain: Ekkami), handles routes to Pattaya, Rayong, Chantaburi and Trat.

ORIENTATION

There is no obvious central focus to Bangkok. The nearest the city gets to having a centre is the area around the junction of Phloenchit Rd and Ratchadamri Rd, dominated by the **World Trade Center** and Siam Square one block west. The nearest Skytrain stations are Siam and Chit Lom, and a number of bus routes converge on the roads that make up the junction.

Taking this area as the centre, **Sukhumvit Rd** runs eastwards out of the city, while to the south lies the more commercial **Silom Rd** area. Over to the west of the city is the railway station, the backpackers' **Khao San Rd** (page 60), and the **Chao Phraya River**. Thonburi, to the west of the river, is rarely visited by travellers.

BANGKOK MAPS

If staying in the capital for more than a couple of days then a good city map showing bus routes and the Skytrain stations is indispensable. There are plenty to choose from, all in colour and all claiming to be 100% accurate (although they never are when it comes to bus routes). Our favourite for a general overview is the Bangkok Groovy Map & Guide, with colour-coded but selected bus routes. Good hotels usually have a rack of tourist literature and often include free maps like Thaiways with its detailed area maps.

INFORMATION

CITY AND TRANSPORT MAPS inside back cover

i There is no **Tourist Authority of Thailand (TAT) Office** conveniently located in the city. It pays to collect maps and information from the TAT office at the airport when you arrive, tel: (02) 523-8972, (02) 535-2669, open 0800–2400.

The TAT office in town is situated at 4 Ratchadamnoen North Rd, tel: (02) 281-0422, (02) 282-9773, open daily 0830-1630.

TAT has an emergency phone line, tel: 1155 or 1699, for dealing with problems like theft.

Credit Card Companies Visa and Mastercard, tel: (02) 270-1122 or (02) 252-2712 for lost or stolen cards. American Express, tel: (02) 236-0276 or (02) 273-0044 for lost or stolen cards.

Directory Enquiries Dial 13 for Bangkok numbers and 183 for the rest of the country.

E-mail and Internet Shops and cafés offering e-mail and Internet access are found in all the main visitor areas of the city. The cheapest rates are around Khao San Rd.

Emergencies The tourist police, who speak English, can be reached on 1151 or 1699. The emergency services phone lines are in Thai. Police, tel: 191 or 123; ambulance, tel: (02) 252-2171; fire, tel: 199.

Embassies and Consulates

Australia, tel: (02) 287-2680 Canada, tel: (02) 237-4125 Cambodia, tel: (02) 254-6630

France, tel: (02) 266-8250 Germany, tel: (02) 213-2231 Ireland, tel: (02) 233-0876

Laos, tel: (02) 539-6667 Malaysia, tel: (02) 254-1700 Nepal, tel: (02) 391-7240

Singapore, tel: (02) 286-2111 UK, tel: (02) 253-0191 USA, tel: (02) 205-4000

Exchange Cash and traveller cheques can be changed any time of day or night at the airport or in five-star hotels. Exchange booths stay open until around 2000 in tourist areas like Sukhumvit Rd, Silom Rd and Khao San Rd.

Hospitals There are lots of excellent hospitals in Bangkok, as well as countless clinics that can deal with minor ailments. The top hotels as well as the European embassies can provide details of English-speaking doctors. Some of the more centrally located hospitals include the Bangkok Adventist Hospital, 430 Phitsanulok Rd, tel: (02) 281-1422, and the Bangkok Christian Hospital, 124 Silom Rd, tel: (02) 233-6981.

Immigration Office Visa extensions are available from the immigration office on Soi Suan Phlu off Sathon Thai Rd, tel: (02) 287-1774,

(02) 287-3101 or (02) 286-7880. Open Mon–Fri 0830–1630. Bring two photos and a photocopy of your passport details.

POSTAL SERVICES The GPO, 1160 Charoen Krung Rd, (River Express: Wat Muang Kae), has a poste restante and a packaging service.

TELEPHONES A good place to find plenty of phones for international calls, and an extensive Home Direct service (for reverse charge calls), is in the grounds of the GPO, 1160 Charoen Krung Rd (River Express: Wat Muang Kae).

BANGKOK'S MAIN AREAS

CITY MAPS inside back coverr

These are the main areas of Bangkok that are used in this guide to structure the accommodation, eating and shopping sections. If staying in the city for more than a couple of days, you should end up with a nodding acquaintance with most of them.

WORLD TRADE CENTER AREA This area is formed by the junction of Phloenchit Rd and Ratchadamri Rd. Dominated by the giant block of the World Trade Center building, it is a few minutes on foot from the Skytrain Chit Lom station. There are lots of restaurants here, including an excellent food centre, and plenty of shops. Many buses stop outside the World Trade Center, including No 73 from the train station. Close to all this traffic mayhem is a serene little Thai temple. One of Bangkok's better five-star hotels, the Grand Hyatt, is located right next to the temple.

SIAM SQUARE AREA Only a short distance west of the World Trade Center the futuristic Siam Square is all concrete and glass, aglow with shopping and entertainment centres and popular with impressionable Bangkok teenagers. Skytrain has a station here and most of the time you find yourself walking under its concrete structure. From a shopping point of view, the Skytrain station further west (Skytrain: National Stadium) is more useful because it has a walkway to the MBK shopping centre.

SILOM RD AREA Silom Rd in the south-west of the city runs from close to the Chao Phraya River (Skytrain: Saphan Taksin and Surasak; River Express: Sathorn) up to Rama IV Rd (Skytrain: Sala Daeng) near to the infamous but very touristy Patpong area. Silom Rd has its fair share of hotels and restaurants but it is primarily a commercial and financial area with lots of banks and airline offices. Half way up Silom Rd (Skytrain: Chong Nonsi) is a Thai Airways office. The Silom Rd area also covers the stretch of Charoen Krung Rd near the river where the famed Oriental Hotel rubs shoulders with good-value budget Muslim restaurants.

SUKHUMVIT RD AREA Sukhumvit Rd is a major road running eastwards from the city centre and heading out of town towards Pattaya. The tourist area, full of mid-to-top-range hotels and restaurants, is the stretch between the skytrain stations Nana and Phrom Phong.

KHAO SAN RD AREA The area is Banglamphu, synonymous with cheap accommodation and its defining thoroughfare, Khao San Rd. Many budget travellers never leave the place, partly because many of the city's outstanding attractions are all within walking distance.

GETTING AROUND

The horror stories you may have heard about Bangkok's traffic congestion say more about the past than the present. It can still be a nightmare trying to get somewhere in a hurry, and when a road floods or something snarls up the traffic flow the consequences can be dire. With a degree of planning, however, and the use of buses, boats and skytrains it is possible to get around the sprawling mass of the city in reasonable time.

BUS It would take a lifetime to fathom all the bus routes that weave their way through the city but it certainly makes sense to master a few key routes relevant to the area you are staying in. The same bus number on the same route can be a comfortable air-conditioned vehicle or a sweaty, bumpy non-air-con version. Buses are often crowded so you need to have some idea of where to get off. Bus maps of the city are readily available in hotel shops, bookshops and along Khao San Rd, but try to check the route with your hotel first. Here is a list of some of the more useful routes around town.

SKYTRAIN

Bangkok's new overhead light railway system, the Skytrain, may not add anything to the capital's aesthetic appeal but it has made a tremendous improvement to the task of getting around the city. It does not cover all of Bangkok but where it does run it offers an inexpensive, clean and reliable alternative to buses and taxis.

There are two lines; one runs from Mo Chit in the north to the east of the city along Sukhumvit Rd. The other runs from the National Stadium to the river at the bottom end of Silom Rd at Saphan Taskin. The lines interconnect at Siam station and operate 0600–2400.

Mounted on huge concrete pillars, the Skytrain threads its way above the crowded roads carrrying passengers in air-conditioned comfort.

No 7: Connects the Southern Bus Terminal with Sukhumvit Rd, via Sanam Luang (for Khao San Rd) and Hualamphong railway station.

No 11: Connects the Eastern Bus Terminal with the Southern Bus Terminal, via Sukhumvit Rd, Democracy Document, and Rajdamnoen Klang (for Khao San Rd).

No 73: Useful connection between the World Trade Centre, Siam Square and the railway station.

No 75: Travels between the railway station and Charoen Krung Rd (for Silom Rd).

BOAT The Chao Phraya Express Boat is a very useful boat service that runs up and down the river daily 0600–1840, tel: (02) 623-6342. It isn't fast, but it is reliable and makes a welcome change from road transport. The standard boat doesn't carry a flag which means it will stop at any pier on the route. Between 0600 and 0900, and 1200 and 1900, there are special boats with either a yellow, a red and orange, or a green flag. These boats only stop at the main piers and certain stops indicated by the colour of the flag. A leaflet explaining the colour codes is available from any pier, but the following list indicates some of the more useful stops:

Pra Athit: This is the closest pier to Khao San Rd and the budget accommodation area. It is also useful for the restaurants along Tha Pra Athit, the National Museum and the National Theatre. Standard boat only.

Railway Station: Not the main Hualamphong railway station but Thonburi (Bangkok Noi) station, on the west side of the river, from where trains to Kanchanaburi depart. Standard boat only.

Tha Chang: A short walk from this pier to the Grand Palace. Standard, green and red and orange flag boats.

Tha Thien: For Wat Po. Standard boat only.

Rachavongse: The stop for Chinatown. All boats.

Wat Muang Kae: The stop for the General Post Office. Standard boat only.

Oriental: For Silom Rd and Oriental Hotel. Standard and green flag boat.

Sathorn: The Saphan Taksin skytrain station is next to this stop, and the Shangri La Hotel.

TAXI Metered, air-conditioned taxis can be flagged down anywhere and there are plenty of them. With fares starting at 35B they are generally a very affordable way of getting around, athough there is a surcharge for traffic congestion of around 70B for a 10 km journey. Avoid unlicensed cabs which don't use a meter. Taxis can be booked for an extra 20B, tel: (02) 435-0090, (02) 880-0888.

Motorcycle taxis are used mostly by locals for short journeys. Helmets are usually provided. Agree on a price beforehand.

Taxi fares

For the first 2 km	35B
2–12 km	4.50B per km
13–20 km	5B per km
21 km plus	5.50B per km

When the taxi moves no faster than 6 km per hour, 1.25B is added per minute.

Tuk-Tuk

The quintessentially Thai form of transport in Bangkok is the *tuk-tuk*, a three-wheeled buggy with open sides that weaves its kamikaze way through the traffic. They are incredibly nippy and can beat the jams that hold up taxis and buses. Most of the drivers don't speak much English so you need an obvious destination or a map, and the fare has to be settled beforehand. The usual rate for a short hop, say from the World Trade Center to Pantip Plaza, is around 40B.

Car

Renting a car for city travel is not advisable. The pace is hectic, traffic etiquette non-existent and the complexity of roads and junctions is mind-boggling, never mind the problem of finding somewhere to park.

Airlines

Air France Charn Issara Tower, Rama IV Rd; tel: (02) 233-9477

Bangkok Airways Ratchadaphisek Tat Mai Rd; tel: (02) 229-3434

British Airways Abdulrahim Place, 990 Rama IV Rd; tel: (02) 236-0038

Canadian Airlines Maneeya Centre, 518 Ploenchit Rd; tel: (02) 251-4521

Cathay Pacific Ploenchit Tower, 898 Ploenchit Rd; tel: (02) 263-0606

Eva Airways Green Tower, Rama IV Rd; tel: (02) 240-0890

Garuda Lumphini Tower, 1168 Rama IV Rd; tel: (02) 285-6470

KLM Thai Wah Tower 2, 21/133 Sathorn Rd; tel: (02) 679-1100

Lufthansa Soi 21, Sukhumvit Rd; tel: (02) 264-2400

Malaysia Airlines Ploenchit Tower, Ploenchit Rd; tel: (02) 263-0565

Northwest Peninsula Plaza, Ratchadarmi Rd; tel: (02) 254-0789

Qantas Charn Issara Tower, Rama IV Rd; tel: (02) 267-5188

Singapore Airlines Silom Centre 2 Silom Rd; tel: (02) 236-0440

Thai International 485 Silom Rd; tel: (02) 288-0060. Lan Luang Road, tel: (02) 215-2020

United Airlines Regent House, Ratchadarmi Rd; tel: (02) 253-0558

Vietnam Airlines Ploenchit Centre, Ploenchit Road; tel: (02) 251-4242

HIGHLIGHTS

You could book a place on a city tour but it really is not difficult to visit most of the city's highlights on your own. You will save money and, by going at your own pace, avoid the *wat* syndrome – when exhausted tourists exclaim 'Not another *Wat*! *Wat* for?' Three of the major sites – the **Grand Palace**, **Wat Po** and the **National Museum** – can be taken in on one day by making an early start to Wat Po, walking north to the Grand Palace and finishing off at the National Museum.

The Grand Palace is not to be missed. Despite the crowds and queues it's unlikely you won't be bowled over by the shimmering play of light on the golden structures and its sheer magnificence. The sprawling complex started life in 1782 and now occupies over 60 acres of land. Guided tours at regular intervals help make sense of the various royal buildings – the king and his family reside elsewhere and only turn up for special occasions. Some visitors prefer just to wander around, goggle-eyed at the psychedelic surfeit of golden orange, mosaic-rich walls and pillars, shining spires, intricate murals, and the astonishingly pristine mix of the garish and the grand.

The chief attraction within the Palace is **Wat Phra Kaeo**, the Temple of the Emerald Buddha, the first temple constructed within the Grand Palace. Another notable structure that can be located using the free map is **Chakri-Mahaprasad Hall**. Visitors cannot enter the hall, which functioned as the royal harem, but the exterior is a fairly unique combination of European and Thai styles. Rama V commissioned an English architect in the 1880s who thought of bringing the Renaissance to Siam and got as far as the roof, which would have been a Western-style dome, when he was prevailed upon to add traditional Thai spires instead.

Another highlight, marked on the map, is the airy **Amarindra Vinichai Hall**. This was the main audience hall and court of justice where people petitioned the king. Today its gilded interior is reserved for important ceremonial occasions involving the king.

The **Grand Palace $$$** Naphralan Rd, is open daily 0830–1530. Admission includes a brochure with indigestible text but a handy map. Wearing shorts, sarongs, flip-flops and other casual or revealing clothes is not allowed. Bus No 8 from Siam Square (Skytrain: Siam) is an easy way to reach the Grand Palace, or arrive by water (Express Boat: Ta Chang). There are English language tours at 1000, 1030, 1100, 1300, 1330 and 1400.

The royal palace's website is at: www.palaces.thai.net. A good book on the palace, which has lots of illustrations, is *The Grand Palace Bangkok* by Naengnoi Suksri (Thames and Hudson).

Wat Po is most famous for its colossal **Reclining Buddha**, but it is also home to a noted massage school, tel: (02) 221-2974, (02) 225-4771, as well as novice and experienced monks who are often found strolling in the grounds away from the star attraction. The gold-leafed 46-metre-long Buddha may be all brick and plaster inside, but its serene smile registers the mystical journey into the state of nirvana. The statue's feet are inlaid with mother-of-pearl, depicting 108 auspicious marks that belong to the true Buddha.

Wat Po **$** Maha Rat Rd, is open daily 0800–1700, tel: (02) 222-0933 (River Express: Tha Thien). From the pier, turn right onto Mahathat Rd and left into Soi Chetuphon. From the main entrance/exit of the Grand Palace, turn left on Nha Phra Lan Rd, then left onto Mahathat Rd and Soi Chetuphon. It takes about 15 minutes to walk from the Grand Palace.

WAT PHRA KAEO

The temple is home to the diminutive **Emerald Buddha**, a mere 60 centimetres in length but looming large in the Thai cultural consciousness. It came to life, so to speak, in the 15th century when a bolt of lightning split open an ancient *stupa* in northern Thailand and the figure rolled out. Said to have been cut from a single block of jade, it rapidly acquired a reputation as an auspicious image but was taken as booty to Laos, where it remained for two centuries.

The capture of Vientiene towards the end of the 18th century saw its return to Thailand and Rama I duly placed it in his palace as a symbol of national pride. The king had two royal robes especially made to clothe the image and a third costume was commissioned by Rama III. Even today only the king is allowed to change the costume. It has become the most important Buddha emblem in the country.

Surrounding Wat Phra Kaeo, in the welcome shade of its cloisters, are 178 murals depicting the story of the ancient Hindu epic, the *Ramayana*. Go to the north wall for the first panel at the central gate and proceed in a clockwise direction from here.

The **National Museum** is the largest museum in south-east Asia, and like all large museums there is too much to take in on a single visit. One approach is to arrive on a Wednesday or Thursday morning before 0930 and join the free English language tours. They focus on a selection of the more interesting exhibits and serve as a useful introduction to varied aspects of Thai culture and religion.

Without a tour, you have to choose between a vast collection of sculptures and artefacts from all periods of Thai history, and the overall impact can be bewildering. It

THE HELPFUL TOUT: PART TWO

Around the premier sights like the Grand Palace, Wat Po and Jim Thomson's House you may find yourself on the receiving end of a well-rehearsed script from a tout. Smartly dressed and well mannered, he will persuasively inform you that the place you are about to visit is closed on that particular day. Stop him there, smile and walk away before you find yourself being convinced by his alternative suggestions, which will invariably end up in a shop.

may be worth selecting just a few of the galleries. The main collection follows a chronological approach, starting on the ground floor where there is a rare example of an early Buddha figure from India. It was found at Gandhara, one of the most easterly outposts founded by Alexander the Great, and clearly reveals the influence of ancient Greek artistic forms.

The museum compound also houses the **Buddhaisawan Chapel**, built in the late 18th century to house the **Phra Sihing Buddha**. This highly venerated statue, like the Emerald Buddha in Wat Phra Kaeo, has a legendary history that begins with its miraculous creation in Ceylon. Experts, however, tend to regard it as a classic northern Thai figure. The chapel is also home to a set of well-preserved murals, depicting scenes from the Buddha's life, that date back to the 1790s.

The **National Museum $$**, Na Phra Thad Rd, is open Wed–Sun 0900–1600, tel: (02) 224-1396. Admission includes a very basic sketch of the various galleries.

Jim Thompson's House is actually a group of six traditional Thai teak houses built for the American expatriate Jim Thompson. Their sloping walls channel away hot air and there is an enchanting garden. He furnished them with an eclectic collection of rare antiques and fine examples of craftsmanship from around south-east Asia. Thompson came to Thailand during World War II as an officer in the Organization of Strategic Services, a precursor to the CIA.

He became so earnestly involved in the promotion of Thai silk that he is credited with having resuscitated the industry. During the 1950s he milked his expatriate image to such an extent that famous people coming to the city could feel slighted if dinner with Jim Thompson could not be arranged.

MONUMENT TO DEMOCRACY

Democracy Monument is a landmark statue along Rajdamnern Klang Rd, close to Khao San Rd, that was completed in 1940. It commemorates the establishment of Thailand's constitutional, as opposed to autocratic, monarchy and as such became the focal point of pro-democracy demonstrations in 1992. The protests were bluntly suppressed by the army and many Thais died in the vicinity of this monument.

The address is 6, Soi Kasemsan 2, Rama 1 Rd, tel: (02) 215-0122, open Mon–Sat 0900-1630. Admission **$$$** includes a compulsory guided tour but you can wander around the grounds at will. Take a skytrain or bus to Siam Square and walk westwards along Rama 1 before turning right into Soi Kasemsan 2.

A Chinatown Walk

Bangkok's Chinatown is squeezed in between the river and Charoen Krung Rd, with Hualamphong railway station to the east and the small Indian enclave of Phahurat to the west. This walk through Chinatown is not a shopping trip. It is a fascinating look at Bangkok street life and the perfect antidote to flashy Siam Square.

A good way to reach Chinatown is by the River Express to Rachavongse, from where you can walk up **Ratchawong Rd** to the junction with **Sampeng Lane** (Soi Wanit 1). This main commercial artery is one long rambling outdoor market, selling a vast range of everyday goods from silk pyjamas and other clothes to electronic toys and spices.

Turn right at this junction and wander along the congested Sampeng Lane to **Mangkon Rd**. This junction is fronted by old commercial buildings that date back to the end of the 19th century and are well worth a closer look, both inside and out. Continue walking along Sampeng Rd until you reach **Soi Issaranuphap** (Soi 16) and take a left turn here up this narrow lane. On the right you will pass the entrance to a wet fish market before reaching a crossroads with the main Yaowarat Rd and its countless gold and jewellery shops.

Whatever Happened to Jim Thompson?

Thompson was acquainted with some of the liberal Thai politicos of the 1960s which became grist to the rumour mill when he dramatically disappeared on Easter Sunday in 1967. He was in the Cameron Highlands in Malaysia (see page 283) when he went out for a walk and was never seen again. Extensive searches never found his body. Was he murdered for his political sympathies? Was he still working for American intelligence? Was he eaten by a tiger? Conspiracy theories were never in short supply and an amateur detective recently unearthed fresh evidence suggesting that he was run down in a traffic accident and the frightened driver buried his body.

Continue walking up Soi Issaranuphap to the main junction with Charoen Krung Rd and turn left for the entrance to **Wat Mangkon Kamalawat**. If you associate Buddhism with other-worldly mysticism and abstract meditation, then a visit here will be educational. This is one of the city's busiest temples, with people dropping in whenever they can snatch an hour from work.

You may be exhausted by now, in which case the best way out is to catch a taxi. Alternatively, retrace your steps to the pier. If you're up for more, then continue walking along Charoen Krung Road for nearly half a kilometre to Chakrawat and **Nakhon Kasem (Thieves' Market)**. This labyrinthine bazaar comes into its own after dusk and while it no longer stocks the illicit goods that gave rise to its name, it is always busy with evening shoppers.

Lumpini Park, the largest park in downtown Bangkok, is at the end of Silom Rd, across the road from Robinson's department store (Skytrain: Sala Daeng). An early morning (before 0900) visit to the park – named after the Buddha's birthplace in Nepal – is recommended for a peek at Chinese residents performing t'ai chi in balletic slow motion.

Later in the day, Chinese men play chess and families have fun with the rowing boats on the lake. Look out too for the vendors who slice up snakes for their supposedly medicinal blood and bile. Tables for picnics and an inexpensive restaurant make it a good place to relax after an exhausting session in the Silom Rd shops.

Snake Farm $$$ A visit here sounds more worthy if you refer to it by its proper title, the Queen Saovabha Memorial Institute run by the Thai Red Cross. Corner of Rama 1V Rd and Henry Dunant Rd, tel: (02) 252-0161 (Skytrain: Sala Daeng). Be sure to arrive before 1030 or 1400 (1030 only at weekends) to catch the half-hour slide show that precedes the live demonstration. Trained handlers show how to extract deadly poison from some of the world's most venomous snakes, with disarming ease. This is not just a circus act because the institute collects the poison to make snake bite antidotes. If you want to handle a snake yourself there is an opportunity at the end of the show.

The **Erawan Shrine** to the four-faced Brahma god, Than Tao Mahaprom, has a remarkable setting on the busy corner of Ploenchit Rd and Rajdamri Rd (Skytrain: Chit Lom), diagonally across from the World Trade Center. During the 1950s the government chose to build a hotel on this site but there were so many problems that a shrine was built to appease the spirits.

From morning to night Thais turn up to make ceremonial offerings of floral garlands and fruit, and an air of calmness manages to rise above the surrounding urban cacophony. Shrines to hedonism are all around in the form of five-star hotels and designer-label shops and there is a constant roar of traffic, yet in the midst of this worshippers carry out their rituals oblivious to all, even intrusive tourists with camcorders.

ACCOMMODATION

One reason why more and more travellers are coming to Bangkok is the availability of rooms to suit all budgets. The prices here reflect official rack rates which in the case of budget and mid-range guesthouses and hotels remain fairly constant. In the case of four- and five-star hotels it is usually possible to get discounted rates through an agent, either in your own country or in Bangkok, such as Thai Travel Trade, 557, Silom Rd; tel: (02) 635-0533, fax: (02) 234-0563, e-mail: thaitr@samart.co.th.

WORLD TRADE CENTER AND SIAM SQUARE AREA	**Grand Hyatt Erawan $$$$$** 494 Rajdamri Rd; tel: (02) 254-1234, website: www.bangkok.hyatt.com. A quirky elephant theme in each of the 400 rooms, great fitness facilities and a rooftop pool.
	White Lodge $$ 36/8 Soi Kasem San 1, tel: (02) 216-8867. Clean, basic and friendly with a good café.
	A-One Inn $$ 25/13 Soi Kasem San 1: tel: (02) 215-3029. Around for some time but standards are maintained.
	If these two mid-range places are full there are plenty of viable alternatives in the neighbourhood.
SILOM RD AREA	**Shangri-La $$$$$** 89 Soi Wat Suan Plu; tel: (02) 236-7777. Remains one of the city's classier hotels. Marble lobby and views of the river in some of the rooms.
	Holiday Inn Crowne Plaza $$$$$ 981 Silom Rd; tel: (02) 238-4300, e-mail: admin@hicp-bkk.com, website: www.hicp-bkk.com. Popular hotel at the top of the Holiday Inn chain, offering all the creature comforts.
	Silom Village Inn $$$ 286 Silom Rd; tel: (02) 635-6810, e-mail: silom-village-inn@thai.com. Not in the quietest corner of town but discounted rates make it good value. Clean, comfortable rooms.
	Niagara Hotel $$ 26 Soi 9 (Suksavithaya); tel: (02) 233-5783. One of the few budget places in this area. Long bleak corridors and basic rooms, but clean and with air-con.
SUKHUMVIT RD	**JW Marriott Hotel $$$$$** 4 Sukhumvit Rd; tel: (02) 656-7700, e-mail: jwmarri1@ksc.th.com. One of the better top end hotels in this part of town. Over 400 rooms, each with three telephones, and seven restaurants.
	The Landmark $$$$$ 138 Sukhumvit Rd; tel: (02) 254-0404, website: www.landmarkbangkok.com. Smart business hotel with lots of restaurants, pampering and Thai cooking classes.

Atlanta $$ 78 Soi 2, Sukhumvit Rd; tel: (02) 252-1650. Hard to beat in terms of location and value. Old-style hotel with excellent restaurant and impecunious but sophisticated atmosphere. Rooms to suit different budgets, and evening videos.

Miami Hotel $$ 2 Soi 13, Sukhumvit Rd; tel: (02) 253-5611.Decent rooms, a pool and a café.

THE ORIENTAL

$$$$$ 48 Oriental Ave; tel: (02) 236-0400, e-mail: reserve-orbkk@mohg.co.com, website: www.mandarin-oriental.com (Skytrain: Saphan Taskin River Express Oriental).

Because it is hidden away down a traffic-clogged road, The Oriental's history is more apparent when viewed from the river. Even if you are not a guest, a visit to the place where writers such as Joseph Conrad, Somerset Maughan, Graham Greene and Noel Coward once stayed is a 'must see' for many visitors to Bangkok. Established in 1876, the hotel soon became *the* place for European travellers to reside and to be seen, and its reputation remains undiminished. The original Italianate building survives as the Authors' Residence, with a new wing added in the 1950s and another nearly 20 years later.

It's not quite true that shorts or sleeveless shirts are not allowed in the lobby but in the evening a dress code is an expected part of the ritual here. The lobby is unspectacular but the small lounge area in the Authors' Residence helps create a sense that if Thailand had ever been colonised The Oriental would have adapted to its role with consummate ease.

Joseph Conrad, a young marine officer in 1877, would not have been able to afford the room rates today. They start at US$250 and climb to an astronomical US$2200 for one of the four authors' suites. There are cultural programmes and a Thai cooking school which is open to non-residents for the resident rate of US$120.

KHAO SAN RD AREA

This is the famed territory of the Bangkok backpacker and features in the opening scene of *The Beach*, when Leonardo DiCaprio's character arrives in the city looking for somewhere to stay.

Nana Plaza Inn $$$ off 202 Khao San Rd; tel: (02) 281-6402. A pleasant enough place and its air-conditioned rooms are at the bottom end of the $$$ range. There are lockers, e-mail and Internet access and a pool table.

Khaosan Palace Hotel $$ 139 Khao San Rd; tel: (02) 282-0578. Rooms come in all sizes, with air-con or fan, and although basic they are fine for the rates charged. No pre-bookings are taken.

Running parallel with Khao San Road to the south is Trok Mayom, a narrow lane with some decent guesthouses that enjoy a relatively quiet and relaxing atmosphere. **The Hodder Guest House $** Spartan but clean rooms, some with their own shower. For half the room rate you can stay until 1800. No telephone bookings.

Swasadee Guest House $$–$ in the same road has singles, doubles and dorm beds, with and without air-conditioning.

Sugar Guest House $ Trok Mayom at the top end of Khao San Rd, close by the Gaylord restaurant; tel: (02) 282-8396. A typical example of the rock-bottom accommodation available in this area. Rooms with fan and shared showers. International phone calls can be made here for the lowest price in Bangkok.

DRINKS BY THE POOL ON A SHOESTRING

The guesthouses in Banglamphu don't have swimming pools but there is a small one behind the Buddy Beer Garden, on the right very shortly after entering Khao San Rd from the Democracy Monument end. Open 0900–2100 the pool is not for serious swimming but it's fine for a cool splash, or for children. There is an inexpensive bar, and a white parrot keeps an eye on the scene.

FOOD

Finding a place to eat is never a problem in Bangkok. The quality of the food is astonishingly good, usually regardless of price. There is also a huge variety of cuisines. In many food centres you can enjoy a tasty lunch dish for under 50B and most of the real quality restaurants are remarkably affordable. The skytrain has made many more eating places accessible, and where a restaurant is within easy walking distance of a station this information is given in the entry.

WORLD TRADE CENTER AREA

Thai On 4 $$$$ Amari Watergate Hotel, 847 Petchburi Rd, tel: (02) 653-9000. Speciality dishes from all parts of Thailand. Sleek, non-traditional setting with modern art and suave sevice gives it a post-modernist feel.

FOOD COUPONS

Some of the best food centres in Bangkok use a coupon system and no cash is exchanged. Buy coupons from the counter, in various denominations, to pay for food and drink from any of the stalls. Any coupons left over can be exchanged back for cash, although only on the same day of purchase.

Felice $$$$ The Arnoma Hotel, 99 Rajdamri Rd; tel: (02) 255-3410. Comfortable enclave offering pizzas, other mainstream European dishes and a fair wine list. Across the road, on the 6th floor of the World Trade Center, **Vegeta** $$$ tel: (02) 255-9569, has vegetarian salads, noodles and curries.

On the street opposite the World Trade Centre, look for a signpost for the **NP Food Centre** $$–$ pointing down a lane that leads to a car park. An excellent place for a quick salad or noodle dish while in the throes of shopping. A coupon system operates and most of the stalls have English menus. The coffee counter is first-rate.

DINING BY THE CHAO PHRAYA RIVER

Salathip $$$$ Shangri-La Hotel, Soi Wat Suan, Charoen Krung Rd; tel: (02) 236-7777 (Skytrain: Saphan Taksin, River Express: Sathorn). Reserve an outdoor table for riverside views, Thai classical dancers hopping about 1945–2100 except Mon, and delicate Thai food.

Yor Yor Marina Restaurant $$$ offers a better value dinner cruise than the Shangri-La. 885 Somdejchaophraya 17 Rd; tel: (02) 863-0565 (River Express: Visutkrasat). 2030–2230. Average food but a great way to enjoy flood-lit views of the Grand Palace.

Supatra River House $$$$ 226 Soi Wat Rakhang, Arunamarin Rd; tel: (02) 411-0305 (River Express: Wang Lang). Old Thai residence opposite the Grand Palace, with indoor and outdoor tables and cultural dance evenings on Friday and Saturday nights.

SIAM SQUARE AREA

Siam Square's reputation for yuppie (or tuppie for the home-grown Thai version) materialism means it's no surprise to find it chock-a-block with American fast food joints. More interesting possibilities include Vietnamese food at **Pho Restaurant $$$–$$** tel: (02) 251-8900, 2nd floor, AlmaLink Building, 25 Soi Chidlom (Skytrain: Siam).

Sarah-Jane's $$$–$$ Sindhorn Building, 130 Witthayu Rd; tel: (02) 650-9992 (Skytrain: Phloen Chit). Two stops east on the skytrain from Siam Square and worth the trip for fiery Issan cuisine from the north-east of Thailand.

MBK Food Centre $$–$ Ground floor, MBK building (Skytrain: National Stadium). All Thai food, cooked in front of you. For Western-style food there are plenty of outlets in MBK and there is another food centre on the 7th floor.

PUB FOOD

Bizarrely, British-style pub restaurants are all the rage in Bangkok. **Bobby's Arms $$$$** Carpark Building, Patpong 11; tel: (02) 233-6828 (Skytrain: Sala Daeng). Roast beef and Yorkshire pudding, meat pies, fish and chips, and a set lunch are all on the menu.

Not far away, **Delaney's $$$$** Sivadon Building, 1–5 Convent Rd, tel: (02) 266-7161 (Skytrain: Sala Daeng), offers competing fare from Ireland. The oak beams may be plastic but the beef and Guinness pies are for real, as are the Guinness and Kilkenny on draught.

Another Irish pub just up the main road is **O'Reilly's $$$$** 62 Silom Rd; tel: (02) 632-7515 (Skytrain: Sala Daeng). Shrimp cocktail followed by Irish stew or cod and chips are firm favourites here. Both these pubs often have live music in the evenings.

SILOM RD AREA

There is a wealth of value-for-money places to eat which cater for the many middle-class Thai office workers in the area. Around Charoen Krung Rd there are clusters of inexpensive Indian and Pakistani restaurants. Also in this part of town are farang-frequented pub-restaurants that serve reasonable grub from mid-morning until the early hours (see above).

These pubs are at the Patpong end of Silom Road where you will also find **Trattoria Da Roberta $$$** Plaza Arcade, Patpong 2; tel: (02) 233-6851 (Skytrain: Sala Daeng). No surprises here but reliable staples like fresh pizza, *pollo alla cacciatoria* and *spaghetti alla Bolognese*.

Towards the bottom end of Silom Rd (Skytrain: Surasak), opposite the Holiday Inn Crowne Plaza, **Char Kari $$$** tel: (02) 234-9663. A pleasant little Thai restaurant for lunch or dinner with a large menu.

Across the road, next to the Holiday Inn, **Mario Restaurant $$** 913 Silom Rd; tel: (02) 234-0440, serves only organic food and drinks.

Silom Village Food Centre $$$, a few hundred metres up Silom Rd, has a brightly lit array of restaurants offering seafood and international dishes.

On the other side of Silom Rd, look for a blue signpost to 13 (trok number) almost opposite the Narai Hotel. Down this small street lurks the spartan but good **Madras Café $** 31/10-11 Trok Vaithi, tel: (02) 233-2128, serving tasty curries, *masala dosai* and *roti*.

For the real centre of Indian food just walk to the bottom of Silom Rd (Skytrain: Surasak) and turn right into Charoen Krung Rd to the **Muslim Restaurant $** at No 1356.

On the other side of the road, pass the few fading antique shops. The alley on the right with a signpost for the Centaur Inn is home to the **Indian Biryani Restaurant $$–$**. Tasty vegetarian and non-vegetarian Muslim food is served at its small four tables. Next door, the similar **Madina Restaurant $$** is a little plusher.

ALL-YOU-CAN-EAT BUFFETS

All-you-can-eat buffets are usually offered by the top hotels. Assuming you have a healthy appetite they can provide great value for money. Check the *Bangkok Post* for details and prices of buffets featuring special promotions.

Teio $$$-$$ Monarch Lee Gardens Hotel, 188 Silom Rd, tel: (02) 238-1991 (Skytrain: Chong Nonsi). A traditional Japanese restaurant with a lunch buffet that doesn't skimp on the raw fish, or the green-tea ice cream. At weekends and on Friday nights the buffet is more expensive, but still worth considering, as is the lunch buffet at the **Ti Jing $$** Chinese restaurant on the 38th floor of the same hotel.

The Dining Room, lunch **$$$$**, dinner **$$$$$**. Grand Hyatt Erawan, 494 Rajdamri Rd, tel: (02) 254-1234 (Skytrain: Chit Lom), delivers a feast of international, seafood, Thai, Asian, and Japanese food for gourmands.

SUKHUMVIT RD AREA

You can hardly walk 100 metres along this road and its adjoining sois without finding a pleasant restaurant of one kind or another. Starting from the top of Sukhumvit Rd near the JW Marriott Hotel and heading eastwards, turn down Soi 3 (Nana Nua) for a couple of middle-of-the-road Indian and Pakistani restaurants: **MehMaan $$$** 69 Soi 3, tel: (02) 253-4689, and **Akbar $$$** Soi 3, tel: (02) 650-3347 (Skytrain: Nana). Other good Indian places can be found up and down Soi 11.

If you want to splash out, consider Vietnamese food at the elegant **Le Dalat Indochine $$$$** 14 Soi 23, Sukhumvit Rd, tel: (02) 661-7967 (Skytrain: Asok). Go for cocktails at Le Lotus bar before settling into the plush golden-hued dining room. Across the road, **Le Dalat $$$** 47/1 Soi 23, Sukhumvit Rd, tel: (02) 260-1849, is its less expensive sister restaurant.

What could justly be described as Bangkok's best Indian restaurant is the **Rang Mahal $$$$$** Rembrandt Hotel, Soi 18, Sukhumvit Rd, tel: (02) 261-7100 (Skytrain: Asok).

Reservations are recommended. Ask for a table by the window or at least take your cocktails on the outdoor terrace. Ecstatic live Indian music every night except Monday, buffet brunch on Sunday, and always lots of superbly subtle dishes like the black lentils, *hara kebab* (spinach, cottage cheese, herbs) and chicken tikka.

La Havana $$$ Soi 22, Sukhumvit Rd, tel: (02) 204-1166 (Skytrain: Phrom Phong), uses Thai ingredients to conjure up a variety of Cuban dishes. Tortilla, fried banana or plantain chips, cooling *gazpacho* soup, *chuletas* (pork chops) and *yucca frita* are served until 0200. A salsa dance club is about to open on the floor above.

The Whole Earth Restaurant $$$ 71 Soi 26, Sukhumvit Rd, tel: (02) 258-4900 (Skytrain: Phrom Phong) is great for vegetarians and non-vegetarians alike.

KHAO SAN RD AREA

Not only the prime area for budget accommodation, this area also has some very affordable places to eat. Most of the guest-houses have cafés serving much the same kind of food, and when you tire of these, there are lots of good, unpretentious restaurants.

For Indian and Pakistani food, try the **Gay Lord Restaurant $$** 71 Chakrapong Rd, tel: (02) 281-6302 at the top end of Khao San Road, where it forms a T-junction with Chakrapong Rd. *Thali* meals and other dishes can be enjoyed in the comfort of air-conditioning and if you're staying in the area, home deliveries are free.

Easy to reach by boat, **Pra Athit Rd** (River Express: Pra Arthit) has a string of continental-style cafés and restaurants that attract young Thais as much as Europeans. Typical is **Hemlock $$$—$$** 53 Pra Athit Rd, where the menu features a host of interesting Thai dishes. For excellent vegetarian fare seek out **May Kaidee $** 117 Tanao Rd at the eastern end of Khao San Road. This tiny outlet, tucked away down a *soi*, serves delicious Thai curries using vegetables and tofu.

HOTEL RESTAURANTS

Bangkok is teeming with top quality five-star hotels, all boasting fine restaurants that compete fiercely to attract domestic and foreign customers. Standards are high but prices are not as frightening as one might think, and some of the restaurants offer tremendous opportunities to experience and enjoy a variety of cuisines with a high degree of comfort and style.

At the **White Elephant** **$$$$$–$$$$** JW Marriott Hotel, 4 Sukhumvit Rd, tel: (02) 656-7700, a serene atmosphere accompanies the authentic Thai cuisine, and with sackfulls of ingredients on display this is a place to learn about the food as well as to enjoy eating it. **Kisso** **$$$$$–$$$$** Grand Pacific, 259 Sukhumvit Rd, tel: (02) 651-1000 has a number of set menus that make Japanese food affordable for two people.

Spasso **$$$$$** Grand Hyatt Erawan, 494 Rajdamri Rd, tel: (02) 254-1234 (Skytrain: Chit Lom), is an Italian restaurant serving buffet lunches and a dinner menu of pasta, pizza, fish and meat dishes. Later in the evening there is a live band and dancing. For a quieter Italian-style meal try the **Hibiscus** **$$$$** on the 31st floor of The Landmark, 138 Sukhumvit Rd, tel: (02) 254-0404, (Skytrain: Nana).

A non-five-star hotel serving top-notch vegetarian food is the art-deco **Atlanta** **$$–$** Atlanta Hotel, 78 Soi 2, Sukhumvit Rd, tel: (02) 252-1650 (Skytrain: Nana).

SHOPPING

Shopping is one of Bangkok's great attractions, but it can be a tiring business and is best staggered over the length of your stay. The size of the city and the diversity of goods on offer are what makes shopping so exhausting. For helpful hints on out-of-the-way shops and obscure markets, it pays to buy a copy of *Nancy Chandler's Map of Bangkok.*

WORLD TRADE CENTER AREA

The advantages of shopping centres are the comfort of air-conditioning and the fixed price policy which operates in many of the stores. The disadvantage is that prices tend to be higher, which is not unrelated to the fact that more expensive shops, like brand name stores and designer boutiques, tend to predominate in many of the shopping centres. A good example is the **World Trade Center** (Skytrain: Chit Lom) itself, where there are eight floors of expensive consumer merchandise and clothing, including a fairly useless Duty Free store that is nothing of the sort. Tower Records have a large outlet on the 7th floor.

A shopping centre that is well worth a visit is **Gaysorn Plaza,** across the road from the World Trade Center (Skytrain: Chit Lom), and its **Thai Craft Museum Shop** on the second and third floors, open 1000–2100. Numerous shops are attractively structured around a series of stalls heavily laden with wood-carvings, silk garments, hand-woven fabrics, ceramics, jewellery and a range of knick-knacks and souvenirs. Prices are not always marked but you can expect a 10–15% discount off the price that is first quoted.

SHOPPING: WHERE TO GO FOR WHAT

Arts and crafts: Gaysorn Plaza (page 75), Central Department Store (below), River City and Oriental Place (page 78)

Music CDs: Tower Records in the World Trade Center (page 75)

Computer hardware and software: Pantip Plaza (page 77)

Jewellery: Department stores like Central on Phloenchit Rd (below), the Emporium Shopping Complex (page 78) and the bottom end of Silom Road (page 78)

Japanese: Tokyu department store in MBK (page 77) and Zen department store in the World Trade Center (page 75)

Silk: Jim Thompson's Thai Silk Company (page 78)

Original designer and brand names clothes: Peninsula Plaza, between the Grand Hyatt and Regent hotels on Rajdamri Rd, the Emporium Shopping Complex (page 78), and Siam Centre and Siam Discovery Centre in Siam Square (page 77)

Atmosphere: Chatuchak Weekend Market (page 77) and Chinatown (page 66)

What's wonderful here is the sheer quality of the merchandise, which far excels most of what is found in the art and craft shops out on the street. **Triphum**, Room 26-29/2 on the second floor of **Gaysorn Plaza**, is an independent shop selling beautiful Thai furniture and home accessories. Prices are reasonable, although for larger items the price of shipping them to Europe or North America can double their cost.

Around the corner from Gaysorn Plaza, on Phloenchit Rd right by the skytrain station (Skytrain: Chit Lom) is the **Central Department Store,** where middle-class Bangkokians shop for clothes and consumer items. It is not huge but there is a fair selection of brassware, bamboo work, clothes and decorative items, all at fixed prices. There is also a handicrafts section on the 6th floor. This is a good place to check out standard prices before considering a purchase elsewhere where some bargaining is necessary.

Endless computer hardware and software, including video CDs and music compilations for PCs, fills every available inch of space at the **Pantip Plaza** on Phetburi Road. Computer hardware and software (usually pirated) is cheaper here than in the UK and US. From outside the World Trade Center (Skytrain: Chit Lom), it is a five minute journey by bus or *tuk-tuk*.

A short walk further up Phetburi Rd, past the Indonesian embassy, leads to newly opened **Hollywood Plaza** which is also dedicated to computer technology. Computer games are less expensive here. Pantip Plaza has a terribly overcrowded food centre but for a more restful repast cross the road to the **First Hotel** where the 24-hr Rendevous Café serves a tasty *pad tai goong sod* (fried noodle and shrimp).

SHOPPING TIP

Department stores, open 1030–2100, are a good place to begin shopping. They offer a comfortable environment, hassle-free staff (unlike Malaysia they don't follow you around as if you're a suspect shoplifter), genuine sales and fixed prices that provide useful benchmarks when shopping in stores where nothing is priced. This is particularly useful when it comes to jewellery because the different prices do reflect genuine differences in quality, something you cannot always take for granted elsewhere.

SIAM SQUARE AREA

While **Siam Centre** is a very modern shopping centre full of designer clothing stores, a far more versatile shopping centre lies within walking distance to the west, or one stop on the skytrain (Skytrain: National Stadium). The huge **MBK Plaza** (Mahboonkrong) is probably the best shopping plaza in Bangkok for shoes, watches, clothes and portable electronic goods, and computer software on the top floor. The ground floor has artists who produce uncannily life-like portraits.

CHATUCHAK WEEKEND MARKET

It used to be a long bus ride out to the Chatuchak market but now the skytrain stops right outside (Skytrain: Mo Chit), and no first-time trip to Bangkok is complete without a visit here. Arrive on a Sunday or Saturday morning around 0900 and you will have a good couple of hours before it gets too crowded. There are around eight thousand stalls to wander past, and while some of them sell handicrafts clearly aimed at the tourist the vast majority, like the stalls specialising in second-hand Levis, are aimed squarely at money-conscious Thais.

The stalls are thematically divided into pets, food, plants, clothes, etc., making it easy to lose your bearings. Make a note of some markers – like the central clock tower – when you first enter the fray. Food and drink stalls are dotted around inside, providing essential pit stops.

A neat little shop specialising in traditional fabrics from all corners of Thailand, sold by the metre or ready-to-wear, is the **Prayer Textile Gallery**, 197 Phrayathai Rd; tel: (02) 251-7549 (Skytrain: Siam).

SILOM RD AREA Silom Road is not for general purpose shopping, though for arts, crafts and jewellery there are some very good shops.

Along Charoen Krung Rd (Skytrain: Surasak) there are a few antique shops which never seem busy. **U-Thong Antiques**, on the corner of Silom Rd and Charoen Krung Rd, tel: (02) 234-4767, is stuffed with Buddhas and assorted objets d'art. **Asisra Gallery**, 6 Oriental Ave (River Express: The Oriental), has some beautiful Buddha statues and, while many are too large to fit into a suitcase, shipping can be arranged.

For upmarket art and craft items, paintings and antiques, have a look at **Silom Galleria** next to the Holiday Inn Crowne Plaza hotel on Silom Rd (Skytrain: Surasak). This end of Silom Rd also has a cluster of reputable jewellery shops, like **Rama Jewelery** on the corner of Silom and Mahesak Rd.

For quality arts and crafts consumerism the place to go is **Oriental Place**, Soi 38, Charoen Krung Rd; tel: (02) 266-0186, one block north of the Oriental Hotel. Antiques, carpets, leather, jewellery, silk, paintings, souvenirs and various handicrafts populate this upmarket shopping arcade. A similar establishment is **River City** (River Express: Harbour Department), which is packed with luxury arts and crafts and fabric stores but has few fixed prices.

Surawong Rd runs parallel to Silom Rd, one block to the north and easily reached by walking down any of the interconnecting *sois*. At No 9 **Jim Thompson's Thai Silk Company** is an excellent place to check out Thai fabrics. Silks and cottons are sold by the length or in ready-to-wear garments, and there are little household items for sale that make great souvenirs or presents.

SUKHUMVIT RD AREA Sukhumvit Road is home to a good run-of-the-mill department store, **Robinsons**, next to the Delta Grand Pacific Hotel near Soi 19 (Skytrain: Asok).

Bangkok's most trendy and upmarket mall, **Emporium Shopping Complex** near Soi 24 (Skytrain: Phrom Phong), is also in the area. As well as genuine designer fashion the sleek Emporium mall also has a very good bookshop.

Sukhumvit Rd, especially around Soi 11 (Skytrain: Nana), is the breeding ground for tailors offering apparently amazing deals on made-to-measure garments for men. The more lavish the deal, such as those with half a dozen shirts and various extras thrown in, the more suspicious you should be. Once you have committed yourself to a deal and paid over some money there is not a lot you can do about the final outcome. Insist on at least two fittings, get everything in writing, especially the price, and know exactly what kind of material is being used. It is probably worth paying more at one of the tailors' outlets in a five-star hotel where at least the proprietor wants to avoid complaints.

Tucked away down a *soi* off Sukhumvit Rd is **Rasi Sayam**, 32 Soi 23, tel: (02) 258-4195 (Skytrain: Asok), one of the better independent art and craft shops in the city. Although nothing here is cheap the merchandise is all good quality.

STREET SHOPPING

Sukhumvit Rd (Skytrain: Nana or Asok) is packed with pavement stalls stretching from around *soi* 3 near the Marriott Hotel to around *soi* 30. Best at night, there are the usual clothes, copy watches, belts, dangerous-looking knives and whatever battery-operated gadgets happen to be around at the time.

Patpong (Skytrain: Sala Daeng): The hard-to-miss turning off the top end of Silom Rd has more than just sex shows, and for atmosphere the pavement stalls have more going for them than Sukhumvit Road. The vendors, who have seen tourists of every national character, bear the nightly tumult with dignity, and as long as you bargain hard their prices are competitive. It's all here: clothes, fake watches, CDs, leather goods…

Khao San Rd: The usual mixture of the useful and the useless, including print shops that will produce high quality fake student cards, press cards and even TEFL certificates. The quality of the consumer merchandise is generally poor and there are better places to shop.

ENTERTAINMENT

PATPONG

Everyone, if they don't already know, soon hears about Bangkok's infamous red-light district off the top end of Silom Road, focused around two *sois*, **Patpong 1** and **Patpong 2**. Some of the sex bars are flamboyantly lit in neon but the less brazen ones are hardly difficult to find. Discretion is not the name of the game and passing pedestrians are cajoled by small choruses of skimpily clad girls and their more insistent touts, who brandish sex show menu cards as if they were promoting special offers at a burger joint. The theatricality of the spectacle can be disarming and tourists come here in their droves to be titillated by the illicit performances. But behind – or more literally on the floors above – the standard floor shows, child prostitution is common and AIDS awareness comes tragically too late for many young women.

BARS There are thousands of bars in Bangkok and the trick is to find one that suits your temperament. The big brand-name joints are easy to find but expect to pay up to 150B for a small bottle of local beer in a place like **Planet Hollywood**, Gaysorn Plaza, tel: (02) 656-1358 (Skytrain: Chit Lom), or **Hard Rock Café**, Soi 11, Siam Square; tel: (02) 251-0792 (Skytrain: Siam). In the Amari Watergate Hotel's **Henry J. Bean's Bar and Grill**, 847 Petchburi Rd, tel: (02) 653-9000, live bands perform in a more relaxed atmosphere, and during happy hour you get two drinks for the price of one. The Henry J. Bean outlet at the **Amari Airport Hotel**, tel: (02) 566-1020, has a similar set-up with live music from Thursday to Saturday and a happy hour.

Irish pubs like **Delaney's** and **O'Reilly's** (page 72) have live bands most nights, and **Bobby's Arms** (page 72) has jazz every Sunday night from 2000. They all have happy hours when the cost of a beer becomes more bearable.

The large **Saxophone Pub**, at the top of Phayathai Road near Victory Monument, tel: (02) 246-5472, has a longer history than most popular bars in the city. The music is mostly jazz, R&B, blues and reggae. There is no cover charge. A pool table is on one of the three floors, and beer is more reasonably priced than in any of the other bars mentioned. Another long-standing watering hole that continues to pull in the crowds is **Cheap Charlie's**, Soi 11, Sukhumvit Rd (Skytrain: Nana). The beer really is cheap at 45B, and if you are really lucky there may be an empty seat outside.

SELLING SEX

There are three main haunts for sex tourists of which only Patpong has become a tourist attraction in its own right. The area around *sois* 21 and 23 off Sukhumvit Road is known as Soi Cowboy, described by one tourist publication as offering a more 'authentic environment than Patpong'. The third area is down Soi 4 off the same road, in and around Nana Plaza, a favourite hang-out for expatriate males and not so well known to visitors.

Prostitution is endemic in Thailand, and was so long before the war in Vietnam led to American soldiers' fuelling the sex industry. Many young country girls are sold into prostitution by their poor families and work as little more than sex slaves for their 'owners'.

If you want to observe the rampant sleaze of Soi Cowboy territory then head for the enclave provided by **The Old Dutch**, Soi 23, Sukhumvit Rd (Skytrain: Asik). Dark stained wood gives this pub and restaurant a reassuring air (the *profiteroles* have been recommended), which is just what's needed in this most unsalubrious part of Bangkok.

For some of the best jazz in the city it is still hard to beat **Brown Sugar**, 231/20 Soi Sarasin, tel: (02) 250-1826 (Skytrain: Ratchadamri), on the north side of Lumpini Park. Drinks are expensive but the atmosphere is just right and the music ain't bad. If you prefer rock music, pop around the corner to **Round Midnight,** 106/2 Soi Langsuan.

KHAO SAN RD

This is a good place to meet fellow travellers and feel cool about being in Bangkok. Lots of bars show up-to-date video films from early afternoon onwards. This is also the place to catch a live English premiership soccer game, get your hair plaited and find the cheapest rates for Internet connection. There are a few massage places and reflexology clinics peppered about the place. Trok Mayom, the lane running parallel to the south of Khao San Rd, has some pleasant little cafés, bars and hairdressers along a pedestrianised section of the road.

THAI BOXING

Watching Thai boxing live is a million times more enjoyable than on television, not least because as a real spectator you have the opportunity to be part of the audience. Often the antics of the crowd are much more entertaining than the performance in the ring, and when a lot of money is riding on a bout the temperature rises accordingly.

It is easy to get tickets and there is no need to go through an agent or a tout. Mon, Wed, Thurs and Sun, turn up at the **Ratchadamnoen Stadium ,** Ratchadamnoen North Rd; tel: (02) 281-4205. Bus No 3 from Rajdamnern Klang near Khao San Rd runs past the stadium. On Tues, Fri and Sat evenings the venue is the **Lumphini Stadium**, Rama IV Rd; tel: (02) 280-4550.

The boxing starts around 1800, sometimes an hour earlier, and it is just a matter of turning up and buying a ticket from one of the windows. Tickets start at around 200B and climb to over 800B for front row seats. The less expensive tickets are just as worthwhile in terms of audience participation.

THAI DANCE

Some restaurants, like the Salathip (page 71) and Supatra River House (page 71), feature sessions of Thai dancing as part of the evening's entertainment. The best place to watch traditional Thai dance is the **National Theatre**, Chao Fa Rd, tel: (02) 224-1342 (River Express: Phra Athit), which shows full-length performances as well as more tourist-oriented programmes. Two other theatres worth phoning for their programmes are the **Chalermkrung Royal Theatre**, 66 Charoen Krung Rd, tel: (02) 222-1854, and the **Thailand Cultural Centre**, Ratchadapisek Rd; tel: (02) 231-4257. At the **Erawan Shrine** (page 67) grateful worshippers regularly sponsor short performances of Thai dance with live music.

EXCURSIONS FROM BANGKOK

Good ideas for day trips from Bangkok, with the option of an overnight stay, include a visit to the **Damnoen Saduak floating markets**. This requires an early morning two-hour bus ride from Bangkok (see page 88). Easier to reach, and return from, is the town of **Nathon Pathom** and its famous *chedi* (page 87), connected to Bangkok by bus and train. Nathon Pathom is 60 km north of the floating markets and the two places could be taken in on one excursion with an overnight stay, preferably at Damnoen Saduak.

The most popular day trips from Bangkok are to **Ayutthaya** (page 127) and **Kanchanaburi** and the **Bridge on the River Kwai** (pages 88-89). Both Ayutthaya and Kanchanaburi have inexpensive guesthouses as well as hotels, and an overnight stay is well worth considering, especially if you want a break from high-pressure Bangkok.

WHERE NEXT?

Visit the wats of Phetchaburi (see page 195), 40 km to the south. You could take in Nathon Pathom on the way, stop at the seaside resort of Cha-am and continue on the route to Chumphon (see page 202).

TRAVELLING IN SAFETY

A little bit of planning goes a long way in safe travelling. Before anything else, consider whether you want to **travel alone or with a companion**. Having a friend will reap more advantages in Thailand and Malaysia than in compact, ultra-safe Singapore and, given the kind of world it is, this is especially pertinent to female travellers.

Think of those you are leaving behind – they will worry and reassurance helps. Write down your itinerary for them, however vague, and agree beforehand on how you **plan to keep in touch**. Don't promise to telephone every few days and then make two calls in a month. It might be more practical to agree to telephone once a week and then stick to it. Consider obtaining a call charge card from your telephone company that bills your home account (or your parents' home account!). Shops from where e-mails can be inexpensively sent and received are to be found all over south-east Asia, and not just large cities, so keeping in touch this way is recommended. If you don't have an e-mail address, contact www.hotmail.com or www.yahoo.com and sign up for free.

When it comes to **packing**, the really essential items are passport (with at least six months to run), tickets and money. Once you have arrived, these same vital items need their own security. Some kind of a money belt is worth considering, especially the kind of large wallet that fits behind the belted waistband of trousers or shorts. Photocopies of documents and travellers' cheques are worth keeping in a separate place in your luggage, and leave a spare set at home as well. Other items worth packing include a small padlock for luggage, and perhaps another one for extra security on the inside door of your room at night. A small Maglite-style torch can be useful on beaches.

As a general rule, don't – literally – leave **credit or bank cards** out of your sight. Check with your bank beforehand about what facilities they offer in Thailand, Malaysia and/or Singapore and have relevant PIN numbers memorized. Bring with you the relevant phone number for reporting a lost or stolen card.

Thefts are not as common in Thailand, Malaysia or Singapore as you might think but if something does go wrong be ready to deal with it calmly and don't let it spoil your holiday. If you have travel insurance you will need some record of having reported it to the police. Have a back-up plan just in case the very worst happens and your documents and money are stolen. Embassies can replace a stolen passport (having a photocopy of the lost one is a great help) and money can be wired from home through companies like MoneyGram.

If you are unlucky, something belonging to you will be stolen. Always keep a close eye on your luggage and do not make the mistake of assuming that your fellow nationals can always be trusted. Budget guesthouses may have the odd impecunious traveller who is not averse to rifling through your rucksack. It may be as trivial as a fellow traveller stealing your alarm clock from beside your dorm bed. Certain routes, especially Bangkok to Chiang Mai and the

TRAVELLING IN SAFETY (CONT.)

train between Malaysia and Thailand, have attracted professional thieves. Try not to carry anything valuable in your luggage and use a good padlock if you are carrying something you would hate to lose.

You will be very unlucky to be the victim of **violence** in either Thailand, Malaysia or Singapore. There was a highly-publicized case of a female backpacker murdered in Chiang Mai in 2000 but this was high-profile news simply because it was so unusual. Sexual stereotyping, and the consequent low-level harassment it tends to bring, is busy at work in parts of Malaysia. The eastern coast of peninsular Malaysia, where Islamic fundamentalism has a voice, can be uncomfortable for a female travelling alone but it is usually nothing more than a mild nuisance.

There is more risk of **culture shock** than theft or violence in south-east Asia. After all, you probably don't speak the language and yet you will be immersing yourself in various aspects of a culture that is not your own. When you are in a good mood culture shock can be stimulating and educational but every now and again, and it happens to everyone somewhere along the line, you will feel yourself beginning to snap because someone isn't dealing with your problem in a way that is culturally acceptable. For example, you could find your self getting extremely annoyed at the constant smile of a hotel receptionist as she tries to explain why there is no bed available for you at 10 o'clock at night – not the lost reservation, but that smile ... Even in far less stressful situations than this, there will be times when the Asian way of doing things causes consternation. It is usually trivial matters, concerning bureaucracy or an apparent lack of haste, but just try to think how aspects of your culture probably cause them to raise their eyebrows. Yet usually they don't, so try to act likewise. This is part of what world travelling is all about.

One good piece of advice for coping with culture shock is to take time off and just do something very ordinary for a few hours or more. Go read a book in the shade or visit the local cinema and enjoy a Hollywood film, having first established that it has not been dubbed into the local language. Usually you can take this for granted but you could find yourself settling down to watch *The Beach* and hearing Leonardo DiCaprio speak fluent Thai...

For **more information on safe travel**, there are a number of websites worth checking out. Rec.travel.asia is a useful usenet newsgroup. For the latest information on official travel advice contact the Foreign and Commonwealth Office on www.fco.gov.uk and/or the US State Department travel information service on http://travel.state.gov. A very useful little book for travellers is *Your Passport to Safer Travel* by Mark Hodson, published by Thomas Cook and costing £6.99. The directory of country information it provides is also available on the web at www.brookes.ac.uk/worldwise.

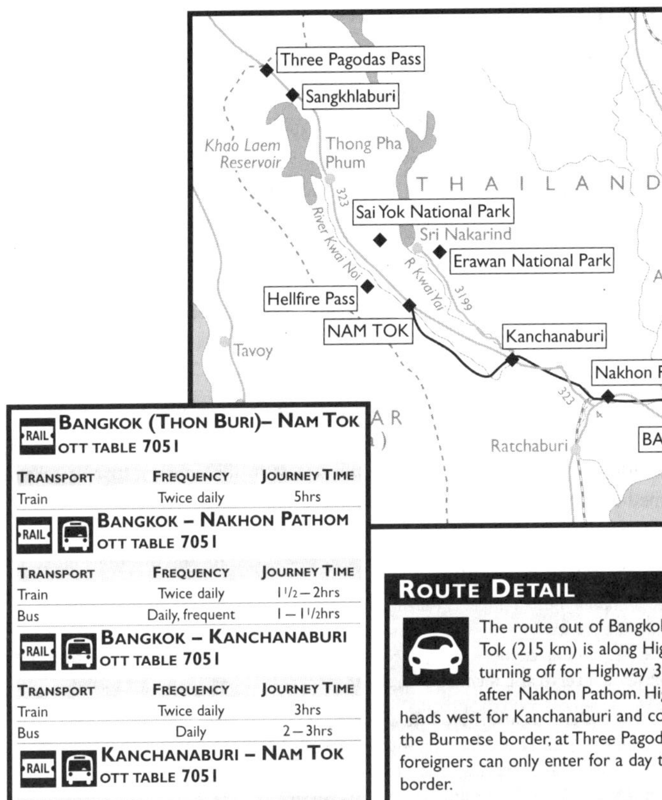

BANGKOK (THON BURI)– NAM TOK
OTT TABLE 7051

TRANSPORT	FREQUENCY	JOURNEY TIME
Train	Twice daily	5hrs

BANGKOK – NAKHON PATHOM
OTT TABLE 7051

TRANSPORT	FREQUENCY	JOURNEY TIME
Train	Twice daily	1½–2hrs
Bus	Daily, frequent	1–1½hrs

BANGKOK – KANCHANABURI
OTT TABLE 7051

TRANSPORT	FREQUENCY	JOURNEY TIME
Train	Twice daily	3hrs
Bus	Daily	2–3hrs

KANCHANABURI – NAM TOK
OTT TABLE 7051

TRANSPORT	FREQUENCY	JOURNEY TIME
Train	Twice daily	1¾hrs
Bus	Daily, frequent	1½hrs

ROUTE DETAIL

The route out of Bangkok for Nam Tok (215 km) is along Highway 4, turning off for Highway 323 shortly after Nakhon Pathom. Highway 323 heads west for Kanchanaburi and continues to the Burmese border, at Three Pagodas Pass, foreigners can only enter for a day trip at the border.

NOTES

Train

Trains between Bangkok and Kanchanaburi cannot be booked in advance in either direction. On Saturday, Sunday and public holidays there is a special tourist train at 0630 from Bangkok's Hualamphong station at 0630 for Nam Tok, stopping at Nathon Pathom and Kanchanaburi. Unlike the trains from Bangkok Thon Buri, this journey can be booked in advance.

Bus

For Nathon Pathom and Kanchanaburi (leaving from Bangkok's Southern Bus Terminal), be sure to board a non-stop bus or your journey will be considerably lengthened by stops along the way. From Khao San Rd in Bangkok it is possible to book a dedicated minibus service to and from Kanchanaburi. It costs more and may be crowded but it saves the hassle of getting out to the Southern Bus Terminal.

WESTERN THAILAND

Western Thailand stretches to the border with Myanmar (Burma), a route which during World War II attracted the Japanese who planned an invasion of India through Burma. They began building a railway line between Kanchanaburi and the Burmese border, using slave labour and prisoners of war captured after the fall of Singapore. The legacy of this painful period in history draws a large number of visitors but it is not the only reason for considering a journey westwards from Bangkok. The town of Kanchanaburi, despite having no beaches, is gradually acquiring a reputation as a relaxed place to hang out.

The territory beyond Kanchanaburi used to be Thailand's Wild West, dangerous to travel through because of various groups of insurgents operating in the region. But in the last twenty years this has all changed and the risk factor today is zero. This accounts for the growing popularity of the region with Thais and overseas Asians who are attracted to the rugged beauty of the forest-clad mountains that form the borderland with Burma. Population density in this part of Thailand is the lowest in the country, farming follows traditional methods and there is no industrialisation or pollution.

TEMPLE ARCHITECTURE

The walled compound of a temple is called a **wat**. Often two walls form a cloistered area where monks have their quarters. In larger temples this may be decorated with Buddhist images and serve as a meditation area for monks.

The inner courtyard area contains the **bot**, also called the *uposatha* or *ubosoth*, a square-like building with sloping tiled roofs. This is a holy area where monastic ordinations take place. There is also likely to be a **viharn**, a building which often looks like a bot and serves as a home for Buddhist relics. Traditionally both the bot and viharn should face water, emulating the position of the Buddha who sat facing water under the bodhi tree whilst achieving enlightenment.

The most conspicuous of the other structures found within a temple is the **chedi**, or **stupa**, recognisable by its typical bell-like shape but subject to a variety of forms in different parts of the country. The chedi is often thought to contain some relic, in the form of a bone, of the Buddha himself.

To make the most of western Thailand beyond Kanchanaburi, it helps to have your own transport. The use of a car or motorbike will overcome problems caused by gaps in the public transport system. Trains and buses all stop at the town of Nakon Pathom, and if you arrive in the morning it is worth stopping off to visit the notable *chedi*. But there is nothing else to see and an overnight stay is unnecessary unless you are planning an early morning trip to the floating markets at Damnoen Saduak.

NAKON PATHOM

It is hard to miss seeing Nakhon Pathom's claim to fame – the shining, gold and ochre, bowl-shaped **Phra Pathom Chedi**. A Buddhist shrine was first built on the site in the early 6th century but it was destroyed in warfare in the 11th century. Building work on the present *chedi*, enveloping the ruins of the ancient shrine, did not begin until 1853, and even though it took 17 years of building to complete the structure there has been more than one rebuilding programme since then. Its height is variously given as 120m and 127m, and a bot and other structures have been added to the complex.

An eight-metre-high Buddha greets visitors approaching the *chedi* from the main entrance's stone staircase. As you walk around the *chedi* you encounter four *viharns* situated at the four points of the compass. Murals, Buddha figures and a model of the original *chedi* are found inside. Wandering around outside can be a peaceful experience in itself.

There are two **museums** on the site. The one most worthy of the name is on the south side of the chedi **$** open Wed–Sun 0900–1200 and 1300–1600. Inside, there is a fair collection of Buddhist statues and artefacts. The other museum, near the east *viharn*, contains a motley assortment of undistinguished finds.

ORIENTATION

The railway and bus stations are close to each other and luggage can be safely left at the railway station. It is a short walk from the stations to the single but singular place of interest, Phra Tathom Chedi.

ACCOMMODATION AND EATING

If you do plan to spend a night in Nakon Pathom – and it only makes sense if making an early morning visit the next day to the Damnoen Saduak floating markets – then head for Rachwithi Rd, which begins south-west of the *chedi*. Along this road there are two good hotels which also offer the most comfortable environment for a meal:

Nakhon Inn $$$$–$$$ Soi 3, Rachwithi Rd, tel: (034) 242-265, offers the best accommodation in town.

Whale Hotel $$$ 151/79 Rachwithi Rd, tel: (034) 251-020, has lots of facilities but less character than the Nakhon Inn.

Mitrsampant Hotel $$ 2/11 Lang Phra Rd, tel: (034) 241-422. A quiet budget place, best reached by taking Ratchadamnoen Rd, which starts at the west side of the *chedi*, and turning right into Lang Phra Rd after about 50m.

For an inexpensive meal before getting back on a train or bus the **fruit market** is conveniently situated between the railway station and the *chedi*, on your right when walking due south from the station.

FLOATING MARKETS – AN EXCURSION

About 60 km south of Nakon Pathom are the **floating markets** of **Damnoen Saduak**, a series of canals laden with boats from which women sell their fruit and vegetables each day between 0600 and 1100. Tourist touts will try to insist that you join one of their motorised boat tours and this is the way most visitors experience the market. But it is just as much fun to wander up and down the narrow walkways and take in the bustling scene as it unfolds. The commercial impact of tourism on these markets is inescapable, and if any place in Thailand could serve as an attraction for the post-tourist then this would be it.

This is a popular day trip for tour groups from Bangkok, but their buses do not usually arrive until about 0900 and it is easy to arrive earlier by taking a public bus from Nakon Pathom. If you are staying on Rachwithi Road you can pick up a bus here without having to go to the bus station. To get there under your own steam from Bangkok, get to the Southern Bus Terminal as close to 0600 as possible and catch bus No 78 to Damnoen Saduak. From the bridge near the bus terminal it is a 15-minute walk along the canal to the floating market, but arrive in style by taking one of the cheap water taxis from the pier at the bridge.

The best way to experience the markets from dawn onwards is to spend the night in Damnoen Saduak. A convenient little hotel, **Little Bird Hotel $$–$** tel: (032) 254-382 or (032) 241-315, is signposted from the bridge near where the bus stops.

KANCHANABURI

Kanchanaburi receives bus- and train-loads of tourists every day, but the vast majority are just passing through and once they have 'done' the Bridge over the River Kwai they're off again. The bridge – its iconic status makes it one of the more photographed sites in Thailand – is especially popular with Asian tourists, while an increasing number of Western visitors are discovering Kanchanaburi as a relaxing destination for a couple of nights' stay in its own right.

Apart from the bridge itself, the main places of interest are the war museums and the war cemeteries. The older of the two war museums, the **JEATH War Museum $** open daily 0830–1630, tel: (034) 515-203, is by the Mae Klong River at the bottom of Wisuttarangsi Road. JEATH is an acronym for six of the countries involved: Japan, England, America and Australia, Thailand and Holland. The museum building is a reconstructed *attap* (woven palm thatch) and bamboo hut of the type lived in by the POWs which houses a small collection of old photographs and drawings. As museums go, it is not particularly special, but it is a far more heartfelt homage to the past than the newer **World War II Museum $** near the bridge itself, open daily 0900–1800, tel: (034) 512-556. The section devoted to the war contains an assorted collection of memorabilia but most of the museum is glossy, tacky and uninspiring.

The **Bridge on the River Kwai** is just over 3 km north of Kanchanaburi and if you stay on the train for Nam Tok you will actually travel across it. You can reach the bridge by hopping on the Nam Tok train at Kanchanaburi or by catching a *songthaew* on Saeng Chuto Road.

The original bridge, the wooden one constructed by prisoners and forced labourers, was completed early in 1943 and a second bridge, built of steel, was added a few months later. Allied bombers attacked the bridges and the one you see today was rebuilt after the war, using parts of the original structure that survived the bombing. The bridge you see today has become a premier attraction for sightseers of all nationalities and the tourist razzmatazz of the place may put you off. For a more authentic insight into the history of the railway, a visit to the town's war museum and cemeteries is worthwhile, and for a very moving and informative introduction to what took place a trip to the Hellfire Pass Memorial Museum is highly recommended.

There are two war cemeteries. The one in town is the **Kanchanaburi Allied War Cemetery**, also known as Don Rak. It is off Saeng Chuto Road, not far from the railway station, and reachable on foot or by any *songthaew* heading in that direction along Saeng Chuto Road. The other cemetery, **Chungkai**, is across the river and best visited as part of a bicycle ride (page 93).

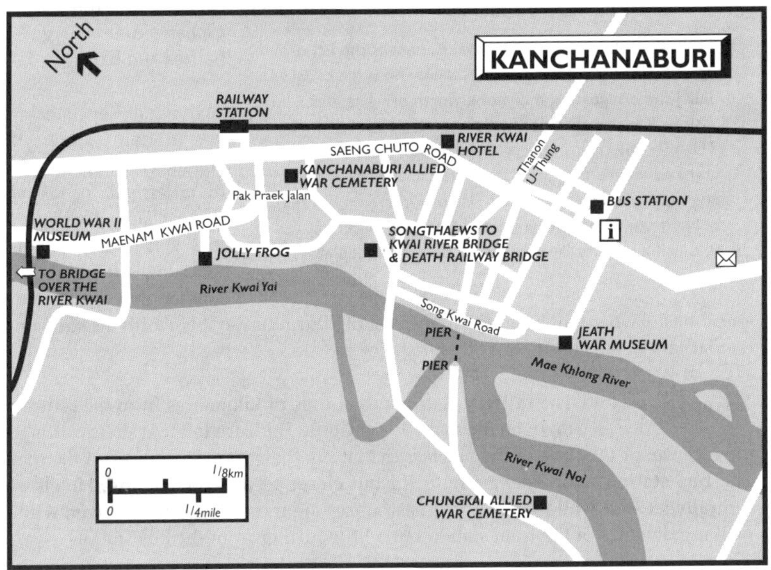

ORIENTATION Kanchanaburi is not a large town and it is possible to get around most places on foot, but this will soon prove exhausting in the heat. There are two main areas for travellers where you will find accommodation, restaurants, Internet cafés, tour agents and places to rent bicycles and motorbikes.

One area, around the River Kwai Hotel on Saeng Chuto Rd, is very central and on the same road as the train and bus stations. Banks are mostly found on and around this road and here too, at the Bangkok end of the road, you will find the tourist office and post office. *Songthaews* run along Saeng Chuto Rd, passing the war cemetery and heading towards the river and the bridge along Maenam Kwai Rd.

FICTION AND NON-FICTION

The Frenchman Pierre Boulle, who made the bridge at Kanchanaburi so famous, was never there himself. This helps to explain his mistake in thinking this part of the Mae Klong River was the River Kwai in the first place. The name has stuck, however, and is now officially called the Kwai Yai River. (This is to distinguish it from the Kwai Noi, the actual river which the main part of the railway line followed and which the Kwai Yai joins just west of Kanchanaburi.) If you want to see the film of the book, drop by the No Name bar (page 92), where it is shown most evenings.

Boulle's book, *The Bridge on the River Kwai*, tells the fictional story of Colonel Nicholson and his men who were ordered to build the bridge. Another book worth bringing with you if visiting Kanchanaburi is *The Railway Man* by Eric Lomax. This tells the true and heart-rending story of how Eric Lomax survived two years of torture and distress after being caught with an illicit radio while working on the railway. He never forgot the voice and face of his interrogator and half a century later discovers the man is still alive.

The other area that is fast developing a modest tourist infrastructure is along Maenam Kwai Rd down by the riverside. Accommodation and restaurants are geared towards budget travellers, bikes can be hired, tours arranged, e-mails collected and travel news exchanged in the guesthouses and bars.

Arriving at Kanchanaburi bus or train station you are likely to be accosted by an armada of *tuk-tuks* and *samlors* all willing to take you to a guesthouse for a low fare. The commission they get from the guesthouse owner will be added to the cost of your room so it is worth insisting on a regular fare to the guesthouse of your choice.

TRAIN AND BUS The **railway station** is a couple of kilometres from the centre of town on the main Saeng Chuto Rd. Turn left to walk towards the town centre or take one of the *songthaews* that ply their way up and down the road. The **bus station** is on Saeng Chuto Rd but closer to the town centre. Hotels are centrally located while the budget guesthouses are mostly close to the river, within walking distance of the train station but a little further from the bus station.

THE DEATH RAILWAY

The railway line was laid down during World War II by forced labour and prisoners of war under the control of the Japanese. Creating a rail link between Burma and Japan was considered essential because it would avoid the risk of travelling by sea, but a 415 km stretch between Burma and Kanchanaburi had to be built completely from scratch. Japanese engineers calculated it would take five years to complete the line: the fact that it was completed by the end of 1943 gives some idea of the forced pace.

The route chosen followed the river valley of the Kwai Noi, and, starting in 1942, some 60,000 Allied POWs worked on the line. Around 20% died as a direct result of the harsh conditions. Food rations were insufficient for the back-breaking work, medical facilities were horrendously inadequate and the treatment of prisoners was often brutal. Around 80,000 civilian labourers are also thought to have died before the railway line was finished in late 1943.

The **TAT Office** is at the Bangkok end of Saeng Chuto Rd, tel: (034) 5110-200, open daily 0830 – 1630. Here you can get a free town map, information on places to stay and useful advice on transport. The **Tourist Police**, tel: (034) 512-795, also operate from the tourist office.

River Kwai Hotel $$$ Saeng Chuto Rd, tel: (034) 513-348, fax: (034) 511-269. OK, it's not by the river but it does offer the most comfortable accommodation in town and there is a small swimming pool.

River Inn $$ Saeng Chuto Rd, tel: (034) 514-635, is directly in front of the River Kwai Hotel and although a little past its sell-by date, this centrally-located place has affordable rooms with air-conditioning.

VL Guesthouse $ Saeng Chuto Rd, tel: (034) 513-546, has clean, tidy rooms with fan and telephone.

Nita Raft House $ 27/1 Pak Phraek Rd, tel: (034) 514-521. One of the least expensive riverside guesthouses, close to the JEATH war museum but definitely not in the quietest part of town. At weekends, especially, the racket from nearby raft discos will keep you awake, but then the rooms are very cheap.

Further up the river, around Maenam Kwai Rd, there is a better choice of accommodation.

Sugar Cane Guest House $ 22 Soi Pakistan, off Maenam Kwai Rd, no tel. One of my favourite places, Sugar Cane is small and friendly and enjoys great views of the river. Bike hire and competitively priced tours can be arranged here.

Jolly Frog Backpackers $ Soi China, off Maenam Kwai Rd, tel: (034) 514-579. A well-known and relatively large guesthouse with a range of bamboo huts close to the river.

River Inn $$–$ Saeng Chuto Rd has very good value meals, like noodle soup with duck for 30B. There are plenty of other inexpensive restaurants along this stretch of the main road.

Punmee Café $$–$ Ban Neura Rd, tel: (034) 513-053. Cornflakes, muesli, toast and marmalade, and a host of Western and Thai meals feature on the menu of this expatriate-run restaurant. It is a good source of information, and bicycles and motorbikes can be rented here and tours arranged. Next door is a useful second-hand bookshop with an exchange service.

Sabaijit Restaurant $ Saeng Chuto Rd. A short way past the River Kwai Hotel there is a cardboard sign in English announcing the inexpensive, clean restaurant, directly opposite the conspicuous Apache Bar. It has large fans and an extensive menu in English.

By the river, places to eat can be found along Maenam Kwai Rd and all the guesthouses have affordable restaurants.

ENTERTAINMENT

A few bars are beginning to spring up along Maenam Kwai Rd near the riverside, and the area has all the signs of developing into the town's hip ghetto for travellers. Look out for **No Name** bar, where you can expect a warm welcome, Aussie style. Open during the evenings for beers, cocktails and snacks, there is a snooker table and photos of inebriated travellers litter one of the walls.

TOURS AND TRIPS

It is possible to see some of the sights around and beyond Kanchanaburi on your own, but public transport is limited and without your own wheels it may be worth considering an organised tour through a Kanchanaburi company.

A Bicycle Ride

Bicycles are easily hired in Kanchanaburi and they open up some of the sights on the other side of the Kwai Noi. There are two ways of fording the river: either by ferry (which takes bicycles) from Song Kwai Rd, or over the bridge further north up the road. Once over the river, stay on the main road for a little over 2 kms and you will come to the **Chungkai war cemetery**. The graves occupy the site of a former POW camp and, like the cemetery in town, there is a quiet dignity about the place that belies the manner in which these men suffered and died.

Stay on the main road and you will encounter the ostentatious cave temple, **Wat Tham Khao Poon**. Fairy lights guide the way through the cave and past a hotchpotch of gaudy images before arriving at the central Buddha figure surrounded by flashing lights. It is all fairly bizarre but anyone prone to claustrophobia will not appreciate the confined space of the cave interior.

Westours, 21 Maenam Rd and Song Kwai Rd; tel: (034) 513-654 or (034) 513-655, is typical of the longer-established and more reliable companies offering a variety of tours. These include popular one-day trips that cover various activities involving an elephant ride, bamboo rafting, visits to a waterfall and Hellfire Pass, and a hot spa. Prices range between 600B and 950B, and include the train ride between Kanchanaburi and Nam Tok, and lunch. Other one-day trips include the floating market at Damnoen Saduak and the Erawan waterfalls, as well as longer hiking trips.

There are quite a few tour companies in Kanchanaburi offering similar trips to Westours. Because a minimum of four persons is often needed, it is well worth shopping around to find a trip that suits you that is actually going to take place.

Other companies to try include **BT Travel Centre**, tel: (034) 624-630, and **AS Mixed Travel**, tel: (034) 514-958 or (034) 512-017. The owner of the **Punmee Café** in Neura Road, tel: (034) 513-053, is also worth checking out for a variety of tours, especially war-related trips and adventure rafting.

SEVEN WATERFALLS

Erawan National Park is about the same size as Sai Yok (page 96) but the waterfalls here are more impressive and enjoy a premier status amongst nature-loving Thais. The acclaim is not unwarranted because the seven falls, spread over 1500 metres, are a beautiful sight and ideal for a splash and a swim, but avoid weekends and holidays if you want to enjoy them all to yourself. There is only one walking trail within the park which leads to the waterfalls, and if you want to reach the higher levels you need decent footwear, not just sandals or flip-flops.

Buses for Erawan depart Kanchanaburi on a daily basis: the journey takes a couple of hours so start early if returning the same day, because the last bus back leaves Erawan at 1600. During peak periods, especially between November and January, minibuses for Erawan depart daily from Kanchanaburi and will collect passengers from the riverside guesthouses.

NAM TOK

The train ride between Kanchanaburi and Nam Tok, at the end of the line, is both dramatic and historical. It begins by crossing the famous girdered bridge on the River Kwai and continues for well over an hour through rural landscapes with knobbly mountains in the background. The train uses the line that was built by the POWs and Asian slave labourers and there is more than one reminder of just how backbreaking their work must have been. At one point the train chugs through an incredibly narrow cutting in the solid rock and a little further on it gingerly makes its way over a trestle bridge that looks as if it could have been built 60 years ago.

The station at Nam Tok, whose name literally means waterfall, was not the original station. The present station is situated at the village of Thasao but the station originally lay 1 km further along the line at a waterfall. It was moved to its present location because part of the line was damaged by heavy rains.

There is nothing to do or see in Nam Tok itself; it is merely the end of the line. Visitors either return to Kanchanaburi – the same train begins the return journey after ten minutes – or travel on to either the museum and Hellfire Pass or the Sai Yok National Park.

HELL FIRE MEMORIAL MUSEUM

The memory of those who died working on the Japanese railway line is preserved at the **Hell Fire Memorial Museum**, free admission, tel: (01) 210-3306, open daily 0900–1600, 18 km from Nam Tok station. If you walk 500 metres from the station through the village of Thasao and onto the main road, Route 323, you can catch an orange-coloured bus to the museum. Apart from arriving on a tour, you could also hire a motorbike in Kanchanaburi or take a *songthaew* from Nam Tok.

The museum has various exhibits, archive photographs and a 7-minute video that tells the story of the railway line using war footage and testimonies from prisoners who survived the ordeal.

Two paths, a concrete stairway and a path through a bamboo forest, lead the way to **Hellfire Pass**, only 250 metres from the museum entrance. Take the forest path because this follows the route that POWs took and also offers a memorable view looking down on the narrow channel cut through the solid limestone and quartz.

From the Pass there is a 4 km walking trail that follows the line laid down by the POWs. It passes a vantage-point from where the prisoners could view the whole valley and the various sections where prisoners worked like ants digging and shifting the soil with primitive tools. In places it is still possible to see the mounting bolts for the timber beams and the embankments that were constructed. The trail also passes the site of the Pack of Cards Bridge, named by the prisoners because it was such a precarious structure and collapsed on them more than once.

HELLFIRE PASS

One of the largest cuttings that had to be made through solid rock during the construction of the railway line has come to be known as Hellfire Pass. A crew of 400 Australian POWs began the work in April 1943, supplemented by British, Tamil and Malay groups. The men worked for up to 18 hours a day, digging the 17 metre deep and 110 metre long cutting in only 12 weeks. They nicknamed it the Hellfire Pass because of the eerie lighting effects created at night by the carbide lamps, bamboo torches burning oil and the open fires that illuminated the construction site. Nearly three-quarters of the men who built this pass died in the undertaking.

DEATH TOURISM

The rail journey between Kanchanaburi and Nam Tok, with its camera-toting tour groups charging on and off the train for a short hop before rejoining their coaches, is the closest you will get to the unpalatable phenomenon of 'black spot tourism', or 'death tourism'. These attractions — the sites of mass killings or deaths of celebrities — include Auschwitz, the highway junction in California where James Dean was killed, and the Paris underpass where Diana, Princess of Wales, died.

SAI YOK NATIONAL PARK

A few miles further up Highway 323 is the start of the 500 sq km Sai Yok National Park, which stretches as far as the Burmese border. Its main attractions are the Sai Yok Yai waterfall, limestone caves, and short walking trails that begin from outside the visitor centre. The chilling scene in *The Deer Hunter* involving a game of Russian roulette was filmed in the park.

Tour companies in Kanchanaburi organise visits to the park and use a stretch of the river here for rafting trips (page 92). To get here on your own, take a bus in Kanchanaburi going to Thong Pha Phum and ask to be dropped off at the park entrance. From here it is a 3 km walk to the visitor centre. There are also direct buses to the park from Kanchanaburi.

Accommodation in the park is available in Forestry Department bungalows, most suitable for small groups, and floating guesthouses by the river.

Pung-Waan Resort $$$$$ Thasao (Nam Tok), tel: (034) 591-017, fax: (034) 591-017, e-mail: pungwaan@samart.co.th. There are a surprising number of resorts tucked close to the banks of the River Kwai Noi, around Nam Tok. Pung-Waan enjoys one of the most tranquil settings, with waterside rooms with balconies, a pool and restaurants.
Kitti Raft $$ tel: (034) 591-106. Pleasant floating rooms with bathrooms. You could walk here from Tam Nok station but it's worth calling for a pick-up.
Saiyok View Raft $$ tel: (034) 514-194. The nicest place in the park and good value as rooms have air-con and bathrooms. At weekends rooms are often at a premium. Other places to try include **Kwai Noi Rafthouses** and **Ranthawee Raft**.

All of the places above have their own small restaurants and there are lots of food stalls near the visitor centre.

BUSES

There are daily buses between Kanchanaburi and Sangkhlaburi, including some air-conditioned vehicles, with the journey taking anything from four to six hours. The speediest way to reach Sangkhlaburi is by a three-hour minibus ride from Kanchanaburi. The minibuses travel fast and stops are infrequent. It is best

TAXI-METER
TAXI-METER

THE BURMESE BORDER

Beyond Nam Tok, Highway 323 continues all the way to the **Burmese border** at Three Pagodas Pass, reaching the market town of Thong Pha Phum after 30 km. The last town on Highway 323 is actually Sangkhlaburi and a couple of miles before it a road branches off for the 20 km trip to Three Pagodas Pass. To be truthful, there is precious little to see or occupy one's time at Three Pagodas Pass and seeing the pagodas themselves is certainly not worth the journey but, as is the case with many terminal points, it is the journey itself that provides the justification for going there. An overnight stay is required and **Sangkhlaburi**, 200 km from Kanchanaburi, is the place to head for in this respect.

The dramatic scenery on the route is the highlight of the journey, especially along the 70 km stretch between Thong Pha Phum and Sangkhlaburi. The road skirts the huge Khao Laem reservoir and opens up an alien landscape of submerged trees with forested mountains gathered in the background.

The human landscape, made up of a mix of Thai, Karen and Mon people, is also an attraction, and there are a number of Mon refugee camps around Sangkhlaburi. The Mon straddle the Burmese-Thai borderlands and for long have been the victims of persecution directed by the Myanmar military regime. A stopover in Sangkhlaburi is recommended because it provides an opportunity to wander around the town's morning market where you are more likely to hear Burmese being spoken than Thai. There is also an elongated wooden bridge that leads across the lake to a visitor-friendly **Mon settlement**.

Sangkhlaburi has a reasonable spread of accommodation, and some of the guesthouses can arrange day trips into the surrounding countryside with elephant ride and adventure rafting options.

to reserve your seat the day before travel because they often fill up, especially the morning ones from Kanchanaburi. Non-air-conditioned buses for Sangkhlaburi can also be picked up in Nam Tok. To reach Three Pagodas Pass you need to hop on a *songthaew* in Sangkhlaburi. They run regularly throughout the day, but bear in mind that the last one back to town departs around 1800. Confirm the time when you arrive.

Somjaineuk Hotel $$$-$ Thong Pha Phum, tel: (034) 599-067. Centrally located, this hotel has two wings: an older quarter with fans and a new wing with air-con, showers, and a degree of comfort.

Burmese Inn $$-$ Sangkhlaburi, tel: and fax: (034) 595-146. Not far from the wooden bridge to the Mon settlement, less than 1 km from the bus station, with a variety of rooms. The English-speaking proprietors know the local area well and can advise and arrange tours into the countryside.
P Guest House $$-$ Sangkhlaburi, tel: (034) 595-061, fax: (034) 595-139. Another well-run operation with a variety of rooms in a scenic location overlooking the lake. Tours can also be arranged and bicycles and motorbikes hired.
Three Pagodas Pass Resort $$$ Three Pagodas Pass, tel: (034) 595-316. The only place to stay here. The wooden bungalows are pleasant enough and a very good room rate can sometimes be negotiated.

EATING There is nothing wrong with the food at either of the Sangkhlaburi guest-houses, although the restaurant at the **P Guest House $$-$** has a more attractive setting. In Sangkhlaburi itself the air-conditioned restaurant at the **Phornphalin Hotel $$-$** is not bad, and there are a few inexpensive restaurants down the same street.

WHERE NEXT?

DAY TRIP TO BURMA

Until quite recently it was not possible for foreigners to cross into Burma. This was a sensible precaution on the part of the Thai authorities at a time when the Burmese military were engaged in fighting with Mon and Karen rebels very close to the border. The rebels are no longer trying to capture the Burmese side of the border and, unless the situation changes dramatically, it is now quite safe to venture across.

At Three Pagodas Pass it is possible to cross the border and enter the Burmese village of Payathonzu (literally, three pagodas) for a payment of US$5 or the baht equivalent. Payathonzu is hardly a village and more an excuse to set up stalls and indulge in a spot of cross-border shopping. There are places to eat and a varied selection of Burmese handicrafts and fabrics on sale, as well as Burmese face powder, inexpensive jewellery, and cheroot cigars. Bargaining is usual and no one expects you to pay the first asking price.

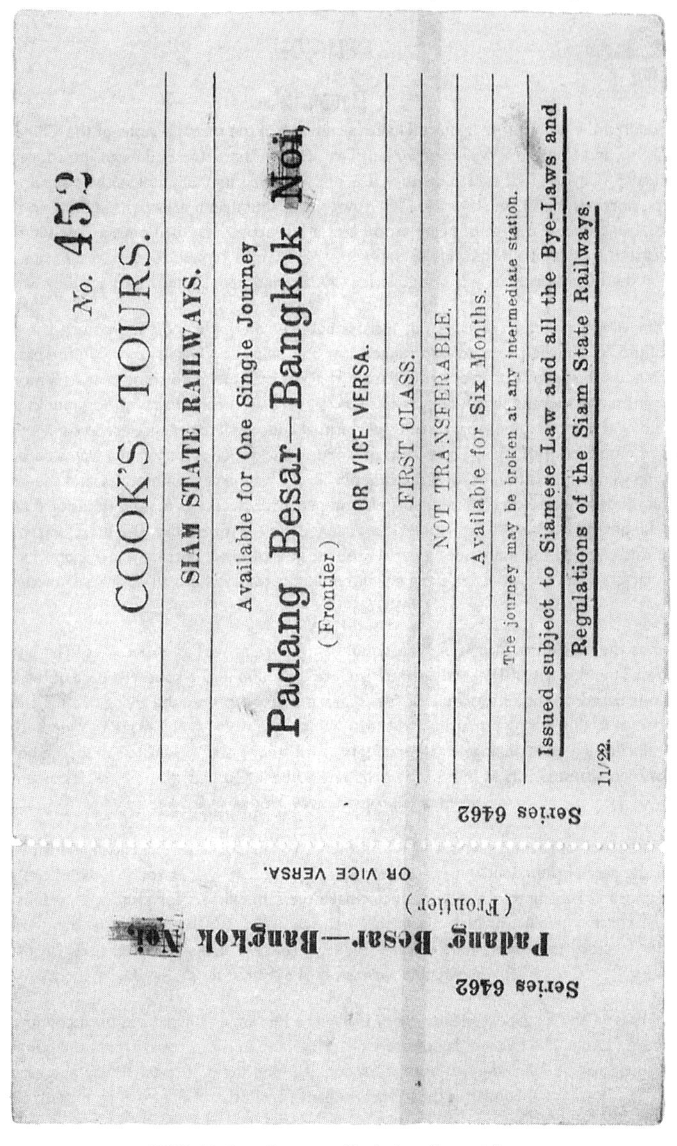

No. 452

COOK'S TOURS.

SIAM STATE RAILWAYS.

Available for One Single Journey

Padang Besar—Bangkok Noi,

(Frontier)

OR VICE VERSA.

FIRST CLASS.

NOT TRANSFERABLE.

Available for Six Months.

The journey may be broken at any intermediate station.

Issued subject to Siamese Law and all the Bye-Laws and Regulations of the Siam State Railways.

11/22.

Series 6462

Series 6462

Padang Besar—Bangkok Noi.

(Frontier)

OR VICE VERSA.

1920s Padang Besar – Bankok railway ticket

RELIGION

Buddhism

Buddhism is the main religion of Thailand and one of the main religions of the Chinese in Malaysia and Singapore. Well over 90% of Thais follow Theravada Buddhism, introduced from Sri Lanka (Ceylon) in the 13th century. It is not nearly so metaphysical as the popular stereotype portrays it and your average Thai is not going about on a daily basis seeking some ultimate, transcendental state of being. Good acts are practised and bad ones avoided in order to increase the odds of a decent life in the next world. Good *karma* (deed or act) means a better life in the next world but it is not governed by fate and people choose to act they way to do.

Every village community has its *wat*, a cross between a temple and a monastery. The number of monks attached to a *wat* can range from one or two to well over 500 in the case of a large and prestigious *wat*. Every young male Thai expects to spend some time as a monk, averaging a few months, which helps explain why there are nearly half a million monks in the country at any one time. Apart from the spiritual and social merit that accompanies this period of monkhood, for many Thais from poor, rural backgrounds a spell in a *wat* is an opportunity to gain an education beyond the primary level. This mixture of motives, and the impact of the modern world on traditional beliefs and practices, accounts for the occasional tales of sexual peccadilloes and other scandals associated with some monks. The most extreme case like this involved the murder of a female tourist in a cave *wat* outside Kanchanaburi in 1996. A far cry from the aim of seeking enlightenment, *nirvana*, where all desire is transcended.

Islam

Islam is the religion of Malays in Malaysia and Singapore as well as about 4% of Thailand's population. The Muslims of Thailand are nearly all to be found in the southern part of the country. Islam is based on the observance of five pillars: the creed, prayer, the giving of alms, the observance of fasting during ramadan, and the endeavour to make a pilgrimage to Mecca. The religion includes a belief in angels and prophets as messengers of God. The Koran, the holy book of Islam, names Jesus as one of the prophets and the Gospels of the New Testament are viewed as prophetic revelations of God.

The influence of Islam is not keenly felt in the east Malaysian states of Sabah and Sarawak but in the rest of the country it is a potent force, political as well as social. In cities like Kuala Lumpur and Penang the religion does not have the same impact for visitors as it does on the east coast of peninsular Malaysia. In this area you will see Malay children learning Arabic in order to study the Koran in its original language. There is also a Malay religious language, Jawi, which is written in the Arabic script.

In Malaysia and Singapore, nearly every Malay is a Muslim and Indians in both countries may also be Muslim. The Muslim day of prayer is Friday and in every town across the country the mosques will be full and lunch hour is extended. Along the east coast, Friday operates like a traditional Sunday in the West and banks and other offices will be closed.

TAOISM

Taoism is the religion of the Chinese in Thailand, Malaysia and Singapore. Taoism, like Buddhism, shows the influence of earlier animist beliefs and practices. Taoism includes an element of ancestor worship and a form of animism lies behind the Taoist belief in *feng shui*. Worship takes place at a temple but most homes will also have a small altar display. Taoism is a very down-to-earth religion that concerns itself with the practical side of life. A person will go to a temple to pray for success in school exams or for luck at a forthcoming job interview. There is a keen element of plain, old-fashioned superstition and particular gods are worshipped because of their association with specific professions or areas of life. Trying to divine the future can become a preoccupation in the search to avoid bad luck and fortune-tellers are often found around a temple complex.

HINDUISM

The majority of Indians in Malaysia and Singapore are Hindus. The Hindu religion shares with Buddhism a belief in reincarnation, both sets of adherents seeking a state of understanding that escapes the endless cycle of birth and death. There is the same notion of *karma*, a belief that what you do in this life will have consequences for a future existence. *Dharma* is the set of rules to be followed by those who seek to live a good life. Traditional Hinduism carries with it a caste system but this is not so observable in Malaysia or Singapore. When the British were keen to attract Indians to Malaya and Singapore they only wanted unskilled labourers to work on rubber plantations and the like. The result was that most Hindus who came were from the lower classes and caste never became an issue.

The multiform variety of Hindu gods is often baffling to monotheistic Westerners. The different gods are best viewed metaphorically, as manifestations of particular aspects of the one omnipresent god. The one central god has three main forms: Vishnu, Shiva and Brahma. All three are usually depicted as having four arms but Brahma, the creator, also has four heads.

TRADITIONAL RELIGION

Most of the ethnic groups living in Sarawak and Sabah practise forms of animism, also called traditional religion. Ancestor worship is another key characteristic of the religion of the Dyaks, the Ibans, the Bidayuh and the various smaller tribes that make up the population of east Malaysia. A factor that is having a negative effect on these traditional religions is the proselytizing activities of evangelical Christians. In peninsular Malaysia, such groups are kept firmly under control and would not dare to encroach on Muslim sensibilities but in east Malaysia it is a different story.

Bangkok – Pattaya

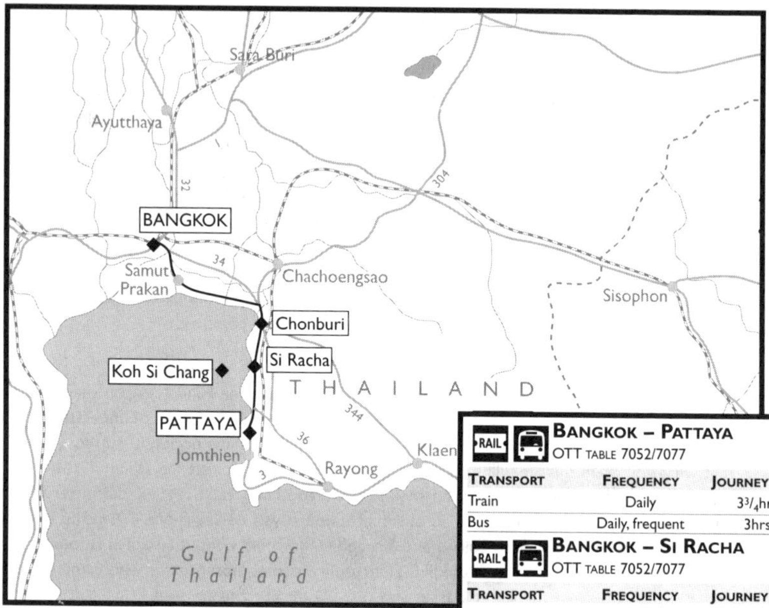

Bangkok – Pattaya
OTT TABLE 7052/7077

Transport	Frequency	Journey T
Train	Daily	3¾hrs
Bus	Daily, frequent	3hrs

Bangkok – Si Racha
OTT TABLE 7052/7077

Transport	Frequency	Journey T
Train	Daily	3hrs 20mi
Bus	Daily, frequent	2hrs 20mi

Si Racha – Pattaya
OTT TABLE 7052/7077

Transport	Frequency	Journey T
Bus	Daily, frequently	½hr
Train	Daily	26mins

Notes

The Pattaya train, No 365/283, leaves Bangkok's Hualamphong station at 0655 and calls at Si Racha. Buses for Pattaya depart from Bangkok's Eastern bus terminal, best reached by the skytrain. Ekkamai station is right outside the bus station.

There are no flights between Bangkok and Pattaya but Bangkok Airways do have a daily 1hr service between Ko Samui and U-Tapao airport, which is a little under 30 km south of Pattaya.

Route Detail

Highway 3, leading to Pattaya from the capital (147km), is the continuation of Sukhumvit Road in Bangkok, and is often still called Sukhumvit Road as it weaves its way through towns along the east coast. Traffic is heavy from Bangkok until Samut Prakan; there is little scenery to admire along the way and the only place worth stopping at is Si Racha. If you are keen on exploring east Thailand by car it might be more worthwhile to hire a car in Pattaya. Avis, tel: (038) 361-6278, have an office at the Dusit Resort Hotel and there are plenty of smaller companies offering car hire.

EASTERN THAILAND

The eastern region of Thailand stretches over 400 km from Bangkok to the town of Trat close to the Cambodian border. The most popular destination remains the beach resort of Pattaya, first made famous during the Vietnam War when it served as a major getaway for American troops. When the soldiers left the resort evolved into a sleazy destination for mostly sex tourists. Now, as a result of the robust and partly successful attempts to improve this image, Pattaya enjoys a wider range of visitors than ever before.

Ko Samet, like Pattaya, is close enough to Bangkok to attract jaded city visitors during weekends and public holidays. Even on Ko Chang, further east and close to the Cambodian border, the atmosphere is very different at weekends and holiday periods. If you want a peaceful time, travel during the week and avoid public holidays.

SI RACHA

Nearly all travellers in Si Racha are passing through on their way to or from the offshore island of Ko Si Chang, but as small Thai towns go there is nothing wrong with spending a night here. Affordable and pleasant hotels and seafood restaurants are strung out attractively along the seafront, called Choemchomphon Rd, and there is a long causeway north of the ferry pier that leads out to an islet, Ko Loi, with a modern Thai-Chinese temple perched on it. As with Ko Si Chang, Si Racha receives its fair share of visitors from Bangkok at weekends and holidays, but during the week the place is invitingly relaxed and unhurried.

Samchai $$$$ Soi 10, Choemchomphon Rd, tel: (038) 311-134 has a choice of aircon rooms. **Srivichai $** Soi 8, Choemchomphon Rd, tel: (038) 311-212, and the adjacent **Sri Wattana $** tel: (038) 311-037 are equally good budget hotels but without air-con.

All the best restaurants are spaced out along the seafront. Current favourites can be judged by their number of customers. Prices **$$–$** are competitive and what you pay has more to do with the kind of fish you choose than the actual restaurant. Whatever you eat, be sure to try the chilli-flavoured ketchup, *nam phrik Si Racha*. It is found all over Thailand but is made right here in Si Racha, and will most certainly be on your table.

BANGKOK – PATTAYA

KO SI CHANG

The first of Thailand's east coast islands, Ko Si Chang would have been quickly passed over as a possible location for *The Beach.* DiCaprio could hardly be seen cavorting on a rocky beach with cargo ships sulking in the offshore, not-quite-turquoise waters. Ko Si Chang has its own charms, though, and plenty of nooks and crannies to explore. The island has enough of a range of reasonable accommodation to make it worth considering as a lazy excursion from Bangkok, or as the first stop on a route that ends with the most easterly island of Ko Chang, near the Cambodian border.

A surfaced road rings the island and motorised *samlors* are easy to find for short trips $ or for a leisurely tour of the island **$$$**. The only beach with a decent bit of sand is **Hat Sai Kaew**, reached by taking the road south from Tiew Pai Guest House. You pass a Marine Research Centre before following a path west to the ruins of a summer palace built by Rama V at the end of the 19th century. The site was soon deserted, after trouble with the French who occupied the island, but what couldn't be dismantled and taken back to Bangkok was left to nature. Renovation work of sorts is going on, but visitors can wander at will amongst the frangipani-clad ruins. From here, a path heads south to the beach at Hat Sai Kaew.

Boats for Ko Si Chang depart from the pier at the end of Soi 14, Jermjophon Rd in Si Racha from early morning until 1700. The last return boat is at 1630. If you are planning to catch this, confirm whether it can be boarded at one or both of the island's piers.

Si Chang Palace $$$$–$$$ Atsadang Rd; tel: (038) 216-276. A first-rate place, within walking distance of the piers, with a pool and rooms with superb sea views.
Tiew Pai Guest House $$–$ Atsadang Rd; tel: (038) 216-084. The best-known guesthouse on the island, with a range of air-con and non-air-con rooms and a reasonable restaurant.

PATTAYA

American GIs looking for more than a suntan turned the name of what was a sleepy fishing village in the early 1960s into a synonym for sex holidays by the beach. The war in Vietnam came and went but the legacy for Pattaya remains the dense concentration of raunchy bars, discos and 'massage parlours' peopled by prostitutes and fuelled by planeloads of sad men from Europe.

Surprisingly, Pattaya also caters for families and regular tourists, and the result is a bizarre mix of the downright seedy and trappings of a conventional holiday resort. There are tattooists, gyms, countless stalls selling fake watches and other goods, and bars and eating places everywhere. Watersports are popular in Pattaya and numerous agents and specialist shops cater for the excellent offshore diving opportunities. All this rubs shoulders with the non-stop sex industry that bedevils the town's attempt to reinvent its image as a more wholesome destination for foreign visitors.

ORIENTATION

Beach Rd, which follows the curve of crescent-shaped Pattaya beach, is linked by a series of *sois* to the parallel Pattaya 2 Rd. Central Pattaya, occupying the area between *sois* 5 and 12, is the main commercial area, while the area to the south of *soi* 12 is the red-light district which comes into its own after dark. Jomtien Beach, lying south of Pattaya, is a far more sedate area, dedicated to watersports rather than sex.

GETTING AROUND

Songthaews ply Beach Rd and Pattaya 2 Rd. It's best not to ask the fare if you are only going a short distance; just hand over 10B at the end of the journey.

i The **TAT Office**, tel: (038) 427-667, on Beach Rd between *sois* 7 and 8. Open daily 0830–1630, it is well organised, with maps and accommodation information.

Pattaya Taxi Centre offers a 24-hr taxi service with English-speaking drivers. Tel (038) 427-523 or 361-075.

Malibu Travel, 485 Pattaya 2 Rd, tel: (038) 423-180, fax: (038) 426-229, e-mail: malibu@chonburi.ksc.co.th, website: www.malibu-travel.com. Situated next to the Vientiane restaurant, at the top of Soi 13, this is a well-established and reliable travel agent for tours, transport and hotel reservations.

The Soi **Post Office**, Soi 15, is the main post office and a telephone office for international calls, although better rates are often obtainable from private phone offices around town.

First-rate **hospital** treatment is available at the 24-hour Pattaya Memorial Hospital on Central Pattaya Rd, tel: (038) 429-422, and the Pattaya International Hospital on Soi 4, tel: (038) 428-374.

The **Tourist Police** can be contacted on Pattaya 2 Rd, near Soi 6, tel: (038) 429-371.

Motorbikes, **scooters** and **jeeps** can be hired from any of the countless touts along Beach Road. **Cars** can be rented from Avis in the Dusit Resort Hotel, tel: (038) 361-627.

The **Amari Orchid Resort $$$$$** Beach Rd, tel: (038) 428-161, fax: (038) 428-165, e-mail: orchid@amari.com. One of the best hotels in town, situated at the quieter north end of Beach Road, with ten acres of grounds, tennis courts, a large pool, and good restaurants.

Lek Hotel $$$ 284 Soi 13, on corner with Pattaya 2 Rd, tel: (038) 425-550, fax: (038) 426629. A reliable mid-range hotel, with its own small pool, rooms with fridges and phones. Centrally located for shopping and tour agents.

A.A. Pattaya Hotel $$$ 182 Soi 13, tel: (038) 428-656, fax: (038) 429-057. Rates drop if you're staying more than one night. Comfortable clean rooms and a small outdoor pool; well, more of a large bath really.

There is no real budget accommodation in Pattaya but the *sois* in central Pattaya are chock-a-block with the cheapest guesthouses.

Apex Hotel $$ 216 Pattaya 2 Rd, between *sois* 10 and 11, tel: (038) 429-233, fax: (038) 421-184. This remains a firm favourite with travellers because its air-con rooms are inexpensive. The place is clean and well run and even has a small pool. The nearby **Diana Inn**, tel: (038) 429-675, is fine if the Apex is full.

Finding western food is no problem in Pattaya. The difficulty lies in finding places serving interesting Thai cuisine. Restaurant prices are noticeably higher than most other parts of Thailand, especially the seafood places in south Pattaya and Jomtien. **Vientiane $$** 485 Pattaya 2 Rd, tel: (038) 411-298, is centrally located not far from Soi 13. The large menu featuring dishes from Laos and Thailand is available daily 1100–2400. Another alternative to fast-food joints and overpriced western meals is **PIC Kitchen $$** Soi 5, which serves excellent Thai dishes in an attractive setting. On the top floor of the Royal Garden Plaza, mid-way along Beach Road, there is a pleasant food centre using a coupon system.

SHOPPING At night Beach Rd and Pattaya 2 Rd are packed with stalls selling the usual mix of fake watches, wallets, fashion and souvenirs. **Royal Garden Plaza** in Beach Rd is a modern shopping plaza with boutiques, a Tower Records store, a cinema and a Boots chemist. On Pattaya 2 Rd there is the similar **Central Festival Centre**.

ENTERTAINMENT **Transvestite cabaret shows** are very popular at two establishments in north Pattaya: **Tiffany's**, tel: (038) 421-700, opposite Amari Orchid Resort, and **Alcazar**, tel: (038) 428-746, 78 Pattaya 2 Rd. These colourful shows are decidedly unraunchy and attract families with children as well as tour groups seeking titillation.

OUTDOOR ACTIVITIES IN PATTAYA

Pattaya is full of surprises, not least in its provision for sports and outdoor activities. For watersports head for **Jomtien Beach** where windsurfing, parasailing, jet-skiing and sailing with Hobie Cats, Prindles and Lasers all are fully catered for. Pattaya's off shore islands provide good opportunities for scuba diving and snorkelling. There are a number of professionally run and PADI-licensed dive centres like **Mermaid's Dive Centre** on Beach Road, tel & fax: (038) 710-918, e-mail: divesite@loxinfo.co.th. These places offer courses for novices, as well as experienced divers seeking speciality training in areas such as wreck or deep-sea diving.

Land-based activities include a safe go-kart circuit, tel: (038) 423-062, good bowling and snooker at the **Pattaya Bowl** near Soi 5 on Pattaya 2 Rd and horse-riding at the **Pattaya Riding Club**, tel: (038) 302-0814.

South Pattaya is ablaze with **bars and discos** and awash with young Thai girls waiting to attach themselves to a European male. **Hopf**, on Beach Rd just south of Soi 13, is a huge bar and restaurant with comfortable seating and a salubrious atmosphere. A little further south a left turn into South Pattaya Rd brings you to the lively **Bamboo Bar** where the live band thumps out a nightly session.

Pattaya – Ko Samet

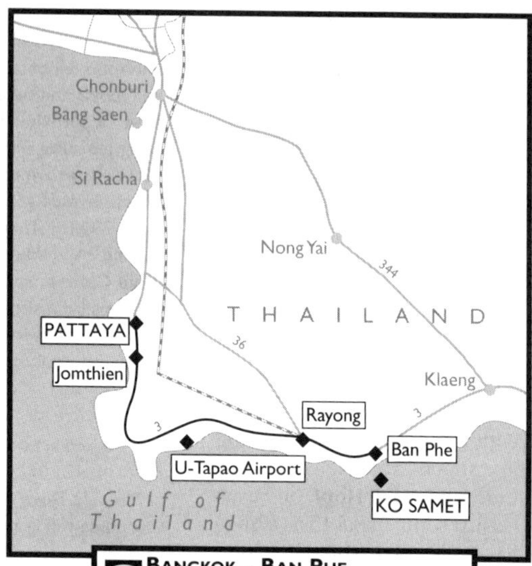

Bangkok – Ban Phe

Transport	Frequency	Journey Time
Bus	Daily, frequent	3–4hrs

Pattaya – Ban Phe

Transport	Frequency	Journey Time
Bus	Daily, frequent	1½hrs

Bangkok – Rayong
OTT Table 7077

Transport	Frequency	Journey Time
Bus	Daily, frequent	2¼hrs

Pattaya – Rayong

Transport	Frequency	Journey Time
Bus	Daily, frequent	1¼hrs

Songthaew: Rayong – Ban Phe

Transport	Frequency	Journey Time
Songthaew	Daily, frequent	½hr

Ban Phe – Ko Samet

Transport	Frequency	Journey Time
Boat	Daily	½–¾hr

Notes

Buses for Rayong and Ban Phe, with and without air-conditioning, depart from Bangkok's Eastern bus terminal, which is best reached by skytrain to Ekkamai station.

Tour agents in Bangkok and Pattaya run package deals to Ko Samet, with or without accommodation on the island. These cost more but offer the convenience of being picked up from your hotel and driven to Ban Phe for the ferry.

There is little to detain the traveller between Pattaya and Ko Samet. Commercial activity, especially around the deep-sea port of Sattahip to the South of Pattaya, has left its blot on the landscape. The Thai military also has a strong presence in the area and there was an incident in 2000 when a couple of their jets accidentally strafed a length of beach and its holiday bungalows. The town of Rayong is famous for its fish sauce, *nam pla*, which is bottled and destined for just about every dining table, public or private, across Thailand. From Rayong it is 17 km by road to the village of Ban Phe, the jumping-off point for the ferry ride to Ko Samet. The destination island of Ko Samet, with clear, clean sand and an absence of crowds, is well worth the short hop from either Pattaya or Bangkok.

RAYONG

There is little reason to stay in Rayong, but the town does have a usefully frequent bus link with Khorat that connects with the Bangkok–Nong Khai route (see page 177). Also, given that boats from Ban Phe stop around 1600–1700, you may wish to stay a night in Rayong and reach Ko Samet the next morning. There are a few inexpensive hotels close to the bus terminal, and the **Rayong Otani** $$–$ 59 Sukhumvit Rd, tel (038) 611-112, is typical of what's available. Turn left outside the station onto Sukhumvit Road. Alternatively, if you miss the last boat to Ko Samet, there is also accommodation at Ban Phe itself.

BAN PHE

Ban Phe is the ferry point for Ko Samet and most travellers see little more of the fishing port than the pier that takes them to a waiting boat. There is a bank west of the pier, with better rates than those available on the island, and shops to stock up on perishables for Ko Samet, where everything costs more. If your accommodation on the island has not been arranged in advance, you may be assailed by touts offering various deals and contradictory information. It makes sense to have made a phone call ahead and have somewhere in mind for the first night at least.

ACCOMMODATION

Last departure for most boats is 1600–1700. If an overnight stay is unavoidable there are budget hotels **$** close to the pier.

One good mid-range hotel metres from the pier is the **Diamond Hotel $$** 286/12 Moo 2, Tambol Pae, Amphur Muang; tel: (038) 651-826, fax: (038) 651-757.

If you are travelling in style, chill out at the well-run though expensive **Rayong Resort $$$$$**186 Laem Tarn, Ban Phe; tel: (038) 651-000, fax: (038) 651-007, e-mail: rayongrr@infonews.co.th. From Ban Phe, where there is a free pick-up, it is ten minutes by road to the resort with its private beach, evening cruises, day trips to Ko Samet, and the best European-style restaurant east of Pattaya.

KO SAMET

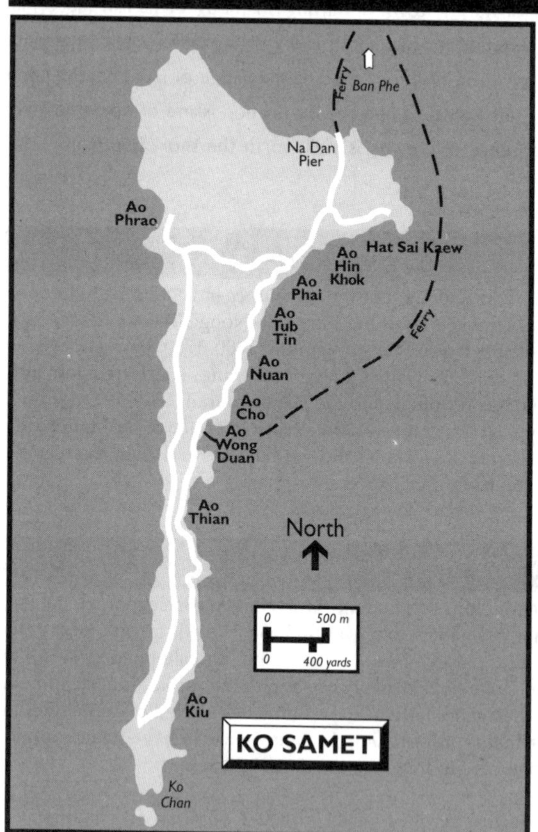

Lovely Ko Samet remained firmly off the tourist track until well into the 1980s, but now this tiny island - only 6 km long - receives daily boatloads of both domestic and foreign visitors. During Thai public holidays (see page 450), especially over long weekends, there are more visitors than hotel rooms, and the island feels grossly overcrowded. Even ordinary weekends attract busloads of stressed-out Thais looking for a break. By avoiding these times Ko Samet can offer a relaxing getaway for a couple of days, but it does partly depend on which beach you choose for your stay.

GETTING THERE Boats ply their way between Ban Phe and more than one beach on Ko Samet. As well as the regular scheduled services a number of resorts have their own boats, which will also take passengers not staying with them. **Na Dan pier** in the north-east of the island is the main arrival point and from here *songthaews* run south as far as Ao Wong Duan. Boats to Na Dan depart from Saphaan Nuan Tip pier in Ban Phe 0800–1600 $.

Boats also go direct to **Ao Wong Duan** and two of the resorts on this beach also run their own boats here. Boats for **Ao Phrao** depart from Saphaan Sri Ban Phe pier, as do some of the other resort boats as well.

From Khao San Road in Bangkok, and other tour agents in the capital, it is easy to book a combined bus and boat ticket **$$$** to Ko Samet. In Pattaya, Malibu Travel, tel: (038) 423-189, run a daily bus and boat service **$$**.

DEPARTURE Boats depart regularly for Ban Phe from Na Dan, but unless you are staying at Hat Sai Kaew or one of the other nearby beaches it is more convenient to catch one of the resort boats that depart from Ao Wong Duan, Ao Chao and Ao Phrao. It is also possible to book bus trips to Bangkok or Pattaya through some of the bungalow operators.

BEACHES The best known beach is **Hat Sai Kaew** in the north-east of the island. It is within walking distance of Na Dan Pier, which makes it the most overdeveloped on the island. Bungalows are cheek by jowl, there are noisy videos in the restaurants at night, lots of bars and discos, and a plethora of plastic tables and deckchairs which do their best to disfigure what is a truly beautiful stretch of soft, sandy beach. Definitely worth avoiding at busy times, but fine if you want to be in the thick of the action.

Due south, and separated by a low rocky promontory that is easily walked around, **Ao Hin Khok** offers another very attractive, though smaller, beach. Good budget accommodation can be found here, the food is much better than Hat Sai Kaew and there is a post office service from one of the bungalows.

The next beach south is **Ao Phai.** With resorts catering specifically for westerners, the place is rarely free from crowded pockets of sun-seekers clustered around umbrella shades. South of here is a string of three small beaches, separated by rocky patches with a trail through them, before you reach the larger Ao Wong Duan beach.

Ao Tub Tim, the first of the three beaches, is the busiest. **Ao Nuan** and **Ao Cho** are delightfully peaceful and free of upmarket resorts. You can stay here and enjoy the tranquility during the day, while a short tramp with the help of a torch at night will take you to the more sociable nightlife of the beaches to the north and south.

Ao Wong Duan is the second most developed beach on Ko Samet and boasts some of the plushest accommodation anywhere on the island. The resorts have their own boats that pull in to the beach daily, and the place does become crowded at times.

Further south is another string of small, very quiet beaches with limited, budget accommodation. **Ao Thian**, usually called Candlelight Beach, is a five-minute walk from Ao Wong Duan. Along with Ao Nuan this is the most convenient location for a secluded getaway. If you want to feel really isolated head for **Ao Kiu,** the most southerly beach, from where it is a short walk over to the west side for romantic views of the setting sun.

Accommodation The cost of a room on Ko Samet can vary enormously, depending on supply and demand. The price ranges indicated here refer to normal times and not holiday weekends, when prices can easily double or even treble. The telephone numbers are mobiles and use the prefix 01.

Hat Sai Kaew	It is hard to distinguish between one bungalow and the next as most of them offer a similar choice, between rooms with a fan and those with air-conditioning. **Diamond Beach $$** tel: (01) 239-0208 and **Coconut House $$** tel: (01) 943-2134, are typical of the better places.
Ao Hin Khok	There are three bungalow operations on the beach. **Naga $** tel: (01) 218-5372, **Tok's Little Hut $** tel: (01) 218-5195 and **Jep's Inn $$** no telephone. All three places serve excellent food.
Ao Phai	Budget accommodation is offered at **Ao Phai Hut $** tel: (01) 353-2644. **Sea Breeze $$–$** tel: (01) 239-4780 and **Samed Villa $$$–$$** tel: (01) 494-8090 offer more comfortable rooms in attractive bungalows.
Ao Tub Tim, Ao Nuan and Ao Cho	**TubTim Resort $$–$** tel: (01) 218-6425, e-mail: tubtimresort@yahoo.com has a range of bungalows. Buses for Bangkok and Pattaya can be booked here, and cash advances on credit cards are available. **Tiewe $** Ao Nuan is a quiet little retreat, shaded by greenery, offering budget rooms and shared showers.
Ao Wong Duan	Perhaps the best bungalows on the island's east coast, with air-conditioning and hot water, are at **Malibu Garden Resort $$$$–$$** tel: (038) 651-292, fax: (038) 426-229.
Ao Thian	There is a choice between **Candle Light Beach $$$** tel: (010 218-6934 which has doubles with fan right by the beach and **Lung Dum Bungalow $$** tel: (01) 458-8430, with better value rooms.
Ao Kiu	The only place to stay is at **Coral Beach $$$–$$** tel: (038) 652-561 or (01) 218-6231. When you phone check when their boat departs from Ban Phe; otherwise it's an hour's walk from Ao Wong Duan.
Ao Prao	This is the only beach on the west coast. Good for snorkelling, it boasts the upmarket **Prao Resort $$$$$** tel: (038) 651-814, fax: (02) 438-9771 which has smart bungalows and watersports.

FOOD All the bungalows and resorts have their own restaurants. It's just a matter of wandering from one to another and seeing what takes your fancy. The menus, all in the $$-$ range, are very similar, offering fresh fish waiting to be barbecued, steaks, Thai curries, salads, soups and sandwiches. Ao Wong Duan has a far more laid-back atmosphere at night than Hat Sai Kaew. The **Vongduern Villa** restaurant at the southern end of the beach has an attractive night-time setting over the rocks, while the Malibu restaurant has some tempting desserts. **Naga's** at Ao Hin Khok has a well-deserved reputation for above-average food.

Ko Samet – Ko Chang

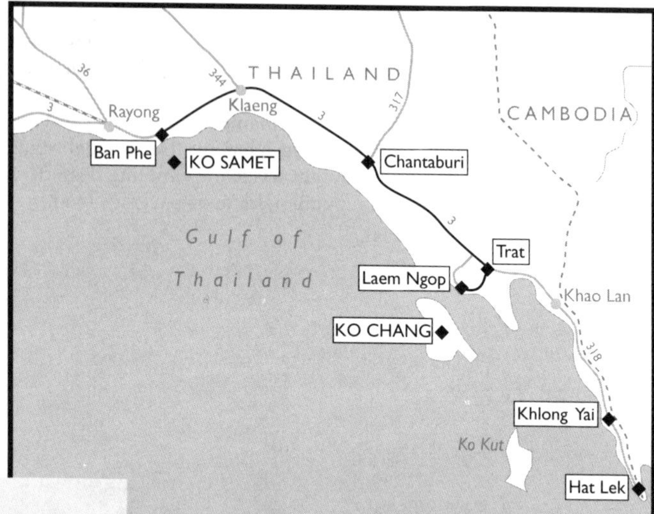

Notes

Getting to Ko Chang from Bangkok in a day is possible, but only if you get to the Eastern Bus terminal before 0800 for a bus to Trat to catch the last boat from Laem Ngop at 1700. If departing from Ko Samet, catching an early boat to Ban Phe is also recommended. Both Chantaburi and Trat suggest themselves as places to bed down for a night.

As well as the above routes, there are also daily buses between Chantaburi and Khorat (6 hrs) which offers a useful link with the Bangkok–Nong Khai route (see page 177) while avoiding a return to the capital.

Bangkok – Trat

Transport	Frequency	Journey Time
Bus	Daily, frequent	6–8hrs

Bangkok – Chantaburi

OTT Table 7077

Transport	Frequency	Journey Time
Bus	Daily, frequent	5–7hrs

Ban Phe – Chantaburi

Transport	Frequency	Journey Time
Bus	Daily, frequently	1½hrs

Chantaburi – Trat

Transport	Frequency	Journey Time
Bus	Daily, frequent	1¼hrs
Shared Taxi	Daily, when full	1hr

Songthaew: Trat – Laem Ngop

Transport	Frequency	Journey Time
Songthaew	Daily, frequent	½hr

Laem Ngop – Ko Chang

Transport	Frequency	Journey Time
Boat	Daily	1hr

Ko Samet – Ko Chang

While the Pattaya—Ko Samet route is now well tavelled, the number of visitors continuing east to Ko Chang is a trickle by comparison. But the trickle is an interesting one because the route attracts more independently minded travellers seeking unspoilt corners of the country. Ko Chang itself is rapidly developing its tourist potential – in five years time it may even be a place to avoid – but the area around Trat has an inviting laid-back character. There is a lot to do in terms of conventional tourist attractions but it is an enjoyable area to explore in a lazy kind of way. Adventurers will be drawn to the narrow strip of Thai territory between the Gulf of Thailand and Cambodia. The tourist infrastructure is virtually non-existent as one approaches the Cambodian border and you need your own transport to visit the small beaches dotted along the coastline. Ko Chang, on the other hand, has a host of white sand coves and beaches and new accommodation and visitor facilities are being developed all the time.

CHANTABURI

Chantaburi does not receive a lot of tourists but the town has enough character to justify a half-day visit. Although there are no 'must see' sights the town has retained an appealing sense of its social history. Chantaburi's charm comes from its ethnic mix, its vernacular architecture, and the buzz of specialist activity from the gem trading that dominates the town's commerce.

Chantaburi's Gems

Rubies and sapphires are mined around Chantaburi but the town's fame as a gem-trading centre now goes well beyond the local market. Mynamar (Burma) is the most important source, as well as Cambodia and Vietnam, and the men seen peering intently through a magnifier at their heap of coloured stones are usually engaged in the fine art of classifying each and every gem.

Rubies and sapphires are varieties of the mineral corundum. Subtle variations in colour are caused by impurities like chromium, titanium or iron in the aluminium oxide that mostly constitutes the corundum. Less prosaically, the gemstones are among the most valuable precious stones on the planet and are far more expensive than diamonds of an equal size. While all rubies are red, the most sought after colour is a deep purplish hue known as pigeon's blood. All other non-red gemstones of corundum are sapphires, although the classic sapphire is a deep cornflower blue.

Highlights From the bus station walk along Sartidet Road until it comes to an end on the west bank of the Chantaburi River. Turn right and wander along Rim Nam Road as it follows the course of the waterway. This is the most interesting and **photogenic part of town**, with dilapidated and occasional ornate shops and houses that reflect the mixed cultural influences of China and Vietnam. The Vietnamese presence in

Chantaburi is pervasive, dating back to the end of the 19th century and continuing into the 1970s, when a fresh wave of refugees decided life in communist-controlled south Vietnam was not to their liking.

The French have also made their presence felt in Chantaburi, having occupied the town for ten years at the tail end of the 19th century, when the borders between Siam and her neighbours were open to 'negotiation' and some coercion. As you walk along the river you will soon reach the footbridge that leads directly to the French-designed **cathedral** built in 1880. Remarkable simply by being here, the cool interior is far more aesthetically pleasing than the outside of the building.

The **gem-dealing area** is not far away, back on the west side of the river around Sri Chan Road, which runs parallel with the river one block inland. This is not the place to go shopping for sapphires and rubies, unless you can really assess their worth, but observing the gem-dealing scene can be fascinating. The gem shops are open to the street and the plainly dressed people who patronise them, like the undistinguished-looking experts who sit nonchalantly at a table before a small pile of precious gems, are masters of understatement.

GETTING THERE Buses from the east, west and north-east of Thailand all pull in at Chantaburi's bus station on Sartidet Rd, less than 1 km west of the town centre. If coming from Ko Samet, the easiest way to reach Chantaburi is by *songthaew* from Ban Phe to Rayong and then a regular bus from there.

Kasemsan I $ 98/1 Benchama-Rachutit Rd, tel: (039) 312-340. The easiest budget guesthouse to get to from the bus station. Walk along Sartidet Rd and, one block before the river, turn right at the main junction with Benchama-Rachutit Rd. Air-con rooms are in the quieter part of the building.

For standard hotel accommodation **KP Inn $$$–$$** Trirat Rd, tel: (039) 311-756, delivers creature comforts at a moderate price.

Chantaburi's local food includes the delicious Vietnamese spring rolls (*chao gio*). The best place to find them is down by the river where **food stalls** next to the river serve them piping hot. The riverside stalls also sell the town's famous noodles with a variety of seafood.

Standard Thai and Chinese dishes can be found in the **Chanthon Phochana** restaurant at the Kasemsan I guesthouse, although reports of the quality of the food here are mixed.

TRAT

Nearly every traveller in Trat is on their way to or from Ko Chang. The town serves mainly as a transit point for the journey to Laem Ngop from where the boats depart. It is also a useful place to stock up on provisions because everything costs a little more on Ko Chang. There are banks on Trat's main road with a far better exchange rate than anywhere on the island. A night's stay may be necessary here if you miss the last boat to Ko Chang at 1600.

HIGHLIGHTS

There is not a lot to do in the town although the budget guesthouses can arrange a river trip and one of them, the Windy Guesthouse, has free canoes for paddling up and down the canal. With time to spare, a more recommended activity is an excursion to Khlong Yai near the Cambodian border (see box below).

ARRIVAL AND DEPARTURE

There are a few companies running buses between Bangkok and Trat but they all have their stations along Trat's main road, still called Sukhumvit Rd, with their timetables and prices clearly marked. There are VIP buses, regular air-con buses, and ordinary non-air-con buses. There are also buses between Trat and Chantaburi, Ban Phe, Rayong and Pattaya. *Songthaews* for Laem Ngop depart from behind the shopping centre in Trat.

There are two good budget places, close to one another, and both reached from the bus stations by walking south down Sukhumvit Road in the opposite direction from Bangkok. After 200 metres, before the canal, turn left down Thoncharoen Road.

Windy Guest House $ 64 Thoncharoen Rd, tel: (039) 511-923 is on the right, and almost opposite is **Foremost Guest House $** 49 Thoncharoen Rd; tel: (039) 511-923.

Owned by the same family, both guesthouses offer simple, clean rooms with shared bathrooms. Best of all, these are excellent places for picking up current information about accommodation on Ko Chang and onward travel across the border to Cambodia. If both are full ask directions to the nearby **NP Guest House $** Soi Luang Aet, tel: (039) 512-270. This is another friendly place to stay, with a convenient small restaurant.

For more comfort and a shorter walk, turn left off Sukhumvit Road by the night market building. On the corner a sign points to the Trad Hotel, which is in fact the **Trat Hotel $$$–$$** Meuang Trat; tel: (039) 511-091. There is a choice of rooms, some with air-con and all with their own bathrooms.

The **Trat Hotel restaurant $,** only open 0600–1730, but is conveniently close to the bus stations and enjoys air-conditioning. The menu is an unexciting list of rice, noodle and fried chicken dishes; few locals eat here because of the proximity of the day and night markets. Next door, the **Jiraporn**'s small menu in English is about half the price of the hotel restaurant.

The best places for good local food are undoubtedly the markets. The night market is north of the Trat hotel, while the day market is one block to the south beneath the town's shopping centre.

Excursion to the Border

A slither of Thai territory slips down to the south-east of Trat as far as Hat Lek at the border with Cambodia, reaching the fishing town of Khlong Yai along the way. *Songthaews* **$** depart regularly to Khlong Yai from behind the shopping centre in Trat, and from Khlong Yai there are *songthaews* and motorbikes that continue on to the border.

There is little to do at Hat Lek but the journey to Khlong Yai is worth the trip because of the spectacular beauty of the Cambodian mountains and forests, and the deep blue sea of the Gulf of Thailand. The **Suksamlan Hotel $$–$** tel: (039) 581-109 in Khlong Yai has decent rooms.

Travelling to Cambodia

It is currently legal and safe to travel across the border into Cambodia at **Hat Lek**. However, this was not the case until quite recently and circumstances may change. A visa for Cambodia may be obtained in Bangkok (see page 58) but it is currently possible to travel into Cambodia and return to Thailand on your Thai visa, as long as it is still valid when you return.

Unless you are planning onward travel to Vietnam it is not necessary to obtain a Cambodian visa; just pay the border police at Hat Lek. The budget guesthouses in Trat are excellent sources of up-to-date information on travel into Cambodia and it is worth calling in even if you are not staying there.

Laem Ngop

Laem Ngop, 17 km south-west of Trat, is the departure point for Ko Chang and there is no other reason to travel here. There used to be only one pier in the town itself but two new piers have now been completed outside of town.

The **TAT office** is near the town pier, tel: (039) 597-255, open daily 0830 – 1630. All the piers have 'tourist information offices' which are just fronts for particular resorts on the island. If you arrive in high season with no accommodation they can serve a purpose.

A favourite with travellers is **Chut Kaew $** tel: (039) 597-088 on the main road, five minutes on foot from the pier. Rooms are basic and bathroom facilities are shared, but it is a friendly place. The **restaurant** is worth a visit in its own right while waiting for a boat: the food is fine and information on Ko Chang is available from the owner and guests.

KO CHANG

Considering its size – it is Thailand's second largest island after Phuket – Ko Chang has been a late developer on the tourist scene. Proximity to Cambodia and previous lack of safety probably contributed to the island's isolation, but it is now rapidly establishing itself as an idyllic island retreat. It boasts beautiful sandy beaches and, compared to Phuket and Ko Samui, remains unspoilt.

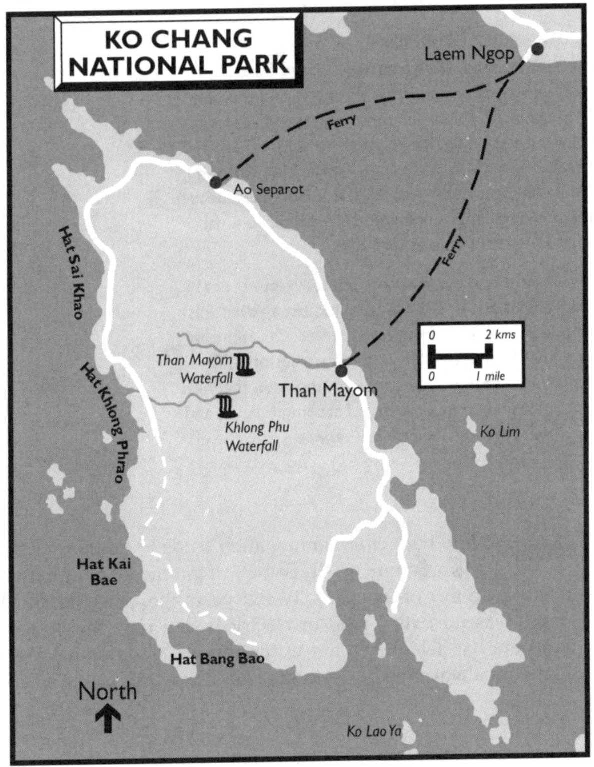

Highlights Compared to Ko Samui and Phuket, the nightlife is low-key. In fact, whatever the time of day, there is not a lot to do but relax, enjoy a massage on the beach, swim, snorkel (snorkelling trips to nearby islands can be arranged through some of the bungalows) and let time pass idly by. Having said that, when the road that winds its way around the island has been completely paved there will be easier access to some of the more isolated beaches, and new developments will spring up.

Getting There **Boats $$** leave from Laem Ngop throughout the day from 0900 until 1600 or 1700, with the most frequent service between December and April. Most boats go to Ao Saparot on the island's north-east coast and from here there are ***songthaews* $** waiting to take passengers to any of the west-coast beaches. There is also at least one boat a day to Than Mayrom on the east coast.

The Beaches

The main beach is **Hat Sai Khao**, White Sand Beach, with the largest cluster of bungalows and resorts, and the only nightlife to speak of. This is the most convenient resort in terms of having a good choice of places to stay and eat. The next beach, 5 km south, is the lovely, quiet **Hat Khlong Phrao**, while further south again **Hat Kai Bee** has a beautiful stretch of sand which unfortunately shrinks to a narrow strip at high tide.

On the south of the island the most attractive sandy beach is **Hat Bang Bao** but unless the road has been paved this far south it is a 5 km walk from Hat Kai Bee. Occasionally, there is a boat from Laem Ngop but don't bet on it. The east coast has no beach to compare with those on the west coast, which is reflected in a paucity of accommodation and an infrequent *songthaew* service.

Accommodation While budget accommodation tends to be more expensive than on Ko Samui or Ko Samet, accommodation for most budgets means there is a good mix of travellers. Twelve years ago, when the first beach huts appeared, there was no paved road or electricity, but now the best resorts have rooms with a mini-bar, telephone, hot water and air-conditioning. Weekends and public holidays are always the busiest time, and it is worth trying to arrive during the week.

HAT SAI KHAO

New places are springing up all the time but the following gives a good idea of what is available. As the *songthaew* reaches the white sand of Hat Sai Khao one of the first places on the right is the venerable **KC $** tel: (01) 211-5607. A pioneer in Ko Chang's tourist development, KC has simple thatched huts virtually on the beach with shared facilities and no electricity.

On the other side of the road **Jinda Bungalow $** has rooms with a fan and indoor bathroom, and discounted rates for stays of more than a couple of nights. There are lots of other budget joints dotted around this stretch of beach and it is easy to walk from one to the other checking them out.

Mac Bungalows $$$ tel: (01) 219-3056, an example of the good mid-range accommodation available right on the beach.

One of the nicest places to stay has to be **Banpu Koh Chang Hotel $$$$$** tel: (01) 314-8763 or (039) 542-355, fax: (039) 542-359. The bungalows, popular with Germans, are set in tropical gardens with carefully crafted rooms and stone-decorated bathrooms.

Moonlight Resort $$$ tel: (01) 212-6036 or (039) 597-198, on a rocky beach but within walking distance of a sandy stretch and a choice of rooms.

Another nearby place with a stony beach, and a good five minute walk to the sand of Hat Sai Khao, is **Changtong Resort $** tel: (01) 823-0991. Its wooden huts only have a fan but are adequate considering the price.

HAT KHLONG PHRAO

The northern stretch of Hat Khlong Phrao, called Chaiyachet Beach, is the location of the upmarket **Koh Chang Resort $$$$$** tel: (01) 948-8177, fax: (01) 912-0738, e-mail: rooksgroup@hotmail.com. Further south there are a few budget choices like **KP Bungalows $** tel: (01) 219-1225 and **Magic $** tel: (01) 219-3408.

HAT KAI BEE

Once a remote location, the beach area is developing fast. **Coral Resort $$** tel: (01) 219-3815 now has a spread of wood and concrete bungalows close to the sea.

Siam Bay Resort $$–$ tel: (01) 452-7061 at the southern end of the beach has a wider range of bungalows and huts.

Lagoona Koh Chang $$$ tel: (01) 848-5052, fax: (039) 511-429. Finishing touches were being put to this new operation at the time of writing and it looks like it is going to be a smart place to stay. Substantial reductions for stays of four days or more will bring it into the $$ category. Worth checking out.

Hat Bang Bao At the moment there are only a few places to stay, though this will soon change. **Bang Bao Blue Wave $** tel (01) 439-0349 has huts with shared facilities and some larger ones with their own shower. During the low season (May–Oct) telephone ahead to make sure it is open.

Virtually every resort or bungalow operation has its own restaurant and it's easy to wander from one to another checking out their menus. Some places which look drab during daylight come into their own at night, especially those close to the water's edge. Look for fresh seafood on display in layers of crushed ice waiting to be selected and grilled on the spot.
At Hat Sai Khao the **Little Miss Naughty Restaurant $$–$** serves the usual Thai stir-fried fare, as well as fried tofu with sweet peanut sauce and a choice of pizzas.
The Banpu Koh Chang Hotel restaurant $$$–$$ has a large choice of soups, sandwiches, noodles, salads, fried meat dishes and tempura, as well as Thai favourites like *tom yam* and curries.
On the left side of the road, approaching Hat Kai Bee from Hat Sai Khao, **Piggy's Delight $$** is a pleasant vegetarian restaurant serving tofu dishes and lots of salads.
At Hat Kai Bee the restaurant at the Coral Resort has a well-chosen site on the rocks and an above-average menu featuring some Thai specialities among more commonplace dishes.

Entertainment

Compared to Ko Samui or Phuket, the entertainment infrastructure is in its infancy on Ko Chang. This can be a blessing for those who enjoy quiet evenings undisturbed by noisy videos, and anyway there is usually a sociable bar within walking distance. At the time of writing the bar next to Mac Bungalows was the liveliest place at night. At Hat Hai Bee the **Kai Bee Pub**, with music, food, pool table, and cocktails, has a grand entrance off the main road.

Shopping

There are no real shops on Ko Chang, although on Hat Sai Khao, opposite the Banpu Koh Chang Hotel, there is a minimarket with a small selection of garments and beachwear. There is also a small bookshop with a second-hand exchange facility. E-mail and Internet access is available upstairs, although the rate is high due to the use of a satellite connection.

Highlights

Motorbikes, scooters and bicycles can be hired from a few places at Hat Sai Khao. This is the best way of exploring the island and reaching some of the pretty waterfalls in the interior. **Than Mayom waterfalls** could be the focus of a trip to

DIVING AND SNORKELLING

At the Banpu Koh Chang Hotel **Eco-Divers** tel: (01) 982-2744 offers PADI diving courses and trips out to sea. A four-day open water course with four dives is US$280. The average cost of a diving trip by boat with a dive-master is US$45, including equipment and two dives. A snorkelling trip by boat is US$15.

the east side of the island. It is about an hour's walk from the settlement of Than Mayom to the first of the three falls. The stones, inscribed with initials, are said to be the calling cards of Rama VI and Rama VII. If you go on to the furthest fall, another hour's walk, the initials of the more energetic Rama V, King Chulalongkorn, await you.

On the west coast the **Khlong Phu waterfalls** can be reached by taking the turn-off signposted Nam Tok Khlong Phu on the main road south of Hat Sai Khao. Hard work on a bicycle, easier with a motorbike, a rough track leads up to the falls through tropical trees, and your reward is a sparkling pool safe for swimming.

Most of Ko Chang is undisturbed **primary forest,** and there are numerous paths that head into the interior, including a trail that leads across the centre of the island. However, it is easy to get lost on the trail and locals recommend the use of a guide.

ISLAND EXCURSIONS

Ko Chang is the largest island in the Ko Chang National Park, but there are other smaller islands, mostly off the south coast, which are mostly visited for their snorkelling and diving opportunities.

Ko Mak can be reached by a daily boat service from Laem Ngop that only operates regularly during the dry months (Nov–May). Most of the island is devoted to rubber and coconut plantations, but there are beautiful white sand beaches and a handful of places offering accommodation. An affordable and fun place to spend a night is **Ko Mak Resort $$–$** tel: (02) 319-6714 or (01) 219-1220.

If you want a really small island, head for **Ko Kham** off the north coast of Ko Mak. There is only one place to stay, **Ko Kham Resort $$$–$** tel: (039) 597-114. Their boat leaves daily each afternoon from Laem Ngop, but only during the dry months (Nov–May).

The largest island after Ko Chang is **Ko Kut.** Most of the accommodation is handled by upmarket resorts, like **Ko Kud Sai Khao Resort $$$$** tel: (039) 511-429, that manage their own transport. To visit the island on your own take one of the boats from Ko Mak that make the journey each day in the dry season. The beaches are sparkling white and the water an inviting transparent turquoise.

Ko Samet – Ko Chang

Boat trips from Ko Chang can be organised through some of the bungalows. Piggy's Delight restaurant at Hat Kai Bee takes bookings for a twice-weekly trip. Other tour organisers, tel: (039) 597-242 or (01) 868-2648, offer a night camping on one of the tiny islands before moving on to another island on the second day.

Bangkok – Ayuttaya

OTT Tables 7060/7076

Transport	Frequency	Journey Time
Train	Daily, frequent	1½hrs
Bus	Daily, frequent	1hr
Boat	Daily	All day cruise

Bangkok – Bang Pa-In

OTT Tables 7060/7076

Transport	Frequency	Journey Time
Train	Daily	1hr 10mins
Bus	Daily, frequent	1½–2hrs
Boat	Sunday only	All day cruise

Bang Pa-In – Ayutthaya

OTT Tables 7060/7076

Transport	Frequency	Journey Time
Train	Daily	15mins
Bus	Daily	30-50mins

Notes

If hopping between Bang Pa-In and Ayutthaya, the buses and *songthaews* are a lot more frequent than the trains.

North to South

Siam's royal capital for over 400 years is close enough to Bangkok to make it a popular day excursion. Ayutthaya and Bang Pa-In are both on the main railway line from the capital to Chiang Mai so it is possible to take them in while leisurely making your way up to northern Thailand.

Bang Pa-In is hardly worth a trip for its own sake, though if time allows it is easy to drop off for a quick visit before moving on to Ayutthaya.

Bangkok trains to Ayutthaya travel on to Chiang Mai and northern Thailand. It is possible to catch these trains from Don Muang railway station directly opposite Bangkok's international airport. You could visit Ayutthaya and move on to the north, leaving Bangkok for the last leg of your trip.

Cruising the Chao Phraya River

Bangkok's Chao Phraya Express Boat Co's **Sunday boat cruise** to Bang Pa-In stops at an arts and crafts centre at Bang Sai, and Wat Pai Lom temple and a bird sanctuary on the return journey. Departs 0800 from the Maharat pier and returns 1730. The fare is 300B return, 200B one way. Tel: (02) 623-6001 or 225-3002.

The Oriental Hotel organises **daily day trips to Bang Pa-In and Ayutthaya.** Trips depart 0800, travelling one way by boat and the other by coach. Cost, including lunch and a tour guide, is 1800B. Tel: (02) 236-0400.

Luxury cruises to Ayutthaya, which make the Oriental Hotel's operation seem cheap, are conducted through the Marriott Royal Garden Hotel. Tel: (02) 476-0021.

BANG PA-IN

In the middle of the 17th century, when the royal capital was at Ayutthaya, the king built a country retreat for himself a few miles downstream on the Chao Phraya River. When the royal seat of power shifted to Bangkok, the Bang Pa-In pad gracefully declined until Rama IV, quick to take advantage of the new steamboat technology, began a restoration programme. But it was his son, Rama V, who set about commissioning the eccentric mixture of architectural styles that make the **Royal Palace $$**, open daily 0830–1530, such a novelty.

Using the free brochure that comes with your admission ticket, begin by identifying the **Warophat Phiman Hall**, a colonial-style private residence built in 1876 and containing a throne hall as well as private rooms. A covered bridge leads from here to the inner palace grounds, where the king and his retinue were left to their own devices and the only commoners allowed to enter were the ladies in his harem.

As you cross the lake it is impossible to miss the **Isawan Thipay-art Hall**, the only purely Siamese structure in the palace. Its elegant oriental curves contrast shockingly with a European-style country chalet in the inner palace painted in lurid shades of green. Behind the country house lurks a lovely Chinese creation, the **Palace of Heavenly Light**, which was brought here from China as a gift to the king from grateful merchants in the capital. The rich and lush interior is open to visitors.

The only other structure of note is the **memorial stone** to one of Rama V's wives, who accidentally drowned in the river in 1887 even though there were servants around who could have easily rescued her. An edict forbade any commoner from touching a royal, under pain of death, so she was left to drown.

From Bang Pa-In's railway station it takes about half an hour to walk to the Royal Palace, though *samlors* are readily available.

AYUTTHAYA

The city was the Siamese capital from 1350 until 1767, when it was attacked and virtually destroyed by invaders from Burma. The historic ruins, which have World Heritage status, stand as testimony to this eventful period in Asian history. Ayutthaya traded with Malaca, Java, China, Japan, India and Persia, and diplomatic ties were established with many European countries. What you see today – fading red-brick ruins dotted about a flat expanse of land – do not so much evoke a rich imperial past as capture a sense of a lost era.

A good way to start a tour is with a visit to the tourist office (see below) to collect a map. Across the road stands the **Chao Sam Phraya National Museum $** Rotchana Rd, open Wed–Sun 0900–1600. There are various finds from the temples and information about Buddha figures and their iconography.

It takes less than ten minutes to walk along Rotchana Road to the **Historical Study Center $$$** open 0830–1630. This museum recreates historical Ayutthaya using models, offering a good introduction to its subject. The admission charge includes entry to an annexe situated some distance away – ask for directions. It has well-researched material on Ayutthaya's relations with foreign states around the 16th century, when

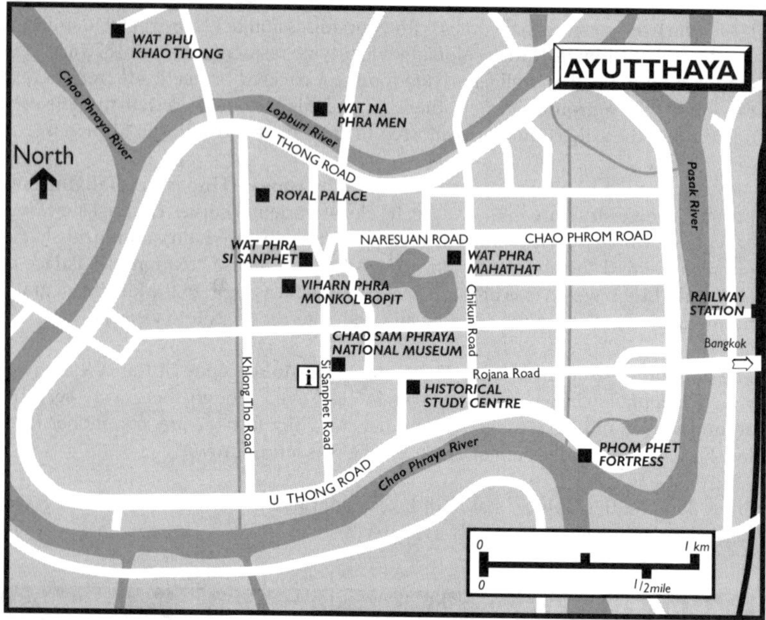

scores of nationalities were living in and around the city, and its population was bigger than London's.

The main reason for any visit to Ayutthaya is to view the ruined temples. As there are too many to take in on one day, choices have to be made. The temples covered in the box opposite start with Wat Phra Mahathat, which can be visited on foot. To reach the others it is best to avoid the hot part of the day and hire a bicycle or use a *tuk-tuk*. Between 0800 and 1830, the official opening hours, there is an admission charge $.

TAT Office, Sri Sanphet Rd, tel: (035) 246-076. If only all TAT offices were like this one. It has a map of all the sites, up-to-date information on transport, suggested walking itineraries with maps and even a list of *tuk-tuk* fares.

The tourist office is next to the City Hall, opposite the Chao Sam Phraya National Museum.

Ayutthaya's Wats: An Itinerary

This route begins at Chao Phrom Rd, facing west away from the river near the railway station. Walk or cycle up Chao Phrom Rd for less than 2 km to the junction with Chee Kun Rd. Just past it are two temples on either side of the road.

Wat Phra Mahathat, on the left, dates back to the 14th century. You can clamber up the remains of the *prang* for a good view of the compound. Assorted ruins and Buddha heads lie around the grounds, including a photogenic one that has become inextricably tied up with the roots of a bodhi tree.

Continue west along what is now Naresuan Rd to **Wat Phra Si Sanphet.** This was once the richest and grandest of all Ayutthaya's *wats.* Now its most distinguished feature is the three central *chedi* containing the ashes of once-illustrious kings. Looking north from here you can see the foundations of the **royal palace** that was destroyed by the Burmese in 1767 and where the stables alone could accommodate 100 elephants.

Head due south instead to find **Viharn Phra Monkol Bopit**, built in the 1950s to represent the original 15th century structure that was destroyed by the Burmese. It is now home to one of the world's largest bronze Buddhas, over 12 metres high and thought to date from the 16th century.

Reaching **Wat Na Phra Men** involves crossing the Lopburi River by the bridge on the north side of the royal palace. It is worth the journey because this *wat* managed to avoid Burmese vandalism and the main bot, the largest in the city and much restored since, survives from the 16th century. Inside, under a resplendently decorated ceiling, sits an imperious six-metre-high Buddha.

If you are on a bicycle it is worth travelling a couple of km north-west to **Wat Phu Khao Thong.** This monastery was constructed in 1387 and, although there is little left to appreciate now, the journey there takes you into scenic countryside and rice paddies.

Orientation The ancient capital was built on an island around the meeting of three rivers and enclosed by a high wall. Accommodation and eating options tend to be clustered at the east side of the island, around Chao Phrom Road and within walking distance of the railway and bus stations.

Bicycles are the best way to visit the temples. The least expensive rates are found along the road from the railway station to the ferry jetty. *Tuk-tuks* are plentiful for short hops between ruins – or negotiate a price for a tour.

Ayothaya Hotel $$$$ Tessabarn Say Rd, tel: (035) 232-855, fax: (035) 251-018. Centrally located just off Chao Phrom Rd, but hardly worth the rack rate. Modern rooms and a swimming pool though, so try for a hefty discount.

Tevaraj Tanrin Hotel $$$ Rochana Rd, tel: (035) 243-139. Turn left out of the railway station and this hotel is a few hundred metres down the road. Handy in this respect, but not for sightseeing across the river. Large rooms with air-con and fridge, views of the river, and a snooker table.

Phaesri Thong Guest House $$–$ 8/1 U Thong Rd. Attractive location by the river, dorm beds and rooms with air-con make this one of the better places for a one night stopover.

T.M.T. Guesthouse $ 14/4 Soi Tro Kkro Sor, off Naresuan Rd, tel: (035) 251-474. Typical of the budget accommodation available in this *soi* off Naresuen Rd. Dorm beds and rooms with shared bathroom and one en-suite room.

Good Luck Café $ Soi Tro Kkro Sor, off Naresuan Rd. A pleasant street-side café with the usual array of Thai dishes, plus a vegetarian menu with dishes like tofu with lotus stems and mushrooms.

Across the road the **Moon Café $**, more of a bar than a café, opens late in the evening for light meals and beers. Guesthouses in this area all have their own restaurants, which are worth checking out.

Krung Si River Hotel Restaurant $$$–$$ 27/2 Mu 11, Rochana Rd. One of three floating restaurants near the railway station. A large menu featuring salads, steaks, fish, curries, and Chinese and Japanese dishes.

NOTES

Six trains a day run between Bangkok and Chiang Mai. Four stop at Ayutthaya.

Berths to Chiang Mai from Bangkok are often sold out and reservations should be made as far in advance as possible.

AYUTTHAYA – CHIANG MAI

OTT TABLES 7060/7076

TRANSPORT	FREQUENCY	JOURNEY TIME
Train	4 daily	12hrs
Bus	Daily, frequent	9hrs

BANGKOK – CHIANG MAI

OTT TABLES 7060/7076

TRANSPORT	FREQUENCY	JOURNEY TIME
Train	6 daily	11-15hrs
Bus	Daily, frequent	9-12hrs

BANGKOK – CHIANG MAI

TRANSPORT	FREQUENCY	JOURNEY TIME
Air	Daily	1hr

AYUTTHAYA – LOPBURI

OTT TABLES 7060/7076

TRANSPORT	FREQUENCY	JOURNEY TIME
Train	12 daily	1hr 10mins
Bus	Daily, frequent	2hrs

LOPBURI – PHITSANULOK

OTT TABLES 7060/7076

TRANSPORT	FREQUENCY	JOURNEY TIME
Train	13 daily	4-5hrs
Bus	Daily, frequent	3hrs

BANGKOK – PHITSANULOK

TRANSPORT	FREQUENCY	JOURNEY TIME
Air	3 daily	45mins

PHITSANULOK – CHIANG MAI

OTT TABLE 7060

TRANSPORT	FREQUENCY	JOURNEY TIME
Train	7 daily	5-6hrs
Bus	Daily	5½hrs
Air	Daily	35mins

NOTES

Cheap buses to Chiang Mai from Bangkok's Khao San Rd may be cramped, uncomfortable and take you to an inconveniently located guesthouse.

From Lopburi, Phitsanulok, Sukhotai and Mae Sot there are possible transport links with other parts of the country. Details are given below under the towns.

Ayutthaya – Chiang Mai

This is a long route and many visitors cover the ground in one 12-hour rail journey. Travelling the route in short hops brings the advantage of being able to observe the transition, geographic and cultural, between central Thailand and the north of the country. The central plains around the valley of the River Chao Phraya are not scenically exciting but they function as the country's breadbasket in terms of rice production. By the time you reach Phitsanulok the plains have been left behind and the distinctive character of northern Thailand begins to make itself felt. The accent of the language is different, people prefer sticky rice to the ubiquitous white rice of the south and there seems to be more variety in the culture of everyday life. Chiang Mai is the capital of northern Thailand, cosmopolitan in nature yet surrounded by various hill tribes whose traditional ways of living are inexorably succumbing to the march of 'progress'. Expect a pleasant suprise if stepping off the train in Chiang Mai after a night's sleep since departing Ayutthaya.

LOPBURI

Lopburi is a very old town dating back to the 6th century. It came under Khmer influence in the 10th century, but after 300 years fell into obscurity until King Narai started rebuilding work in the second half of the 17th century. Lopburi was to be his second capital and his palace, built with the help of European architects, is the best reason for stopping off at Lopburi on your way north. A more frivolous motive would be to see playful monkeys in an urban environment; they are all over the old part of town.

The King's Palace

The palace's main entrance leads to the **outer courtyard**, now mostly composed of ruins, where the food stores, stables for elephants and horses, and a reception hall for visitors were located. The ruins of another reception hall, once lined with elegant French mirrors to impress foreign dignitaries, can be seen in the **middle courtyard**, but the main interest here now is the **museum** $ open Wed–Sun 0830–1530. Housed in a colonial-style building built in the 1860s by King Rama IV, the museum has an impressive display of Thai art across the centuries as well as plenty of monumental art from Lopburi. The **inner courtyard** was reserved for royalty, but only ruins remain of **Suttha Sawan Pavilion**, the king's private residence and where King Narai died in 1688.

HIGHLIGHTS One of the city's more minor attractions is waiting to be seen immediately after leaving the railway station, **Wat Phra Si Ratana Mahathat** $ open daily

0830–1630. It is noted for its refined, slender Khmer *prang* made of laterite which may date back to the 12th century. It has little in common with the nearby ruined *viharn* with its distinctly Gothic aspects, but King Narai's interest in European forms reappears in the King's Palace.

The King's Palace, **Phra Narai Ratchaniwet,** free, open daily 0730–1730, is not far away on Sorasak Rd. Built between 1577 and 1665 with the help of French and Italian architects, there are three courtyards to the palace complex.

The north entrance of the king's palace leads onto Rue de France on the other side of the main Ratchadamnern Rd. Halfway down this road, on the left, stands the white **Wat Sao Thong-Thong**, another example of Narai's penchant for mixing Thai and European architectural styles. Inside, tucked into niches along the wall where lamps were once placed, are some good examples of dragon-headed Buddhas.

ROUTE DETAIL

Rail

Catching an early train from Bangkok (0705 or 0745) and leaving luggage at Ayutthaya station leaves enough time to see Lopburi before catching the 2123 or 2346 night train to Chiang Mai.

Bus

Buses run between Lopburi and Suphanburi, from where there are regular buses to Kanchanaburi which allows you to link up with the Bangkok–Nam Tok route (page 85) in western Thailand. A link with the Bangkok–Nong Khai route (page 177) in the north-east of the country is possible by taking one of the regular buses between Lopburi and Khorat (Nakhon Ratchasima).

The **TAT Office** is inconveniently located in the new part of town on Narai Maharat Rd, open daily 0830–1630, tel: (036) 422-768. For years there has been talk of moving to a new office in the old part of town, close to the Wat Phra Si Ratana Mahathat.

Asia Lopburi Hotel $$–$ Sorasak Rd, tel/fax: (036) 411-892. A short walk from the railway station and overlooking the King's Palace, this is the obvious place to stay for one night. Avoid rooms on the noisy main road.

Nett Hotel $ 17/1-2 Soi 2, Ratchadamnern Rd, tel: (036) 411-738. This neat little hotel offers the best budget accommodation.

White House Garden Restaurant $$–$ Praya Kumjud Rd. The best place for a good value meal in the old part of the city, conveniently close to the palace and hotels. The Thai food has some flair and the alfresco setting is pleasing.

The main road outside the railway station, **Na Phra Karn Rd**, has a number of inexpensive Chinese-style restaurants. Worth seeking out along this road is the **Boon Bakery**, especially if you step off a morning train feeling hungry. Turn right outside the station, walk up Na Phra Karn Rd to junction with Ratchadamnern Rd and the bakery is next to the Indra Hotel.

PHITSANULOK

Journeying north, there are good reasons for considering an interruption at Phitsanulok. There is enough to see to easily justify one night's stay, and the town also serves as the beginning of an interesting route that heads due west to Sukhothai, Mae Sot and Umphang (page 145). Sukhothai is close enough to be taken in on a day trip from Phitsanulok, which itself has a fair range of places to stay. Especially good value in Phitsanulok are the competitively priced top-end hotels, and there are some excellent restaurants.

HIGHLIGHTS

Wat Phra Si Ratana Mahathat, on the east bank of the Nan River and known locally as Wat Yai, is the town's most important temple and worthy of a visit to view one of the most highly revered Buddha images in the country. The 14th century haloed bronze figure is dramatically positioned with the help of interior lighting in its *viharn*. The low-ceilinged *viharn* itself is a work of art in itself, with mother-of-pearl doors and marble flooring. The whole temple is so highly regarded that visitors are expected to dress appropriately. This is not the place for flip-flops, tatty shorts or sleeveless shirts.

ROUTE DETAIL

Rail

All but one of the six daily trains to Chiang Mai from Bangkok make a stop in Phitsanulok, as do six out of the seven that make the return journey.

Bus

Phitsanulok is well connected by bus with Bangkok, Chiang Mai and Chiang Rai, as well as smaller towns in between.

Phitsanulok's **Folk Museum** is at 26/43 Wisutkaset Rd, open Tue–Sun 0830–1630, admission by donation. You will not see a better ethnographic collection in Thailand, and a visit here is recommended because there are so many artefacts and items on display that are fast disappearing from Thai culture. Traditional rooms in a village home have been reconstructed and there is a wealth of clever little home-made devices that bear testimony to Thai ingenuity. The museum is within walking distance of the youth hostel, or take bus No 8 from the town bus station.

Cross the road from the folk museum and a short distance south is a **Buddha-casting Foundry** that welcomes visitors who wish to watch the production process. The statues are made using the 'lost wax' process, which is explained with the help of photographs.

i There is a good **TAT office** on Sithamtraipidok Rd open daily 0830–1630, tel: (055) 252–742. From the railway station walk south on Ekathosarot Rd for 1/2 km and turn right onto Sithamtraipidok Rd.

FLYING VEGETABLES

Phitsanulok is famous for its flying vegetable shows – culinary acrobatics involving the humble morning glory (*phak-bung*). The cook stir-fries the vegetable as normal but then hurls the *phak-bung* up and through the air to land on a plate held by a balancing waiter some distance away. The act is turning into a bit of a tourist show but is still fun to watch.

Topland Plaza Hotel $$$ 68 Ekathosarot Rd, tel: (055) 247-800, fax: (055) 247-815. A multi-storey hotel that deserves its name if you take a room on the higher floors. A swimming pool, restaurants, fitness centre and adjoining shopping centre combine to make this great value for money.

Amarin Nakhon Hotel $$$ 3/1 Chaophraya Rd, tel: (055) 258-588, fax: (055) 258-945. Reliable, run-of-the-mill establishment with a good restaurant.

Phitsanulok Youth Hostel $$–$ 38 Sanam Bin Rd, tel: (055) 242-060. For the most pleasant budget accommodation in town take a *samlor* or *tuk-tuk* $ from town or the station, or bus No 4 which runs past the hostel. Dorm beds, and rooms with air-con.

For budget rooms closer to the town centre, take the first turning right after leaving the train station and turn left. Sailuthai Road has a number of similarly-priced $ hotels and guesthouses that are fine for a one night stay.

Phitsanulok Youth Hostel Restaurant $$–$ 38 Sanam Bin Rd. Open-air restaurant serving Thai and Western food in a very relaxed setting. There are a number of other restaurants along this stretch of road, most with air-conditioning and menus offering a good selection of Thai and Chinese meals.

Song Khwae Floating Restaurant $$$–$$ Buddhabucha Rd. Close to the post office on the east bank of the Nan River are a number of floating restaurants serving seafood and a mix of Chinese-style dishes. Not cheap, but good food and a lively atmosphere.

Follow the river to the south of these restaurants for a lively **night market** where a multitude of food stalls compete for business and where the 'flying vegetable' show is most likely to be seen.

For American fast food, head for the shopping complex at the Topland Plaza Hotel. Along Ekathosarot Rd, the road that runs past the railway station and up to the Topland Plaza, there are a number of food stalls and small restaurants.

Chiang Mai

A trip to moated Chiang Mai is a highlight of any visit to Thailand. By no means typical of Thai towns, Chiang Mai combines quaintness with modernity and has the best of everything the country has to offer, except for white sandy beaches. In terms of tourist infrastructure the place is hard to beat. It has an exemplary choice of places to stay and eat, undoubtedly the best shopping opportunities outside of the capital, and its compact size makes it a pleasure to get around. On top of this, Chiang Mai has pleasingly cooler evenings than many other parts of Thailand and is the nicest place to enrol in a course on Thai cooking, Buddhism, or a host of other learning programmes. However long your intended stay, the chances are you will consider staying longer.

The old part of the city is a neat square surrounded by moats. Moonmuang Rd, Chiang Mai's chic version of Khao San Rd in Bangkok, is a centre for inexpensive accommodation in and around Soi 9, and a good place to meet other travellers. There are plenty of good-value places to eat, tour agents, genuine massage centres, cookery schools and ice-cream parlours. There isn't a designer café there yet, but watch this space.

GETTING THERE AND GETTING AROUND

Bus The long-distance bus station is called the Arcade Bus Station, tel: (053) 242-664, on Kaeo Nawarat Rd about 4 km out of the city centre. The following list of destinations does not cover every route but gives an idea of what is available. Chiang Rai 3–4 hrs $$, Khorat 12 hrs $$$, Mae Sot 6 hrs $$$, Sukhothai 5–6 hrs $$$, Udon Thani 12 hrs $$$.

Air As well as Bangkok, flights from Chiang Mai go to Chiang Rai, Mae Sot and Phuket. There are international connections with Kuala Lumpur and Singapore, as well as Vientiane, Mandalay, Yangon and Kunming.

Getting Around

A Bicycle is ideal for temple-hopping trips. Along Moonmuang Rd there are places to rent bicycles and motorbikes such as Mr Kom just past the Shuffle restaurant at No. 131, tel: (053) 419-114, and another operator right next door. There is also a place renting bicycles next to the tourist office on the east side of the river.

Tuk-tuks are useful when arriving and departing but always bargain for around 40B to or from the bus or train station or 50B to the airport.

Songthaews run up and down the main streets of Chiang Mai, just flag one down and check it's going your way. The standard fare is about 10B.

GETTING AROUND

CAR HIRE places are not in short supply. Always ask to see evidence of any insurance paid for, especially when dealing with smaller companies. Avis have a desk at the airport, tel: (053) 201-574, and in town at the Royal Princess Hotel, tel: (053) 281-033, e-mail: avisthai@locxinfo.co.th. National are also at the airport, tel: (053) 793683, and on Charoenmuang Rd, tel: (053) 245-936, e-mail: smtcar@samart.co.th. Two local firms with good reputations are Queen Bee, Moonmuang Rd, tel: (053) 275525, and North Wheels, tel: (053) 418-233, e-mail: sales@northwheels.com.

INFORMATION

CITY MAP
inside back cover

MEDICAL SERVICES

There are lots of well-equipped hospitals with English-speaking doctors. Two that are well used to foreigners are McCormick Hospital, Kaew Nawarat Rd, tel: (053) 241-311, and Chiang Mai Ram Hospital, Bunreuangrit Rd, tel: (053) 224-861.

i The **TAT office** is at 105/1 Chiang Mai-Lamphun Rd, open daily 0830–1630, tel: (053) 235-334 or 248-604. Offers free town maps, general information and a list of approved tour operators. A few doors down is the **Tourist Police** office, tel: (053) 248-974 or 248-130.

Chiang Mai Municipal Tourist Information Office at 135 Praisanee Rd, open Mon–Fri 0830–1630, tel: (053) 252-557. Has a good free map of town showing all the hotels and guesthouses, and if that's all you want it is closer to the town centre than the TAT office.

Look out too for various free publications, like the monthly *Welcome to Chiang Mai & Chiang Rai* and *Chiang Mai Newsletter*, which are useful sources of information. Nancy Chandler's *Map of Chiang Mai* is worth buying if you're staying in the city for more than a couple of days.

Websites worth consulting are: **www.chiangmai-chiangrai.com**, **www.chiangmai-online.com** and **www.chiangmainews.com**. As well as general information, these sites can be used to reserve rooms at a variety of hotels (and not just the five-star ones). Sometimes the rates are well below the quoted rack rates.

ACCOMMODATION

Chiang Mai has a terrific range of accommodation possibilities but at peak times it still pays to have something arranged for at least the first couple of nights. The peak period is Dec–Feb and during the Songkhran festival in April.

Imperial Mae Ping $$$ 153 Sri Dornchai Rd, tel: (053) 270-160, fax: (053) 270-181. The place to stay for comfort and luxury. Good restaurants and a swimming pool in this well-managed, busy hotel.

River View Lodge $$$ 25 Charoen Prathet Rd, Soi 4, tel: (053) 271-109, fax: (053) 279-019, website: www.riverviewlodgch.com. In an attractive areas of green by the river with lots of shade and a small pool.

Traveller Inn $$$ 66 Loi Khraw Rd, tel: (053) 208-484, fax: (053) 272-078. Good, clean, value-for-money accommodation. Mediocre restaurant but lots of cafés and restaurants along the road. Centrally located and close to night bazaar.

Galare Guest House $$$ Soi 2, Charoen Prathet Rd, tel: (053) 818-887, fax: (053) 279-088. Comfortable rooms in a pleasant setting and appealing restaurant overlooking the river.

Montri Hotel $$$–$$ 2 Rajdamnern Rd, Thapae Gate, tel: (053) 211-069, fax: (053) 217416, e-mail: am-intl@cm.ksc.co.th. One of the smarter hotels in this area, with an inviting bakery in the lobby. Free airport transfer.

Green Lodge $$–$ 60 Charoen Prathet Rd, tel: (053) 279-188, fax: (053) 279-188. Functional but perfectly adequate for a short stay.

Libra $$–$ 28 Soi 9, Moonmuang Rd, tel: (053) 210-687, fax: (053) 418-053. Well-established guesthouse with cooking school and trekking options that gathers a hip crowd.

SP Hotel $$ corner of Soi 7, Moonmuang Rd, tel: (053) 214522, fax: (053) 223042. Zero atmosphere in this large, nondescript block but you get what you pay for.

Daret's House $ 4, Chaiyaphum Rd, tel: (053) 235-440. Centrally located with lots of cheap rooms.

FOOD

The Gallery $$$ 25 Charoenrat Rd, tel: (053) 248601. For a romantic, candle-lit dinner, reserve one of the riverside tables under lantern-lit trees. Delicious meat and vegetarian Thai food. Live music most evenings from 2000 and last orders around midnight.

Oriental Style $$$ 36 Charoenrat Rd, tel: (053) 245-724. A stone-paved courtyard between two mid 19th century Chinese merchant houses has classical music, cocktails by candelight, a choice of fish and imported steaks alongside many less expensive Thai dishes and a little surprise ceremony.

Piccola Roma $$$ 144 Charoen Prathat Rd, tel: (053) 820-297. Chiang Mai is not noted for its European food but this restaurant has superb Italian food and a wine list to match. Free transport.

The Riverside $$ 9 Charoenrat Rd, tel: (053) 243-239. The mother of all menus has Thai, European and vegetarian food, pizzas, curries, burgers, noodles, salads, sandwiches and breakfast. Live music nightly with an unfortunate bias for country and western. Open 1000–2400.

Whole Earth Restaurant $$ Si Donchai Rd, tel: (053) 282-463. Dine indoors or on the pleasantly shaded balcony from a menu which features Indian food alongside shrimp tempura and minced bean curd with chilli.

Thae Prae Gate $$ Moonmuang Rd. Tasty pizzas from a large wood-fired oven. Open 1100–0300, no air-conditioning.

Anusran Market $$–$ Chang Khlan Rd has numerous food stalls and small restaurants at night to choose from.

Indian Restaurant $ Soi 9, 27/3 Moonmuang Rd. Small Indian place offering very inexpensive dishes and a choice of thalis. The proprietors also run cookery classes.

Vihara Liangsan $ off Chang Khlan Rd. A little tricky to find but worth the effort for the very cheap vegetarian Thai food. Walk south down Chang Khlan Rd from junction with Si Donchai Rd for about 1 km and turn left after a low-level white plaza to the restaurant less than 100 m away. Pile up your plate from ten or so dishes and take it to be weighed and priced. Rice and soup is included.

COOKING COURSES

Numerous hands-on Thai cookery courses are available, but they usually require a minimum number of participants so ring around to check what is available. Some take you to a local market for ingredients, some have their own gardens and all throw in a recipe book of one form or another.

Noi's Kitchen, tel: (053) 247-379, e-mail: noi@northernthailand.com. One and two day courses in traditional Thai cooking in the comfort of the chef's home and garden outside the city.

Sompet Thai Cookery School, Sompet Travel, Chiang Inn Plaza, 100 Chang Khlan Rd, tel/fax: (053) 280-901, website: www.infothai.com/sompet/. Easy to find, near Pizza Hut. A range of courses, including special fruit and vegetable programmes, 800–1500B.

Thai Kitchen Cookery Centre, tel/fax: (053) 219-896. Well-established courses: one to three days (700–2000B).

Indian Vegetarian Courses 27/3 Moonmuang Rd, Soi 9, tel: (053) 223-396. Enquire at the Indian restaurant.

Galore Food Centre $ on Chang Khlan Rd has half a dozen outlets. Mostly Thai and some seafood and a very average Indian place. A nightly show of music and dance is a plus.

Aum Vegetarian Food $ 65 Moonmuang Rd, tel: (053) 278-315. Low, Japanese-style and regular tables. Vegetarain Thai dishes like fried pumpkins with mushrooms and tofu. Decent coffee but disappointing desserts. Open 0830–1400 and 1700–2100, closed last Sun of month.

HIGHLIGHTS

If you are interested in the culture and art of northern Thailand it may be worth visiting the **National Museum $** open Wed–Sun 0900–1600, although it warrants a journey in itself because it is stuck out on Highway 11. Apart from the usual collection of Buddhas there are exhibitions on pottery and artefacts of ethnographic interest. Coming this far, it makes sense to walk west for ten minutes to **Wat Jet Yot** and its distinctive seven-spired *chedi*. The temple dates from the 15th century and its bas relief stucco work has been well preserved.

Chiang Mai's Wats

The old city is littered with temples but one that should be top of your list is **Wat Phra Singh** in Ratchdamnoen Rd. This delightful complex of buildings includes the photogenic **Lai Kham Viharn** which houses the much-revered Phra Singh image of the Buddha. Equally interesting are the late 18th century **murals** with all sorts of fascinating details of past life in northern Thailand.

On the way back to town along Ratchdamnoen Rd, turn right into Phra Pokklao Rd for the ruins of **Wat Chedi Luang**. Even the remains of this huge *chedi*, which once stood some 90 m high, are impressive, and when the present restoration work is completed the sight should be quite something.

A third *wat* worth seeing is **Wat Chiang Man**, off Ratchaphakhinai Rd in the old city. This is the city's oldest temple, founded in the late 13th century, with lovely gilded woodwork and fretwork that typifies northern Thai temple architecture. The *viharn* on your right, after entering the temple, contains two highly regarded Buddha images. The small one carved in stone is the Phra Sila, thought to come from India, while the really tiny crystal one from Lopburi is carried in procession through the streets during the Songkhran festival.

The most interesting museum is the **Tribal Museum**, Ratchamangkhala Park, open Mon–Fri 0900–1600, especially if you are planning a trek into the countryside. There are models of villages, exhibitions on agriculture, costumes, musical instruments, as well as useful general information on the cultures of the various tribes living in northern Thailand. A video is shown at 1000 and 1400. Food is not available at the museum but the nearby park makes a good picnic site.

EXCURSIONS **Hill trekking** (see page 152 for details and tour operators) is the main activity undertaken by visitors to Chiang Mai but there are plenty of other options. One of the best is the trip to **Doi Suthep**, a mountain 16 km north-west of the city. From the top of the mountain there are breathtaking views and a delightful temple. *Songthaews* travel the paved road to the top of the mountain and leave Bangkok along Huai Kaeo Road; they can be picked up outside Chiang Mai University. Most tour companies include a Doi Suthep trip in their itineraries.

Chiangmai Green Tour & Trekking 29 Chiangmai-Lamphun Rd, tel/fax: (053) 247-374, e-mail: cmgreen@hotmail.com have tours that are typical of those available from the better companies. Choose from **daily sightseeing tours** (Doi Suthep, elephant camp, handicraft factories, river cruise), mountain bike tours (half to two days), nature tours, elephant rides, bamboo rafting and an 'organic-agro tour'.

Tour companies can be found everywhere in Chiang Mai but Moonmuang Rd is a good hunting ground because they are all within walking distance of one another. Expect to pay around 450B for Doi Suthep and 900B for elephant riding and bamboo rafting.

Every day on the hour between 1000 and 1500 a **boat** leaves the pier at the Navaratt Bridge for a slow ride to Wat Tahlug Market and an agricultural centre. Guided **microlight flying trips** give an aerial perspective on the ancient city, tel: (053) 868-460, e-mail: flying@cmnet.co.th.

SHOPPING

Many visitors to Chiang Mai skip the museums and only see a *wat* from the seat of a *tuk-tuk* because **shopping** takes up all their time. There is a great variety of handicrafts at prices that are generally affordable, and the whole experience of looking around shops is infinitely more enjoyable than anything Bangkok can offer.

The **night bazaar** starts mushrooming every evening on every night of the year on the pavements of Chang Khlan Rd between Loi Khraw Rd and Nawarat Bridge. This

Yoga

Courses that could change your life abound in Chiang Mai. Take promises of metaphysical alchemy with a pinch of salt and establish exactly what is being offered, course numbers, duration and the tutor's experience.

Hatha Yoga Centre, tel/fax: (053) 271-555, e-mail: marcelandyoga@hotmail.com. Marcel claims 20 yrs' experience. Weekday sessions 0530-0730 and 1700-1900.

Meditation and martial art **Tai Chi Chuan** classes start on the 1st and 16th of each month at Naisuan House, 3/7 Doi Saket Kao Rd, Soi 1, Room 201, tel: (053) 306012 ext. 201, website: http://go.to.taichi.

Breath of Life, Eurosia Travel, Huay Kaew Rd, tel: (053) 223-1192, e-mail: eurosiatravel@hotmail.com. Pranayama yoga and yoga-jungle tours.

Yoga Centre, 65 Arak Rd, tel: (053) 277-850, e-mail: yogacntr@chmai.loxinfo.co.th, web: www.infothai.com/yogacenter/.

is the scene of Thailand's busiest tourist night market and a visit here should not be missed. A lot of the merchandise is the usual tourist junk consisting of counterfeit designer items and cheap handicrafts, but there is plenty to see and some of the clothes are very good value.

The permanent shops on both sides of the street are also buzzing at night and have better quality goods and clothes. A few shops have a fixed price policy, which can be a welcome relief, but hard bargaining is the usual name of the game. Have a good look around to establish prices and work towards a hefty discount of anywhere between 20% and 60% off the first quoted price.

Export Co-Op, 9 Chang Khlan Rd, is a large store full of wonderful handicrafts, all with clearly displayed fixed prices. A shipping service is available; expect to pay around 8000B per cubic metre.

The non-market end of Chang Khlan Rd has a fair sprinkling of art and craft shops and some, like **Ishikawa Trading** at No 185/1, have fixed prices. Ishikawa Trading has a neat collection of bags, hemp cloth sold by the metre and basketry.

Moonmuang Rd has a selection of mid-range shops like **Baan Welcome** at No 155. It's at the north end of the road, just before the fruit market, and has fixed prices for its silk sold by the yard. Thapae Rd is similar, with shops like **City Silk** at No 336 and its modern display of silk items.

Loi Khraw Rd, to the south, is well worth a look. **Nanthakan Chantarar** at No 69 has a small but elegant selection of women's clothes at reasonable prices. **Earth Tone** is a similar kind of place about 100 m up the road on the other side. As well as clothes shops, this is a good area for handicrafts and souvenirs. **Chiangmai Hemp Store** at No 15/3 is typical of the smaller stores along this road.

The **shopping plaza** opposite the Galore Food Centre on the night market street offers a quieter environment and better quality goods than the street outside. Good wood carvings, more serious art and craft shops selling 'antiques', and some talented artists can be found here.

Jewellery making: **Nova Collection** 27 Thapae Rd, Soi 4, tel/fax: (053) 206-134, e-mail: nova@thaiways.com, website: www.thaiway.com/nova. Workshops in jewelry making, weekdays 1000–1530. A full five-day programme is US$100, excluding the cost of materials.

A good book makes all the difference on long journeys. The very useful **Lost Bookshop** 34/3 Ratchamanka Rd has a good selection of second-hand books and a discount if the book is returned. The best regular bookshop in town is the **Suriwong Book Centre,** 54 Si Donchai Rd.

NIGHTLIFE

Moonmuang Rd has lots of pubs, cafés and restaurants. At No 47 **True Blue**, tel: (053) 278-503, opposite the restored ancient wall, is open 0700–2400 for drinks, conversation, darts and pool. There is a garden area and food is served.

Kafe, next to the Shuffle restaurant at Soi 5, has a happy hour from 1600 to 1900 for beer by the pitcher.

Life Bar, on Loi Khraw Rd near Charoen Prathet Rd, is a roadside watering hole with a pool table which stays open until the last customers leave.

Joe's Place next door is open until around 0100, dishing up hamburgers and steak and chips.

For a bit more bar space than Life Bar can manage, try around the corner on Charoen Prathet Rd where the **White Lotus Bar and Restaurant** has been serving reasonably priced cocktails for more than ten years.

The Good View, 13 Charoenrat Rd, tel: (053) 302-764, is a well-stocked bar and restaurant with music from 2000 to 0100.

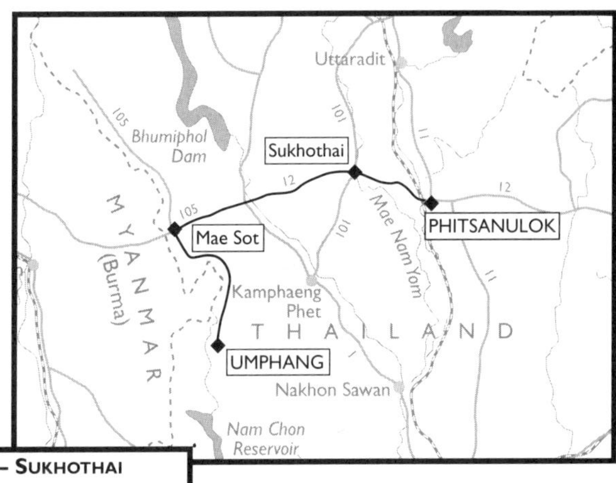

PHITSANULOK – SUKHOTHAI

TRANSPORT	FREQUENCY	JOURNEY TIME
Bus	Daily, frequent	1hr

SUKHOTHAI – MAE SOT

TRANSPORT	FREQUENCY	JOURNEY TIME
Bus	Daily, frequent	3hrs

PHITSANULOK – MAE SOT

TRANSPORT	FREQUENCY	JOURNEY TIME
Bus	Daily	5hrs

PHITSANULOK – MAE SOT

TRANSPORT	FREQUENCY	JOURNEY TIME
Air	4 weekly	5hrs

MAE SOT – UMPHANG

TRANSPORT	FREQUENCY	JOURNEY TIME
Bus	Daily, frequent	5–6hrs

Notes

Sukhothai can also be reached directly by bus and air from Bangkok and Chiang Mai and by bus from Khon Kaen.

There are buses to Mae Sot from Bangkok (10hrs) and Chiang Mai (8hrs)

Phitsanulok – Umphang

The **Phitsanulok–Umphang route** appeals to different people for quite different reasons. Visitors interested in Thai art and culture are drawn to Sukhothai's ancient ruins, and the nearby town of Mae Sot and the Burmese border with their appealing mix of living cultures. Travelling south from **Mae Sot to Umphang** is of primary appeal to travellers seeking outdoor activities. Trekking and rafting are being developed to cater for foreign visitors, and this is a chance to visit a region in its tourist infancy.

SUKHOTHAI

Between 1238 and 1376 the city of Sukhothai reigned as the first capital of a unified Thailand. The ruins of that golden age have been restored to form Sukhothai Historical Park. This is the focus of any trip here but there are other ancient sites and scenic spots in the vicinity. The more enterprising guesthouses organise affordable tours to the various attractions.

Sukhothai Historical Park, open daily 0600–1800, covers a large area and is divided into five zones, each of which charges a separate entrance fee **$** plus a small fee for a bicycle, motorbike or car. The central zone charges a little extra **$$**.

There are so many ruins that there is a high risk of temple fatigue. It pays to select just one or two of the more interesting temples. Begin with a quick visit to the **museum $** open daily 0900–1600 near the entrance to the central zone. There is not a lot to see but it introduces King Ramkhamhaeng and his famous stele.

Inside the entrance to the central zone is the 13th century moated **Wat Mahathat**, the most important site in the Park and well worth seeing. This was the kingdom's spiritual capital and the central *chedi* dominates the complex. It is the epitome of the lotus-bud style of *chedi* architecture that Sukhothai has come to represent.

A short way west is another fine example of the lotus-bud style in the *chedi* of **Wat Trapang Ngeon**. The *bot's* remains stand on a small island which you can walk to and the well-preserved stucco reliefs alone are worth a visit here.

Of the remaining four zones, all of which are spread out and best visited by bicycle, a visit to the north zone is the most fulfilling. There is a small information centre with a model of the whole site and the Khmer **Wat Phra Phai Luang**, converted into a Buddhist temple. Half a kilometre away, **Wat Sri Chum** boasts the largest Buddha in the Park, a fine example of monumental art.

GETTING TO AND AROUND SUKHOTHAI HISTORICAL PARK

Songthaews run regularly throughout the day from New Sukhothai to the central zone. Once there, the best way to get around is to hire a bicycle from the vendors who congregate close to the museum. Be warned that during the hot months between March and October cycling around Sukhothai can be gruelling. Carry lots of water and consider turning up early in the morning. This also gives you an edge over the tour coaches and buses that start arriving after 0900. Alternatively, use the trolley bus that departs regularly from near the museum $ and shuffles visitors around the central zone.

A HISTORY LESSON

In the past it was the Khmer Empire, based at Angkor in what is now Cambodia, that ruled the land of what is modern Thailand. Early in the 13th century, however, two Thai generals overthrew the waning Khmer power and established the kingdom of Sukhothai.

Ramkhamhaeng, the son of one of the generals, Intradit, has a leading role in Thai nationalism because he is regarded as having established the modern Thai alphabet and encouraged the spread of Theravada Buddhism. His most famous inscription, known as the Ramkhamhaeng Stele, resides in Bangkok's National Museum. By the second half of the 14th century Sukhothai was losing out to the growing power of the Ayutthaya kingdom and the glorious childhood of Thailand was coming to an end.

Modern historians dispute this simple narrative and the whole role of King Ramkhamhaeng, and the stele may be a piece of political myth-making, but there is no doubting the significance of Sukothai and the richness of its artistic culture.

Lotus Village $$–$ 170 Ratchathani Rd, tel: (055) 621-484, fax: (055) 621-463). One of the most attractive places to stay. Gardens, lotus ponds, rooms to suit different budgets and a stylish restaurant.

Number 4 Guest House $ 140/4 Soi Khlong Mae Lumpung, off Jarot Withithong Rd, tel: (055) 610165. Eight thatched bungalows surrounded by greenery, with private bathrooms. Thai cooking courses available. Charming setup. Although 20 mins on foot from town, it is on the road to the Historical Park.

Sukothai has a very good **night market $** in the centre of town, where stalls serve up simple but delicious rice and noodle dishes.

Some of the hotels around the night market have decent restaurants. One of the best is the **Chinawat Hotel Restaurant $$–$** Nikhon Kasem Rd. Thai and Western dishes at very reasonable prices.

Dream Café $$–$ opposite the Bangkok Bank on Singhawat Rd, has a touch of class. It serves up good ice creams and coffees as well as a fair range of meals.

MAE SOT

The town of Mae Sot is only 6 km from the Burmese border and, although there is not a great deal to do here, it is a relaxing and interesting place to break the journey from Phitsanulok or Sukhothai to Umpang. Mae Sot has a cultural mix of inhabitants - Burmese, Thais and Karen with their respective religions of Islam, Buddhism and Christianity - and there is still a perceptible sense of a border region that has only recently come in from the cold. Ten years ago, when black-market traders almost openly carried guns, only the reckless traveller would have dreamt of spending time in this corner of the country.

Songthaews run throughout the day to the **Burmese border** at Rim Moei. The short journey is worthwhile if you have the time. The border is formed by the Moei River and, depending on the current political situation, you may well be able to take the ferry across for a day visit to Myanmar. The **border market** on the Thai side of the river is the main focus of interest, and although most of the merchandise takes the form of dried foods and domestic items there is always a smattering of Burmese goods that may take your fancy.

ARRIVAL AND DEPARTURE

When travelling by bus to Mae Sot from Phitsanulok it is sometimes quicker to change buses at Tak rather than wait for a through bus.

Mae Sot is a friendly little town. When arrriving by bus, mention your guesthouse to the driver and the chances are he will drop you off close by.

The main bus station is right in the centre of town on Indharakiri Rd, although sometimes minibuses depart from around the nearby First Hotel. State your destination and you will be directed to wherever your bus leaves from.

Mae Sot Hill Hotel $$$ 100 Asia Rd, tel: (055) 532-601, fax: (055) 532600, website: www.centralgroup.com. A touch of luxury amidst jungle hills. Swimming pool, massage service, two tennis courts, comfortable rooms and a shuttle bus into town.

First Hotel $$ off Indharakiri Rd, tel: (055) 531-233. Conveniently located for public transport. Non-air-con rooms are good value, although air-con rooms are also available.

Mae Sot Guest House $ Indharakiri Rd, tel: (055) 532745. A ten minute walk from the bus station. Very cheap but spartan rooms, some with air-con.

Pim Hut $$ Tang Kim Chang Rd (turn left out of the bus station onto Indharakiri Rd and then right). The menu in this sociable place is a surprising blend of Asian and western cooking, with steaks and pizzas served alongside fried noodles and green curries.

Chez John $$, 656 Indharakiri Rd, tel: (055) 547-206, offers an equally surprising combination of French and Thai dishes.

UMPHANG

The journey to Umphang from Mae Sot is a memorable one, as befits one of the most off-the-beaten-track destinations in the country. The road from Mae Sot climbs high into the mountains and follows a dizzying course up, down and through valleys until it drops into the soporific backwater of Umphang. It is more of an overgrown village than a town, where the streets have no names. Once you've had a look around you may well wonder what you are doing here. The answer should be trekking, because there is little other reason for making the journey.

The usual **trek** takes four days and three nights, and is usually a combination of rafting down the Mae Khlong River, three to four hour jungle walks, overnight camping and an elephant ride thrown in somewhere along the route. Cynics might say that this is just a copycat of the treks based around Chiang Mai, but at least you are not walking in the footsteps of many thousands of previous trekkers, which gives the whole experience a degree of novelty. Equally important, perhaps, you are less likely to encounter other groups using the same route.

Nearly every trek involves a visit to the **Thilawsu Falls**, a particularly memorable sight after the rainy season. Day trips to the falls are available through guesthouses in Umphang.

TREKKING FROM UMPHANG

Some of the larger tour companies in Bangkok can arrange treks from Umphang, but they will probably subcontract the work to a local operator. The extra money you are paying is purely for the convenience of having the whole thing arranged in advance. Even with companies in Mae Sot you will end up paying the extra cost of private transport from there to Umphang.

So if you want to keep costs to a minimum just turn up and be prepared to spend a day or two asking around the guesthouses. At least this way you can be sure of determining exactly where you are going and the modes of transport – raft, elephant, jeep, whatever – involved.

The costs quoted here are based on trips arranged in Umphang and work out at around 3000B each for two people on a four day/three night trip, or 2000–3000B in a larger group of four people or more. These prices should cover transport, accommodation, meals and guide.

EN ROUTE

Most buses depart from both Mae Sot and Umphang in the first part of the day and the bumb-numbing journey usually involves a lunch break along the way.

Umphang Guesthouse $ tel: (055) 561-021. On the left down the road that leads to the river. Cheap, adequate rooms with their own shower and toilet in a large wooden longhouse. This guesthouse is owned by BL Tours, one of the main trekking companies.

Phu Doi Campsite $ tel: (055) 561279. There is a campsite, but stay in one of the wooden bungalows overlooking a pond. Clean rooms and a proprietor well versed in the trekking scene. Less than a ten minute walk from the centre.

Umphang Hill Resort $ tel: (055) 561063, fax: (055) 561-065. This is the prettiest location for accommodation. There are large expensive chalets $$$$ for groups as well as simple folksy bungalows for budget travellers. On the southern bank of the river, across from Umphang Guesthouse.

Umphang's new entry into the trekking scene is reflected in the scarcity of places to eat. Give it a few years and all will have changed but for the moment there is only one decent restaurant.

Phu Doi Restaurant $ on the main street, west of the *wat*. Thai rice, noodle and curry dishes make up the bulk of the menu but the meals are good. Without the Phu Doi life a trip to Umphang would be dismal indeed.

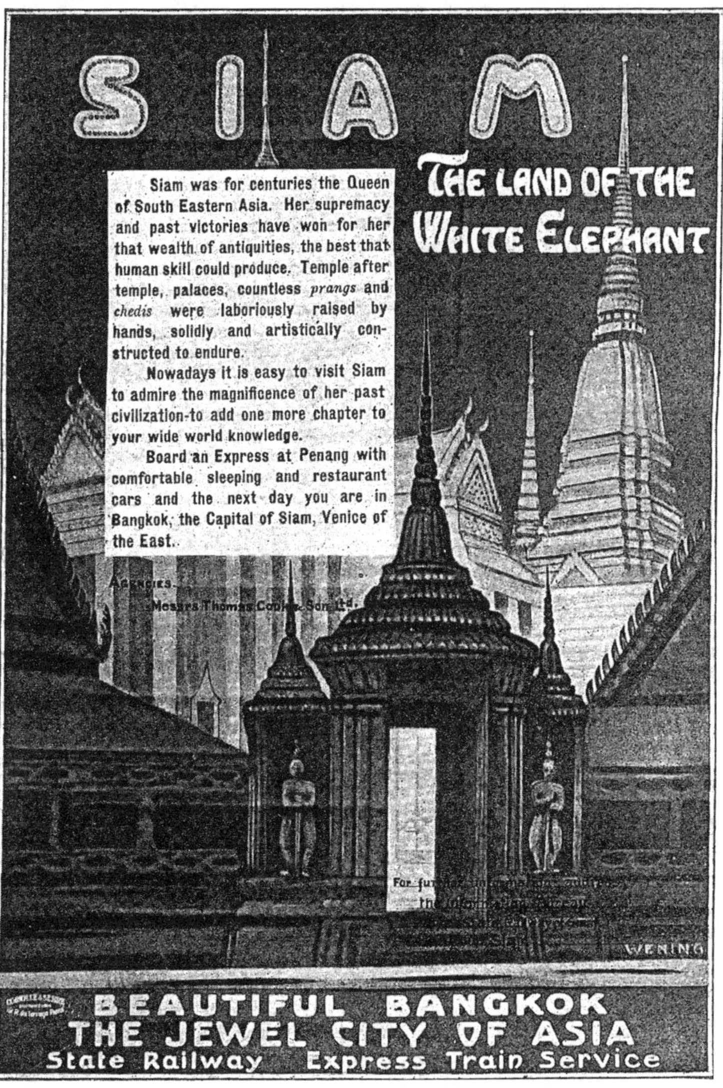

Advertisement from 1926 Thomas Cook *Malaysia and Indo-China* brochure

TREKKING

Trekking in northern Thailand is not the same as trekking in Nepal, North America or most other parts of the world. The emphasis is not on day long walks through rugged landscapes, testing one's stamina and being rewarded with magnificent views of scenery or opportunities to observe wildlife.

The highlight in the north of Thailand are the hill tribes that inhabit the countryside. The people-spotting nature of some treks is something worth considering before setting off in the first place. Not everyone who goes on a trek enjoys playing the role of earnest western traveller poking their nose into other people's cultures. Fortunately, the treks come in all shapes and sizes and you should be able to find one that suits your needs.

With the number of annual trekkers now approaching one hundred thousand (about one for every eight tribespeople) and the majority travelling within relatively small and defined areas, it should be obvious that the experience is not one of adventure exploration in virgin territory.

Different companies offer different types of treks. The trick is to know what you want and find a trek that can deliver. There is a multitude of companies promoting treks. The tourist office in Chiang Mai has a list of those belonging to the Northern Thailand Jungle Tour Group. This group aims to maintain certain standards, use qualified guides and practise an awareness of the social impact of trekking on the tribes people and their culture.

Costs vary but expect to pay between B1500 and 2000B for a three day/two night trek with elephant riding and rafting. Many of the more popular treks hardly justify the name because the actual amount of walking is minimal. Transport in four-wheel drive jeeps, elephant riding and river rafting only leave time for as little as three or four hours' walking a day.

A good tour company will provide all the essentials, including food, water and sleeping bags, but still bring some

Trekking Companies

One company that offers genuine, long-distance treks operates through the **Libra Guesthouse** (page 138), tel: (053) 210-687.

Companies that specialise in visits to hill tribes include **Trekking Collective**, tel: (053) 419-079, fax: (053) 419080, and **Siam Adventures**, tel: (053) 842-595, fax: (053) 842-589.

Queen Bee Travel Service, tel: (053) 275-525, fax: (053) 275-525, is another reputable company that offers both long-distance treks and visits to hill tribes.

water of your own and perhaps a sheet. Stout walking shoes are not essential in the dry months. Bring a small amount of cash but leave documents and valuables in a safe deposit box at your hotel or guesthouse. Only do this, of course, if you feel you can trust the place, and get a signature on your inventory.

CHOOSING A TREK

Establish what you will be doing and how long will be spent on each activity.

Shop around, ask lots of questions and if possible talk to people who have just returned from a trek.

Find out how many people will be in the group. This is crucial because it affects the price and, even more importantly, the whole nature of the experience.

Try to speak to the guides who will be leading you and go over the route with them, preferably with the aid of a detailed map.

The chemistry of the group is one variable that is hard to predict or control but try to find out something about those whose company you will be sharing the days and nights with.

You are paying for what you get but you are still a guest of the hill tribes and some rules of etiquette should be observed. While staying in a hill tribe settlement dress modestly and do not assume you can go anywhere and photograph anyone. It is not necessary to take gifts. Smoking opium appeals to some travellers but, while it undoubtedly provides something to talk about about back home, it probably only encourages young villagers to take up the habit. Often the opium given to tourists is not of a quality to get anyone high. Needless to say, a drug-addicted guide hardly enriches the experience and many companies are able to guarantee a drug-free trek.

Chiang Mai remains the main centre for organising treks but Chiang Rai is rapidly developing in this respect. It is also possible to organise treks in Mae Sot and Umphang and other small towns. While some of these will usually work out to be less expensive they will also be less organised. The best time to trek is between November and February when the climate is cool, but it is possible anytime of the year.

HILL TRIBES

The word 'tribe' has all sorts of unfortunate connotations and it is not the best term to describe the ethnic minorities living in the northern highlands of Thailand. In the Thai language they are 'mountain people', and each ethnic minority has its own language and culture. None of the tribes are exclusively Thai and they can be found in various parts of south-east Asia and southern China. To find out more about them, a visit to the museums in Chiang Mai and Chiang Rai is recommended.

KAREN (KARIANG OR YANG IN THAI) Karen people form the single largest group in Thailand, with a population of about 350,000 living west of Chiang Mai and along the border with Myanmar (Burma). They are engaged in a long-running guerrilla war against the military government in Myanmar. In Thailand they live in settled villages with their own small farms. Their homes look familiarly Thai, thatched and built on stilts, and although animism is their traditional religion the influence of Buddhism is making itself felt. Christian missionaries have also made a significant impact on their forms of worship and belief system. Unmarried females wear white, characteristically V-shaped, dresses with brighter colours reserved for those who marry.

HMONG (MEO) The Hmong are the second largest group, numbering somewhere in the region of a hundred thousand in Thailand. Many still live in south China from where they originally came. Strongly associated with opium farming in the past (and today to a lesser degree), their homes are built at ground level in high altitudes. They make batik and their dress is highly distinctive with colourful embroidery and heavy silver jewellery worn by the women. On special occasions the wearing of multi-tiered neck rings, chains and rings is a striking sight.

LAHU (MUSSUR) More so than other groups, the Lahu have been converted by missionaries to Christianity and their traditional culture is steadily eroding. Their dress is colourful but varied and it is hard to recognise them by their clothes. Famous for their embroidered shoulder bags, most Lahu now wear factory-produced clothes. At around eighty thousand in number, they make up the third largest ethnic minority in the country.

MIEN (YAO) The only group with its own written language, their Chinese origins are apparent in the use of Chinese characters in their writing. In addition, their traditional religion is a form of Chinese Taoism. Mien houses are built on the ground and are large enough to accommodate extended families of 20 or more members. More so than any other hill tribe, the Mien women can be instantly recognised by their customary large black turbans and striking red woollen ruffs. The embroidery work that characterises both male and female dress is wonderfully intricate and an opportunity to visit a Mien village when a ceremony like a wedding is taking place should not be missed.

AKHA (KAW, EEKAW) Originally from Tibet and in Thailand mostly living near Chiang Rai, the Akha have a lower standard of material life than most other tribes but have also preserved their traditional cultural forms more stubbornly than others. They still follow a shifting system of cultivation, and the fields that are fixed are commonly devoted to the cultivation of poppies to produce opium. Akha people smoke the opium themselves as well as using it as a cash crop.

Their forms of dress are distinctive, particularly the women's headdresses made up of their finest jewellery. Akha children wear colourful caps, also decorated with beads, silver coins and tassles, while the men's dress tends to be more restrained.

LISU (LISAW) Only numbering about thirty thousand, the Lisu inhabit high lands north-west of Chiang Mai where they still grow opium. Their dress is very colourful. Tassles are a major feature, hanging from the waist or from turbaned headgear. Women wear knee-length tunics and skirts with bright reds and greens and a wide black sash around the waist.

1926 Thomas Cook brochure cover

LANGUAGE

It really pays to learn a few words and phrases in Thai and Malay because the pleasure it will cause and its immediate gain in breaking down barriers far outweighs the time spent memorizing them. Your first efforts in situ will probably sound way off the mark but take note of the corrections offered and you will soon have a few phrases off pat.

THAI

GENERAL

hello	sawat-dii
thank you	khawp khun
I don't understand	mai khao jaiw
where is the ...?	yuu thii nai ...?

GETTING AROUND

bus station	sathaanii khon song
train station	sathaanii rot fai
left	saai
right	khwaa

ACCOMMODATION

How much is it per night?	kheun-la thao rai?
toilet	hawng naam
towel	phaa chet tua
hot	rawn

SHOPPING

How much?	thao rai?
Too expensive	phaeng pai

EMERGENCY

A doctor is needed	tawng-kaan maw
Go away!	bai si!
Stop!	yut!

FOOD

tea	chaa
curry	gaeng
chicken	kai
rice	khaaw/khao
egg	khai
toast	khanom pang ping
salt	kleua
crab	kung
knife	mit
pork	muu
bottled water	nam kuat
sugar	nam taan
milk	nom

LANGUAGE (CONT.)

vegetables	phak
fish	pla
sweet and sour	priaw waan
salad	yam
I am vegetarian	phom/dii (male/female) chan kin jeh

MALAY

GENERAL

good morning	selamat pagi
good night	selamat malam
thank you	terima kasih
I don't understand	saya tidak faham
where is the ...?	di mana ...?

GETTING AROUND

What time does the bus leave?	pukul berapakah bas berangkat?
train	keretapi
left	kiri
right	kanan

ACCOMMODATION

How much is it per night?	berapa harga satu malam?
toilet	tandas

SHOPPING

How much?	berapa?
Too expensive	mahal

EMERGENCY

A doctor is needed	panggil doktor
Go away!	pergi!
Stop!	berhenti!

FOOD

tea	teh
chicken	ayam
fried rice	nasi goreng
boiled rice	nasi putih
pork	babi
sugar	gula
milk	susu
vegetables	sayur-sayuran
fish	ikan
beef	daging lembu
crab	ketam
prawns	udang
fried noodles	mee goreng
I don't eat...	saya tidak mau ...

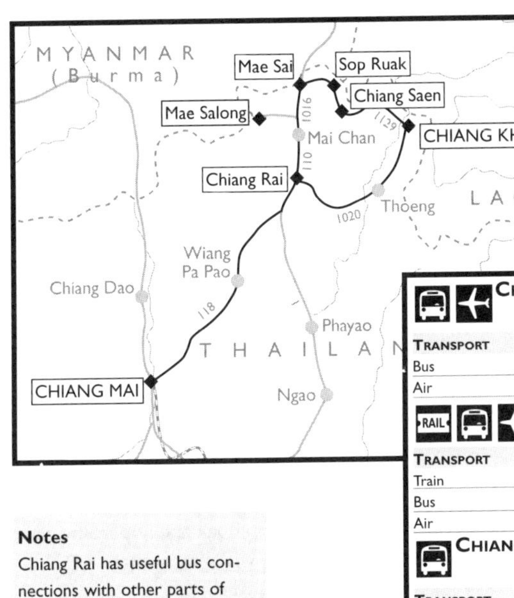

CHIANG MAI – CHIANG RAI

TRANSPORT	FREQUENCY	JOURNEY TIME
Bus	Daily	3–4hrs
Air	2 daily	40mins

BANGKOK – CHIANG RAI

TRANSPORT	FREQUENCY	JOURNEY TIME
Train	5 daily	5½–6½hrs
Bus	Daily, regular	12hrs
Air	5 daily	1¼hrs

CHIANG RAI – MAE SAI

TRANSPORT	FREQUENCY	JOURNEY TIME
Bus	Daily	1½hrs

SONGTHAEW: MAE SAI – SOP RUAK

TRANSPORT	FREQUENCY	JOURNEY TIME
Songthaew	Daily	45mins

SONGTHAEW: SOP RUAK – CHIANG SAEN

TRANSPORT	FREQUENCY	JOURNEY TIME
Songthaew	Daily	40mins

CHIANG SAEN – CHIANG KHONG

TRANSPORT	FREQUENCY	JOURNEY TIME
Bus	3 daily	2hrs

SONGTHAEW: CHIANG RAI – CHIANG SAEN

TRANSPORT	FREQUENCY	JOURNEY TIME
Bus	1 daily	2hrs
Songthaew	Daily, am only	2hrs

CHIANG SAEN – CHIANG KHONG

TRANSPORT	FREQUENCY	JOURNEY TIME
Bus	Daily	3hrs

Notes

Chiang Rai has useful bus connections with other parts of Thailand, besides Chiang Mai and Bangkok. There are daily buses to Khon Kaen (see page 182), taking 11–12 hours, and Phitsanulok (see page 134), taking 5–6 hours.

There are good transport links between Chiang Saen and other towns, including direct buses to and from Chiang Rai and Chiang Mai.

CHIANG MAI – CHIANG KHONG

Route 118 connects Chiang Mai (see pages 136-144) with Chiang Rai and takes the visitor from well-heeled cosmopolitanism to workday earthiness. Chiang Rai may be the tourist centre for trips around the self-acclaimed Golden Triangle area but it is also recognisable as a working town which looks as if it could survive a collapse in tourism less painfully than Chiang Mai. A lot of visitors spend a couple of nights in Chiang Rai before heading off on a hill tribe trek.

Another activity worth considering is hiring a car and heading further north to meander along the banks of the River Mekong. This is the Golden Triangle region, with Myanmar (Burma) and Laos on the other side of the river, luridly evoked in films about drug running. There is no danger for the traveller but it adds and enjoyable frisson and local Thais have sensed its commercial potential, retailing a whole line of T-shirts featuring opium plants and the like.

Travellers who are pressed for time and cannot complete all of this Chiang Rai–Chiang Khong route should consider skipping out Mae Sai and Sop Ruak and hop from Chiang Rai to Chiang Saen and then return by way of a direct bus to Chiang Mai.

CHIANG RAI

Not so many years ago, Chiang Rai was the ultimate northern outpost for intrepid travellers but now it is more of a centre for tourists who look down on Chiang Mai as passé. The generally high standard of accommodation is attracting an increasing number of visitors and Chiang Rai is steadily beginning to rival Chiang Mai as a centre for organising ethnographic treks into the countryside.

If this is your thing, a good place to start is the **Hilltribe Museum & Education Centre**, 620 Tanalai Rd, open daily 0900–2000, tel: (053) 719-167. A big new centre, six times the size of the old one, is currently being constructed next door to the existing museum. This will mean more of everything: handicrafts, jewellery, tapes of tribal music and so on. There are useful

TRIPS TO LAOS

A typical one-day trip from Chiang Rai involves a boat crossing to Huaixai-Bokaew in Laos and a shopping-oriented visit to a hilltribe village, followed by a visit to a sapphire mine or a disused airport used during the Vietnam War. A couple could expect to pay between 4000B and 4500B for this package, and the price should include all transport, a guide, lunch and the visa fee.

TOURS FROM CHIANG RAI

As in Chiang Mai the tourist office has a list of approved tour companies which includes a guide to average prices for different types of tours and treks.

One of the companies, **PDA Tours** tel/fax: (053) 740-088, e-mail: crpda@hotmail.com, is based at the Hilltribe Museum & Education Centre. Profits go directly to support community development projects amongst the hill tribe communities.

A company that caters for long-distance treks is **Golden Triangle Tours** 590 Phaholyothin Rd, tel: (053) 711-339, fax: (053) 713-963. It is worth comparing their deals with PDA who can also organise serious treks.

Chat House 3/2 Soi Saengkaew, Trirat Rd, tel: (053) 711481, has been recommended for backpackers seeking good deals. Its treks in the Chiang Rai area cover Amphoe Muang, Amphoe Mae Suai and the banks along the Mekong River.

Many tour companies also offer one-day visits into the countryside with either no trekking at all or very easy walks lasting a couple of hours at most.

Maesalong Tours 882 Phaholyothin Rd, tel: (053) 716-505, fax: (053) 711-011, e-mail: msltour@loxinfo.co.th, for example, organise a one-day trip using *tuk-tuk*, speedboat and elephant to visit a Mien village before a splash at a waterfall and then an Ahka village. The cost for one person is 600B.

Dits Travel 144/2 Moo 1, Baan Doo, Phaholyothin Rd, tel: (053) 702-681, fax: (053) 716-222, e-mail: ditscei@loxinfo.co.th, website: www.diethelm-travel.com offer tours which include a longboat cruise along the Mekong River to Chiang Khong and visits to Mien and Hmong villages. A couple should expect to pay between 3500B and 4000B per person.

exhibits on the six major hill tribes and a slide show in various languages.

During the day Chiang Rai takes on a desultory mood and there is little to do, but at night the place livens up a little as the shops come alive, stalls appear on the street pavements and the night bazaar gets going. The town itself is not particularly attractive and, despite its situation on the south bank of the Kok River, little is gained by the riverside setting.

There is not much to see about town but a temple that is worth a visit during daylight hours is **Wat Phra Kaeo**, on Trairat Rd within easy walking distance of the tourist office (see below). The story goes that a bolt of lightning in the 15th century split open the *chedi* and out popped the Emerald Buddha, the country's most revered image which is now in Bangkok (page 64). In the 1990s an imitation of the figure was commissioned by a local Chinese millionaire and although not an exact replica – that would break temple protocol – the differences are minor. A new shrine built for the new image stands behind the temple's *bot* by the ponds.

ARRIVAL AND DEPARTURE

Bus: There are two bus routes between Chiang Mai and Chiang Rai, designated old route and new route. Make sure you take the new route to avoid stopping at various towns along the way and lengthening the journey considerably.

The bus station is a couple of blocks south of Phaholylothin Rd in the centre of town, which is fine for some of the hotels that are within walking distance but an exhausting trek in the heat to some of the guesthouses.

The free map provided at the TAT office lists bus routes, schedules and prices.

Air: Chiang Rai's airport is 10 km north of town, off the main highway to Mae Sai. Car hire desks are at the airport, taxis run into town and many of the hotels have minivans waiting for passengers.

Thai Air's office in town is at 870 Phaholyothin Rd, tel: (053) 711-179.

Angel Air, tel: (053) 793-981, fax: (053) 793-983, at the airport also fly direct between Chiang Rai and Bangkok on Wed, Fri, Sat and Sun. Two flights from Bangkok depart on these days in the morning and return in the afternoons. On Wed, Fri, Sat and Sun they also have one afternoon flight to Singapore. Flights from Singapore to Chiang Rai depart in the mornings.

TAT Office 448/16 Singhaklai Rd, tel: (053) 744-674, open daily 0830–1630. Provides useful map of Chiang Rai which includes little maps of Mae Sai, Chiang Khong and the Golden Triangle region as a whole. Accommodation and tour company lists and general information are also available.

PDA Tours at the Hilltribe Museum and Education Centre function as a general tour agency and can provide travel information, from booking hotels and air tickets to elephant rides and treks.

Wiang Inn $$$$ 893 Phaholyothin Rd, tel: (053) 711-533, fax: (053) 711-877. Set back from the main road, this is the plushest hotel in the town centre, with a swimming pool.
Wangcome Hotel $$$$ Pemavip Rd, tel: (053) 711-800, fax: (053) 712-973. Not the most beautiful of exteriors but centrally located with comfortable rooms and good service.
Pintamorn Guest House $$–$ 509/1 Rattanaket Rd, tel: (053) 715427, fax: (053) 713-317. A good all-purpose

guesthouse with a spacious restaurant area, choice of rooms with and without air-con, motorbikes for hire and the chance to meet travellers returning from treks. Close enough to the centre of town to reach on foot from the bus station.

Chat House $ 3/2 Soi Sangkaew, off Trairat Rd, tel: (053) 711-481. Well known to veteran Thai travellers, laid-back Chat House is still going strong and continues to offer a good deal to budget travellers. Some rooms have air-con and dorm beds are also available. Bicycles and motorbikes can be hired and competitively-priced trekking tours can be arranged.

Cabbages and Condoms $$ Hill Tribe Museum, 620 Tanalai Rd. Still one of the most pleasant places in town for a Thai meal with dishes like *tao hoo song kreung* (stir-fried chicken with tofu and eggplant). Few vegetarian options.

Aye's Place $$–$ on Phaholyothin Rd near the bus station is Chiang Rai's best western-style restaurant. Service can be slow but the menu has a cheering variety of cocktails and non-alcoholic drinks, a vegetarian selection, the usual Thai dishes and a set of 'world dishes' like goulash, wiener schnitzel, chilli con carne and lasagne. Like the similar but smaller **Funny House Restaurant** a few doors down, Aye's Place is a good place to meet fellow travellers and swap stories.

Pintamorn Restaurant $ 509/1 Rattanaket Rd, is the dining area of the guesthouse of the same name. Very American, with Confederate flags decorating the walls and pancakes on the breakfast menu. A sociable place.

The **night food market $** near the bus station has the best selection of inexpensive food in town and is well used to tourists. Tables are laid out in a central square and the food brought to you from whatever stalls you order from. Or you can sit on the balcony at **Ratanakosin Restaurant $$** and watch the hoi polloi eating in the market below. The menu is Thai and there are reasonably-priced set dinners.

The two roads that run into each other, Jet Yod Rd and Suksathit Rd, parallel to Phaholyothin Rd behind the Wangcome Hotel, have half a dozen inexpensive eating places and small bars. It is worth a stroll after dark to see which ones are the most lively. **Moom-Thammachat $** 897/2 Jed Yod Rd is a quiet little place with tables tucked away in the shade of trees and plants with art work for sale on the walls. The food is good, including some spicy vegetarian dishes.

SHOPPING The **night bazaar,** off Phaholyothin Rd and near the bus station, can't compare with Chiang Mai's in terms of size or variety, but prices are considerably lower and there isn't as much pure tourist junk. This is probably the cheapest place in northern Thailand for handicrafts and souvenirs, spread out on stalls and the pavements by importuning but friendly tribes people. Amongst the trinkets and bric-a-brac there is enough of interest – shoulder bags, gorgeous picture frames, hand-made cushions, bags, brass – to warrant buying another piece of luggage to carry it all.

Phaholyothin Rd has a few shops selling wood sculptures, small mobiles and other handicrafts. **Silver Birch** at No 891 is fairly typical. **Lily's Handicrafts**, opposite the Wangcome Hotel on Pemavip Rd, is not worth visiting for its handicrafts but there is a large selection of ethnic-style clothes, mostly for women. There is a small department store along this road.

GETTING AROUND THE MEKONG AREA

Taking an organised tour (page 161) is one way to get around the border area along the Mekong River to places like Mae Sai, Sop Ruak, Chiang Saen and Chiang Khong. But hiring a car or motorbike gives you a lot more freedom and control over your time and itinerary. The roads are good, generally well marked and there is little traffic, making driving in this corner of northern Thailand a leisurely and enjoyable experience.

Expect to pay between 900B and 1500B for a jeep or 200B to 500B for a motorbike. A reputable company that won't pull any insurance scams is Avis, at the airport and Dusit Island Resort tel: (053) 715-777. Other reputable companies include Budget 590 Phaholyothin Rd, tel: (053) 740442 and KM Car Rent 869 Pemavip Rd, tel: (053) 715-136.

EXCURSION TO MAE SALONG

The unique village of Mae Salong, now officially called Santikhiri but no one calls it that, lies north-west of Chiang Rai. The origins of Mae Salong's strangeness go back to Mao Tse Tung's victory over the Chinese Kuomintang nationalists in 1949. The main body of nationalists fled to Taiwan under Chiang Kai-shek, where they still defy mainland China, but another group found refuge in northern Thailand and Burma.

As hopes of toppling the communists faded, the nationalists turned to the opium trade and became a permanent presence. After being expelled from Burma, Mae Salong became their main settlement and the isolated location – the road from the highway has only been paved in the last few years – made it difficult for the Thai military to impose their authority. Even today you are just as likely to hear

Yunnanese – the Chinese dialect of the Kuomintang nationalists – being spoken as Thai, although the opium trade is now restricted to land across the border in Burma.

The Thai government has worked assiduously to deal with the situation and replace opium growing with other forms of agriculture. This has been largely successful, hence the change of name to mark Mae Salong's new identity. But the Chinese character of the village remains and a visit here is well worth considering because it really is a very singular place.

There is no particular sight or site to justify a visit but the Chinese flavour of the place is remarkable, making it enjoyable just to wander around and take in the obvious and not-so-obvious reminders of Chinese culture.

If you are here early in the morning, check out the **morning market** near the Shin Sane guesthouse when Akha, Mien and Lisu people display their produce. Also worth visiting is the tea factory in town. On some of the pavement stalls and at the traditional Chinese medicine store near the Shin Sane guesthouse there are curious bottled concoctions of whisky made from local corn. Look closely and you will see some unlikely pickled ingredients, including the odd centipede. At weekends especially, Thai people flock here in groups to sightsee and buy local goods, but if you stay overnight you will have the place to yourself.

The surrounding countryside presents **trekking** opportunities. The Shin Sane guesthouse can organise day treks to nearby hill tribe villages, including horseback journeys.

GETTING THERE Take any bus from Chiang Rai heading north to Mae Sai and ask for Ban Basang (also spelt Ban Pasang), just north of Mae Chan village on the highway. This leg of the journey takes about 40 minutes. From Ban Basang there are *songthaews* running the 36 km to Mae Salong. It takes about an hour to climb up to an altitude of 1200 metres.

By car, drive north from Chiang Rai on Highway 110. After Mae Chan look for the turn off left for Mae Salong on road No 1130. After a short while this becomes the 1234 road to Mae Salong.

You could visit Mae Salong as a day trip from Chiang Rai but the last *songthaew* back to Ban Basang leaves in the late afternoon and then you have to wait on Highway 110 for a late bus travelling south from Mae Sai. Better to spend a night and set off early the next morning, because there is reasonable accommodation in the village and the hotels and guesthouses are all easy to locate.

Mae Salong Resort $$$$–$$ tel: (053) 765-014, fax: (053) 765-135. This is the best place to stay, but only when the rack rates are heavily discounted – usually whenever demand is low, especially during the week.

Mae Salong Villa $$$–$$ tel: (053) 765-114, fax: (053) 765-039). Good value bungalows with moody views of Burma just a short distance away.

Shin Sane Guest House $ tel: (053) 765026). The best deal for budget accommodation. Friendly, well-informed management.

The places to stay all have restaurants. The one at Mae Salong Villa has an especially attractive setting. Well worth sampling from any of the numerous food stalls in town is the tasty Yunnanese chicken noodle dish.

MAE SAI

This is the northern end of the line as far as Thailand's territory goes, and Mae Sai thrives on its proximity to Myanmar, more familiar as **Burma**, which is just across the river. The town would be a dusty backwater without its border crossing, but the constant coming and going of people and cross-border trade give it a degree of atmosphere. Travellers hang out here for days because the place feels foreign and ever so slightly illicit. Tourists do not arrive in their thousands, and because Mai Sai gets along fine without them the place has a likeable authenticity.

It is easy to cross from Mae Sai into Burma, which is another attraction of being here. Even if you stay on the Thai side of the border, there are constant reminders of Burma's closeness. Cafés and restaurants serve Burmese food, characteristically Burmese handicrafts like the shining lacquerware are displayed on pavements stalls, and every morning and evening there is a constant flow of human and vehicular traffic across the bridge.

For a good view of Mae Sai walk south from Top North Hotel down Phaholyothin Rd and turn right to **Wat Phrathat Doi Wao**. The temple itself is definitely not worth the journey but from the top of the hill there are great views of the town and the languid Sai River, with Myanmar stretching away on the other side of the water and Laos visible in the east.

ARRIVAL AND DEPARTURE

Car: Highway 110 from the south makes its way into Mae Sai and leads right up to the border bridge. If arriving by car stay alert or you'll find yourself in the queue for cross-border traffic, though just before the bridge a turning on the left leads to Sawlongchong Rd, the main drag for inexpensive accommodation and eating.

Bus: The main bus station is 4 km south of town but every 15 mins a minibus leaves from opposite the Leo Hotel, outside the Mail Boxes Alliance Co Ltd office. (This office, incidentally, is a good little setup from where you can send e-mails and faxes.)

The most frequent bus connection is with Chiang Rai but buses also depart for Chiang Mai (5 hrs) and Bangkok (around 14 hrs).

Air-con buses to Chiang Mai can also be picked up from the Mae Sai Plaza Guesthouse at 0715 and 1400 daily. The buses from here to Chiang Rai leave every 15 mins 0600–1830. Buses from here also go to Chiang Saen every hr 0900–1500.

Wang Thong Hotel $$$$ 299 Phaholyothin Rd, tel: (053) 733-388, fax: 733-399. The most ostentatious and expensive hotel in town, with a pool, bar and restaurant. Room rates are dropped when business is slack.
Top North Hotel $$ Phaholyothin Rd, tel: (053) 731-955. Near the bridge and better than it looks from the outside. Comfortable rooms with or without air-con, all with own bathrooms.
Mae Sai Plaza Guesthouse $ 386/3 Sawlongchong Rd, tel: (053) 732-230. This photogenic place could win a prize for its location, with tiered shack-like bungalows hanging to a hillside overlooking the river. The upper levels have terrific views across to Burma and there is a useful choice of rooms ranging from singles with shared bathroom to doubles with private facilities.
Northern Guest House $ Sawlongchong Rd, tel: (053) 731-537). Right by the river, this crazily designed place has rooms with balconies, and bungalows with shared outdoor facilities.

The best place for a meal for comfort and service is the **Wang Thong Hotel Restaurant $$** (see above) but if you're unlucky a tour bus will turn up and disgorge its passengers just as your appetiser arrives. There are a few decent eating places along **Phaholyothin Rd** and some inexpensive restaurants in the various guesthouses along **Sawlongchong Rd**. **Northern Guest House Restaurant $**, for example, has a pleasant setting and a large menu featuring omelettes, salads, chips, chicken and fish.

TRIPS INTO BURMA

There are two types of trips across the Mae Sai international bridge into Burma. For a day trip over to **Thakhilek** (also spelt Tachilek), the town directly opposite Mae Sai, all you need is a US$5 note at the border crossing on the bridge.

There is nothing exotic about Thakhilek, in fact it looks just like Mae Sai, and you pay for everything using baht. The handicrafts and 'antiques' for sale are indistinguishable from what's displayed back on the Thai side but the food is Burmese and there are lots of cheap places to enjoy a quick meal. Westerners can even spend a night down by the river in fairly cheap, basic bungalows.

A longer trip into Burma, for up to two weeks, means travelling past Thakhilek to the town of **Kengtung** (Chiang Tun in Thai), over 160 km away. From here, it is not a huge distance to the Chinese border but foreigners are not yet allowed to travel past Kengtung. To arrange this trip enquire at any of the guesthouses in Mae Sai.

Bear in mind, though, that Myanmar is a military dictatorship and Burmese human rights groups argue that foreigners should not visit the country until the present state of affairs shows some improvement.

EXCURSION TO DOI TUNG

The journey to the 1800 metre summit of Doi Tung is half the fun of the trip but when you do arrive there are spectacular views of the Chiang Rai region from **Wat Phrathat** on the summit. The border with Myanmar is very close indeed and poppy cultivation is going on within a few miles of where you stand. The *wat* is supposed to date back to the early 10th century and Thai pilgrims earn spiritual brownie points by ringing its row of bells. The story goes that when the *wat* was completed in 911 the local king unfurled a huge flag from the twin *chedis*. The Thai word for a flag is *tung*, hence the name of the summit.

There is a Thai **royal villa** near the summit. The idea was that royal patronage would encourage government endeavours to wean villagers off poppy growing and into alternative forms of agriculture. The project seems to have been at least partly successful to judge from the dense woods of planted trees and cash crops.

From Mae Sai travel south by car on Highway 110 for around 25 km to Ban Huai Klai or, from Chiang Rai, travel north on the highway for about 35 km. A paved road leads from a turn off on Highway 110 at Ban Huai Klai. From here it is only 24 km to the summit, but the road follows a torturously winding road and due care is required if driving. The journey is an exciting one as the road gropes its way through Akha and Lahu villages, passing what were once poppy plantations.

Tours to Doi Tung can be arranged in Chiang Rai or Mae Sai. Public transport is also available by asking the driver of a Mae Sai–Chiang Rai bus to drop you off at Ban Huai Klai, from where *songthaews* travel to Doi Sai. *Songthaews* only make the run during the mornings and afternoons, mostly taking Thai pilgrims to the temple at Doi Tung, and at weekends are always more regular. It is possible to hitch a ride or consider paying the full whack, about 500B, to hire an empty *songthaew.*

OPIUM'S GOLDEN TRIANGLE

The northern most province of Chiang Rai is part of the infamous poppy producing Golden Triangle formed by the converging borders of Mynamar, Laos and Thailand and southern China not far away. The amount of opium being cultivated in the Chiang Rai province today is so insignificant, mainly as a result of government policy and law enforcement, that locals resort to conjuring up suitably enticing images from its recent past to entice tourists.

Hill tribe people cultivated opium mainly because it can flourish at high altitudes, climate permitting, and it can be readily converted into cash. Attempts to dissuade farmers from growing poppies were doomed to failure until grants backed up campaigns to switch to more benign crops like tea, coffee and cabbage. Opium addiction is still a fact of life among some of the hill tribes, especially the Hmong. To find out more on the subject a visit to the small opium museum at Sop Ruak is recommended.

SOP RUAK

GETTING THERE

There is no bus service to Sop Ruak, but *songthaews* travel every 20 mins or so from Mae Sai. *Songthaews* also travel regularly between Chiang Saen and Sop Ruak.

Sop Ruak, where two rivers and three countries meet, has become the designated tourist centre of the Golden Triangle, especially for tour groups who are not always dissuaded from thinking fierce bands of drug-dealing bandits are lurking behind trees. A reassuring line of stalls selling T-shirts and tourist junk should help remove this misapprehension.

What does lend some romance to the location, apart from the fact that Thailand, Laos and Myanmar do converge exactly at this spot, is the broad but sluggish sweep of the Mekong River and its confluence with the Ruak River. Sop Ruak itself is very much an invented tourist destination, by and large constituted by an excess of tourist stalls and a number of large hotels along and around the main road west of Mae Sai.

Roadside signs constantly proclaim that visitors are now in the Golden Triangle but the only evidence of this is a small museum, the **House of Opium** $ open daily 0700–1800. The museum, clearly signposted on the road in Sop Ruak, is far more engaging than one might suspect, given the tourist hype about the subject. There are well-presented displays and many fascinating exhibits, including farming tools, decorated and crafted weights, and delicate scales and pipes.

Sop Ruak's drawback is the scality of mid-range and budget accommodation and places to eat, adding argument to the value of hiring a car or motorbike in Chiang Rai or Mae Sai and touring the region (see page 164). From Chiang Saen it is quite feasible to travel here by bicycle and take a picnic to enjoy on the banks of the Mekong.

CRUISING THE MEKONG

From the pier in Sop Ruak there are longtail boat trips along the Mekong River. They are expensive unless a small group of at least four people can share the cost. Some of the tour agents in Chiang Rai and Mae Sai organise boat trips. Dits Travel, for example (page 161), run a package from Chiang Rai for 625B per person for two people, dropping to about half that for a group of four and 305B for a party of six.

Le Meridien Baan Boran $$$$$, tel: (053) 784-084, fax: (053) 784-095, e-mail: lmbboran@loxinfo.co.th. Clearly signposted, this elegant hotel has a swimming pool and stirring views in all directions. Mountain bikes and elephant rides are available.

Imperial Golden Triangle Resort $$$$ tel: (053) 784-001), fax: (053) 784-006. A hillside location but a blot on the landscape geared to tour groups. Try for a hefty discount.

S.V. $$–$ tel: (053) 784-026, (01) 950-0994, fax: (053) 784-027. The only decent place to stay apart from the two expensive hotels. Easy to find on the main road, just past the opium museum in the direction of Chiang Saen. Clean, large rooms with air-con and bathrooms and a small restaurant next door.

Jang's Place $ no tel, is a series of bamboo huts on the bank of the river when leaving Sop Ruak in the direction of Chiang Saen.

Le Meridien Hotel's **Opium Restaurant $$$** is the most comfortable and enjoyable place for a meal, and it has an **Opium Den** pub.

The restaurant at the **Imperial Golden Triangle Resort** is periodically invaded by coach parties and the usual evening meal is a buffet.

CHIANG SAEN

This small town by the side of the Mekong River has a lot more going for it than commercial Sop Ruak. As well as better accommodation – although sadly the same cannot be said for the food – the town itself has a faded charm, having grown up haphazardly amid the crumbling ruins of a more glorious past.

The ancient kingdom of which Chiang Saen was the capital goes back a thousand years; the town itself was founded in 1328. It was conquered by Burmese forces in the 16th century and remained under foreign rule for 300 years until Rama I recaptured it. Fearing that the town might later fall back into enemy hands, the king ordered its destruction and it was only in the last century that it started coming back to life.

Chiang Saen is another one of those delightful places in Thailand where there are no compulsory sights but where the mood and character of the place prove intrinsically interesting. Old wooden shop-houses blend seamlessly with the scattered ruins and extant ramparts of the ancient city.

This is a place to wander aimlessly, seeking shade near a dusty temple and enjoying a picnic lunch. The centre of activity is where the main Sop Ruak - Chaing Khong road meets the town's main street from Chiang Rai at the river. From early morning onwards, all along this stretch of river there is a buzz of mercantile activity as boats from southern China and Laos load and unload their wares. There is a lot more to see and do here than Sop Ruak, during the day at least, and tour coaches tend to trundle past without stopping.

At the end of Phaholyothin Rd on the left, just before the end of the ramparts, there is a small **national museum $** open Wed–Sun 0900–1600 with a small but significant collection of Buddha images, various local finds and some ethnographic exhibits.

THE GIANT CATFISH

What is said to be the largest freshwater fish in the world, the giant catfish *(pla beuk)*, is only found in the Mekong River. In Thailand at least it is fished primarily in the stretch of the river that flows past Chiang Khong. Growing in length over a period of many years, it reaches up to three metres and can weigh as much as 300 kilograms.

The fishing season is very brief, from mid April to the end of May, when the river is shallow and the fish are moving upstream to spawn. Before the fishing boats cast their first nets a ceremony is held, invoking the assistance of the appropriate goddess, and much acclaim is accorded to those who get the first catch.

Up to 60 fish are caught each season and are immediately sold at up to 500B per kilo. By the time it reaches the restaurants in Bangkok and Chiang Mai the price has increased many times. The danger of over-fishing to the point of extinction has been recognised for decades, and a system of artificially induced spawning has been perfected by the Thai Fisheries Department.

Of the many crumbling *wats* around town. **Wat Phrathat Chedi Luang**, opposite the museum, is one of the more noteworthy ones. Built in the early 14th century, this was once the city's main temple, and its distinguishing feature is the 60 metre high *chedi* rising from its octagonal base.

The most impressive *wat*, not least because it has benefited from restoration work, is **Wat Pa Sak**. From the museum, walk down Phaholyothin Rd beyond the ramparts and cross the road after 200 metres. It is always open but 0900–1600 there is likely to be a charge $. Again, it is the *chedi* that captures one's attention, and art historians have written monographs on the cultural influences that might account for its odd shape. The stucco work is also worth admiring.

ARRIVAL AND DEPARTURE

Chiang Saen's transport hub, just west of the T-junction on Phaholyothin Rd, is where *songthaews* for Sop Ruak congregate and the station for Chiang Rai and Chiang Mai buses.

By car from Mae Sai simply follow road 1290 to Sop Ruak and continue, with the Mekong River still on your left, to Chiang Saen. From Chiang Rai stay on Highway 110 for 30 km to Mae Chan, and bear right on road 1016 for about the same distance to Chiang Saen.

River Hill Hotel $$$ Tambon Wiang, tel: (053) 650-826, fax: (053) 650-830. A block from the river, south from the main T-junction, this is easily the nicest place to stay. Attractive Thai décor, friendly service and rooms with air-con, fridge and telephone.

Gin's Place $$–$ tel: (053) 650-847. A pleasant, laid-back establishment. Car, motorbike and bicycle rental and tours arranged. Overseas call box, Thai massage, laundry service and visas for Laos. 2 km out of Chiang Saen towards Sop Ruak. Free transport from the Eng. Cent (English Centre) from where you can send e-mails.
JS Guesthouse $ off Phaholyothin Rd, tel: (053) 777-060. Basic, simple rooms with shared bathrooms. Signposted from the post office.

Wieng Saen Phu Restaurant $$ at the River Hill Hotel wins hands down as a place to eat. Food is average, but there is air-conditioning, pleasant service and attractive décor.
Keaw Varee $ has a menu of familiar Thai dishes. Near the police station. Food stalls can be found nearby and sometimes down on the bank of the river.
At Gin's Place **The Cowboy Restaurant $** has a Wild West theme, with breakfasts of muesli and pancakes and meals like fried garlic chicken and a good selection of curries.

SLOW BOAT TO CHINA

In 1992 the first boat in a very long time made an official trip from Yunnan down the Mekong River to Chiang Saen. Following an ancient trade route, the success of the '92 trip heralded a new era in Sino-Thai trade in this corner of the world. Thai entrepreneurs looked forward to a bustling tourist trade only to be suddenly shattered by the collapse of the baht. Now that the country's economic health seems to be recovering, there is a possibility that this route will be resuscitated for travellers.

CHIANG KHONG

Thailand's most easterly town on the Mekong is the end of this route and, unless you are planning a trip across the river into Laos, it is a matter of heading back to Chiang Rai. There is not a lot to do here. Cross-border trade, which more or less accounts for the town's existence, generates a certain amount of activity. The 13th century **Wat Lunag** was restored in the late 19th century and one result of this is the fiery murals decorating the *viharn*. Near Baan Golden Triangle hotel, at the northern end of town, there is a cemetery on a hill with graves of nationalist Chinese soldiers and panoramic views.

ARRIVAL AND DEPARTURE

Car: The 1129 road from Chiang Saen brings you to a T-junction at Chiang Khong. A left turn leads to the bridge to Laos. To the right, the town's single main street, Saiklang Rd, becomes Highway 1020 heading south to Chiang Rai.

Bus: There are only three buses a day between Chiang Saen and Chaing Khong but the Chiang Rai service is a lot more frequent. Four or five buses daily run to and from Chiang Mai (6 hrs) and three daily to and from Bangkok (13 hrs). It is also possible to take a *songthaew* to or from Chiang Saen.

Baan Golden Triangle $$$ Tambon Wiang, tel: (053) 791-350. Large air-con bungalows with bathrooms are at the bottom end of this price category. High on a hill (on the left before the T-junction on the 1129 from Chiang Saen), with atmospheric views of Laos across the sluggish Mekong.
Ruan Thai Sophaphan $$–$ Soi 1, Saiklang Rd, tel: (053) 791-023. Agreeable accommodation close to the river.
Ban Tam Mi La $ Soi 1, Saiklang Rd, tel/fax: (053) 791-234. Next door to the Ruan Thai Sophaphan, a deservedly popular guesthouse. Attractive riverside setting and huts with and without shared facilities. Catch the proprietor for information on short walks in the neighbourhood.

There are cheap rice and noodle stalls along Saiklang Rd but the eating places attached to the guesthouses and hotel are the best bet for a decent meal.

The riverside restaurant at **Ban Tam Mi La $** has more than just token vegetarian dishes.

There is little to do in the evenings so it is worth wandering down the sois that lead to the river and checking out the small restaurants here. The road that hugs the river at the southern end of town, from Soi 5 off the main road, has a couple of places worth looking at. The **Rimkhong $** has a menu in English but if you see something good on another table just point to it.

TRAVELLING TO LAOS

Chiang Khong is one of the few places where foreign travellers can legitimately cross the border into Laos, though the crossing at Nong Khai (page 178) is a lot more convenient if Vientiane is your main destination. Agents who handle the paperwork for visas are easy to find along the main road, and many of the guesthouses can also do this.

One of the more well-established agents is Ann Tour 6/1 Moo 8, Saiklang Rd, tel: (053) 655-198, fax: (053) 791-218. The standard rate for a 15-day visa is US$60 or the baht equivalent. Ann Tour can obtain a visa in one day if you turn up when the office opens at 0800. You could have the visa in time to make the crossing the same day, but this entails a late afternoon crossing and little time to arrange onward travel once you disembark in Laos.

Getting across the Mekong River is by way of one of the cargo boats that make daily crossings. A good agent should be able to arrange this and accompany you to the boat to ensure visa formalities are completed. The Laotian town across the river is Ban Huai Sai (Huay Xai), and from here boats depart for Luang Prabang. There is also a small airport at Ban Huai Sai with flights to Luang Prabang and Vientiane on certain days of the week. Again, a good agent will be able to provide details and current timetables for onward travel in Laos. There are places to stay in Ban Huai Sai, so staying there overnight is not a problem.

BANGKOK – NONG KHAI

BANGKOK – NONG KHAI
OTT TABLES 7065/7079

TRANSPORT	FREQUENCY	JOURNEY TIME
Train	3 daily	12hrs
Bus	Daily, frequent	11–12hrs

BANGKOK – KHORAT (NAKHON RATCHASIMA)
OTT TABLES 7065/7079

TRANSPORT	FREQUENCY	JOURNEY TIME
Train	11 daily	5½–6½ hrs
Bus	Daily, frequent	4hrs
Air	2 daily	30mins

BANGKOK – KHON KAEN
OTT TABLES 7065/7079

TRANSPORT	FREQUENCY	JOURNEY TIME
Train	5 daily	9hrs
Air	4 daily	1hr

BANGKOK – UDON THANI
OTT TABLES 7065/7079

TRANSPORT	FREQUENCY	JOURNEY TIME
Train	3 daily	11hrs 15mins
Air	3 daily	1hr

KHORAT (NAKHON RATCHASIMA) – KHON KAEN
OTT TABLES 7065/7079

TRANSPORT	FREQUENCY	JOURNEY TIME
Train	3 daily	4hrs
Bus	Daily, frequent	3hrs

KHON KAEN – UDON THANI
OTT TABLES 7065/7079

TRANSPORT	FREQUENCY	JOURNEY TIME
Train	5 daily	2hrs
Bus	Daily, frequent	2hrs

UDON THANI – NONG KHAI
OTT TABLES 7065/7079

TRANSPORT	FREQUENCY	JOURNEY TIME
Train	3 daily	1hr
Bus	Daily, frequent	1¼hrs

NOTES
For the 12-hr Bangkok – Nong Khai journey, consider Express 69 night train departing 2030 (Express 70 in reverse).

ROUTE DETAIL

Highway 2 (Friendship Highway) stretches from the outskirts of Bangkok to the banks of the River Mekong at Nong Khai (615km). Take Highway 1 from Bangkok to Saraburi. Here, take a right turn onto Highway 2, which goes straight to Khorat. Avis car hire is available at Khon Kaen airport, tel: (043) 344-313, and Udon Thani airport, tel: (042) 244-770.

Bangkok – Nong Khai

North-east Thailand

Every year the north-east of Thailand, known as Isaan, receives less than 2% of the total number of visitors to the country. This alone makes it one of the country's more attractive destinations. The big cities along this route – Khorat, Khon Kaen and Udon Thani – have no major visitor attractions but their busy and bustling natures capture the everyday rhythms of urban life in Thailand in a way that touristy Bangkok and Chiang Mai have long lost.

At the end of the cool season (Nov/Feb), landlocked Isaan begins to bake and with temperatures of 40°C it is hard to expend energy during much of each day. The searing heat combines with an infertile soil to make the north-east the poorest part of Thailand. The Thais you see in Bangkok engaged in menial jobs or backbreaking hard labour are very likely to be seasonal immigrants from Isaan.

In the decades after the end of World War II, the poverty of the north-east made many farmers sympathetic to communism, and the US-supported government poured money into the making of new roads in an attempt to defeat insurgents. During the Vietnam War, American purchasing power fuelled the development of 'massage parlours' as towns like Khorat and Udon Thani became large bases for American forces intent on bombing Thailand's eastern neighbours.

Reasons for travelling this route include the imposing Angkor ruins at Phimai, opportunities for buying silk and other cloths at relatively low prices, and the enticing vista of Laos across the River Mekong at the attractive border town of Nong Khai. It is easy to cross the river into Laos, and Vientiane is a mere 24 km away.

You will need a US$50 note (other bills not accepted) with your passport to pay to cross into Laos from Nong Khai (see also page 189).

Route Detail

A visit to the north-east could join with the Chiang Mai – Mae Sai Route (see p. 159) by a 9hr bus journey from Chiang Rai to Khorat, or a 12hour bus ride between Chiang Mai and Khorat. The Bangkok – Pattaya Route (see p. 102) can be linked via a 6hr bus journey from Pattaya to Khorat, or with the Pattaya–Ko Samet Route (see p. 108) by a 4hr bus journey to Rayong. There are also buses between northern Thailand and Udon Thani.

KHORAT (NAKHON RATCHASIMA)

The official new name of this large commercial city is Nakhon Ratchasima but everyone still calls it by its old name, Khorat (aka Korat). During the Vietnam War the Americans had a large airbase outside the city, although the military fatigues you'll see about town belong to members of the Thai armed forces who now have their own important base here.

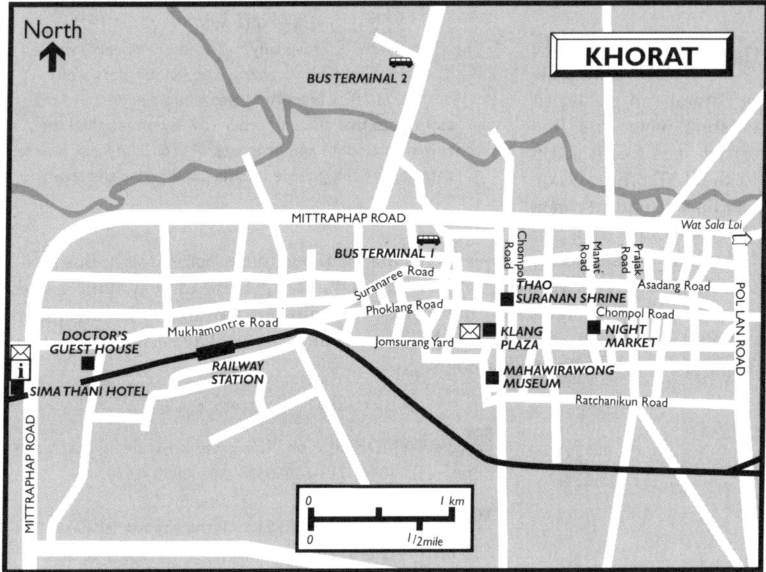

Nakhon Ratchasima, which translates literally as 'Frontier Country', is the transport gateway to the north-east, and the main reason for stopping off here is to visit the nearby Khmer ruins at Phimai or for an overnight stay after a day's travelling.

Khorat is not a compact city. The railway station and some of the better accommodation is situated in the older, western half, while shops, banks and amenities are mostly clustered in the busy eastern part of the city.

There are no must-see attractions, but the **Thao Suranari Shrine** is centrally located on the western side of the moat and if anything is happening in town it will take place here. Evening devotions often include performances of folk songs and at the end of March/early April there is a 10-day festival celebrating the Thao Suranari.

The nearby strip of grass is the town's public park, a good place to while away time and observe Thai social life. South of the shrine, just outside the moat, the **Mahawirawong Museum $** open daily, 0900–1600, has a modest collection of local Khmer art, mostly Buddha statues. An evening stroll from the north-east corner of the moat leads to the architecturally interesting Wat Sala Loi, built in the 1970s and representing the heavenly boat journey to nirvana.

THE BRAVE LADY

The Thao Suranari, 'brave lady', was the braveheart who led the people of Khorat against Laotian invaders from Vientiane in 1826. Her name was Khun Ying Mo and the story goes that she and other townswomen plied the enemy with alcohol and promises of sensual delight before slaughtering the gullible invaders and saving the town.

ORIENTATION The size and scale of Khorat can be disorientating when you first arrive. It is worth a trip to the TAT office to collect their useful city map that pinpoints transport links, hotels, restaurants, temples, plus the main bus routes across town. Bus Nos 1, 2 and 3 all travel between the tourist office in the west, via the railway station, to the eastern part of Khorat inside the moat. The main bus terminal is inconveniently situated in the north of the city on Highway 2, and *tuk-tuks* have a standard fare $$. The train station is on Mukhamontre Rd.

The **TAT Office** is on Mittraphap Rd at the western end of town, tel: (044) 213-666, open daily 0830–1630.

Sima Thani Hotel $$$$$ Mittraphap Rd, tel: (044) 213-100, fax: (044) 213122, e-mail: sales@simathani.co.th. Best hotel in town, with good restaurants and full-sized snooker table.
Chumsurang $$$ 2701 Mahadtthai Rd, tel: (044) 257-088, fax: (044) 252-897, has air-con rooms and a small pool. Easy to find on the road that goes east from Klang Plaza, near the night market.
Anachak $$ 62 Jomsurangyard Rd, tel: (044) 243-825 is a good value hotel with air-con rooms in the centre of town. From the Klang Plaza it is just past the post office. There is a 24hr café and a Thai restaurant next door where you can point at whatever takes your fancy. Almost as good value is the **Farthai Hotel $$** 3535 Phoklang Rd, tel: (044) 267-390, with a choice of rooms. The café is fine for breakfast but not much more.

Doctor's Guest House $ 78 Soi 4, Suebsiri Rd, tel (044) 255-846. Leafy Soi 4 runs parallel with Mukhamontre Rd, off which Suebsiri Rd runs. A quiet, clean place which shuts up nightly at 2200; a little English spoken.

If the hustle and bustle of Khorat are too much to bear, consider spending a night at peaceful Phimai instead.

Two good places to eat are near the tourist office.
Nat Ruen $$ at the Sima Thani hotel has an excellent lunch buffet of Asian and European food.
Cabbages and Condoms $$ just past where Soi 4 meets Suebsiri Rd, near the Doctor's Guest House, is not as green as the name might suggest and vegetarians will be frustrated. A good choice is *gung phun oil* (spring rolls), followed by *kai pud mermamuang* (cashew nuts with chicken and garlic).
Around **Klang Plaza** is the usual cluster of western-style donut, chicken and burger fast-food joints and there is a Swensen's here as well as a supermarket.
Around the corner, at 698 Ratchadamnoen Rd, there is a small but adequate **vegetarian restaurant $** next to a bakery.
The **night market $** has the usual array of stalls serving good Thai food.

EXCURSION TO PHIMAI

A day trip to Phimai, 60 km from Khorat, is easily managed by catching an early No 1305 bus from Bus Terminal 2 and returning to Khorat in the late afternoon.

Thailand's best-preserved Khmer ruins are well worth the journey.

The dusky pink sandstone **Prasat Hin temple complex $$**, open daily 0730–1800, has been well restored, and hours can be spent admiring the ancient carved Buddhist and Hindu motifs that adorn the lintels and pediments. The 12th century complex was linked by a road to Angkor Wat, though it predates the Cambodian site and may even have served as an inspiration for it. There is an **open-air museum $**, open daily 0900–1600, with more superb examples of carved stonework. Stalls sell neat little sandstone reproductions of the more graceful carvings.

Old Phimai Guesthouse $ tel (044) 471-918, off the main street, is the backpackers' favourite haunt and a good place to meet and chat. **Phimai Hotel $$** Haruethairome Rd, tel (044) 471-306, is equally close to the ruins and has a restaurant, though there are plenty of places for an inexpensive lunch or dinner. If overnighting in Phimai, rent a bike from Old Phimai Guesthouse and get directions to Thailand's largest and most ancient **banyan tree**. It really is colossal.

KHON KAEN

Khon Kaen is another large commercial town but with a far more relaxing sense of space than Khorat. If you just want to rest for a day, enjoy some creature comforts and check out some quality shopping for silk and cotton fabrics, then Khon Kaen is the place to go.

The town's **Museum $**, open Wed–Sun, 0830–1630, half a km north of the tourist office on Lungsun Rachakhan Rd, is a branch of the National Museum and ranks as one of the best anywhere outside of Bangkok. Carved stonework, artefacts from the Ban Chiang site (see p. 184) and an ethnographic collection make up the exhibits.

The **TAT Office** is at 15 Prachasamoson Rd, 5 mins east of the bus station, tel: (043) 244-498, open daily 0830 – 1630.

A very good range of hotels is spread out along Klang Muang Rd, around the corner from the tourist office.
Kaen Inn $$$ 56 Klang Muang Rd, tel: (043) 236-866, fax: (043) 239-457, has decent rooms with air-con and fridge, and plenty of amenities on the premises.
Roma $$–$ 50 Klang Muang Rd, tel: (043) 236-276, may lack a touch of style but is very good value and has a choice of rooms.
Sansumran $ 55 Klang Muang Rd, tel: (043) 239-611, is a popular budgt place but some rooms are better than others. No hot water.

Parrot $$–$ Si Chan Rd, opposite Kosa Hotel. Open 0730–2200 for popular fried breakfasts, real coffee, tasty pizzas and other standard western food.
Pizza and Bake $$–$ Klang Muang Rd is just as good as Parrot, with similar food.
Krua We $$ 1 Klang Muang Rd has authentic Vietnamese food.

Local Isaan cuisine is best enjoyed from the **food stalls $** that spring up at night along the top end of Klang Muang Rd around Kaen Inn.

SHOPPING Khon Kaen has the best shopping in the north-east. A good place to start is the huge **Prathamakant Local Goods Centre** 81 Ruen Rom Rd. All the Isaan arts and crafts are represented here, including triangular-shaped pillows, *mut mee* (see box) fabrics, jewellery, basketry and small furnishings. Klang Muang Rd has a number of small shops specialising in silks and other textiles.

EXCURSION TO CHONNABOT Chonnabot is a silk-weaving town 50 km south-west of Khon Kaen. It can be reached by *songthaew* from the regular bus terminal in about an hour, or by bus or train to Ban Phae and then a *songthaew* for the 10km hop to Chonnabot.

Visitors are welcome to stroll into the town workshops to watch the women skilfully manipulating their wooden machines. Prices for silk are always negotiable, and always lower than what you would pay in Bangkok.

FOOD AND FABRICS SPECIALITIES

Even by Thai standards the food of Isaan is noted for its spicy pungency. One of the most popular dishes is *som-tam*, a piquant salad of grated papaya over a mix of fish sauce, lime, chillies and other spices.

Mut mee is the name of the weaving method that is especially characteristic of Isaan culture. It describes the process of tie-dying cotton thread in bundles before it is woven by hand. The dye is a paste extracted from the indigo plant, and the depth of colour depends on how often the yarn is dipped in the solution. The traditional pattern is a geometric one, using chevrons, lozenges and human figures.

UDON THANI AND BAN CHIANG

The town of Udon Thani is not as cosmopolitan as Khon Kaen, over 100 km south, but it is an easy place to spend a day or two. The atmosphere is friendly and unhurried and the roundabouts are encircled by palm trees as if to emphasise the laid-back mentality of the town. While there is little to do in Udon itself, an excursion to the archaeological site of Ban Chiang, 50km to the east, can be managed as a day trip.

A shopping trip to the weaving village of Ban Naka, about 20 km north of town, is a chance to buy silk, *mut me* fabrics and ready-made clothes at prices that are less than half those of Bangkok. A *tuk-tuk* ride **$$** can also be taken to visit an orchid farm in the north-east of the town.

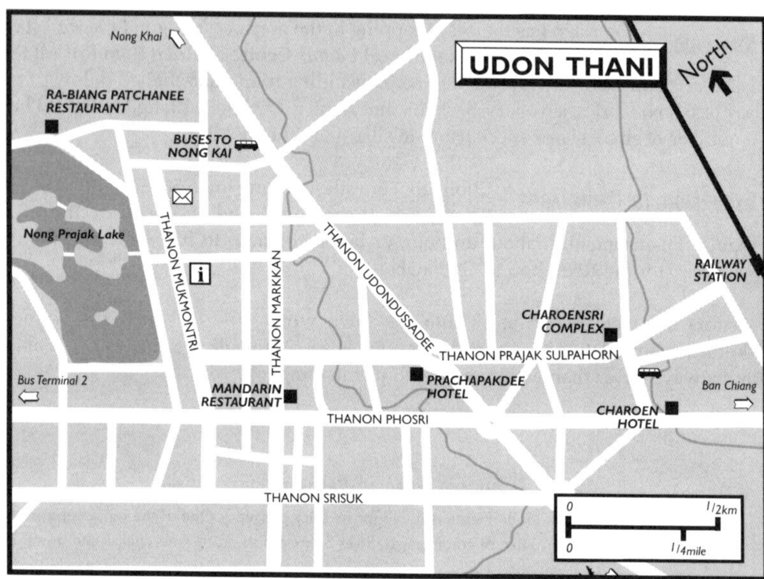

An area of the archaeological dig at **Ban Chiang** can be visited, but the main focus is the exemplary **museum $** open daily 0900–1600 with its attractive displays of artefacts from the local site. Check opening days on tel (042) 261-351. Getting to Ban Chiang is easy because *songthaews* regularly make the 50km journey from Udon Thani. Returning is not so straightforward because the *songthaews* tend to peter out in the afternoon, but take a *samlor* or *tuk-tuk* for the ten-minute journey to Ban Pulu and from here wait for any bus travelling to Udon Thani from Sakon Nakhon.

WHO STARTED THE BRONZE AGE?

Orthodoxy was overturned when bronze finds at Ban Chiang were first dated as being earlier than 3000 BCE, the accepted date for the origins of the Bronze Age in ancient Mesopotamia in the Middle East. The dates have since being revised but grounds remain for questioning the orthodox view that bronze was first discovered in the Tigris and Euphrates basin. Ban Chiang has also revealed that bronze metallurgy spread from Thailand to China and not the other way around.

The **TAT Office** is at 16 Mukmontri Rd, tel: (042) 325-406, open daily 0830–1630.

Charoen Hotel $$$ 549 Phosri Rd, tel: (042) 248-115, fax: (042) 241093. Built during the Vietnam War for Americans, today it offers comfortable rooms and good facilities, including a pool. Best value hotel in town.
Prachapakdee Hotel $ 156 Prajak Sulpakorn Rd, tel: (042) 221-804, is right in the centre of town. This friendly, old-fashioned hotel has clean, well-kept rooms and a 24hr convenience store next door.

Ra-Biang Patchanee $$ is tucked away by the Nong Prajak lake, but every *tuk-tuk* driver knows the way to Udon's best restaurant for authentic Thai and Isaan dishes.
Mandarin $$-$ Mak Khaeng Rd for breakfast, inexpensive noodle dishes, appetisers, steamed crab, curries and steaks. Air-conditioned.
Charoensri Complex $$ eastern end of Prajak Sulpakorn Rd is huge, with an array of familiar franchises for Pizza Hut, Swensen's and the like.

ENTERTAINMENT There is a string of little bars opposite the Charoensri Complex and two e-mail shops are also located here. The Charoen Hotel has the **Cellar Pub** with a Filipino band performing nightly from 2130, and a nightly disco with no cover charge.

NONG KHAI

Nong Khai is an interesting destination in itself, while offering the tantalising prospect of further travel across an international border. Thailand's main north-east railway line and its US-financed Friendship Highway terminate at the riverside town of Nong Khai, where the broad Mekong sweeps by as another reminder that this is indeed the end of the line. The best places to stay are huddled close to the river, with the land of Laos beckoning and its capital city a mere bus ride away.

Nong Khai's appeal is based on its frontier status and riverside setting, a few stylish dilapidated wooden houses that hint at the influence of French colonialism from across the river, and an almost romantic air of having arrived at a terminus. It's an easy place to hang out for a couple of days, the kind of place where you could conjure up an Asian version of Casablanca with an ex-pat Bogart type running a bar and guest house for *farangs* with dubious pasts.

To soak up the atmosphere take the **evening boat ride $** (excluding food or drinks) that departs around 1700 from a floating restaurant between the Mutmee and Mekong guesthouses. The boat keeps to the Thai side of the river and opens a window on riverside life in what is still a quiet backwater.

Wat Pho Chai, an exception to the mostly undistinguished *wats* dotted around town, is near the bus station. The spacious interior is remarkably glossy and ornate, with the burnished gold head of Buddha taking pride of place on the lustrous altar lit by a large chandelier. Murals decorate the *bot* and tell the story of how the Buddha image was taken from Laos and sank in the Mekong before miraculously reappearing.

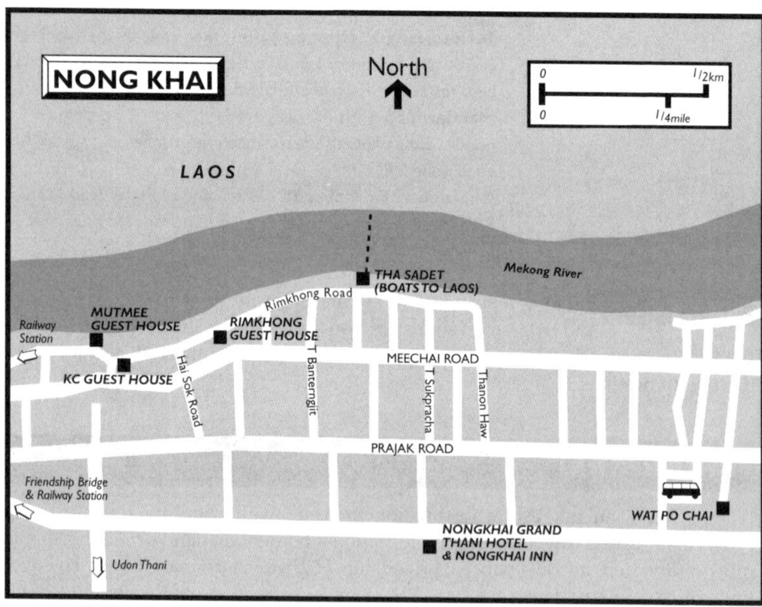

Bicycles and motorbikes can be hired from guesthouses, and a 2km trip brings you to the **Friendship Bridge**, open for foreigners wishing to visit Laos.

It is hard to beat Nong Khai for value for money accommodation.

Sawasdee Guest House $$-$ 402 Meechai Rd, tel: (042) 412-502, fax: (042) 420-259. Quaintly restored, well-managed townhouse. Hot water, laundry service and bikes for hire.

Mutmee Guest House $ 111 Kaew Worawut, tel/fax: (042) 460-717, is deservedly one of the most popular budget places. Friendly, well-informed management, excellent restaurant, good travel info and bikes for hire.

Rimkhong Guest House $ Rimkhong Rd. Not on riverside, but pleasant garden.

Along Rimkhong Rd there is a good choice of small Thai eating places offering inexpensive local and Vietnamese dishes, including:

Mae Khong $$–$ with a large riverside balcony overlooking the river and wild boar with chilli on the menu.

Fish Restaurant $ offers a large menu in its wooden shack. Good views of the river and dusty wind chimes lend the place some charm.

At the **Mutmee Guesthouse** the food lives up to the promise of its superb setting among bamboo and green plants. Vegetarian choices and daily specials.

Danish Baker $$–$ Meechai Rd has hearty breakfasts, hamburgers and Thai food.

Nobbie's $$ Meechai Rd serves pizzas and other European favourites.

SHOPPING

Village Weaver Handicrafts 1151 Chitapanya Lane, tel: (042) 411-236, is a self-help project created to promote an income for local weavers. The weaving process can be watched in situ behind the shop and there is a good selection of *mut mee* cotton, clothes and woven bags. Prices are marked but a discount is usually available.

To find the shop, walk east from the bus station along Prajak Rd. After about half a kilometre, turn left down Chitapanya Lane at the Honda bike shop opposite the Esso station. The shop is on the right past the school.

Shops and stalls along Rimkhong Rd sell a miscellany of inexpensive Thai and Lao items, including filigree (silver wire) jewellery. The **Wasambe Bookshop** near the Mutmee Guesthouse has arty T-shirts and cards as well as new and second-hand books. A fax and e-mail service is also available here.

Nong Khai Walkabout

This walk begins at the ferry crossing point in the centre of town by the riverside. The ferry is only for locals, but there is an observation platform where you can watch the river traffic and gaze across the expanse of the Mekong for picturesque and enticing views of Laos.

Wander westwards along Rimkhong Rd past the shops and restaurants until the road becomes a narrow lane. Enjoy a cup of Laos coffee at the Fish Restaurant, gazing upriver to the Australian-financed **Friendship Bridge** which spans the Mekong.

Walk south from the restaurant to Meechai Rd and turn right to pass the hospital and the delightful flower garden in front of the public library. Take the first turning right back towards the river and look for the lane on the right with a sign to the Mutmee Guesthouse. This lane, with the useful Wasambe Bookshop and places offering meditation courses and the like, is developing an inviting hippy atmosphere. Check out the menu and daily specials at the Mutmee before returning to Meechi Rd, and turn left to walk back towards the town centre.

Along Meechi Rd you pass the Danish Baker, banks and shops. Pass the Sawasdee Guest House and then take the sixth turning on the right, Phochai Rd, that cuts down to Prajak Rd. Cross Prajak Rd and continue to **Wat Pho Chai** (see page 186), where the walk ends.

Departure Tips

At the Sawasdee Guest House there is a hot shower room, metered for 10 mins at a time, that can be used before setting off on a long train or bus journey. Nobbie's on Meechai Rd sells large, tasty, takeaway sandwiches, ideal for that long journey back to Bangkok.

WHERE NEXT?

All you need to enter Laos via the Friendship Bridge is a US$50 note and your passport, but make sure that your Thai visa has enough days left for you to return to Thailand. The Laos visa is valid for 15 days but you can apply for a 30-day visa at the Laos consulate in Khon Kaen, tel: (043) 223-698, or Bangkok, tel: (02) 539-6667. This takes from one to three days.

ROYALTY

Royalty is a feature of Thai and Malaysian life and in both countries it is treated with a very high degree of respect. In Thailand especially, saying or doing anything that might be interpreted as disrespectful towards the royal family carries a maximum jail sentence of 15 years. In 1995 a French visitor was arrested on landing at Bangkok airport, having been heard to express anti-royal sentiments on the plane (a Thai princess was on the same flight).

The present Thai king, Bhumibol Adulyadej, was born in the US and it is very much his efforts that have maintained a high profile for royalty within the country. He is a cosmopolitan individual, a fan of jazz music, a noted saxophone player and the winner of a yachting gold medal in the Asian Games. He has handled political minefields with finesse and emerged as a popular people's king. In both 1973 and 1992, when political turmoil raged in Bangkok, the king made decisive interventions that were welcomed by ordinary people. Whether this success will be maintained by his eldest son and successor remains to be seen, although his daughter has achieved noted public relations success in representing and promoting royalty.

Various semi-compulsory practices endorse the unquestioned role of the royals in Thai society and visitors will see some of these for themselves in public places. People stand for the national anthem in bus and train stations at 0800, as they do in small towns and villages across the countryside. Any visit to the cinema is incomplete with an obligatory standing to attention while the anthem is played. Visitors are often expected to join in with these observances.

In Malaysia they go one better, or rather nine times better, and enjoy the spectacle of nine different royal families. The Malaysian head of state is the *yang di-pertuan agong*, the 'king', who is elected every five years from amongst the nine sultans attached to nine of the peninsular states. All nine royal sultans are immune from the normal workings of the law and all are above public criticism, a fact that visitors should bear in mind. Their position and privileges are enshrined in the constitution and are likely to remain unchallenged for the foreseeable future. The sultans are seen as custodians of traditional Malay, Muslim culture and, given the sensitive nature of multicultural Malaysia under firm Malay political control, no public figure would take the risk of questioning the status quo.

While the Thai royals have managed to avoid the whiff of scandal and slander, their Malay peers have not been quite so successful. The most notorious cases have involved the Johor royal family and even in the mid-1980s scandalous stories about the son of the Johor sultan were still common currency. In 1976 the son was actually convicted of manslaughter before being pardoned by his father who was the sultan of the state. Less serious shenanigans have surrounded the sultan of Kelantan and his passion for expensive, European cars.

Series 6463 C. COOK'S TOURS *No.* 3326

The Royal State Railways of Siam

Hotel Service

To the Restaurant Car Attendant

Please provide M. ....

with one AFTERNOON TEA

[Beverages not included]

Issued subject to Siamese Law and all Rules and Regulations of the Royal State Railways of Siam.

[No refund shall be made on this coupon.]

Series 6463 C.

Meal Coupon. 1 Afternoon Tea.

Royal State Railways of Siam.

Meal coupon, issued by Thomas Cook, 1930s

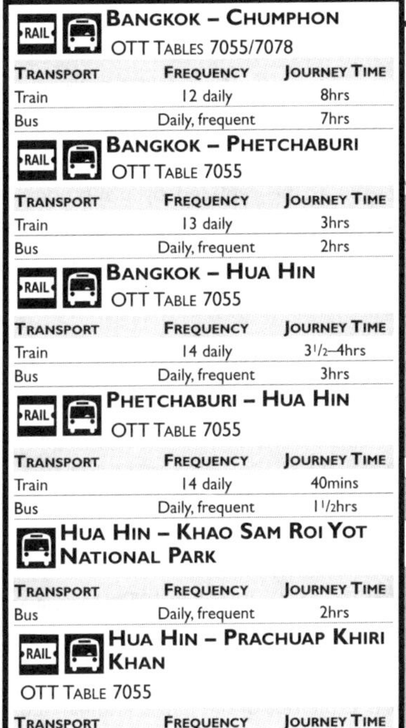

BANGKOK – CHUMPHON
OTT TABLES 7055/7078

TRANSPORT	FREQUENCY	JOURNEY TIME
Train	12 daily	8hrs
Bus	Daily, frequent	7hrs

BANGKOK – PHETCHABURI
OTT TABLE 7055

TRANSPORT	FREQUENCY	JOURNEY TIME
Train	13 daily	3hrs
Bus	Daily, frequent	2hrs

BANGKOK – HUA HIN
OTT TABLE 7055

TRANSPORT	FREQUENCY	JOURNEY TIME
Train	14 daily	3 1/2–4hrs
Bus	Daily, frequent	3hrs

PHETCHABURI – HUA HIN
OTT TABLE 7055

TRANSPORT	FREQUENCY	JOURNEY TIME
Train	14 daily	40mins
Bus	Daily, frequent	1 1/2hrs

HUA HIN – KHAO SAM ROI YOT NATIONAL PARK

TRANSPORT	FREQUENCY	JOURNEY TIME
Bus	Daily, frequent	2hrs

HUA HIN – PRACHUAP KHIRI KHAN
OTT TABLE 7055

TRANSPORT	FREQUENCY	JOURNEY TIME
Train	11 daily	2hrs
Bus	Daily, frequent	2hrs

PRACHUAP KHIRI KHAN – CHUMPHON
OTT TABLE 7055

TRANSPORT	FREQUENCY	JOURNEY TIME
Train	10 daily	4hrs
Bus	Daily, frequent	3hrs

PHETCHABURI – CHUMPHON
OTT TABLE 7055

TRANSPORT	FREQUENCY	JOURNEY TIME
Train	10 daily	6hrs
Bus	Daily, frequent	6hrs

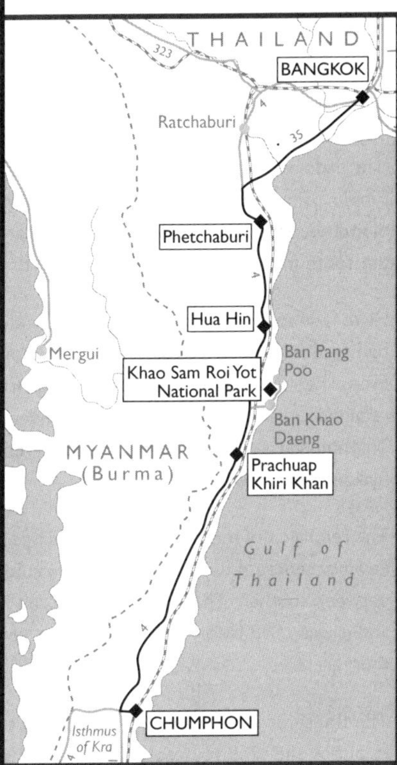

Notes

Trains All Bangkok – Phetchaburi trains from Hualamphong have sleeping cars except the 2230 and 2250.

The Bangkok – Butterworth Southern Line: This Bangkok – Chumphon route forms part of Thai Railways' main Southern Line. The ten trains that depart daily from Bangkok's Hualamphong station go through Surat Thani (page 223) while Train 35 which departs early afternoon goes all the way to Butterworth in Malaysia.

Buses Although buses are faster than the trains, they leave from Bangkok's Southern Bus Terminal which takes longer to get to.

Bangkok – Chumphon
Southern Thailand

Travelling south on this route means seeing a slow shedding of many of the characteristics associated with Thailand. Buddhism starts giving way to Islam and the call of the mosque becomes more common than the sight of colourful *wats*. The familiar view of rice paddies from train and bus windows begins to be replaced by plantations of rubber, palm oil and coconut trees. The further south one travels, the more Malay the mood becomes, and the feeling grows that it is more than kilometres that separates the south from Bangkok and the rest of the country.

History, it seems, is to blame. Until around the 13th century the south was culturally tied to the Malay peninsula, and traded more with China than with land to the north. Even when the emerging kingdom of Sukhotai began to be more influential, the south retained considerable de facto independence. As late as the 1970s, when the rest of Thailand had a cultural and political coherence, in the south Thai communists were still making their presence felt.

The remnants of the communist opposition that fought the British in 1950s Malaya and never accepted the new Malaysian government had its strongholds in the borderlands between southern Thailand and northern Malaysia. They outlasted their Thai comrades and it was 1990 before the last of the guerrillas came out of the jungle and handed in their arms.

The transition from 'mainland' Thailand to southern Thailand is not sudden or dramatic, but by the time you reach Chumphon the differences are apparent.

PHETCHABURI

Commonly shortened to Phetburi or Petchaburi, this ancient town has about 30 *wats* but the number worth seeking out can be counted on one hand. The best ones can be taken in on a walking tour, outlined below. It starts from the railway station where most visitors arrive. To skip the first leg of the walk take a *samlor* from the station to Wat Yai Suwannaran.

If temple fatigue takes the shine off this idea, an alternative destination is **Khao Wang**. This 95-metre-high hill to the west of town is admittedly crowned with a host of *wats, chedis* and *prangs,* but they are architecturally insignificant and the view from the top, best enjoyed as the sun starts to go down, is the sole reason for making the ascent.

It is a stiff climb but a tram **$$** Mon–Fri 0800–1730, Sat–Sun 0800–1800, saves the legwork. The hilltop **Phra Nakhon Khiri**, built by Rama IV as a summer pad, is now a museum **$** Wed–Sun 0900–1600, filled with a miscellany of artefacts collected by the king.

A WALKING TOUR

Coming out from the railway station, turn left and follow the road past the night market for almost half a kilometre until you see the bus station on your left. The road turns right here, passing Siam Commercial Bank on your left, and reaches a busy crossroads. Turn right here to the Chomrut bridge that crosses the river.

On the other side of the bridge walk straight ahead past the Chom Klao Hotel on Phongsuriya Rd until **Wat Suwannaram** looms on your right. Two points of interest here are the graphic murals decorating the *bot* and the elegant old library building in the middle of the pond. Two other *wats* a little further down the road hardly merit attention. When you reach them, turn right instead into Phokarong Rd and after a five-minute walk turn right into Phrasong Rd for **Wat Kamphaeng Laeng**.

This 12th century temple was built to honour Hindu deities. Its ancient lineage helps explain its unspectacular appearance. Continue on Phrasong Rd, passing two undistinguished *wats* on either side of the road. At the crossroads with Matayawong Rd you can either turn left for three *wats*, stretched out along the left side of the road, or walk straight across the junction, still on Phrasong Rd, back towards the river and a bridge.

Cross the bridge for the important and hard to miss **Wat Mahathat** on Damnoenkasem Rd. Extensive restoration work on the five *prangs* and the *bots* have turned this into the town's most visited temple. There is plenty to see and lots of detailed art work to admire, especially the *bot's* imaginative murals.

A short way north up Damnoenkasem Rd brings you back to the junction near Chomrut Bridge.

ARRIVAL AND DEPARTURE

Bus: The main bus station is near Khao Wang, too far from the town centre to walk with luggage in the heat, but *samlors* are always on hand. Buses to and from Hua Hin and Chumphon, however, use another bus station more conveniently located in the centre of town (see walking tour on page 195).

Chom Klao $ 1–3 Phongsuriya Rd, tel: (032) 425-398. The best of fairly dismal choices in the town. Centrally located at least, next to Chomrut Bridge, and service with a smile. Some rooms with bathrooms, some with river views.

Phetkasem Hotel $$–$ 86/1 Phetkasem Rd, tel: (032) 425-581. Convenient for Bangkok bus station and the better rooms have air-con, hot water and bathrooms.

Rabieng restaurant **$** Damnoenkasem Rd, tel: (032) 425-707, in the town centre at Chomrut Bridge. Open-fronted riverside location. English menu with a good mix of inexpensive seafood and meat dishes.

If you are staying at the Phetkasem Hotel, there are a number of inexpensive restaurants along the road which are also useful when arriving or departing by bus.

LAZY SEASIDE DAYS

The small seaside resort of Cha-am, between Phetchaburi and Hua Hin, is best avoided at weekends and during school holidays unless you thrive on crowds and noisy families. Arrive during the week, though, and the sandy beach is all yours. There is nothing to see or do, so only drop by if you want to do simply nothing but lie on a beach and work on your tan. Getting to Cha-am is a breeze, with buses and trains from Bangkok running every day.

There are lots of places to stay that are horrendously busy with families over the weekends, but during the week are so empty that generous discounts of up to 50% should be available. Unless they appeal to you, skip the condo-style apartment blocks that line the main drag by the sea, Ruamchit Rd, and pick out the beachside wooden bungalows that can be found in between them. Here are a couple to consider, but there are plenty more.

Santisuk $$$–$$ 263/3 Ruamchit Rd, tel: (032) 471-212. A terrific range of accommodation, from inexpensive wooden huts to regular rooms.
Kaenchan $$$–$ 241/3 Ruamchit Rd, tel: (032) 471-314. Another place with wooden bungalows and air-con rooms. Also a small rooftop pool.

i There is a **TAT Office** at the southern end of town, open daily 0830–1630, tel: (032) 471-502, with information on accommodation and Hua Hin.

HUA HIN

The first royal palace at Hua Hin was built in the early 1920s. Ever since Rama VII chose the site for another summer palace at the end of that decade, Hua Hin has been a premier domestic beach resort and possibly the oldest in Thailand. The king named his palace Klai Kangwon, 'Far From Worries'. Current tourist literature continues his tone: 'Long, sandy beaches, unspoilt and uncluttered'. Well, sort of. Hua Hin's beach is 5 km long and there is sand, but there are also countless deckchairs, lurid beach umbrellas and lines of sailing boats, ski jets, and vendors touting horse rides.

Most weekends see an invasion from Bangkok. On quieter days, Hua Hin is worth a short visit because it has a good tourist infrastructure, local seafood with a deservedly high reputation and a safe beach for swimming. Also, there is the wonderful renamed Railway Hotel, which is always worth nosing around. In addition, Hua Hin is conveniently close to Khao Sam Roi Yot National Park (see page 200).

The best stretch of Hua Hin's **beach** is at the end of the main road that begins once you step out of the railway station. This explains the location of the famous old **Railway Hotel**, now unglamorously renamed the Sofitel Central. The railway line was extended to Hua Hin because of the royal palace, and when Thailand's social elite followed the king's example and started holidaying here the railway company began construction of the hotel in 1923.

By the 1980s it had failed dismally to move with the times (although it was used in the filming of *The Killing Fields* in 1983) but by the end of that decade a French company had moved in on a long lease and helped finance a major renovation project. The restoration work proceeded with loving attention to detail, and what you see today fairly accurately creates the character of the original open-fronted, colonial-style hotel.

The extensive grounds and airy lobby are a pleasure to walk around, and a visit is recommended. It does not radiate the social snobbery that afflicts the Oriental in Bangkok and it also helps to show just how hollow the restored Raffles in Singapore is by comparison.

WHAT'S IN A NAME?

Rama VII (1925–1935) may have called his palace 'Far From Worries' but it hardly lived up to its name. While he was staying here in June 1932 news reached him of a coup d'état in Bangkok. It was not a popular people's revolution (although there was general discontent at the economic consequences of the Great Depression), and there was no attempt to topple the monarchy. But it did result in a constitutional monarchy, and presumably spoiled the king's seaside summer holiday.

TRAIN Hua Hin is on the main Southern Line and all trains on this line from Bangkok stop here. Hua Hin's quaint railway station is at the west end of town and within walking distance of the centre.

Most trains from Bangkok arrive in the late evening or late at night, so it pays to have the first night's accommodation booked in advance. Trains travelling up from the south, on the other hand, arrive early in the morning.

The **local tourist office** is just east of the railway station, at the corner of Damnoenkasem Rd and Phetkasem Rd, open daily, 0830 – 1630, tel: (032) 511-047. General information, details of hotels and restaurants, and local transport information available. The post office is on the other side of the junction, across from the tourist office.

Chiva Som $$$$$ 73/4 Phetkasem Rd, tel: (032) 536-536, fax: (032) 511-154. A visit to this health resort begins with a brief consultation with the resident nurse, prior to choosing from the various forms of treatment on offer (paid for separately). Two pools, health-conscious restaurant (meals included in the room rates), gym, spa, tai-chi pavilion and a stretch of beach directly outside.

Hotel Sofitel Central $$$$$ Damnoenkasem Rd, tel: (032) 512-021, fax: (032) 511-014, e-mail: sofitel_central@hotmail.com. The restored Railway Hotel, complete with polished wood panelling, industrial-sized ceiling fans, large rooms and lovely grounds. Expensive but worth inquiring about discounts for mid-week.

Ban Boosarin $$$ 8/8 Poonsuk Rd, tel: (032) 512-076. Still one of the best mid-range hotels in Hua Hin. Fridge, phone and television in rooms and no weekend surcharges.

Jed Pee Nong Hotel $$$-$$ Damnoenkasem Rd, tel: (032) 512-381. Nondescript, functional hotel but reliable. A choice of rooms and a swimming pool.

Bird $$ 31/2 Naretdamri Rd, tel: (032) 511-630. One of the very best guesthouses in this price range. All rooms have bathrooms and while not spacious they have outdoor space overlooking the sea.

All Nations $ 10 Dechanuchit Rd, tel: (032) 512-747, fax: (032) 530-474, e-mail: gary@infonews.co.th. The best of the really budget places. Shared facilities, fan, balcony, informative and helpful management.

Pattana Guest House $ 52 Naretdamri Rd, tel: (032) 513-393, fax: (053) 530-081. Basic rooms in two wooden traditional style houses. Tucked down a *soi*.

OTHER TOP HOTELS

Outside of Bangkok, Hua Hin has one of the best concentrations of top-notch hotels anywhere in Thailand. They are expensive of course, but the competition means healthy discounts during quiet periods, and it is worth shopping around.

Apart from the Hotel Sofitel, and the Chiva Som (which doesn't discount), other four- and five-star hotels worth checking out are:

Melia Hua Hin, off Naretdamri Rd, tel: (032) 512-879, fax: (032) 511-135.

Royal Garden Resort, 107/1 Phetkasem Rd, tel: (032) 511-881, fax: (032) 512-422.

Sirin Hotel, Damnoenkasem Rd, tel: (032) 511-150, fax: (032) 513-571.

Mercure Resort, Damnoenkasem Rd, tel: (032) 512-036, fax: (032) 511-014.

Royal Garden Village, Phetkasem Rd, tel: (032) 520-250, fax: (032) 520-259, e-mail: royalgardenvhh@minornet.com..

Chatcahi Market $$ off Dechanuchit Rd and Phetkasem Rd near the bus station. A great place for seafood in the evenings and inexpensive Thai dishes during the day. There is another night market specialising in seafood near the train station.

Naretdamri Rd, which runs north off the beach end of Damnoenkasem Rd, has a good choice of restaurants for international and European food as well as excellent seafood eateries at its northern end. Pasta, pizzas, lasagne and the like appear with a monotonous regularity on too many of the menus, but they are some honourable exceptions serving quality continental cuisine.

Le Chablis $$ 88 Naretdamri Rd. French food, but also some good Thai dishes. A restaurant that works hard to create an enjoyable and entertaining atmosphere.

SEAFOOD

Hua Hin is justly famous for its seafood and enjoying good food at moderate prices is one of the resort's main draws. All kinds of fish appear on the menus – crab, mussels, squid, cottonfish (kingfish), shrimp, garoupa, perch – and many of the seafood restaurants display their fresh catch wrapped in ice outside their premises. Methods of cooking are equally varied. You can have your fish raw (Japanese style), grilled, fried, steamed or served in a classic Thai spicy sauce.

KHAO SAM ROI YOT NATIONAL PARK

Khao Sam Roi Yot ('Mountain of Three Hundred Peaks') National Park borders the Gulf of Thailand. Its 98 square kilometres support a variety of habitats and are rich in wildlife. There are forest walks, caves, two beaches, and well over 200 species of birds. The only drawback is the relative difficulty of getting there by public transport. The best solution is to either hire a car or motorbike in Hua Hin or take a day tour from there.

Western Tours, 11 Damnoenkasem Rd, Hua Hin, tel: (032) 512-209, run day trips and also rent cars. **Avis** have outlets at the Sofitel Central Hotel, tel: (032) 512-021, and the Chiva Som Resort, tel: (032) 536-536.

From the **visitor centre**, there are two marked trails. One leads through a forest and the other winds through a mangrove environment. The kind of wildlife you are most likely to spot includes long-tailed macaques, dusky languor monkeys, barking deer, monitor lizards and perhaps dolphins cruising off the coast. To appreciate the birdlife either bring your own binoculars or rent them from the park headquarters.

Accommodation: $$$-$$ at the park is organised by the Forestry Department and either arranged at the visitor centre when you arrive or through the Bangkok office, tel: (02) 561-4292.

GETTING THERE

Bus/Train: To reach the park by public transport, take a bus from Hua Hin to Pranburi, and from there hire a *songthaew* all the way to the park headquarters.

Car: From Huan Hin travel south on Highway 4 for 25 km to Pranburi before turning left at the signposted junction. It is another 36 km to the park headquarters and visitor centre.

EN ROUTE

PRACHUAP KHIRI KHAN

This small town on the route between Hua Hin and Chumphon does not receive a lot of foreign tourists but suggests itself as a quiet destination for an overnight stay. The beach is poor and the most enjoyable activity is a climb up the 400 plus steps to Khao Chong Krajok at the north end of town.

From the summit there are views of Myanmar, only a few miles away, and of the coast to the east. I first came here some years back to visit Ao Manao, a beach about 5 km south of town, where the Japanese landed in December 1941 as part of their co-ordinated invasion of Thailand and Malaya. The beach is actually more appealing than the main one in Prachuap, and there are a couple of places to stay.

There is a small **tourist office**, reached from the bus or train station by walking down Kong Kiat Rd and turning left into Sarachip Rd.

Buses depart regularly throughout the day from Hua Hin, as do the **trains** that nearly all stop at Prachuap Khiri on their journey south to Chumphon.

Yuttichai Hotel $ 115 Kong Khai Rd, tel: (032) 611-055, is easy to find on the right side of the main road that leads from the railway station to the beach.

CHUMPHON

The town of Chumphon has little or no intrinsic appeal to the traveller, but it does mark an important junction. One route continues directly south to Surat Thani, the jumping-off point for Ko Samui, and on to the border with Malaysia. The other route heads down the west coast of southern Thailand to Ranong and Phuket.

Chumphon, in a slowly developing endeavour to be more than a mere junction, is also marketing itself as the gateway to the island of Ko Tao. There are two good tour agents in town, both close to the bus station, where bus and train information can be obtained as well as details for onward travel to Ko Tao.

Infinity Travel Service, 68/2 Tha Taphao Rd, tel: (077) 501-937, also organise tours to local beaches and caves. **Songserm Travel**, tel: (077) 502-023, is on the same road. All the guesthouses that have got their act together have information on local trips and ways to occupy a day or two in the vicinity.

Jansom Chumphon Hotel $$$–$$ 118/138 Sala Daeng Rd, tel: (077) 502-502, fax: (077) 502-503. Run of the mill town hotel, but perfectly adequate for a night's stay and a modicum of comfort. The attached disco may be either a distraction or irritant at weekends.

Tha Taphao Hotel $$ 66/1 Tha Taphao Rd, tel: (077) 511-479. If using buses, more convenient than Jansom Chumphon, though very similar.

Mayaze's Resthouse $ tel: (077) 504-452, fax: (077) 502-217. Down a quiet *soi* between Tha Taphao Rd and Sala Daeng Rd. Handy for the bus station and travel agents. Good reputation for friendliness and cleanliness. Shared bathrooms but the welcoming and homely atmosphere makes this a cut above other budget guesthouses and a good place to meet fellow travellers.

New Chumphon Guest House $ Soi 1, off Krom Luang Chumphon Rd, tel: (077) 501-242. Another friendly guesthouse with lots of experience of catering for backpackers.

Sarakrom Wine House $$ Tha Taphao Rd. Only open in the evening. Refreshing change for anyone seeking respite from rice and noodles. Thai food and a wine list. **Sala Daeng Rd**, where the Jansom Chumphon hotel is situated, has a number of inexpensive options for an evening or lunch-time meal. **Tha Taphao Rd** is another good hunting ground.

KO TAO

The small island of Ko Tao is just over 20 square km, with an established reputation as a centre for scuba diving. During the peak tourist season Dec–March there are more travellers arriving than the island can support, and the appeal of being here during those months is questionable.

At other times, though, it has its charms, and for non-divers the fun of snorkelling in the clear, clean water is a reason for making the long journey from Chumphon.

The drawback for non-divers, however, is that the bungalow operators aren't extracting as much money from you and have a tendency to downgrade you to second-class status.

The plus side is that Ko Tao offers a good opportunity to learn scuba diving at competitive rates. Expect to pay around 8500B for a complete four-day course leading to a PADI certificate, including all costs.

There are dozens of places to stay, all more or less the same in terms of facilities and most in the **$$–$** price range. If arriving in the high season it's advisable to have your accommodation booked in advance through one of the travel agents in Chumphon. At other times you can wander along the beaches and check out the options. All the bungalow operations have their own restaurants and expect guests to use them at least some of the time.

Boats for Ko Tao depart daily in the morning from Pak Nam, 14 km south of Chumphon. The journey takes about four hours, depending on the weather. You can also reach the island from Ko Pha Ngan.

Chumphon – Ko Lanta

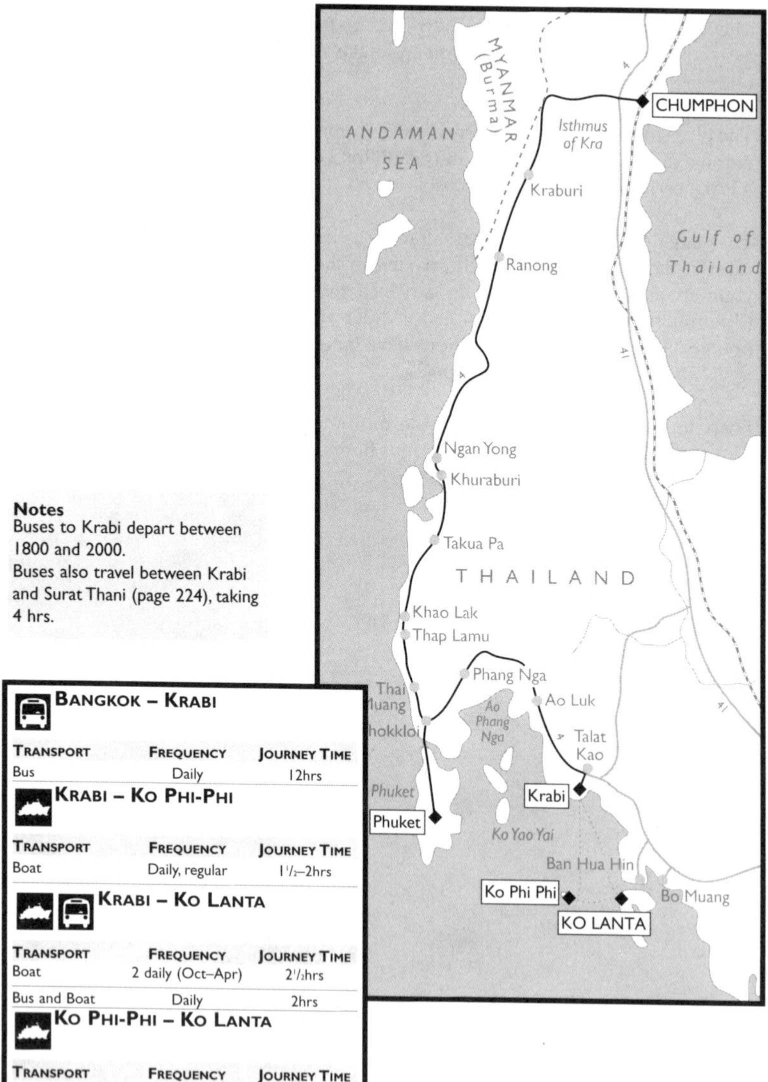

Notes
Buses to Krabi depart between 1800 and 2000.
Buses also travel between Krabi and Surat Thani (page 224), taking 4 hrs.

Bangkok – Krabi

Transport	Frequency	Journey Time
Bus	Daily	12hrs

Krabi – Ko Phi-Phi

Transport	Frequency	Journey Time
Boat	Daily, regular	1½–2hrs

Krabi – Ko Lanta

Transport	Frequency	Journey Time
Boat	2 daily (Oct–Apr)	2½hrs
Bus and Boat	Daily	2hrs

Ko Phi-Phi – Ko Lanta

Transport	Frequency	Journey Time
Boat	2 daily (Oct–Apr)	1hr

The long Andaman Sea coastline of southern Thailand has scores of idyllic offshore islands that offer hedonism without the grossness of Phuket or the gloss of Ko Samui. Krabi is fast transforming itself into the main departure point for visits to the islands of Ko Phi Phi and Ko Lanta. The Chumphon – Ko Lanta route will attract travellers in search of an activity holiday as well as those who are content to chill out on pristine beaches shaded by gently swaying palms. Trips by inflatable sea canoe open up the hidden lagoons and mangrove forests, and scuba divers and snorkellers are spoilt for choice as regards coral reefs teeming with marine life. Local agents in Krabi also cater for rock climbers who want to try their skills on the challenging limestone cliffs. If all this sounds too much like hard work, head for Ko Lanta. It sounds like a cliché but Ko Lanta really is unspoilt and the perfect place to just do nothing for a couple of days.

KRABI

Although not well known yet, the small, tidy town of Krabi is fast developing into an important transport hub for travel in the region. Krabi is still a pleasant place, and is a possible base for excursions to nearby beaches. It is also the place to catch a boat to Ko Lanta and other islands.

The town has plenty of **travel agents**. All take bookings for boats and buses as well as accommodation on the beaches. They can be a good source of information, and during the high season it is not a bad idea to have your first night's accommodation booked in advance. Information and tickets for onward travel to Malaysia can also be obtained. Two well-established travel agents, **Jungle Book** and **Chan Phen**, are next to each other on Utarakit Rd.

MANGROVE TOURS

A boat trip to the mangrove forest in the estuary of the Krabi River is one of the most worthwhile tours available. It offers an opportunity to view the weird architecture of mangroves close up as well as a chance to see fiddler crabs and mudskippers.

The agents also offer a variety of **local tours**. Boat trips to local mangrove swamps are well worth considering, although the trips to nearby islands, hidden lagoons and coral reefs may seem more instantly appealing.

The accommodation in Krabi town is mixed, with lots of cheap guesthouses offering claustrophobic rooms that quickly exhaust their charm after one night's stay. There are a couple of exceptions, listed below. While hotels are a better bet they hardly earn their room rates for a short stay.

The **TAT Office** on Utarakit Rd, tel: (075) 612-740, has useful maps of the town and area, and up-to-date information on accommodation.

Krabi Meritime Hotel $$$$$ tel: (075) 620-028, fax: (075) 612-992. 2 km out of town on the bus station road, this is the upmarket place to stay. Rooms with a view, pool, fitness centre and restaurant.

City Hotel $$$–$$ 15/2–3 Sukhon Rd, tel: (075) 621-280, fax: (075) 621-301. Good, centrally located hotel with clean rooms and the option of air-con.

Grand Tower $$–$ 73/1 Utarakit Rd, tel: (075) 611-741. Calls itself a hotel but is basically a guesthouse with nondescript but adequate rooms, a restaurant, a roof-top balcony and a reliable travel agent.

KR Mansion $ 52/1 Chao Fah Rd, tel: (075) 612-761. One of the best budget places, a ten-minute walk from the centre. Airy rooms, friendly management and a roof-top balcony to watch the sunset. Tours and tickets can be booked here, and there is a decent restaurant as well.

Thammachart $$–$ Kong Ka Rd. Easy to find by the riverside and close to the piers. One of Krabi's more interesting places to eat, with an imaginative menu and delicious vegetarian food.

Barn Thai Issara $$ Maharat Soi 2. Another great place but it closes at 1600, so come for breakfast or lunch. Home-baked breads, imported cheeses, and delicious fresh pasta and Thai dishes.

Ruan Phae $$ Utarakit Rd. Like most floating restaurants in Thailand, the food plays second fiddle to the concept. Still, it's a pleasant place to relax and take in the views.

Muslim Restaurant $ Pruksa Uthit Rd. Rotis and curries – everyone's favourite for a quick but tasty and filling meal. Walk west on Utarakit Rd. Turn left into Phattana Rd just before Chan Phen Travel and right into Pruksa Uthit Rd.

KRABI'S BEACHES

The beach at **Ao Nang**, 18 km west of Krabi, is reached by a 30 to 45 min *songthaew* journey. It is the most developed of Krabi's beaches, with a host of dive shops and a raft of tour agents offering kayaking expeditions, snorkelling trips, boat rides through the mangrove swamps, and tours to idyllic looking islands. Between December and February the hotels are packed with Western holidaymakers, and rates are at a premium. Outside the high season discounts on rooms are hefty, but between June and October high winds make swimming inadvisable, and the beach tends to collect wind-borne rubbish.

Laem Phra Nang is the headland south of Ao Nang, reached only by boat. This does not diminish the crowds, because the dramatic limestone cliffs, soft, white sand beach and crystal clear water make up everyone's fantasy of a tropical paradise. You can have fun just being here for a day or two, enjoying the beauty of it all, but there is plenty of scope for activities as well.

The **snorkelling** is great and **rock climbing** is beginning to develop into a major attraction because of the proximity of limestone cliffs. Tour agents and guesthouses can all handle bookings for short introductory courses. Prices range from 500B to 1000B for a half- or full-day course, and up to 3000B for a full three days. These courses are run by professionals and include insurance and all equipment.

There are two main beaches at Laem Phra Nang. The one on the west side, called variously Hat Tham Phra Nang, Princess Cave Beach, or Ao Phra Nang, is the most stunningly beautiful. Most visitors are awestruck by its picture-postcard perfection. The beach to the east, East Railae, is less attractive but a lot more developed, and only a ten-minute walk to the west beach.

Boats for Laem Phra Nang depart from Krabi and Ao Nang at regular intervals throughout the day.

KO PHI-PHI

Ko Phi-Phi is the name for two islands, Phi Phi Le and Phi Phi Don, 40 km south of Krabi. Both islands are beautiful, with soft sand beaches and transparent water full of colourful fish, but they are not undiscovered. This is painfully obvious between mid December and early March, and in July and August. Accommodation is only available on Phi Phi Don, and rooms are at such a premium during the high season that it is advisable to have somewhere booked in advance.

Diving, snorkelling and **kayaking** are the most popular activities on Phi Phi Don. Dive operations in Phuket and Krabi run trips to Ko Phi-Phi, and there are also dive shops on Phi Phi Don. Most of the guesthouses and tour agents run snorkelling trips to the neighbouring coral reefs and uninhabited islands.

Boats to Phi Phi Don run daily from Krabi, taking two hours, and from Phuket, which take a little longer. During the high season there are also some boats from Ao Nang and Ko Lanta. The only way to reach Phi Phi Le is by boat from its sister island.

All the boats pull in at Ton Sai, where a lot of the accommodation is based as there are no roads on the islands. The places to stay listed below are the tip of a burgeoning accommodation iceberg but it is still essential to have something reserved in advance, especially over Christmas when demand pushes room rates even higher.

Ton Sai Village $$$$ Ton Sai, tel: (075) 512-434, fax: (075) 612-196. Comfortable beach bungalows with air-con. Overpriced, but that goes without saying on Phi Phi Don.

Phi-Phi Hotel $$$$ Ton Sai, tel: (02) 941-7184, (01) 230-3138, fax: (02) 579-5764, e-mail: phiphi@samart.co.th. Low-rise hotel set back from the main drag, with similar amenities to Ton Sai Village.

Phi Phi Pavilion $$$ Lo Dalam, tel: (075) 620-633. Picturesque wooden bungalows, with the sea on your doorstep. Lo Dalam beach is a ten-minute walk from Ton Sai and a little quieter.

Charlie Beach Resort $$-$ Lo Dalam, tel: (01) 229-0495). Thatched bungalows similar to Phi Phi Pavilion next door. Close to the sea, with a beach bar.

Every resort and bungalow operation has its own restaurant, and their prices tend to reflect the kind of accommodation they offer. In Ton Sai there are a number of independent restaurants with menus that have evolved to satisfy tourists. A well-established place that has maintained its high standard of cooking is **Mama Resto**. Multilingual menus feature a good range of western favourites as well as Thai food.

DiCaprio's Beach

The filming of *The Beach,* based on Alex Garland's novel, began at the end of 1998 on Phi Phi Le's Maya beach, with heart-throb Leonardo DiCaprio as the big star. By the time of the film's premiere in Bangkok in early 2000, environmental activists were staging a mock ritualistic suicide. They urged the public to boycott the film, claiming that 20th Century Fox had ruined the fragile eco-system of Maya Bay. It is true that 100 palm trees were planted on the beach and sand dunes had been bulldozed.

'I think to alter a natural treasure just for the benefit of 15-year-old American movie fans is not a very good idea,' voiced a tourist at the protest event. The irony is that *The Beach* — a mediocre film that begins with a pimp's words, 'Do you want a girl?' — bombed in America and Europe, and will only make a profit from ticket sales in Thailand and other parts of Asia.

KO LANTA

Ko Lanta is the generic name for a large group of islands south of Krabi. One of the largest, 25 km long Ko Lanta Yai, has been developed to offer inexpensive beach accommodation. Transport to the island and accommodation is easy to arrange through tour agents in Krabi, Ao Nang and Phuket.

Ferries for Ban Sala Dan, on the northern tip of Ko Lanta, depart from the pier in Krabi and from Ko Phi-Phi, but note that regular transport is only available between October and April. At other times of the year the journey from Krabi involves travelling over 40 km south to Ban Hua Hin for a ferry over the narrow waterway to Ko Lanta Noi, and then continuing south to Ko Lanta.

Ko Lanta Yai has nice beaches on its west coast, interspersed with rocky outcrops. The further south you walk the more the Robinson Crusoe effect kicks in. Although the beaches are not as spectacularly beautiful as those on Phi Phi or Laem Phra Nang, they do not attract mass crowds and large tour groups. Ko Lanta is still an island where you can see normal life going on, unlike most of the other big resort areas in this part of Thailand. This means there is not a lot to do except sunbathe and swim and generally relax, though dive operators have set up shop at Ban Sala Dan and snorkelling trips to smaller islands are readily available.

Transport on the island is by motorbike taxi from the beaches to the pier, but service is haphazard. Motorbikes can be rented but Ko Lanta is very much an island where visitors hang out rather than feel the need to organise something active. Anything that is going to happen will start at **Ban Sala Dan**, the pier and village at the north of the island.

Bear in mind the lack of transport when choosing where to stay. Luckily, the most attractive beach, **Hat Khlong Dao**, is only half an hour's walk from Ban Sala Dan. It also has the widest choice of bungalows and places to eat. When you step off the ferry many of the guesthouses will have minivans waiting. The places listed below are only a selection, and new places are popping up all the time.

Kaw Kwang Beach Bungalows $$$–$ Hat Khlong Dao, tel: (01) 228-4106. A good range of bungalows on the best stretch of beach. Snorkelling trips can be arranged.

Golden Bay Cottages $$–$ Hat Khlong Dao, tel: (01) 229-0879. Clean, comfortable bungalows on another lovely stretch of beach.

Deer Neck Cabana $ Hat Khlong Dao, tel: (01) 723-0523. Not the best bit of beach but friendly management and inexpensive rooms.

Lanta Palm Beach $ Ao Phra-Ae, tel: (01) 723-0528. Bamboo huts and coconut trees on a lovely beach. Peaceful Ao Phra-Ae is a couple of kilometres south of Khlong Dao.

Lanta Coral Beach $ Hat Khlong Khoang, tel: (01) 228-4326. Thatched huts, some with bathrooms. This beach is further south again, not as sandy but ok for snorkelling and very quiet.

Every bungalow has its own restaurant, but there is no pressure to eat where you are staying. Prices and menus are fairly standard. In Sala Dan there are a few independent restaurants. One that serves quite good food is **Danny's Bar**.

Pronounced 'Pooket', the island is Thailand's largest and every year well over a million overseas visitors arrive here. Tourism has made a huge impact on the island and its culture, and anyone arriving here for their first trip to Thailand will receive a rather distorted view of the country and what it can offer.

Phuket is the most un-Thai place in the country, and it is not too much of an exaggeration to say that some Thai restaurants in London offer a more authentic glimpse of the country's culture than parts of Phuket's west coast. On the plus side, the island offers wonderful beaches, a wealth of watersports and years of experience in catering to the needs and whims of holidaymakers.

The capital of the island is **Phuket town** on the south-east coast, and, because it is not close to the airport, 32 km away, many people never visit it. The town is well worth seeing and can make a welcome break from the beaches. Travellers counting their bahts, or anyone who wants to see Phuket without being holed up in a resort, could consider staying in town and making day trips to the beaches. The differences between the various beaches are not as pronounced as on Ko Samui, although **Ao Patong** is definitely the most developed and **Ao Kata** the quietest.

No matter where you are in Phuket, the price of just about everything is significantly higher than anywhere else in the country.

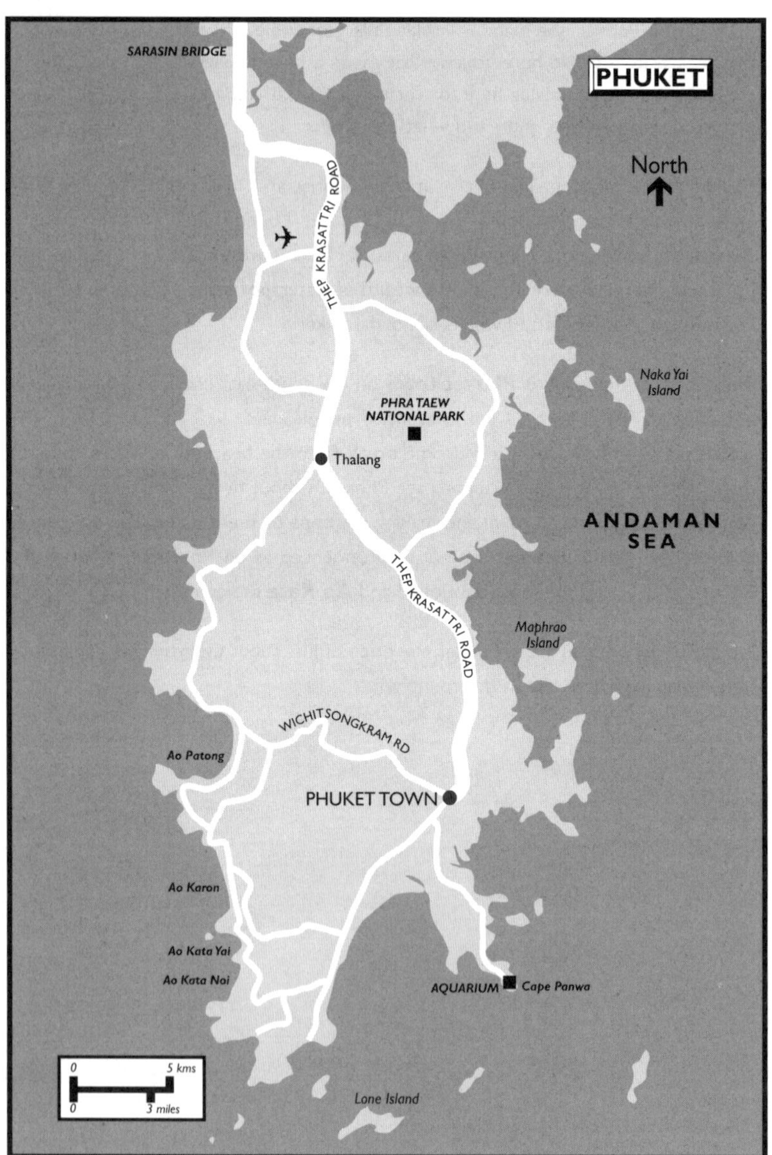
SARASIN BRIDGE
PHUKET
North
THEP KRASATTRI ROAD
PHRA TAEW
NATIONAL PARK
Thalang
Naka Yai
Island
ANDAMAN
SEA
THEP KRASATTRI ROAD
Maphrao
Island
WICHITSONGKRAM RD
Ao Patong
PHUKET TOWN
Ao Karon
Ao Kata Yai
Ao Kata Noi
AQUARIUM
Cape Panwa
0
5 kms
0
3 miles
Lone Island

ARRIVAL AND DEPARTURE

AIR Thai Airways operate numerous daily flights between Bangkok and Phuket, taking just under an hour and a half. There are also flights to Chiang Mai, Hat Yai and Surat Thani. The office is at 78/1 Ranong Rd, tel: (076) 211-195).

Bangkok Airways flies daily between Phuket and Ko Samui. The office is at 2-3 Yaowarat Rd, tel: (076) 225-033.

International routes connect Phuket with Kuala Lumpur, Langkawi, Penang and Singapore. There are also flights to other Asian and European cities. Malaysia Airlines (MAS) have an office in Thungkha Rd, tel: (076) 216-675. Singapore Airlines and Silk Air have their offices in Thungkha Rd as well.

Phuket international airport, tel: (076) 327-230/5), has money exchange facilities and a tourist office.

A minibus service runs between **the airport** and all the main beaches. Tickets are bought at a central counter, and the bus driver will usually drop passengers off at their hotel or guesthouse. Taxis, more expensive, are also readily available.

Transport to your hotel can be booked through most of the hotels. There is also a less expensive airport service run by Tour Royal Enterprises, tel: (076) 222-052, 235-268. The buses depart 0700–1800 from a station on Wichit Songkhram Rd, the continuation of Ranong Rd in Phuket, and within walking distance of the town centre.

BUS Air-con buses and minibuses link Phuket with Bangkok, taking 14 hrs and departing from the Southern Bus Terminal in Bangkok. Other destinations include Hat Yai (7 hrs), Krabi (4 hrs), Nakhon Si Thammarat (8 hrs) and Surat Thani (6 hrs).

The bus station is at the eastern end of Phang Nga Road in Phuket town, within walking distance of the road where *songthaews* depart for the beaches. The tourist office has a useful brochure listing all routes, journey times and fares.

INFORMATION

Tune In

Every night between 2030 and 2100, and 2130 and 2200, daily news from the *Phuket Gazette* is broadcast on FM 89 MHz.

The **TAT Office** is at 73 Phuket Rd, Phuket town, open daily 0830 – 1630, tel: (076) 212-213, 211-036. This very well-run office supplies a useful map of the town and the island, information on local transport, and schedules and fares for long-distance buses. From the fountain roundabout near where the songthaews from the beaches congregate, walk along Ratsada Rd to a junction near the river and turn right into Phuket Rd.

A few doors down from the tourist office there is a good **bookshop** with a small **Internet café**. E-mails can be sent and collected from a number of places around town, but this is one of the more comfortable and competitively priced places.

Maps And Mags

The free *A-O-A Phuket Map* has good inset maps of Patong, Karon, Kata and Phuket town, showing accommodation and places to eat. It's useful for drivers because it shows petrol stations.

There is a lot of other free literature on Phuket which can be picked up in hotel foyers, most of it containing maps. Look for the advertising-fuelled monthly pocket-size guide to food, shops and entertainment and the monthly *Phuket Guide*. The 20B fortnightly *Phuket Gazette* is worth dipping into for local current affairs and a round-up of the music and pub scene.

Useful Telephone Numbers

Tourist Police: 1699

Phuket International Hospital: 210-935, 249-400

Bangkok Phuket Hospital: 254-421

Lost Credit Cards: American Express, (02) 273-0022. Master and Visa, (02) 299-1990

Overseas Phone Service: 100

GETTING AROUND

There are good roads around the island, and *tuk-tuks* make their way from one beach to the next for what is by Thai standards an extortionate amount. Expect to pay *at least* 100B for a *tuk-tuk* between Patong and Karon, 120B between Patong and Kata. The best deal on public transport is by *songthaew* from Phuket town to the main beaches for around 20B.

Motorbikes and mopeds are available for hire everywhere, and provide the best means of getting around. Cars and jeeps can be hired at the airport and from countless agents in the beach areas. Avis have a desk at the airport, tel: (076) 351-243, and at Le Meridien Hotel, tel: (076) 340-480. Budget, tel: (076) 205-396, website: www.budget.co.th have competitive rates. One-way rentals to Ko Samui and other parts of Thailand are possible.

ACTIVITIES

Watersports, diving, fishing, speedboat excursions to the Phi Phi islands (page 207), bamboo rafting, horseback riding, Thai boxing, target shooting, jungle and elephant treks, 'eco' tours, bungy jumps, golf, canoeing and anything else an entrepreneur can come up with are available on Phuket.

A few of the more well-established companies, most with websites that you can check out before you arrive, are listed here, but pick up any of the free literature in your hotel and their advertisements fill the pages.

Sea Canoe, tel: (076) 212-252, website: www.seacanoe.com. Sea-caving in kayaks is their speciality.

Khao Lak Safari, tel: (076) 225-522, website: www.phuketunion.com. All sorts of day trips in and around Phuket.

Siam Safari, tel: (075) 280-116. Jungle safaris and elephant treks.

Andaman Divers, tel: (076) 321-429, website: www.andamandivers.com.

Coral Seekers, tel: (076) 345-074, website: www.coralseekers.com.

West Coast Divers, tel: (076) 341-673, website: www.westcoastdivers.com.

Bungy Jump, tel: (076) 321-351, website: www.phuket.com/bungy.

Elephant Treks, tel: (076) 290-056, website: www.phuketdir.com/kalimtrek.

Big Game Fishing, tel: (076) 214-713, e-mail: wahoo@phket.loxinfo.co.th.

PHUKET TOWN

Only in Phuket town is there any sense of a community not dependent on tourism for its livelihood. It also boasts some lovely examples of Chinese urban buildings of a lost era – Hokkien merchants' houses in pastel colours with shutters, small balconies and fading sculpted woodwork. Wandering around Talang Rd, Yaowarat Rd, Ranong Rd and Damrong Rd you will come across some unexpected **architectural treasures**. If you have been to Georgetown in Penang or Ipoh the buildings will come as no surprise, but they are still classics and only now are some of them being restored.

For a glimpse into Phuket's 20th century history, stroll around the lobby and bar of the **Thavorn Hotel** on Ratsada Rd. This veritable museum is packed with old photographs and artefacts from the past, and the bar has some great photos of 1940s Phuket.

SHOPPING IN PHUKET TOWN

There is no shortage of shops lining the beach roads in the west of the island, but the merchandise tends to be the usual assemblage of tacky 'handicrafts' and poor quality fabrics that look good on display but won't last many spins in the washing machine. A day trip to Phuket town at least offers a chance to look at some more interesting shops and Yaowarat Rd is a good place to start.

Just up from the fountain roundabout, **Ayoraya** at No 27 has an assortment of fabrics and home furnishings. At No 51, **Ban Boran Textiles** has a small but select range of quality cotton clothes for women. At No 43, **China House** has clothes for both sexes and assorted objets d'art but nothing very special.

The Loft, 36 Talang Rd, displays artefacts and antiques from south-east Asia on two floors of a converted Hokkien merchant's house. It is a pleasantly stylish shop with some lovely Burmese and Thai antiques, as well as carpets and items of furniture. A shipping service is available, but the cost of transporting some of the larger items exceeds their shop price. **Touch Wood**, 12 Ratsada Rd, next to The Circle café, also sells furniture, fine arts and ornaments.

Phuket Reminder, 85 Ratsada Rd, tel: (076) 213-765, retails raw silk by the yard and a collection of cutlery and crockery made from coconut shells. This shop also conducts **Thai cooking classes,** and recipe sheets are sold in the shop. Across the road from the tourist office, **Phuket Unique Home** has a varied display of items for the home, such as ceramics, glassware, crockery and wood carvings.

Imperial Hotel $$$ 51 Phuket Rd, tel: (076) 212-311, fax: (076) 212-894. A few doors down from the tourist office, this is a neat, modern hotel with hot water and air-con.
Thavorn Hotel $$$–$ 74 Ratsada Rd, tel: (076) 211-333. Large rooms with fan and bathrooms or more modern rooms with air-con. The lobby certainly has character.
On On Hotel $ 9 Phang-Nga Rd, tel: (076) 211-154. Terrific period piece of a building, dating back to the late 1920s. Some air-con rooms.

Sawadee $$$$-$$$ 8/5 Maeluan Rd, tel: (076) 234-804. Colonial-style restaurant with wooden floors and live music. European (including steaks and fondue) and Thai food.
The Circle $$ at the fountain roundabout. This delightful café has a European touch. Good coffee and tea, a breakfast menu that includes strawberries and cornflakes, with meals like beef stew, tuna pie and beans on toast. Britain's *The Guardian* is among the newspapers and magazines for patrons to peruse.
On On Hotel Café $ on Phang-Nga Rd, open 0730–2000, has a full menu of fish and meat dishes. Next door is an ice-cream parlour and a few doors down an inexpensive Thai place.
Ooh-Khao $ Opposite Thavorn Hotel on Ratsada Rd, this little Thai restaurant makes elegant use of newspaper for tablecloths. Open 0930—2130 Mon—Thurs only.
For **vegetarian food $** walk past the line of *songthaews* on Ranong Rd and the caged bird shop until you see two restaurants on the left with yellow signs. The second one is the best, with both white and brown rice and a good selection of dishes. Just point and enjoy.

ENTERTAINMENT

The town does not try to compete with the beaches in terms of big bands and rowdy pubs, but the **Bepob Rock Pub and Restaurant,** Takuapa Rd, tel: (076) 236-137, does its best. Open at 1800, the music gets going after 2200 and finishes around 0300.

AO PATONG

Fifteen kilometres west of Phuket town, Ao Patong is the heart of Phuket's beachland. Its 3 km of sandy beach filled with deckchairs and bodies barbecuing on the sand can be a surreal sight, until it starts to pass for normal. Ao Patong is packed with hotels, restaurants, and an increasing number of bars with hostesses that suggests the direction this resort area might be heading in – if it hasn't already arrived.

At night the beach road turns into one long market of stalls selling cheap clothes, cheap music, cheap batik from Indonesia, and junk knick-knacks. Bargain hard.

What Patong has going for it is a sociable nightlife, a beach that is safe for swimming and suitable for children, a centre for diving operators who every year introduce the sport to complete novices, and a complete holiday environment. All it lacks is a sense of being in Thailand.

Amari Coral Beach $$$$$ Trai Trang Rd, tel: (076) 340-105, fax: (076) 340-115, e-mail: coralbea@loxinfo.co.th. Enjoys one of the more secluded spots in Patong. Suitably expensive.
Phuket Cabana Resort $$$$$ 41 Patong Beach Rd, tel: (076) 340-138, fax: (076) 340-178. Centrally located and artfully designed set of bungalows very close to the beach.
Neptuna $$$$ Rat Uthit Rd, tel: (076) 340-824, fax: (076) 340-627. Good location, a little tight on space but good value.
Safari Beach $$$ 83/12 Patong Beach Rd, tel: (076) 340-230, fax: (076) 340-231. Small pool, restaurant, good value given its location in Patong's centre and close to the beach.
Shamrock Park Inn $$$-$$ Rat Uthit Rd, tel: (076) 340-991, fax: (076) 340-990. Adequate rooms with own showers. Roof garden.
PS 2 Bungalows $$$-$$ tel: (076) 342-207, fax: (076) 290-034. Ten minutes from the beach and a choice of rooms. Good value, traveller-friendly.

Baan Rim Pa $$$$ 100/7 Kalim Beach Rd, tel: (076) 340-789. Popular open-fronted Thai restaurant on a hill at north end of beach. Reservations usually necessary.
Karlsson's Steak House $$$$-$$$ Soi Patong Tower, tel: (076) 345-035. Imported steaks and seafood, Swedish chef.
Naurang Mahal $$$-$$ 58/3 Soi Bangla, Patong Beach, tel: (076) 292-280. Vegetarian and non-vegetarian Indian food. Telephone for a free pickup.

ExPat Hotel $$$ Soi Sunset, tel: (076) 342-143. Open 24 hours for hamburgers, hot dogs and Thai dishes. In-house videos.
Ghadafi $$$ 178 Phratharamee Rd, tel: (076) 340-639. Thai Muslim and Arabic food, lovely roasted chicken. Open 24 hrs.
Kwality Indian Cuisine $$$ Soi Kepsab, tel: (076) 294-082. Tables outside or air-con inside, set menus at under 500B for two people and including two beers.

ENTERTAINMENT

The **Banana Pub** beneath the Banana Disco on Beach Rd, tel: (076) 340-301, open 1900–0200. Expats and tourists turn up to display their musical talents, and anyone is welcome to give a musical twirl. There are three Irish theme pubs in Phuket at the last count, and flavour of the month at the moment is **Molly Malones**, on the beach road. Draught Guinness and Kilkenny beer, open from 1100 for food, live music at night.

Most of the big hotels have bands performing live in their bars; the *Phuket Gazette* carries the latest details. The **Novotel Phuket Resort**, tel: (076) 342-777, usually has music every night except Sunday in its Hourglass Lounge. The **Holiday Inn Resort**, tel: (076) 340-608, goes in for safe theme nights three times a week 2200–2400.

The **Simon Cabaret**, tel: (076) 342-114, has nightly transvestite, shows at 1930 and 2130 for which reservations can be made. Like the Pattaya shows, the emphasis is on colour and choreography rather than anything naughty. The **Parkarang Restaurant**, at the Meridien Hotel, has a nightly dinner theatre show with a Filipino troupe; dinner at 2000 and a show at 2100.

Banana Disco, Beach Rd, tel: (076) 340-301. Phuket's oldest disco and still going strong, open until 0200. **The Tin Mine 21** is a disco in the Royal Paradise Hotel, tel: (076) 340-666, with a DJ; open until 0400. For hi-tech, eardrum-bursting noise **The Titanic**, Soi Sunset, gets going around 2300. A new disco is **The Shark Club**, at the corner of Soi Bangla and Rat Uthit Rd, tel: (076) 340-525.

PHUKET FANTASEA

A nightly dinner buffet with a show that claims to blend Thai culture with Las Vegas-style flair. One of the advertised highlights is a disappearing act involving elephants. This is Phuket-style entertainment and some people find it fun. A ticket for the dinner and show is 1500B (1100B for children). Tel: (076) 271-222, website: www.phuket-fantasea.com.

AO KARON

Ao Karon is only a couple of miles south of Ao Patong, but not so crowded and far better in terms of mid-range accommodation. The least expensive places to stay tend to be set back off the road, but this also gives them some privacy. Patak Rd encircles the beach area, and a *songthaew* can be flagged down anywhere along here for a short hop along beach road or into Phuket town. The beach and its talcum powder sand are lovely.

The top end of Karon, sometimes called Karon Noi or Relax Bay, is dominated by the plush Le Meridien hotel but they cannot claim the beach as their own.

Thavorn Palm Beach Resort $$$$$ tel: (076) 396-090, fax: (076) 396-555, e-mail: palm@phuket.com. Plush, large and filled with palm trees, one of the better top-end resorts. A pool and a relatively empty beach across the road.
South Sea Resort $$$$$ Moo 1, Patak Rd, tel: (076) 396-611, fax: (076) 396-618. So-so rooms but with balconies. A pool.
Phuket Ocean Resort $$$ Moo 1, Karon Beach, tel: (076) 396-176, fax: (076) 396-470. Far north end of the beach, pleasant rooms with sea views and balconies, pool. Fair value.
My Friend $$–$ Katong Beach, tel: (076) 396-344. Huts on a terrace, pleasant enough for the price, and a small restaurant.
Lume & Yai Bungalows $$–$ Katong Beach, tel: (076) 396-383, fax: (076) 396-096. Sea views, friendly management. Well worth considering.

The Old Siam $$$$-$$$ Thavorn Palm Beach Resort, tel: (076) 396-090. Thai food in a very scenic setting if you reserve a terrace table.
The Little Mermaid $$$ 36/10 Patak Rd, tel: (076) 396-628. A menu in 13 languages. Popular with Scandinavians. Steaks, free salad bar and open 24 hrs.
Il Pirata $$$ Thavorn Palm Beach Resort, tel: (076) 396-090. Wood-fired pizza, live music in the evening.
Al Dente $$$ 35/7 Patak Rd, tel: (076) 396-569. Pasta, pizza and home-made ice cream.

ENTERTAINMENT **The Phuket Arcadia Hotel**, tel: (076) 396-038, has live music nightly from 1800 until after 2400. A table can be reserved in the Lobby Bar. At **Marina Cottage Resort**, at the south end of the beach, English-language movies are shown on a large screen, tel: (076) 330-493.

KATA YAI AND KATA NOI

Kata Yai lies to the south of Ao Karon, separated by a headland but linked by road. Another headland divides it from Kata Noi further south. The *songthaew* station is outside Kata Beach Resort. There is a little island, Ko Pu, that makes an achievable target for swimmers, and the snorkelling is not too bad here.

Kata Yai, where the water remains shallow for over 20 metres from the shore, is dominated by Club Med, but there are no private beaches in Thailand so use the beach by all means. More peaceful Kata Noi has three top-end resorts who again think the public beach is all theirs, although they do help to keep it clean.

Kata Thani Resort $$$$$ Kata Noi, tel: (076) 330417, fax: (076) 330426, e-mail: katathani@phuket.com. A vast resort that almost takes over the beach. Well-organised and great for families too. A bit of a walk to the main spread of restaurants, as *songthaews* outside the resort like to overcharge.
C Tabkew Bungalow $$$ tel: (076) 330-433, fax: (076) 330-435. Currently the best mid-range accommodation close to the beach.
Pop Cottage $$$ Kata Yai, tel: (076) 330-181, fax: (076) 330-794, e-mail: popcott@loxinfo.co.th. Between Kata Yai and Kata Noi, not as attractive as C Tabkew Bungalow but the next best.

The place for a splurge is **The Boathouse $$$$$** Kata Beach, tel: (076) 330-015. Pricey wine list, Thai, European and seafood, and soft live jazz on Saturday nights from 2100. Samba and bossanova Latin music on Wednesday nights from 2100.
Gung Café $$$ next to The Boathouse, tel: (076) 330-015, serves less expensive Thai food. Lobster is the house speciality.

The main road has a run of small restaurants **$$$–$$** that look their best at night when lit up. One of them, the **Flamingo**, has a good range of pizzas and always seem to attract a steady number of diners. The cul-de-sac opposite the *songthaew* station has a few inexpensive places to eat and a couple of bars like **Club 44** with free use of the pool table.

CAPE PANWA

South of Phuket town, Cape Panwa is easily reached by regular *songthaews* from Ranong Rd in about 15 minutes. There is no beach to speak of, and the only place of interest is the **Phuket Aquarium $** open daily 1000–1600. It is worth a visit with children, and the multicoloured fish might stimulate a newcomer to try snorkelling.

Cape Panwa Hotel $$$$$ tel: (076) 391-123, fax: (076) 391-117. Stay here and you might have the same room that Leonardo DiCaprio or Pierce Brosnan used when filming *The Beach* and *Tomorrow Never Dies* respectively. Watersports, tennis court, gym, and a tram to trundle lazy guests down to what is effectively a private beach.

There are a couple of tourist restaurants **$$$** in the small complex of buildings facing the sea. The friendly **Cat Bar Garden $** at the bottom of the road to Cape Panwa Hotel is a shack with a kitchen inside, but the tables are outside facing the sea.

There are a couple more affordable places **$$** on the road towards the aquarium but nowhere worth singling out.

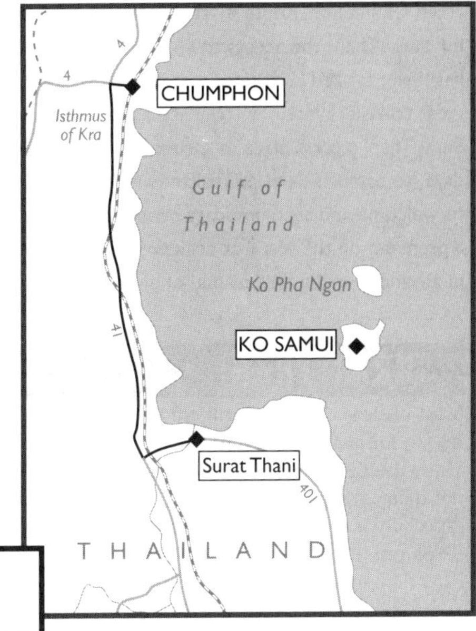

BANGKOK – SURAT THANI
OTT TABLES 7055/7078

TRANSPORT	FREQUENCY	JOURNEY TIME
Train	10 daily, frequent	11hrs
Bus	Daily, frequent	11hrs
Air	2 daily	70 mins

CHUMPHON – SURAT THANI
OTT TABLES 7055/7078

TRANSPORT	FREQUENCY	JOURNEY TIME
Train	10 daily, frequent	$2\frac{1}{4}$hrs
Bus	Daily, frequent	$2\frac{1}{4}$hrs

SURAT THANI – KO SAMUI
OTT TABLE 7070

TRANSPORT	FREQUENCY	JOURNEY TIME
Boat	2 or 3 daily	$2\frac{1}{2}$hrs
Boat	Daily, frequent	$1–1\frac{1}{2}$hrs
Boat	Nightly	6–7hrs

BANGKOK – KO SAMUI

TRANSPORT	FREQUENCY	JOURNEY TIME
Air	Daily, regular	80 mins

Notes

From Bangkok to Surat Thani the 1820 (rapid) and 1915 (express) trains have sleeping carriages. From Surat Thani there are also buses to Krabi (page 205), and Phuket (page 211).

CHUMPHON – KO SAMUI

From Chumphon, Route 41 skirts the coast and follows the railway line as it heads south for Surat Thani, the access town for travel to Ko Samui in the Gulf of Thailand. Ko Samui has never looked back since first it was discovered by backpackers in the early 1970s, and most travellers in Surat Thani are either heading to or back from the island. This makes Surat Thani a good place to garner information, pick up news and organise your next few days. Ko Samui is perhaps Thailand's most sophisticated beach resort, and yet it is still able to welcome and accommodate people on shoe-string budgets. Accommodation can be at a premium on the island at peak times, and it is very advisable to have something booked in advance for the first couple of nights at least.

SURAT THANI

Most visitors in Surat Thani are on their way to or from Ko Samui. There is little other reason for being here other than as a base for a day trip to Chaiya, 60 km north. Surat Thani itself is a busy and prospering commercial town but ideally your travel plans will not delay you here. But you may well find yourself having to spend a night in town, especially if you have not booked a train ticket in advance. If you miss the day boats to Ko Samui there is a useful slow night boat that departs at 2300 (page 227).

ORIENTATION

Talat Mai Rd is the main artery through town, and the two bus stations are helpfully close to it. The departure point for the night boat to Ko Samui is centrally located by the river.

i The **TAT Office** is at 5 Talat Mai Rd, tel: (077) 288-819, open daily 0830 – 1630. Maps of the town and area and general information on the region, including meditation retreats at Chaiya (but not Ko Samui).

Phantip Travel 293/6-8 Talat Mai Rd, in front of the bus station, is more usefully situated for transport and Ko Samui information.

Train: The train station, tel: (077) 311-213, is at Phun Phin, 13 km to the west. Buses to and from town run regularly throughout the day until around 1900, and shared taxis are always waiting during daylight hours to do the same run. Advance train tickets can be booked in town at Phantip Travel, and on Ko Samui Songserm Travel can make reservations.

Air: Thai Airways, 3/27 Karunarat Rd, flies twice a day to Surat Thani, tel: (077) 272-610. Ask here about the minibus to and from the airport, 27 km south of town.

EN ROUTE

PHUN PHIN

If you are in Phun Phin, the chances are you are waiting for a train connection. The station has a left-luggage office, and there are a couple of places for a meal nearby. Buses from the ferry drop passengers off outside the **Queen Hotel $$–$** tel: (077) 311-003, within sight of the railway station. It is easily the best place to stay and where most people eat, although it is not the only option.

Across the road is a 7—11 store, and the road to the railway station takes you past a side street filled with tables. An English menu **$** has standard rice, noodle and chicken dishes. With time to waste, wander around the night market behind the block with the 7—11 store where there are food stalls but no tables.

Wang Tai $$$ 1 Talat Mai Rd, tel: (077) 283-020, fax: (077) 281-007. Best value for money hotel at the top end. Stuck out of town but there's little to do there anyway. Clean, comfortable rooms, swimming pool and restaurant.

Tapi Hotel $$ 100 Chonkasem Rd, tel: (077) 272-575. Another very good value hotel with some less expensive rooms. Within walking distance of the bus stations.

Ban Don Hotel $ Na Meuang Rd, tel: (077) 272-167. Functional but clean rooms and an inexpensive Chinese restaurant.

Eating: The best place for a quick meal is one of the stalls in the **food market** near the long-distance bus station. For more comfortable surroundings, take a *samlor* out to the Wang Tai hotel's restaurant. Closer to the town centre, the Chinese restaurant at Ban Don Hotel is fine for a meal.

MEDITATION RETREATS

The ancient town of Chaiya enjoyed its heyday a thousand years ago when it was the capital of southern Thailand, but there is little to evoke its past glory today. The reason to come here is the temple of **Wat Suan Mokkhb,** 6 km south of town, and its meditation retreats.

The retreats take place at the **International Dhamma Hermitage**, a kilometre from the temple, during the first ten days of each month. Bookings are made in advance at the temple, tel: (077) 431-552. Expect to pay around 1000B to cover accommodation and food for the ten days. The courses are conducted in English but are not a soft option, and participants are expected to help out with chores.

Chaiya is 3 km off Highway 41, the main road between Chumphon and Surat Thani, and any bus travelling this route (an hour from Surat Thani) will drop passengers off at the junction. Motorbike taxis are usually waiting during the day for the short hop into town, and walking is always an option.

In Chaiya buses and *songthaews* run past the temple. *Songthaews* and shared taxis run to the temple from outside the local bus station in Surat Thani. You can also take a north bound train from Phun Phin to Chaiya and then a *songthaew* from the station.

KO SAMUI

ISLAND MAP – inside back cover

Palm-fringed, white tropical beaches first attracted enterprising backpackers in the late 1960s and early '70s, and Ko Samui hasn't looked back since. Thailand's third largest island after Phuket and Ko Chang is now the country's most sophisticated beach resort but can still offer budget accommodation and quiet beaches.

You need to know what kind of a holiday you want on Ko Samui to choose the appropriate beach because different areas offer quite different environments. All in all, it beats Phuket by a mile and although it does become very busy during high season Ko Samui still manages to cope with a smile.

Travel inland and there are literally millions of coconut trees. Many visitors never leave their beach strip, but hiring a vehicle and exploring the less touristy parts is recommended. The south-west is the least visited part of the island where there are some remote and quiet bungalow operations. They are easily reached with your own vehicle but troublesome if relying on *songthaews*. There are also some impressive waterfalls after periods of rain and the well-visited Temple of the Big Buddha.

Accommodation caters for all budgets throughout the year. Costs drop during June and early July, and between October and 20 December. Many top-end places accept Internet bookings. Advance reservations are advisable over the busy months.

KO SAMUI'S BEACHES: THE ESSENTIALS

Chaweng: The longest beach strip and social centre of the island.

Lamai: Labelled seedy and loose by some. Lots of bars, strong on nightlife.

Maenam: Relatively undeveloped but some good places to stay.

Chong Mon: Quiet and subdued, no discos but a choice of accommodation.

WATERFALLS

Within walking distance of Nathon, the popularity of **Hin Lat Falls** sometimes affects the enjoyment of a visit. The falls are 3 km south of Nathon and signposted off the 4169.

The **Na Muang Falls** are in the centre of the island, signposted off the 4169 south of Nathon. At weekends and holidays, the number of other visitors may be off-putting, but there are different levels and it is over a mile to reach the upper one. *Songthaews* travel to Na Muang Falls from Nathon, Chaweng and Lamai.

Temple of the Big Buddah

The temple is on a small island reached by a short causeway at **Bophut**. The Buddha figure, erected in 1972, is colourful and conspicuous but not especially remarkable. Over the last couple of years the area around the temple has developed to cater for the constant stream of tourists. There are stalls selling clothes and trinkets, and one quite pleasant place to eat.

Orientation Ko Samui is 25 km long and 21 km wide, and most people arrive by ferry at Nathon on the west coast. A ring road, the 4169, encircles the island, heading north from Nathon and around to the main beaches of Chaweng and Lamai before striking inland and cutting off the south-west corner of the island. The 4170 road loops off the 4169 to take in this south-west corner before rejoining the 4169 south of Nathon.

The **TAT Office** is at the northern end of Nathon, Chonwithi Rd, tel: (077) 420-504, open daily 0830–1630. Excellent glossy maps of the island are freely available everywhere. There is also a free accommodation, food, shopping and entertainment guide, updated monthly, which carries maps of the beaches. Ko Samui's newspaper is available online at www.samuiwelcome.com.
Websites that are very useful for general information on Ko Samui and for booking accommodation include www.go-siam.com and sawadee.com.

Getting There Flights from Bangkok tend to fill up quickly during the high season, and while flying to Surat Thani from Bangkok on Thai Airways might seem a viable alternative there is still the time and hassle of getting from there to the island.

Night Boat: The cheapest route is by the night ferry from Ban Don pier in Surat Thani, arriving in Nathon the next morning before 0600. The return from Nathon arrives inconveniently at 0300, but passengers can stay on board until 0700 or later. Pillows and mattresses are provided for the journey and it's worth paying the little extra for the upper deck.

Day Boat: These are run by Songserm Travel, and their buses wait at the bus and train station in Surat Thani and Phun Phin for free transfer to the pier for these departures. Tickets include a bus from Tha Thong to the train station at Phun Phin or Surat Thani town.

Train: From Bangkok to Ko Samui it is worth considering the purchase of a combination train/bus/boat ticket from the State Railway at Hualamphong station. It doesn't save money but it does avoid having to arrange the boat connection on arrival at Surat Thani.

Bus: Bus/boat combination tickets are available from the Northern Bus Terminal in Bangkok, and although private companies advertise cheaper deals in Bangkok's Khao San Rd they are generally less comfortable and more prone to delays and irregularities.

Vehicle and Passenger Boat: The car ferry runs between Don Sak, 70 km east of Surat Thani, and Thong Yang, 8 km south of Nathon. These ferries leave every couple of hours during the day for most of the year, and take passengers without vehicles. Travellers buying a combination bus/boat ticket in Hat Yai (page 243) are likely to find themselves on this car ferry, and the price includes a bus ride into Nathon.

GETTING AROUND

Songthaews wait on the waterfront in Nathon, to your right after disembarking, and depart at regular intervals in clockwise and anti-clockwise directions around the island. Their routes are indicated on the front or side of the vehicle, but always double-check with the driver.

Fares are fixed (currently 40B to Chaweng and 30B for a shorter run, like Chaweng to Lamai). The *songthaews* can be hailed down anywhere along their route, but after dusk they are infrequent and tend to charge more. Once you know the fare for a particular journey, or can judge what it should be, just hail down the vehicle and step on without checking the cost. Being asked the fare (always paid at the end of the journey) is an irresistible temptation to some drivers to overcharge.

Jeeps and motorbikes can be hired from scores of places, especially on Chaweng. Most have the annoying habit of trying to retain your passport. This should be strenuously resisted not only on principle but also because you will be in an extremely vulnerable position should there be any problem. Leaving your driving licence should be acceptable, and if it isn't go elsewhere.

Insurance is not usually available for motorbikes but it is best not to hire a car without comprehensive cover; check the small print. Budget, tel: (077) 427-188, have a desk at the airport and one-way rentals to Phuket are an option. **P.K. Tours**, Chaweng, tel: (077) 230-950, almost opposite the Central Samui Beach Resort, asks for a passport but will accept your licence.

ACTIVITIES A trip to the **Ang Thong National Marine Park**, a packed group of over 40 islands some 30 km to the west of Ko Samui, provides the most enjoyable alternative to lying on a beach for a day. The only way to access the Park is on a tour that departs from Nathon pier at around 0830 and returns at 1800.

There are white sand beaches, coral reefs and an opportunity for snorkelling (gear can be hired but bring your own if you have it). The standard tour also includes a chance to walk up the hill on Ko Wua. This is the largest of the small islands, and from the 430 metre summit there are fine views, especially if you can be there around sunset.

Any of the tour agents in Nathon or Chaweng will take a booking for the tour, which costs around 350B. This includes lunch but bring some snacks of your own and plenty of water. The Park authorities, tel: (077) 400-800, manage bungalows for rent and sometimes there are tours that include an overnight stop.

Island Safari, Bophut, tel: (077) 230-709, run daily **'eco-safari tours'** at 0800 and 1400. The programme covers a baby elephant show, elephant 'trek', ox-cart ride, rubber-tapping demo, coconut-picking monkey show and a meal at the end. Phone to check on transport to and from your accommodation or beach.

The **Samui Snake Farm**, off road 4170, tel: (077) 423-247, has shows with snakes and scorpions at 1100 and 1400, and there is a restaurant attached.

DIVING There are lots of dive companies on Ko Samui and most of them have their offices at Chaweng. They conduct courses for complete novices, leading to a recognised PADI (Professional Association of Diving Instructors) certificate that is accepted around the world as proof of basic proficiency. An introductory course costs around 2500B, but many people think it makes more sense to shell out about three times that amount for a basic four-day certification course.

One of the better established companies is **Easy Divers**, tel: (077) 231-190, fax: (077) 230-486, with offices at Chaweng and Lamai. They do everything from a one-day 'discover scuba diving' programme with a supervised fun dive to certificated courses lasting from four days to six weeks.

Other established companies include:
Mui Divers Padi Resort, tel/fax: (077) 233-201, e-mail: info@muidivers.com, web: www.muidivers.com.
Pro Divers, tel: (077) 233-399, e-mail: prodivers@samuinet.com.
Samui International Diving School, tel: (077) 231-242, e-mail: cesareb@samart.co.th.

NATHON Many travellers pass through the island's capital and hardly notice it. The layout of Nathon is straightforward, with the pier abutting Chonwithi Rd and two roads running parallel with it. The third of these roads, Thawiratpakdee Rd, is full of shops and some places to eat. Should the need arise, there are a few places to stay and, indeed, if beach fatigue kicks in, a night in town might seem a good idea.

Songserm Travel, tel: (077) 421-316, have their main office on Chonwithi Rd opposite the pier where their boats arrive and depart from. Also along this road to the south are **banks,** while at the north end near the TAT Office is the **post office**. There are private clinics and hospitals in Chaweng but the perfectly adequate government **hospital**, tel: (077) 421-230, is just outside Nathon. The immigration office, tel: (077) 421-069, is not far away on the 4169 road.

Palace Hotel $$ 152 Chonwithi Rd, tel: (077) 420-079. Large rooms, with and without air-con, close to town centre.
Seaview Guest House $$–$ 67/15 Thawiratpakdee Rd, tel: (077) 420-298. No sea views but easy to reach, close to town, and obliging management.

Mumthong Food Corner $ on the corner of Thawiratpakdee and Na Amphoe Rd is a popular open-fronted restaurant. Good breakfasts, salads, sandwiches, lots of Thai and Chinese dishes, and beer that is not overpriced. If you've just disembarked, cross the road to Songserm Travel and walk left around the first corner.
A few other places are scattered along **Chonwithi Rd** facing the sea and **Thawiratpakdee Rd.** Worth seeking out on this road is **RT Bakery** for its meals and above average breads for taking on the boat.

MAENAM Maenam, 13 km from Nathon, along with Hat Choeng Mon, is one of the quieter beaches on the island. It also has a good supply of budget accommodation. At night there is not a lot of activity on the beach, but on the main road is **Jazzer**, tel: (077) 247-424. The bar has live music, but call to check what is on because without the music there is zero atmosphere.

Paradise Beach Resort $$$$$ 18/8 Maenam Beach, tel: (077) 247-227, fax: (077) 425-290, e-mail:

paradise@loxinfo.co.th, website: www.kohsamui.net/paradise. Villas and bungalows by the beach in a tropical garden setting. Pools, restaurants, and well-equipped rooms in this upmarket resort.

Cleopatra's Palace $ east end of Maenam Beach, tel: (077) 425-486. Basic bungalows with fans and a decent restaurant.

Friendly $ east end of Maenam Beach, tel: (077) 425-484. Clean bungalows with own bathrooms right on the beach,

Home Bay $ west end of Maenam Beach, tel: (077) 247-214. The very cheap huts are nothing special, but the bungalows with bathrooms are worth considering.

Eddy's $$ Main Rd, tel: (077) 245-127. Definitely the best place for an evening meal. Despite its location on the main road (1 km east of turn-off to Paradise Beach Resort) traffic noise is not a problem. The burger meals are great and the jazzy atmosphere of the restaurant makes a welcome change from Ko Samui's usual style.

BOPHUT

Bophut is a quiet beach like Maenam with a modest but adequate infrastructure that includes money exchange facility, tour agents, water-sports, supermarket, shops and restaurants. Budget accommodation is in short supply, but there are quite a few mid-range guesthouses. From the Bophut pier a boat leaves daily for the neighbouring island of Koh Pha Ngan.

Samui Palm Beach Resort $$$$$ tel: (077) 425-494, fax: (077) 425-358. The best of the top-end places, with a beach- front setting, pool and restaurants.

Ziggy Stardust $$$ west end of Bophut, tel: (077) 425-173. Typical of the better quality mid-range bungalow operations on the beach. Wooden chalets with welcoming décor and a good restaurant.

Smile House $$$–$$ west end of Bophut, tel: (077) 425-361, fax: (077) 425-239. A well-maintained operation – not on the beach side of the road but with a fair-sized swimming pool. Rooms to suit different budgets.

Phrayo Restaurant $$–$ Big Buddha, Bophut. The most pleasant place for a meal on a visit to the Big Buddha. Tables overlooking the sea with orchids and other plants growing up the walls. The menu is a mix of good Thai, western-style and vegetarian dishes.

Ziggy Stardust $$ has a great location by the beach and a menu of Thai dishes and seafood.

CHOENG MON

There is no central village to draw in crowds, and a generally peaceful and subdued atmosphere prevails. The crescent-shaped, white sand beach is beautiful. The shallow sea makes it attractive for families, although they don't over run the place. At night the guesthouse restaurants that back onto the beach are lit with fairy lights and oil lamps. Bar staff arrange deckchairs on the sand and a controlled bonfire invitingly encircled by empty slingchairs is about as active as things become. Choeng Mon is our favourite beach, an unhurried place to relax and unwind.

The Tongsai Bay $$$$$ 84 Moo 5, Bophut, tel: (077) 425-015, fax: (077) 425-462, e-mail: info@tongsaibay.co.th, website: www.tongsaibay.co.th. The ultimate luxury accommodation on the island. Private beach, 25 acres of gardens, beach front, and cottage suites and villas. Bathtubs on the balcony and superb restaurants.

The White House $$$$$ tel: (077) 245-315, fax: (077) 245-318, e-mail: whitehouse@sawadee.com, website: whitehouse.KohSamui.net. Smart, Bali-esque décor with two restaurants, a beachside pool, library and a delightful sitting room.

P.S. Villa $$ tel: (077) 425-160, fax: (077) 425-403. Bungalows with fans or air-con in this modest and friendly establishment right on the beach.

It is very much a matter of just checking out the restaurants attached to the various guesthouses and those along the main road, and picking one that takes your fancy. The differences in the food and prices are less important than the setting and the style.

The beachside **P.S. Villa Restaurant $** usually has barracuda and shark on the menu, and is often less busy than some of the bigger restaurants.

Lotus Restaurant $$ at the Chaweng end serves reasonably priced Chinese food.

Kontiki $$, away from the beach, has spaghetti, salads, steaks and curries as well as Thai and Chinese food. A tin-roof but it's pretty enough inside.
Chef Chom's $$$$$ The Tongsai Bay Hotel, tel: (077) 425-015, is the place to go for a special night. Excellent Thai cuisine prepared by the chef who was Keith Floyd's collaborator for the Thai section of his *Far Flung Floyd* TV series.

CHAWENG

Ko Samui's most popular and lively beach, 7 km in length, is still stunningly beautiful despite the rampant tourist developments that threaten to turn Chaweng into Thailand's equivalent of Bali's Kuta. Watersports galore are available on the beach, and although this is easily the busiest beach on the island there is still room to breathe and fling down a towel on the hot sand for some serious sunbathing.

Chaweng has endless bungalows, hotels, bars, restaurants and shops. The accommodation ranges from international-style luxury hotels to thatched huts at under 200B a night. The effect of this is a refreshing mix of people, and eating options to suit all budgets.

After sunset the main street turns into a night bazaar with pavements lined with stalls selling the usual merchandise, including inexpensive pirated CDs. Entrepreneurs have only just sensed the untapped shopping market. The small number of permanent boutiques presently in existence is likely to multiply over the next twelve months.

Central Samui Beach Resort $$$$$ 38/2 Moo 3 Borpud, Central Chaweng, tel: (077) 230-500, fax: (077) 422-385, e-mail: cenguest@samart.co.th, website: www.centralgroup.com. Some 200 rooms, all overlooking the beach, in-house movies, 24 hr room service, good restaurants, tennis courts, pool, fitness centre and spa. A place to spoil yourself.
Tradewinds $$$$$–$$$$ 17/14 Moo 3 Borpud, Central Chaweng, tel: (077) 230-602, fax: (077) 231-247, e-mail: tradewind@sawadee.com. Twenty comfortable bungalows in a garden setting by the beach, pleasantly quiet and well run. The best accommodation of its kind on Chaweng.
The Island $$$$–$$$ North Chaweng, tel: (077) 230-942. Combines attractive accommodation with an excellent restaurant and a 'cool' ambience.

Samui Natien Resort $$$ Central Chaweng, tel: (077) 422-405, fax: (077) 422-309. Good, middle of the road accommodation with a choice of bungalows.
Long Beach Lodge $$ North Chaweng, tel: (077) 422-162). Good value bungalows in a reasonably attractive setting surrounded by coconut trees.
Charlie's Huts $$–$ no telephone, Central Chaweng. Popular, hip accommodation. Straw-roofed huts spread across a lawn that leads down to the beach.

Poppies $$$$$ South Chaweng Beach, tel: (077) 422-419. Reserve a table by the sea under the pandan trees for a romantic setting in this busy restaurant. Salads, pasta, pizza, seafood and meat dishes. A bit pricey.
Beetlenut Restaurant $$$$–$$$ Central Chaweng, tel: (077) 413-370. Chic, Californian-style cuisine in this relatively new restaurant.
Hagi $$$ Central Samui Beach Resort, tel: (077) 230-500. Japanese food at affordable prices. Sitting at the counter can be too hot because there is no air-conditioning.
Chez Andy Restaurant $$$ Central Chaweng, tel: (077) 422-593. Steaks imported from Australia, wine list, open-air dining room.
Oriental Gallery $$$ Central Chaweng, tel: (077) 422-200. The real draw here is not so much the food – Thai, Italian, steaks, salads and seafood – as the stylish interior.
Ali Baba $$ Central Chaweng, tel: (077) 230-253. Vegetarian and non-vegetarian Indian delights. Open for American breakfast at 0900.
Piccola Italia $$ Central Chaweng, tel: (077) 230-026. Opposite the Central Samui Hotel. Large menu of pasta and pizza options, with decent coffee.
Ninja Crepes $ opposite Charlie's Huts on main road. Decent budget-traveller-friendly café serving salads, vegetarian food, crepes and lots of cheap rice and noodle dishes. Open for breakfast.

LAMAI Very quiet during the day, Lamai comes into its own at night when the bars light up and the hostesses materialise. Some travellers find Lamai a bit tacky but the 5 km long beach is lovely, and other visitors find its slightly dishevelled character is more fun than Chaweng. There is a good range of places to stay, but the food scene is a definite drawback compared to the other beaches.

Aloha Resort $$$$$ 128 Lamai Beach, tel: (077) 424-014, fax: (077) 424-419, e-mail: aloha@sawadee.com, website: www.sawadee.com/samui/aloha. Bungalows and rooms, pool, beach bar, tour agent and restaurant. Friendly.
Weekender Resort $$$$–$$$ tel: (077) 424-429. Three types of accommodation in this well-organised resort that caters for tour groups as well as individual travellers.
Spa Resort $$–$ tel: (077) 230-855, fax: (077) 424-126, e-mail: thespa@spasamui.com, website: www.spasamui.com. Eighteen bungalows, all with fan and bathroom, at low prices. A range of rejuvenating health programmes for the body and mind. Classes in shiatsu, reiki, Thai massage and yoga for residents only.
White Sand $ southern end of Lamai, tel: (077) 424-298. A favourite with old Thai hands on a shoestring, beginning to show its age but still a good place to meet other travellers.

There are plenty of places to eat along the road, but nowhere is worth singling out. **Mira Mare $$** has tables fronting the beach and is pleasant enough.
Spa Resort $$–$ has an authentic vegetarian restaurant open 0700–2200. Features dishes like garlic and cashew pesto with spinach fettuccini, salads and special fruit drinks.

Entertainment

Chaweng has the widest range of bars and discos, and attracts a good mix of people. The **Reggae Bar** pub is still a firm favourite and always worth a visit after 2300. A visiting ten-piece band is not unusual, there is no cover charge and the place is fun. **Santa Fe**, opposite Poppies on the main road, gets going around 0300. The **Blues Brothers** pub never seems to be busy and has a poor reputation, but that could change. Lamai has dozens of bars, some of which are clearly pick-up joints.

South and West Coast

The lack of long stretches of sandy beaches has hampered the development that characterises the rest of the island, but this of course is what makes the south and west coast so appealing. It helps enormously to have your own wheels, at least for some of the time.

Laem Set Inn $$$$$ 110 Mu 2, Hua Thanon, tel: (077) 424-393, fax: 424-394, e-mail: inn@laemset.com, website: www.laemset.com. Compared to a Gauguin painting in one magazine, this stylish and ecologically aware resort remains fairly exclusive due to its prices.

Coconut Villa $$$–$$ Phang Ka, tel & fax: (077) 423-151. Tucked away in the south-west corner with a choice of reasonably priced bungalows. A pool, restaurant and motorbikes for hire. A terrific little place.

Wiesenthal $$$–$ Ao Taling Ngam, tel/fax: (077) 235-165. Bungalows with a bit of space around them and an excellent restaurant are two good reasons to stay here.

Big John Restaurant $$ Tang Yang Beach, tel: (077) 423-025. A Thai and European-style seafood restaurant run by an ex-policeman, with good sunset views. A great place, unless the occasional tour group turns up. Taxi service.

SHOPPING

The **Oriental Gallery**, between the Central Hotel and Charlie's Huts on the main road at Chaweng, open 1200–2300, has a range of handicrafts, souvenirs and furniture. This is one of the better outlets in a cluster of shops on this block. Next door **Golden Antiques** plays very loosely with the definition of an antique, but it's worth a look.

FULL-MOON PARTIES

Ko Pha-Ngan is the island and Hat Rin the location for monthly full-moon raves that attract anywhere from between five and ten thousand party people. Unless you arrive at least a day or two before the party the chances of finding somewhere to stay are fairly remote, but that doesn't deter day trippers from Ko Samui. The parties can be a lot of fun but it is advisable not to bring valuables with you. Drugs are readily available but so are plain-clothes policemen, who like nothing better than extracting the standard 50,000B fine.

WHERE NEXT?

Some 20 km from the north coast of Ko Samui, only half an hour by boat, the neighbouring Ko Pha-Ngan is developing with the overspill from Samui. There are now over 150 bungalow operators so the island is hardly a remote tropical paradise but compared to Samui it is still a low-key destination and less expensive as well. Hat Rin, in the south-west of the island, is famous for its raves and full-moon parties.

The main port for boats from Ko Samui is Thing Sala, and on arrival the usual armada of touts are waiting to whisk you off to their selected bungalows.

Songserm Travel, *tel: (077) 377-046, runs boats every day from Nathon to Ko Pha-Ngan, and boats also reach the island from the pier at Bophut. There is a night ferry from Surat Thani at 2300 which takes about seven hours. Around the time of the monthly full-moon party there is a dramatic increase in the number of boats departing from Bophut.*

For more information on Ko Pha-Ngan, check out the website at www.kohphangan.com.

THE BUDDHA AND HIS POSES

Buddha (563?–483? BC) was a Hindu prince named Siddhartha Gautama, born in present-day Nepal. He achieved fame for his holy love of all living creatures and for his meditation upon the meaning of life, suffering and death. Sitting one day in solitude under a tree, he experienced a deep spiritual awakening and became known as the Buddha, a term meaning 'the enlightened one'. He began preaching and teaching over the next 40 years of his life and after his death temples began to appear in his honour. Although his beliefs became a religion, Buddha did not see himself as divine or as in special communication with a divine spirit. He prayed to no higher being and Buddhism remains unique among religions as a belief system without a God, without a Creation and without a Heaven.

There is an entire iconography surrounding Buddha images that goes back to the early centuries of the last millennium. The easiest way for a visitor to appreciate this is by focusing on the pose of the Buddha statue and the position of the hands and feet. The posture of the Buddha is not something that can be freely rendered by the artist. Instead, the pose of the Buddha must be recognizable within the Thai tradition. He is often shown placed on an open lotus flower, itself full of significance because the lotus germinates in mud but blossoms into something beautiful. Strict observance of some of the ancient precepts governing the depiction of the Buddha are harder to achieve. The chin is supposed to resemble a mango, the eyelashes those of a cow.

Bhumisparcamudra is one of the most classic poses and has the right hand of the seated figure resting on the right knee while the tips of the fingers make contact with the ground. The story goes that while the Buddha was meditating, the king of malignant demons, Mara, tried to scupper his concentration by presenting him with various distractions. The Buddha conquered his foe by touching the earth with his fingers, a gesture of calling upon the earth goddess for support.

Abhayamudra is a common pose that signifies the granting of protection and the expulsion of fear. The Buddha is in a standing position, occasionally even a walking position, with at least the palm of the right hand, sometimes both, raised outwards.

The **Buddha calling for rain** also shows a standing Buddha but with both hands held down by the side and the fingers pointing downwards. This pose is most likely to be seen in northern Thailand.

Vitarkamudra sometimes seems to express an oddly modern gesture, that of the thumb and index finger of the right hand touching to form a circle. It signifies the teachings of the Buddha.

Dhyanamudra is a pose of the Buddha that depicts a state of meditation. Both hands rest open in the lap of a seated figure. The palms point upwards, with the right hand always over the left.

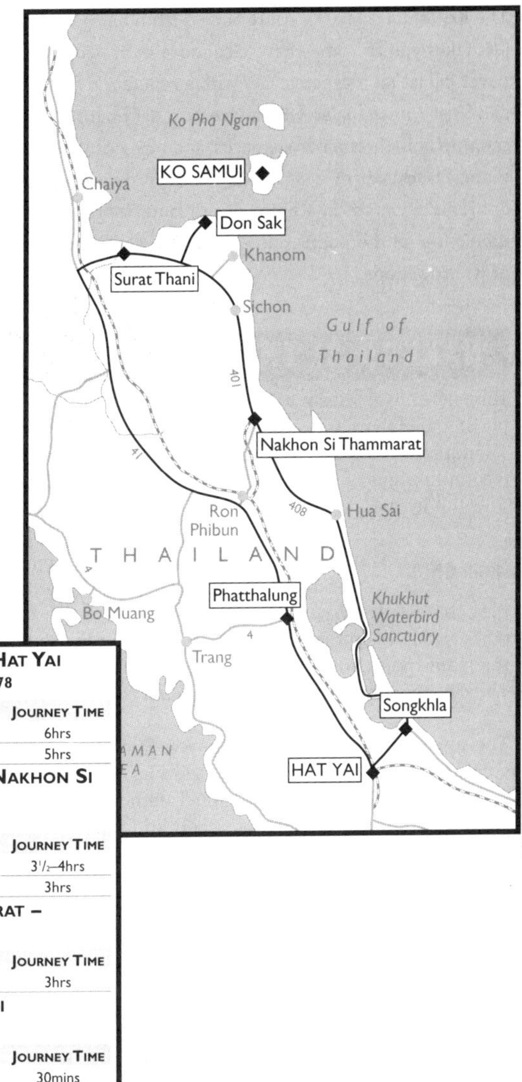

SURAT THANI – HAT YAI
OTT TABLES 7055/7078

TRANSPORT	FREQUENCY	JOURNEY TIME
Train	5 daily	6hrs
Bus	Daily, frequent	5hrs

SURAT THANI – NAKHON SI THAMMARAT
OTT TABLE 7055

TRANSPORT	FREQUENCY	JOURNEY TIME
Train	2 daily	3½–4hrs
Bus	Daily, frequent	3hrs

NAKHON SI THAMMARAT – SONGKHLA

TRANSPORT	FREQUENCY	JOURNEY TIME
Bus	Daily, frequent	3hrs

SONGKHLA – HAT YAI
OTT TABLE 7074

TRANSPORT	FREQUENCY	JOURNEY TIME
Bus	Daily, frequent	30mins

Ko Samui – Hat Yai

The Ko Samui – Hat Yai route suffers from being regarded as a functional journey that just takes you to somewhere else more desirable. Intrinsic attractions are hard to discover in Hat Yai, a dynamic city with a reputation for prostitution the attracts Malaysian and Singaporean males, who arrive on a daily basis. They are easy to recognise, self-consciously noisy in their small packs, and many of the hotels would go bankrupt without them. Places worth a stopover in their own right are Nakhon Si Thammarat and Songkhla. Situated on a mere spit of land, Songkhla's charms are underplayed, and the ethnic mix of the population – Thais rub shoulders with Malays and Chinese – is one of its attractions.

NAKHON SI THAMMARAT

Travellers always seem to have another pressing destination, either Ko Samui to the north or Malaysia to the south, that takes them through or past Nakhon Si Thammarat. This is both a pity and a blessing. The attractive town deserves more recognition but of course its charm is partly dependent on the fact that it remains unspoilt by mass tourism.

Highlights

Wat Mahathat is the town's claim to fame, and a visit here is sufficient justification for stopping off in Nakhon Si Thammarat (if you like temples, that is). At the southern end of the main Ratchdamnoen Rd, any of the numerous *songthaews* on this street will stop nearby. Everything about this *wat* is big, with the main *chedi* almost 80 metres in height and the golden spire a distinctive sight. The cloisters have their share of Buddha images and a quirky little museum.

The town's **national museum** $ Wed–Sun, daily 0900–1200 and 1300–1630, is not spectacular but mildly diverting with its collection of prehistoric artefacts, Hindu and Buddhist images, and regional ethnographic exhibits. To reach the museum continue south along Ratchdamnoen Rd for about half a kilometre.

A **shadow puppet workshop** is also at this end of town, a block east of Wat Mahathat at 110/18 Soi 3 off Si Thammasok Rd. Visitors can see the puppets being made and buy them at reasonable prices, knowing the money is going straight to the producer.

Nakhon Si Thammarat is good for shopping for **handicrafts**. There are shops near the tourist office selling silverware and basket work better than anything found in the tourist shops elsewhere in southern Thailand.

ARRIVAL AND DEPARTURE

Train: The station is centrally located on Yommarat Rd but most of the north–south trains stop at Thung Song, 40 km west of Nakhon Si Thammarat, which means a bus or taxi ride into town.There are, however, two trains from Bangkok that pull into the town station: the Rapid 173 from Hualamphong at 1735 and the Express 85 that leaves at 1915. Trains travelling up from Butterworth only stop at Thung Song.

Bus: The station is outside of town but buses can be picked up at various points, in addition to the private minibuses that cover most of the popular routes. The tourist office has the latest information on pick-up points, fares and schedules, and you can also enquire at your accommodation.

Shared Taxis: These are a good way to travel. There is a large gathering point for the taxis on Yommarat Rd, and as soon as a vehicle is full it chugs off to Krabi, Hat Yai or Phattalung. Shared taxis for Surat Thani and Chumphon use a separate terminus at the north end, past the railway station, of Ratchdamnoen Rd.

The **TAT Office**, Sanam Na Muang, off Ratchdamnoen Rd, tel: (075) 346-515, open daily 0830–1630. From the railway station, walk onto Yommarat Rd and turn right. Continue past the junction with Phaniat Rd that crosses the river to the end of the road near the park and police station.

Grand Park Hotel $$$ 1204/79 Pak Nakhon Rd, tel: (075) 317-666, fax: (075) 317674. The best hotel in town, modern and within walking distance of train station.

Montien Hotel $$–$ 1509/40 Yommarat Rd, tel/fax: (075) 341-908. Conveniently close to train station. Looks dreadful but rooms are a lot better than you might think.

Thai Lee Hotel $ 1375 Ratchdamnoen Rd, tel: (075) 356-948. Singles and doubles with fan and bathroom. Fine for one night.

Nakhon Si Thammarat is full of excellent, affordable places to eat. The restaurant at the Grand Park is worthy but bland compared to the street food and small restaurants along Yommarat Rd and neighbouring side streets.

Bovorn Bazaar, off Ratchdamnoen Rd, not too far from the train station. Food stalls set up here at dusk. Banana rotis and chicken or vegetable pancakes are good, but there are lots of choices and some open-air restaurants as well.

SONGKHLA

The town of Songkhla has an interesting location, perched on a very narrow peninsula between the Gulf of Thailand and a lagoon. Compared with neighbouring Hat Yai it can fairly claim to be sophisticated. If travelling by train through southern Thailand the town is bypassed completely, but it is so close to Hat Yai, with buses running between the two every ten minutes, that it makes for a good day out. Apart from the few sights, there are decent hotels and good restaurants, and just strolling around the waterfront and admiring the Sino-Thai architecture can be enjoyable.

Highlights The main attractions are clustered in the centre of town, and the **National Museum $** is a good place to start. It is on Jana Rd, open Wed–Sun 0900–1600, and even when closed the building itself is a minor work of art. Built originally as the private mansion of a local bigwig in the 1870s, it has been successfully restored. Inside there is an oddball collection of artefacts, furniture, weapons, farm tools and religious art. One of our favourite museums in Thailand, there is bound to be something on display that will catch your interest.

A little south of the museum, on Saiburi Rd, is the photogenic **Wat Matchimawat**. Over 400 years old, the temple is most interesting as an example of Sino-Thai architecture and for its colourful murals. To see more of this hybrid architecture, albeit of the domestic kind, just wander around the small streets near the waterfront. During the second half of the 19th century there was an influx of Chinese immigrants into southern Thailand, hoping to find work as miners, and many settled in Songkhla.

Arrival and Departure Songkhla has good transport connections using buses and shared taxis. Government and private buses run to and from Bangkok, taking 13 hours, but you are more likely to find yourself hopping on or off one of the buses running to and from Hat Yai. They all run down Wichianchom Rd and Saiburi Rd, or just ask your hotel or guesthouse where the most convenient point is to hail one down.

Pavilion Hotel $$$ 17 Platha Rd, tel: (074) 441-850, fax: (074) 323-716. Large rooms, good facilities and fine views from the rooms on the higher floors.

Royal Crown Hotel $$$ 38 Sai Ngam Rd, tel: (074) 312-174, fax: (074) 321-027. Rooms with air-con and fridge at the bottom end of this price category make them very good value.

Amsterdam Guest House $ 15/3 Rong Meuang Rd, tel: (074) 314-890. Deservedly popular budget place. Friendly atmosphere.

EXCURSION TO KO YO

Ko Yo is a small island west of Songkhla that is worth a day trip for shopping and its Folklore Museum. **Ban Nok**, the main settlement, has turned into a permanent market place, with opportunities to purchase top-quality cotton fabrics from the island's weaving villages.

The **Folklore Museum $$** open daily 0800–1800, is at the north end of the island near the bridge, in a park area with terrific views over to Songkhla. Displays and exhibits cover handicrafts, shadow puppets, religious art, domestic and military items and, the pièce de résistance, a set of coconut graters that will surprise you with their imaginative and risqué design.

Transport to Ko Yo is by way of chunky wooden *songthaews* that depart from near Jana Rd's clock tower in Songkhla. On their way to the terminus in Ko Yo they pass the folk museum first and then the cloth market, so passengers can hop off at the museum and then walk the 2 km to the market place in Ban Nok.

There are lots of restaurants in the centre of town, with some pricier seafood places near the beach. **The Skillet**, Saket Rd, is a pub and restaurant serving pizzas and the like, with other western style places close by.

Jazz Pub, opposite the Pavilion Hotel, has an air-con restaurant serving European and Thai food.

HAT YAI

Because of its major transport links with other parts of the country as well as with Malaysia, only 50 km away, many travellers find themselves here. There is no reason to spend any time in this busy, commercial city. Arriving in Hat Yai from Malaysia on a first trip to Thailand can give an unfortunate first impression, but it serves as a good introduction to the intricacies of the country's public transport systems.

i The **TAT Office** is at 1/1 Soi 2, off Niphat Uthit 3, open daily 0830–1630, tel: (074) 243-747. If you have just arrived by

train, walk out of the station and go up Thamnoonvithi Rd straight ahead for four blocks. Turn right into Niphat Uthit 3 and keep walking for 600 metres to Soi 2.
The **immigration office** is on Phetkasem Rd, tel: (074) 243-019.

ARRIVAL AND DEPARTURE

Train: Hat Yai is on the main southern line of Thai Railways, and there are five trains daily travelling to and from Bangkok's Hualamphong station.

Hat Yai has excellent bus connections with other parts of Thailand. Some of the more important routes are:

Bangkok – 14 hrs

Ko Samui – 7 hrs

Krabi – 4 hrs

Nakhon Si Thammarat – 2 hrs

Phuket – 6 hrs

Songkhla – 30 mins

Sungai Kolok – 4 hrs

Surat Thani – 6 hrs

Bus: The bus station is inconveniently located outside of town, and using an agent makes a lot of sense. A useful agent for booking long-distance buses is **Pak Dee Tour**s, tel: (074) 234-535, at the Cathay Guest House. There are plenty more travel agents scattered along Niphat Uthit 2 and Niphat Uthit 3 Rds.

Green-coloured buses for Songkhla depart regularly from near the clock tower on Phetkasem Rd.

Air: The airport is 12 km from town. Thai Airways run a shuttle bus service between the airport and their office at 190/6 Niphat Uthit 2, tel: (074) 234-238.

As well as Thai Airways flights to Bangkok and Singapore, Malaysian Airlines (MAS) fly between Hat Yai and Kuala Lumpur and Johor Bahru. MAS have an office in the Lee Gardens Hotel, tel: (074) 245-443.

Central Sukhontha Hotel $$$$$ 3 Sanehanuson Rd, tel: (074) 352-222, fax: (074) 352-223. Comfortable, relaxed centrally located hotel with 24 hr café, pool and Chinese restaurant. From the station, walk up Thamnoonvithi Rd for five blocks and left into Sanehanuson Rd
Regency $$$$ 23 Prachathipat Rd, tel: (074) 353-333, fax: 234-102. Huge lobby and swimming pool, comfortable and well run, though often very busy.
King's Hotel $$$–$$ 126 Niphat Uthit Rd, tel: (074) 234-140, fax: (074) 236-103. Straightforward hotel with air-con and hot water; fine for an overnight stay.
Indra Hotel $$ 94 Thamnoonvithi Rd, tel: (074) 245-886, fax:

(074) 232-464. Showing its age a little but still good value. Chinese restaurant and coffee shop.

Cathay Guest House $ 93 Niphat Uthit 2 Rd, tel: (074) 243-815, fax: (075) 354-104. Popular because of its cheap rooms, central location and travel service. Range of rooms and dorms. Laundry service, videos in the small lounge where beers can be purchased and inexpensive breakfast. Easy to reach from the train station.

Thai, Chinese, Muslim and Western food is all available in Hat Yai.

Muslim-O $ 117 Niphat Uthit 1 Rd, near the King's Hotel, is a clean and friendly little restaurant turning out curries and rotis. There are more Muslim cafés in the area, including the modest but friendly **Sulieman Restaurant $** on Niphat Uthit 2 Rd, almost opposite the Cathay Guest House.

Nai Yaw $$ corner of Thamnoonvithi Rd and Niphat Uthit 3 Rd, is a popular and often busy restaurant serving very good Chinese and Thai food.

Pee Lek 59 $$ 185/4 Niphat Uthit 3 Rd, on the corner with Niyomrat Rd, is a first-rate open-air seafood restaurant. Western fast-food outlets from all the brand names are on Thamnoonvithi Rd and along Prachathipat Rd near the Regency Hotel. Opposite the Regency there is a **Sizzlers $$** steak house and an ice-cream parlour.

Thailand – Malaysia

Trains between Thailand and Malaysia There is one train a day that travels each way between Thailand and Malaysia. A sleeping berth is necessary unless you want to stay in a seat all night. The station at Padang Besar becomes the border crossing for immigration, where the train waits while passengers disembark with their luggage and clear immigration and customs before getting back on the train.

From Thailand The Express 35 train departs Bangkok at 1420 each day, leaving Hat Yai at 0705 the next morning before reaching Padang Besar fifty minutes later. Two hours later it departs for Butterworth, Malaysia, arriving at 1240.

From Malaysia The Express 36 train departs Butterworth at 1340 and leaves Padang Besar at 1700. It reaches Hat Yai an hour later and departs at 1810, arriving in Bangkok's Hualamphong station at 1100 the next morning.

There is another train route that doesn't actually cross the border with Malaysia but stops within a mile of it, at Sungai Kolok. The crossing point is 1 km away at Golok Bridge, and there are motorbikes and trishaws waiting at the station to take you there. On the other side of Golok Bridge, in Malaysia, it is another 1 km to Rantau Panjang – transport is again waiting to take passengers there – and from there buses and taxis run to Kota Bharu and other Malaysian destinations. Sungai Kolok is a grotty town, but fortunately the train schedules mean there is no need to spend a night there.

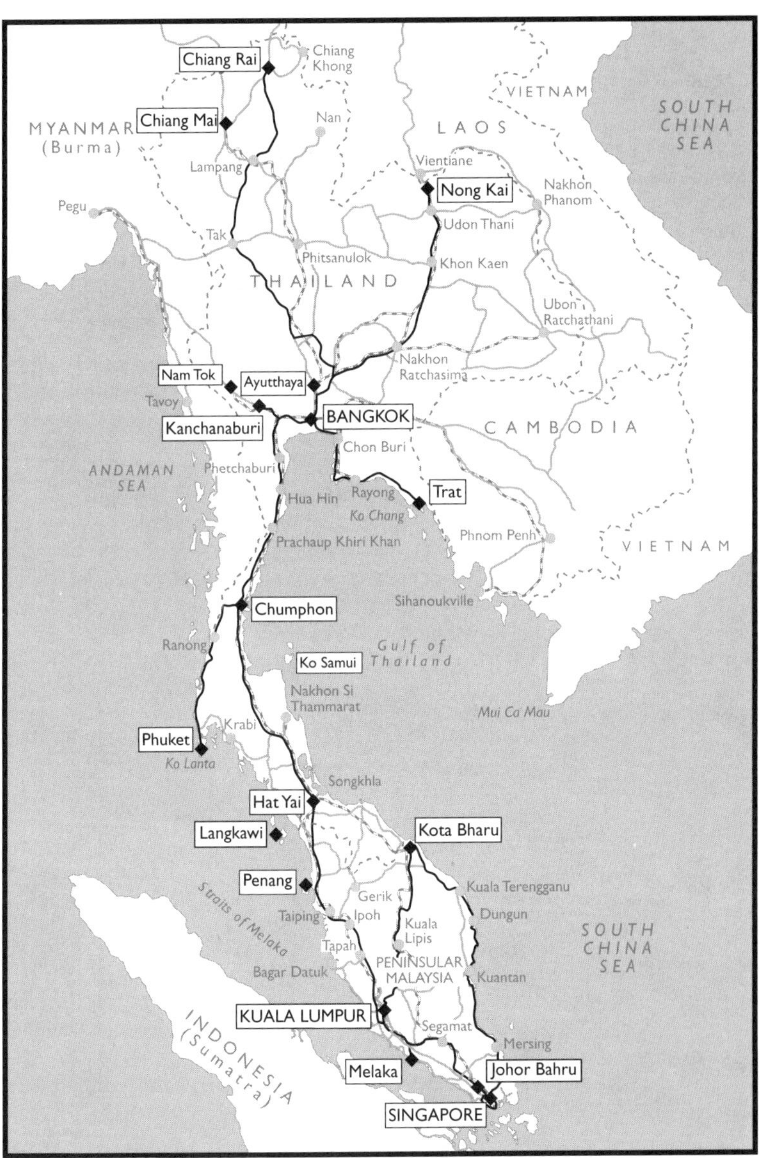
Chiang Rai
Chiang Khong
Chiang Mai
MYANMAR (Burma)
Nan
VIETNAM
LAOS
SOUTH CHINA SEA
Lampang
Vientiane
Nong Kai
Nakhon Phanom
Pegu
Udon Thani
Tak
Phitsanulok
Khon Kaen
THAILAND
Ubon Ratchathani
Nakhon Ratchasima
Nam Tok
Ayutthaya
Tavoy
BANGKOK
Kanchanaburi
CAMBODIA
Chon Buri
ANDAMAN SEA
Phetchaburi
Trat
Hua Hin
Rayong
Ko Chang
Phnom Penh
Prachaup Khiri Khan
VIETNAM
Sihanoukville
Chumphon
Ranong
Gulf of Thailand
Ko Samui
Nakhon Si Thammarat
Mui Ca Mau
Krabi
Phuket
Ko Lanta
Songkhla
Hat Yai
Langkawi
Kota Bharu
Penang
Kuala Terengganu
Straits of Melaka
Gerik
Taiping
Ipoh
Dungun
Kuala Lipis
SOUTH CHINA SEA
Tapah
PENINSULAR MALAYSIA
Bagar Datuk
Kuantan
KUALA LUMPUR
INDONESIA (Sumatra)
Segamat
Mersing
Melaka
Johor Bahru
SINGAPORE

BUSES BETWEEN THAILAND AND MALAYSIA

Between Hat Yai and Malaysia and Singapore there are a number of important bus routes, using modern buses with air-conditioning:

Kuala Lumpur – 12 hrs

Penang – 4 hrs

Singapore – 15 hrs

Pak Dee Tours, tel: (074) 234-535, at the Cathay Guest House (page 245) in Hat Yai is the most convenient way of booking seats on these buses.

Cultural diversity, modern dynamic cities, vast tracts of virgin jungle, accessible wildlife, idyllic beaches, affordable resorts, an amazing variety of food, sleepy towns and laid-back beach communities are all good reasons for visiting Malaysia.

The capital city of Kuala Lumpur is a strange mix of high tech and third world chaos, where great concrete behemoths rise up beside quaint neogothic colonial buildings and where Internet cafés sit beside *roti canai* men flipping their pastries at roadside stalls. From shopping malls to traffic jams this is a modern city in every sense, and yet there is a strong sense of an older culture existing side by side with all the 21st century steel and glass.

Part of this more traditional culture can be found in the western half of peninsular Malaysia. The towns of Melaka, Penang and Ipoh offer historic sites and superb architecture, while close at hand are the beautiful islands of Pangkor and Pangkor Laut. In the towns along the west coast and in the capital the cultural diversity and racial tolerance of this country become apparent. Malays, Chinese and Indians live together while preserving their traditional religions, forms of dress and styles of eating. Georgetown on the island of Penang is the most Chinese city in south-east Asia, and the town has a unique character while remaining one of the most visitor-friendly cities in the region.

The east coast offers hundreds of miles of white, deserted sandy beaches, some magnificent islands with great opportunities for snorkelling and diving, quiet seaside *kampungs* (villages) and the strong Malay culture of the northern states.

Malaysia's national parks are a deservedly major attraction, and Taman Negara, in the middle of peninsular Malaysia, is one of the world's great natural wonders. Days and nights spent in a tropical rainforest provide a memorable experience and there is nothing to match Taman Negara in terms of accessibility and authenticity.

Add to all of this the pleasure of sitting at a roadside stall eating delicious food for a tiny amount of money or even dining in luxury at an affordable city restaurant and you have a multitude of good reasons to visit this tolerant, safe and friendly country.

Peninsular Malaysia

Kuala Lumpur

Kuala Lumpur is the capital of Malaysia and its biggest city. Until a decade ago it slumbered peacefully, unaware that the 20th century was drawing to a close and leaving it behind. Now it has the highest towers in the world, if you include the spires, and buildings of steel, glass and concrete are springing up all the time. Sometimes it seems that all this has happened too fast. Old cultural institutions are disappearing, pedestrians are discounted, road systems and overhead rail systems are multiplying, and the city risks falling into total gridlock.

Although things may seem bad in rush hour on a hot afternoon, in 15 minutes you can get out of the city and into the surrounding forest and plantations. Side by side with the steel and glass, amazing old colonial hotels still serve steak and kidney pudding on the same marble-topped tables that the colonial planters ate at. Curious old shop-houses sell equipment used in Malaysian households for generations, and hawkers cook amazing delicacies on street corners on gas cylinders just as their grandfathers did.

KL, as it is normally called, unlike its neighbouring capital Singapore, has kept much of its lively street life while adding sophisticated shopping malls and architectural wonders. About five days is enough time to get the feel of this city, familiarise yourself with its rail and bus systems, visit the best of its sights and sample some of its excellent and very inexpensive cuisine.

ARRIVAL AND DEPARTURE

Air Kuala Lumpur's KLIA (Kuala Lumpur International Airport), tel: (03)877-7888 or 600-847-747 is 43 km south of the city centre at Sepang, and an airport coach or taxi will take you into town.

The old airport, Subang, is 24 km west of Kuala Lumpur, and still functioning. It handles some internal flights and some of the flights from Sarawak in east Malaysia, tel: (03) 746-1833.

KUALA LUMPUR
North
Sentul Station
Batu Caves
Titiwangsa
Sentul Timur Station
DYNASTY
PEKILLING BUS STATION
PUTRA WORLD TRADE CENTRE
MALAYSIAN TOURISM PROMOTION BOARD
LEGEND
PUTRA BUS STATION
THE MALL
PWTC
Putra
Jalan Putra
JALAN KUCHING
JALAN RAJA LAUT
JALAN TUANKU ABDUL RAHMAN
Chow Kit
Jalan Raja Muda
Jalan Raja Uda
JALAN TUN RAZAK
LABUHRAYA MAHAMERU
Sultan
Jalan Sungai Baharu
CITY SQUARE
AMPANG PARK COMPLEX
MING COURT
Kampung Baru
Jalan Ampang
NIKKO
KLCC
RENAISSANCE
Dang Wangi
MALAYSIAN TOURIST INFORMATION CENTRE
PETRONAS TWIN TOWER
Kuala Lumpur City Centre (KLCC)
Bandaraya
Bank Negara
SOGO
COLISEUM THEATRE & RESTAURANT
SHANGRI-LA
MEMORIAL TUANKU ABDUL RAHMAN
Little India
MENARA KUALA LUMPUR (KL TOWERS)
Jalan P. Ramlee
EQUATORIAL
HILTON
JALAN SULTAN ISMAIL
ASEAN SCULPTURE GARDEN
Golden Triangle
KOMPLEKS BUDAYA KRAF
SELANGOR CLUB
Jalan Tun Perak
Masjid Jamek
JALAN RAJA CHULAN
Jalan Conlay
NATIONAL MONUMENT
MERDEKA SQ
MASJID JAMEK
STAR HILL PLAZA
PANGGUNG ANNIVERSARI
KL MEMORIAL LIBRARY
SULTAN ABDUL SAMAD BLDG
KL PLAZA
MARRIOTT
KL TEXTILE MUSEUM
BUKIT BINTANG PLAZA
RITZ CARLTON
BUTTERFLY PARK
DAYABUMI COMPLEX
JALAN PUDU
LOT 10
CARCOSA SERI NEGARA
Plaza Rakyat
SWISS GARDEN
Jalan Sultan Ismail
SUNGAI WANG
CENTRAL MARKET
MALAYA
PUDURAYA BUS & TAXI STATION
JALAN BUKIT BINTANG
DEER PARK
ORCHID GARDEN
SWISS INN
FEDERAL
Chinatown
JALAN IMBI
IMBI PLAZA
BIRD PARK
Pasar Seni
LAKE GARDENS (TASEK PERDANA)
NATIONAL MOSQUE (MASJID NEGARA)
JALAN HANG TUAH
0
1 km
JALAN DAMANSARA
KL VISITORS CENTRE
KL Railway Station
Hang Tuah
Taman Bangsar
JALAN MAHARAJELA
0
½ mile
NATIONAL MUSEUM
JALAN PUDU
JALAN TRAVERS
KL Sentral
Pudu
Port Kelang & Seremban
Petaling Jaya & Airport
ISTANA NEGARA
Jalan San Peng
JALAN LOKE YEW
Subang-Jaya, KLIA & Sepang
JALAN ISTANA

TRANSPORT TO AND FROM KLIA

TAXI

Taxis come in two classes – luxury and regular. Tickets can be bought at the counters inside the Arrivals Hall at the airport. The fare for regular taxis to central KL should be about RM66. Luxury limousines are around RM88. With four passengers a regular taxi is cheaper than the bus.

AIRPORT COACH

There are several bus and minibus/LRT (light railway) options. The easiest and most expensive is the KLIA – Hentian Duta – Hotel air-conditioned coach. It takes you to the outskirts of the city for transfer to a minibus which drops people off at their hotels. It takes about an hour and a half. Buses depart every thirty minutes. Price is RM25.

Another coach goes to Chan Sow Lin LRT station, from where you take the LRT to your destination. This is not very convenient if your hotel is in the Golden Triangle where the LRT is still under construction. Buses run every hour and take one hour. Price is RM10 plus your LRT fare – about RM2.

A third option is a bus to the Pan Pacific Hotel in KL from where you can make your own way to your accommodation. Journey time is 45 minutes and buses run every hour. Price is RM8.50.

FACILITIES AT THE AIRPORT Malaysians are very proud of their new airport which boasts a post-modernist design with exposed structures and great glass walls. Aesthetically, the airport is very pleasing but look behind the hi-tech decor and everything is not always so wonderful. The 'duty free' shopping is nothing of the sort, and the currency exchange facilities are inadequate.

EATING Inside the departures area the food is terrible, but the food court on the way to the bus station is reasonable and includes an Indian outlet serving *murtabaks* and chicken curries. Alternatively there are Burger King, Delifrance and a few other fast food joints in the Arrivals Hall, as well as a second food court above it.

In the adjoining Pan Pacific Hotel there are three good eating places: the Pasta and Mee Restaurant where a buffet is usually available, the more expensive Pacific Market restaurant and the hotel bar which also serves food.

i A **tourist office** in the Arrivals Hall is open 0900–2100. Next door, a traveller's service centre will book transport and hotels for you.

Left luggage in Arrivals hall. Open 24 hrs.

Post office Level 5 open 0830–1700 Mon–Sat.

Money exchange There is a bank in the Arrivals Hall near to the left-luggage office. Outside of banking hours a booth outside will change cash but not travellers'cheques. In the Departures Hall there is an exchange facility and in the bus station area the exchange facility stays open until 2100.

TRAIN Kuala Lumpur station is in Jalan Hishamuddin, tel: (03) 274-7435. There are trains to and from Thailand and Singapore as well as national destinations. Facilities include left luggage, an information office (open daily 0630–2200), a tourist information office, and an Internet café just outside. Tickets can and should be booked 30 days in advance.

Taxis should be booked at the taxi kiosk outside platform four. Taxis into town cost RM8. If you turn left past the kiosk and walk a couple of hundred yards to the nearest rank (close to the Central Market) the fare will be considerably cheaper.

PANIC IN THE PUDURAYA

Puduraya bus station is completely chaotic. Before you join in the general mayhem, notice the information point, tel: (02) 230-0145, and the police post.

Up one flight of stairs are ticket booths with people clustered around shouting. Men wandering around will offer to help you buy a ticket. What they actually want is to sell you a ticket for their own company, or more likely a shared taxi ride to your destination. They will lie to do this.

Each booth is an independent bus company. Walk around and find one going to your destination at the time you want. As long as you book a day in advance you will have no problem. The biggest company is Transnational (03) 238-4670 and their booth is the most chaotic, but there are any number of other companies competing with them at similar or lower prices.

Long-distance taxis depart from the second floor of the Puduraya bus station. Taxis collect four passengers before they depart and the cost is shared between them. When one passenger is dropped off another may be picked up along the route. Get there early and expect a long wait until there are enough passengers, and negotiate a fare beforehand.

BUS Most long-distance buses, including those from Singapore and Thailand, arrive and depart from the Puduraya bus station, beside the Plaza Rakyat LRT station.

ORIENTATION KL is a city without a centre. Instead, there are clusters of shopping centres and hotels in various locations in the city. With the LRT, getting around is no longer the misery it once was. However, for the next year or so until the third arm of the LRT is built, the Golden Triangle - with most of the shopping centres and hotels - is still a cab ride away.

Taking Chinatown/The Central Market/the railway station as the place you are most likely to start out from, the Golden Triangle is due east by taxi or on foot, and a stroll north brings you to Masjid Jamek, 'Little India', and the LRT.

From here the Star LRT can take you north to the World Trade Centre and the Mall. The Putura LRT can take you west to KLCC, the twin towers and the huge shopping centre below them, or further west to the City Square and Ampang shopping centres. South of the railway station is the National Museum.

INFORMATION

i There are tourist information centres scattered around the city. The biggest is the **Malaysia Tourist Information Complex** at 109 Jalan Ampang, tel: (03) 264-3929, open daily 0900–1800. It has information on the whole of Malaysia as well as counters for the various National Park headquarters and booths for booking long-distance buses.
At The Putra World Trade Centre is the **Tourism Malaysia Office**, tel: (03) 293-5188, open six days 0900–1800. There are also tourist information offices in the underground shopping plaza by Merdeka Square, and at the train station and airport.

INTERNET There are Internet shops in Sungei Wang Plaza, next to the railway station, the Central Market and in the Marrybrown Chicken restaurant, as well as several other shops in Jalan Cheng Lock. Most of them sell computer game time as well, so they are rarely very relaxing places, especially during school lunch hours.

EMERGENCIES

Dial 999 for the police or ambulance service and 994 for the fire service. The tourist police hotline is (03) 249-6590.

EMBASSIES AND CONSULATES

Australia, tel: (03) 242-3122, 6 Jalan Yap Kwan Sweng

Brunei, tel: (03) 261-2800, MBF Plaza, 172 Jalan Ampang

Canada, tel: (03) 261-2000, MBF Plaza, 172 Jalan Ampang

China, tel: (03) 242-8495, 229 Jalan Ampang

France, tel: (03) 249-4122, 192 Jalan Ampang

Germany, tel: (03) 242-9666, 3 Jalan U Thant

Singapore, tel: (03) 261-6277, 209 Jalan Tun Razak

UK, tel: (03) 248-2122, 185, Jalan Ampang

USA, tel: (03) 248-9011, 376 Jalan Tun Razak

EXCHANGE Banks are open Mon to Fri 1000–1600 and Sat 1000–1230. Most banks have an exchange section but you will get a better rate if you shop around for moneychangers, who often do not charge a commission on travellers' cheques and give better rates than the banks. There are moneychangers in KLCC, Sungei Wang Plaza, The Mall and most smaller shopping centres.

HOSPITALS There are 24 hr Accident and Emergency departments at Assunta Hospital, Petaling Jaya, tel: (03) 792-3433, City Medical Centre, 415-27 Jalan Pudu, tel: (03) 221-1255.

IMMIGRATION The immigration office at Block 1, Pusat Bandar Damansara, can supply visa extensions; tel: (03) 255-5077.

POSTAL SERVICES GPO, Dayabumi Complex, Jalan Sultan Hishamuddin. Poste restante counter.

KL'S MAIN AREAS

Chinatown borders the Central Market to the west and the Puduraya bus station on its eastern side. Several budget hotels are in this area, as well as shopping centres and some tourist sights.

The Golden Triangle is home to several of the big hotels, lots of good value budget hotels, an infinity of malls and the amazing Jalan Bukit Bintang, where caffeine levels must be the highest in the world. Running behind this road is Jalan Alor, an incredible strip of hawker stalls at night.

Little India is the area north of Masjid Jamek where there are lots of good, inexpen-

sive Indian restaurants, street markets, some discount stores and historic Merdeka Square nearby.

Jalan Ampang and KLCC is another area of interest to tourists, with the 1,475-foot-high twin Petronas Towers (1996), the vast shopping complex and old colonial style bungalows and hotels along Ampang Road.

To the west of the Central Market are the **Lake Gardens**, bird park, orchid garden and several other places of interest worth an afternoon's wandering.

GETTING AROUND

Once upon a time KL was a nightmare of slow buses, taxi drivers with unmetered taxis, crazy traffic and lunatic *trishaw* drivers. The LRT and the introduction of taxi metres have got rid of the worst excesses of the system, although the city still snarls up during rush hour.

Drivers will very quickly realise that there is very little lane discipline in KL and driving is defensive to say the least. There are few pedestrian-friendly areas of the city, crossing some of the major junctions means taking your life into your hands and pavements are really only parking spaces for mopeds.

LIGHT RAILWAY (LRT)

There are two LRT systems, chiefly running along elevated lines. The **STAR** system runs from Sentul Timur in the north of the city, through Little India, and divides into an eastern line going towards the suburb of Ampang and a southern line going towards the suburbs of the south. The section of most use to tourists is the northern end which accesses several good hotels, the World Trade Centre, the Mall and south as far as Plaza Rakyat.

The **PUTRA** system, using driverless trains, runs roughly east-west and meets the STAR system at Masjid Jamek (you have to leave one station and go into the other – there is no connection). Trains travel eastwards to KLCC and Ampang Park and continue south-west to the railway station. By the time you read this there may be a stop at the Central Market.

BUS

Fares are around RM1. Make sure you have the right money as no change is given. Destinations are clearly displayed on the outside of buses but ask the staff in your hotel or guesthouse for information on how to get somewhere by bus.

TAXI

These are plentiful and metered. If a driver suggests a fare in advance find another cab and make sure the driver switches the metre on. Fares start at

RM2 and go up ten sen per 200 metres. Drivers can charge another ringgit for the use of the boot and for going to a hotel. There are taxi stands all over the city and you should not try to flag down a cab on the street.

Several hotels and especially KLCC have cabs lurking about outside. Drivers here want an airport trip or a minimum RM10 fare and aren't interested in short journeys. Also avoid the large maxicabs which park outside the big hotels. Their flag charge is RM4 and they have a higher rate per metre.

Don't be alarmed if your cab takes off in the opposite direction to your destination – it's often quicker to get outside the city and go back in than to shuffle through blocked city streets. A regular cab fare to the airport should be around RM60. Long-distance taxis are not metered so agree a fare beforehand.

AIRLINES

Aeroflot, tel: (03) 261-3231, Wisma Tong Ah, 1 Jalan Perak 50450

Air India, tel: (03) 242-0166, Agksa Raya Building, Jalan Ampang

Air Lanka, tel: (03) 232-3633, MUI Plaza, Jalan P Ramlee

British Airways, tel: (03) 2167-6188, See Hoy Chan Plaza, Jalan Rajah Chulan

Canadian Airlines International, tel: (03) 248-8596, Lot 25 Bang Angkasaraya, Jalan Ampang 50450

Cathay Pacific, tel: (03) 238-3377, UBN Tower, 10 Jalan P Ramlee

China Airlines, tel: (03) 242-7344, Amoda Building, 22 Jalan Imbi

Egypt Air, tel: (03) 245-6867, Plaza Berjaya, Lot 325, 12 Jalan Imbi, 55100

Japan Airlines, tel: (03) 261-1722, 20th floor, Menara Lion, Jalan Ampang

Lufthansa, tel: (03) 261-4666, 3rd Floor, Pernas International Building, Jalan Sultan Ismail

Malaysia Airlines (MAS), tel: (03) 230-5115, Ground Floor, UMBC, Jalan Sultan Sulamein

Pakistan International, tel: (03) 242-5444, Angkasa Raya, Jalan Ampang

Quantas, tel: (03) 2167-6188, UBN Tower 10, Jalan P Ramlee

Singapore International Airlines (SIA), tel: (03) 292-3122, Wisma SIA, 2, Jalan Dang Wangi.

ACCOMMODATION

Kuala Lumpur is awash with grand hotels whose rates compare favourably with much more modest accommodation in Europe. The five- and even six-star hotels often have discounted rack rates and special offers. You may get a better deal through an agent in your home country in KL than from the hotels directly. The mid-range hotels, chiefly in the Golden Triangle area and Chinatown, compete with each other for special offers, so shop around. Real budget places are a bit thinner on the ground. The price brackets below are for room rates before any discount.

THE GOLDEN TRIANGLE

EXPENSIVE

The Ritz Carlton $$$$$ 168, Jalan Imbi, 55100, tel: (03) 242-8000, fax: 243-8080. Stylish boutique hotel, with individually designed rooms and special butler and business service. Small enough to make you feel at home.

J W Marriot $$$$$ 183, Jalan Bukit Bintang, tel: (03) 925-9000, fax: 925-7000. Centrally located, lovely rooms, great views. All the amenities you could ask for.

The Federal $$$$$ 35, Jalan Bukit Bintang, 55100, tel: (03) 248-9166, fax: 248-2877, e-mail: fedhot@po.jaring.my. Inquire about special offers. All the facilities, including pool and revolving restaurant, at often quite modest prices.

MID-RANGE

Bintang Warisan Hotel $$$ 68, Jalan Bukit Bintang, 55100, tel (03) 248-8111, fax: 248-2333, e-mail: warisan@tm.net.my. Children under 12 free, nice coffee shop and comfortable rooms.

Hotel Capitol $$$ Jalan Bulan, tel: (03) 243-7000, fax: (03) 243-0000, e-mail: capitol@capitol.po.my. Busy, functional hotel, modern and centrally located.

Sungei Wang Hotel, 74–76 Jalan Bukit Bintang, tel: (03) 248-5255, fax: 242-4576. Look for special offers which put this well into the economy range. All mod cons and good location. Ask for breakfast included.

BUDGET

Cardogan Hotel $$ 64, Jalan Bukit Bintang, tel: (03) 244-4883, fax: 244-4865, e-mail: cardogan@po.jaring.my. One of several busy good value hotels with lots of special offers along this road. Check them all out first for the best rates. The higher rooms are less noisy and more expensive. Good value coffee shop/restaurant.

Hotel Imperial $$ 76–80 Cangkat Bukit Bintang, 50200, tel: (03) 248-1422, fax: 242-9048. All the basics, central location. Nice Chinese fast-food place downstairs.

Hotel Seasons View $$ 59–61 Jalan Alor, tel: (03) 245-7577, fax: 243-3532. Good value rate includes breakfast. Right in centre of Jalan Alor food stalls, so a lot of coming and going.

Hotel Nova $$ 16–22 Jalan Alor, 50200. tel: (03) 243-1818, fax: 242-9985. New, stylish place near Jalan Alor food stalls. Very good value.

Cheng Traveller Lodge $ 46–48 Jalan Utara, tel: (03) 243-3960. Dorms and choice of rooms. Garden, barbecue area, laundry, shared bathroom.

CHINATOWN AREA

MID-RANGE

Swiss Inn $$$ 62, Jalan Sultan, 50000, tel: (03) 232-3333. Warren-like corridors and small, spartan, but clean, rooms. Good coffee shop in heart of Petaling St night market but with expensive beer. Very busy hotel so few discounts.

Hotel Malaya $$$16, Jalan Hang Lekir, tel: (03) 261-1111, fax: 230-0980. Good sized, clean rooms, 24 hr restaurant.

Heritage Station Hotel $$$$–$$$ Railway station, Jalan Sultan Hishamuddin, tel: (03) 2273-5588, fax: (03) 2273-2842. The Moorish-Colonial architecture of the railway station makes staying here seem like a wonderful idea. Unfortunately the character of the place doesn't rub off once you are inside.

BUDGET

Excel Inn $ 89, Jalan Petaling, tel: (03) 201-8621. Clean but windowless en suite rooms.

Hotel City Inn $$ 11, Jalan Sultan, tel: (03) 238-9190. Quiet hotel, small comfortable rooms, a little above budget rates but worth it.

JULAN TAR

There are lots of hotels in this area, some sleazier than others, but one or two whose history makes them worth staying at.

Coliseum Hotel $ tel: (03) 292-6270, 100, Jalan TAR. Large spacious rooms and original bar, restaurant and menu from 1921.

Rex Hotel $ 132 Jalan TAR, tel: (03) 298-3895. Fan and shared bathroom but lots of 1920s atmosphere.

Central Hotel $ 510 Jalan TAR, tel: (03) 442-2981. Doubles with air-con and en suite bathroom.

OTHER AREAS

Although farther out of town, hotels in Jalan Ampang to the east and near the World Trade Centre in the north are close to the LRT, which puts them in prime shopping and sightseeing territory.

EXPENSIVE

Hotel Nikko $$$$$ 165 Jalan Ampang, 50450, tel: (03) 2161-1111, fax: 2161-1122, e-mail: reservation@hotelnikko.com.my. Grand, Japanese-owned hotel with everything you could wish for. Close to LRT.

Mingcourt Vista Hotel $$$$$ Jalan Ampang, 50450, tel: (03) 2161-8888, fax: 2161-2393, e-mail: minvista@tm.net.my. Four-star hotel close to LRT, recently renovated, great breakfast buffet, pool, pleasant rooms.

The Legend $$$$$ Putra Place, 100 Jalan Putra 50350, tel: (03) 442-9888, fax: 443-0700. Popular, busy hotel close to LRT, good restaurants.

Dynasty $$$$ 218 Jalan Ipoh, 51200, tel: (03) 443-7777, fax: 443-6868, e-mail: resvn@dynasty.com.my. Big rooms, close to LRT and the Mall. Lots of five-star facilities but not as pricey as one might expect.

AIRPORT

Pan Pacific Hotel $$$$$ KLIA, tel: (03) 8787-3333, fax: (03) 8787-5555. If your flight is seriously delayed then hope the airline puts you up here. Bars, restaurants, outdoor pool, indoor tennis court, 24-hr fitness centre, and some rooms looking out on the main runway.

FOOD

Ten years ago you'd have been hard pressed to spend a week eating out in KL, but now places to eat are tripping over each other in their rush to make their mark on an affluent and discerning public. If you want quick, cheap tasty meals try one of the indoor food courts or hawker centres, or if you want to flash your diamonds check out the restaurants in the five-star hotels. In between are thousands of small independent bistros, fast food joints and cafés, with every type of cuisine you care to mention. The list below is a fraction of what is available at amazingly reasonable prices.

CHINESE

The Museum $$$$ The Legend Hotel, tel: (03) 442-9888. Excellent, innovative Cantonese food in serene and attractive surroundings.

Old China Café $$ 11, Jalan Balai Polis. Traditional Chinese nyonya seafood, highly recommended by locals. Furnished with feng shui mirrors, bentwood chairs and marble topped tables. Try the *laksa*, fish head in assam and *sago gula melaka*.

INDIAN

Bombay Palace $$$ 388, Jalan Tun Razak. Excellent north Indian cuisine served by waiters in moghul warrior dress. Lovely setting in a detached Chinese merchant's house. Quality of the food so well known that reservations are essential at weekends and a good idea anytime.

Bharath's $$ Lot 415 Level 4 KLCC, tel: (03) 263-2631. South Indian cooking, lots of style.

Kampong Pandan $ Lot M2 Mezzanine Floor, Central Market, tel: (03) 274-6595. Indian Muslim place serving stacks of barbecued seafood, roti, masala dosa, huge fish-head curries. Very busy and popular.

Bintang Corner $ in lane behind Metrojaya, Jalan Bukit Bintang. Open-air roti café, very popular and open late.

Restoran Ramzaan $ Jalan Bukit Bintang. Old-style Malay-Indian restaurant of the kind that is fast disappearing (like Irish theme pubs, mock versions have started appearing in hotels). Rotis, murtabaks, six types of *nasi goreng* and vegetable naans. Useful for a cheap bite in between shopping, and the *nasi lemak* with egg is ok for breakfast as well.

ITALIAN

Piccolo Mondo Gastro $$$–$$ Wisma Peladang, Jalan Bukit Bintang, tel: (03) 244-7806. Sprawling pizza place with open-air seating in the heart of the Golden Triangle area. Try La Tagliatelle Alla Lady Diana (spinach noodle and mushroom) or order a pizza to share for a cheap lunch. Big screen inside shows English Premiership soccer.

JAPANESE

Kampachi $$$$ Equatorial Hotel, tel: (03) 2162-7777. Classy, very popular place with excellent, fresh food in functional surroundings.

Kamogawa $$$ Mingcourt Vista Hotel, tel: (03) 2161-8888. Relatively inexpensive, prettily designed and extensive authentic menu.

MALAY/INDONESIAN ASIAN

Equatorial Coffee Shop $$ Jalan Sultan Ismail. A mix of lots of different cuisines but the Malay buffets are particularly good. Claims to be the first designer coffee bar in KL.

Ginger $$$ Central Market, M12A, tel: (03) 2273-7371. Very popular Asian cuisine based around the eponymous herb. Vegetarian options.

House of Sundanese $$$ 4th Floor, KLCC, tel: (03) 2166-2272. The fourth floor of KLCC is full of restaurants but this is the most interesting because Sundanese food (from west Java) is not readily available in Malaysia. Try *ikan nila goreng*, a delightful fish dish, or *sedap ikan snapper bakar*, a house specialty of charcoal-grilled fish with a mild spicy sauce.

Senja $$ 4th Floor, KLCC, tel: (03)382-0780. Malay home-cooking in pleasant surroundings.

WESTERN/INTERNATIONAL FUSION

Carcosa Seri Negara Hotel $$$$ Taman Tasek Perdana, tel: (03) 282-1888. The grandest place to eat in KL. The old governor's residence, now a very classy hotel, bar and restaurant. Small, classical western menu and attentive waiters. If you can't afford the dinner menu, go for the afternoon high tea.

FIC's $$$$–$$$ Hilton Hotel, Jalan Sultan Ismail, tel: (063) 244-2157. Refreshingly informal restaurant with a menu organised around small/medium/large plates of food. Choose from white grape gazpacho, salmon marinated in sake and lamb shank with saffron mash. Open daily for dinner and Sun–Fri for lunch.

Revolving Bintang Restaurant $$$ Federal Hotel, tel: (03) 248-9166. Great fun, 18 storeys high and revolving a little nervously above the building sites of the Golden Triangle. Good, western-style food with a spicy Asian twist.

Riverbank $$$ G14 Central Market, tel: (03) 274-6651. American fusion cuisine in a spacious restaurant.

Coliseum Café $ Jalan TAR. Mostly English menu, including sizzling steaks and baked crab, barely changed since planters took lunch here in the 1930s. You might sit in a chair once used by Somerset Maugham.

Le Coq d'Or $$ 121 Jalan Ampang, tel: (03) 261-9732. Old millionaire's mansion with steaks, grills, Malay home cooking and some Chinese dishes. If the plaster is crumbling the food is still good and surprisingly inexpensive.

THAI

Chakri Palace $$$ 417B 4th Floor, KLCC, tel: (03) 382-7788. Haute Thai cuisine in ethnic surroundings.

HAWKER STALLS

The best, most atmospheric place to eat on the street in KL is in **Jalan Alor**, in the Golden Triangle. Mostly Chinese hawker stalls cook wonderful things for very little, and all you have to do is wander along, take your pick and find an empty table. Behind the stalls are cafés and more restaurants so you really could eat here every night.

At **Jalan Hang Lekir**, near Petaling St, night market stalls spread out from the cafés, cooking satay and barbecued fish, but the prices and atmosphere are much more touristy than Jalan Alor. On the street you have to side-step waiters who thrust menus under you nose and almost drag you to a seat.

Near Jalan TAR is the **Chow Kit market,** where in rather seedy surroundings you can choose from the myriad of options at the *nasi campur* stalls. On Sunday mornings in the Golden Triangle there are *roti canai* stalls in the street behind Jalan Sultan Ismail.

At **BB Park** in Jalan Bukit Bintang is an upmarket open-air hawker centre. It has prices to match the jazzy style, traditional dance performances on some evenings and souvenir stalls. The Chinese, seafood, Indian tandoori and Western food stalls are popular with locals.

FOOD HALLS

Under cover and usually with the comfort of air - conditioning, there are several food halls that provide excellent value for money. In the Golden Triangle area the best option is the non-air-con but covered-roof area of **Sungei Wang**. It has a Buddhist vegetarian place, several *roti canai* and chicken rice stalls, and lots of Chinese buffet places where you collect what you want and the owner eyes it up and names a price. There is a particularly good Indian vegetarian restaurant to the left of the lift from KFC on the ground floor. On the same floor is an air-con place with a few lacklustre food stalls, nothing so lively as those outside.

In the basement of **Lot 10** there is another air-con and fast food place with plenty of great options from Japanese sushi to chicken rice, *nasi campur*, fish and chips and lots more. In KLCC the **Scotts Food Centre** is equally good, with north Indian, Thai, Malay, Hainanese, Japanese and Western food to choose from. It has less background noise, too, than other food courts. **Warong Food Centre** is another KLCC food centre, on the fourth level, where the choice of food is not so good. Upstairs in the **Central Market** are several good places, especially Kampung Padang, an Indian Muslim restaurant piled high with seafood options.

A CAFFEINE FIX

The latest craze to hit KL is the open-air designer coffee bar. Not so long ago locals wouldn't have been seen dead in the open air when there was air-con available, but now hanging out on the sidewalk is the thing to do. Some places even have machines blasting cold air onto the seating areas.

The area between Lot 10 and Bintang Walk must have the densest concentration of caffeine in Asia. Every imaginable combination of coffee and other ingredients, are available along this stretch of pavement. Linger long enough and you may find yourself an unwitting extra in a Malay soap, or see a wannabe pop star with entourage slinking past. Some of the coffee is pretty good too.

ENTERTAINMENT

In this drug-free, alcohol-free society it sometimes seems that the biggest buzz you're likely to get is from a Starbuck's iced cappuccino, but when KL'ers decide to go out there are places to see and to be seen in.

Barn Thai, 370B Jalan Tun Razak. Really an excellent Thai restaurant but people go there for the jazz and atmosphere as much as for the food.

El Nino Latin Café, 21, Jalan Mayang. Hacienda-style club with lots of Latin music and dancing. Wednesdays free margaritas for women. RM25 cover charge at weekends. Mexican and banana leaf food. Open till 0100.

Embassy, 26, Jalan Ampang. An entertainment centre including an Italian restaurant, Thai restaurant, dance club, wine bar and more.

BANGSAR

You won't have been in KL long before somebody tells you about Bangsar. It's the place where all the people who want to enjoy themselves and not be packed into an expensive Golden Triangle bar go. Pick up a copy of *Vision KL* magazine which has a map of Bangsar and up-to-date listings of shops and restaurants. There's lots to do, especially on Sundays when the night market gets going around 2100. If you plan your departure from Malaysia for Monday morning, go to Bangsar for your last night in Malaysia and stay till dawn. You'll be so tired the next day that you won't notice the 28 inches of space you're crammed into for your 13 hr flight home.

SHOPPING

Some people say the best thing to do in KL is shop. The prices are dramatically lower than Singapore which is why so many Singaporeans are here. Clothes and shoes are cheaper than home by a long way, except of course British imports like M&S, and there are some amazing computer software bargains to be had. Computers are cheaper than Europe and electronics are cheaper than Singapore if you shop wisely, but a good duty-free shop at Changi on the way home is probably cheaper.

Fake items are everywhere but they are cheaper and more readily available in Thailand or even Penang. Although it sounds obvious, bear in mind that fakes aren't as good quality as the originals. KL is a centre for crafts but they are cheaper in the areas where they are made – batik in Terrengganu or Khota Bharu, kites in Khota Bharu, basketware in Sabah and Sarawak, silver in the north, 'antiques' in Melaka. The following is a list of the malls and streets with suggestions for what to look for.

Markets

Night markets take place all over the city on different nights. Check in *Vision KL*, with your hotel reception or with the tourist board for details. **Jalan Petaling** is nightly but very tourist-oriented. **Bangsar** is more for locals and usually takes place at Jalan Telawi on Sundays. An excellent non-touristy night market is on Saturday at **Jalan TAR**. On Sunday mornings the backstreets around Jalan TAR see an unusual array of herbal and animal remedies, along with some gory before and after pictures.

KLCC, Suria Floors and floors of upmarket shops, especially clothes. Lots of chain stores, an excellent food hall, supermarkets, restaurants, moneychangers, Isetan department store and Marks and Spencer. There's a large Times bookshop on the third level, and a couple of good craft shops like Arch on Level 2, 229-A, selling framed woodcuts of traditional buildings using ramin-wood. KLCC is designed for spend-happy locals rather than tourists, but it's still a place to wonder at. Stand outside House of Sundanese restaurant on the fourth floor and look up at the Twin Towers.

Sungei Wang, Jalan Sultan Ismail This vast place links up with the BB Plaza which is almost as big. Those of a nervous disposition should get a floor plan before venturing inside. Its once spacious atrium and halls are now crowded with stalls selling belts, jewellery and mobile phones and it can get very noisy. There is a cheap and cheerful Parkson Grand Department store and an IT centre on the third floor, including a noisy Internet café. Scattered throughout are some good restaurants, a multiplex cinema two flights up from the main entrance, an excellent and cheap hawker centre and good moneychangers. BB Plaza links up with Sungei Wang and has Metrojaya as its anchor department store. **The Mall** has a wonderful glass wall, as well as small clothes shops and a couple of interesting furniture/craft shops. **Lot 10** has a good food hall and all the same stores as KLCC, and a few more. At **Plaza Ampang** and **City Square** at the end of Jalan Ampang there are designer and upmarket clothes shops. In Jalan TAR is **Sogo**, big as a shopping complex but just one department store. **Imbi Plaza** in the Golden Triangle sells computer software and hardware, and if you know what you want and its price at home you should save some money here.

Crafts The **Central Market** is a good place to browse and buy if you are good at bargaining. A fixed price alternative is the **Craft Complex** in Jalan Conlay open 0845–1800 daily. It is a huge park where you may be able to watch people making batik or throwing pots or weaving or painting. The real reason to go there is to visit the two huge craft shops which have goods from all over Malaysia. There are no bargains but just about everything you are likely to see in the rest of the country is here. It might be an idea to inquire about guided tours, tel: (03) 2162-7459, since the place seems to fall asleep between tour bus visits.

HIGHLIGHTS

Kuala Lumpur is not really a city dedicated to tourists. Its attraction lies in its fascinating contrasts of old Malaya and hi-tech, high-rise steel and plate glass. There are a number of museums, the Lake Gardens, Menara Kuala Lumpur, the telecommunications tower and the local markets. At night KL comes alive with street vendors, trendy coffee shops and cafés, and restaurants sprawl out across the streets.

MENARA KUALA LUMPUR

This 421 metre telecommunications tower is the fourth highest in the world, and it provides stunning views of the city and its surrounding hills for RM8. Kuala Lumpur is only 150 years old, a fact that is visually brought home when you see the entire city spread out before you from the observation platform. High-rise tower blocks are popping up everywhere, many of them ugly and badly designed and with little thought for their surroundings. The distant hills are shrouded in smog from the city, and you can see thunderstorms looming towards you. Open 1000–2130 daily, the tower is best approached by taxi since it is on a steep hill. Taxis wait around at the top to carry visitors down, and consequently charge a RM3 waiting surcharge.

COLONIAL KL

Merdeka Square is at the heart of colonial Kuala Lumpur. It was once a swamp, then a police training ground and later the Padang, the field where colonial types played cricket, sipped their gin and tonics and gossiped with their friends. During World War II bananas and tapioca were grown on what is now a neatly manicured green. Independence was celebrated here on 31 August 1957. The Tudor style building is the **Royal Selangor Cricket Club**, still as exclusive as it was in colonial times.

The square is used for state occasions, most notably the annual celebration of independence. Below the square is Plaza Putra, an underground shopping centre with a tourist information office, theatre, shops and restaurants.

Around the square are several of KL's famous Moorish buildings. Mostly built by the British architect A.C. Norman, they are a fascinating mix of fantasy Middle Eastern architecture and Victorian Gothic. To the east across the road is the **Sultan Abdul Samad** building, looking like a Christmas tree at night and like some magnificent sultan's palace during the day. New Year is celebrated here as its 40 metre high clock strikes midnight.

North of Merdeka Square is another late 19th century creation of A.C. Norman, **St Mary's Cathedral**, built in 1894 for the British community. It still contains the original pipe organ made by the famous organ maker Henry Willis.

On the south side of the square at 29, Jalan Rajah, tel: (03)-294-4590, is another colonial building, now the **National History Museum**. Open daily 0900–1800, free, it's worth a brief look inside if you have nothing better to do. Next door is another Norman building, the old City Hall, now a **textile museum $** with displays of batik, songket and pua, open daily 0930–1800.

Further south looms the **Dayabumi building**, all soaring concrete and Islamic arches. Another little masterpiece in Gothic Moorish fantasy is the **railway station**, designed by British architect A.B. Hubbock. Inside pure Victorian station platforms are hidden by extravagant Moorish minarets.

Opposite the station on Jalan Sultan Hishamuddin are the **KTM Offices**, another Hubbock fairytale extravaganza. Beside it is the **National Art Gallery**, once the Majestic Hotel, open 1000–1800 daily.

To the north east of Merdeka Square at the confluence of the Kelang and Gombok rivers is **Masjid Jamek**. It marks the spot where the first Chinese tin prospectors set foot on what was to be the capital city. The mosque is a pretty, quiet spot in the middle of a raging traffic jam. It is all pink and white stripes and domed minarets, again designed by Hubbock, with a walled courtyard complete with palm trees and views of the river. For an overhead view of the mosque you can climb the stairs to the STAR LRT, or the main entrance is in Jalan Tun Perak.

CHINATOWN

This area is best visited during the evening when the quiet daytime streets come alive with market traders, restaurants and coffee shops. The centre of activity is **Jalan Petaling** where from about 1700 market stalls are set up. By around 2000 the place is a hive of bargaining with streams of tourists wandering between the copy watch, T-shirt and odds and ends stalls.

In **Jalan Hang Lekir** live seafood is displayed on barrows so you can choose your evening meal as it wriggles about. Beware starting negotiations if you don't intend to buy. Bear in mind also that most things are cheaper in Penang.

In Jalan Tun H S Lee, south of **Jalan Hang Lekir**, is the **Sri Mahamariammam Temple**, originally built in 1873 by Tamil contract labourers and funded by wealthy Chettiar traders. The building you see is much more recent, dating from 1985, and positively glows with gold leaf, precious stones and elaborate tiles. The temple is the starting point for the Thaipusam festival when the silver chariot dedicated to Lord Murugan is taken in procession to the Batu Caves.

To the west of Chinatown is the refurbished **Central Market**, now a dedicated arts and crafts and 'antiques' venue where serious bargaining needs to be done if you want to buy anything. Most things are going to be cheaper in the provinces than here. Upstairs in the Central Market are some good inexpensive restaurants.

LAKE GARDENS

A popular place with Malaysians at weekends, the **Lake Gardens** are a man made, 91.6 hectares of jogging tracks, lakes, bird and butterfly collections and statuary. In the south end is the **National Museum $**, tel: (03) 282-6255, open daily 0900–1800. Well worth a visit, the museum includes exhibits on the country's history, culture, natural history and much more.

Moving northwards into the park you can enjoy the lakes with pedal boats for hire, a hibiscus garden, an orchid garden and a deer park. At the north end is the **National Monument**, designed by Felix de Weldon, creator of the famous Iwo Jima statue in Washington, to represent Malaysia's recovery from the threat of Communism. An attempt was made in 1975 to blow it up.

Beside it is the **ASEAN Sculpture Garden**. The garden contains a huge enclosed park with many local and foreign birds **$**, open daily 0900–1700, and a butterfly park **$$** where butterflies are bred on site and released into the rainforest setting, open daily 0900–1800.

EN ROUTE

On the way to the park, about 8 km before it, is **Kampung Kuantan**, a small village where millions of fireflies can be seen, attracted to the berembang trees that hang over the river. The best time to make the brief river trip is just after dark, around 1930. The females flash their lights and the males synchronise their flashing.

Local people run river trips from the village, or you can have the entire trip organised by one of the KL tour agencies. The Nature Park can also arrange the Kampung Kuantan trip and has chalet accommodation **$**, tel: (03) 889-2294.

DAY TRIPS

A few kilometres outside the city are two major places of interest: **Batu Caves** and **Templer Park**. The park is about 10 km beyond the turn-off from Highway 1 for the caves, so both places could fit into a day trip.

Situated in a vast limestone outcrop 13 km north of KL, **Batu Caves** were discovered in 1881 and quickly became a Hindu shrine dedicated to Lord Subramanian. For most of the year the rather shabby shrines and soot-caked walls are silent and empty. But during the Thaipusam Festival in February thousands of people come here, and visitors can watch penitents wearing vast metal *kavadis* with their bodies pierced with metal spikes.

The main cave is 272 steps up into the limestone outcrop, where fairy lights illuminate the various cave formations. Below is a museum dedicated to Hindu mythology. During the war the Japanese used the caves as munitions factories, and the cement floors and machinery bases can still be seen. Take bus No. 11 from Central Market.

Templer Park $ is 21 km north of the city with 1200 hectares of forest, the 3000 m Kanching waterfall and several limestone outcrops. Very busy at weekends, the park is quiet during the week and there are lots of walks and picnic spots. Take bus Nos 66, 78, 83 or 81 from Puduraya bus station.

Kuala Selangor Nature Park, 250 hectares of mud flats and river estuary, as well as forest reserve, is 65 km north west of KL, entrance RM2. Several trails run out from the entrance, some a considerable walk and others a brief stroll. All lead to hides where typical estuary and wading birds of the region can be seen, as well as migratory birds making their way from Siberia, China and Russia to Australia. The park keeps captive birds too. Milky Storks, extinct now in Cambodia and Thailand, are being bred here in captivity in an effort to save the species.

THE ORANG ASLI MUSEUM

This little museum 25 km north of KL is dedicated to the culture and life of the original inhabitants of Malaysia, the Orang Asli. There are about 60,000 Orang Asli living in 18 tribes in remote areas of the mainland. The museum displays artefacts still in use, such as blowpipes, traps and fishing equipment. Open Sat–Thur, 0900–1730, free. Take bus No174 from Lebuh Ampang.

How to See

SINGAPORE

The Malay Peninsula and Penang

Express Train Leaving Kuala Lumpur Station.

Programme of

Sightseeing Arrangements

Under the Management of

THOS. COOK & SON, LTD.,

Generol Foreign Passenger Agents, Pennsylvania Railroad,

18, BATTERY ROAD, SINGAPORE.

Tel. Nos: 3016 & 3017. Cable Address: "COUPON"

1928 Thomas Cook brochure cover

KUALA LUMPUR – TAMAN NEGARA

KUALA LUMPUR – KUALA TEMBELING

TRANSPORT	FREQUENCY	JOURNEY TIME
Bus	1 daily (0800)	3hrs

KUALA TEMBELING – TAMAN NEGARA PARK HQ

TRANSPORT	FREQUENCY	JOURNEY TIME
Boat	2 daily	2–3hrs

KUALA LUMPUR – JERANTUT

OTT TABLES 7005/7006

TRANSPORT	FREQUENCY	JOURNEY TIME
Bus	Hourly	3hrs
Train	1 daily	5hrs

JERANTUT – KUALA TEMBELING

TRANSPORT	FREQUENCY	JOURNEY TIME
Bus	4 daily	45mins
Minibus	Daily	45mins

Notes

The easiest, if not cheapest, way to Taman Negara is the bus organised by resort to the Park HQ via Tembeling.

Trains from KL link badly with an express train from Singapore at Gemas, and are hardly worth the effort, while the buses to Jerantut necessitate another bus or cab ride to Tembeling in time to catch one of the two boats into the park. There is now a road all the way into the park, and Jerantut hotels organise bus rides for about RM25 per person, but this cuts out one of the best aspects of the visit to the park.

ROUTE DETAIL

It takes around 3 hrs to drive to Kuala Tembeling (170km). Take the Kuala Lumpur–Karak highway east to Mentakab and 3km after Mentakab take the turning for Kuala Krau which leads to Jeantut. There is a car park at the jetty that costs RM5 a day.

Kuala Lumpur – Taman Negara

The medium is the message and the recommended way to reach Taman Negara is by means of an eight-seater perahu, a timber boat with an outboard motor. It takes nearly three hours to travel up the Sengai Tembeling, but it's a memorable experience and puts you in the right frame of mind to enjoy the National Park. Kampong life unfolds on the banks of the river with children, women and water buffalo all taking advantage of the water to wash clothes, take a dip or just enjoy nature. A sudden flash of blue as a kingfisher darts across the river, or a two-metre, lazy monitor-lizard (*varanus salvator*) sliding off a mudbank, is a sign of the glorious wildlife yet to come. In the summer months, keep an eye open for the majestic blue-throated bee-eater.

TAMAN NEGARA

MAP – inside back cover

If you only make one journey in peninsular Malaysia, make the trip to Taman Negara. The forest here is probably the oldest in the world. The area was never affected by assorted ice ages by volcanic eruptions so besides man there has been little interference with the 4343 sq km of virgin jungle in the last 130 million years.

Designated a National Park in 1938, this place is home to Malaysia's 300 or so tigers, elephants, civet cats, tapir, wild ox, sambar and lots more. Unfortunately the most dangerous creature in the park is *Homo sapiens*. They poach, hunt (the indigenous Orang Asli people are allowed to hunt in the forests), wear out forest trails and generally encroach on the lives of the animals which subsequently become less accessible each year. Nonetheless, leave the resort and its paths behind and even if you don't see a tiger you'll see and hear the forest and its birds, maybe a flying fox, macaques and the monitor lizard as well as a billion mosquitoes and leeches.

Ecopolitics

Taman Negara was a well-kept secret for many years, visited by hardy souls who didn't mind roughing it a bit. Then someone saw the tourist dollars to be made and it was privatised in 1991. Expensive accommodation was built and prices for boat hire and guides shot up.

Although the thousands more people who visit the park every year bring in much needed revenue, they also cause erosion and damage. In addition, the huge expansion of towns and villages around the perimeter is reducing the space available to animals which once roamed beyond the park boundaries.

Now a road has been built all the way into the park, access is no longer dependent on river water levels. The park, once closed for the rainy season, is now open all year. It is just a matter of time before there is more development of tourist accommodation and the Orang Asli and the animals are driven even deeper into the forest.

JERANTUT

There is little reason to visit this town except as a stopping point on the way to Taman Negara. It is possible to book your trip into the park from here, and it is a good stocking-up point if you plan to do your own catering there.

GETTING THERE

Buses from KL to Jerantut leave from the Pekeliling bus station in Jalan Tun Razak in the north of the city, tel: (03) 442-1256. There are several buses a day, but you should enquire about times and book the bus in advance.

Buses for Kuala Tembeling from Jerantut bus station are designed to catch the boat to the national park, although with delays they do not always do so. Private buses to the jetty or even all the way to the national park headquarters are organised by several of the hotels in town.

Share taxis for Jerantut leave from the Puduraya bus station in Kuala Lumpur and cost RM20 per person. Taxis from Jerantut to Kuala Tembeling should cost about RM18, and are a much more reliable way of getting the boat than a local bus.

Boats to Taman Negara park headquarters are operated by the Resort and the Nusa camp in the park.

A travel agent close to the railway station takes bookings and has information about the national park resort.
At the bus station is a booking office for the Nusa camp, tel: (09) 266-2369.
Several of the town's guesthouses also offer information to guests and will book transport into the park for them.

Sri Emas Hotel $ Jalan Besar, tel: (09) 266-4499. Nothing to shout about, but lots of park info and bookings taken.
Hotel Jelai $ Jalan Besar, tel: (09) 266-7412. Clean air-con rooms.

Coffee shops in Jalan Besar, food stalls between the market and the railway station and Chinese restaurants in Jalan Besar. Also, KFC near the bus station.

KUALA TAHAN

Kuala Tahan is both the national park HQ and a small village which has built up budget accommodation and places to eat to serve the thousands of travellers who want to enjoy the park but can no longer afford the prices at the resort. In either the village or the resort there is a good week or more of enjoyment to be had.

HIGHLIGHTS

Hardier visitors can spend a week **trekking** to the farthest reaches and back or even trek all the way out of the park to Merapoh on the border of Pahang and Kuantan. There are also lots of hides and salt licks close to the resort or within a short boat journey.

Very close to the HQ is **Bumbun Tahan** which overlooks a clearing and waterhole. Deer, macaques and various birds are quite regular visitors. The best time to look is in the evening.

Further away from the HQ and a morning's walk or an excellent river-boat ride away are several more hides. **Bumbun Blau** and **Yong** are south of the HQ and about a 2 hr walk or a boat journey. They are close to **Gua Telinga**, a cave system with a river running through it where bats and snakes are often spotted.

Bumbun Tabing and **Bumbun Cegar Anjing** are both accessible by river-boat or by a hot hour or so's walk, and look out on salt licks in clearings. **Tabing** has a toilet and washing facilities, and clean water nearby. **Bumbun Kumbang**, 11 km from the HQ and a 45 minute boat ride followed by a 45 minute walk, is the place where lucky people have spotted elephants.

WHAT TO BRING

The hides are very basic with earth toilets. If you stay overnight you must take all provisions and a sleeping sheet with you. The jungle never really cools down so a sheet and mosquito net are a better choice than a sleeping bag. Basic first aid in terms of iodine and sticking plasters and something to clean up minor wounds is important.

Long-sleeved clothes and long trousers made of thin cotton keep off the insects, and a good pair of canvas jungle boots are protection against leeches. Mosquito repellent and insect repellent for the leeches are vital, as is a torch. You should also bring a string bag to hang up your food. Rats invade the shelters at night and will carry away anything they can get their paws on. Water-purifying tablets or a gas stove to boil water are also important.

WALKING

Those who come to Taman Negara in the hope of seeing a tiger or elephant may well go away disappointed. Others will realise that the true beauty of the place isn't the exotic creatures but the amazing jungle itself. Walking around it is like being inside a great, heaving living creature. At every step there is some outrageous life form teeming away inches away from you. Walking in the rain-forest is both safe and exhilarating, and you should spend every day on one of the walks.

The 3 hr **Bukit Indah Trail** is the best introductory walk. It follows the course of the Sungei Tembeling to the canopy walkway, which has an entrance fee. From there follow the signs to Bukit Terasek where there are fine views.

Alternatively you can follow the signs to Lubok Simpon from the walkway and spend some time in a swimming area before returning to the park HQ. Or from the canopy follow the Bukit Indah trail for more fine views over the forest canopy.

LONGER TREKS

For all longer treks a guide must be hired which increases the cost. Trips can be planned around the various lodges and camping grounds in the park so that you have accommodation for the night, but it is best to try to join a group rather than take on the cost of boat rides and guides on your own. The park HQ organises and has details of longer treks which include:

OTHER SHORT WALKS

Kuala Trenggan, about 5 hrs, 9 km along the river bank. You can stay at the lodge (book 2 days in advance at the park HQ) or get the river boat back to the resort.

Gua Telinga, about 2hrs from the resort. Then you can crawl through the cave system itself; about half an hour following a rope guide. Take a torch.

Latah Berkoh: about 4 hrs, 8km north of the resort, on the Gunung Tahan trail. Latah Berkoh is a series of cascades on the river which are good for paddling and picnics. There is a very basic lodge nearby which can be booked for the night. You must bring supplies. There is also a camp site en route at Kemah Lameh to stay overnight, or you can book a ride back on one of the boats to the waterfall.

Gunung Tahan: 9 days. Fifty-five kilometres to the summit of Gunung Tahan and the same distance back. A guide and supplies are essential for the full nine days. Not to be undertaken lightly. Camp sites en route have water and firewood.

Rentis Tenor trail: 3–4 days, depending on your route. Only 15 km from park HQ. A guide may not be necessary as all the trails are marked. Crossing the Tahan River, the trail goes to Kemah Yong on the banks of Sungei Yong and makes a brief, 570 metre ascent up Bukit Guling Gendang. Nights are spent at the Yong campsite. The third day is a day-long trek to Kemah Lameh beside the Sungei Tenor. The last day is spent retracing your steps back to the resort.

THE CANOPY WALKWAY

Walking along the forest floor means you miss out on much of the rainforest activity taking place high above you in the canopy of huge trees which form the top layer of the forest. The canopy walkway leads you along 400 metres of rope bridge suspended from the biggest of the trees at a height of about 25 metres from the ground. Probably the noise of all the other walkers has driven anything interesting away, but it's a good experience and gives a different view of the forest. Entrance to the walkway is RM5 and it is open daily 1100–1445.

ORGANISED ADVENTURES Long gone are the pioneering, make-your-own adventure days of Taman Negara. The resort and park headquarters organise trips into the jungle at night, into the caves, up the rivers and into the Orang Asli settlements. You can ride the rapids in an inflatable raft, fish in the rivers and even hold a conference or banquet here. All of it costs, especially boat and guide hire, which unfortunately prevents some people doing some of the more exciting activities.

INHABITANTS OF THE FOREST

You won't see tigers peering out of the jungle at you or rampaging herds of elephants. But you may catch sight of the laughably ungracious hornbills who honk their way around the jungle. Or the primeval monitor lizards, looking like great logs rolling down the river until they open an eye to give you a stare. Or the pink coral snake, which is deadly poisonous except that its jaws are only wide enough to bite the bit of skin between your fingers.

Then there's the teeming insect life. Great trails of ants carrying huge butterflies that they've killed back to their nests. Flocks of exotic butterflies attracted to the sweat on your boots. Even the leeches have a certain comic dignity as they slip out of your boots, three times the size they went in and drunk on your blood. Especially rewarding are those unsought moments. You glance up to see a flying fox, an orchid is growing on the path beside your foot, or an entire colony of bats surges out of the hillside at dusk. You can see tigers at the zoo. Taman Negara is special.

Taman Negara Resort $$$$ tel: (09) 266-3500, Kuala Tahan. KL sales office Lot G O1A, Ground Floor, Comp. Antarabangsar, Jalan Sultan Ismail, tel: (03) 245-5585, fax: 245-5430. Dorms and simple guesthouse rooms. **Terenggan Lodge** and **Keniam Lodge** are more basic and a little cheaper than accommodation at park HQ.

Nusa Camp $–$$ No 5, Jetty Taman Negara, tel: (09) 266-3034; (booking office) Kuala Lumpur office MATIC, 109 Jalan Ampang, tel/fax: (03) 2162-7682. Dorms and chalets, much more basic than the resort, but affordable. Packages work out cheaper and include boat fares, trips etc.

Teresek View $ Kampung Kuala Tahan, tel: (011) 911-530. Chalets and dorms, some attached bathrooms. In village on bank opposite park HQ.

There are several other paces to stay in Kampung Kuala Tahan, none with phone or much in the way of facilities.

The resort has two restaurants with set meals or an a la carte menu, from **$$$$–$$.** There is also a restaurant at Nusa Camp, with a more restricted menu and lower prices. In Kampung Kuala Tahan are lots of restaurants in boats and barges along the bank of the river. Any one of them will ferry you over to the village. The resort has an expensive supermarket so if you want to save money, bring as much food in as you can.

WHEN TO VISIT

Taman Negara is at its driest between February and September which is the best time for walking. But if the rivers get too dry much of the fun of the place is lost. During school holidays the place gets very crowded and winter brings Europeans escaping their climate. In July is the Taman Negara Festival, with traditional dance shows and handicrafts made by the Orang Asli and Batek tribe, which is generally good fun.

BOAT The Resort leaf-lets warn that only people with reservations at the resort can book seats in their boats from Kuala Tembeling. Their fares are RM19 one way. They also operate a speedboat (twice daily) which takes only 45 minutes, but loses much of the joy of getting there.

The Nusa Camp runs boats (twice daily) from Kuala Tembeling to the park HQ and then on to their camp for RM38 return. Nusa also offers a regular riverbus service to many of the locations in the park, at much lower prices than chartering a boat at park HQ. This includes a service every 2 hours to and from the park HQ to Nusa Camp and a twice-daily service to the canopy, to some of the caves in the park and to some distant campsites.

Kuala Lumpur – Taman Negara

Bus SPKG Tours operates a shuttle bus service between KL and Kuala Tembeling which can be booked through the Nusa Camp offices in KL and Kuala Tembeling. The resort also arranges a daily shuttle bus to meet the Kuala Tembeling ferry. Enquire about prices and pickup point at the KL office.

KUALA LUMPUR – BUTTERWORTH (FOR PENANG)

OTT TABLES 7006/7043

TRANSPORT	FREQUENCY	JOURNEY TIME
Train	3 daily	7hrs
Bus	Several daily	8hrs
Air	Daily, frequent	2hrs

KUALA LUMPUR – TAPAH

OTT TABLES 7005/7043

TRANSPORT	FREQUENCY	JOURNEY TIME
Train	3 daily	2hrs
Bus	Hourly	3hrs

TAPAH – CAMERON HIGHLANDS

OTT TABLE 7046

TRANSPORT	FREQUENCY	JOURNEY TIME
Bus	Hourly	1hr

KUALA LUMPUR – CAMERON HIGHLANDS

OTT TABLE 7046

TRANSPORT	FREQUENCY	JOURNEY TIME
Bus	Daily	5hrs

KUALA LUMPUR – IPOH

TRANSPORT	FREQUENCY	JOURNEY TIME
Train	3 daily	3½hrs
Bus	Frequent	4hrs

TAPAH – IPOH

OTT TABLES 7046/7005

TRANSPORT	FREQUENCY	JOURNEY TIME
Bus	Hourly	1½hrs
Train	3 daily	1hr

IPOH – LUMUT

TRANSPORT	FREQUENCY	JOURNEY TIME
Bus	Hourly	2hrs

LUMUT – PANGKOR

TRANSPORT	FREQUENCY	JOURNEY TIME
Boat	Half hourly	30mins

LUMUT – KUALA KANGSAR

TRANSPORT	FREQUENCY	JOURNEY TIME
Bus	Hourly	2hrs

IPOH – KUALA KANGSAR

OTT TABLES 7005/7043

TRANSPORT	FREQUENCY	JOURNEY TIME
Train	3 daily	1hr
Bus	Hourly	1hr

KUALA KANGSAR – TAIPING

OTT TABLES 7005/7043

TRANSPORT	FREQUENCY	JOURNEY TIME
Train	4 daily	50mins
Bus	Hourly	1hr

TAIPING – BUTTERWORTH (FOR PENANG)

TRANSPORT	FREQUENCY	JOURNEY TIME
Train	3 daily	2hrs
Bus	Hourly	2hrs

ROUTE DETAIL

The north–south expressway, a toll road, takes you to Tanjung Malim on the Selangor/ Perak border and then on to Tapah. From Tapah route 59 leads to the Cameron Highlands. From Tapah to Ipoh the route again follows the north–south highway. From Ipoh to Lumut, take route 5. Ipoh – Kuala Kangsar is again the north–south highway, as are Taiping and Penang.

The Scenic Route

The north–south highway is an easy road to drive but it could be anywhere in the world with its multiple carriageways, toll booths and rest stops. If you would rather see a little more of the country on your trip it is possible to get off the highway at Tanjung Malim and take old highway 1.

This passes Selim River where the British fought a battle against the encroaching Japanese forces, Teluk Intan with its pagoda-style leaning clock tower and Kampung Pasir Salek where the first British Resident of the state was assassinated in 1875. The town is also home to some traditional style houses given over to museums of history and culture.

En Route

Tapah

Of little interest except as a staging post on the journey to the Cameron Highlands, Tapah is, nonetheless, an interesting example of small town Malaysia. It has rail links with Thailand in the north and Singapore in the south, a few small hotels, and coffee shops, but generally a sense that life goes on without it. You may well spend an hour or so here on the journey to the Cameron Highlands, in which case you could hang out for a while at the coffee shop in the Hotel Timuran.

The train station is 9 km west of town with links to Penang and Kuala Lumpur, and there is a half-hourly bus service to and from the town.

Long-distance buses leave from outside the Caspian restaurant in Main Rd or from the bus station. Buses for the Cameron Highlands leave from the bus station in Jalan Raja. Close to the bus station is the taxi station where you can get a share taxi to Tanah Rata, the first village in the Cameron Highlands.

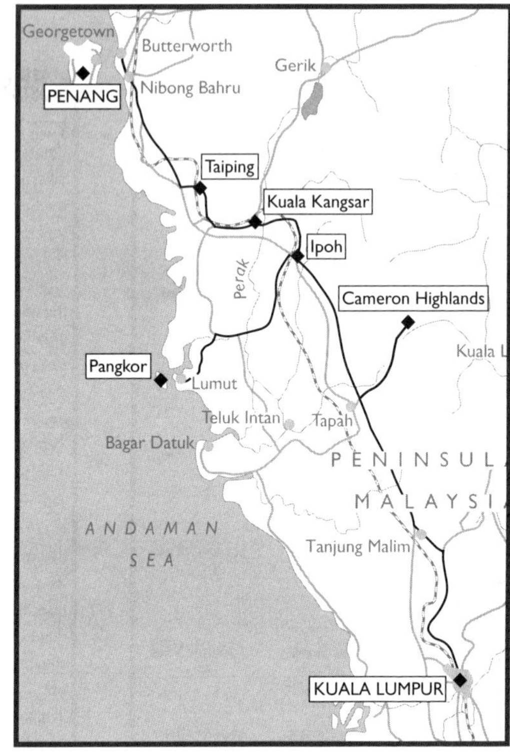

Perak

The great north–south highway has made a trip to Penang from KL a brief morning's drive through the state of Perak rather than a major undertaking. It has also opened up the 21,000 sq km of the state once dedicated to tin mining and rubber plantations to visitors, with Ipoh as the major attraction. The Cameron Highlands are a gentle reminder of the old days of colonial life. Pulau Pangkor, with its burgeoning beach resorts, shows the new side of the state, while the historical town of Kuala Kangsar has its famous black ceramic pottery.

TRAVEL SICKNESS

Travelling by bus or even by car along the winding mountain road to the highlands can cause travel sickness. Sufferers should take motion sickness pills beforehand and try to sit at the front of the bus.

Part of the attraction of the Cameron Highlands is the cool climate. When evening comes holidaymakers in the old government bungalows light unnecessary log fires just to remember what it feels like. In between tea plantations you can visit strawberry farms and in gardens see roses, honeysuckle and lupins side by side bougainvillea and hibiscus.

THE CAMERON HIGHLANDS

Sixty km off the main north-south highway, 1300 to 1800 metres above sea level, miles of tea plantations, golf courses and tourist resorts make up the Cameron Highlands. Unlike the heady 30°C or more in the rest of Malaysia this place rarely gets above 24°C.

The area was unknown to the world until 1885 when a surveyor, Cameron, discovered it. Its potential as a hill resort was spotted straightaway, and clearance of the wooded slopes began. For a hundred years or more it has remained fairly inaccessible except by a slow grind up winding hills.

ORIENTATION The narrow mountain road leads through Ringlet, a working Malay town. It passes the man-made and nearly choked up lake beside the Lakehouse Hotel before reaching Tanah Rata, where most of the tourist interest is centred. The road continues to the golf course and upmarket hotels, and on to Brinchang, a more Chinese town. Beyond that the road goes to tea estates and another small road winds its way up Gunung Brinchang.

WALKING IN THE HIGHLANDS

Walkers should be aware that it is very easy to get lost in the hills here. Every year search parties end up looking for lost walkers. Tell someone which trail you are going on and when you intend to be back. Carry a whistle and lots of water as well as matches, wet-weather gear, food and warm clothing. For missing walkers contact the District Office, tel: (05) 491-1222.

There is a lot to do in the highlands and the mild climate encourages activity. There are many clearly marked walking trails, details of which can be found at the tourist office. Two easy and popular trails are No 4 to the **Parit Falls** and No 9 to the **Robinson Falls**. Much more strenuous but worth the effort is trail No 10, climbing up **Gunung Jasar**, which takes about three hours.

TEA AND THE CAMERON HIGHLANDS

Tea comes from the evergreen shrub *Camellia sinensus*, and is suited to hill slopes in the tropics where regular rainfall on acid soil can be expected. It has been cultivated for thousands of years in India, south-east Asia and the Far East and today the main producers are India, Sri Lanka and China. *Camellia sinensus* means 'Chinese camellia' and, as the Chinese writer of the 8th century observed, there are 'a thousand and ten thousand teas'. In terms of world production Malaysia's contribution is infinitesimal but Boh tea, the product of the Cameron Highlands, has its own followers and is widely regarded as a very respectable tea.

The Highlands owe their name to William Cameron, a British surveyor who mapped the region in the late 19th century – though the actual Highlands were first mapped by a Malay, Kulop Riau. In the 1920s the British began building bungalows for colonials who could afford this means of escaping the heat and humidity. At 1,524 metres above sea level, the Highlands were ideal for tea plantations and in 1926 the first tea was planted.

Techniques of tea-gathering, as you will discover if you visit one of the working plantations, have not changed much since the days of the British in India. Modern technology comes in the form of electric clippers but the shoots are still collected in large baskets which are adroitly carried on the head. The tea workers themselves are mostly Indian, many being descendants of those who were first brought over from Ceylon (Sri Lanka) in the 1920s.

It requires about 5 kilograms of leaves to make one kilogram of tea and the largely mechanical process can be seen at close quarters in the Highlands. The key concept here is mechanical, for tea making is a process that has no truck with computers and miniaturized circuit boards. The first stage is a drying process that reduces the moisture in the leaves by simply blowing hot air underneath the now soft and pliable leaves.

The next step is a vigorous shaking of the leaves in a special rolling machine that was developed in India in the 1880s. The fermenting juices are released when the cell structure of the leaf is fractured by the rolling machine and it is these juices that give tea its flavour. When the leaves have fermented there is another drying stage to remove moisture and it is at this stage that they take on their characteristic black colour. It is basically a process of oxidation that produces this colour. Unfermented tea is green tea while the semi-fermented variety is oolong tea. The last stage at the Cameron Highlands plantations is a selection procedure that grades the tea according to its quality. The criteria for this is explained during the tour and tea of differing qualities can be purchased at the plantation.

A brief walk off the main road near Brinchang brings you to the huge **Sam Poh Temple**, dedicated to the Lord Buddha with a giant golden Buddha inside. Beyond Brinchang there are lots of fruit farms and apiaries to visit, which can be organised by local tour companies in Brinchang. Titiwangsa, tel: (05) 491-1200, or CS Travel, tel: (05) 491-1200.

Look out for **Uncle Sam's** which grows kaffir lilies, strawberries, apples and cacti. Beyond that is **Kea Farm** which grows tomatoes, cauliflowers and other vegetables more common in moderate climates. Continuing along the main road past the turn-off to the Kea Farm are two **butterfly parks** competing with one another. They sell dead butterflies and insects, but in the gardens, as well as exotic butterflies, there are some classic European plants.

There are two rose gardens along this stretch of road. One, **Rose Valley**, entrance RM3, has hundreds of roses, including a green and a black rose and a thornless rose. Not to be missed are the **tea plantations**. The best one to visit is the Boh factory and estate, signposted from the main road north of Brinchang. It has a visitor's centre, regular tours of the factory and estate and tea for sale.

Arrival and Departure

Bus: An hourly bus leaves Brinchang via Tanah Rata for Tapah where there are connections to KL and Penang.

Car: 158 km north of Kuala Lumpur turn off the north–south highway at Tapah. The 59 km to Tanah Rata take an hour at least.

i A small **tourist office and museum** are at the western end of Tanah Rata, open Mon–Thur 0800–1615, Fri 0800–1216 and 1445–1615, and Sat 0800–1245.

The Cameron Highlands are very popular with both Malaysians and Singaporeans. During school holidays in April, June and December accommodation gets very booked up and very expensive, with prices sometimes doubling.
The Old Smokehouse $$$$ Tanah Rata, tel: (05) 491-1215, fax: 491-1214. Deliciously olde worlde ex-colonialist mock Tudor residence. Each room beautifully individually furnished. Lovely gardens, bric-a-brac everywhere and a natural genteel feel to the place. Centrally located with views over the golf course.

The Lakehouse $$$$ Ringlet, tel: (02) 495-6152. 2 miles above Ringlet opposite the lake. Not quite as authentically British Malaysia as the Smokehouse but a close second. Individually furnished rooms, lots of luxury, log fires etc.
Strawberry Park Resort $$$$ Tanah Rata, tel: (05) 491-1166, fax: 491-1949. Huge resort with apartments as well as rooms. Pool, great views.
Hotel Rosa Passadena $$$ Brinchang, tel: (05) 491-2288, fax: 491-2688. In main street of Brinchang, modern, mock Tudor. Out of season, bargain a little.
Cool Point Hotel $$$–$$ 891, Pesiaran Dayang Endah, tel: (05) 491-4914, fax: 491-4070. Good value out of high season. Lots of facilities.
Jurina Resort $$$–$$ Tanah Rata, tel: (05) 491-5522. Good value rooms, use of kitchen and sitting room.
Hill Garden Lodge $$ 15–16 Jalan Besar, Brinchang, tel: (05) 491-2988, fax: 491-2226. The main street can get noisy, but good rooms with en suite bathroom and TV. Low season discounts.
Cameronian Holiday Inn $ 16, Jalan Mentingi, tel: (05) 491-1327. Nicely furnished rooms in a quiet side street. Hot showers, garden, restaurant. Dorm beds available.

There are foodstalls at Tanah Rata serving good inexpensive Malay and Chinese food. Brinchang has a night market with stalls serving mostly Malay food, as well as a permanent food centre at the southern end of the street.
Smokehouse $$$$ traditional English dishes, speciality beef Wellington, cucumber sandwiches, cream teas.
Lakehouse $$$$ same as above, slightly different setting.
Bala's $$ outside Tanah Rata on road to Brinchang. Vegetarian options, cream teas, good breakfasts.
Thanum $ 25 Jalan Besar. Indian food as well as Hainanese chicken rice. Seating outside.
Kwan Kee $$ Brinchang. Steamboat at very reasonable prices.

IPOH

The capital of Perak state and Malaysia's third largest city sits in the Kinta valley between two mountain ranges, the Keledang Mountains and the Main Range. Ipoh made its fortune in the 19th and early 20th centuries from tin mining, and many of the mansions of the Chinese tin miners still stand to tell the tale. The economic boom here hasn't been as big as other cities in Malaysia, and many of the town's old features still survive.

The oldest part of town, and the one most worth visiting, is to the west near the railway line. The **train station** and **Majestic Hotel** were built as a piece in 1917. They have the same Moorish domes and minarets combined with Victorian Gothic that characterise the colonial architecture of KL. The hotel in particular is magnificent in its recall of the old days of punkah wallahs, with its huge marble balconies and planter's chairs and tables ready to hold the mandatory colonial gin and tonic. From the balcony you can see neoclassical **Edwardian Town Hall**, white as a Christmas cake.

Along Jalan Dato Maharaja Lela is the ornate **Hong Kong and Shanghai Bank** with its Corinthian pillars and tower. Opposite it is the **Birch Memorial Clock**, built in memory of the state's first president, assassinated in 1875 at Pasir Salak.

The town has two museums. The **Darul Ridzuan Museum** open daily 0930–1700, free, on Gantang Wahab is a converted tin millionaire's house full of old photographs of the town and the history of tin mining and logging. The **Geological Museum** open Mon–Fri 0800–1600, free, is a little out of town to the east on Jalan Harimu, and is full of minerals and precious stones.

A few miles out of town are some good places to visit which can be done in a half day's taxi hire or with your own transport. **The Perak Tong Temple**, open daily 0900–1700, free, but make a donation. A cave temple 6.5 km north of Ipoh, this is on several levels with huge statues of the Buddha and walls painted by various pilgrims over the years. At certain points openings in the limestone rock reveal views of the surrounding countryside. Bus Nos 3, 41 or 141 to Kuala Kangsar.

The **Sam Poh Tong Temple,** open daily 0730–1530, free, but make a donation. This is another converted limestone cave with one large cave and several smaller ones. It has a vegetarian restaurant and a turtle pool where thousands of the creatures thrash about hoping to gain a little more space in the sickly green water. In front of the temple are pretty Chinese gardens. No 66 or 73 bus.

Three km north of town on the Taiping road is a **Thai Buddhist temple** where you can see the difference between Thai and Chinese Buddhism in the figure of the highly elaborate reclining Buddha.

i The **tourist office** is at Jalan Sambathan, tel: (05) 241-2957, open Mon–Fri, 0800–1245, 1400–1615.

ARRIVAL AND DEPARTURE

Train: Train timetables change every six months so inquire at the station about times, tel: (05) 254-7987.

Bus: The long-distance bus station is in Jalan Tun Abdul Razak in the south west of the city. Opposite it is the Perak Roadway bus depot for buses to Lumut. From the bus station buses depart regularly for all areas of Malaysia, including Kuala Kangsar, Kuala Lumpur, Penang, Taiping, and Tapah.

Air: Malaysia Airlines has four flights a day into Ipoh from KL. The airport is 15 km south of town. A taxi should cost around RM12.

Casuarina Parkroyal $$$$$ 18, Jalan Gopeng, tel: (05) 255-5555, fax: 255-8177. Big rooms, spacious gardens, swimming pool, a little way out of town.

Syuen Hotel $$$$ 88, Jalan Sultan Abdul, tel: (05) 253-8889, fax: 253-3335. Big modern concrete and glass edifice. Close to town, small, rooftop pool.

Hotel Seri Malaysia $$$ Lot 10406, Jalan Sturrock, tel: (05) 241-2936, fax: 241-2946. At the very bottom end of this price range, one of a chain of inexpensive, basic hotels with big rooms and very good value family rooms.

Ritz Kowloon $$ 92-96 Jalan Yang Kalson, tel: (05) 254-7778, fax: 253-3800. Good basic hotel, TV and coffee making facilities. Ask about discounts.

Majestic Station Hotel $$ Bangunan Stesen Keratapi, tel: (05) 255-5605, fax: 255-3393. Beautiful old hotel, recently renovated. Basic, big rooms are good value, and rates include breakfast on the balcony. Ask about discounts.

New Hollywood Hotel $$–$ 72, Jalan Yussuff. Bottom of this price range, air-con, clean, restaurant.

Golden Inn $ 17, Jalan Che Tak, tel: (05) 253-0866. Clean, well organised, air-con rooms with bathrooms.

Ipoh has a reputation for its Chinese food with dishes such as *char kway teow* (flat rice noodles in black bean sauce with seafood) particularly associated with the town.

VKK Madra $ 38 Medan Istana, tel: (05) 241-9139. South Indian cuisine with a vast range of dosai, black pepper mutton, chicken biryani. Clean, pretty dining room.

LUMUT

This is the departure point for **Pangkor Island** and has little to interest tourists. It is a major navy base and has a naval museum, and a good beach. Teluk Batik, 7 km south of town. It is also the venue for the August sea carnival each year.

The tourist office is in Jalan Titi Panjang, open irregular hours, near the jetty.

Car: Lumut is accessible from Ipoh, 101 km to the north east. There is a long-term car park at the Shell petrol station. RM6 per day.

Bus: Lumut has a bus station from where there are direct buses to Ipoh and Butterworth.

Boat: In the high season ferries leave from the Lumut jetty for Pulau Pangkor every 20 mins from 0645–2100, RM3. At other times ferries are less frequent. The ferry for the two northern resorts leaves every 2 hrs. A separate ferry leaves for Pangkor Laut every 2 hrs or so but this is for residents only.

PANGKOR ISLAND

Small and pretty with several white sandy beaches, Pangkor Island is a major Malaysian holiday destination. At peak times, especially the Malaysian and Singaporean school holidays in April, June and December, it is probably well worth avoiding unless you head for one of the more exclusive beach resorts. Off peak it's a nice little island with places to visit, cycle rides and some good food.

ORIENTATION

Most people in Pangkor live on the east side of the island, which is basically a single inhabited strip of land fronting the beach, occupied by fishermen and boatbuilders.

Motorbikes can be hired for about RM20–30 a day in Pangkor village from several places, including Soon Seng Motor, 12 Main Rd, near the jetty, tel: (05) 685-1269. There are also hire places at Pantai Pasir Bogak. Many of the hotels rent **bicycles** at around RM10 a day.

From Pangkor a bus service goes to the first of the tourist areas on the west coast, Pasir Bogak, the most developed, crowded and often dirty beach. The more northerly beach, Teluk Nippy, where most of the budget accommodation is, is accessible by taxi only.

The ferry from Lumut lands at two places along this strip, Sungei Pinang Kecil and Pangkor Village. At the north end of the island are two quite exclusive resort hotels which are served by a separate ferry which lands at Tele Dalam.

HIGHLIGHTS The size of the island and shortage of reasonably priced taxis make cycling a good option. Many of the resorts hire bikes to their guests. From **Pasir Bogak** there are lots of little bays and empty beaches along the western side of the island, with hotels where you can stop for lunch.

Passing the Pan Pacific Resort and the northern headland of the island, head downhill and south to the village strip where there are lots of little shop-houses, boat-building yards, coffee shops and temples. At the south end of the island there are the remains of a Dutch fort, dating back to the 16th century.

Other activities include hiring a boat to go around the island or for a day trip to smaller uninhabited islands, or even for a quick visit to Pulau Pangkor Laut where for a large fee you can enjoy the very exclusive resort's facilities. The clear waters are good for snorkelling and the resorts have sailboats and other water sports.

Prices at all these places can double at peak times which include the school holiday months in Malaysia (April, June and December) and weekends. During term time, weekdays are quiet and cheap but you must ask for a discount.

Pan Pacific Resort $$$$$ Teluk Balanga, tel: (05) 685-1399, fax: 685-2390. Very exclusive, beautiful resort with all facilities and a glorious beach watched over by great hornbills.

Pangkor Laut Resort $$$$$ Pulau Pangkor Laut, tel: (05) 699-1100, fax: 699-1200. Beautiful, exclusive, expensive.

Teluk Dalam Resort $$$$ Teluk Dalam, tel: (05) 685-5000, fax: 685-4000. All the facilities of the other hotels but not such a good location.

Nipah Bay Villa $$$ Teluk Nipah, tel: (05) 685-2198. Air-con chalets, price includes meals.

Seagull Beach Resort $$$–$ Teluk Nipah, tel: (05) 685-2878, fax: 685-1050. Simple huts with a fan to air-con chalets. Water sports equipment available.

Sri Bayu Beach Resort $$$$$ Pantai Pasir Bogak, tel: (05) 685-1929, fax: 685-1050, e-mail: sbbr@po.jaring.my. Pool, sports, several restaurants, but right in the middle of all the beach accommodation.
Khoo's Holiday Resort $–$$ Pantai Pasir Bogak, tel/fax: (05) 685-1164. Chalets with fan or air-con set on hillside. Good value.
Pangkor Village Beach Resort $$$–$ from basic huts to air-con bungalows right on the beach. Prices include meals.

Most people tend to eat in their hotels as part of a package or, in the case of the resorts, out of necessity. There are food stalls on the beach at Teluk Nipah, as well as the hotel restaurants and one or two cheap places. In Pangkor village there are lots of seafood places and roti shops where for very little you can enjoy good fresh food.
Bayview Café $$–$ Teluk Nipah, tables outside, good food, pleasant atmosphere.
The Hornbill Hotel Restaurant $$$ Teluk Nipah. Western food, wine list.
No 1 Seafood Restaurant $$$ Teluk Bogak. Chinese seafood, children's menu.
Sea View Hotel $$ Pantai Pasir Bogak. Nice setting with a garden overlooking the sea.

KUALA KANGSAR

Now a small sleepy little backwater halfway between Ipoh and Taiping Kuala, Kangsar was once the capital city of Perak and home to the state's sultans for over 500 years. It lies on the Kangsar River beside whose banks the sultan's palace sits. One of the most interesting things to see in Kuala Kangsar is Malaysia's official **first rubber tree**, beside the District Office, surrounded by a protective fence and a little plaque.

Kuala Kangsar's other sights are all slightly out of town along the river and then up Bukit Chandan. The **Ubadiah Mosque** was completed in 1917 and really stands out from the many other mosques in the country with its glimmering gold onion dome and elegant minarets. It is surrounded by the graves of the Perak royal family, the living members of which live in the Istana on the top of the hill. This was built in 1930 and is a glorious mix of Art Deco and Islam. This palace is not open to the public but the old one next door is.

RUBBER

In the early 19th century most people were getting around on steel rimmed wooden carts and carriages, blissfully unaware that deep in the forests of South America were trees, *Hevea brasiliensis*, that would change the world. Once the Brazilian government discovered the uses of latex from the trees, they banned their export and kept the source of their amazing new product a secret.

But, like all good capitalists, the British stole some of the seeds and germinated them at Kew Gardens. From there seeds went to Singapore and an industry was born. Mad Rubber Ridley, the Director of the Botanic Gardens in Singapore, persuaded Hugh Low, the then Resident of Perak, to try some out in Kuala Kangsar.

By the time pneumatic tyres were in demand in the west around 1905 a rubber plantation was producing latex in Perak, and within ten years there were plantations in every state. Today, with Indonesia, it produces half of the world's rubber, all from some seeds stolen from Brazil.

It is a **museum** open Sat–Thurs 0930–1900, free, dedicated to the history and insignia of the state and the royal family. More interesting is the exterior of the building, which is wooden and built entirely without architectural plans or nails. Close to the Padang with its pavilion from which the sultan once watched the cricket matches is the **Malay College**, still a prestigious school with beautiful architecture. Anthony Burgess, author of *A Clockwork Orange,* taught here.

THE JAPANESE LEGACY

There are two signs of the Japanese years of occupation in this area. In Taiping the town's prison was built by the Japanese on the site of an earlier one of 1885, and the road up to Maxwell Hill, now seriously returning to the soil it was carved out of, was built by Japanese prisoners of war.

Rumah Rehat, Kuala Kangsar $$ Bukit Chandan, tel: (05) 777-3705. Big airy rooms with air-con with great river views. Good Malay restaurant.
Mei Lai $ 7 Jalan Raja Chulan, tel: (05) 776-1729.

There are food stalls and cafés close to the bus station. Two Indian Muslem cafés serve roti in Jalan Kangsar: **Restoran Muslim** and **Restoran Rahmaniah**. The rest house has a good Malay place.

TAIPING

At one time visitors to Taiping, or Larut as it was known in the 19th century, would have come across a Chinese Wild West, full of tin miners working in a harsh and lawless land and rival groups of Chinese clans breaking out into open warfare. The British put a stop to that, confidently renaming the place 'Everlasting Peace'.

Economic booms and swings quietly made Taiping a backwater, but like Kuala Kangsar it has retained lots of Malay and colonial architecture, and is a quiet place for a day's visit or a night's stay, especially if you want to take a look at the hill station of Maxwell Hill.

Highlights Centred around the **Lake Gardens** are several places to visit. The gardens themselves were once the site of an opencast tin mine. Beside them is an **allied war cemetery**, full of the graves of men who fell under the Japanese onslaught of December 1941. On the north side of the Lake Gardens is the **Museum**, built in 1883 and the oldest in Malaysia. Its architecture, like many of the country's museums, is more interesting than its displays. Nearby is the Anglican **All Saints church**, built in 1889.

In town are the **Ling Nam Temple** and the colourfully painted **Hindu temple**, both worth a look around.

Seri Malaysia $$ 4, Jalan Sultan Mansor, tel: (05) 806-9502, fax :806-9495. Good value, big, family-sized rooms, coffee shop.
Panorama Hotel $$ 61–79 Jalan Kota, tel: (05) 808-4111, fax: 808-4129. Big rooms, all mod cons, coffee shop, good value.
Town Rest House $$$–$$ 101 Jalan Stesyen. The old governor's residence, its colonial style buildings recently renovated.
Rumah Rẹhat Bahru $–$$ Taman Tasik, tel: (05) 807-2044. Set in the Lake Gardens with lovely views and huge fan-cooled or air-con rooms.

The best places for food in Taiping are the food centres near the taxi station and in Jalan Tupai. The night market also has lots of good food.

MAXWELL HILL

Maxwell Hill, or Bukit Larut, is the wettest, oldest and smallest of Malaysia's hill stations. It makes an excellent day trip, especially since there is very little in the way of accommodation except bungalows, and these are always booked up especially during the school holidays.

It has very little in common with the other hill stations – no golf, casinos, smoke houses, or even much in the way of eating places (only the Surau Kanteen, near the land rover office or some of the guesthouses, if you book in advance). The only way up the crumbling road, with its 70 or so hairpin bends, is by government land rover (bookable on tel: (05) 807-7243), or a 4-hour walk.

At the top there are gardens and some trails into the jungle, but for long walks you need a guide. You will almost certainly see macaques, amazing butterflies and leeches. Land rovers depart hourly from the bottom of the hill near the Taiping Lake Gardens for a RM2 fare. Remember to book your return journey as soon as you get to the top or be prepared for a pleasant but long walk down.

ARRIVAL AND DEPARTURE

Bus: Buses on the Penang-Kuala Lumpur highway stop at Kamunting, 7 km outside Taiping. Buses are frequent to KL, Ipoh and Butterworth. From Kamunting there are regular buses into Taiping. From Taiping it is possible to get buses directly to Ipoh, Lumut and Kuala Kangsar, but for Butterworth you need to take the No 8 bus back to Kamunting.

TRADITIONAL MALAY CULTURE

Traditional Malay cultural forms like top spinning and shadow puppets are an endangered species, despite their vigorous promotion in states like Kelantan and Terengganu in Malaysia. Indeed, the chances of seeing a performance outside of this region is diminishing all the time so if you want to see a show then head for the east coast of peninsular Malaysia. On the plus side, these performances are not tourist-fuelled and what you see will be a genuine show that finds meaning purely within the culture of the local community.

Top spinning, *gasing*, may not be an Olympic sport but it is very popular in parts of peninsular Malaysia. There are two areas of competition, the 'spinning' contest and the 'striking game'. With spinning, the object is simply to keep the top spinning for as long as possible and the current record is around two hours. The 'striking game' is a little more aggressive because competitors use their tops to try and unbalance their opponent's efforts. It may all sound a bit silly but it requires expertise to launch a powerful spin using a long rope wound around the top and secured to a nearby tree. Once the top is furiously spinning, the player has to scoop it off the ground and position it on a post so that an exact timing is achieved when the spinning stops.

Shadow puppets, *wayang kulit*, are made from buffalo hide and set up on rattan sticks. The puppeteer is supported by a small orchestra that plays a musical accompaniment to the enactment of traditional takes from venerated sources like the *Ramayana*. The link with India can be traced back to the 14th century when the Javanese are thought to have introduced the Hindu epics to the Malay peninsula.

Kite flying, *wau ubi*, is most likely to be seen in the state of Kelantan and in the logo of the national airline, MAS. As with top spinning, the rules are fairly simple and the objective is to keep the kite as high in the air as possible and for as long as possible. The activity of kite flying has an honourable place in Malay history and there are accounts of it as a pastime with the royal nobility in the 15th century. Modern competitions can be tense affairs, with marks being awarded for skill in manoeuvring (i.e. avoiding attempts by opponents to knock your kite off course) as well as height and duration.

Drumming, as in Africa, has its origin as a means of communication. It is now a highly colourful spectacle that creates a great deal of noise. The wooden drums, *rebana*, are about 60 centimetres in diameter and covered in animal hide before being painted in as dramatic a design as possible. There is also the *kertok* drum, made from extra-large coconuts with a special string obtained from the sago plant stretched across its mouth to form the sounding board.

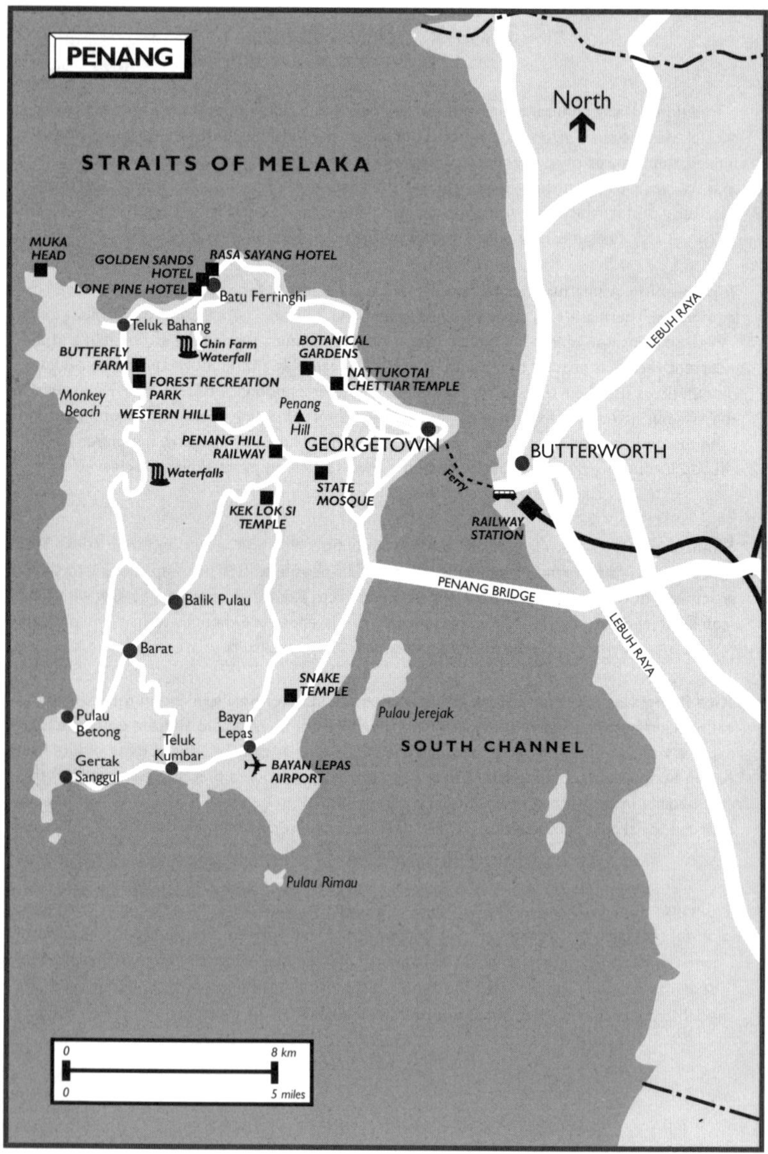
PENANG
North
STRAITS OF MELAKA
MUKA HEAD
GOLDEN SANDS HOTEL
RASA SAYANG HOTEL
LONE PINE HOTEL
Batu Ferringhi
Teluk Bahang
BUTTERFLY FARM
Chin Farm Waterfall
BOTANICAL GARDENS
NATTUKOTAI CHETTIAR TEMPLE
FOREST RECREATION PARK
Monkey Beach
WESTERN HILL
Penang Hill
GEORGETOWN
PENANG HILL RAILWAY
Waterfalls
STATE MOSQUE
KEK LOK SI TEMPLE
Ferry
BUTTERWORTH
RAILWAY STATION
LEBUH RAYA
PENANG BRIDGE
LEBUH RAYA
Balik Pulau
Barat
SNAKE TEMPLE
Pulau Jerejak
Pulau Betong
Bayan Lepas
Teluk Kumbar
SOUTH CHANNEL
Gertak Sanggul
BAYAN LEPAS AIRPORT
Pulau Rimau
0
8 km
0
5 miles

PENANG

Penang is an island, a state and a town. The entire state includes a strip of mainland once known as Province Wellesley after Lord Wellington (Arthur Wellesley), more commonly known as Sebarang Prai. Penang also refers to Pulau Pinang, the 300 sq mile island and the centre of interest for visitors. The main town on the island is Georgetown, and people often have the urban centre in mind when referring to Penang.

WHAT'S IN A NAME?

Penang comes from the Malay for the areca palm, *pokok pinang*, used by the Portuguese when they arrived in the 16th century. When the British turned up in 1771 they renamed it Prince of Wales Island, but somehow it didn't stick. Georgetown, after the same Prince of Wales, became the principal settlement, and the name has stayed attached to the town even after Malaysian independence.

As you wander around the island you will notice that there is also some confusion about street names. Many of them have been changed from the old colonial ones honouring assorted British dignitaries to lengthy titles involving sultans, datos, maharanis and Malaysian figures. The trouble is that people still use the old names, so that while the street signs say one thing locals say another.

Modern Penang is a vibrant Chinese city with its share of office blocks and apartment buildings, but much of its past has survived. This is partly because of the efforts of Penang's conservation societies and clan groups, but mainly because of a system of rent control that kept Georgetown's rents so low that owners lacked an incentive to renovate or rebuild.

The rent control system has now been scrapped and it will be interesting to see what happens to the many old buildings that give Georgetown such character. The Chinese vernacular architecture is so impressive that some hope to turn Georgetown into a World Heritage Site.

The rest of the island also has lots to offer the visitor, especially Batu Ferringhi where there are resort hotels, beach sports, good food and a vast market which puts KL's in the shade.

ARRIVAL AND DEPARTURE

AIR Penang has worldwide connections, usually via Kuala Lumpur. There are direct flights, mostly with Malaysia Airlines, to KL, Langkawi, Singapore, Johor Bahru, Phuket and Bangkok. As well as Malaysia Airlines, (04) 262-0011, Air Asia (04) 262-9882, Cathay Pacific (04) 226-0411, Singapore Airlines (04) 226-3201 and Thai Airways (04) 226-6000 also operate out of Penang. Several travel agents in Penang, many of them along Lebuh Chulia and around Komtar, have good value discounted fares.

BUS Most long-distance buses stop at the bus station beside the ferry terminal in Butterworth. Butterworth has frequent, long-distance buses to most large towns in Malaysia with connections to smaller destinations. Because of the distances involved many of these are night buses. From Georgetown a limited number of buses to KL, Kota Bharu and Terengganu depart from the Komtar Centre where there are ticket offices. There are also buses for Hat Yai, Krabi, Phuket, Surat Thani and Bangkok. The travel agents in Lebuh Chulia or hotel travel desks or receptions can arrange bookings.

TRAIN Trains from Thailand, Kuala Lumpur and Singapore stop at Butterworth station beside the ferry terminal. Besides the train stops within Malaysia there are trains to Bangkok, Hat Yai, Surat Thani (for Ko Samui) and smaller towns in Thailand. This means getting off at Padang Besar on the border for immigration, and usually returning to the same train for the onward journey.

CAR There is a toll of RM7 on the bridge into Penang but none on the return journey.

BOAT A 24 hour ferry operates between Butterworth and Georgetown. Journey time is 15 minutes and the 60sen fare is paid once when embarking at Butterworth. A car ferry also operates between the two towns.

There are ferry services to and from Penang from Sumatra, in Indonesia, run by the **Kuala Perlis Langkawi Ferry Service**, tel: (04) 264-3088, and **Ekspress Bahagia**, tel: (04) 263-1943. Langkawi Ferry Services also run a daily service to Langkawi and to Pulau Payar, a marine park. The booking office is at 8, Lebuh King.

GETTING AROUND

Bayan Lepas Airport is on Penang Island, 18 km south of Georgetown. Taxis are operated on a coupon system and a journey into Georgetown is RM20. Journey time is 45 minutes. Bus number 83 operates to and from the airport at hourly intervals, RM1.40. Journey time is an hour.

Taxis in Penang do not use metres. You must determine a price before you get in.

BUS It is worth taking the trouble to use the buses in Penang since its various sights are spread out around the island. Most start at Pengkalan Weld beside the ferry terminal. Many of them can also be picked up in the bus station in the Komtar building which has an information desk for assistance.

Bus Nos 93 and 202 go to Batu Ferringhi and Teluk Bahang from the Komtar station, No 7 to the Botanic Gardens, No 78 or minibus No 32 to the snake temple. Bus Nos 136, 93 and 94 go to Gurney Drive. Bus Nos 1 and 91 and minibus No 21 go from Pengkalan Weld to Air Hitam, from where it is a five-minute walk to the funicular railway up Penang Hill. Bus No 321 is a handy service for zipping between Lebuh Chulia and Komtar.

CAR Hiring a car is a good way to explore the island, and there are several places offering inexpensive car hire. All the main companies are represented but there are better prices at some of the smaller places. For a very inexpensive sightseeing tour, or just a good taxi service try **Thomas Chin**, mobile, tel: (017) 477-8895.

INFORMATION

GEORGETOWN MAP – inside back cover

i **Malaysian Tourist Promotion Board** in Jalan Tun Syed Sheh Barakbah, open Mon–Fri 0800–1700, Sat 0800–1300.
More useful is **Penang Tourist Guides Association** at Level 3 in the Komtar building, open daily 1000–1800. They have little literature to hand out, but useful and accurate information from volunteer tour guides.
Another useful place is the **Penang Tourist Centre** in Pesara King Edward, open Mon–Fri 0830–1300, 1400–1630, Sat 0830–1300.

PENANG

MONEY There are moneychangers along Lebuh Chulia and in various locations around town. They are open longer hours and have better rates than the banks. Shop around before you change money and ask what the fee is for travellers' cheques if you have them.

POST AND PHONES There is a small post office at street level in the Komtar centre and another branch in Lebuh Buckingham. The main post office in Lebuh Downing has a telecentre from where you can make international calls and there is a Telecom Centre in Jalan Burma which opens 24 hours. E-mail is available all over town with several places in the Komtar Centre and lots of Internet cafés in Lebuh Chulia. The cheapest but least salubrious are those in the Komtar Centre.

ACCOMMODATION

GEORGETOWN

Eastern and Oriental Hotel $$$$ 10 Farqhuar St. Recently renovated, beautiful old colonial hotel with pretty gardens rolling down to the waterfront.

Sheraton Penang $$$$$ 3 Jalan Larut, tel: (04) 226-7888, fax: 226-6615. Five-star facilities in the centre of town, good restaurants.

Hotel Equatorial $$$$$ 1 Jalan Bukit Jambul, Bayan Lepas, tel: (04) 643-8111, fax: 644-8000. More an inland resort than a city hotel, this place has everything, including a golf course. Next door to a huge shopping and entertainment centre and close to the airport. Japanese restaurant is excellent, especially for lunch.

Shangri-la Hotel $$$$$ Jalan Magazine, tel: (04) 262-2622, fax: 261-5967. Very central with an entrance into Komtar centre. Good restaurants, pool, laundry service and breakfast included in rates. Free shuttle bus to Ferringhi beach.

The Oriental $$$–$$ 105 Jalan Penang, tel: (04) 263-211, fax: 263-5395. Centrally located near to Lebuh Chulia, big rooms, coffee shop, restaurant. Good value.

Cathay Hotel $$ 22 Lebuh Leith, tel: (04) 262-6271. Old colonial building, big rooms, often fully booked.

Waldorf $$ 13 Lebuh Leith, tel: (04) 262-6140. Anonymous building but good value en suite and air-con rooms.

Honpin Hotel $$ 273B Lebuh Chulia, tel: (04) 262-5234. Centrally located, popular café, basic, quiet, air-con and en suite rooms.

THE E AND O

Brothers Martin and Tignan Sarkie built the Eastern Hotel on the seafront in Penang in 1884. When they built another, the Oriental next door, it wasn't long before the two combined to become Penang's biggest and classiest hotel. In 1903 they added a ballroom and after 1918 a Victory wing, and the hotel quickly gained a reputation as the finest in the East.

Writers Somerset Maugham, Noel Coward and Herman Hesse and film stars Douglas Fairbanks and Mary Pickford all stayed here. The hotel was in the grand style with a huge copper dome, gardens running down to the seafront and one of the earliest lifts to be installed in a hotel. The Planter's Bar served stengahs to colonial types discussing the price of rubber, and powdered European ladies dressed up for the grand balls that were held here.

The Sarkies went out of business in the 20th century and, like its sister hotels Raffles in Singapore and the Strand in Rangoon, the place gradually slipped into a state of crumbling grandeur. It now has a 21st century new look, having been nearly gutted and rebuilt according to the old design, preserving the huge copper dome and other architectural features. What has emerged is a modern version of what the hotel was like in its heyday.

Swiss Hotel $ 431 Lebuh Chulia. Very basic, rooms with toilet and shower.

Broadway Hostel $ 35F Jalan Masjid Kapitan Keling, tel: (04) 262-8550. Family size and cheaper fan–cooled rooms as well as dorm beds. The hostel organises buses to Hat Yai, Ko Samui and Bangkok.

FERRINGHI BEACH

There is little in the way of budget or hotels at Ferringhi Beach. Most of them are small, old tin–roofed houses close to the food stalls on the beach.

Penang Parkroyal $$$$$ tel: (04) 881-1133, fax: 881-2233. Pleasant family resort hotel, with big rooms overlooking the beach, free use of non-motorised water sports and good Japanese restaurant.

Shangri La Golden Sands Resort $$$$$ tel: (04) 881-1911, fax: 881-1880. Busy, popular resort hotel with all facilities. Pretty gardens leading down to the sea. Fairly quiet.

Casuarina Beach Resort $$$$$ tel: (04) 881-1711, fax: 881-2788. Smaller, older hotel, pleasant gardens, all rooms with balconies, beach sports.

Lone Pine Hotel $$$$ tel: (04) 881-1511, fax: 881-1282, e-mail: info@lonepinehotel.com. Very different from the other places at Ferringhi Beach. Small, quiet, almost Bali-esque. Some rooms have private gardens, and hotel gardens include hammocks, pool and an animal farm.

Popular Ferringhi $$ tel: (04) 881-3454, fax: 881-3458. Small rooms but with most things you need. Off the beach, central for night market, restaurants etc.

Ali's $ tel: (04) 881-1316. A few small rooms with fans, some with bathrooms. Nice garden.

Ah Beng Guesthouse $ tel: (04) 881-1036. Rooms with balconies and good sea views.

FOOD

GEORGETOWN

The Emperor $$$$$ Sheraton Hotel, tel: (04) 226-7888. Haute Cantonese, with items like soon hock fish taken from tanks on display. Turn up before 2000 for happy hour in the Traders Lounge bar, with free use of the Internet. Dim sum lunch $$$ is very popular.

Dragon King $$$–$ Lebuh Bishop. 23 years old, specialising in Penang version of nyonya cuisine: hot and sour rather than sweet with coconut. 16 tables only, very basic decor.

Hot Wok $$ Tanjung Tokong. Well out of Georgetown on the road to Ferringhi Beach, another good nyonya place occupying two shop–houses and crammed with Peranakan antiques. Try *otak otak* (fish in coconut cream paste) curry Kapitan or Assam prawns.

Subahan's $$ Junction of Burmah Rd and Tavoy Rd. Double storey shop–house serving vast range of curries and roti. Open till 0400.

HAWKER FOOD

The best places to get good, authentic food in Georgetown are the hawker stalls and coffee shops. Gurney Drive, 1 km of stalls along the promenade, is the most well known and the most expensive. Stalls and coffee shops start to open around 1730, and by about 2100 it is impossible to find a seat. Chinese, Malay and Indian stalls all do a roaring trade.

Another good collection of stalls has a pleasant location at The Esplanade, near the Padang and right on the seafront. It is chiefly Malay but there are Chinese stalls too. Around Chulia St are lots of stalls along the five-foot ways. In Tamil St is a series of Nasi kandar and roti stalls which are very popular. A good though raucous place is the Food Court in the Komtar Centre, which is very busy at all times of the day. There are some good Indian Muslim stalls here.

Yasmeen Restaurant $ 177 Jalan Penang. Tiled floor and walls and industrial-size fans. Biriyani, roti, murtabaks and fresh juice drinks.

Line Clear $ Junction of Penang Rd and Chulia St. Excellent 24 hr *nasi kandar* and roti stall.

Roti canai stall $ Argyll Rd. On the street in the shade of a tree. Excellent roti with choice of curries, mornings only.

FERRINGHI BEACH

Ferringhi also has its share of hawker places. **Long Beach** is a collection of inexpensive stalls that come alive in the evenings. There is an unnamed collection of stalls on the beach close to the cheaper accommodation, and all along the beach strip are open-air cafés **$$$–$$** doing western, seafood and Indian dishes. There are also some restaurants that combine good food and service with a comfortable and pleasant setting.

Sigi's by the Sea $$$$–$$$ Golden Sands Resort, tel: (04) 881-1911. Bistro which spills out onto hotel pool side. Familiar menu of Californian style dishes with some east–west fusion.

Il Ritrovo $$$$$ Casuarina Beach Resort, tel: (04) 881-1711. Dark, very Italian place with extensive classic Italian dishes. Live guitar combo serenades you as you eat.

Gion $$$$ Park Royal Beach Resort, tel: (04) 881-1133. In the Park Royal hotel. Sit at the teppanyaki bar to watch the chefs at work. Reasonably priced, good Japanese food.

The Ship $$$$** tel: (04) 881-2142. A life–size Portuguese galleon. Seafood and steaks in nautical setting, wine list. Open daily 1200–2400. Reservations often essential to avoid queuing. Set lunch **$$.

Popular Ferringi Motel $$$$–$$$ Just past The Ship, a road side restaurant serving seafood, steaks and Chinese meals in a sociable setting.

HIGHLIGHTS

A COLONIAL ERA WALK

This walk begins in the heart of colonial Penang, where the town's white rulers paraded their wealth on Sunday afternoons. It ends where they ended, in the city's Protestant graveyard.

The **Victoria Clock Tower** was built to commemorate the queen's Diamond Jubilee (1837–97), with each foot representing a year of her reign. Strangely, it wasn't erected by loyal colonialists, but by a Chinese tin millionaire, Cheah Chin Gok. Beside the clock tower are the remains of **Fort Cornwallis** (1808). Little is left but the remains of the Christian chapel and the storeroom. The ramparts of the fort are home to a series of cannons.

West of the fort is the **Padang**, where the city's elite played bowls and cricket and walked in the cool of the evening. **The Esplanade** was, and is, used for parades and festivals. On the night of the full moon during Chinese New Year young Peranakan girls would throw oranges into the sea in the hope of getting a good husband. Really it was an opportunity for them to be paraded in front of the young men in their community.

West again are the **Town Hall** (1880) and the **City Hall** (1903), both emblems of the grandiose Victorian confidence of the time. The Town Hall was an all-white social club with a ballroom and stage for theatrical productions.

Walk south away from the Town Hall along Lebuh Pitt (Jalan Masjid Kapitan Kling), past the **Court Buildings** (1905), another example of the grand colonial style, to **St George's Church** (1818), Malaysia's oldest Anglican church. In the grounds is a **memorial** to Francis Light, the man who arranged for the East India Company to take control of Penang, then a deserted jungle. The church is locked up most of the week and should be seen on Sundays when the shutters are opened. Today there is a full congregation made up of all races, rather than just the white people for whom it was built.

Next door to the church is the **Penang Museum and Art Gallery $** open Mon–Sun 0900–1700, closed 1215–1445, tel: (04) 261-3144. Formerly a school and recently renovated, it has good displays about the history of Penang's appealing multi culturalism. There are also exhibits about the East India Company and the Japanese occupation, although no mention of the ignoble evacuation by the British that they kept secret from the rest of the island's population.

Next door again is the **Cathedral of the Assumption**, named after the day that the first Eurasians arrived in Penang. The Eurasian community who once lived in bungalows here built the church in 1860. Opposite the cathedral is the **Convent of the Holy Infant Jesus**, a former girls' school and convent. In its grounds is the 1790 bungalow which Francis Light built for himself. Stamford Raffles is said to have worked in the bungalow after it became the offices of the East India Company.

Pass the grand old **E and O** hotel to the **Protestant cemetery** in Jalan Sultan Ahmad Shah. It is well worth a wander around to see the names of the early European pioneers. One of the graves marks the burial place of Thomas Leonowens, husband of Anna, who later became the inspiration for the movie *The King and I*. Oddly, its remake, *Anna and the King*, was filmed just a few streets away.

A Georgetown Walk

Lebuh Pasar, Penang, Queen and Chulia make up the area known as **Little India**. It is a vibrant, thriving area full of tiny shops, banana leaf restaurants and mamak stalls selling *roti canai* and *teh tarik*.

Start the walk in Jalan Masjid Kapitan Keling (also known as Lebuh Pitt). This road was designated by Light specifically for places of worship, and was to be known as the **Street of Harmony**. On the corner of Lebuh Farquhar is **St George's Church**.

Streets in Georgetown

When Francis Light first had the streets of Georgetown laid out, he designated certain areas for different ethnic groups. Chulia St was for the Indian community, Bishop St for the church of the Eurasian community, Lebuh China for the Chinese and Lebuh Pasar for the market. Lebuh Light was reserved for the officers and their families.

But by 1908 the British had moved to the suburbs, and these streets were given over to the 'natives'. Because of this the streets of Georgetown are probably the most intact and diverse record of 19th century colonial architecture in the world. They incorporate not only the British Raj at its most arrogant, but a corresponding history of the Chinese clans, Indian temple architecture and the styles of the other ethnic groups that settled in Penang.

A few blocks south at the junction with Lebuh China is the **Kuan Ying Teng temple** (1801), dedicated to the Goddess of Mercy and built by the Cantonese and the Hokkien. Its huge courtyard is always full of visitors, hawkers and beggars. During festivals, puppet shows and dances are held here. Opposite the temple is a newspaper office which was once a government storage depot for opium. The British made much of their revenue from the trade of this drug.

Further south is the **Sri Mahamariamman temple** (1833), with its modern entrance on Queen St. Outside in the street is usually a painted *kolam*. The *gopuram*, or entrance sculpture, consists of 38 statues of gods and goddesses and four swans.

Inside, a statue of Lord Subramaniam is encrusted with precious stones and gold and silver leaf. It is paraded through the town during the Thaipusam festival.

Parallel with Lebuh Queen is **Lebuh King**. A diversion down here will reveal amazing street architecture where almost every building is a clan house or temple of some sort, each with its own distinctive roof design.

Further south again on the corner of Lebuh Buckingham and Lebuh Pitt is the **Kapitan Kling mosque**, in the middle of the Indian Muslim community. The current building retains part of the 1905 Moghul structure but is largely a construct of the 1930s.

South along Lebuh Pitt at the junction with Lebuh Armenian is the **Yap Khongsi clan house and temple**, a modest, modern pair of buildings. Further along the street, which has now become Lebuh Cannon, is the alleyway entrance to **Cannon Square,** where the most elaborate city clan houses can be found. Founded in 1851 by immigrants from Xiamen in Fujian, China, the square consists of houses let by the Khoo clan to its members. At the time they were built there were great wars going on between the various clans, hence the very few, narrow entrances.

A Tip for the Top

There are great views from the observation level on the 58th floor of the Komtar Tower, but it costs RM5. Instead, take the lift to the 60th floor (not the same lift that accesses the 58th floor). Buy an ice cream or a drink at the restaurant serving Malay and western food and keep the receipt. Walk down two floors to the viewing level and flash your receipt for free admission.

Leaving Cannon Square head for Lebuh Aceh, the road originally designatd for Achinese Sumatrans. At the road junction is the **Acheen St Mosque**, built by a wealthy Arab merchant to serve the Achinese community, which settled here in 1808. Its minaret is Arab in style rather than Moghul, and the story goes that the round window halfway up was actually made by a cannonball during the Penang Riots of 1867.

Turning right brings you first to the former home of Dr Sun Yat Sen at No 120 and then to the **Syed Atlas Mansion** $ once the home of a wealthy pepper trader and now open to the public Mon–Sat 0900–1700. The street is also a centre for stoneworkers who you can see carving inside some of the shop-houses.

The Cheong Fatt Tze Mansion $ in Leith St was built by a 19th century Richard Branson called Cheong Fatt Tze. He left China a penniless young man and ended up as economic advisor to the Empress of China. Involved in shipping, banking and railways, he decided in the 1880s to build a mansion that would befit his status in life. The result is this house with 38 rooms, seven staircases and five courtyards in an amalgam of classic Chinese design, art nouveau and Victorian cast iron. The house crumbled for a few decades but is now open to the public Mon, Wed, Fri and Sat.

Wat Chayamangkalaram in Jalan Burma on the Ferringhi Beach road is a Thai temple, open early morning until 1730, dedicated to the reclining Buddha. In the complex is also a nine-storey pagoda. Opposite it is the **Dhammikarama Burmese Buddhist temple**, with an upright Buddha and a pagoda built in 1905. In the same street a third Buddhist temple, the **Penang Buddhist Association temple**, is very different to the first two, with lots of Italian marble and chandeliers.

SHORT EXCURSIONS

The **Nattukotai Chettiar temple** on Waterfall Rd is the biggest Hindu temple on the island. One stop further along on bus No 7 are the **Botanic Gardens**, open daily during daylight hours, an excellent afternoon's entertainment, especially if the macaques are in fighting mood.

A short bus ride west of Georgetown brings you to **Air Hitam**, supposedly the largest Buddhist temple in Malaysia. 20 years in the building, it has gardens, a turtle pond, lots of tourists as well as followers of the Lord Buddha and a pagoda with 10,000 Buddhas.

Nearby is the 1923 **Penang Hill** cable railway, open daily 0630–2115, 830 metres high and much cooler than the city. The railway is good fun and the hill has lots of foodstalls, walks and a Sarkies hotel, now a government building.

Not to be missed is the **Snake Temple**, dedicated to Chor Soo Kong, on the road to the airport. The temple itself is nothing special but the snakes inside it are. They are mostly harmless green tree snakes, but there are also Wagler's pit vipers, which you wouldn't want to step on accidentally. In the entrance are stalls selling 'I touched a pit viper' T-shirts and other objects.

Penang has many other attractions, including **fruit farms**, a **butterfly park** and **cultural centre** at Teluk Bahang, lots of beaches to explore if you have transport, and walks through the **Pantai Acher Forest Reserve**. Teluk Bahang itself is home to the fabulous **Mutiara Beach Resort**, lots of good cafés and several inexpensive home-stay places.

SHOPPING

Ferringhi is always worth a stroll at night when stalls line either side of the road and diplay their fake designer gear. Music CDs, watches, T-shirts, sunglasses, belts and jeans sit alongside items from Thailand, beautiful pieces of batik and dresses from India.

The **Komtar complex** has all the big names as well as local department stores. The top floor has a few Internet places. One of them, Lot B2, 4.02, has a better choice of computer software than the operators on the bottom floor.

A big new shopping centre, **Pragin Mall**, is due to open in 2001 just behind the Komtar building.

Chulia St, where little open-fronted shops sell clothes and some bric-a-brac, is worth a bit of window-shopping. There is a good second-hand **bookshop** on this street next to the Swiss Hotel.

FESTIVALS

Penang celebrates most of Malaysia's big festivals. **Thaipusam** is a Hindu festival usually held in February when penitents skewer themselves and carry huge metal frames embedded into their skin. **Chinese New Year** is big in Penang, with lion dances and cultural shows all over the island and displays by the *khongsis*. June sees the international **Dragon Boat Festival**. There is a **Lantern Festival** in September and in November is **Deepavali**, the Hindu festival of light.

NIGHTLIFE

Chulia St has a nice collection of bars and cafés which come alive at night. Opposite Cheong Fat Tze Mansion is the renovated row of shophouses called **Leith St** which is very fashionable at the moment. At Ferringhi beach there is the **Reggae Club**, open till 0300 nightly, with an emphasis on Bob Marley hits and a nice atmosphere. Several of the big hotels have good happy hour rates until late.

PENANG – LANGKAWI – ALOR SETAR – PENANG

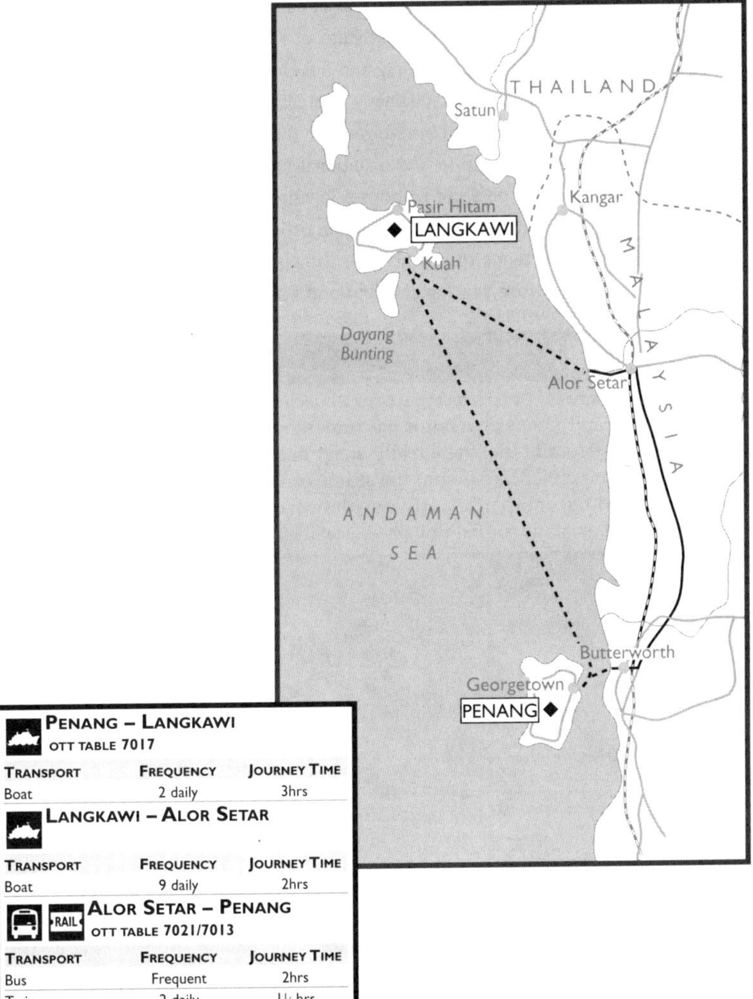

PENANG – LANGKAWI
OTT TABLE 7017

TRANSPORT	FREQUENCY	JOURNEY TIME
Boat	2 daily	3hrs

LANGKAWI – ALOR SETAR

TRANSPORT	FREQUENCY	JOURNEY TIME
Boat	9 daily	2hrs

ALOR SETAR – PENANG
RAIL
OTT TABLE 7021/7013

TRANSPORT	FREQUENCY	JOURNEY TIME
Bus	Frequent	2hrs
Train	2 daily	$1^1/_2$hrs

The two destinations in this route, the island of Langkawi and the town of Alor Setar, are what take visitors to the north-west state of Kedah. It is one of the most Malay and the most rural states in the country, and not the kind of place where tourists die of excitement. Alor Setar has a distinctly Thai flavour, reflecting the fact that this corner of Malaya was under Siam sovereignty for the most of the 19th century. British colonialism hardly got its nose in and traditional Malay culture was left undisturbed. Langkawi island produces different responses in visitors because some people enjoy its lazy appeal and low-octane atmosphere, while other, grow bored with the package-holiday syndrome that tends to characterise the place. It is a good place to relax but not a destination for those seeking activities and variety.

LANGKAWI

In theory, Langkawi is the perfect place for a beach holiday, with resorts, restaurants, places to visit and blue skies. But it has undergone such massive tourist development in the last decade that there really aren't many more sites for resorts, and the existing ones are either bursting at the seams or going under. Many of the people who run the tours, and particularly the Mafiosi cab drivers, seem intent only on getting hold of as many tourist dollars as possible.

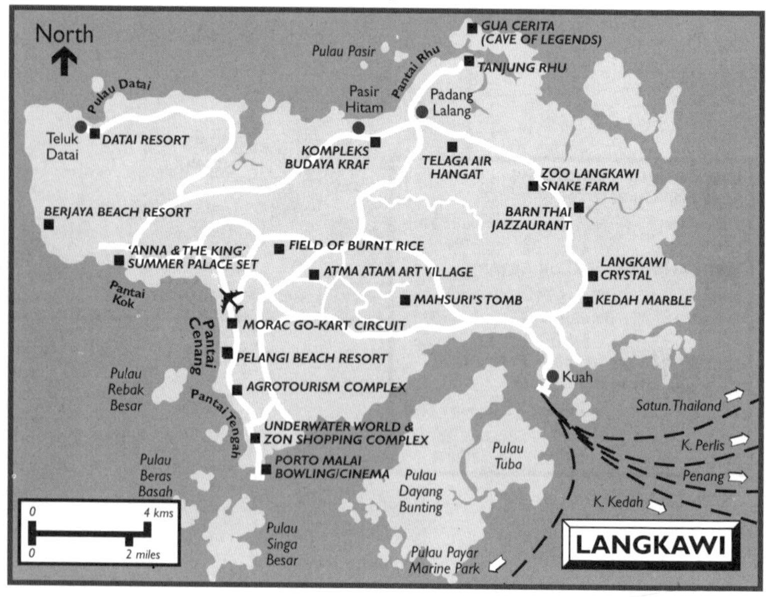

ARRIVAL AND DEPARTURE

Boat: Boats to Langkawi travel to and from Kuala Kedah west of Alor Setar at least nine times daily. An alternative route into Langkawi is via Kuala Perlis, further north on the mainland where there are more frequent boats. A daily ferry connects with Penang and there is a connection with Satun in Thailand. The ferry offices are all located at the ferry terminal. **Langkawi Ferry Services**, tel: (04) 966-6929, operate the Penang, Perlis and Kuala Kedah trips.

Air: Langkawi International Airport is 20 km from Kuah, about RM20 by taxi. There are daily connections with KL, Singapore, JB and Penang.

Car: Most beach resorts have cars for hire or they can be hired from one of the loud touts at Kuah. Rates should be around RM85 a day. There are places all over the island to hire mopeds or bicycles. The rate is around RM25 per day for a moped, RM12 for a bike. A taxi costs around RM50 for a couple of hours, which is all you need to 'do' all the sights.

i The **tourist office**, tel: (04) 966-7789, open daily 0900–1300, 1400–1700, is in Kuah, near the Al Hama mosque. All Government offices close on Fridays.

The only **banks** are at Kuah and at the beaches the only places to change money are the resorts where the rates will not be the best. Try to change what you need before you arrive.

There is an **Internet** shop at Cenang beach.

Langkawi is a **duty free zone** which means that you can buy very cheap beer as well as some more unusual items. You will see groups of Chinese people hauling giant cardboard boxes on to the ferries. These are Chinese herbal remedies and medicines which come under the duty free label.

HIGHLIGHTS

Go to Langkawi to lie on the beach, eat reasonable food and spend a day whipping round the island on a moped. Don't go to find out what life in Langkawi is like or experience Malaysia, because you won't.

The island has a few sights, some of them spectacular in ways that were never intended. The first is the jetty with its hysterical screaming touts and the nearby landscaped theme park, which boasts the biggest, ugliest fibreglass eagle you've ever seen.

Pantai Cenang is the most pleasantly relaxed part of the island, full of little cafés, shops, budget accommodation and obligatory big resorts. The white sand beach is huge and mostly underused, as most people sit around their hotel pools. But between November and January you can walk out to the island of Pulau Rebak Kecil from a sandbar which appears at low tide. Along the main drag at Pantai Cenang is **Underwater World**, a series of fish tanks and some gardens. Open daily 1000–1800, RM15.

MAHSURI

A few kilometres west of Kuah, the main town, is Mahsuri's tomb, the final resting place of a Malay princess unjustly accused by her mother-in-law of adultery. She was put to death by being buried up to her waist in sand and a kris knife shoved through her shoulder blades. White blood poured from her wound and in her dying breath she cursed the island so that it wouldn't prosper for the next seven generations. Some say this is why the island paradise has never been quite as profitable as the government hopes. The mausoleum has the regulation genuine Malay house on stilts beside it flogging artefacts.

At Kuala Muda, north of Pantai Cenang is **Aquabeat**, a swimming complex with wave machine. North again is **Pantai Kok**, a lovely white strip of beach dominated by resorts but with a few food stalls. **Telalga Tujuh**, a huge waterfall inland from Pantai Kok, is definitely worth hiring a moped for. At Padang Lalang a major road junction in the north of the island is Compleks Budaya Craf a very big **craft centre** and shop selling Malaysian crafts. No bargains though. There is a **cultural village** nearby at Air Hangat where there are nightly cultural shows with **hot springs** close by.

DAY TRIPS

Pulau Payar Marine Park makes an excellent day's outing. It consists of several small islands, all with crystal clear waters and vast numbers of very tame, colourful fish. Lots of tour groups organise trips to the marine park. **Langkawi Coral**, tel: (04) 966-7318, RM220, has a good tour to a platform anchored off the main island from where you can snorkel to the shore, take a trip in a glass-bottomed boat, view the fish from an underwater viewing platform, or take scuba diving lessons. The platform has a bar and lunch is included in the price. The main island has pleasant sandy beaches from where you can venture into the interior.

OTHER ACTIVITIES

The island is dotted with caves, many of which can be visited on a tour. There is also a mangrove swamp trip, which takes a boat out in the evening as the bats begin to emerge for the night. Other trips include an island tour and island hopping to the many smaller islands of Langkawi. Your hotel will gladly arrange any of these activities for you, or you can try a company like SALA Travel and Tours, tel: (04) 966-7521.

Tanjung Rhu Resort $$$$$ Mukim Ayer Hangat, tel: (04) 959-1033, fax: 959-1899. If you can afford it, this place is everything you ever wanted in a beach resort and it's well away from the tourist traps. All day beach café, Mediterranean restaurant and miles and miles of countryside.

Pelangi Beach Resort $$$$$ Pantai Cenang, tel: (04) 955-1001, fax: 955-1122. A huge spread of pretty wooden, two-storey chalets with golf cart transport.

Berjaya Langkawi Beach and Spa Resort $$$$ Pantai Kok, (04) 959-1888, wooden chalets. Very busy, nice beach and a health spa.

Langkawi Holiday Villa Beach Resort $$$$ Pantai Tengah, tel: (04) 955-1701, fax: 955-1504. Moderately priced, yet all the necessities of a resort. Bring your own tea and coffee. Accommodation in rooms, not chalets, but all overlook the sea.

Grand Beach Hotel $$$–$ Pantai Cenang, tel: (04) 955-1457. Beach front rooms with fan and bathroom are good value. Also more luxurious air-con rooms.

Since the vast majority of people on holiday here come as part of a package they tend to eat in their hotels. Most of the resorts have good but pricey restaurants.

Pelangi Beach Resort has a particularly good buffet dinner, but if they are busy you should make a reservation (see accommodation).

Pantai Cenang is the best source of good quality, inexpensive food.

Fat Mum's at the Pantai Tengah end of the built up strip of beach comes highly recommended.

Eagle's Nest in Pantai Cenang has tables in a sheltered garden. It serves basic Western style food with nice desserts. **Bon Ton** is a new restaurant with good food north of Pantai Cenang, set up by the people who opened the famous Bon Ton in Kuala Lumpur.

Along Pantai Cenang are small grocery stores where you can stock up on things for lunch or fresh fruit for breakfast. Kuah has several places to eat if you can bear the shouting. In the terminal itself is McDonald's and KFC as well as a very nice Indian Muslim place which serves roti until about 1100.

ALOR SETAR

There's no real reason to visit Alor Setar. It's a sleepy little town with a few interesting places. But it's pure northern Malaysia, utterly unused to tourists or even non-Malays, and it makes a change for locals to be rubbernecking at you rather than the other way round.

The town has several Thai temples and a padang, where there are some interesting buildings including the Muzium de Raja, once the **royal palace**. Open daily 1000–1800, it is full of regalia and photos of the sultan with important people. Also here is the **Balai Seni Negeri**, in another old colonial building. It contains some interesting local painters' work and is open during the same hours. Also on the square is the **state mosque**, all domes and spires and epic outlooks.

Two kilometres north of the town centre is the **National Museum** which contains the royal barges used in ceremonial occasions, plus lots of archaeological material found around Alor Setar. There is also a museum dedicated to Dr Mahathir, in his one-time family home at 18 Lorong Kilang.

ARRIVAL AND DEPARTURE

Bus: From the bus station in Jalan Langgar buses leave half hourly to local destinations including Kuala Kedah and to Butterworth.

For towns to the north and the Thai border buses leave from a different bus station on Jalan Sultan Badlishah.

Long-distance internal buses leave from a third bus station in Jalan Mergong, north of the town centre. From here there are buses to Melaka, KL, Johor Bahru and the east coast.

Train: More fun and less fuss is the KTM line from Singapore to Thailand with stops at Butterworth, Padang Besar (for Thai immigration), Hat Yai, Surat Thani (for Ko Samui) and Bangkok. Train timetables tend to change so collect a current timetable in KL. For information tel: (04) 733-1798.

Hotel Grand Continental $$$ 134, Jalan Sultan Bandishah, tel: (04) 733-5917, is very central.

Hotel Grand Crystal $$$ 40 Jalan Kampung Perak, tel: (04) 731-3333, has a pool.

Hotel Seri Malaysia $$$ Lot 005127, Mukim Alor Malai, Jalan Stadium, tel: (04) 730-8737, fax: 730-7594, is a little out of town. Big rooms with a public pool next door and a coffee shop with a very Malay buffet breakfast.

There is a KFC opposite Hotel Seri Malaysia and several sleepy but functioning Indian Muslim places in Jalan Tunku Ibrahim and Jalan Badlishah. Beyond the Thai temple is an outdoor nameless café and some food stalls which are usually crowded. Hai Choo on Jalan Tunku Yaakub must be doing something right, as it's been around for over 100 years.

Kota Bharu – Johor Bahru

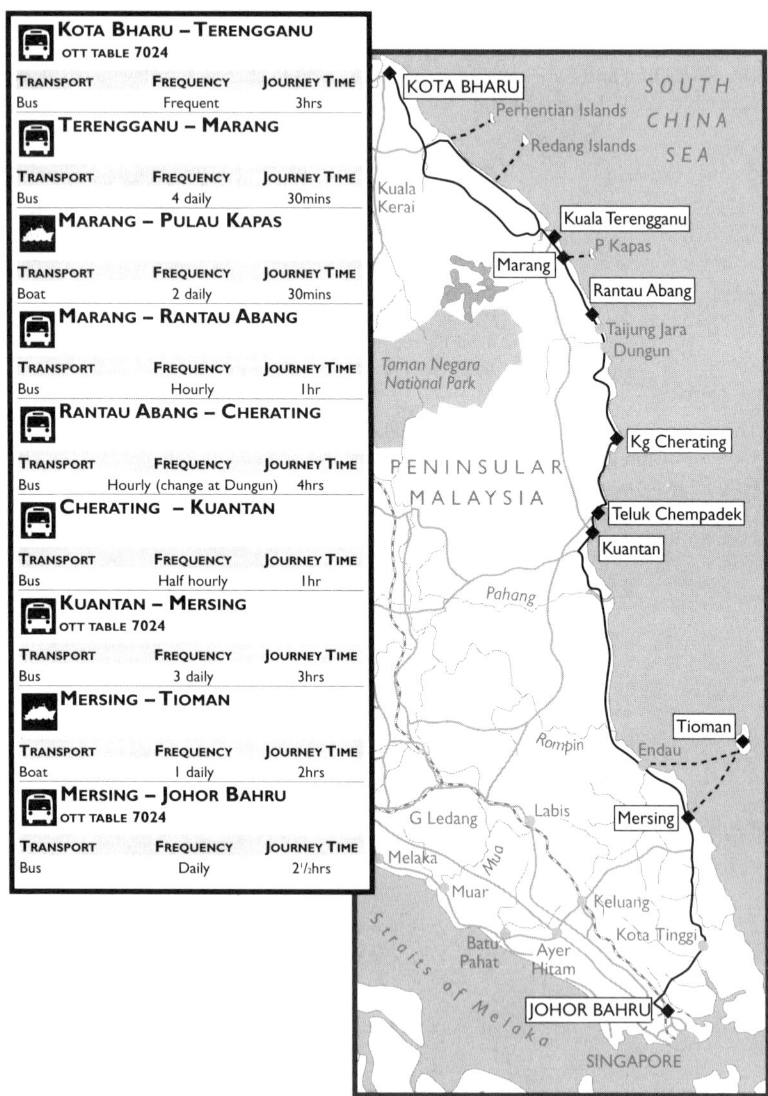

Kota Bharu – Terengganu
OTT TABLE 7024

Transport	Frequency	Journey Time
Bus	Frequent	3hrs

Terengganu – Marang

Transport	Frequency	Journey Time
Bus	4 daily	30mins

Marang – Pulau Kapas

Transport	Frequency	Journey Time
Boat	2 daily	30mins

Marang – Rantau Abang

Transport	Frequency	Journey Time
Bus	Hourly	1hr

Rantau Abang – Cherating

Transport	Frequency	Journey Time
Bus	Hourly (change at Dungun)	4hrs

Cherating – Kuantan

Transport	Frequency	Journey Time
Bus	Half hourly	1hr

Kuantan – Mersing
OTT TABLE 7024

Transport	Frequency	Journey Time
Bus	3 daily	3hrs

Mersing – Tioman

Transport	Frequency	Journey Time
Boat	1 daily	2hrs

Mersing – Johor Bahru
OTT TABLE 7024

Transport	Frequency	Journey Time
Bus	Daily	2½hrs

This route along the east coast of peninsular Malaysia is a fine introduction to the country's attractions. There are magnificent beaches and delightful fishing villages where the pace of life has slowed down to an imperceptible crawl. This is not a route to travel in a hurry and only by adjusting to the local tempo will some of the magic begin to rub off. Four states share the coastline – Kelantan, Terengganu, Pahang and Johor – and our favourite is Terengganu. Historically, it was cut off from the rest of the peninsula because Europeans found little of economic value there, and so never built roads into the state. Ethnically, it is overwhelmingly Malay in tone and character. Some of the best beaches in south-east Asia are to be found here, especially a short way off-shore on the Perhentian islands, where white-sand beaches and snorkelling possibilities draw in a constant stream of discerning travellers.

ROUTE DETAIL

Highway 3 runs the entire route from Kota Bharu to Johor Bahru (550km). For the most part it is a single carriageway road with no overtaking lane, passing through each town rather than bypassing them. In the north it is scenic as it closely follows the coast, offering lots of opportunities for stops.

KOTA BHARU

MAP – inside back cover

Probably the most foreign place you will visit in Malaysia, KB has a distinctly different atmosphere from the south of the country. Part Wild West frontier town and part electronic superhighway, KB is still sleeping under a durian tree yet at the same time charged with excitement about the future.

The town sits in the valley of the Kelantan River and is still relatively undeveloped. It is dominated by its rural surroundings, with rice its biggest export. Although the women are all covered, they wear shockingly gaudy clothes in fine silks, often with long slits in the skirts and bright makeup. If the sexes have to keep apart for fear of an unholy thought entering men's heads there is enough flirting going on to keep the air seriously charged. Islam and Malay culture are a strange mix, and they are at their strangest in this interesting little town.

ARRIVAL AND DEPARTURE

Bus: KB has three long-distance bus stations: beside the night market, on Jalan Pasir Puteh and on Jalan Hamzah. The main bus company is SKMK and most of its routes begin at the central bus station. Other companies operate out of Langgar or Hamzah. Buy tickets in advance and ask where the bus departs from.

SKMK has a ticket office at the central bus station and is easier to deal with. It runs buses to and from Butterworth (8 hrs), Penang (about 8 hrs), Melaka, and most towns on the route southwards, as well as KL (10 hrs) and Singapore (12 hrs).

Air: Malaysia Airways operate direct flights to KL from where there are connections to international destinations. The airport is 8 km north–west of town. A taxi costs about RM15, or bus No 9 leaves from the old central market.

Train: The KTM jungle railway connects Wakaf Bharu, a few km outside KB with Kuala Lumpur, Kuala Lipis, Jerantut, Gemas and Singapore. There are evening trains which connect with KL and Singapore, arriving at their final destinations in the early morning. Both have the advantage of allowing you to sleep through a very long journey, but the disadvantage that you miss most of the amazing jungle scenery that you travel through. All day–time journeys are slow and tedious, stopping at local stations and involving changing trains.

AN ISLAMIC STATE

Like its southern neighbour, Terengganu, KB's state government is dominated by the Islamic Party which seeks to introduce the Shariah or Islamic law. Penalties include dismemberment for 'crimes' such as intoxication, extra-marital sexual intercourse and theft.

As about a third of the population of the state is non-Muslim this has caused considerable discord with the federal government which seeks to practise a liberal, tolerant Islamic regime. In terms of the affect it might have on visitors it doesn't add up to much – separate counters at supermarket for men and women which are universally ignored, a ban on alcohol in state-run hotels and a general disapproval of foreign women travelling alone and uncovered.

Rather more serious is the belief among some men in KB that all western women are available, otherwise their menfolk would have them stored safely away somewhere. Muslim women are expected to, and for the most part do, wear the *baju kurung* traditional Malay dress, as well as a headscarf, and the state is seeking to enforce the wearing of a headscarf for all female state employees. During Ramadan things get a bit stickier. Party officials go into cafés and any Muslims found eating or drinking there are publicly shamed.

HIGHLIGHTS The Padang Merdeka was once the town's marketplace, where in 1915 the British government displayed the body of Tok Janggut, a local elder who had led a failed rebellion against British land taxes. Around the outskirts of the padang are several museums, all worth a quick glance.

HANDICRAFTS

Because of its cultural associations with Thailand, Kelantan has some craft skills more naturally associated with that country. There is a tradition of woodcarving which can be seen in the two *istanas* and in the new handicraft village. Wooden buildings are highly decorated with fretwork, and craft items such as wooden frames and furniture find their way into tourist shops all over the country.

Silver work is another skill inherited from the north. Fine filigree jewellery is common and more cumbersome epoussé items abound. Silver workshops can be visited in Jalan Sultan Zainab or at Kampung Badang on the way to PCB Beach. Along the same road are *songket* weaving work–shops, where silver and gold thread is worked into ceremonial cloth, and many batik factories, often in someone's backyard, where you can watch the entire process of mass producing intricate patterns using wax. There are bigger factories at Kampung Puteh and Kubor Kuda.

The **World War II Museum** $ is housed in the town's oldest brick building, the former Mercantile Bank. During the Japanese occupation it became their headquarters and today houses old photos, weapons and a bicycle which may have been used in the so–called bicycle invasion. Open Sat–Thurs, 0830–1645.

Next door is the **Muzium Islam**, showing a collection of Islamic art and its influence on everyday life in the state. Open Sat–Thurs, 0830–1645, free. The **Istana Jahar** was once the sultan's palace. Its exterior is almost as beautiful as the royal artefacts inside. Open Sat–Thurs, 0830–1645, free.

DRUMMING

While you are in KB you may see an exhibition of the giant drums which are a traditional form of communication between *kampungs* isolated by dense jungle and rivers. Nowadays it is quite a spectacle. The drums, called *rebana*, are made from hollowed out logs, 60 cm in diameter and covered in a taut buffalo hide. In July there is a drum festival when teams of drummers compete. There is one of these drums in the lobby of the Perdana hotel.

Next is the bright blue **Istana Batu**, another, later royal palace, this time containing royal possessions, clothes, replicas of the crown jewels, furniture and old photos. Open Sat–Thurs 0830–1645, free. Behind is the **Balai Getam Guri**, or handicraft village. It is beautifully built, showing that the skills used to build the two previous palaces are still alive in Kelantan, but unless you visit on a busy day you may be disappointed. On quiet

WATS

Wat Phothivihan at Kampung Berak, 12 km east of KB, is a relatively new (1973) Buddhist temple with a huge reclining Buddha statue. It is inaccessible without your own transport. Others are less impressive but more accessible. **Wat Kok Seraya** and **Wat Phikulthong** are north of KB at Chabang Empat and can be reached by bus Nos 27 and 19. All are interesting for the simple fact that such temples should even exist in this Muslim dominated state.

days, instead of people actually making the handicrafts and displaying their uses in the village, the place is deserted. Open daily Sat–Thurs, 0830–1645, free.

The **Cultural Centre** in Jalan Mahmud, opposite the Perdana Hotel, has displays of drumming, top spinning, cultural dances and shadow puppetry on most days. Collect a schedule from the tourist office.

Pantai Cahaya Bulan, or Pantai Cinta Berahi as it was known in pre-Islamic times, is the most easily accessible and popular of KB's beaches. The original name meant the beach of passionate love, which is why the government wanted to change it. En route are any number of silversmiths and batik factories.

The beach itself is a fine, vast sandy strip with Malay fishing villages dotted along it and lots of places to eat including the Perdana Resort with a very reasonable café. **Pantai Irama** is 25 km south of KB but is reputed to be the most beautiful beach in the state. It is backed by landscaped gardens; bus 2A or 2B. **Pantai Seri Tujuh**, 7 km north of KB, is the site of the annual kite–flying festival.

TOURS AND TRIPS

Lots of people stay much longer in KB than they intended because there are so many activities to be organised from here. Several tour companies offer homestay packages where you live with a local family in a *kampung* and watch handicrafts being made. There are good trips up the Sungei Kelantan to the rainforest and to Dabong village upstream, as well as trips to the many waterfalls which grace the mountains close to KB.

Sampugita Holidays Lot 1 Perdana Hotel, tel: (09) 748-2178, fax: 748-5000, organises tours of the countryside around Tumpat to the *wats* and batik factories, river trips and visits to boatmaking and woodcarving centres. **Hedaco** Lot 3 Hotel Perdana, tel: (09) 746-2178, runs similar tours, as well as homestay packages which include cooking lessons and craft work.

i The **tourist information office** is in Jalan Sultan Ibrahim, beside the State Museum, tel: (09) 748-5534, open Sun–Thurs 0800–1245 and 1400–1630.

E-mail is available in McDonald's and at KB Backpackers' Lodge, 2 Jalan Padang Garong.

Perdana Hotel $$$$ Jalan Mahmood, tel: (09) 748-5000, fax: 744-7621. Quiet, pleasant place with well-equipped rooms, good coffee shop, restaurant, swimming pool, but alcohol free.
Perdana Resort $$$$ Jalan Kuda Pa' Amat, PCB, tel: (09) 774-4000, fax: 774-4980. A pleasant alternative to staying in town, this place has a pool, fishing pond, horses and lots of other activities. Accommodation in spacious chalets. Fills up at weekends and school holidays but ask for a big discount during the week.
Safar Inn $$$ Jalan Hilir Kota, tel: (09) 747-8000, fax: 747-9000. Close to the padang, a small quiet place with good value rooms.
Kencana $$ Jalan Doktor, tel: (09) 744-0944 Jalan Padang Garong, tel: (09) 744-7944, Jalan Sri Cemerlang, tel: (09) 747-7222. Three branches of the same hotel. Basic but good value, TV, en suite bathrooms, air-con and breakfast included.
KB Backpackers' Lodge $ 2981F Tkt 2 Jalan Padang Garong, tel: (09) 743-2125. Dorms and private rooms, kitchen, rooftop garden, and Internet access. It also organises tours and bus tickets.
Menora Guest House $ Jalan Sultan Zainab, tel: (09) 748-1669. Rooftop terrace and air-con.

BAZAAR BULU KUBU

A good place to wander around and buy batik, this three-storey market is full of drapery stores, jewellers and stalls selling other basic items. Once you have seen what you want, start bargaining by offering half the price asked and work upwards.

The most exciting place to eat is the night market where there are lots of Malay foodstalls selling *nasi kerabu* (rice with coconut sauce) and *ayam percik* (barbequed chicken marinated in coconut milk and spices). There are also some roti stalls here, and several curry places.
Meena Curry House $ in Jalan Gaja Mati serves *daun pisang* meals in a dilapidated setting.
Razak and Hamid's are two *daun pisang* and roti places close to the market. Razak's is the more organised of the two. At the west end of the padang by the river are a series of attractive places selling Malay food, some with pleasant seating beside the river. There are foodstalls in the old market and beside the stadium in Jalan Mahmood. On Sunday morning a whole series of Chinese coffee houses come alive along Jalan Kebun Sultan.

ISLAND TRIPS

Off the coast between KB and Terengganu are three popular islands with resorts, opportunities for snorkelling and golden beaches. All of them are more easily accessed from Kuala Terengganu because of bus services and because the infrastructure for packages is better there. It is possible, however, to get tour companies in KB to organise the trips. (See tour groups on page 320).

TERENGGANU

MAP – inside back cover

Sitting on a little promontory jutting out into the South China Sea and bordered to the west by the Sungei, Terengganu has grown in the last decade from sleepy fishing village into a city. It has fewer sights than KB and fewer ethnic minorities to balance out the strong Islamic tendencies of the north, but it is friendlier, the old part of town is less frenetic and it too has good nightmarkets and some excellent places to shop for local crafts.

HIGHLIGHTS The **central market** is the liveliest place, especially in the early morning when fishing boats deliver their catch at the jetties just behind the market. Downstairs the market sells fresh food while upstairs is a good source of craft items.

South of the market is **Chinatown**, full of little shops selling strange things, and a very brightly coloured **Chinese temple**. Near to the central market is **Bukit Puteri**, a hill with fine views of the city and some ancient remains.

From the jetty opposite the tourist office you can get a boat to **Pulau Duyung**, where you can still see boatbuilders making the traditional shaped local fishing boats. The ferry $ goes whenever it has enough passengers. On the way out of town is **Pantai Batu Buruk**, the city's beach, dominated by the Park Royal Hotel but with a good promenade and excellent foodstalls nearby. Under reconstruction in 2000, there will soon be a huge new cultural centre along here with cultural shows. Ask at the tourist office for details.

The **State Museum $** is a few kilometres south west of the city at Losong, accessible by minibus No 6 from the central bus station. The museum is housed in the old sultan's palace and has displays of local craftwork, kris knives and a boat museum. Open daily 1000–1800.

Seven kilometres south of town at Cendering is **Kraftangan Malaysia**, a craft centre with beautiful crafts on display and for sale. Open Sat–Thur 0830–1700, free. Next door is **Nor Arfa** batik factory where you can watch batik being made and buy some as well. Also nearby is **Sutera Semai** silk factory where you can watch the entire process of silk production.

The **tourist office** is on Jalan Sultan Zainal Abidin, tel: (09) 622-1553, open Sat–Thurs 0900–1600
There are no moneychangers in Kuala Terengganu so money can only be exchanged at **banks**.
There is an **Internet** shop at 46, Jalan Masjid.

Permai Park Inn $$$$ Jalan Sultan Mahmud, tel: (09) 622-2122, fax: 622-2121. Modern hotel with pool and fitness centre and an excellent, popular coffee shop. Rates include Malay breakfast. Out of town on road to Marang, but free minibus into town.
Hotel Seri Malaysia $$$ Lot 1640, Jalan Hiliran, tel: (09) 623-6454, fax 623-8344. Very central and good value rooms.
Hotel Sri Hoover $$ 49, Jalan Sultan Ismail, tel: (09) 623-3833, fax: 622-5975. Very good value and very central.
Ping Anchorage $ 77A Jalan Dato Isaac, tel: (09) 622-0851. Rooms with fan and bathrooms, rooftop restaurant, bar (with alcohol), café and excellent tour agent on premises.

Café in the Park at the Park Inn has an excellent buffet dinner of local specialities every night, as well as good lunch offers and a pizza delivery service: tel: (09) 622-2122 ext 611.
Along the beach front at **Pantai Batu Buruk** are lots of foodstalls which get going in the evening, as well as fast food places.
In **Jalan Air Jernih** are two or three reasonable *daun pisang* places. **Restoran Kari Asha** is particularly good and very popular. Along **Jalan Sultan Ismail** are more foodstalls in quite pleasant surroundings. Opening at the end of 2000 is a new shopping complex in **Jalan Dato Isaac** which promises more fast food.

SHOPPING The central market is a good source of crafts, as are the places at Cendering. In Jalan Sultan Ismail is a good state run craft shop with fixed prices. **Teratai** in Jalan Bandar is an excellent little craft shop selling lots of unusual things, not all of them from Malaysia but worth a look.

TOURS Several agencies organise trips into the interior and to the offshore islands. **Nawar Travel and Tours**, Hotel Grand Continental, tel: (09) 624-7449, fax: 624-7349, organises tours to Kapas island, Sekayu Waterfall, Kenyir Lake, Tenggol, Redang and Lang Tengah islands, as well as local tours of the city and handicraft places.

Ping Anchorage (see accommodation) has the largest range of trips, and at very competitive prices, including jungle trekking, the islands, river trips, turtle watching and more. Most tour agencies will know which island resorts have vacancies and can get better prices than the walk-in rates. In addition, transport and food, which can be difficult for an independent traveller, will be part of the tour.

THE PERHENTIANS The easiest way to make a trip to the Perhentians is with one of the tour agencies. There are resort offices in Jalan Bandar in Kuala Terengganu but each one deals only with its own resort. The resorts are pretty much fully booked weeks in advance between February and November, particularly at weekends, and are closed the rest of the year. Any vacancies are held by the agencies, particularly Ping Anchorage.

Both islands are still the cleanest, most beautiful and most unspoilt in Malaysia, and the effort of making the trip is well worth it. The larger island, **Perhentian Besar**, has accommodation of around 16 resorts and collections of chalets on the west side. The biggest and most luxurious is the **Perhentian Resort** $$$, tel: (09) 691-0946 for the resort office in Kuala Besut, while the cheaper places have beach chalets for around RM25 for a

PULAU REDANG

Redang is part of a marine park consisting of nine islands with white sandy beaches and wonderful opportunities for snorkelling. It is easier to go there with a tour company than on your own since most places are fully booked and there is little in the way of food outside the resorts. An agency will also get you a better rate and be able to find available rooms.

In most places a twin air-con room with meals, return transfer to the island and snorkelling trips is about RM280 per person. Boats to Redang are operated by the biggest resort, Berjaya, and will only take independent travellers if there is room. They leave from Merang and there are daily buses from Kuala Terengganu. Taxis cost about RM10. Close by is Pulau Lang Tengah which has two resorts, both quite expensive, and again a package is far easier and possibly cheaper than just turning up.

chalet with a fan and shared bathroom. Most places have their own restaurants and there are a few foodstalls and cafés. Camping is possible on the beaches.

The smaller island, **Kecil**, has much more basic accommodation, chalets with primitive bathrooms and mosquito nets, and it is possible to go to the island without accommodation and find some there. Ferries run to the two main beaches and it is possible to walk between them. There are some cafés and a shop, and you can rent snorkelling equipment and boats to explore the coastline.

Impiana Beach Resort $$$, on the south coast (no phone), has air-con chalets. Both speedboats and slower boats depart regularly from Kuala Besut for various destinations on both islands. If you have booked a chalet you must make sure you are being taken to the right place. From Kota Bharu buses go to Jerteh on the main road, from where you can get another bus or taxi to Kuala Besut.

MARANG

Once a laid–back little backpackers' haven, Marang is now a suburb of the city. It succumbed badly to developers who knocked down the old wooden houses and built a concrete precinct, but it still has some advantages as an alternative to Kuala Terengganu. It has some good beaches and in the evenings fishing boats bring in their catches. It is also the stepping–off point for Pulau Kapas, a pretty island well worth a day trip or a few nights' stay.

ARRIVAL AND DEPARTURE

Long–distance buses stop on the main road at several different places, so you must ask at your hotel or when you buy your ticket where to wait. For Rantau Abang take the Dungun bus.

Hotel Seri Malaysia $$ Lot 3964, Kampung Paya, tel: (09) 618-2889, fax: 618-1285. Outside the main village and facing the sea, this place has excellent value rooms and frequent special offers.

Marang Guesthouse $$–$, tel: (09) 618-1976. Well organised with a good restaurant with Western and Malay food. Sea views and island and river trips offered.

Anggulia Beach House Resort $$ Km 20, Kampong Rhu Muda, tel: (09) 618-1322. Right on the beach with a good if expensive restaurant.

This place is popular with Singaporean weekenders, so there are a whole series of seafood places up on the main road. There are also some foodstalls along the waterfront near the jetty.

RANTAU ABANG This is in the centre of a long strip of sandy beaches, good for a stop at any time but especially popular in August, the turtle egg–laying season. There is little to do here – a trip into busy, noisy Dungun is about the most exciting things get – but the water is clear and the beach is clean. The **Turtle Information Centre**, 13th mile, Jalan Dungun, tel: (09) 84-1533, is right on the beach and full of information about the four types of turtles that lay their eggs here.

PULAU KAPAS

Only 6 km offshore, this is still a pretty unspoiled island with fine sandy beaches. It is good for a day trip as long as you avoid the school holidays and weekends, and there is accommodation on the island if you want to stay. Rooms or chalets cost about RM50 for a fan and attached bathroom. Speedboats to the island depart at 0800 and 0900 and charge RM25 return. You must arrange when to be picked up for the return journey.

LEATHERBACK TURTLES *Dermochelys coriacea*, the giant leatherback turtle, lays its eggs in five known places in the world, and one of them is the beach at Rantau Abang. The turtles are 3 metre long, 350 kg monsters that live deep in the Pacific Ocean all their lives except when the females struggle their way ashore to lay their eggs. The males' only contact with land is when they hatch out of their eggs.

Although these turtles have a family tree dating back 150 million years, there are now thought to be only about 60,000 females left in the world, and the Rantau Abang sightings are about 5% of what they were 30 years ago. They live on a diet of jellyfish and spend most of their day seeking out their own bodyweight of them. The females probably come ashore to the place where they hatched, and are thought to navigate their way around the oceans by means of magnetite in their brain.

A female lays about 150 eggs each time she comes ashore and lays about nine batches each season. Of those, about two-thirds hatch out and face the challenge of the rush down to the sea and the shallows where they can be picked off by gulls or other predators. Their worst enemy is man who dumps plastic and rubbish into the sea or traps them in nets. Their shells are used for decoration and their flesh is a delicacy in many cultures.

Awang's $$–$, tel: (09) 844-3500. Beside the Turtle Information Centre. Guides here will wake you up to take you to where a turtle has been spotted.
Ismail Beach Resort $$–$, tel: (09) 983-6202. Next door and similar in style to Awang's.
Dahimah's $$$–$, tel: (09) 845-2843. 1 km south of the centre, signposted from the road. Restaurant.
Merantau Inn $$–$, tel: (09) 844-1131. 3.5 km north of the turtle centre, restaurant, big rooms, close to village of Kuala Abang.

Most of the accommodation has restaurants and there are stalls near to the bus stop and in Plaza R&R.

CHERATING

Another of the east coast's sleepy villages, Cherating is tolerant and laid–back. It has also given way to developers, but if the big resorts have moved in and fenced off their land there are still quiet places to hang out, practise batik making and just enjoy the beach. There are two good travel agents in the village and you can make lots of the inland trips from here as easily as from Kuantan. Alcohol flows freely and there are fewer stares for bare–shouldered foreign women than in the north. The really big resorts are a couple of km south of the old village and don't really have much connection with the village atmosphere, but they are good places to stay.

ARRIVAL AND DEPARTURE

Local buses stop along the main road at designated bus stops and basically wherever someone hails them. Buses run every half-hour between Kemmamam north of Cherating and Kuantan to the south. They are not air-conditioned and the journey is a slow one, stopping every few minutes. Long–distance buses can be booked at the two travel agents in the village, and you must arrange when and where they will stop for you on the main road because there is no designated stop at Cherating. They can arrange direct buses to the Thai border, Kota Bharu, Jerteh, Terengganu, Marang and Rantau Abang.

HIGHLIGHTS

Activities include batik printing classes, exhibitions of martial arts, top spinning, kite flying and trips up the **Cherating River**. You can also watch trained monkeys collecting coconuts and small turtles which come ashore here to lay their eggs. The **Cherating Cultural Village** puts on shows in the restaurant with traditional musicians and dancers.

Two travel agents in the village will book onward journeys, local and more distant trips and change cash and travellers' cheques, but at a poor rate.

Badger Lines, tel: (09) 581-9552, is in the centre of the village and **Travel Post**, tel: (09) 581-9825 is opposite the Rhana Pippin. Both offer **tourist information**, **Internet** service, car rental, international calls, poste restante and more, including trips to local night markets, Pulau Ular, upriver, Lake Cini, and the Chara Caves.

The Legend Resort $$$$ Lot 1290, Mukim Sg, Karang, tel: (09) 581-9818, fax: 581-9400. Big sprawling resort, two pools, right on the beach, two good restaurants, lovely big rooms with sea views, some chalets on the beach. A public bus runs half–hourly to the village or a cab is RM20.

Residence Inn Cherating $$$$ Lot 826–Mukim Sg Karang, tel: (09) 581-9333, fax: 581-9252. Big resort on village outskirts, restaurant and café, architecturally interesting, special offers, but away from the beach. Rates go up at weekends.

Rhana Pippin $$$ right on beach in centre of the village. Café, organised river trips and water sports.

Cherating Cottage $$–$ tel: (09) 581-9273, opposite Matahari's. Wooden chalets on a well–maintained site, nice café, rooms with bathroom, TV and hot water.

Green Leaves Inn $ tel: (09) 337-8242, beside river in quiet location, very basic accommodation in mangroves.

Matahari Chalets $ no phone. On road in from the highway, close to the river. Pleasant garden setting, nicely spaced chalets and a longhouse, kitchen and TV room.

There are lots of places to eat in Cherating, all offering variations of Chinese seafood and some western dishes.

Blue Lagoon $$ is a typical neon–lit roadside place with a long menu which includes quail, squid and stingray.

The Dragon Seafood Restaurant $$$$–$$ is another simple roadside place at the crossroads in the village, with a vast seafood menu.

Mimi's $$ close to the Rhana Pippin does good inexpensive Indian food. The café at the Rhana Pippin also has a good reputation for western dishes.

NIGHTLIFE Unusually in this part of the world, Cherating has a good, active nightlife.

La Blues Bar is very popular, situated right on the beach and getting going at about midnight.

Pop Inn is close to La Blues Bar, so if you get bored of one place you can try the other.

The Moon at the chalet resort of the same name close to the main road is also good.

TOP SPINNING

Gasing, or top spinning, is a sport practised seriously by adults in Malaysia. There are two kinds of games. In one, the person who can make a top spin the longest is the winner. The wooden tops, made from *merbau* wood, can weigh up to 5 kg, be spun by a 5 metre rope and spin for as long as two hours. The other game is a little like conkers where one person sets a top spinning and the other tries to knock it over.

KUANTAN

The end of the huge 300 km long beach strip, Kuantan and its suburb Chempadek, are good places to stop for a day or two after days of beach and island. Kuantan is a busy Malaysian town with a population of about 100,000, relatively liberal, with predominantly Chinese and Indian communities.

ARRIVAL AND DEPARTURE

Bus: The long–distance bus station is in Jalan Stadium. Buses leave from here for most larger towns in Malaysia. The ticket offices are all two floors above street level where you can wander around choosing the best time and price for you. KL is 5 hrs and buses leave hourly, Mersing is 3 hrs and buses leave twice a day, JB is 5 hrs and Singapore 7 hrs.

The local bus station for buses to Cherating is beside the river. Look on the front of the bus for its destination and pay once on board. Buses to Teluk Chempadek, Jalan Besar, the Mosque and the long–distance bus station. Look for Buses 39A and 39B.

Air: Sultan Ahmen Shah Airport is 20 km south of Kuantan. Malaysian Airways flies direct to KL and Singapore. The MAS office is in Wisma Bolasepak Pahang, Jalan Gambut, tel: (09) 515-7055.

HIGHLIGHTS

The river in town is a good place for a stroll and the **mosque**, in the centre of town near the padang, is quite a sight - modern, airy and marbled. The main tourist focus is **Chempadek Beach** where there is a good sandy beach, rocks to clamber over, lots of good foodstalls and a Vietnamese refugee boat made into a beach bar.

EXCURSIONS

Tasek Cini is a series of freshwater lakes in the heart of the rainforest. The area is inhabited by Orang Asli people called Jakun who live in simple *kampungs* and believe, or so they say, that a serpent inhabits the lakes. The area is good for fishing, walks in the jungle and wildlife spotting. The lake is covered in lotus flowers between June and September. It is almost impossible to do this trip without going through a tour agent who can arrange overnight stays, river trips, trekking etc. Try **Malaysian Overland Adventures**, tel: (03) 241-3569, or **East Coast Holidays**, 33 Teluk Chempadek, tel: (03) 510-5228.

Gua Charas (Charas caves) $ is 26 km north of Kuantan at Panching, a limestone outcrop sitting in a palm plantation. Inside is a reclining Buddha carved out of the cave wall, as well as lots of shrines and other statues. The cave system goes on beyond the main lit caves and you can explore if you have a torch. Again a tour is the easiest option but it is possible to get there by bus No 48 to Panching and a 4 km walk or hitch–hike to the caves.

i The **tourist office** is in Jalan Mahkota, opposite the Kompleks Terantum, tel: (09) 513-3026.
A good place to change **money** and travellers' cheques is Hamid Bros, 71 Jalan Mahkota, marked on some maps as Jalan Abdul Aziz. The **post office** is further east along the same street.
There is an **Internet** shop, Network 21, two floors up from street level in the Berjaya Megamall in Jalan Tun Ismail.

Hyatt Regency $$$$ Teluk Chempadek, tel: (09) 566-1234, fax: 567-7577, e-mail: hyatt_kuantan@hrktn.com.my Two pools, beach bar made from an old Vietnamese refugee boat, water sports, fine rooms with garden or sea view, tennis, health centre, popular coffee shop on beach which fills up for Sunday buffet lunch, Chinese restaurant.
Hotel Grand Continental $$$$ Jalan Gambut, tel: (09) 515-8888, fax: 515-9999. A good, newish city hotel close to the Megamall with pool, Chinese restaurant and coffee shop.
Shazan $$$–$$ 240 Jalan Bukit Ubi, tel: (09) 513-6688, Fax 513-5588. Another new hotel close to the mosque, overlooking the padang, all mod cons, coffee shop.
Megaview $$ Lot 567, Jalan Besar, tel: (09) 555-1888, fax: 555-3999. Very new, right beside the river with excellent views, nice rooms, coffee shop. Rate includes breakfast.
Hotel Classic $$ 7, Bangunan LKNP, Jalan Besar, tel: (09) 555-4599, fax: 513-4141. Big rooms with TV and fridge, rate includes breakfast, coffee shop.

In the **Berjaya Megamall** there are lots of fast food places, plus a good food court dominated by a Chinese steamboat restaurant with one of those signs warning that people who leave food on their plates will be fined.
Near the local bus station and beside the river are a whole strip of **Malay stalls** well worth checking out if only because you can watch the river while you eat. There are banana leaf places along Jalan Bukit Ubi and an excellent roti place, **Restoran Mubarak**, next door to the long–distance bus station.

TELUK CHEMPADEK

Four kilometres east of Kuantan, this is really a much nicer place to spend your time than the city. The foreshore is paved and there are lots of hawker stalls in the area behind. There is a cliff walk around to the next beach, **Pelindung**, as well as longer walks into the **Teluk Chempadek Forest**.

In the row of shop–houses leading down to the beach are several good restaurants and a shop selling handicrafts and batik. Accommodation is either the Hyatt (see page 331) or the **Kuantan Hotel $$** opposite, tel: (09) 513-0026. In the row of shop–houses leading down to the beach are the **Country Ranch**, an Indian place, and the **Checkers Pub**, also serving Indian food.

MERSING

A wacky little place, Mersing is really only a stepping–off point for Tioman but it has a scruffy beach of its own and that Wild West atmosphere that is so attractive in some Malaysian towns. There are lots of places to stay and most of the cheaper places are used to independent travellers passing through on their way to find a perfect beach.

The government rest–house is a little wonder and has the beach behind it with a long walk possible around the shore. Nine kilometres north of town is **Air Papan**, a good beach, and 6 km south is **Sri Pantai**, less well known but almost as good.

ARRIVAL AND DEPARTURE

Bus: Most buses depart from the R&R Plaza bus station. There are departures for KL, 3 times a day; Kuantan, twice a day; Terengganu, Rantau Abang and Cherating, 3 times a day; and Melaka once a day. In addition, the north- and south-bound buses sometimes stop outside the **Restoran Malaysia** on the main road. The restaurant sells bus tickets and will provide information.

Boat: There are ferries from Mersing for Tioman, Pulau Rawa and Pulau Sibu. There are no hard–and–fast sailing times for any of the ferries, which depend on the tides, the number of bookings and the weather. For Tioman the big boats usually depart twice a day at high tide and the faster boats which are not dependent on the tide depart several times a day depending on bookings. At the bus stop beside the Malaysia restaurant is **Island Connection Travel and Tours**, which will be able to give you sailing times and book accommodation for you.

i The **tourist office** is in Jalan Abu Baker on the way to the jetty. It is open daily and closes at 1630.

Several of the offices for the resorts are at the R&R Plaza beside the jetty. Travel agents and bus and ferry **booking offices** are also here.

There are two **banks** in Jalan Ismail where you can change travellers' cheques.

Cyber World **Internet** shop is at 36, Jalan Abu Bakar.

Government Rest House $$–$ 490 Jalan Ismail, tel: (07) 799-2102. Huge, shabby rooms, great restaurant, pretty gardens overlooking the beach, big common balcony with views.
Hotel Timotel $$$ 839 Jalan Endau, tel: (07) 799-5888, fax: 799-5333. Special offers bring the cost right down. Newly built, all essentials, coffee shop popular with locals, bar with alcohol, on main road opposite bus stop.
Hotel Embassy $ 2 Jalan Ismail, tel: (07) 799-3545, fax: 799-5279. Very basic air-con rooms with simple bathroom and hot water. Good coffee shop.
Mersing Hotel $ Jalan Ismail, tel: (07) 796-1004. Same standard and rates as the Embassy.

There are good seafood restaurants in town, notably the **Mersing Seafood Restaurant** in Jalan Ismail, which is air-conditioned.
The **Golden Dragon** is the café below the Embassy Hotel and is popular with locals. There are several good Indian Muslim places doing roti in the mornings and evenings.
Try **Zam Zam**, near **Omar's backpacker's Hostel**.
At the jetty are lots of **nasi kandar stalls** selling reasonable curries.
There is also a **KFC** in Jalan Abu Bakar for fast air-con eating.

PULAU TIOMAN

Once a magical, innocent, beautiful island hideaway, Tioman has succumbed to the developers but still has lots to offer visitors. One of its biggest attractions is its accessibility – it is easy to bus it to Mersing, jump on a boat, get out there and find a good place to stay. The island is excellent for diving and snorkelling, particularly the beaches on the west side and Pulau Rengis, the little rock just offshore from the Berjaya Resort.

ARRIVAL AND DEPARTURE

Boat: High–speed boats leave at around 0700 and 1330 while the Seagull Ferry, which is a slower boat, leaves around midday and 1630 depending on the tide. More boats run according to demand and all of these times vary from day to day. The slower ferries charge RM45 return while the faster boats charge RM30 one way.

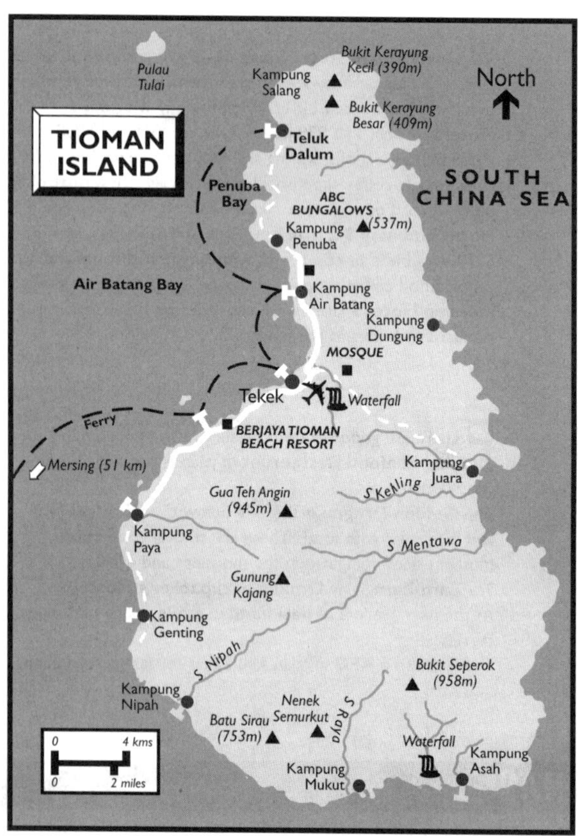

SANDFLIES

These evil little creatures can ruin a holiday if you are at all sensitive to their bites. Go to Tioman equipped with mosquito coils and insect repellents because on a bad day you can be badly eaten up by them.

Boats call first at Genting, then in the following order: Paya, Berjaya Resort, Tekek, Air Batang and Kampung Salang. A round-island ferry leaves Tekek at 1630, stops at Air Batang and Salang, and goes on to Juara. It costs RM420, takes a little over an hour for the full journey and returns from Juara at 1500. It is possible to hire boats for journeys around the island and to other islands but these are very expensive.

Air: There is an airport on the island, which was serviced by Pelangi Air from Singapore, KL and Kuantan, which has now gone out of business. It isn't yet clear if a service will replace it.

HIGHLIGHTS

There are **good walks** around the coast from Berjaya to Paya and Genting, and northwards from Tekek to Salang, into the hills and across the island to Juara (2–3 hrs) through virgin rainforest. In season **turtles** lay their eggs around Nipah Beach and there is lots of other **wildlife** to see.

The number of expensive resorts has multiplied but there are still simple fan–cooled beach chalets to be found. From late August to the monsoon season in November you are in a buyer's market and should visit each office getting the best rates. The beaches are as follows:

KAMPUNG TEKEK

This is the main village on the island, with shops and some places to eat. The best place to stay here is **Swiss Cottage $$–$** tel: (07) 224-2829. Small chalets close to the beach with its own restaurant. The resort offers packages inclusive of board and transport. Round the headland from Tekek beach is the **Berjaya Resort $$$$$** with all mod cons, sea sports, a pool, tennis, horse riding and an excellent beach. Between November and February when there are few visitors you can get big discounts.

AIR BATANG

This is the major traveller's place to stay and has mostly fan–cooled chalets. The better places are **Mawar's $** with its own restaurant, tel: (09) 419-1153, **Bamboo Hill Chalets $$** tel: (09) 419-1339, very small and often full, and **Nazri's Beach Cabanas $$** tel: (011) 333-486, with big bungalows and its own restaurant.

KAMPUNG PENUBA

North of Air Batang, the best place here is **Penuba Inn Resort $$$–$** tel: (011) 952-963 with air-con chalets for RM58. The resort sits on a hill overlooking the sea and is often booked up so phone ahead.

SALANG

North again is Salang with a pretty beach with restaurants but lots of resorts. The **Salang Indah $$** tel: (09) 413-1406, with fan–cooled and air-con chalets, its own restaurant, a bar and shop.

FINDING ACCOMMODATION

There are many offices in town selling accommodation and packages at the various resorts. Check these out before you go over to the island or book a trip with Seagull, Island Connection or one of the other tour agencies. Do not be persuaded at the jetty by touts that the cheaper places are full; this rarely happens.

Salang Beach Resort $$$ tel: (07) 799-3607 has a restaurant with reasonable prices and offers packages including transport and food which work out cheaper.

PAYA South of the resort is Paya beach, where there are some expensive resorts. **Tioman Paya Resort $$$$** has its own restaurant, coffee shop, bar and karaoke lounge. Packages include full board and transport and work out cheaper. Inquire at **Sea-Gull Express**, 26 Jalan Sulamein, tel: (07) 799-4297.

GENTING This beach is less accessible than the others and has fewer eating options outside its resorts. Try **Genting Damai Resort $$** tel: (07) 799-1200 which has a restaurant and minimarket. It too offers packages with full board and trips. **Yacht Resort $$$** can be booked through Seagull and has air-con rooms.

NIPAH Very isolated with a glorious beach great for snorkelling, a stay here needs to be organised through Island Connection (see page 332) because there is no transport unless a trip is arranged. Nipah consists mostly of small guesthouses where rooms cost RM35 and there are no air-con places. With only one restaurant, food and drinks are more expensive than elsewhere on the island.

RAWA, BESAR, SIBU, TENGGAH

Other islands are also accessible from Mersing. Rawa and Sibu both have resort hotels where packages can be arranged.

Rawa is surrounded by a coral reef. The island is dominated by the **Rawa Safari island Resort $$$** which has fan–cooled and air-con rooms. Outside food is not allowed on the island but there is a restaurant. The only way to the island is via its own boat, RM40 per person, which can be booked on tel: (07) 799-1204 at Plaza R&R.

Besar has several resorts, is close to the mainland and is accessible by a regular ferry service. It is possible to go to the island without accommodation and find somewhere to stay there. Sibu is also easily accessed and much less crowded than Tioman. There is a good range of accommodation from simple beach huts to the **Sibu Island Resort $$**. Tenggah has no resorts and so no regular service, but it can be visited by joining **Omar's Island Hopping Tour** available from Omar's Hostel in Mersing.

JOHOR BAHRU

Capital of the state of Johor, JB suffers a little from being placed so close to the wonders of Singapore. Just over the causeway is everything you could ever ask for in terms of food, shopping, tourist attractions, public transport, hotels and more. JB, on the other hand, is chaotic, unregulated and dirty.

Most travellers arriving here from Singapore stop long enough to sort out immigration and move on. But JB is worth more than a glance out of a bus or train window. In a way its chaos is a welcome antidote to 'Fine City', as Singapore has come to be called, and as the last stop on the east coast trip it can seem a little oasis of shopping malls, seafood restaurants, and fast food delights.

Singaporeans come to JB when the regulations over the causeway get them down. Many of them live here: housing, petrol, clothes, food, beer and entertainment are all cheaper. Lots of tour groups even arrange their clients' stay in JB and bus them over the causeway each day to save on accommodation and eating costs.

GETTING THERE

Air: There are direct flights between JB and KL, Kota Kinabalu, Kuching, Penang, and Surabaya in Indonesia. The Malaysian Airways office is in the Menara Pelangi building on Jalan Kuning. **Sultan Ismail** airport is 32 km north of the city at Senai. A bus service leaves from the **Pan Pacific Hotel** and is timed to meet incoming and outgoing flights. A taxi should cost about RM25. Most taxis are metered.

Bus: There are buses between JB's **Larkin bus terminal**, 5 km north of the city and Queen St bus terminal in Singapore leaving at 15 minute intervals. It is also possible to get the SBS service 170 at Larkin or at the causeway where you can buy tickets on the bus. Coming from Singapore buses go to Larkin or you can disembark at immigration and walk into the city.

At Larkin buses depart to all major cities on Malaysia. None of them need to be booked in advance although it might be advisable for Melaka. There are a series of long–distance bus booking offices on the second storey of the Merlin Tower facing the railway station.

Train: There are direct links with KL and the west coast. Change at Gemas for the jungle railway to Kota Bharu. The railway station is on Jalan Siu Nam in the city centre. The booking office is open 0900–1800 and it is best to book in advance for longer journeys.

Boat: East of JB is a ferry terminal at the Stuland Duty Free Trade Zone from where there are connections to Singapore and Sumatra. From Tanjung Belungkor, near Desaru, a car ferry goes to Singapore.

GETTING AROUND

Taxis have meters for the most part but make sure that the driver switches it on or gives you a price before the journey begins. Most of the big car–hire companies have offices in JB.

There are two **tourist offices** in the JOTIC building, on Jalan Air Molek west of the causeway. The state tourist office is more useful for information about the state of Johor, while the Tourism Malaysia office on the fifth floor deals with the city. Both are open Mon–Sat 0900–1700. They don't officially close for the lunch hour but everyone disappears then.
Moneychangers litter the street in the roads around the causeway. All have competitive rates but don't change small Singaporean bills when the rates are poor.
The **post office** is in Jalan Ibrahim.
There are **Internet** shops in JB City Centre and Plaza Kotaraya.

HOURLY ROOM RATES

The seedier side of JB nightlife means that quite a lot of the less classy hotels rent rooms by the hour. The five–star hotels offer all the facilities expected at prices to match, so the cheaper hotels offer good value accommodation despite all the coming and going. Those listed here are the more respectable ones. Rates in the cheaper hotels go up at weekends when the Singaporeans hit town.

Hyatt Regency $$$$$ Jalan Sungei Chat, tel: (07) 222-1234, fax: 223-2718. Two km west of town on a hill overlooking the Straits of Johor and Singapore. Pool, sculptured gardens, good restaurants, excellent buffet breakfast. Large rooms with luxurious bathrooms.
Crowne Plaza $$$$ Jalan Dato Sulamein, tel: (07) 332-3800, fax: 331-8884. Pool, coffee shop, Italian and Szechuan restaurants, free local calls, free shuttle service, some excellent full–board packages. In northern outskirts of the city centre, close to the Holiday Inn Plaza.
Mercure Ace $$$18, Jalan Wong Ah Fook, tel: (07) 221-3000, fax: 221-4000, e-mail: mercure@po.jaring.my. Right in the centre of things, this modern hotel has stylish rooms, a wholefood café and attentive service.
Gateway Hotel $$ 61, Jalan Meldrum, tel: (07) 223-5048, fax: 223-5248. All the basics, at a reasonable rate.
Top Hotel $$ 12, Jalan Meldrum, tel: (07) 224-4755. All the basics, next to a good coffee shop, right in centre of town.

There are two restaurants among the many in the five–star hotels which are worth a look.
Selasih $$ in the **Pan Pacific** serves a Malay buffet along with some traditional music and dancing. You can try lots of local specialities here and have things explained as you eat.
Meisan $$$$ is at the Crowne Plaza and serves Szechuan food.

Foodstalls are good and popular, especially with Singaporeans who flock here at weekends to eat the seafood. Right beside the drain and outside the Hindu temple is the very popular **night market $** where you can try Malay Chinese and Indian food.

Along the waterfront running west of the Causeway are lots of Chinese seafood places. Close to the hospital is the **Tepian Tebrau hawker centre** where all the stalls have similar seafood menus.

For a more expensive Chinese seafood meal you could try **Eden Park Seafood Garden** in Jalan Gelam, noticeable for its huge sign on the hillside. It is open 1730–0100 daily.

JB City Centre, a huge new shopping complex, has an excellent food court on its top floor with Thai, Japanese, western, and *nasi padang* stalls and a good *laksa* stall serving heavily coconut–flavoured *laksa johor*. There is also a fairly rare *yong tau fu* stall where you select the all-vegetarian food items for the stallholder to dunk in gravy to cook for a few minutes.

In City Square and Holiday Plaza are branches of the excellent and very popular **Restoran Hameed's,** serving Indian Muslim food, roti and dosa.

HIGHLIGHTS

The main attraction is the **Royal Abu Bakar Museum $$$**, open daily 0900–1800. It is well worth the high price and is a good afternoon's visit. The building is the old royal palace (built 1864–1866) which is no longer used by the sultan, except on state occasions. The architect was British and much of the furniture on show is European.

The place is an amazing mixture of everyday items and great wealth. The treasury contains all the gifts given to the sultans including silver kris. Special women's *kris* were kept on their persons in case of attack when they could commit suicide rather than be violated. Also on display are execution swords with which murderous or adulterous criminals were stabbed through the back. Other gory relics include various dismembered animals made into ashtrays and doorstops.

Sultan Abu Bakar Mosque (built 1892–1900) is one of those curious mixtures of Islamic and English Victorian architectural styles common in KL. The minarets have a distinctly colonial feel and would not be out of place on, say, Manchester City Hall.

The **Sultan Ibrahim** building is another very distinctive style and dominates the JB skyline. Built in the 1940s, it looks almost mediaeval.

The **Istana Bukit Serene** is not open to the public but it too has an imposing appearance with beautiful gardens and a private zoo. Its 1930s tower was used in November 1941 by General Yamishita, the commander of the 25th Army, to watch the invasion of Singapore. When his troops signalled that they had established a bridgehead on Singapore soil, the general wept from the window here.

Entertainment

JB has a distinctly sleazy element to its nightlife, but this is easily avoided. There are lots of karaoke places and late–opening nightclubs and discos. Just wander around and the person at the door will lure you in.

Qudos in Plaza DNP, Jalan Datuk Abdulah Tahir, is a new and very trendy place. It plays some interesting music, has a dance floor and pool table, lots of happy hour offers and is open late. A similar place is the **Blues Café,** 55 Jalan Kuning, open till 0200.

For something a little different you can join the **Amusement World Cruise** package, tel: (07) 222-9898. It is an all–night boat party with karaoke, cinema, disco and live bands – all for RM50 including a room and three meals.

Shopping

The other thing that Singaporeans flock here for is the shopping. Many of the plazas cater almost entirely for Singaporean tastes and only really come alive at weekends. JB is probably a little more expensive than other places because of this.

The best of the malls is **JB City Centre**, newly opened and bursting with expensive shops. **Holiday Inn Plaza** is cheaper and has more small places and bargains.

Jason's Bay

Also known as Teluk Mahkota, this is an isolated and rather muddy beach. Apart from some wandering cattle it is utterly deserted. The foreshore is lined with palms and casuarina trees and macaques swing boldly over the approach road to stare at passing cars. Apart from **Jason's Bay Beach Resort** tel: (07) 891-8077 there is little else. Come for a picnic to an unusual black beach but don't stay here. There is no public bus service and you really need your own transport.

EXCURSIONS **Desaru** is full at weekends with Singaporeans heading for the first bit of sand they can find. The beach is good but the waves are very strong, and the entire place has one resort after another. Prices match the high demand and the only places to eat are the resorts. Take a bus to Kota Tinggi and then another to the beach. Taxis cost about RM100.

EN ROUTE

30 km south of Mersing and still fairly inaccessible is **Tanjung Leman**, a promontory a few km off the Kota Tinggi–Mersing road. It has pretty white sandy beaches but very little in the way of accommodation. It is, however, the only way to get to several rather pretty offshore islands, all of which were once accessed via Mersing. Conspiracy theorists might think that it is all a plot to make tourists dependent on tour agencies.

A good place to visit is **Gunung Ledang**, or Mount Ophir, 38 km north–east of the town of Muar. There are waterfalls at the foot of the mountain and trails going up it. At the base is accommodation in the form of chalets, campsites and longhouses, all very basic, including the **Gunung Ledang Resort**, tel: (06) 977-2888. Take the bus to Segamat and ask to be dropped off at Sagil, from where it is a 1 km walk through rubber plantations to the falls.

Seafood and Singaporean food lovers must make the trip to **Kukup**, 40 km south west of JB on the Straits of Melaka. It is a Chinese *kampung* which has gained a huge reputation for its seafood dishes, especially chilli crab and chilli prawns. The restaurants are mostly stilt buildings leaning out over the water at the shoreline. They tend to cater for Singaporean coach parties which come in droves at the weekends. Take the bus to Pontian Kecil, then change for Kukup.

Kota Tinggi, 42 km north east of JB, is a stop on the route to Mersing, but it also has the Lumbong Falls set in a pretty country park with some chalet accommodation. The falls start on Gunung Muntahak and descend via a series of pools. They are good for dips and there are nice walks in the area, but the place is to be avoided at all costs at the weekend when it heaves with people. Take bus No 41 or 227 from Larkin to Kota Tinggi, one of several express buses, or bus No 43 from the town.

Pulau Tinggi, an extinct volcano and a marine park, has miles of sandy white beaches, great diving and snorkelling and a few resorts. **Nadia's Inn island Resort $$** tel: (07) 799-5582 has air-con rooms, while **Tinggi Island Resort $$$** tel: (07) 223-3698 is a little more upmarket. There are no regular ferries to Tinggi since most people book the whole package at one of the resorts, which is probably the easiest and cheapest option. The boat journey to the island is 2 hrs.

Pulau Sibu is much more accessible, although still only from Tanjung Leman which has its own access problems. There are good beaches and coral banks as well as jungle walks. Again the easiest option is to book the whole trip through an agent, but it is possible to turn up at the island and find accommodation. **Rimba Resort $$$** tel: (011) 711-528 is a very relaxed place and operates largely through full-board packages. It is probably the best place to stay as it has a private beach and its own transport.

Pulau Pemanggil and **Pulau Aur** are also accessed via Tanjung Leman. Both are big resorts catering for large diving parties. Packages tend to run from Friday evening to Sunday afternoon, with little going on during the week. Try **Dive Atlantis Singapore**, tel: (Singapore) (02) 295-0377. To get to Tanjung Leman from JB take the Mersing bus and ask to be dropped off at Tenggaroh Junction. From here taxis wait (but only before a boat is due to leave) to make the journey to the jetty.

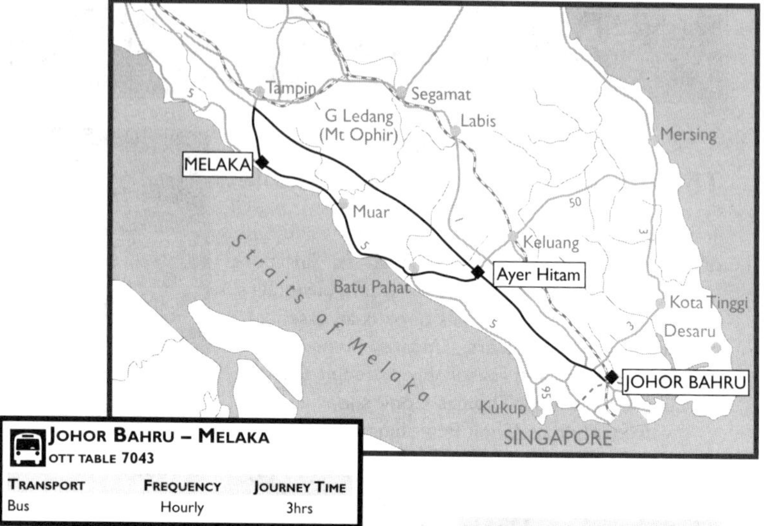

Johor Bahru – Melaka
OTT table 7043

Transport	Frequency	Journey Time
Bus	Hourly	3hrs

Notes

Several bus companies operate this route and there is little need to book ahead.

Johor Bahru – Melaka

This route offers a contrast of two very different Malaysian towns, and along the way you will see dramatic evidence of what fuels the country's economy. Thousands of acres of land, clearly visible from the roadside or the air, are devoted to huge estates of rubber, pineapple and palm oil. They seem to go for ever and account for the relative prosperity of the Johor state. There was a time, half a millennium ago, when the small state of Melaka was a big player on the international economic stage. Its status as the trading port of south-east Asia was unchallenged, and successive waves of Europeans washed up on its shores. It is their cultural legacy that makes Melaka the favourite destination of historically minded travellers. Under the British, Melaka was one of the Straits Settlements along with Penang and Singapore.

MELAKA

Melaka spent many years as a sleepy town and is now in the middle of a massive development project which has seen the beachfront give way to land reclamation, and new man-made islands appear off the coast. Fortunately, all this development is on reclaimed land and the amazing winding old streets and ancient shophouses have been left relatively intact.

Batu Pahat

If you are driving through, this place is good for Chinese food and has some interesting architecture.

En Route

Muar, on the west coast, was once a busy centre and is very Malay in character. The mosque is another Victorian Moghul mixture and there are some old colonial buildings. The rest of the coastal road between here and Melaka has lots of *kampung* villages with traditional Melaka style houses, built on blocks with elaborate tiled fronts and a space underneath the house.

Six hundred years ago traders spotted the economic value of this small town in the Straits of Melaka, halfway between China and India, and sheltered from the monsoons by the island of Sumatra. It became a natural refuelling and resting stop for great trading ships where ships from China would later bring goods to trade with vessels from India.

Ayer Hitam

This little town at a major road junction is worth the stop for its many roadside pottery stalls. Much of the work here is made in potteries along the road, which is not available in other craft shops in Malaysia. Pottery animals, jugs, bowls and much larger pieces can be bought here at very reasonable prices.

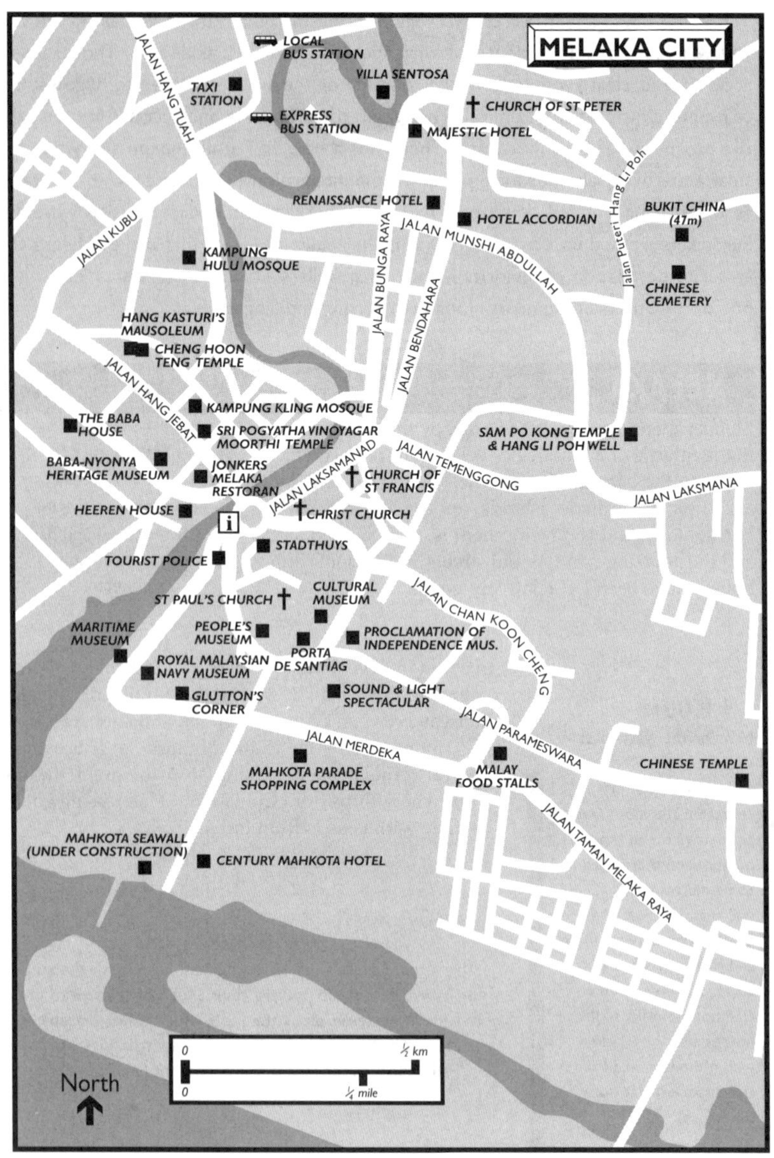
MELAKA CITY
LOCAL BUS STATION
VILLA SENTOSA
TAXI STATION
EXPRESS BUS STATION
CHURCH OF ST PETER
MAJESTIC HOTEL
JALAN HANG TUAH
Jalan Puteri Hang Li Poh
RENAISSANCE HOTEL
HOTEL ACCORDIAN
BUKIT CHINA (47m)
JALAN KUBU
JALAN MUNSHI ABDULLAH
KAMPUNG HULU MOSQUE
JALAN BUNGA RAYA
CHINESE CEMETERY
JALAN BENDAHARA
HANG KASTURI'S MAUSOLEUM
CHENG HOON TENG TEMPLE
JALAN HANG JEBAT
KAMPUNG KLING MOSQUE
THE BABA HOUSE
SRI POGYATHA VINOYAGAR MOORTHI TEMPLE
SAM PO KONG TEMPLE & HANG LI POH WELL
BABA-NYONYA HERITAGE MUSEUM
JONKERS MELAKA RESTORAN
JALAN LAKSAMANAD
JALAN TEMENGGONG
CHURCH OF ST FRANCIS
JALAN LAKSMANA
HEEREN HOUSE
CHRIST CHURCH
STADTHUYS
TOURIST POLICE
ST PAUL'S CHURCH
CULTURAL MUSEUM
JALAN CHAN KOON CHENG
MARITIME MUSEUM
PEOPLE'S MUSEUM
PORTA DE SANTIAG
PROCLAMATION OF INDEPENDENCE MUS.
ROYAL MALAYSIAN NAVY MUSEUM
GLUTTON'S CORNER
SOUND & LIGHT SPECTACULAR
JALAN PARAMESWARA
JALAN MERDEKA
MAHKOTA PARADE SHOPPING COMPLEX
MALAY FOOD STALLS
CHINESE TEMPLE
JALAN TAMAN MELAKA RAYA
MAHKOTA SEAWALL (UNDER CONSTRUCTION)
CENTURY MAHKOTA HOTEL
0
½ km
0
¼ mile
North

Eventually someone realised that whoever controlled Melaka governed all the trade of the East and people began to fight over it. At first Chinese controlled, the town attracted first the Portuguese and then, in the 17th century, the Dutch and finally the British. In 1824 Melaka became part of the British Empire. But then irony struck – the port silted up, Singapore and Penang took off as trading centres and Melaka sank into obscurity and remained a little dinosaur until the tiger economy of the 1980s took hold.

ARRIVAL AND DEPARTURE

Bus: Long–distance buses travel between Melaka and most of the major towns in peninsular Malaysia as well as Singapore. The long–distance bus station is by the river off Jalan Tun Mamat and there are booking offices around the bus station.

Boat: Four ferry companies run regular trips to Dumai in Sumatra: Astoria, tel: (06) 282-9888; Indomai Express, tel: (06) 281-6107; Tunas Rapat, tel: (06) 283-2506; and Madai Shipping, tel: (06) 284-0671. Ferries travel to Pulau Besar from Umbai jetty, tel: (06) 261-0492, and to Pulau Upeh from the TIC jetty.

GETTING AROUND

Melaka is small enough to walk around. Local taxis are rare but there are plenty of *trishaws*. They charge a minimum of RM6. Negotiate a price before beginning a journey. Bus No 17 goes to Medan Portugis and No 10 to Air Keroh from the local bus station beside the river.

The **tourist office** is in Jalan Kota at the roundabout opposite Christ Church. Open 0845—1700 daily, closed Fri 1215—1445. It should have a map of the town. Many of the hotels have similar maps.

The **post office** is at street level of Mahkota Parade where there are several banks.

Renaissance $$$$$ Jalan Bendahara, tel: (06)284-8888, fax: 284-9269. Stylish, big hotel in the old part of town. Wonderful views of Chinatown and the river mouth, popular coffee shop, pool, fitness centre, disco and poolside bar.

City Bayview $$$$$ Jalan Bendahara, tel: (06) 283-9888, fax: 283-6699. Facilities include pool, health centre, night club, coffee shop and restaurant.

The Emperor Hotel $$$–$$ 123 Jalan Munshi Abdullah, tel: (06) 284-0777, fax: 283-8989. With its special promotion, the best value in town. Pool, fitness centre, sauna and steam bath, nice rooms, Chinese restaurant, coffee shop.

Hotel Puri $$$–$$, 118 Jalan Tun Tan Cheng Lock, tel/fax: (06) 282-5588. Restored Peranakan shophouse with ancient marble tables and carved panels. Café, garden, e-mail service, pleasant rooms. Ask for promotional rate.

The Baba House $$ 125-7 Jalan Tun Tan Cheng Lock, tel: (06) 281-1216, fax: 281-2168. Good, basic rooms in a pretty renovated Peranakan house complete with antiques.

Lucky Inn $$ 116.3 and 116.4 Jalan Bendahara, tel: (06) 281-0070, fax: 284-4636. All the basics at a competitive rate.

Hotel Accordion $$–$ 114A Jalan Bendahara, tel: (06) 282-1911, fax: 282-1333. All the basics for RM50 plus breakfast.

The Majestic Hotel $ 188 Jalan Bunga Raya, tel: (06) 282-2367. Still sporting the same cushion covers it had 20 years ago, this classic Chinese hotel has a big central lounge, loads of atmosphere, nice bar.

FOOD

Melaka is most famous for its Peranakan style of cooking, a mix of Malay slow cooking with coconut and lemon grass and Chinese fast frying. Most famous and widely available is *laksa,* not the hot, red spicy stuff from Penang but a mellow thick creamy soup, full of coconut and mildly spiced. It is sold in most hawker centres and food courts.

Another influence on cooking in this area is the legacy of the Portuguese who settled here and intermarried. Try the spicy, seafood-based dishes like 'devil curry' at the restaurants at Medan Portugis. For a quick cheap meal, visit the food court in Mahkota parade where there are good *laksa* and *yong tau fu* stalls as well as Malay and western places.

PERANAKAN	**Nancy's Kitchen $$** 15, Jalan Hang Lekir. Old shop–house with lots of Peranakan dishes.
	Ole Sayang $$ 198, Jalan Melaka Raya. Air-con and good, authentic nyonya dishes.
	Ole Ole Peranakan Baba Nyonya $ Lot C Jalan Merdeka. Modern shop–house in the reclaimed land area of town.
	Heeren House $ 1, Jalan Tun Cheng Lock. Coffee shop in Peranakan style guesthouse, serving Peranakan and Portuguese dishes.
PORTUGUESE	**Restoran de Lisbon $$** Medan Portugis. Good seafood and devil curry. Bands most night and cultural dances in the square.
	San Pedro $$ 4, Jalan D'Aranjo. Portuguese seafood dishes served in an intimate atmosphere.
INDIAN	**Selvan $** on main junction of Jalan Bandaraya and Jalan Bandahara. Very busy banana leaf restaurant serving vegetarian and meat curries, dosa and roti.

Restoran Vazhai $ 40 A, Jalan Munshi Abdullah. Small, elderly banana leaf restaurant. Good dosa for a light breakfast.

OTHER **Iguana $$**, **The Riverfront Café $$–$** and **Looney Planet $$–$**, in Jalan Laksamana, are all geared to tourists and do western and local dishes. Iguana has a pleasant banana fringed yard with tables.

Another café in this street is **Kim Swee Huat $**, doing good breakfasts and other Western dishes.

Rock & Roll Grill $$ 34, Jalan Melaka Raya does very meaty, grilled dishes. Will collect you if you call, tel: (06) 284-9652. Live music in the evenings.

HIGHLIGHTS In the old city is the beautiful **Stadthuys**, built between 1641 and 1660 by the Dutch in a very different style to much later British colonial buildings. It is now a **museum $**, open Sat–Thurs 0900–1800, closed 1245–1445. The ethnography section is the most interesting, with its displays on the ceremonies and customs of Melaka's ethnic groups from the Peranakan, the Chittys and the Portuguese, to the dominant culture of the Malays.

Close by and just as red is **Christ Church**, made from real Dutch pink bricks and not just painted. Built as a Dutch reformed church to commemorate 100 years of Dutch rule, it was made Anglican by the British. The bell tower, porch and vestry are later English additions. Open Sun–Fri 900–1700.

SIR STAMFORD RAFFLES

By the early 19th century Melaka was past its prime as a trading post and the governor, Mr Farquar, decided it would be a good idea to abandon Melaka and to blow up the walls rather than have a rival empire make use of them. The walls were 4.5 metres thick and 18 metres high, so this was no easy task. He was halfway through the job, sending huge pieces of masonry sky high, when Sir Stamford Raffles, then a minor secretary in Penang intervened. He persuaded his government not to abandon Melaka and the explosions stopped, but much of the damage had been done.

The **People's Museum $** on Jalan Kota has exhibits on local economic development and a more interesting section about international ideas of beauty. This includes mutilations practised for vanity, such as foot binding, piercing, neck rings and scarification as well as cosmetic surgery. A strange display but worth a look. Open Sat– Thurs 0900 – 1800; closed 1245 – 1445.

The stone archway of **Porta de Santiago** is all that remains of extensive Portuguese fortifications. Once, a four-walled fort here running along the bank of the river protected the Portuguese settlement. There was a four-storey-high keep, 120 big guns protecting the walls, and inside were palaces, schools, hospitals, and churches including St Paul's – the remains of which can be seen on the hill. The walls were never impregnated. The Portuguese gave the fort up to the Dutch who extended it. When the British arrived in the 19th century they blew it up rather than maintain an expensive colony here. Through the gateway and up the steps is what remains of **St Paul's Church**. The first church on this site was built by the Portuguese in 1521 on the site of a sultan's palace. St Francis Xavier preached in this Catholic church before the Dutch made it Protestant and named it St Paul's. The British built their own churches and made the old building into a weapons store. Today you can walk among the ruins and admire the headstones. The empty tomb in the church once held the body of St Francis Xavier.

THE LEGEND OF HANG TUAH

According to the Malay poem *Hikayat Hang Tuah*, Hang Tuah and his three companions were martial arts experts who in the 17th century saved the life of the Prime Minister. They were awarded positions in the Malay court and pledged themselves to the service of the sultan. Hang Tuah became very influential and as a court official was awarded his own special *kris* (knife) which was said to have magical powers.

Like all closed communities jealousy set in and rumours began that Hang Tuah had seduced one of the sultan's wives. The Bendahara whose life he had saved hid Hang Tuah away and put it about that Hang Tuah had been executed. When Hang Tuah's friend, Hang Jebat, heard of his death he ran amok, killing people and could not be stopped. When the sultan's life was threatened Hang Tuah came out of hiding and a terrible battle raged between the two friends, ending in Hang Jebat's death.

Hang Jebat's mausoleum is in Jalan Kampung kull, while Hang Tuah's soul is in a well on the road to Muar. He is said to appear from time to time in the form of a white crocodile which only the holy can see.

THE MALACCA CLUB

The early 20th century saw the opening of a fine new club for the white rulers of the settlement and their wives and daughters. Carriages, and later automobiles, pulled up in front of the padang where games of bowls and cricket regularly took place. Planters fresh from upstation would drop in to pick up the gossip and do a bit of trade while they sipped their stengahs. Later still, famous world travellers would call in and gather ideas for their next novel, like Somerset Maugham who set his short story 'Footprints in the Jungle' partly in the building.

The **Malacca Sultanate Palace $** is more attractive from the outside. Inside are dioramas and information about the structure of the sultan's court. One interesting display tells the story of Hang Tuah and his group of Malay musketeers who went around doing good deeds and serving the sultan. Open Sat–Thurs 0900–1800, closed 1245–1445.

THE FLORA DEL MAR

This Portuguese ship sank off Melaka loaded with tons of gold in the early 16th century. It has never been found, or at least no one has ever claimed to have found it. Its cargo is estimated to be worth about US$9 billion.

Close to the Sultanate Palace is the **Memorial of the Proclamation of Independence $,** open Sat–Thurs 0900–1800. Closed 1245–1445. This very British-looking building was once the exclusive Malacca Club and it is fitting that it should hold exhibits on the Malaysians' struggle for independence. Outside is a 1957 Chevrolet used in the elections of that year.

The **Maritime Museum** in Jalan Laksamana next to the river is a reconstruction of a Portuguese ship the *Flora Del Mar*. Inside are displays of spices that the ship carried and models of other ships, as well as bits and pieces salvaged over the years. Across the street is **The Royal Malaysian Navy Museum**, which has salvaged items from the *Diana* which sank in the shallow waters of Melaka in 1817. The ship was salvaged in 1993 and huge quantities of pottery were recovered.

The streets of **Chinatown**, the roads around Jalan Tun Cheng Lock, Jalan Hang Jebat and the roads between are a living museum to the history of the people who lived here. Jalan Tun Cheng Lock is full of the life of the Peranakans who built these shophouses and lived in them.

THE PERANAKAN

The early Chinese settlers in Melaka were all men and so when they married they took Malay wives. These women held on to their own customs of dress and cooking but adopted Chinese religion, and a strange amalgam of the two cultures emerged. The second generation of these now wealthy merchants were married into similar families and the Peranakan or 'locally born' culture emerged.

The women taught their children their own language but adopted the marriage and funeral practices and religious rites of the Chinese. As they grew wealthier and more distant from their cultural roots in China they adopted western habits, sending their children to English schools, and choosing western styles in furniture, playing billiards and above all avoiding the more recently arrived Chinese.

The **Baba and Nyonya Heritage Museum $$** at Nos 48 and 50 is a faithfully reconstructed Peranakan home. Built 1896 in the Chinese Palladian style, it has Roman pillars, Chinese roof tiles and ornate Malay–style carved shutters. Inside are furniture, clothes, porcelain and old photographs of the family that lived here. Inside is an internal courtyard open to the sky where water was collected in a little pool. Open daily 1000–1230, 1400–1600. Admission includes a very informative tour of the house.

Still in Chinatown, the **Cheng Hoon Teng Templ**e in Jalan Tokong is probably the oldest in Malaysia. Its name means the Merciful Cloud Temple and it is dedicated to Kuan Yin, one of the acolytes of the Lord Buddha who subsequently entered the pantheon of Taoist deities. Originally built in 1646, all the materials used in its construction were imported from China.

Inside, beside Kuan Yin is Tin Hau, the Goddess of Seafarers. In front of the two deities worshippers tip out little pots of *chim* (bamboo sticks) to see what their future holds; the way the sticks fall indicates the future. In the courtyard, huge incinerators burn offerings to ancestors, usually 'hell money' sent to them so that they pay their way in heaven.

Opposite this temple is another - a more modern temple dedicated to the Lord Buddha. In the shops around here you can see paper products which people burn to send to their ancestors. The paper windmills are blessed by the priests and are taken home. As the wind turns them the house is blessed.

In the same street is the **Masjid Kampung Kling**, built in 1748 in the Sumatran style, with a tiered roof rather than the typical onion dome. Both the roof tiles and the minaret are reminiscent of Chinese architecture, and the tiles around the water baths are European. An English chandelier hangs in the prayer hall. You may not enter the prayer hall itself but it is possible to stand in the courtyard if your shoulders are covered.

Another mosque nearby in Jalan Kampung Pantai is the **Masjid Kampung Hulu**, the oldest mosque in Malaysia, built in 1728. It too has a pagoda style minaret.

St Peter's Church in Jalan Tun Sri Lanang was built in 1710 during the Dutch occupation, but by Portuguese settlers. Their original church, Christ Church, was then Protestant and until this time all Catholic worship had been banned. It is a quiet place, unused except at Easter when the Portuguese community celebrate Good Friday.

BAV3403

MELAKA'S PORTUGUESE CUISINE

Very much Malay in style, the cooking of the Portuguese relies on the typical Malaysian flavourings of lemon grass and chilli as well as candlenuts and coconut milk. Vinegar, onions, ginger and star anise give the food its distinctive flavour. The famous devil curry gets its peculiar taste from the ground, fried spices in which the meat is slowly cooked. Another type of Portuguese curry, *curry seku*, is drier with the meat baked in the sauce.

In the new roads beside Mahkota Parade is the **Jade Museum**, a private collection of about 200 pieces of jade. Some of them are over 2,000 years old and include carved mythical creatures, drinking vessels and even a large phallic symbol drinking cup used by newlyweds. The collection is changed regularly from a larger collection of thousands of pieces. You need to be deeply interested in old jade to visit as the entrance fee is a steep RM20.

Medan Portugis, 3 km east of town, was created in 1933 for the descendants of the first European settlers in Melaka. Unlike the Dutch, the Portuguese intermarried with the local Malay people and a cross–cultural community evolved just as the Peranakan had. The Portuguese in Melaka have their own language, their own cooking style and traditional dances which owe much to the culture of Portugal.

Today, there are only about 500 people of Portuguese descent living in the medan. The modern square only dates back only to 1985 and survives because of its attraction to tourists. There are regular dance performances in the square and several restaurants serving Portuguese/Malay food. Bus Nos 17 and 25 go to the square.

SHOPPING

Melaka is famous for its **antique shops** along Jalan Hang Jebat and the adjacent streets. There are some genuine antiques here but most of them are huge old pieces of furniture badly in need of restoration. The smaller 'antique' shops sell craft items from Malaysia and Indonesia at quite high prices, but you can haggle if there is something you really like.

Along the streets here are art galleries such as **Malaqua House**, 70 Jalan Tun Cheng Lock, decorated like a Peranakan home and selling some beautiful but expensive things. In Jalan Laksamana **Karyaneka Handicrafts Emporium** sells clothes, batik and crafts from around Malaysia and at No 9, opposite the Stadthuys, **Dulukala** has some excellent pottery, jewellery and handicrafts from Indonesia.

NIGHTLIFE

The **Sound and Light Show** near the Porta de Santiago is held nightly at 2000 in Malay and 2130 in English. It is quite a powerful event, illuminating the ruins and telling the story of the history of Melaka. The show lasts an hour and costs RM5. At Medan Portugis there are cultural shows on Saturday nights from 2000, which you can watch while you eat your Portuguese meal. During the week there are live pop bands.

TOURS There are daily river trips through the city which depart from behind the tourist office. They go past old warehouses to kampung Morten, a Malay style area with old kampung houses. The tours last 45 minutes and depart at 1100, 1200 and 1300, but only leave if there are at least six passengers.

EXCURSIONS **Ayer Keroh**, 12 km north of town, is a tourist development aimed at locals. The **zoo $** is popular with children and has some rare Asian creatures such as Malayan sun bears and rhinos from Sumatra. Nearby is a **crocodile farm $**, the largest in the country according to the tourist literature. The collection includes albinos and hunchbacks, although you have to wonder if the hunches are due to cramped conditions rather than genetics.

More worthwhile is the **Orang Asli Museum $** containing artefacts and displays on the culture of the indigenous people. The **Air Keroh Recreational Forest** is the best reason to go to Ayer Keroh and has well signposted trails going off into the secondary forest. Cabins can be rented for an overnight stay and there is a campsite. **Taman Mini Malaysia** and **Mini Asean $** has reconstructions of the various styles of houses common in Malaysia and its ASEAN neighbours. Like the forest park it is worth the trip.

PULAU BESAR

Five km off the coast of Melaka, Pulau Besar is a pretty island with pleasant beaches and wooded hills which can be explored. It has resort hotels and a golf course, and like Malaysia's other islands is most easily accessed by booking a trip with one of the resorts. It is accessed from Umbai, 10 km south east of Melaka. (See page 347 for details of the ferry.)

Last but by no means least is the **Butterfly Farm $$** with 200 local species of butterfly, including the Rajah Brooke, a huge creature, and the birdwing butterfly, another king-sized lepidoptera. The farm also has a collection of snakes, stick insects, spiders and other creatures that children love.

TANJUNG BIDARA Twenty-five km north–west of Melaka on the road to Port Dickson is this pleasant and as yet unspoiled beach, a little dirty from the passing tankers but with lots of hawker stalls along the shore. A large part of the beach is taken up by the Tanjung Bidara Beach resort but there is still plenty of room for everyone. Bus Nos 51, 42 and 18.

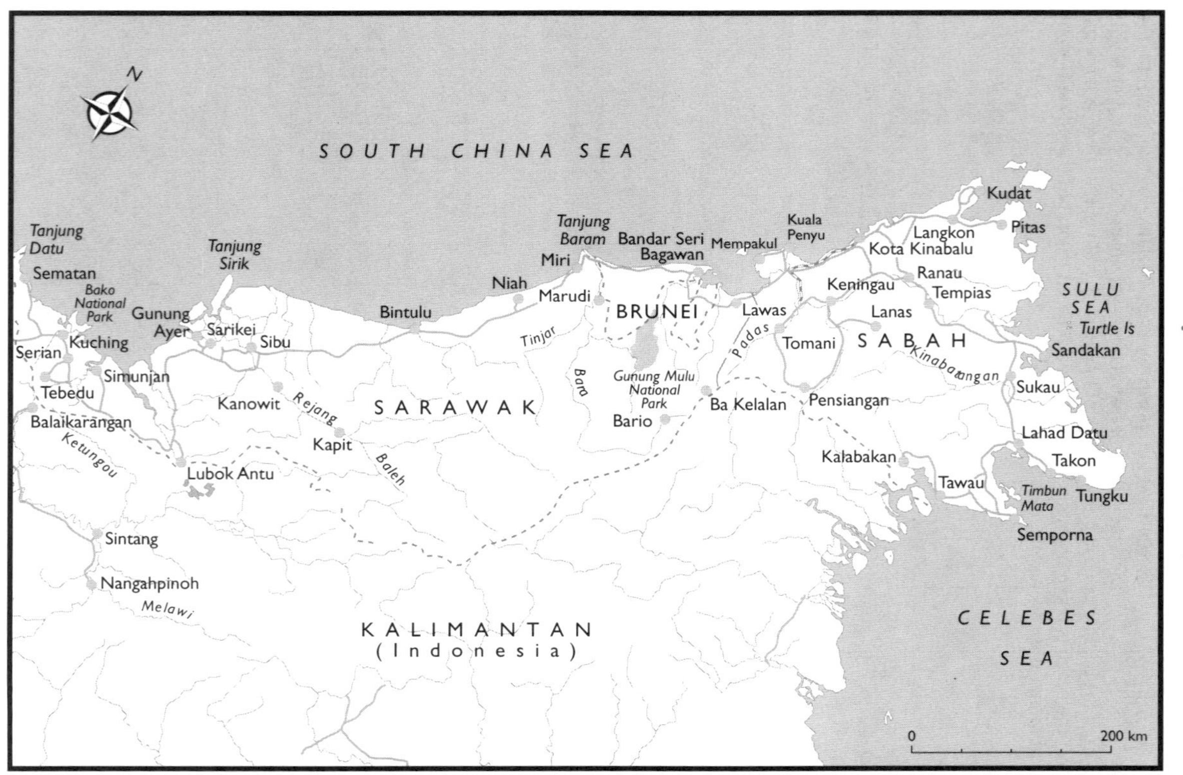
N
SOUTH CHINA SEA
Tanjung Datu
Sematan
Bako National Park
Kuching
Serian
Tebedu
Balaikarangan
Ketungou
Simunjan
Gunung Ayer
Tanjung Sirik
Sarikei
Sibu
Kanowit
Rejang
Kapit
Baleh
Lubok Antu
Sintang
Nangahpinoh
Melawi
Bintulu
SARAWAK
Niah
Tanjung Baram
Miri
Marudi
Tinjar
Baram
Bandar Seri Bagawan
BRUNEI
Gunung Mulu National Park
Bario
Mempakul
Kuala Penyu
Lawas
Padas
Ba Kelalan
Tomani
Pensiangan
Keningau
Lanas
Kota Kinabalu
Langkon
Ranau
Tempias
SABAH
Kinabatangan
Kudat
Pitas
SULU SEA
Turtle Is
Sandakan
Sukau
Lahad Datu
Takon
Timbun Mata
Tungku
Semporna
Tawau
Kalabakan
KALIMANTAN (Indonesia)
CELEBES SEA
0
200 km

Sarawak and Sabah, East Malaysia

The two east Malaysian states of Sarawak and Sabah, occupying a small part of the island of Borneo, are separated from mainland Malaysia by hundreds of miles of sea. The distance between east and peninsular Malaysia, though, is far more than one of nautical miles. They are also divided by history, culture and geography. The result is an almost unique destination and one of the world's best-kept secrets in terms of natural wildlife habitats.

Sarawak served as the personal fiefdom of the Brooke family from the 1840s until the outbreak of World War II in 1939. Sabah also had a separate identity because it was owned lock, stock and barrel by the British North Borneo Chartered Company from 1880 until the war. Both states have a rich variety of ethnic groups. Malays are just one of many minorities that include Ibans, Bidayuhs, Chinese, Kadazans, Bajaus, Filipinos and a host of smaller tribes, like the forest-dwelling nomads called the Penans.

The lifestyle of the Penans has been virtually destroyed by a combination of logging and government inducements to abandon the forest, but other cultural groups have been more successful in preserving aspects of their traditional way of life. Visiting an ethnic tribe and spending a night or two in their longhouses is one of the highlights of a visit to Sarawak.

Underlying the separate history and culture of Borneo is a distinctive geography characterised by mighty rivers, jungle and forest which offers unique travel opportunities for the intrepid tourist. A visit to Sarawak and Sabah requires a bit more organisation and advance planning than peninsular Malaysia, Thailand or Singapore, but the rewards are more than compensation for anyone with an interest in activity holidays, nature and wildlife. Transport involves a combination of internal flights on Malaysia Airlines and turbo-charged boats that ply up and down the rivers. Transport costs are not high, and while the cost of tours needs budgeting for there are still great places, like Mount Kinabalu and Bako National Park, that can be visited independently.

Malaysia's largest state can seem like another country. On arrival you need to fill out a separate immigration form and have your passport stamped. This act of officialdom reflects the cultural independence of Sarawak. Islam is a minority religion here and the state has a distinct geographical identity as a part of Borneo.

Historical sights and sandy beaches are secondary to Sarawak's wildlife and national parks, while the state's indigenous cultural groups are a major reason for leaving peninsular Malaysia and flying to the state capital of Kuching.

An Unlikely History

From the 14th century Sarawak was part of the powerful kingdom of Brunei, but by the 18th century there was signs of discontent from the Malay population. Malays had first moved north from Kalimantan (the main land mass of Borneo, now part of Indonesia) into Sarawak around 200 years earlier and now, as Brunei's power started to wane, they flexed their muscle. In 1836 the Sultan of Brunei sent his uncle to quell disorder and protect the valuable trade in *serawak*, the Malay word for antimony.

James Brooke sailed into this volatile situation in 1839. Brooke was an English adventurer keen to emulate Raffles' achievement in Singapore. When the sultan's uncle offered him the title of Raja (ruler) of Sarawak in return for crushing the Malay rebels he jumped at the chance, and an astonishing offshoot of Britain's colonial conquests began. Brooke gradually acquired more and more territory by slaughtering the native Ibans so that by the time he died in 1867 he owned more than half of what is now Sarawak.

His son, Charles Brooke, took over the title in 1863 and before he died in 1916 he passed the throne to his son, Charles Vyner Brooke, who held power until the Japanese rudely interrupted this imperial idyll in 1941. Britain took over after the war, in acrimonious circumstances, and remained in charge even after Malaya's independence in 1957. It was 1953 before the state became part of the federation of Malaysia.

Transport within Sarawak is also different from peninsular Malaysia. Malaysian Airlines internal flights and turbo-charged river boats are the main forms of long distance travel. Overland routes are possible but are very time consuming, and the affordable fares for internal flights are difficult to resist. Travellers also usually find themselves using tour operators at least once, primarily because they offer the best way of getting to some of the most interesting places.

Sarawak's People

More than 30% of the population are **Ibans**, the famed headhunters of a bygone era and now a remarkably laid-back and friendly people who live throughout the state. Most still live in longhouses and earn a living as farmers. The **Malays** make up 20% of the population, and along with the

Melanau (6%) mostly live along the coastal area, as opposed to the **Bidayuh** people (8%) who are found inland. Around 30% are **Chinese** people, found in all major towns. The various other indigenous tribes, including the endangered **Penan,** who were once all nomadic forest dwellers, are referred to generally as the **Orang Ulus**.

Kuching

Despite rampant economic development over the last ten years, Kuching retains a tangible sense of history that makes it the most unique town anywhere in both Sarawak or Sabah. The town still has some quaint touches that date back to the era of the Brookes, and its multi-ethnic identity may come as a blessing if you're just arriving from the monocultural east coast of peninsular Malaysia.

Outside of Penang and Ipoh, the west side of Kuching has the best pre-war vernacular Chinese architecture in Malaysia, and there are good examples of colonial architecture as well. Kuching's many museums are nearly all worth a visit and most are free. Another good reason for lingering in Kuching is the excellent food scene, easily the best in Sarawak.

ARRIVAL AND DEPARTURE

Air The most common route is on a Malaysian Airlines (MAS) flight from KL but there are also direct flights from Singapore using Singapore Airlines. The least expensive way of reaching Kuching from Singapore or the south of peninsular Malaysia is on a MAS flight from Johor Bahru. MAS in Singapore encourages this by running a direct bus from the Novotel Orchid Hotel to the Malaysian airport.

MAS have their office at Lot 215, Jalan Song Thian Cheok, tel: (082) 246-622, and Singapore Airlines at Wisma Bukit Mata Kuching, Jalan Tunku Abdul Rahman, tel: (082) 240-266.

Air Asia operates a daily flight between KL and Kuching. Some restrictions apply. Air Asia flights operate from the old KL Subang airport, not the new KL International, so allow plenty of time if you have a connecting flight.

Transport to and from the Airport Kuching International Airport, tel: (082) 454-255, is 11 km from town. Bus No 8A, blue and white in colour, runs between town and the airport 0600–1935 at roughly hourly intervals. The green and cream bus No 12A does the same run 0630–1915 on a similar schedule. These buses can be picked up near the tourist office on Main Bazaar or around the corner, outside the main post office.

A coupon system operates at the airport for taxis into town. See Getting Around below for taxis to the airport from town.

DOMESTIC FLIGHTS MAS flies to Sibu, Miri and Bintulu in Sarawak, and Kota Kinabalu in Sabah.

BUS Long–distance buses leave from the Regional Express Bus Terminal on Penrissen Rd, 5 km out of town. There are many longdistance bus companies and the local newspaper carries the schedules, as well as the tourist office. Leaving Kuching, it is quicker to get a boat to Sibu and then a bus from there.

Borneo Highway Express, tel: (082) 427-035, run buses from Kuching to Miri at 0630, 1000 and 1300 for RM70. Biaramas Express, tel: (082) 452-189, do the same route from Kuching at 0630 and 1000. So does Lanang Road Bus Company, tel: (084) 335-973 at 0800 and 0930.

BOAT It's about four hours on a high-speed boat from Kuching to Sibu, and tickets should be bought in advance at the jetty. The main company, Ekspres Bahagia, tel: (082) 421-948, has a daily departure at 1230 and the fare is RM35. Bus Nos 17 and 19 from the market on Main Bazaar and No 1C travel to the jetty at Pending, 6 km out of town.

ORIENTATION Kuching is mostly spread out along the south side of the Sarawak River in a schizophrenic manner. The west side of town has all the history, the main museum, and bus stations, while the east side has modern hotels and shopping centres. A riverside road, with a promenade for part of the way, connects the two halves of the city and the distance is easily walkable.

The north side of the river is not very developed but it does house Fort Margherita (currently closed due to renovation work) and the **Cat Museum**.

MAPS

There is one excellent, free colour map available from the Visitors' Information Centre, entitled *Sarawak & Kuching*, that is well worth getting hold of. As well as providing a good overall map of Sarawak and a detailed street map of Kuching, it also contains inset maps of the Kuching area, Damai, Sibu, Kapit, Miri and Bintulu.

INFORMATION

MAP – inside back cover

RIVER CRUISE

There is a daily 2hr sunset cruise on the M.V. *Equatorial* that usually departs at 1730 from behind the Sarawak Plaza. The cost is RM25 which includes a welcome drink, tel: (082) 240-566.

If only all tourist offices in Malaysia were like those in Sarawak and Sabah. Kuching has two exemplary **tourist offices**, both centrally located and full of useful and detailed information.

The **Visitors' Information Centre**, tel: (082) 410-944, Padang Merdeka, opposite the Merdeka Palace Hotel, is open Mon–Fri 0800–1800, Sat 0800–1600, and Sun 0900–1500.

The **National Parks and Wildlife office**, tel: (082) 248-088, for booking accommodation at Bako, is in the same building.

The **Sarawak Tourist Association** (STA) Main Bazaar, tel: (082) 240-620, is open Mon–Thur 0800–1245 and 1400–1615, Fri 0800–1130 and 1430–1615 and Sat 0800–1245. There is also a small STA office at the airport, tel: (082) 456-266.

Tourism Malaysia have an office on Jalan Song Thian Cheok, tel: (082) 246-775, only worth a visit if you need information on Sabah or peninsular Malaysia.

From the tourist offices and hotels look for a free copy of *The Official Kuching Guide*, packed with useful and reasonably accurate information on accommodation, places to eat and local tours.

The **immigration office** is part of the government offices on Jalan Simpang Tiga, 4 km south of town on the road to the airport, which can be reached by bus Nos 8, 8A, 8B, 14, 14A, 14B or by taxi.

GETTING AROUND

Most places of interest in Kuching can be visited on foot, and those that can't can be reached by public bus. There are five bus companies, each with differently coloured buses. The Visitors' Information Centre dispenses a useful map of the town with all the relevant destinations reachable by bus and their colours, fares and schedules listed on the back. There is no central bus terminal.

Kuching has taxis but hailing them down on the street is not common because they are only empty when returning from somewhere. Instead, taxis gather at the open-air market at the end of Gambier Rd, the long–distance bus station and the big hotels at the east end of town.

Car rental is available through various companies, including Pronto, tel: (082) 236-889, fax: (082) 236-889, Mayflower, tel: (082) 410-110, fax: (082) 410-115, and Wah Tung, tel: (082) 616-900. Some have desks at the airport. Expect to pay around RM120 to RM140 per day.

A Town Walk

This walk takes in many of Kuching's places of interest and begins outside the Sarawak Tourist Association office on Main Bazaar. Firstly, enquire at the office whether **Fort Margherita** has reopened and, if so, consider taking the cross-river **sampan $** from the jetty along the waterfront. The fare is payable on leaving. From where the boat pulls in on the other side of the river, it is a short walk to the fort built by Charles Brooke in 1879 on the site of an original fort built by his father, which was burnt down by Chinese miners. Before its closure in 2000, the fort was an interesting police museum with assorted memorabilia and well worth a visit.

From outside the tourist office, pause to look at the splendid examples of **Chinese shop–house architecture** across the road. Resist the temptation to cross because this walk will bring you to them later. Instead, with your back to the tourist office, turn right and walk along Jalan Gambier with its historic buildings from the 1920s and '30s and the town's fish market. The sacks of dried fish, spices and rice and flour spilling out onto the pavement hark back to the time when merchants set up shop here to be close to the river where boats unloaded their cargoes.

On reaching the busy junction and taxi station, turn left and first left again into pedestrianised **Jalan India**. Despite the name, this street is unmistakably Chinese and there is often a Chinese medicine 'stall' spread across the pavement. Notice how prominent the Chinese characters on the shop signs are; in peninsular Malaysia they are not allowed to be written large. Notice too the Muslim restaurants and money –changer on the left.

At the end of Jalan India, walk across Jalan Barrack and through the **Courthouse**, first built by Charles Brooke as his lawcourt and still fulfilling that judicial function today. It is an elegant structure that uses its space to create maximum shade, with a memorial to Brooke outside that was added in 1924. The bronze panels at the bottom are in recognition of the state's four main ethnic groups: Ibans, Chinese, Malays and Orang Ulu.

From the other side of the Courthouse from where you entered the impressive **General Post Office** on Jalan Haji Openg is clearly visible. Built in 1931, its neo-classical and imperious style was presumably chosen by the last rajah, Vyner Brooke, to express the power of the white man. The building opposite, the **Pavilion**, has been undergoing renovation for years. It was originally a hospital and then the education department before being used by the occupying Japanese as an 'information bureau'.

Cross the road and head down **Jalan Carpenter** with its unmistakably Chinese goldsmiths and pawnshops and a colourful Chinese temple on the right. Some of the shops are worth nosing into, particularly the one on the left selling old coins from the Brooke era and banknotes from the Japanese occupation. At the junction with Jalan China, with the temple-like facade of the Kuching Hainese Association across the road, turn left and walk up Jalan China to the craft shops on Main Bazaar. If you turn right at the top into Main Bazaar, the shops are in the order they appear below.

SHOPPING

Shopping on Main Bazaar

Galleri M, 26 Main Bazaar (and in the lobby of the Hilton hotel), has the sort of tribal artefacts that will be seen in every shop on Main Bazaar, plus paintings and prints. Next door, **Bong Gallery** has some Chinese work in amongst the chiefly Iban craftwork. There are some great wooden frames and a shipping service can be arranged. Next door is a more regular souvenir shop with colourful T-shirts, batik, and Penan-style basketry.

Kelvin's Gallery, at No 32, is perhaps a little pricier but bargaining might iron out the differences. **Arts of Dyaks** at No 34 is a friendly little shop with reasonable prices. Further along, at the corner with Jalan Bishopgate, a shop retails jars of Sarawak peppers, sago biscuits and laksa mixes. At No 57, **Sin Ching Loong** has a good selection of inexpensive batik from Indonesia as well as fabrics from Malaysia.

By the time all these shops have been checked out, it will be a time for a drink and a gourmet sandwich in the old Chinese coffee shop now converted into **Denis' Place**.

All of these shops are closed on Sunday.

Cat Museum

Petra Jaya, north of the river, free, open daily 0900–1700. Kuching has a thing about cats, as this museum shows. A motley and modern set of exhibits looking at cats from all angles. There are stuffed cats, cats in music, cats in ancient Egypt, cats in theatre posters, cats in medieval society... Bus Nos 6 and 2B will take you there.

HIGHLIGHTS

The **Sarawak Museum,** which claims to be the best museum in south-east Asia, is spread out in two buildings on Jalan Tun Haji Openg. Admission is free, open daily 0900–1800. The new wing, closed throughout 2000 for renovation work, is due to reopen sometime in 2001.

The museum was inspired by the socialist scientist Alfred Russell Wallace (1823–1913) whose travels in this part of the world led him to develop the theory of evolution by natural selection. It was his letter to Darwin announcing his theory that scared the more famous scientist into finally publishing his own views.

The **old wing** is the original museum, with the floor on street level devoted to stuffed animals and birds and the floor above largely given over to a re-created longhouse (complete with authentic shrunken skulls) and a room packed with ethnographic artefacts. Look for the Melanau *blum* images and the description that explains their purpose, though the pagan totem-like ceremonial poles are the most dramatic exhibits.

The **new wing** may have changed when it reopens but the floor at street level was devoted to Sarawak's singular history. The next floor had superb displays on Iban cotton-weaving, birds' nest collecting and a Bidayuh longhouse. There was also a section that disguised the government's cultural genocide of the Penans.

The **Islamic Museum**, Jalan P. Ramlee, is accessible from the new wing of the Sarawak Museum, free, open Sat–Thurs 0900–1800. Seven galleries, each with a separate theme, set about a central courtyard. More interesting than anything comparable in peninsular Malaysia and well worth a visit.

Chinese History Museum, on the waterfront, free, open Sat–Thurs 0900–1800. Built in 1912 as a courtroom for the Chinese (spot the scales of justice over the entrance), this is another great little museum covering all the immigrant groups: Cantonese, Chao Ann, Foochew Hainan, Hokkien, Luichew and Teochew.

ACCOMMODATION

Merdeka Palace $$$$$ Jalan Tun Haji Openg, tel: (082) 258-000, fax: (082) 425-400, e-mail: mpalace@po.jaring.my. Facing the *padang*, this top–of–the–range hotel houses an Italian restaurant, the **Seattle Coffee Company**, a popular English pub and all the usual amenities.

Crowne Plaza Riverside $$$$$ Jalan Tunku Abdul Rahman, tel: (082) 247-777, fax: (082) 425-858, e-mail: cprk@tm.net.my. Luxury hotel in heart of the city, tastefully decorated rooms with an ethnic touch. Chinese and Malay restaurants, poolside bar, gym, shopping centre and bowling alley attached.

Hilton Kuching $$$$$ Jalan Tunku Abdul Rahman, tel: (082) 248-200, fax: (082) 428-984. The most peaceful and classy of the five-star Kuching hotels. Rooms overlook the Sarawak River and a stay here can be combined with a night or two at the sister hotel at Batang Ai (see page 374).

Telang Usan Hotel $$$ Ban Hock Rd, tel: (082) 411-433, fax: (082) 419-078, e-mail: tusan@po.jaring.my. Famously friendly hotel with laundry service, safety deposit boxes, café and Chinese restaurant. Good rooms, some of which creep into the $$$$ category.

Laila Inn $$ Jalan Datuk Ajibah Abol, tel: (082) 420-930, fax: (082) 238-960. Air-con rooms with telephone, bathroom, fridge and TV. Safety deposit boxes and laundry service.

B&B Inn $ 30–1 Jalan Tabuan, tel: (082) 237-366, fax: (082) 239-189, e-mail: gohyp@po.jaring.my. Dorms and rooms with fan or air-con. Central, well run and helpful to travellers.

FOOD

Ristorante Beccari $$$$ Merdeka Palace Hotel. Elegant restaurant, excellent Italian food.

Steak House $$$$ at the Hilton Hotel has top quality European food. The hotel also has the best pastry outlet in town.

Denis' Place $$$–$ 80 Main Bazaar. Sandwiches, salads and steaks. Good coffees, happy hour for beer 1600–1800.

Benson Seafood $$ east of the Holiday Inn. Great place for an al fresco seafood meal. All the fish are on the display. Prawns are a speciality but also try the 'bamboo snails'.

National Islamic Café $ Jalan Carpenter. Been here for as long as I can remember and still serving excellent vegetable biryani and idli, as well as chicken and murtabak dishes. Airy and clean.

Briyani Café $ opposite the tourist office on Man Bazaar, serves similar Muslim food.

Malaya Restaurant, **Jubilee** and **Abdul Rashid $** are a cluster of restaurants on Jalan India that are always reliable for an inexpensive meal.

FOOD CENTRES

For sheer value for money and freshly cooked food, it is hard to beat Kuching's food centres.

Open Air Market $ Jalan Market. Not open-air, good selection of Malay and Chinese food.

Top Spot Food Centre $ Jalan Bukit Mata Kuching. Open-air, on top floor of a car park, with a wide range of Malay and Chinese food.

Taman Sri Food Centre $ behind Parksons Department store at Crowne Plaza Riverside hotel. Block of Malay and Chinese foodstalls popular with office workers during the day. At night the little cafés and bars around here come alive.

ORGANISED TOURS

Joining a tour at some stage is fairly inevitable in Sarawak, because a visit to a longhouse and to some of the parks (although not Bako) is a lot more practicable this way. Eco-tourism is a familiar oxymoron that pops up in some of the brochures but the good news is that many of the tour companies are sophisticated and reliable operations, and one or two are clued up about the ecological and cultural implications of mass tourism.

The downside is what tends to be an inverse relationship between the quality of the experience and the cost of the tour. The least expensive ones involve short visits to commercialised longhouses that are hardly worth it; the time would be better spent looking at the ethnographic exhibits in the Sarawak Museum. Expect to pay around RM50 for a city tour, less than RM150 for day trip to a local longhouse, and a minimum of RM230 for a two day/one night trip involving a stay in a longhouse. A more interesting visit to less touristy longhouses will cost more. (See page 380 for more on visits to longhouses.)

Singai Travel Service, Lot 257 Jalan Chan Chin Ann, tel: (082) 420-918, fax: (082) 258-320, e-mail: manfred@pc.jaring.my, web: www.singai.com. This is probably the most responsible tour company in Sarawak. While they offer standard city tours and local excursions they also organise programmes covering traditional Chinese medicine, therapy massage, *feng shui*, acupuncture, and Malay and Indian cooking. Their longhouse tours last from half a day to four or five days, and they also run safari-type treks on foot or by car, river safaris and trips to Mulu Caves, Sibu, Miri and Sabah.

Borneo Adventure, 55 Main Bazaar, tel: (082) 245-175, fax: (082) 422-626, e-mail: bakch@po.jaring.my, website: www.borneoadventure.com. Well-established company with a reputation for some of its longhouse trips.

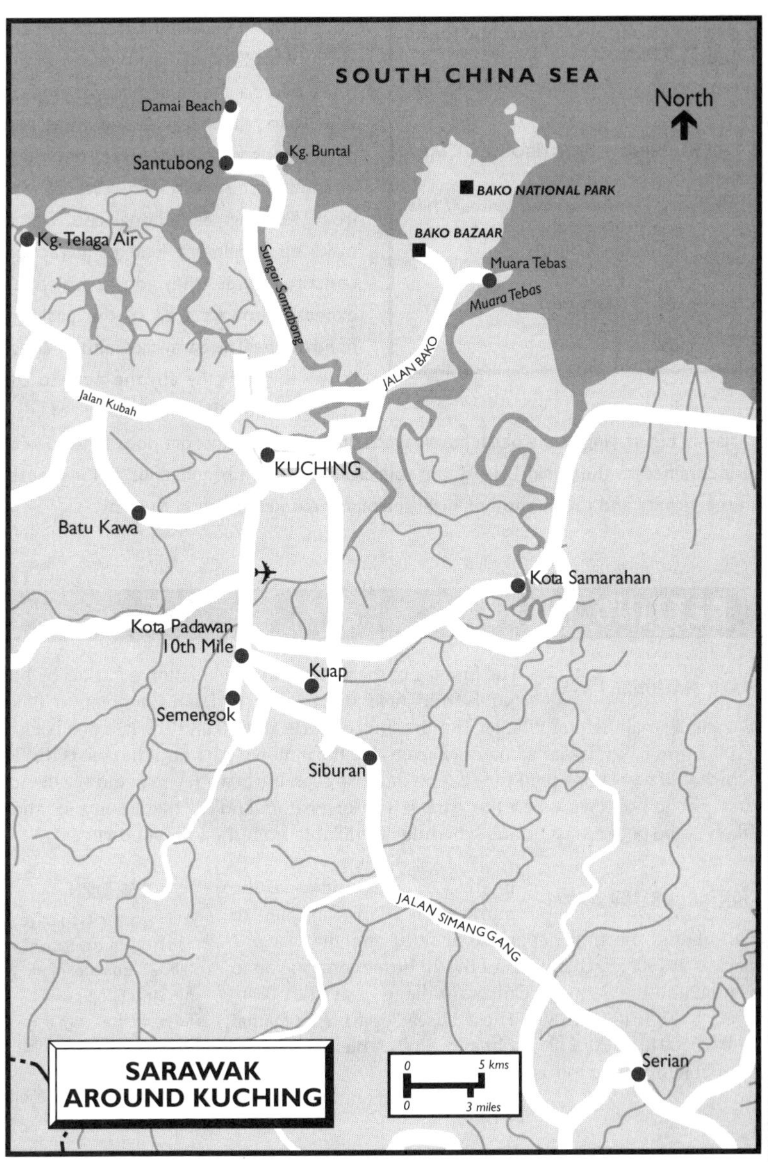
SOUTH CHINA SEA
North
Damai Beach
Santubong
Kg. Buntal
BAKO NATIONAL PARK
Kg. Telaga Air
BAKO BAZAAR
Muara Tebas
Muara Tebas
Sungai Santobong
JALAN BAKO
Jalan Kubah
KUCHING
Batu Kawa
Kota Samarahan
Kota Padawan
10th Mile
Kuap
Semengok
Siburan
JALAN SIMANG GANG
Serian
SARAWAK
AROUND KUCHING
0
5 kms
0
3 miles

Around Kuching

Kuching – Bako National Park

Transport	Frequency	Journey Time
Train	Daily, frequent	45mins
Boat	Daily, regular	30mins

Kuching – Santubong & Damai

Transport	Frequency	Journey Time
Bus	Daily, regular	40mins

Kuching – Serian

Transport	Frequency	Journey Time
Bus	Daily, regular	1hr

Kuching is an excellent base for experiencing what Sarawak has to offer and this route offers a choice of different kinds of trips. Bako National Park, one of the best destinations for nature lovers anywhere in south-east Asia, is very easy to visit from Kuching. Santubong and Damai make up a different kind of attraction, constituting as they do a relatively expensive tourist area of the package-holiday type. The Sarawak Cultural Village is worth a visit by anyone new to the cultural and ethnic diversity of east Malaysia, but staying at the plush hotels without your own transport does tend to keep you confined to the peninsula. All the tour agents in town handle trips to longhouses in the vicinity and this is another highlight of any extended stay in Kuching.

Getting There

Bako National Park

The first leg of the journey to Bako National Park is by bus No 6 from near the market in Jalan Gambier to Bako Bazaar, a small fishing village. The first bus departs at 0640 and the last one back is 1700. From Bako Bazaar a boat is chartered to the national park and the cost is RM30, which will have to be paid in full if no one else is on the boat. Try to avoid weekends and public holidays when the park is full of visitors and all the accommodation likely to be booked up. A bus schedule is available from the tourist office.

Santubong and Damai

Bus No 2B goes from near the market in Jalan Gambier to Santubong, the first departure at 0640 and the last one back is at 1900. Each day six of the 2B buses continue on to Damai and the Sarawak Cultural Village – at 0720, 0840, 1000, 1320, 1640 and 1800. These buses depart from Damai at 0820, 0940, 1100, 1420, 1740 and 1900. A bus schedule is available from the tourist office.

Car Hires

Hiring a car (see page 363) for a day would allow you to explore the Santubong peninsula and make for easy transport to the two fishing villages of Santubong and Buntai and their seafood restauraunts.

All the tour companies run organised trips to Bako and Sarawak Cultural Village and there is a shuttle bus from the Holiday Inn in Kuching to the sister hotel at Damai which can be booked by non-residents.

BAKO NATIONAL PARK

A visit to Sarawak's most interesting and most accessible park is highly recommended. Day trips are possible but an overnight stay would be more rewarding. Bako contains almost every type of vegetation found in the state, including beach, mangrove, dipterocarp forest, grassland, and swamp forest.

Jungle trails access the different eco-systems and there are opportunities to see five species of **pitcher plants** as well as a variety of **wildlife**. Around the park headquarters wild bearded pigs and macaque monkeys scavenge for food, while deeper into the park look out for otters, monitor lizards and some of the 150 species of birds. The star attraction is the proboscis monkey, most likely to be seen early in the morning or at dusk. Stay overnight and you might see mouse deer, flying lemurs, bats and fireflies.

All the **walking trails** are colour-coded and easy to follow without a guide, as long as you plan to get back to park headquarters before dusk at around 1830. The **Lintang trail** is a good one to start with because it passes through all of Bako's vegetation types and pitcher plants will certainly be seen after a climb up to a barren plateau where the plants lie among the shrubs. You should be able to find *Nepenthes gracilis* hanging from trees, the pot-shaped *Nepenthes ampullaria* and the distinctive *Nepenthes rafflesiana* with red and white stripes around its bowl.

The **Telok Delima** and **Telok Pako trails** are the best places to see proboscis monkeys. A walk to the **Tajor waterfall** includes a detour to **sandy beaches**, a rare sight in Borneo and far more inviting than those at Damai.

ORIENTATION

The park headquarters, **Telok Assam**, has the park accommodation and a central office where all visitors sign in and pay a small entry fee. Free maps showing the walking trails are available and there is an information centre with displays covering the park's ecology. A slide show on Bako's wildlife is shown in the evening.

ACCOMMODATION

Park accommodation is not luxurious and was probably left to deteriorate when it seemed that the park might be privatised.

This now seems unlikely and hopefully some funds will be found to improve the lodges. A lodge for two people **$** has a fan; there are also dorm beds in a hostel and camping.

Accommodation must be booked in advance through the National Parks and Wildlife office, Padang Merdeka, Kuching, tel: (082) 248-088, fax: (082) 256-301, in the same building as the Visitors' Information Centre. Reservations may be made in advance by telephone or fax but payment must be made before the first night's stay.

FOOD There is a park café, open 0800–2100, serving adequate but dull rice and noodle dishes. Definitely consider bringing some food with you to make it a more enjoyable experience. Packed meals are necessary for lunch when out walking. Bring lots and lots of water, as well as snacks and goodies for breaks along the way.

SANTUBONG AND DAMAI

The Santubong peninsula, at the mouth of the Sarawak River, is dominated at its northern end by Mt Santubong (810 metres). It has a beach at Damai which has been turned into an up - market beach resort dominated by two Holiday Inn hotels.

The main attraction out on the peninsula is the **Sarawak Cultural Village $$$** open daily 0900–1715, tel: (082) 846-411. It can be reached by public transport or a package offered by the Village for RM60, which includes transport from your hotel, entrance fee and lunch for RM60. Given that the entrance fee alone is RM45 this is quite reasonable.

The Village is a living museum, consisting of examples of Iban, Bidayuh and Melanau longhouses and other traditional habitations, with tribespeople demonstrating aspects of their lifestyle. The Penan dwelling, for example, has an animal trap, and elsewhere are displays of weaving, sago processing and basketry.

Visitors are invited to try their luck using a blow pipe, and there are scheduled performances of traditional dance with an element of audience participation, which is either good fun or plain embarrassing, depending on your point of view. Unavoidably touristy but managed with a degree of authenticity, a visit may well whet your appetite for a trip into the interior and a night at a genuine longhouse.

Jungle treks are possible on the peninsula. There is also a marked walking trail that begins near the Holiday Inn Resort Damai Beach and takes little over half an hour to complete. An ascent of Mount Santubong is a stiffer proposition which takes a whole day. A guide is recommended for this - enquire at the tourist office in Kuching.

Holiday Inn Resort Damai Beach $$$$$ Teluk Bandung Santubong, tel: (082) 846-999, fax: (082) 846-777, website: www.holidayinn-sarawak.com. On the beach, with all amenities. Fine if you only want to sunbathe, eat and drink; otherwise you may feel like a prisoner.
Holiday Inn Resort Damai Lagoon $$$$$ Teluk Penyu, Santubong, tel: (082) 846-900, fax: (082) 846-901, website: www.holidayinn-sarawak.com. Not so much a sister hotel as an identical twin. The beach is smaller but the restaurant has a sea view.
Santubong Resort $$$ Jalan Pantai Damai, Santubong, tel: (082) 846-888, fax: (082) 846-666, e-mail: skresort@pd.jaring.my. A useful alternative to the Holiday Inn near-monopoly, with frequent package deals. Pool, restaurants; ten-minute walk to beach.

The **Sarawak Cultural Village restaurant $$–$** has a menu service but most visitors have the buffet at lunch time. The restaurant closes around 1700 after the last dance show.
There are various restaurants at the three hotels but the food is mediocre, considering the prices. The only one worth mentioning is the circular **Peninsula Terrace $$$$–$$$** at the Damai Lagoon hotel. It overlooks the sea and there are tables outside but only about half the seating area gives a view of the sunset. Every Thursday there is an outdoor seafood buffet.
The best food is from the seafood restaurants at Buntai, but as there is no public transport in the evenings you need a car to get home unless you are staying at one of the hotels. Typical of these restaurants is **Beach Sea Food Restaurant $$$** tel: (082) 846-701, on stilts over the water and offering a car service from the hotels. Prawn, crab, lobster and plenty of other fish feature on the menu, as well as beef, chicken and deer.

SERIAN

Although this town south-east of Kuching can be visited as a day trip from Kuching, most visitors are likely to make a stop here as part of an organised tour to a longhouse on one of the tributaries of the Lupar River. Along the way, look out for the rich agricultural produce that is most of the inhabitants' livelihood. Cocoa plants are common and small pepper plantations are readily identifiable because of the way they are grown up four-foot sticks planted in rows close to the road.

Serian, one of the first inland settlements populated by Chinese immigrants, is full of roadside restaurants and small shops. The main point of interest, and usually included in longhouse trips taking this route, is the **food market** behind the main street.

ACCOMMODATION

Accommodation usually takes the form of a night in an Iban longhouse (see page 380) on the Lemanak or Skrang rivers, but there is one notable exception.

Hilton Batang Ai Longhouse Resort $$$$$ tel: (083) 584-338. A traditional longhouse with Hilton-style amenities. There is a small pool, a slide show at night, and activities such as fishing and trips to a local longhouse. It is a 4-hour drive from Kuching, followed by a 15-minute boat ride, so a one-night stay is hardly worth the trouble. Reservations and transport are arranged through the Hilton in Kuching (see page 366).

EATING

Typical of the eating places in Serian is the **Shin Fug Café $** opposite the Shell garage on the main street. Chicken, vegetables, rice and noodles make up the standard menu, along with some interesting drinks like peppermint tea and sweetish, green wheat–grass juice.

Sarawak Markets

A visit to a market in Sarawak can prove a fascinating experience, and both Kuching and Serian have interesting ones. At **Kuching's Sunday market** on Satok Rd villagers start arriving on Saturday afternoon, so everything is up and running by sunrise the next morning. **Serian's market** is busy everyday of the week.

Some of what you see at a market will be familiar enough – dried fish, pumpkin, bananas, mangoes – but there will also be lots of strange exotic fruits and vegetables. Round aubergines, spinach-like ferns, bags of *gula apong* (a brown sugar) and *mengkuang*, the essential ingredient in *rojak* salads, are nearly always available. Occasionally there will be some illicit produce for sale, like the bud of the rafflesia plant (see page 402) in its pre-flowering stage, which is credited with medicinal properties for women after childbirth.

The benefit of visiting a market as part of a tour is the opportunity to quiz your guide about what you can see. But even on your own it should be possible to identify and purchase *salak*, a brown palm–tree fruit with a scaly skin that needs to be peeled before its sweet taste can be enjoyed. Another common fruit is *keranji* which comes in two flavours: honey and sour.

Sibu – Kapit

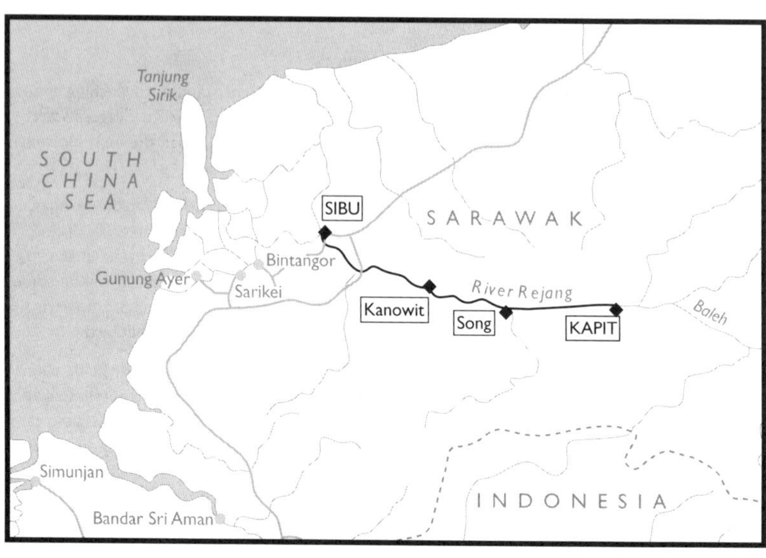

Sibu – Kapit

Transport	Frequency	Journey Time
Boat	Frequent, regular	2½hrs

Kuching – Sibu

Transport	Frequency	Journey Time
Boat	Daily, regular	4hrs
Bus	Daily, regular	7hrs
Air	Daily, regular	35mins

This route introduces the traveller to the characteristic mode of transport in Sarawak, very fast steel-bottomed, submarine-like boats that jet through the water at more than 30 km an hour. If your attempt at conversation is not drowned out by the sound of the engine then it will certainly be extinguished by the non-stop videos that play at maximum volume on all the trips up river. The journey to Kapit takes you past down Kanowit, a settlement on the River Rejang where Charles Brooke built a fort to assert his authority and enforce his ban on headhunting. The fort is still there but hardly worth stopping off to see. Boats also stop at Song, where during World War II Ibans were allowed to renew their headhunting pastime, as long as it was against the Japanese. By the time Kapit is reached, you should feel like an intrepid adventurer ready to enjoy a night or two in a longhouse.

SIBU

Sibu is the second largest city in Sarawak and it is situated on the mighty 563 km long Rejang River, the longest river in Malaysia. A busy commercial centre, Sibu is not a city that invites lingering. Travellers find themselves here because it is the jumping-off point for travel on the Rejang and for tours to **Iban longhouses** along its tributaries.

There is not a lot to see in Sibu, but worth a visit while waiting for transport is the Taoist **Tua Pek Kong Temple**, often marked on maps as the Chinese Pagoda or the Seven Storey Pagoda. Situated close to the jetty, the site dates back to before 1871. A stone-built temple appeared in 1897 but was destroyed by Japanese aerial bombing in 1942. The present structure was built in 1957; renovation work in 1987 added the seven-storey pagoda. When the caretaker is around, which he is most of the day and early evening, you can climb to the top of the pagoda for Conradian views of the river.

ORIENTATION Sibu lies on the north bank of the Rejang, 60 km from the sea. The centre of all the action is down by the waterfront where boats for Kuching and Kapit congregate at their jetties and issue piercing whistles to announce an imminent departure. Hotels and places to eat are all within walking distance of the waterfront.

BOAT There are two jetties on Sibu's waterfront, one handling boats to and from Kuching, via Sarikei, and one for trips up the Rejang to Kapit. Destinations and departure times are all clearly marked, and passengers can buy their ticket and leave their luggage on board for up to an hour or more before departure. **Ekspres Bahagia's** boats, tel: (084) 319-228, depart for Kuching at 1300, and boats to Kapit depart roughly every two hours between 0600 and 1500. Most of these boats stop at Kanowit and Song along the way.

A CHINESE CITY

Sibu's unmistakable Chinese character goes back to the early 20th century, when Wong Nai Siong from China's Fukien province came to an agreement with Charles Brooke to develop land along the Rejang basin. He quickly brought seventy immigrant families from China and more followed. Many changed from rice farming to rubber farming, and the settlement developed into a thriving town.

The city was largely destroyed by fire in 1928 and occupied by the Japanese in 1942, forcing thousands of Chinese into slave labour. The timber trade took off in the 1950s. Logging convoys on the Rejang are constant reminders that this remains the mainstay of Sibu's economy.

AIR Malaysia Airlines flights connect Sibu with Kuching, Bintulu, Miri in Sarawak, Kota Kinabalu in Sabah and Kuala Lumpur. Malaysia Airlines have their office at 61 Jalan Tunku Osman, tel: (083) 326-166. Sibu airport, tel: (083) 307-899, is 25 km from town and best reached by taxi.

BUS The local bus station is by the waterfront, a short distance west of the jetties, but the long-distance station is west of town at Sungai Antu, easily reached by bus No 7 from the local station which takes 15 minutes. There are various bus companies at the long-distance bus station and their ticket offices display their routes and prices. The 418 km journey to Miri takes about eight hours, and while there are also buses to Kuching the journey by boat takes half the time but costs more or less the same.

i The **Visitors' Information Centre** is at 32 Jalan Cross, open Mon–Thurs 0800–1645 and Sat 0800–1615, tel: (084) 340-980. Here you can obtain detailed information on travel within Sarawak and a useful colour map of the town that also lists all local and long-distance bus routes, their schedules and fares. The **tourist office** is just over half a kilometre from the waterfront, in the centre of town.

ORGANISED TRIPS UP THE REJANG There is nothing to stop you boating up the Rejang and enquiring in Kapit about a local longhouse that will accept you for a night's stay. In practice, though, it can be less fun than going in a group through a tour company and having all the transport arrangements organised for you with an interpreter on hand.

PREPARING FOR A BOAT RIDE

Don't choose a seat near TVs at the front unless you enjoy extremely loud videos featuring good guys kickboxing bad men into a state of unconsciousness. Even if you sit away from them, the volume will still reach you so bring a good book, a mini-disc player or ear plugs.

The air-conditioning results in continuous blasts of freezing cold air against which a T-shirt is poor protection. Consider buying a cheap blanket or at least bring a long-sleeved garment. You have been warned.

As with any tour, it pays to ask all the questions about the package before you commit yourself. Some tours using the Rejang spend a day and night in Sibu and use the Regency Pelagus Resort as the accommodation base with only a day trip to a local Iban longhouse. Another typical three-night trip uses a hotel in Kapit for the first night and continues on to Belaga for the second day, spending the night at a Kejaman or Kenyah longhouse, with the last night in a hotel back in Belaga.

All the tour companies in Kuching (see pages 367–368) offer trips like these. **Sarawak Adventure Tours**, 4 Central Rd, Sibu, tel: (084) 336-017, fax: (084) 338-031, e-mail: sazhong@tm.net.my is a company based in Sibu.

Tanahmas Hotel $$$$ Jalan Kampung Nyabor, tel: (084) 333-188, fax: 333-288. Within walking distance of the waterfront, with a pool and some rooms facing the river.
Sarawak Hotel $$ 34 Jalan Cross, tel: (084) 333-455. In the centre of town near the tourist office. Large, clean rooms and good value for money.
Hoover House $ Jalan Pulau, tel: (084) 332-973. The best budget place, but telephone in advance to check availability.

The **Premier Hotel Restaurant $$$** Jalan Kampung Nyabor, tel: (084) 323-222, two blocks north of the Tanahmas Hotel, is the place for a comfortable and enjoyable meal.
The **New Capital Restaurant $$$–$$** is a good Chinese restaurant with air-con, across from the Premier Hotel.
There is a **food centre** at the end of Jalan Market, one block north of the Tanahmas Hotel.

Overnight in an Iban Longhouse

On arrival at a longhouse, guests are normally introduced to the families and the chief. A tour of a guesthouse and its surroundings is as stimulating as you make it by asking the sort of questions that interest you. Looking around the vegetable gardens can be educational, as sugar cane, tapioca, papaya, pepper and aubergines are grown in a small space.

In the evening, guests are served with a meal, which can be surprisingly good. The women then display their handicrafts for sale, but there is no obligation to buy. Rice wine, *tuak*, is normally served before a gong announces the performance of a traditional dance in ceremonial dress. More *tuak* follows, usually with an element of audience participation, so that the residents have a chance to gawk at you for a change.

Depending on the arrangements made by your tour company, your bed will either be outside on the *ruai* or in a separate room. Some longhouses have guesthouses built next to the longhouse for tour groups. If you don't expect hot–water showers in a tiled cubicle and enter into the spirit of things, you will have a very enjoyable time.

The Iban Longhouse

The Iban longhouse is traditionally made of wood, built close to the banks of a river and raised off the ground by stilts. On entering you see a long vacant gallery between the bedrooms and the balcony, traditionally called the *ruai*. This is the social centre for the various families, typically about 15, who have their own private bedrooms but share the *ruai*. This is where the men and women do their work, making mats, baskets and farming apparatus, and where children play when not outside. At night, this is usually the sleeping area for young men and visiting male guests.

The *ruai* and the balcony command a view of the river and function as the front of the house, harking back to the days when anything that happened, such as hunting trips or enemy raids, took place on the river. Headhunting is a thing of the past but the river is still the lifeblood of any longhouse settlement.

The lifestyle here is communal. Any gifts brought will be divided equally by the chief between families, although property isn't shared. Each family has its own land and living space and is responsible for the area outside their apartment.

KAPIT

Kapit was an obscure outpost on the Rejang until the blistering pace of Malaysia's economic boom made it into a thriving little town. But arriving here after more than two hours travelling upriver, there is still a satisfying sense of a frontier settlement. Kapit might have the trappings of a town but the roads don't lead anywhere because the jungle surrounds it and the river is the only way in or out. Redmond O'Hanlon's book *Into the Heart of Borneo* describes his trip up one of the tributaries of the Rejang, the Batang Balleh, reached from Kapit.

To your left, stepping onto the jetty, is **Fort Sylvia.** It was built in 1880 to deter the Ibans and named after Vyner Brooke's wife in 1925. The tabulated high-water marks on the outside give some idea of how much the river can rise during heavy rain. A plaque records the signing of a big peace treaty here in 1924 between the Ibans, the Kayans, Kenyahs and Kajongs, supervised by the white rajah himself. The fort is well preserved as it is built of belian (ironwood), but is not open to the public.

A small **museum**, free, open Sat–Thurs 0900–1200 and 1400–1600, in the civic centre on Jalan Hospital is not especially interesting, though it does have some old photographs.

Greenland Inn $$ Jalan Teo Chow Beng, tel: (084) 796-388, fax: (084) 796-708. A smart, modern hotel with a range of rooms with air-con. Best value in town.
New Rejang Inn $$ Jalan Teo Chow Beng, tel: (084) 796-600. A little less expensive than the Greenland Inn. Decent rooms with fridge, phone and bathroom.
Dung Fang $$–$ Jalan Temenggong Jugah, tel: (084) 797-779. Not as bad as it sounds. Rooms with fan or air-con, adequate for a night's stay.

The Orchard Inn $$ 64 Jalan Airport. (Kapit used to have an airstrip, hence the street name.) An air-conditioned, comfortable restaurant with good food.
Kah Ping Restoran $$ Jalan Teo Chow Beng at the town square. Standard Chinese-style meals at reasonable prices.

TURTLES

Sea turtles, stretching back 150 million years into the past, are a truly ancient species. Of the seven species that swim the world's seas, four of them visit the coasts of south-east Asia, especially the east coast of peninsular Malaysia and the eastern coast of Sandakan. These are the leatherback, hawksbill, green turtle and the olive ridley. The largest, the 3-metre-long leatherback *(Dermochelys coriacea)* weighing around 350 kilograms, can be seen at Rantau Abang on the east coast while the green turtle inhabits Turtle Island National Park in Sandakan, Sabah.

Turtles, living off a diet of jellyfish, roam the world's oceans but the females periodically touch land in order to lay eggs. A male, once hatched, heads for the sea and never returns to dry land again. There are about 60,000 leatherbacks left in the world, mostly swimming alone and, as with the green turtle, the female lays between 50 and 150 eggs in one night. A hole is dug in the sand and covered up with sand once the eggs are in place. After about two months of incubation, the hatchlings emerge from their shells and hurry for all they are worth to the safety of the sea. Most will fall prey to marine predators and gulls and those that survive this ordeal live to face the danger posed by the human world. Plastic bags and oil slicks are modern threats, added to the age-long practice of hunting turtles for their shells and meat. Their eggs are also sold for consumption and, although this is now illegal in Malaysia, it is not difficult to find them on sale in the market at Sandakan in Sabah. Turtle shells are still used to make ornaments and turtle meat is still eaten across south-east Asia.

Leatherback turtles live to be a hundred or more and ones tagged in Malaysia have turned up off the coasts of Japan and China. They live nearly all their life in the sea, and your best chance of seeing one in open water is when they periodically surface to replenish their store of oxygen. Their time in the sea is spent looking for food – they need to consume at least their own weight in jellyfish every day – but how they navigate in the water remains a mystery. Females are thought to return to the island where they were born in order to lay their own eggs but how exactly they do so remains unclear. Scientists have identified magnetite in turtles' brains and this, being highly magnetic, may make up some kind of navigational device that taps into the earth's magnetic waves. The best way to find out more about turtles is by visiting the east coast of peninsular Malaysia or by spending a night on Turtle Island off Sabah. If you are lucky you will have an opportunity to watch a female laying her eggs and enjoy the spectacle of newly hatched turtles making their frantic rush for the sea. This rush for the sea occurs within minutes of breaking through the surface of sand above the egg, although the young will take up to two days making it from the egg to the surface.

Around Miri and the Kelabit Highlands

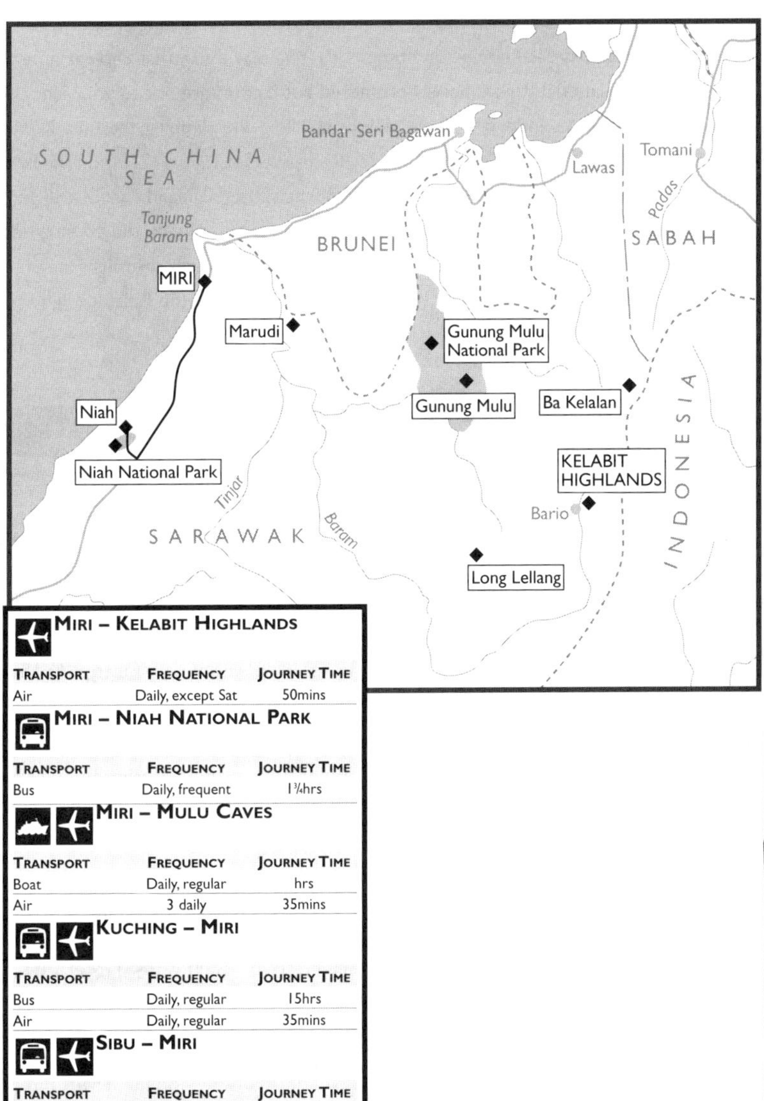

Miri – Kelabit Highlands

Transport	Frequency	Journey Time
Air	Daily, except Sat	50mins

Miri – Niah National Park

Transport	Frequency	Journey Time
Bus	Daily, frequent	1¾hrs

Miri – Mulu Caves

Transport	Frequency	Journey Time
Boat	Daily, regular	hrs
Air	3 daily	35mins

Kuching – Miri

Transport	Frequency	Journey Time
Bus	Daily, regular	15hrs
Air	Daily, regular	35mins

Sibu – Miri

Transport	Frequency	Journey Time
Bus	Daily, regular	8hrs
Air	Daily, regular	35mins

Around Miri and the Kelabit Highlands

Miri, like Kuching, is an ideal base for excursions into the surrounding area. There are a number of possible destinations, and time budgeting may mean that choices have to be made. Mulu National Park is heavily promoted but if caves are not to your fancy, or you're not the type to undertake some serious trekking and climbing, then the Kelabit Highlands suggest themselves as an enjoyable alternative. Set high (1127m) on the floor of a valley in the highest inhabited region of Borneo, the Highlands are a delightful suprise for visitors who welcome fresh air and invigorating walks in the countryside. The Niah Caves are best visited as a day trip from Miri, although overnight stays are possible. If time is pressing, our recommendation is to go for the Kelabit Highlands simply because it is a unique place.

MIRI

With a population of over 100,000, Miri emerged from obscurity in 1910 when oil was discovered in the region. The city is still on an economic roll with hundreds of wells, on land and offshore, pumping out some 80 million barrels of oil a year. Plans are well under way to transform the city into a major resort centre, evidence of which can be seen on the ride from the airport into town.

There is not a lot in the town itself to detain the traveller but the developing tourist infrastructure and the ease of getting about makes it a pleasant base for trips to **Niah National Park**, the **Mulu Caves**, and the **Kelabit Highlands**.

Miri has a beach to the south, **Hawaii Beach**, easily reached on bus No 13 from the local bus station in less than 15 minutes. Popular at weekends, during the week it suggests itself as a place to enjoy a picnic because there are barbecues and picnic tables to rent, as well as accommodation in beach chalets.

Getting There

Air: Malaysia Airlines has non-stop flights between Miri and Sibu, Kuching, Kuala Lumpur and Kota Kinabalu. The MAS office is at Lot 239, Halaman Kabor off Jalan Yu Seng Salatan, tel: (085) 414-144, open Mon—Fri 0830—1600 and Sat 0830—1600. The airport, tel: (085) 417-906, is 5 km from town, from where a coupon system $$ operates for taxis into town.

Bus: The long–distance bus station is about 5 km north of town on Jalan Miri Pujut. The local bus station is in the centre of town across from the tourist office and a regular bus service operates between the two.

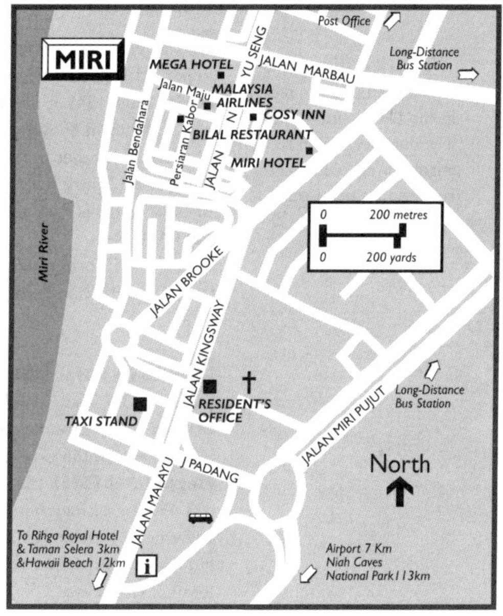

To Kuching and Sibu

Borneo Highway Express, tel: (082) 427-035, runs buses from Miri to Kuching via Sibu at 0630, 0730, 1330 and 2100. **Biaramas Express**, tel: (085) 434312, does the same route at 0630 and 1330. So too does **Lanang Rd Bus Company**, tel: (084) 335-973 at 0630, 0830 and 1130, and they also run buses just between Miri and Sibu. **Borneo Amalgamated Transport**, tel: (084) 654-308, run a night bus from Miri to Kuching via Sibu at 2100.

To Niah National Park

Syarikat Bas Suria run buses to Batu Niah from 0630 and then roughly every hour until 1600. These yellow and light–blue buses depart from behind the Park Hotel, close to the local bus station.

Tune In
On 94.4 FM you can pick up the UK station Radio London, beamed in to neighbouring Brunei and received clearly around Miri.

The **Visitors' Information Centre** is centrally located on Jalan Malayu, tel: (085) 434-181, open Mon–Fri 0800–1700 and Sat 0800–1245. It is worth calling in for their free colour map of the town, showing places to stay, restaurants, bus schedules, and other useful information. The Visitors' Information Centre is also where permits and accommodation for Niah National Park and the Mulu Caves are arranged, tel: (085) 434-184.

Bintang Plaza, north of the tourist office, has an **Internet** café as well as a Parkson department store.

RIHGA Royal $$$$$ on the beach south of town, tel: (085) 413-877. This is Miri's plushest hotel, with a pool and all facilities, but it is too far to walk into town and for a short stay is hardly worth the expense.

Mega Hotel $$$$$ Jalan Marbau, tel: (085) 432-432, fax: (085) 433-433, e-mail: megahot@po.jaring.my, website: www.megahotel.net. The brochure speaks of 'affordable luxury' but if so a substantial discount should be available. Centrally located, 17 storeys.

Miri Hotel $$ 47 Jalan Brooke, tel: (085) 421-212. Good mid-range hotel with clean rooms and reliable service.

Cosy Inn $$ Jalan Yu Seng Selatan, tel: (085) 415-522. One of a few mid-range hotels down this road and more or less living up to its name. Small but clean rooms.

Thai Foh Inn $ 19 China St, tel: (085) 418-395, e-mail: thaifoh@hotmail.com. Near the local bus station, rooms with and without air-con, bathroom and free Internet use for the first 30 mins.

Bilal Restaurant $$–$ Jalan Persiaran Kabor. Excellent, long-standing establishment at the corner of a pedestrianised street in centre of town. Tandoori chicken, curries, rotis and murtabaks served against a background of Indian videos.

Insaf Restaurant $$–$ is a similar restaurant across the road.

Chatterbox Coffee House $$$–$$ in the Mega Hotel can be relied on for its local and Western food. The hotel also has a Chinese restaurant, **Lotus Court $$$** and a lounge bar with live music in the evening.

Taman Selera Food Centre $$–$ out at the beach has a good variety of stalls selling Malay and Chinese dishes and seafood at night.

Tour Operators for Niah, Mulu and the Kelabit Highlands

Virtually all the established tour companies in Sarawak handle trips and package deals for Niah, Mulu and the Kelabit Highlands, and if they don't they will sub-contract the work to a company that does.

Kuching-based tour companies have already been mentioned (see pages 367–368) and there are some more good companies based in Miri. They all offer the same type of standard trips to Niah and Mulu and they should also be able to tailor-make an itinerary to suit particular interests.

Seridan Mulu has an office at the RIHGA Royal Hotel, tel: (085) 414-414-300, fax: (085) 416-066, e-mail: gracie@pc.jaring.my. As well as day trips to Niah and two/three/four/five-day packages to the Mulu Caves, the Pinnacles and Mount Mulu, they also have some interesting treks in the Kelabit Highlands.

A three-day/two-night trip covers a flight to Bario from Miri, a local longhouse visit and a three-hour, 10 km trek to Pa' Lungan for lunch with a trek back to Bario for the night. This costs RM600 per person for a minimum of two people. A five-day trip with three days trekking over the border into Indonesia and back costs RM1000 per person in a group of two. A more demanding ten-day trek up and down hills and crossing rivers over a total distance of around 50 km is also possible.

Tropical Adventure, tel: (085) 419-337, fax: (085) 414-503, e-mail: hthee@pc.jaring.my, website: www.ecoborneo.com. A typical three-day/two-night package departs for the Mulu Caves with the first night at the Royal Mulu Resort and the second night in less plush accommodation. The cost covers all transport, one picnic lunch, two set dinners, and guides for RM430 per person in a group of two. The same kind of package for two days and one night is RM295.

NIAH NATIONAL PARK

The Niah National Park, situated near the coast between Miri and Bintulu, is most famous for the **Niah Caves**. They may be geologically insignificant compared to the Mulu Caves but more than make up for this by their human interest. Tom Harrison (see page 394), the curator of the Sarawak Museum in 1957, led an archaeological dig at the mouth of the largest cave and the following year a human skull estimated to be 40,000 years old was unearthed. Rock paintings confirmed that early man had lived in the caves.

But the human interest that draws visitors to the caves today has more to do with bats and swiftlets than prehistoric man. Hundreds of thousands of bats (naked bats and Cantor's roundleaf bats) and swiftlets live in the caves and drop about one tonne of guano (dung) on a daily basis.

The guano forms a living carpet on the ground of the caves, supporting a colony of cockroaches and scorpions, and approaching the caves along the walkway you may well encounter men carrying away sacks of it for sale as fertiliser. The caves' swiflets (*Collocalia fuciphaga*) – white-bellied and black-nest birds – provide a more dramatic means of livelihood for local workers.

The 3 km long walkway to the caves takes you through primary forest. Towards the end of the walk bear right to reach the main cave. If you don't have your own torch, it is worth hiring one at the park headquarters. When you arrive at the **park headquarters** at Pangkalan Lubang there is an entrance fee $ to pay before heading down to a small river, the Sungai Niah, where a boatmen waits to ferry you across in a sampan for a small fee. The wooden walkway begins on the other side of the river and it takes about half an hour to reach the main cave.

DEADLY WORK

The swiftlets glue their nests onto the walls of the caves using an edible saliva and their nests are highly sought after by the Chinese for their medicinal properties. The nest–collecting season lasts from August to December (before eggs are laid, thus forcing the birds to rebuild) and from January to March (when the young have flown away and the nests are empty).

At these times if you crane your neck you can see the acrobatic, death-defying skills of the collectors as they scale fragile bamboo poles to scrape away the nests using 10 metre poles with torch lights attached. Even if you reach the caves outside the collecting season, some of their climbing equipment can still be seen. Safety nets have not been removed because they are never used, and serious accidents and fatalities do occur.

GETTING THERE People spend good money on a day tour to the Park from Miri but it is not difficult to make the journey using public transport. Syarikat Bas Suria runs nine buses, $$ from the local bus station in Miri, tel: (085) 434-317, to Batu Niah at 0630, 0730, 0915, 1020, 1200, and then on the hour until the last bus leaves at 1600. The return buses from the Batu Niah bus station, tel: (085) 737-179, depart at 0630, 0710, 0800, 0900, 1000, 1200, 1320, 1430 and 1530.

From Batu Niah boats $ wait to ferry passengers to the park headquarters and taxis $$ are waiting by the bus station for the short journey. You could also walk to the park in less than an hour by following the track by the side of the river.

National Park Chalets and Hostel $$$$–$ Pangkalan Lubang, reservations made either at the Visitors' Information Centre in Miri, tel: (085) 434-184, fax: (085) 434-179, or at the National Park headquarters, tel: (085) 737-450, fax: (085) 737-918. VIP chalets **$$$$** and regular chalets **$$$** with air-conditioning, dorm beds **$** and rooms with four beds **$$**.
Niah Cave Inn $$ Batu Niah, tel: (085) 737-333. Rooms with a fridge as well as air-con and telephone.
Park View Hotel $$ Batu Niah, tel: (085) 737-021. Probably the best value for money, comfortable rooms with air-con and bathroom.
Niah Caves Hotel $ Batu Niah, tel: (085) 737-726. Close to the river for access to the Park; plain rooms with air-con and a small restaurant attached.

National Park Canteen $ serves rice and noodle dishes. There is also a kitchen for the use of guests in the chalets and hostel with crockery, cutlery and cooking equipment provided. Some provisions in cans can be bought on the premises but it is better to bring your own food from Miri or use the supermarket in Batu Niah.
The restaurant at the **Niah Caves Hotel $** is always an option, and the small restaurants/food stalls **$** along the road leading to the river are OK for rice, noodles and chicken.

GUNUNG MULU NATIONAL PARK

Sarawak's largest national park has been open to the public since 1985 and the Mulu Caves, their main attraction, are so effectively advertised that they receive a constant stream of visitors from around the world. The spectacular cave system, the largest limestone **cave system** in the world, was first explored and mapped in the late 1970s and only four caves, the so-called Show Caves, are always open to the public.

Lang Cave, open afternoons daily, has a visually exciting variety of stalactites, stalagmites, helicites (branched stalactites) and rock formations, and an ever so tiny cave worm that you need a torch to see. A visit to **Deer Cave**, open daily in the afternoon, begins inauspiciously with a three-foot-deep carpet of guano covered with wriggling cockroaches at the entrance (don't worry, the walkway protects visitors).

After a short distance inside the cave look back to see the Lincoln profile at the cave's entrance. Try also to spot the centipedes on the ground that give off a luminous green glow when touched. Every evening between 1700 and 1830 a million bats fly out of the cave in sinuous waves, and there is a viewing platform outside where people gather to view the spectacle. Look out, too, for the hawks that turn up to pick off an easy meal of batmeat.

Wind Cave, open mornings daily, is probably the least interesting of the Show Caves. Halfway along the walkway there is a viewing platform with steps down to the entrance to a 7 km long tunnel that links up with Clearwater Cave. It takes between four and five hours to work your way along this linking passage, and a guide for this caving trip costs RM88 for a group of one to five cavers.

From the entrance to Wind Cave there is a boardwalk that hugs the rock as it follows the course of the river to **Clearwater Cave**, open mornings daily, where there is a lovely pool safe for **swimming**. Many of the tour groups organise a picnic lunch at this spot.

The crystal–clear water of Clearwater Cave certainly earns the cave its name and brings home the impact of logging in Sarawak when compared to the murky and muddy brown colour of the Rejang. Some 200 steps lead up to Clearwater Cave and at the top, near the entrance on the left, look out for the *Monophylaea glauca*, the one-leaf plant that is shown in a photograph in the display room at Park headquarters.

The **walking trail** that leads to the Wind and Clearwater Caves from the Park headquarters takes about half an hour and can often reveal fascinating glimpses into the micro–wildlife of the jungle. Raja Brooke's birdwing butterfly can often be seen fluttering about (scarlet head and green margins on the wing), and you may spot a feathery innocuous looking caterpillar on the handrail, which shouldn't be touched as it produces a terrible itchy skin rash.

About three-quarters of the way along, coming from the Park headquarters, there is a fine specimen of the *Antiaria toxicaria* tree on the right, clearly labelled. Also called the Ipoh tree, it once provided the Penans with poison for their blow darts.

There are three main options for **trekking** in the Park. In order of difficulty these are the **Headhunters' Trail**, a climb of the **Pinnacles** (see page 392) and an ascent of **Mt Mulu**. All take a minimum of three days, with overnight stays in longhouses and hostel-type camps, and can be expensive for just one or two people. Guides are compulsory, and necessary, for these treks. Full details are available at the Park headquarters.

Useful Gear for the Mulu Caves

A torchlight is useful, and essential if there is no guide waiting at the entrance to Deer Cave, plus swimming gear and a towel for a dip in the pool at Clearwater Cave. Binoculars are helpful when observing the mass exodus of bats from Deer Cave. Lots of water is essential (and far cheaper if purchased in Miri than in the Park). When walking through the Deer Cave, resist holding onto the railings because they tend to be covered in slimy bats' droppings. If you are keen to try some caving it is advisable to bring your own helmet and torches because hiring them at the Park is very expensive.

Getting There

Air: Malaysia Airlines flies to a small airstrip close to the Park headquarters, and if the weather permits the pilot will often fly in low over the Pinnacles for a breathtaking view of the Park's natural beauty. From the airstrip it is a 2 km walk to the Park headquarters, though guests at the Royal Mulu Resort will have a minibus waiting.

Bus and Boat: Not much money is saved and a lot of time is spent making it to Mulu by bus and boat. The first leg of the journey is the 0600 bus from Miri to Kuala Baram and then a three-hr boat journey to Marudi. From Marudi another boat goes to Long Terawan, sometimes involving a change of boat if the water level is not high enough, and then a third boat to the Park. The moral of the story is book ahead and get a seat on the plane.

GUIDES AND FEES There is a small $ entry fee to the Park and visiting the caves entails a compulsory RM18 charge for Deer and Lang caves and another RM18 for Wind and Clearwater. Guides are supposed to be waiting at the cave entrances but sometimes demand outstrips supply and you are left to go around on your own (your guide fee will not be reimbursed).

All the caves can be reached on foot from Park headquarters but it takes about an hour to reach Wind and Clearwater caves, and a boat there and back costs RM20 per person if five or more people want to go. Otherwise it is RM85 to charter the whole boat.

The charges for a guide on a trek depend on the destination. For the Headhunter's Trail it is RM24 for a group of up to five people, RM110 for the Pinnacles and RM264 to climb Mt Mulu.

All charges for guides, boats and accommodation are set out on schedules available at the Park headquarters.

THE PINNACLES TRIP

The Headhunter's Trail is a manageable trek for anyone who is reasonably fit. The Pinnacles trip is a little more demanding but no special skills are required, just stamina. It takes three days and two nights, and could be organised as an independent trip by just paying for a guide and the various fees for the boat trip and camp fees.

However, by the time you throw in the cost and trouble of buying your own food, cooking utensils and fuel it is very tempting to have a guide organise the food. The cost per person is RM600 (RM800 if you book through the resort hotel), and you need to come prepared with walking boots, wet gear, sufficient water and a sleeping bag.

Royal Mulu Resort $$$$$ Sungai Melinau, tel: (085) 790-100, fax: (085) 790-101, website: rihgamulu.com. This much-touted luxury accommodation, with an admirable design that blends in with the environment, might be worth considering as a package but is not worth the money when most of your time is going to be spent out and about. The restaurant is poor value for money and drinks are outrageously priced.

National Park Accommodation $$$$$–$ VVIP and VIP rooms **$$$$$** which are not worth the extra money when compared to the perfectly adequate chalets **$$** and rainforest cabins **$$**. There are also beds in the hostel **$** with lockable storage space.

Booking Park accommodation should be done at the Visitors' Information Centre in Miri. It is advisable to get some proof of room reservation just in case the booking is not relayed.

The food at the resort's restaurant is disappointing and most guests sooner or later discover the **canteen** just across the bridge at the entrance. The meals are inexpensive **$$–$** and the drinks almost a third of the resort's prices.
At the Park headquarters the **canteen $$** does adequate set lunches and set dinners. It opens at 0300 for breakfast for travellers departing at 0500 to return to Miri, and closes at 2340. Across the road is a new canteen, the **Buyuu Sipan** (literally 'salt lick') **$$–$** serving beer, rice and noodle dishes and a set lunch.

KELABIT HIGHLANDS

The Kelabit Highlands, the highest inhabited area of Borneo, are refreshingly cool and highly recommended for anyone interested in trekking. The only way to get here is by plane from Miri to Bario, a tiny settlement adjoining the airstrip.

Although tour companies all run **trekking** expeditions it is not difficult to organise something for yourself when you are there. Shorter half-day and whole-day treks are possible without a guide and it only takes two hours to reach a longhouse at Pa Umor, from where a path continues over a small bridge to a salt spring.

For a real adventure it is well worth organising a longer trip and spending a couple of nights in jungle huts and longhouses. Expect to pay around RM50 a day for the services of a local guide. The most enjoyable trek I ever experienced in Malaysia was a four-day return walk to Pa Tik. Although this is no longer possible as a direct trek from Bario, due to the encroachment of logging operations, it is still possible to take a more roundabout route. One of the longer treks is to Long Lellang from where MAS runs a rural airstrip with flights back to Miri on Thursdays and Saturdays.

Another possibility for an adventurous trek through the jungle is a walk to Ba Kelalan, with a night's stay at Pa Lungan in a longhouse. From Ba Kelalan MAS runs a daily rural air service to Lawas, and from there MAS has flights to Miri and Kota Kinabalu. The journey from Bario to Ba Kelalan takes four or five days and leads through a landscape of lush paddy fields, and up and down steep hills in the jungle.

There is only one place to stay in Bario. The proprietor can put travellers in contact with local guides and offer suggestions and advice on the trekking possibilities. A journal records some of the treks undertaken by guests in the past which provide lots of ideas for walking trips. If you organise a trip with a local guide this will include food provisions, but it makes sense to bring your own food too. A small store in Bario sells tinned and dried food but Miri offers a far wider range.

Officially, permits are required to visit Bario and although no one seems to bother about inspecting them it is a mere formality to obtain one from the Resident's Office on Jalan Kingsway in Miri. The tourist office in Miri should also be able to offer some help planning a trek from Bario. The best time for highland trekking is before and after the rains, between September and November, and between March and May.

Getting There

Malaysia Airlines flies between Miri and Bario, via Marudi, every day of the week except Saturday, departing between 1020 and 1220. The Bario airstrip is tiny and there are delays in the service caused by bad weather, something that is most likely in the rainy months between October and March. The service at Bario is managed through the Co-operative Society, no telephone.

Accommodation and Food

Tarawe's $ no telephone, short walk from the airstrip. This is the only place to stay and have meals in Bario, but this is not a drawback because it is a friendly place and can provide help and information to travellers.

The World Within

Tom Harrison, an English anthropologist, was parachuted down to the Kelabit Highlands with a small group of men towards the end of World War II. His mission was to organise local resistance to the Japanese, who had not reached the Highlands. His sojourn in Bario gave him a unique opportunity to study the people and their lifestyle.

His book, *The World Within*, is an account of the Kelabit culture. It is a fascinating read because it records the culture before Christian missionaries arrived in the 1950s and effectively destroyed many of the traditional beliefs and customs. A few senior citizens in Bario still remember Tom Harrison and in one of the longhouses outside the village I spotted an old black and white photograph of him, next to a colour picture of the Blessed Virgin.

SABAH

The north-east corner of the large island of Borneo was known as British North Borneo until it became part of Malaysia in 1962. Once covered by primary rainforest, the trees have all been logged. The survival of one part of the original forest has more to do with public relations on the part of commerce than any genuine regard for the natural environment.

Fortunately, no way has yet been found of making money out of destroying a mountain and Mount Kinabalu, the highest mountain in south-east Asia at 4100 metres, is waiting to be climbed by any reasonably fit person. The other main natural attractions of Sabah are mostly in the south near the town of Sandakan. Here there is an orang-utan settlement and offshore, close to the Philippines, a tiny island where turtles come to nest. To the south of Sandakan, along the Kinabantangan River, the rare proboscis monkey can be seen.

The capital, Kota Kinabalu, is where most visitors to the state arrive. All of Sabah's tour companies have offices here and many visitors use them, or are passed on to them via tours originally booked in Kuching. However, independent travel is more feasible around Sabah than Sarawak, and most places of interest can be visited on your own.

Books on Sabah's Wildlife

If you are travelling to Sabah to see some of the wildlife, there are some good books that can be bought in Kota Kinabalu which are difficult to find in bookshops elsewhere. They are published by Natural History Publications and can be purchased in Borneo Books on the ground floor of Wisma Merdeka. All but one of the following are paperbacks and affordable. (For bird books see page 411.)

Mount Kinabalu, K.M. Wong and C.L. Chan. The natural history of the mountain, and its plant and animal life.

The Natural History of Orang-Utan, Elizabeth Bennet. Lots of colour illustrations and sound text.

Proboscis Monkeys of Borneo, Elizabeth Bennet and Francis Gombek.

A Walk through the Lowland Rainforest of Sabah, Elaine Campbell.

National Parks of Sarawak, Hazebroek & Morshidi. Hardback and lavishly illustrated, RM150.

Kota Kinabalu – Tenom

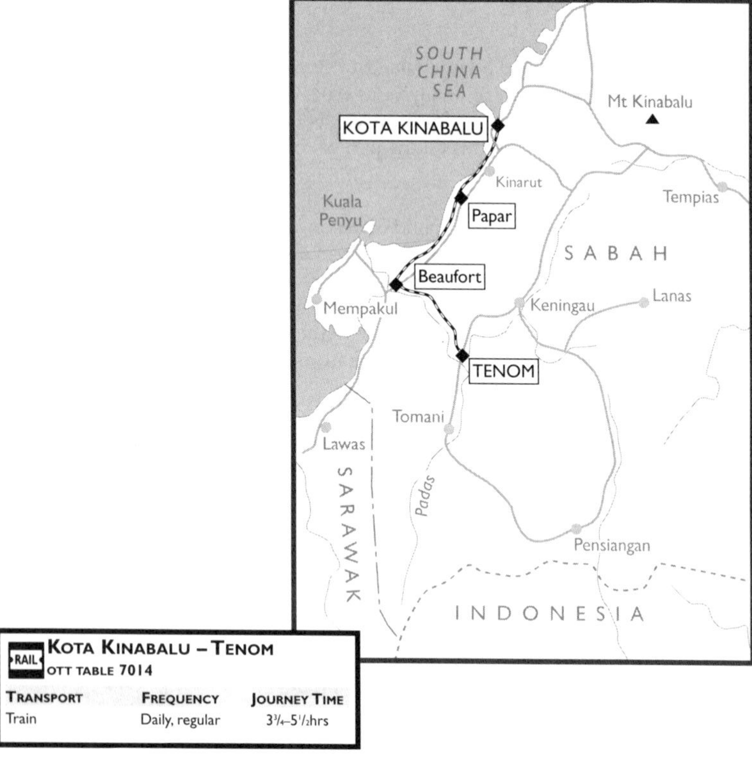

RAIL **Kota Kinabalu – Tenom**
OTT TABLE 7014

Transport	Frequency	Journey Time
Train	Daily, regular	3¾–5½hrs

Kota Kinabalu's urban feel can soon become tiring and an excursion suggests itself. The Rafflesia Forest Reserve is one possibility while the Tunku Abdul Rahman National Park is conveniently reached by a short boat trip from the centre of town. A journey by rail seems unlikely in east Malaysia but it makes for a far more relaxing experience than that provided by the cacophony on the river boats. The line runs through dense jungle, following the course of the River Padas. At Beaufort it turns inland across the Crocker mountain range, and views from the windows make this most definitely the highlight of the route. The local people are the Murut, easy-going and friendly, but there is not a lot to do in Tenom and even a one-night stay will exhaust the tourist facilities around town.

KOTA KINABALU

Completely razed during World war II, the tourist office, formerly the post office, is one of less than a handful of pre-war buildings here.

The only place to find some history is the **Sabah Museum**, free, open Mon–Thurs 1000–1630, Sat and Sun 0930–1700, Jalan Tunku. A bit too far to reach on foot from the town centre, catch any bus heading south along Jalan Tunku Abdul Rahman and ask to be let off the stop before the mosque. Built in the style of a longhouse, there are interesting archaeology, history and ethnography sections. An adjoining **Art Gallery**, with the same opening hours, has some appealing folksy paintings. There is a restaurant and pleasant garden grounds that are worth a stroll.

While visiting the museum, it is worth looking at the nearby **State Mosque** (1975), a successful example of modern Islamic architecture. The impressive exterior is composed of a dozen broad columns, each topped with a small golden dome. Visitors are allowed inside the huge interior if they remove their shoes.

It doesn't take long to tire of Kota Kinabalu's drab town centre but **Tunku Abdul Rahman Park** is the perfect diversion, consisting of five islands a few kilometres off the coast, with lovely sandy beaches and transparent water suitable for snorkelling. Best avoided at weekends and public holidays, **Pulau Manukan** has especially good coral, accessible to snorkellers with gear that can be hired from the island's small shop. There is also a restaurant **$$$–$** here that stays open until late in the evening.

Boats depart for Pulau Manukan from behind Wisma Merdeka, on the hour between 0800 and 1200 and then 1400 and 1630. There are chalets for rent on the island $$$$ that sleep four people, booked through Nature Resorts (see below).

NORTH BORNEO STEAM TRAIN

Colonial-style carriages pulled by a mid-20th century steam engine chugs and puffs its way from Kota Kinabalu to Papar (with plans to extend the service to Beaufort) and back, on Wed, Thurs and Sat at 1000, returning by 1430. The fare is RM160 which includes a tiffin-style lunch and soft drinks on board. Popular with British tourists and train buffs. Tickets and departures from Tanjung Aru railway station, tel: (088) 263-933.

ARRIVAL AND DEPARTURE

Air: The airport is 7 km outside of town at Tanjung Aru, and a coupon system operates for taxi transport into town $$. From the bus station behind Centre Point, minibuses run past the airport. Malaysia Airlines have their office in the Kompleks Karamunsing, tel: (088) 213-555, which is south of the town centre and a bit too far to reach on foot.

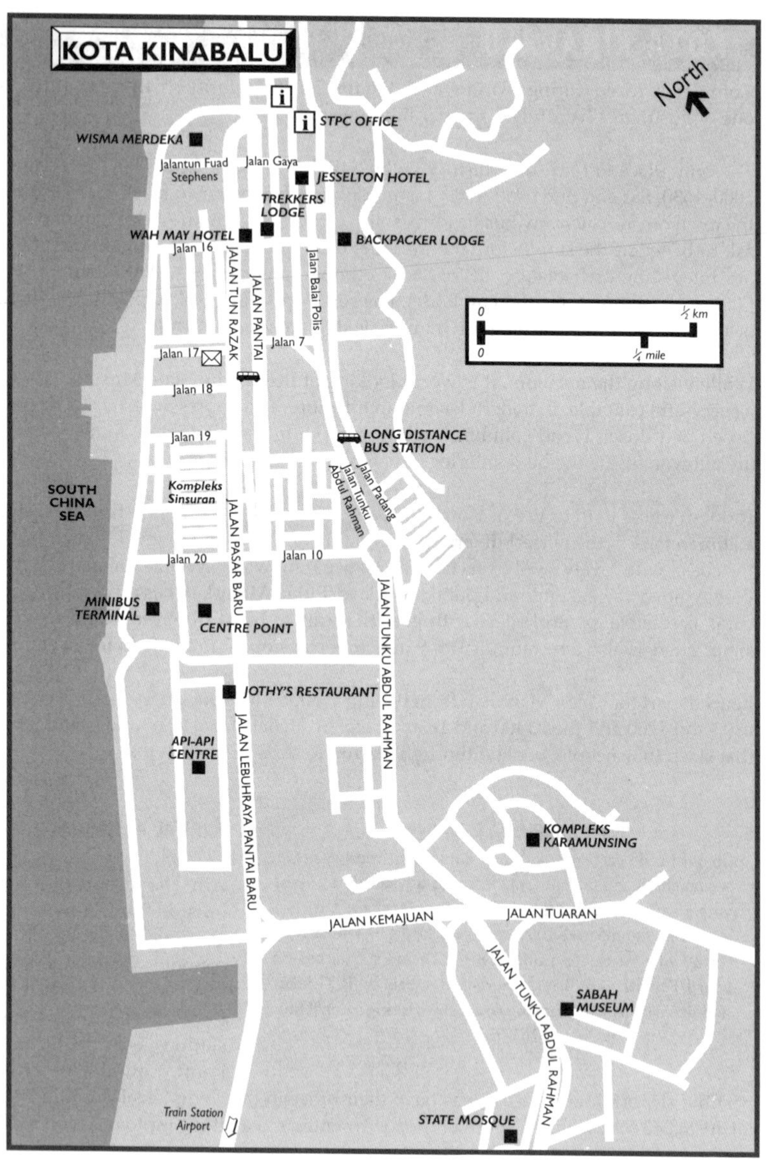
KOTA KINABALU
North
STPC OFFICE
WISMA MERDEKA
Jalantun Fuad Stephens
Jalan Gaya
JESSELTON HOTEL
TREKKERS LODGE
WAH MAY HOTEL
BACKPACKER LODGE
Jalan 16
JALAN TUN RAZAK
JALAN PANTAI
Jalan Balai Polis
0
½ km
0
¼ mile
Jalan 7
Jalan 17
Jalan 18
Jalan 19
LONG DISTANCE BUS STATION
Jalan Padang
Jalan Tunku Abdul Rahman
SOUTH CHINA SEA
Kompleks Sinsuran
JALAN PASAR BARU
Jalan 20
Jalan 10
JALAN TUNKU ABDUL RAHMAN
MINIBUS TERMINAL
CENTRE POINT
JOTHY'S RESTAURANT
API-API CENTRE
JALAN LEBUHRAYA PANTAI BARU
KOMPLEKS KARAMUNSING
JALAN KEMAJUAN
JALAN TUARAN
JALAN TUNKU ABDUL RAHMAN
SABAH MUSEUM
Train Station
Airport
STATE MOSQUE

To and from Kota Kinabalu, there are direct flights connections with Johor Bahru, Kuala Lumpur, Kuching, Lahad Datu, Miri, Sandakan and Singapore. Some of these flights sometimes involve a stop at Kuching.

Bus: Long–distance, air-con buses for Kinabalu, Sandakan and Lahad Datu use an area of open ground off Jalan Tunku Abdul Rahman. It is a matter of turning up and taking a seat until there are enough passengers, and the best time for a quick get-away is from 0700 to 0900. Minibuses travel to towns like Beaufort and Tenom, and the station is the empty ground behind Centre Point. They are usually over-crowded, and the train is preferable.

Train: The train station, tel: (088) 254-611, is 5 km south of town at Tanjung Aru, and the line runs to Beaufort and Tenom. Trains depart Mon–Sat at 0756, 1001 and 1340 and Sun at 0745 and 1350. The first–class fare from to Tenom is RM22.80 and economy is RM7.50.

i The **Sabah Tourism Promotion Corporation** is at 51 Jalan Gaya, tel: (088) 212-121, fax: (088) 212-075, e-mail: sabah@po.jaring.my, website: www.jaring.my/sabah. Open Mon–Fri 0800–1700, Sat 0800–1400. This is the office for information on Sabah only. Try not to get fobbed off with a photocopy of the town map, but ask for the colour brochure that has a detailed town map. An adjoining shop retails some craft items.

For enquires regarding other parts of Malaysia, cross the road to **Tourism Malaysia** on the floor at street level of the Wing On Life building on Jalan Sagunting, tel: (088) 211-732. Open Mon–Fri 0800–1245 and 1400–1615, Sat 0800–1245.

Bookings for accommodation in Mt Kinabalu and on Pulau Manukan are made through **Nature Resorts**, tel: (088) 257-941, 243-629, fax: (088) 242-861, 242-862, e-mail: nature@kinabalu.net, website: www.nature.kinabalu.net/. The company is at present located at Komplex Karamunsing but a change of address is imminent. Telephone, fax and e-mail information should remain the same.

Car rental, which makes more sense in Sabah than Sarawak, will cost around RM120 a day from companies like Aband-D, tel: (088) 722-300, fax: (088) 721-959.

The best deal for the **Internet** is K.K. Internat opposite the Merdeka Plaza, but the Jesselton Cyber Café in Gaya Street, near the Rasa Nyonya restaurant, offers more privacy and quietness.

SHOPPING

Wisma Merdeka is the most convenient place for general shopping. There are moneychangers on the floor at street level, as well as Borneo Books which has a good selection of material on Sabah wildlife, arts and ecology, as well as guidebooks to the region. Next door, **Rafflesia Gift Centre** sells souvenirs and gift items, and there are a few shops like this in the centre. Also worth seeking out is **Borneo Page**, Lot BG 58 B, a tiny shop selling *pareos*, a general–purpose type of sarong.

Centre Point has a department store and floors of shops selling shoes and clothes. There are moneychangers and a food centre.

Pacific Sutera and Magellan Sutera **$$$$$** Sutera Harbour, tel: (088) 318-888, fax: (088) 317-777, e-mail: sutera.po.my, website: www.suteraharbour.com. Nearly 1000 rooms, a ten-minute free shuttle bus drive from the city. Throw in 15 eating outlets and bars, a bowling alley, fitness centre, three pools and tennis courts, and you have one huge tourist complex. Pacific Sutera is the more subdued and business-like but less expensive.

The Jesselton $$$$$ 69 Jalan Gaya, tel: (088) 223-333, fax: (088) 240-401, e-mail: jesshtl@po.jaring.my, website: www.jaring.my/jess. A lovely place, with a colonial accent that befits the oldest hotel in the city. Modern, cosy rooms.

Hotel Wah May $$$ 36 Jalan Haji Saman, tel: (088) 266-118, fax: (088) 266-122. Rooms with air-con and bathrooms. Laundry service and safety deposit boxes.

Trekkers Lodge $$–$ Sinsuran Complex, tel: (088) 252-263, fax: (088) 258-263, e-mail: trekkerslodge@hotmail.com. Another Trekkers Lodge is at 46 Jalan Pantai (entrance at rear of building), tel: (088) 231-888, fax: (088) 258-263. These two centrally located places have dorm beds $ and double rooms **$$** with fan or air-con. Breakfast is included, and there is Internet connection, safety deposit boxes, and a laundry service as well as a booking service for all the regular Sabah tours.

Food Centres

Kota Kinabalu has plenty of food centres, usually located in the shopping centres, which are convenient for inexpensive food. The **SEDCO Complex $$–$** in the town centre is particularly good for seafood but only opens at night.

The street level of Kompleks Sinsuran is not especially appealing but the **Restoran New Arafat $** is OK for curries and murtabaks and **Restoran Anuar $** opposite has a good choice of Malay dishes set out cafeteria style. The **Wisma Merdeka Food Centre $** has a self-service food court with a choice of meats, vegetables and rice.

Backpacker Lodge $ Australia Place, tel: (088) 261-495, e-mail: lucychong@backpacker.com, website: www.sabahnet.com.my/backpacker. Dorm beds for RM18, laundry facilities and plenty of travel information.

Spice Islands $$$$$** Magellan Sutera Hotel, tel: (088) 312-222. Asian fusion is one of the more imaginative menus in the many restaurants at the two Sutera hotels. Starters like minced prawns on sugarcane sticks and main courses of garoupa with tempura lobster and spiced sirloin with yam cakes. Far quieter, too, than the more popular Italian-style Ferdinand's **$$$$$.

Gardenia Restaurant $$$$ The Jesselton Hotel, 69 Jalan Gaya, tel: (088) 223-333. Elegant, candlelit tables and fine food that includes snails from Spain, oysters from Australia and steaks from the US and Scotland.

Tam Nak Thai Restaurant $$$–$$ Street level, Api-Api Centre, tel: (088) 257-328. Pleasant and popular place, serving Thai favourites like green curry, papaya salad, *tom yang goong*, and lots of seafood.

Rasa Nyonya $$$–$$ 50 Jalan Gaya, tel: (088) 218-092. A short walk from the tourist office, a café-style place doing dishes like stir-fried beef with celery, chicken with ginger, steamed fish, lamb curry, plus a Western menu with steaks from New Zealand.

Jesselton Hotel $$$–$$ has a café-style restaurant popular with locals who come here for dishes like beancurd and seafood in a claypot and curry *laksa*.

Jothy's Curry $ Api-Api Centre, is reached from the main road outside the Centre. A limited menu of masala, chicken tandoori and fish–head curry.

Tour Companies

The standard tours offered by all the companies include city tours of Kota Kinabalu (RM45) and Sandakan (RM45), Kinabalu National Park (RM120), Sepilok Orang Utan Centre (RM100), the Rafflesia Centre (RM120) and the Kinabatangan River (from RM400). These prices are per person and based on a minimum of two people, but they are only approximate. All companies should be able to offer combinations of most of these tours with appropriate discounts.

Suniland, Jalan Oantai Sembulan, tel: (088) 291-500, fax: (088) 291-1530, e-mail: suniland@tm.net.my
Wildlife Tours, Tanjung Aru Resort, tel: (088) 246-000, fax: (088) 231-578.
Kinabalu Nature Resorts, 3rd Floor, Block C, Karamunsing Complex, tel: (088) 257-941, fax: (088) 242-861, e-mail: nature@kinabalu.net, website: www.nature.kinabalu.net/
Borneo Wildlife Adventure, tel: (088) 213-668.

EXCURSION TO RAFFLESIA FOREST RESERVE

This is where visitors have a chance to see the world's largest flower, the rafflesia. The plant does not flower to order and it is worth telephoning the reserve, tel: (087) 774-691, to ask if one is in bloom.

The reserve, 60 km south-east of Kota Kinabalu, can be reached by taking any minibus to Tambunan or Keningau from the station behind Centre Point, and asking to be dropped off on the main road outside the reserve. Getting back to Kota Kinabalu means waiting on the main road for a minibus, though it may be worth hitching while waiting.

From the reserve's information desk it takes between 30 and 60 minutes to reach a flower site, and you can ask the staff to draw a rough sketch showing the nearest location. Bring plenty of food and perhaps a picnic lunch because there are places to rest along the paths.

RAFFLESIA

There are 14 species of the flower, three of which are found in Sabah. The most common is *Rafflesia pricei* which grows to a maximum of 30cm in width. (*Rafflesia arnoldii*, in Sumatra, grows to over one metre in diameter.)

The rafflesia is a leafless parasite that grows and feeds off a vine. After a growing spell of up to 18 months, the buds emerge from inside the vine's roots and the flower opens during the night. Within a couple of days the flower has faded, producing a rancid smell that attracts carrion flies who carry the pollen from male to female plants. The rafflesia's fruit holds the seeds which are distributed by the rodents that eat the fruit.

TENOM

This is the end of the passenger railway line from Kota Kinabalu, which is the main reason for being here. The really interesting part of the railway line is the 50km between Beaufort and Tenom, best enjoyed from a seat on the right side of the carriage. The train follows the Padas River and trundles across wooden bridges and through thick jungle. It is a terrific journey, one of the best rail trips in Malaysia and comparable to the train ride from Bangkok to Kanchanaburi (see page 85).

Taking the first train from Tanjung Aru and arriving in Tenom around midday would allow three hours (half an hour less on Sunday) to look around town and have lunch before returning on the afternoon train. Although there is little to do in Tenom at night, you could stay overnight and return the next morning.

The railway station, tel: (087) 735-514, is right in town and places to stay and eat are all within easy walking distance. Departure times for the return trip to Tanjung Aru are Mon–Sat 0800, 1015 and 1450, and Sun 0800 and 1430.

Hotel Sri Jaya $ Jalan Padas, tel: (087) 735-669). A standard mid-range hotel with rooms with bathroom and TV. From the railway station, walk to Jalan Padas and turn left.
Sabah Hotel $ Jalan Padas, tel: (087) 735-534. Less expensive than the Sri Jaya but the clean rooms have either fan or air-con.

The Bismillah Restaurant $ at the Sabah Hotel can be relied on for tasty, fresh rotis and murtabaks, and is a good place for lunch although it is also open in the evening.

If staying overnight, a **night market** sets up in the car park further down the main road.

CLIMBING MOUNT KINABALU

Climbing Mount Kinabalu, half the height of Everest, is one of the highlights of a visit to Sabah and afterwards, when the muscle aches have subsided, you will undoubtedly regard it as *the* highlight. Anyone who is reasonably fit can make it to the top and children under ten and people in their sixties have proudly collected their certificates after a successful climb. However, large reserves of mental and physical stamina are needed, because it is a steep climb and there will probably be times when you wish you had never started. Take plenty of rests, start off slowly and develop a steady pace to suit your constitution.

It takes two days to reach the summit and your rucksack should include some warm clothing for the early morning start on day two. No special equipment is needed, even climbing boots are not essential, but bring plenty of water, some food for snacks and wet weather gear. Suntan lotion is essential and a torch is needed for the early morning start on the second day.

The ascent starts with a minibus ride from the Park headquarters to the power station at 1830 metres, where the eight-kilometre walk begins. The first bus leaves around 0700, and it pays to make an early start because that gives a whole day to reach Laban Rata at 3300 metres. The thought of accommodation, hot showers and a restaurant at **Laban Rata** should keep you going as the first day's climb draws to an exhausting end. Getting to sleep early should not be a problem.

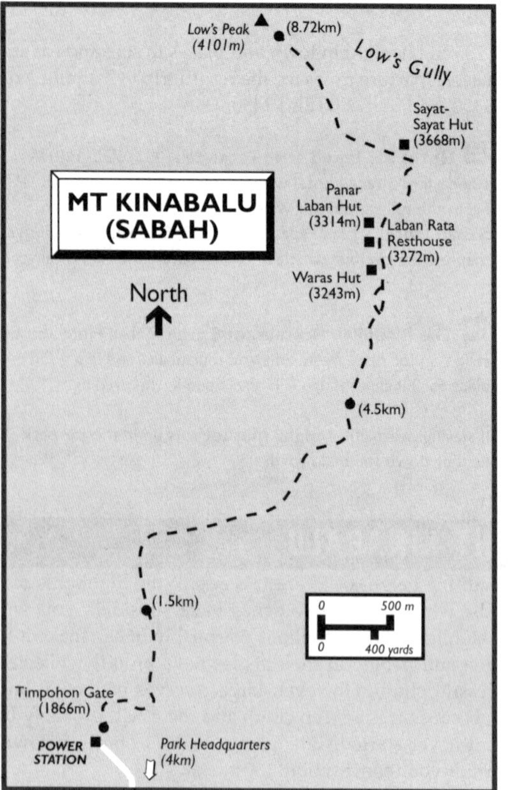

Day two begins around 0400, to allow for the ascent before clouds set in. The first hour is spent crossing and climbing bare rock in the dark, with the help of ropes and hand rails. This is the most exciting part of the climb, making everyone feel like a professional mountaineer, but when it is over it takes at least another two hours to get to the top.

This is when you may need to draw on your emergency supply of stamina but all is worth it when you finally reach the tiny perch that constitutes the summit. It is a forlorn spot and few climbers linger here for long; the view down into the black depths of **Low's Gully** can be quite frightening.

It takes about six hours to make your way down and there is no bus waiting at the power station so it is a long haul. This is when your leg muscles really get stretched, although it will be the next morning before you begin to feel the effect.

Kinabalu's Flora

The first day's walk up the mountain can be, and should be, regularly interrupted by opportunities to look at pitcher plants along the way. Most common is *Nepenthes villosa*, found at the base of trees or on the ground, identified by its peristome that points down inside its cup. Also look for *Nepenthes tentaculata* which can be seen along the sides of the trail between the power station and an hour before Laban Rata. Bring a guidebook (see page 395) with colour photographs to identify other pitcher plants that you might spot.

Accommodation

At Park Headquarters

All accommodation at the park headquarters should be booked as far as in advance as possible, through Nature Resorts in Kota Kinabalu (see page 399). It is more expensive at weekends, the eve and day of public holidays and school holidays.

Menggilan and Medang Hostels

Dorm beds $ with cooking facilities and a dining area with a fireplace. **Twin bed cabins $$$–$$** come with attached bathrooms and hot–water showers, costing RM92 at weekends and RM58 weekdays. The **annexe suite** costs RM184/115, weekends/weekdays, and sleeps up to four with a shared bathroom. **Duplex cabins**, a **single storey cabin** and a **double storey cabin**, all **$$$$**, sleep up to six, five and seven people respectively. **Nepenthes Villa**, **Kinabalu Lodge** and **Rajah Lodge**, all **$$$$$**, sleep up to four, eight and ten people.

On the Mountain

Laban Rata Resthouse $ shared bathroom facilities, a bed in a four-bedroom heated room costs RM29. There is one two-person room with attached bathroom for RM115 and a four-person room for RM230. **Panar Laban Hut $** and **Waras Hut $** are huts near Laban Rata and, while they only cost RM12 (half that on weekdays), there is no heating. Accommodation is also available at **Sayat-Sayat $**, an hour's climb from Laban Rata, but there is no electricity and it is very basic.

Near Park Headquarters

If the Park accommodation is completely booked out, there are some alternatives nearby. **Rina Rina Lodge $$$$–$** tel: (088) 889-282. A range of rooms from dorms to private doubles, a ten-minute walk from the turn-off for the Park on the main road. **Kinabalu Resort Hotel $$** tel: (088) 889-781, is not very attractive but it is equally close to the Park.

There are two restaurants at Park headquarters. **Kinabalu Balsam $$–$**, with a variety of Chinese, Malay and Western dishes at fair prices, receives the bulk of business. The **Mt Kinabalu Restaurant $$$–$$** is a little more expensive but has a wider choice of food. There is also a shop selling drinks, canned food and provisions.

The **Laban Rata Restaurant $** serves simple rice and noodle dishes (you are halfway up a mountain) and after you collapse into a seat here after the first day's climb the food will taste wonderful. There is also a shop selling drinks and snacks; consider calling in here on the way down for one of the walking sticks.

ARRIVAL AND DEPARTURE

An air-con bus departs from Kota Kinabalu (see page 399) for the Park every morning around 0700 and until 0900 you can also catch a bus for Sandakan and ask to be dropped off outside the Park on the main road, from where it is a short walk. Coming from Sandakan, any bus going to Kota Kinabalu will drop you off at the turn-off.

To return to Kota Kinabalu or to travel on to Sandakan, wait on the main road and hail down a minibus. This is no problem until noon, but the service becomes infrequent as the afternoon goes on. Hitching is not uncommon.

Kota Kinabalu – Sandakan

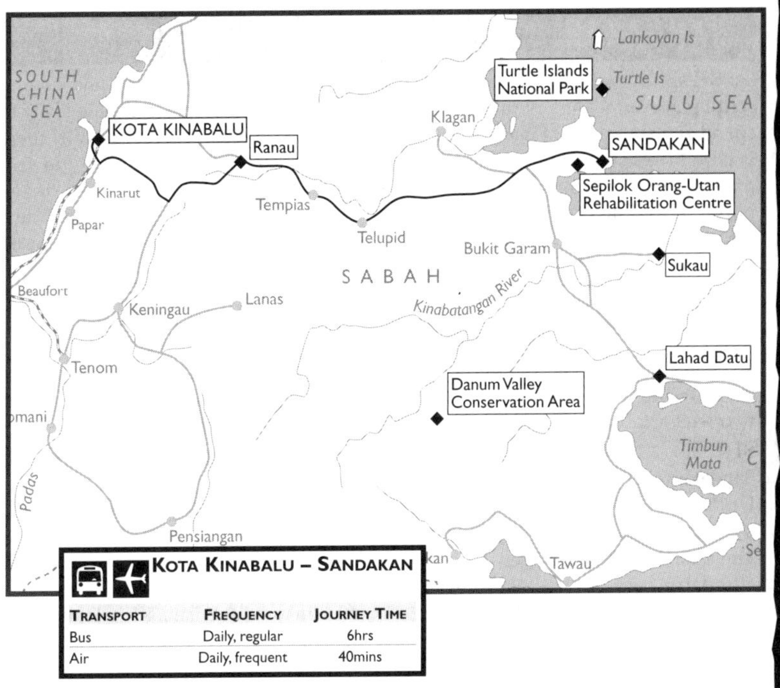

Kota Kinabalu – Sandakan

Transport	Frequency	Journey Time
Bus	Daily, regular	6hrs
Air	Daily, frequent	40mins

There is little point in travelling to Sabah without undertaking at least one leg of this route. Climbing Mount Kinabalu, the first stop along the way, is a manageable challenge for anyone who is reasonably fit, and the ascent may well turn out to be one of your most memorable experiences in south-east Asia (see page 403). The town of Sandakan has little intrinsic appeal but it is the jumping-off point for trips to the well-known Turtle Islands, the even better-known orang-utan sanctuary, and the unknown Lankayan Island, the latter being one of Sabah's best-kept secrets. Sandakan is also the starting point for more nature-loving journeys, this time across land to the south. The state's longest river, the Kinabatangan, provides the focus of an environment that supports a rich diversity of wildlife, including the proboscis monkey. Unlike the exclusively priced Danum Valley Conversation Area, the Kinabatangan region caters for all budgets.

SANDAKAN

Sandakan town, completely destroyed during World War II, is a drab and nondescript place but it has a number of nearby places of interest so you are quite likely to spend at least one night here. All the tour companies offer a city tour but really there is little to see apart from the market down by the riverside, and this is easy to visit on your own. You can save money by visiting the orang-utan centre on public transport, but for Turtle Islands you have to go through the private company that runs the park (see pages 409-410). Visits to the Kinabatangan River need to be organised through a tour company.

ORGANISED TOURS

All the tour companies, in Kuching and Kota Kinabalu as well as Sandakan, offer city tours, trips to Sepilok, Turtle Islands, and the Kinabatangan River and various combinations of some or all of them. For Turtle Islands and Kinabatangan River, the only places you can't visit on your own, two well-established Sandakan tour companies are worth checking out.

SI Tours, tel: (089) 673-503. Reliable and experienced company, with an office at Sandakan airport.

Uncle Tan (see page 410), tel: (089) 531-917. Offers the least expensive tours to the Kinabatangan River.

Travellers' Rest Hostel (see page 410), tel: (089) 216-454. Like Uncle Tan, the most affordable tours to the Kinabatangan River.

Wildlife Expeditions, tel: (089) 219-616. An office in town at Wisma Khoo Siak Chiew and at the Sandakan Renaissance Hotel, tel: (089) 273-093.

A major attraction is the **Sepilok Orang-Utan Rehabilitation Centre $$** open daily 0910–1100 and 1410–1530, easily reached by public transport. Barbara Harrison, the wife of Tom Harrison (see page 394), suggested the idea of a rehabilitation centre for orang-utans raised in captivity. A year after the 1963 law that made it illegal to keep the animals, the centre was established to help released orang-utans learn how to adapt or re-adapt to jungle life. Now most of the animals are there as the result of jungle logging.

Feeding time is 1000 and 1500, but try to turn up as early as possible to secure your place. Sepilok is very popular and large, video–camera-toting groups are often impossible to avoid, but seeing the animals is so much fun that it is worth putting up with it. There is a restaurant $ serving basic meals and snacks from 0700 until mid-afternoon.

Coming from Kota Kinabalu, you can ask the driver to drop you off at the turn-off to the Centre. From Sandakan, take the bus showing Sepilok as its destination from the local bus station or one of the minibuses, and check with them the return times to

Sandakan. The budget guesthouses will advise on the easiest and cheapest way to reach the centre.

ARRIVAL AND DEPARTURE

Air: The airport, tel: (089) 660-525, is 13 km from the city, and there is an airport bus into the city as well as taxis **$$$**. The Malaysia Airlines office is on the corner of Jalan Pelabuhan, just south of the town roundabout, tel: (089) 273-966.

Bus: The long-distance bus station is off Lorong Empat, west of the town roundabout and within walking distance of the town centre. For Kota Kinabalu turn up early in the morning because most buses depart between 0600 and 1200.

SANDAKAN MEMORIAL PARK

The Sandakan Memorial Park occupies the site of the Prisoner of War camp where 2700 Australian and British prisoners, mostly captured at Singapore, were held by the Japanese. Early in 1945 they were forced to march 260 km west into the mountains to Ranau: between January and June some 500 prisoners died on the three forced marches, and the remainder mostly died at Ranau or the camp itself. By the end of August only six men were still alive: two escaped on one of the marches and four escaped from Ranau.

The exhibition room at the Park, open daily with free admission, tells the story of the POW camp and the Death Marches through a moving set of photographs and survivors' memories. In the Park itself there is rusting machinery that the prisoners sabotaged, and the whole place is disturbingly empty of visitors.

To get there, take any bus going to Sepilok on the main road to Ranau and ask to be dropped off. Look for an Esso garage on the right, after the airport roundabout, on the corner of the road that leads up to the park. The Sri Rimbawan restaurant is across the road on the other corner. A large residential block is being built nearby which will probably affect the peaceful atmosphere that presently prevails.

TURTLE ISLANDS NATIONAL PARK The Park comprises three islands around 40 km north of Sandakan and very close to Philippine waters, but only one of them, Pulau Selingan, is open to visitors. Day trips are not possible and visitors stay the night to watch the turtles nesting and hatching. The green turtle is the most common. The female leaves her mate out at sea while she comes ashore and digs a metre-deep hole in the sand to bury her eggs. A hatchery on the island allows visitors to see the baby turtles emerge from their eggs, and it is not only children who delight in watching them being released on the sand and scurrying bravely into the sea to face a very uncertain future – only 1% will survive marine predators.

All trips to the island are organised through Crystal Quest, tel: (089) 212-711, in Wisma Khoo Siak Chiew in Sandakan. The cost, nearly RM400 for two people, includes transport, accommodation for one night in a chalet and meals.

Renaissance Sandakan $$$$$ tel: (089) 213-299. Not worth the quoted room rates but all the tour companies get healthy discounts and like to show it off on their itineraries.
Hotel London $$ Lebuh Empat, tel: (089) 216-371. From the bus station, walk up Jalan Tiga to Lebuh Empat and turn right. Decent mid-range place, though one traveller told me he could hear rats in the ceiling of the top floor.
Hotel New Sabah $$ Jalan Singapura, tel: (089) 218-711. Just west of the town roundabout, clean rooms with air-con and bathroom.
Travellers' Rest Hostel $ Block E, Bandar Leila, tel: (089) 216-454. From the town roundabout walk west along Lebuh Tiga, which becomes Jalan Leila, for about 1 km. The best budget place, with dorms and spartan double rooms. Good source of information and travel advice.
Uncle Tan $ Jalan Labuk, tel: (089) 531-917. Inconveniently located outside town, a couple of miles from Sepilok. Buses from Kota Kinabalu should be able to drop you off nearby, otherwise take bus No 19 from the local bus station in Sandakan. Bikes can be hired for visiting Sepilok.

There are lots of cheap places to eat around the waterfront but more salubrious establishments are not so common. The Renaissance hotel has the **Ming Restaurant $$$–$$** serving Cantonese and Szechuan food. For Western food try the **XO Steak House $$$–$$** opposite the Hsiang Garden Hotel on Jalan Leila. Along Jalan Tiga, the road that runs up from the market place has a few affordable restaurants with a degree of comfort: try the **Fairwood Restaurant $$** or **The Boss 2 $$–$**.

Lankayan Island

The most famous diving resort in Sabah is at **Pulau Sipadan**, 36 km off the south-east coast. It was from here that a group of 21 tourists and staff were kidnapped by the Abu Sayyaf Muslim separatists from the Philippines in April 2000. A little known alternative is Lankayan Island, the only dive resort in the Sulu Sea, managed by Pulau Sipadan Resort and Tours. They are also one of the companies operating on Pulau Sipadan but they have Lankayan Island all to themselves.

This idyllic little island is too small to accommodate more than one setup, and the result is a near perfect diving resort. Unless a large group of macho divers turns up, which is unlikely, the island is a haven of tranquillity and, unlike Pulau Sipadan, a non-diver could enjoy a couple of nights here just snorkelling, sunbathing and taking in a Robinson Crusoe experience (albeit with creature comforts). For details of inclusive package deals contact Pulau Sipadan Resort and Tours, tel: (089) 228-081, 765-200, fax: (089) 763-575, 271-777, e-mail: sepilok@po.jaring.my.

Bird-watching in Borneo

Bird-watching is one of the real delights of any visit to Borneo. A good guidebook makes all the difference. The affordable *Pocket Guide to the Birds of Borneo*, by Charles Francis, is readily available in Kota Kinabalu (published by the Sabah Society, website: sbs-online.com/sabahsociety). The *Field Guide to Birds of Borneo, Sumatra, Java & Bali*, published by Oxford University Press, has far better colour prints and may be worth the extra cost.

If you want to spoil yourself fork out RM270 and buy the just-published fourth edition of B.E. Smythies' great classic *Birds of Borneo*, published by Natural History Publications, 9th Floor Wisma Merdeka. In the UK it can be ordered through Natural History Book Services, Devon (e-mail: iaustin@nhbs.co.uk), and in the USA through The Borneo Company, Cincinatti (e-mail: rs888@aol.com, website: www.theborneocompany.com). The fourth edition is an astonishing achievement and should remain the definitive guide.

Kinabatangan River

Wildlife lovers should not miss a trip to the lower reaches of the Kinabatangan River, 80 km south-west of Sandakan, and its tributary, the Menanggul. The most unusual animal to see is the bizarre proboscis monkey, and the chances of not seeing one are virtually nil. There are also long-tailed and pig-tailed macaques, silver langur, red and silver leaf monkeys, the occasional wild orang-utan and dozens of species of birds, including the beautiful hornbill.

For bird-watching, the Oxbow lake is a prime area. Ask your guide to point out any birds and if you are lucky you should see the rhinoceros hornbill (*Buceros rhinoceros*), the largest and most flamboyant of the species. The pied hornbill and bushy-crested hornbill are also

ORANG-UTANS

The Malay word for 'man of the jungle' is orang-utan. It is their very human behaviour that fascinates the crowds of visitors that flock every day to the rehabilitation centre at Sepilok. Perhaps, too, Borneo's orang-utans played a part in the development of Alfred Russell Wallace's theory of evolution quite independently of Darwin.

I still cherish the memory of walking through the Park at Sepilok when a young orang-utan strolled out of the bush and casually took my hand to escort me down the pathway. The power of the juvenile's grip was tremendous; an adult has the strength of half a dozen men. But orang-utans are not aggressive animals. They are solitary creatures, sleeping alone in the branch of a tree, sharing an area of around 2 sq km during the day with others, and only coming together when sharing food or mating. At around the age of five the young orang-utan leaves the mother and wanders off alone into the jungle.

common, as are flocks of oriental darters (*Anhinga melanogaster*), the Chinese egret, Jerdon's Baza, the broad-billed roller, white-chested babbler, stork-billed kingfisher and the black-naped monarch.

Although travel and accommodation have to be booked in advance through a tour company, there are packages to suit most budgets. All the tour companies in Sandakan handle trips and most of them have their own lodges on the river. At the budget places, run by Uncle Tan and the Travellers' Rest Hostel in Sandakan, expect to pay around RM150 per person for a package that includes transport, accommodation and meals. At one of the more up market lodges, the rooms have a fan and attached bathrooms: expect to pay from RM260 at least, per person, for a package covering transport, accommodation and meals. All the packages include boat rides on the river and a guide.

DANUM VALLEY

Danum Valley is privately owned by the Sabah Foundation, the innocuous name for a large logging company. A part of their concession has been turned into a conservation area of primary rainforest. It is unique to Sabah because every other corner of forest has been logged, which is what makes a visit here so memorable. The big drawback is the prohibitively expensive rates charged for visitors.

But, apart from Taman Negara in peninsular Malaysia, Danum Valley is the best opportunity to experience the wildlife of the rainforest firsthand. The Borneo Rainforest Lodge is in the heart of the forest, where around 1800 each evening the imperial cicada (aka the 6 o'clock cicada) responds to the change in the light. It emits its alarming ruckus by vibrating a membrane across a cavity in the side of its body which acts as a sound box.

The guided tours conducted from the Lodge include a night ride in the open back of a truck when visitors can hope to see a flying squirrel gliding up to 100 metres across the night sky. Wild elephants are often seen between May and July when the hot weather encourages them to come out of the jungle to seek more open, cool space and eat the plants by the side of the road. There are good opportunities to observe wildlife very close to the Lodge itself, including bands of acrobatic gibbons, orang-utans, bearded pigs and sambal deer.

GETTING THERE The nearest town is **Lahad Datu** and it takes well over an hour's drive from there to reach the Danum Valley Conservation Area where the only accommodation is located. Malaysia Airlines flies direct between Kota Kinabalu and Lahad Datu, and buses from Sandakan take three hours to reach Lahad Datu.

Borneo Rainforest Lodge $$$$$ Danum Valley Conservation Area, tel: (088) 243-245, fax: (088) 262-050, e-mail: tourism@ysnet.org.my, website: www.ysnet.org.my/icsb/brl. Over 20 bungalows with their own balconies and bathrooms. Rates of RM350 per person for a standard room include meals and guided jungle activities. It is another RM230 per person for transport from Lahad Datu and entry permit.

The Executive Hotel $$$$–$$$ Lahad Datu, tel: (089) 881-333, fax: (089) 881-777. The best place to stay and the most comfortable place to eat in town.

Hotel Ocean $$ Lahad Datu, tel: (089) 881-700. Just past the KFC between the two roundabouts, this modest hotel has clean rooms with attached bathrooms.

The Executive Hotel's **Plantation Coffee House $$$$–$$** has a good menu of salads, grills, steaks, chicken satay, burgers, seafood and Chinese dishes.

The **Azura Restaurant $$–$** Jalan Bunga, opposite the minibus station, serves tasty Malay-Indian Muslim food like murtabaks, rotis and chicken.

If you arrive by air and are going to Danum Valley, the chances are you will be taken across the road from the airport to Borneo Nature Tours who handle transport to the Borneo Rainforest Lodge. A few doors down from their office, **Restoran Tarhamiza $$–$** does Muslim food of the chicken murtabak kind.

Further down, **Serai Wangi $** has a menu in Malay, but it is easy to see what is available.

SINGAPORE

Singapore arouses strong reactions from people. Unnervingly clean, organised and high tech, it sometimes seems as if there isn't a square inch that isn't regulated, sorted, tidied up and smoothed over, like a Sim City project done by a headmaster. But there is much more to the place than this.

The city has anything a tourist could ask for, from excellent food to enough sights to keep you for much longer than you intended to stay. There are beautifully renovated colonial buildings, thousands of good places to eat from hawker stalls to five-star restaurants, museums, boat rides, offshore islands and acre upon acre of shops. A tolerant, truly multicultural society with distinct areas dedicated to different ethnic groups and a multiplicity of cuisines, this tiny city–state's few square miles are packed with places of interest.

Best of all, considering its size and population, it has some wonderful green areas consisting of wetlands, primary rainforest, manicured parks with plants from all over the world and even uninhabited sandy islands. Coming from the relative chaos of Johor Bahru, the order and regulation of Singapore can be very welcome, even if you know that after a while it will wear thin and you will long for a bit of litter and a wily cab driver.

'The handiest city I ever saw'

'Singapore is certainly the handiest city I ever saw, as well planned and carefully executed as though built entirely by one man. It is like a big desk, full of drawers and pigeon-holes, where everything has its place, and can always be found in it.'

W. Hornaday, 1885

GETTING THERE

Air Singapore is a major transit point and connected by direct flights to many of the world's capitals. **Singapore** and **Malaysia Airlines** do a joint walk-on service between Changi Airport in Singapore and Kuala Lumpur's KLIA airport. Flights leave roughly every half-hour 0630–2130.

Singapore is also connected by direct flight with **Malaysia Airlines** to Kota Kinabalu (1 daily), Kuantan (2 daily), Kuching (2 daily), Langkawi (5 daily) and Penang (2 daily).

Angel Air, tel: 541-3210, has direct flights between Singapore and Chiang Rai (2 weekly), Bangkok (3 weekly) and Phuket (3 weekly), all in Thailand.

Bangkok Air has a direct flight between Singapore and Ko Samui (daily). Thai Airlines has direct flights between Singapore and Bangkok (7 daily).

Silk Air, the domestic arm of Singapore Airlines, does flights to Chiang Mai, Hat Yai, Phuket and Langkawi.

Taxis from the airport are metered with a S$3 supplement. A trip into town should cost about S$15. There are shuttle buses, tel: 542-1721, into town leaving at half-hourly intervals 0700–2300 which deliver passengers to their individual hotels. Tickets cost S$7 and can be bought at the shuttle kiosks in either terminal.

Facilities at Changi Airport

You could almost spend a pleasant holiday in Singapore without ever leaving the airport. Terminal 1 handles most international flights and terminal 2 Malaysia Airlines, Ansett Australia, Air New Zealand, Philippine Airlines, Royal Brunei Airlines, Silk Air and Singapore Airlines, Air France, Finnair and Lufthansa.

Accommodation

Each terminal has its own transit hotel, on level 3 of the transit lounges. There are also recliner chairs along the windows of the departure transit lounges.

Food

Both terminals have fast food places as well as regular restaurants, from sushi bars to Chinese seafood places, with a similar range of places to eat. In addition there is a 24 hr minimarket on level 3 of terminal 2. In the rooftop of the car park outside terminal 2 is a good hawker centre and there is another in the basement of terminal 1. Both are much less expensive than the outlets inside the terminals.

Entertainment

There is a cinema on level 3 of terminal 2 as well as a video games room on the same level. There are rooms for watching sport (level 2 terminal 2) and the news (level 2 terminal 1) on TV, a fitness centre, showers and swimming pool (level 3 terminal 1).

Post, Phones and Internet

There are Singapore Telecom outlets in the transit and public areas of level 2 in both terminals. They have postal services. Internet facilities are on level 3 of terminal 1 and level 2 of terminal 2. Both are in the transit areas.

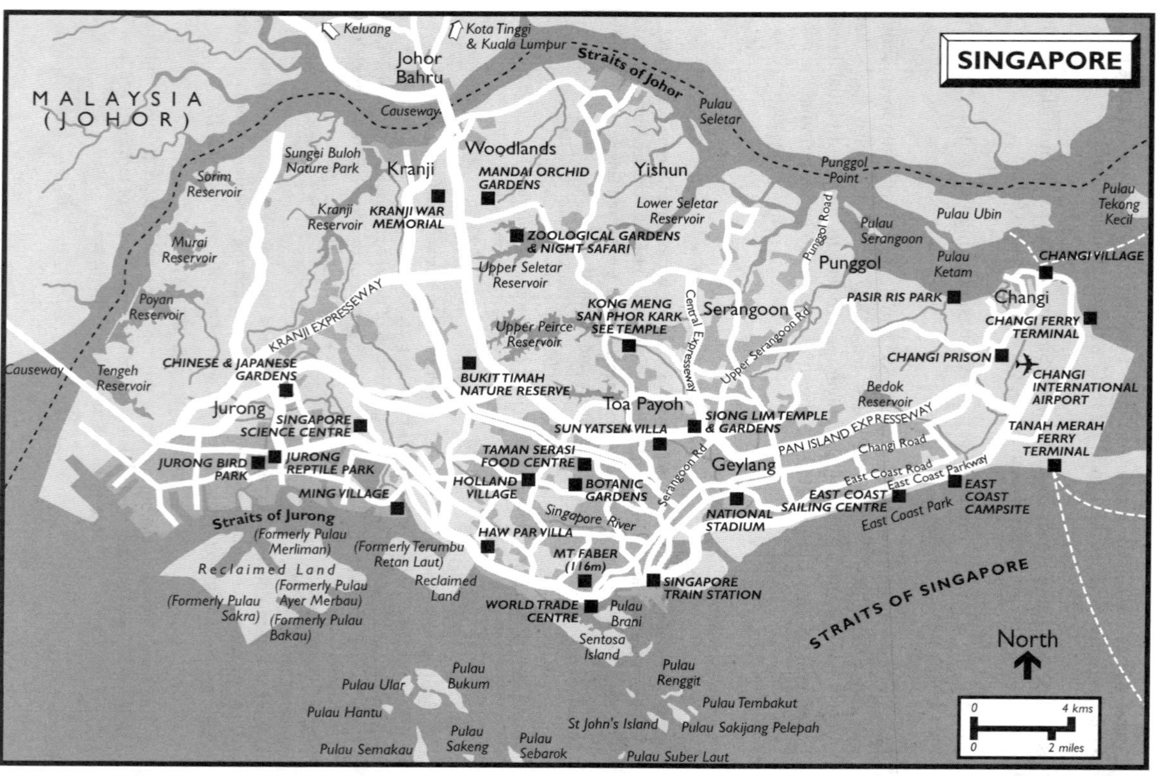
SINGAPORE
MALAYSIA (JOHOR)
Keluang
Kota Tinggi & Kuala Lumpur
Johor Bahru
Causeway
Straits of Johor
Pulau Tekong Kecil
Pulau Ubin
Pulau Seletar
Pulau Serangoon
Pulau Ketam
Punggol Point
Punggol Road
Punggol
Changi
CHANGI VILLAGE
CHANGI FERRY TERMINAL
CHANGI INTERNATIONAL AIRPORT
TANAH MERAH FERRY TERMINAL
CHANGI PRISON
PASIR RIS PARK
Bedok Reservoir
PAN ISLAND EXPRESSWAY
Changi Road
East Coast Road
East Coast Parkway
East Coast Park
EAST COAST CAMPSITE
EAST COAST SAILING CENTRE
STRAITS OF SINGAPORE
North
0 4 kms
0 2 miles
Upper Serangoon Rd
Serangoon
SIONG LIM TEMPLE & GARDENS
Geylang
NATIONAL STADIUM
Serangoon Rd
Central Expressway
Yishun
Lower Seletar Reservoir
ZOOLOGICAL GARDENS & NIGHT SAFARI
KONG MENG SAN PHOR KARK SEE TEMPLE
Toa Payoh
SUN YATSEN VILLA
BOTANIC GARDENS
Singapore River
SINGAPORE TRAIN STATION
Pulau Brani
Sentosa Island
MT FABER (116m)
WORLD TRADE CENTRE
Woodlands
MANDAI ORCHID GARDENS
Upper Seletar Reservoir
Upper Peirce Reservoir
BUKIT TIMAH NATURE RESERVE
TAMAN SERASI FOOD CENTRE
HOLLAND VILLAGE
HAW PAR VILLA
Kranji
KRANJI WAR MEMORIAL
Kranji Reservoir
Sungei Buloh Nature Park
KRANJI EXPRESSWAY
CHINESE & JAPANESE GARDENS
Jurong
SINGAPORE SCIENCE CENTRE
JURONG REPTILE PARK
JURONG BIRD PARK
MING VILLAGE
Straits of Jurong
Sarim Reservoir
Murai Reservoir
Poyan Reservoir
Tengeh Reservoir
Causeway
Reclaimed Land (Formerly Terumbu Retan Laut)
Reclaimed Land
(Formerly Pulau Merliman)
(Formerly Pulau Ayer Merbau)
(Formerly Pulau Bakau)
(Formerly Pulau Sakra)
Pulau Renggit
Pulau Tembakut
Pulau Sakijang Pelepah
Pulau Subar Laut
St John's Island
Pulau Sebarok
Pulau Bukum
Pulau Sakeng
Pulau Ular
Pulau Hantu
Pulau Semakau

TOURIST INFORMATION

There are information desks located throughout both terminals. Moneychangers are in the transit areas of level 2 of both terminals and in both arrivals halls. There are 24 automatic left–luggage lockers throughout both buildings.

TOURS

There is a free tour of Singapore available for transit passengers with five hours or more to spare, 1000–1900. It is also possible to book trips to various locations in Singapore but these are not free.

TRAIN Singapore is connected by KTM, the Malaysian rail service, to JB, Kuala Lumpur and stations along the west coast. There is a direct train service into Thailand (see page 21). There is also a route via Gemas to Jerantut for Taman Negara and Kota Bharu in the north east. The train station is in Keppel Rd, tel: 222-5156.

BUS Air-conditioned express buses leave for Johor Bahru from the Queen St bus station every 15 minutes. Price is S$2.40. There is also a local bus SBS 170 which can be picked up along the route, which costs S$1.10. At the Singapore immigration point passengers disembark, retaining their ticket, and go through immigration.

TICKET PRICES

Bear in mind if buying air tickets to Malaysian destinations from Singapore that it is often much cheaper to fly from Johor Bahru airport. JB also has more direct flights to Malaysian destinations than Singapore.

The Express bus usually waits for passengers to reboard but if it has gone, you can get on the next one. The 170 doesn't wait but keep this ticket and get the next one. Passengers disembark a second time at Malaysian immigration and from there you can either get back on the bus and go to the bus station at Larkin, 6 km north of town, or walk out of immigration into the city.

For destinations beyond JB there are direct buses to Melaka and the east coast of Malaysia from **Lavender St bus station**. For Kuala Lumpur there is a choice between Lavender St and Queen St. For other destinations north of Melaka and Kuala Lumpur buses leave from the **Golden Mile Complex** in Beach Rd. Tickets for all routes can be bought at the bus stations concerned or from travel agents. For Thailand, buses leave from the Golden Mile Complex. Most departures are in the afternoon and travel overnight. Tickets can be bought at the bus station.

TAXI Taxis to Johor Bahru cost around S$30 for the whole cab, more if there are queues at the causeway. They depart from Queen St bus station.

BUS FARES

It is considerably cheaper to go to Larkin bus station in Johor Bahru from Singapore and buy a ticket to your Malaysian destination from there rather than taking a direct bus from Singapore.

BOAT From **Tanah Merah Ferry Terminal** on the east coast there are ferries to Batam and Bintan islands in the Riau Archipelago, part of Indonesia. There are ferries every half-hour 0730–2000 to Batam, taking about 45 minutes. Ferries to Bintan cross four times a day with a journey time of about an hour. From the same terminal there are daily ferries to Johor Bahru. Ferries to Pulau Tioman leave daily at 0830 outside of the rainy season (early Nov–Mar). Tanah Merah ferry terminal is accessed by MRT to Tanah Merah and then bus No 35. Tickets are available from the ticket offices at the terminal or through a travel agent.

THE CAUSEWAYS

There are two causeways between Singapore and Malaysia. A recently built one links Tuas with Geylang Patah in Malaysia and is really only used by long–distance lorries, or people heading up the west coast. Most people travel on the older causeway between Woodlands and Johor Bahru. The new link has improved things but there are still huge traffic jams and long queues at immigration at rush hour and at weekends. It is possible to walk over the causeway.

From **Changi Village** ferries go to Tanjung Belungkor, for Desaru in Johor state. Journey time is 45 minutes and there are four ferries a day. Small, 12-person ferries also go to Pengerang in Malaysia when they fill up with passengers.

GETTING AROUND

TRAIN The MRT travels across the south of the island from Pasir Ris in the east to Boon Lay in the west. A second line runs from Marina Bay in the south to Jurong via Woodlands in the north. Single–fare tickets are available from vending machines at the station entrances and cost from S$0.70 to S$1.60. You need the exact change but there are change machines. There is also an elevated light rail system, the SLRT, which connects with the metro.

You can also buy a stored value card which allows you to make several journeys until the stored value is used up. It can be recharged. Singaporeans save their last few stored cents for long journeys. The cards can also be used on buses. The S$7 tourist ticket gives you S$6 of trips and is not rechargeable.

BUS Singapore has a vast network of buses which travel all over the island. For S$1.40 you can buy the pocket–sized Transitlink Guide which lists all the bus routes. Fares range from S$0.60 (non-air con) to S$1.50 and you need the exact fare or your transitlink card.

The Singapore Trolley which you see scooting about town costs S$14.50 per day. That's the equivalent of 8 trips across the island on a regular bus, but it has the advantage of a route that covers most tourist attractions, and you can hop on and off as you like.

TAXIS All taxis in Singapore are metered, air-conditioned and very clean. Fares start at S$2.40 and go up S$0.10 for every 240 meters after the first 1 km. There are surcharges for a call out, for journeys beginning in the Central Business District (CBD) and a 50% surcharge after midnight. Some taxis accept credit cards.

THE CBD AND ERP (ELECTRONIC ROAD PRICING)

In order to ease the huge traffic congestion at peak hours, and to gain income, the Singapore government has introduced a toll system for certain areas of the city and some of the highways. These tolls only operate during peak hours and are levied via a little black box that sits on everyone's dashboard.

Machines on overhead gantries read the messages emanating from the black box and charge the driver's account with the toll, S$2.50 0800–0900 and S$3 0900–1930 Mon–Fri and 1015–1400 Sat. If you are in a cab some, but not all, of this charge will be reflected in your fare. Taxi companies have negotiated different deals with the government. It should never be more than S$1.

CAR Traffic drives on the left in Singapore. The speed limit is 50 km per hour, 80 km on expressways. Parking is by a coupon which you can buy in shops. Car hire is much more expensive in Singapore than JB and it is even more expensive if you plan to take the car over the causeway. It is cheaper to bus over to JB and hire one. There are tolls on both causeways, and petrol tanks must be three–quarters full on leaving Singapore.

INFORMATION

CITY AND TRANSPORT MAPS – inside back cover

The main tourist office is at **Tourism Court** 1 Orchard Spring Lane, tel: 736-6622, Mon–Fri 0830–1700, Sat 0830–1300. There are smaller offices at **Liang Court** 177 River Valley Rd, open daily 1030–2130, and **Sentosa** and **Suntec City** 3 Temasek Boulevard, 01-35/37/39/41, open daily 0800–1830.

E-MAIL AND INTERNET

There are Internet cafés in the Funan Centre, Tanjong Pagar Rd, Boat Quay and many other shopping centres. There are also two at Changi airport.

EMBASSIES AND CONSULATES

Australia, tel: 737-9311, 25 Napier Rd
Brunei, tel: 733-9055, 325 Tanglin Rd
Canada, tel: 325-3200, 15th floor IBM Tower, 80 Anson Rd
China, tel: 734-3080, 70-76 Dalvey Rd
France, tel: 466-4866, 5 Gallop Rd
Germany, tel: 773-7135, Far East Shopping Centre, 545 Orchard Rd
Indonesia, tel: 737-7422, 7 Chatsworth Rd
Malaysia, tel: 235-0111, 268 Orchard Rd
Philippines, tel: 737-3977, 20 Nassim Rd
Thailand, tel: 737-2644, 370 Orchard Rd
UK, tel: 473-9333, 100 Tanglin Rd
USA, tel: 476-9340, 27, Napier Rd

EMERGENCIES

For police, phone 999, for ambulance and fire 995. Lost property tel: 733-0000 (Tanglin Police Station). Lost and stolen credit cards: American express tel: 1800 732-2244, Diners tel: 1800 294-4222, Mastercard tel: 1800 110-0113, Visa tel: 1800 345-1345.

EXCHANGE

There are licensed moneychangers in all of the big shopping centres. They are open longer hours than banks and do not charge a fee for changing travellers' cheques. Banking hours are 0930–1500, Mon–Fri, 0930–1130 Sat. Singaporean ATMs (auto teller machines) accept a range of credit cards.

HOSPITALS **Singapore General Hospital**, tel: 222-3322 in Outram Rd has an Accident and Emergency department.

POSTAL SERVICES The main **post office** is in Robinson Rd but there are many smaller branches in the shopping centres. Most post offices are open 0830–1700 Mon–Fri, 0830–1300 Sat. Robinson Rd has a post restante service.

ACCOMMODATION

Singapore has a good range of accommodation, from five-star designer hotels to dorm beds in flats in Geylang. Prices are higher than over the causeway, and one way of offsetting the cost of your stay in Singapore is to stay in JB and bus over. But the expensive Singapore hotels have much to offer in terms of design and luxury, and the more moderate ones are very central and well regulated. Hotels add 13% to their bills in taxes and service charges, and where the room rate has a series of pluses after it you can add the 13% on the bill. Cheaper places include that in the room rate.

EXPENSIVE

Goodwood Park $$$$$ tel: 737-7411, fax: 732-8558, 22 Scotts Rd. Almost as grand as the Raffles, 1 Beach Rd, but not as expensive. Vast grounds, two pools, lovely big old rooms and a new modern wing.

Oriental $$$$$ tel: 338-0066, fax: 339-9537, 5 Raffles Ave. Built in a fan shape, with a huge cathedral-like atrium. Big rooms and pretty harbour views. Big pool, excellent restaurants, jogging track, fitness centre.

Marina Mandarin $$$$$ tel: 338-8388, fax: 339-4977, 6 Raffles Boulevard. Another vast atrium, festooned with plants and songbirds. Lovely rooms, good river views, pool, all above an excellent shopping centre.

Westin Stamford $$$$$ tel: 339-6633, fax: 336-5117, 2 Stamford Rd. The highest hotel in the world, according to the *Guinness Book of Records*, but for how long? If you have a head for heights the top floors have the most amazing views and balconies. Nice rooms, great series of pools, 13 restaurants.

Hilton $$$$$ tel: 737-2233, fax: 732-2291, 581 Orchard Rd. Singapore's third oldest hotel, developing a historic style of its own as all the other 1970s buildings bite the dust. Small pool but nice rooms, excellent restaurants and great cheesecake in the deli.

New Otani $$$ tel: 338-3333, fax: 339-2834, 177 River valley Rd. Close to Boat Quay in pleasant part of the city. Excellent Japanese restaurant, nice rooms, vaguely Japanese ambience, good pool, above shopping centre.

Plaza Parkroyal $$$ tel: 298-0011, fax: 296-3600, e-mail: plazahtl@mbox2.singnet.com.sg, 7500A Beach Rd. Comfortable hotel with pleasant rooms in quiet area. Good coffee shop, Chinese restaurant, excellent fitness centre with rock climbing, nice pool, pub with dance floor.

Amara $$$ tel: 224-4488, fax: 224-3910, e-mail: reserv@amara.com.sg, 164 Tanjong Pagar Rd. In Chinatown, this place is well maintained with an excellent Thai restaurant, launderette, good sports facilities.

Golden Landmark $$$ tel: 297-2828, fax: 298-2038. Islamic-looking tower block near Arab St and Serangoon Rd. Good value.

MODERATE

City Bayview $$ tel: 337-2882, fax: 338-2880, 30 Bencoolen St. Part of a chain, all facilities in the rooms and price includes breakfast.

RELC, International House $$ tel: 737-9044, fax: 733-9976, 30, Orange Grove Rd. Ugly building, a little out of the way but huge rooms with all the basic requirements, launderette, kitchen.

Hotel Bencoolen $$ tel: 336-0822, fax: 336-2250, e-mail: bencoolen@pacific.net.sg, 47 Bencoolen St. Good location, TV, safe, minibar and a spa pool on the roof.

Perak Lodge $$ tel: 299-7733, fax: 392-0919, 12 Perak Rd. Restored shop-house close to Serangoon Rd with all room facilities of Bencoolen at a slightly cheaper rate. Good security, price includes breakfast, bar and coffee shop.

Dickson Court Hotel $$ tel: 297-7811, fax: 297-7833, 3 Dickson Rd. Close to heart of Serangoon Rd this newly renovated building has good rooms and a popular open-air coffee shop.

Broadway Hotel $$ tel: 292-4661, fax: 293-6788, 196 Serangoon Rd. Well-maintained older hotel with all requirements in air-con rooms at much lower rate than others in this category. Downstairs is a very good Indian restaurant.

Damenlou Hotel $$ tel: 221-1900, fax: 225-8500, 12 Ann Siang Rd. Nicely renovated Chinese shop-houses. All facilities in room, coffee shop downstairs.

South East Asia Hotel $$ tel: 338-2394, fax: 338-3480, e-mail: seahotel@singnet.com.sg, 190 Waterloo St. Very clean, basic place in the newly pedestrianised Waterloo St. Café, vegetarian restaurant, all mod cons in room. Excellent value for two people sharing. Payment in cash and on daily basis.

BUDGET Most of the accommodation in this price range of $40 or less for an air-con room with attached shower is in Geylang to the east of town. They accept cash only and are between 10 and 15 mins' walk from the MRT. Others are closer to the centre but poorer in quality.

Sun Hotel $$–$ tel: 338-4911, 260-2 Middle Rd. Very clean pleasant rooms, some with balconies. Air-con puts some of the rooms up a category but there are discounts for longer stays.

Alana Hotel $ tel: 745-9909, fax: 743-9033, 9 Lorong Ten, Geylang. TV, attached bathrooms, air-con, tea and coffee making facilities, 15 mins from MRT.

Princeton Hotel $ tel: 745-1515, fax: 746-0515, 15 Geylang Lorong Rd. Same facilities as above, 10 mins from MRT.

Kam Leng $ tel: 298-2289, 383 Jalan Besar. Old and run-down with very basic rooms with air-con.

San Wah $ tel: 336-2428, 36 Bencoolen St. Wacky old Chinese house with large untidy front yard. Some air-con rooms but not in this price range. Shared showers. Next door is an excellent 24 hr coffee shop.

FOOD

One could write a two-volume tome on places to eat in Singapore. It is a constant topic of conversation among Singaporeans, and when food reviews in the newspapers mention a place its customers quadruple overnight for about a week until the next issue. The following list scrapes the surface and you would need a couple of years of eating out several times a week to do the place justice.

Singapore has fewer of the chaotic-looking hawker places that still survive in Malaysia but there are a few. Most people eat cheaply in air-conditioned food halls in the big shopping malls. Food here is about twice the price of food in Malaysia, taking the exchange rate into account, which is amazing when you consider that it all comes from the same fields in Malaysia.

Indian roti and banana leaf places flourish, and the east coast is famous for its Chinese seafood. At a much higher price bracket the big hotels make a large portion of their income from their F&B (food and beverage) outlets. There are hundreds of little bistro type places coming and going as areas go in and out of fashion. This year it's Boat Quay, last year it was Clarke Quay, before that Holland Village and there was a brief spell when Chijmes was the place to eat. The next place will be the hyped up multimillion-dollar conservation project.

HAWKER FOOD Hawker stalls are alive and well and situated in the many wet-fish markets all around Singapore. The centres have a series of stalls cooking their own versions of fast food with communal tables and chairs. You can order dishes from several different stalls and eat it all together. The plates are colour coded and everyone seems to get their own utensils back without too much fuss.

An exception to this is the thoroughly nasty Newton Circus, a tourist trap, where if you try to sit at a table claimed by one of the hawkers, he'll chase you off. Two of the older ones that survived the big clean-up of the last 20 years are great places to eat.

The **Taman Serasi** hawker centre is on Cluny Rd, at its junction with Napier Rd, opposite the Botanic Gardens. It is very Malay both in its relaxed atmosphere and cooking styles. There are two or three stalls which make the increasingly rare *tahu goreng* (see page 51), some roti john places and an excellent fresh fruit stall where you can get soursop and sugarcane juice.

The **Maxwell Rd Food Centre** looks even scruffier than Taman Serasi and it may not have many years left before its gets Singaporised, but many people claim it has some of the best food in Singapore. It is very Chinese, and one of the stalls sells herbal and pig's brain soup. Another stall sells quite a rarity nowadays – *yew tao*, a kind of Chinese deep fried croissant.

A real suburban hawker centre to visit is **Tiong Bahru** wet fish market which has lots of foodstalls downstairs, including a very popular pau stall selling Chinese sweet buns.

ROTI PLACES These are in tiny shops scattered all over the island. Two or three of them are in North Bridge Rd near the Sultan mosque.

The Islamic Restaurant $ at No 791 was established in 1921. It serves roti, murtabak, biryani chicken and mutton and fish-head curry in a pleasantly unreconstructed shop-house.

Zam Zam $ at No 699 and **Victory $** at No 701, are similar in style and slightly shabbier.

A **24 hr Indian Muslim place $** in Bencoolen St beside the San Wah hotel serves very good roti and biryani.

Holland Village has an excellent roti and biryani place in Lorong Mambong, behind the main road.

Shahee $ at 63 Tiong Bahru Rd, close to the birdsong area, is is a good suburban version of the Indian Muslim place, with tables on the street and very good roti.

FOOD COURTS

Most of the fun of hawker centres has been lost in these clean, sanitised, muzaked places, but the food is good and if you can keep from going mad from the constant noise you can enjoy cheap food in air-conditioned surroundings.

In Orchard Rd the best places are in the basement of **Lucky Plaza**, where there are Indian Muslim and *yong tau fu* stalls, and **Scott's Food Court** which has a *nyonya*, a *laksa* and a north Indian stall, amongst others.

Over in the colonial part of town the **Funan Centre** has a good food centre on the 7th floor. In Telok Ayer St and aimed at lunchtime office workers is **China Square,** which has two floors of stalls selling everything imaginable at slightly higher than usual prices.

Opposite, in Far East Square, **Food Opera** has collected several very famous producers of good street dishes – Liang Seah St prawn noodles, Stamford fish-head noodles, Hock Lam Beef noodles and Nam Seng Wanton noodles – all named after the original shop-houses that sold the dishes before they were relocated here.

A selection of restaurants is provided below:

CHINESE

Cherry Garden $$$$$ tel: 339-3740, Oriental Hotel. Haute cuisine with an eclectic mix of Cantonese, Szechuan and Hainanese styles. The Peking duck is excellent as is the chef's special, shark's fin and abalone parcels in consommé.

Lei Garden $$$$$ tel: 339-3822, Chijmes, Victoria St. Rub shoulders with the rich and famous and enjoy some very high-class Cantonese-style food.

Teochew City Seafood Restaurant $$$–$$ tel: 733-3338, Centrepoint Shopping Centre. Reasonable prices, braised meats and seafood. Air-conditioned and oriental setting.

Prima Tower Revolving restaurant $$$$–$$$ tel: 272-8822, 201 Keppel Rd. Book in advance for this strange revolving restaurant perched on top of a grain silo, with views over the city and Sentosa. Beijing cuisine.

INDIAN

Annalakshmi $$$–$$ 02–10 Excelsior Shopping Centre. Vegetarian restaurant. Nightly changing menus. Lovely atmosphere, nice but expensive food. Closes at 2130.

Muthu's Curry House $$–$, 78 Race Course Rd. The speciality is fish-head curry. Don't believe the stories about the eye being the best bit – it's the cheek. Lots of other curries too.

Banana Leaf Apolo $$–$ 56 Race Course Rd. Very famous banana leaf restaurant frequented by Singapore's movers and shakers as well as ordinary folk. Fish-head curry, massive prawns, lots of vegetables.

Delhi Restaurant $$–$ Broadway Hotel, 195 Serangoon Rd. Sit out on the porch and watch Serangoon Rd activity. Banana leaf, roti, naan, tandoori dishes. Inexpensive and good food.

Taj $$ 214 South Bridge Rd. Air-conditioned Indian Muslim place right beside the Jamai Mosque.

Komala Vilas $ 12–14 Buffalo Rd and 76–8 Serangoon Rd. A banana leaf vegetarian place – lovely *dosa* and south Indian style *thalis*, on steel trays, not banana leaves.

Woodlands $ 14 Upper Dickson Rd. Vegetarian restaurant with enormous range of breads and set *thalis*. There is an upmarket air-con branch of this place **$$** at B1-01 Tanglin Shopping Centre.

Komala's Restaurant $ 3–9 Upper Dickson Rd, 111 North bridge Rd, B1-07E Peninsula Plaza, 6 Scott's Rd, #B1-05 Scott's Shopping Centre. It had to happen. This is the Indian equivalent of McDonald's, only the food is freshly cooked and tasty. Tell the cashier what you want, pay for it, give your receipt to the girls by the kitchen and out pops a sumptuous banana leaf meal only on a plastic tray. Lovely breads.

THAI

Thanying $$$ tel: 222-4688. Amara Hotel, 165 Tanjong Pagar Rd. Royal Thai cuisine cooked by women who trained at the royal palace in Bangkok. Reservations essential. There is a second branch at Clarke Quay.

Sukothani $$$ tel: 467-4222, Lorong Mambong, Holland Village.

MALAY AND INDONESIAN

There are very few Malay restaurants in the city but around **Geylang Serai** market several small coffee shops serve *nasi padang*, the Malay style buffet, as well as the hawker centre in the market.

Sanur $$$–$$ Ngee Ann City, Suntec City, Centrepoint. A mixture of Malay and Indonesian cooking. *Tahu telor*, fish-head curry, very spicy grilled chicken and fish. Geared to shoppers rather than romantic evening dining.

House of Sundanese $$ 55 Boat Quay. Cuisine from west Java. No air-con. Barbecued fish, curries, even the salad is spicy. Another branch is at Suntec City.

PERANAKAN

Nonya and Baba $$ 262 River Valley Rd. Open-air dining and good Peranakan food. *Otak otak, laksa,* nice desserts.

Blue Ginger $$$$ 97 Tanjong Pagar Rd. Good *nyonya* food in a relaxed atmosphere. A second branch is in the Heeren shopping centre, 260 Orchard Rd.

INTERNATIONAL

Harbour Grill $$$$$ tel: 730-3393, Hilton Hotel, 581 Orchard Rd. Classy international restaurant whose speciality is oysters and caviar. Lovely nouvelle cuisine menu, pleasant atmosphere. Vegetarian options. Try the ice-cold oyster shooters – served with a shot of vodka.

Nutmegs $$$$$ tel: 730-7112, Hyatt Regency, 10–12 Scott's Rd. Californian cuisine at its most innovative. Food is served from an open kitchen so you can watch it being cooked. Menu changes with each guest chef.

Morton's $$$$$ tel: 339-3740, The Oriental, 5 Raffles Ave. The latest place to eat steak in style. Very American menu, from Cajun ribeye steak to hash browns and baked Idaho potatoes and New York cheesecake. Reservation always necessary.

El Filipe's Cantina $$$$ Lorong Mambong, Holland Village, 02-09 International Building, 360 Orchard Rd. Innovative, long established Tex-Mex place serving good Mexican food and deadly margaritas.

Pasta Fresca $$$ 30 Boat Quay, Shaw House, 350 Orchard Rd. Good value, tasty Italian food. A Boat Quay branch is open 24 hrs.

HIGHLIGHTS

A COLONIAL WALK

Lots of old Singapore bit the dust before the government realised the buildings were marketable, but around the old colonial core of the city lots of the old British Empire buildings remained and have been beautified in the last few years. Some have even survived the beautification.

This walk starts, as it should, outside that bastion of colonial social life, the **Raffles Hotel**, 1 Beach Rd. Once a small beachfront bungalow owned by a merchant from the Middle East, the Sarkie brothers, who also owned the Strand in Rangoon and the E and O in Penang, bought it in 1886. When the Sarkies went out of business in the early years of the 20th century the hotel, like its sisters, grew dilapidated, until in the 1970s real riff-raff like backpackers could afford to stay here for weeks on end. Its renovation wasn't so much a facelift as major reconstructive surgery, and what emerged was the gleaming edifice you see before you. The hotel has a museum which you can visit 1000–1900, free.

Two left turns into North Bridge Rd and then Coleman St bring you to **St Andrew's Cathedral** on the left, built in the 1850s in the Victorian Gothic style by convict labour to a design by Colonel Ronald Macpherson.

Ahead of you is the **Padang** and to the right is the **City Hall**, both steeped in history. The Padang was once a seafront playing field where in the early days of empire British troops were quartered, and in more peaceful times the ruling classes gossipped and strolled and watched cricket matches. At one end of the Padang is the Singapore Recreation Club, where the Eurasians fraternised, and at the other is the Singapore Cricket Club, for whites – both still as exclusive as they were a hundred years ago. In 1942 the Japanese lined up the British on the Padang, men on one side and women and children on the other, and marched them off to Changi prison.

Over to the left you can see the **War Memorial Park** which remembers the hundreds of civilians who died during this time. On the steps of the City Hall, Lord Mountbatten accepted the Japanese surrender in September 1945. Fourteen years later Lee Kwan Yew stood on the same steps to declare Singaporean independence. Next door to the City Hall is the **Supreme Court Building**, built in 1939 and one of the last of the great colonial buildings. In the lobby is a display area with information on the history of the building.

Crossing the Padang towards the sea you come to the **cenotaph**, which remembers the war dead of the two world wars. To the left is the **Tan Kim Seng fountain**, erected in 1882 with money donated by the eponymous benefactor. To the right is the **Indian National Army Monument** remembering the many Indian soldiers who died in the war. Another memorial is the **pagoda** in the Esplanade Park dedicated to Lim Bo Seng, one of the leaders of the resistance movement between 1942 and 1944.

Following the curve of the Padang round to the right you can see ahead the **Victoria Theatre and Concert Hall**, originally the town hall and only converted in 1905. Behind it is the parliament building, now no longer used and about to become an arts centre. It was designed by the man who gave Coleman St its name, George Coleman, an Irishman. The early building was erected in 1821 but very little of it is visible since it was constantly added to over the years.

Walking towards the **river** brings you to the place where it all started – Raffles' landing place. Across the river is Boat Quay, once a series of shop-houses and ware-houses, and now a trendy night spot. To the left is the Empress Place Building, now the Asian Civilisations Museum. Follow the river along to Hill St and turn right.

ST ANDREW'S CATHEDRAL

The gleaming white walls of the cathedral are the result of some inventive plaster work made from crushed eggshell, egg white, lime, sugar, coconut husks and water. The original church bells were donated by Maria Revere Balastier, daughter of Paul Revere and the wife of Singapore's first American consul. In the days of bombardment leading up to the surrender to the Japanese in 1942 the cathedral became a makeshift hospital, the pews serving as beds and the vestry an operating theatre.

SIR STAMFORD RAFFLES

Born at sea in 1781, Stamford Raffles joined the East India Company at the age of 14. When Britain gained some colonies in the east, he was sent first to Java and then to Penang. Raffles saw the importance of the west coast of Malaya as a means of controlling the sea trade, and in 1819 he was allowed to seek out a site for a new base of operations.

He sailed up the Singapore River and landed in what was to be Singapore that year. The island was largely marsh, ruled by the sultan of Johor but effectively controlled by pirates. The island's ownership was in dispute between two warring sultans so Raffles went to one, Hussein Mohammed Shah, and offered him support in his war with the other sultan and a huge sum in rent for sole trading rights on the island.

The Dutch also wanted to control Singapore and things grew very nasty between the two colonial powers until a deal was struck in 1824. Raffles got Singapore and in exchange ceded Bencoolen on the west coast of Sumatra. Melaka was thrown in as part of the deal.

Singapore became part of the Straits settlements, with Penang in the north, Melaka in the middle and Singapore in the south. Raffles oversaw the development of the colony, laid out the areas in which each ethnic group were to live and built himself a bungalow on Fort Canning Hill from where he could keep a weather eye on the sea.

Singapore quickly boomed, immigrants flooded in from India and China to work in plantations and the docks, and in 1867 the island became a crown colony. Steamships followed and the opening of the Suez Canal led to even more trade links.

THE BELLY OF THE CARP AND BAD CHI

The six-storey building on the corner of Hill St was the Hill St Police Station, built in 1934 and believed by most of the residents of Boat Quay to have very bad chi (energy). The curved river area was known to the Chinese as the belly of the carp, its shape bringing great good luck to the merchants who operated in the area. When the building was erected people believed that it loomed full of policemen over the river and blocked the healthy flow of chi into the belly of the carp and brought about the area's economic decline.

Further along Hill St is the **Armenian Church of Gregory the Illuminator**, designed by George Coleman and built by public subscription in 1835. It is Singapore's oldest church and its design is based on St Martin-in-the-Fields church in London. Turning up Loke Yew St brings you to the **Asian Civilisations Museum**, once the Tao Nan Secondary school, built in 1910 and the first school in Singapore to teach in Mandarin. Nowadays this beautiful old colonial, style building is home to a collection of artefacts telling the story of the development of Asian civilisations.

From the Asian Civilisations Museum turn up Canning Rise to Fort Canning Park, once known as Bukit Larangan, the sacred burial ground of the Malay kings. The path goes past an old colonial graveyard, now the spice garden, to the **Battle Box** (see page 432), the recently opened Fort Canning HQ from where General Percival oversaw the fall of Singapore.

Heading down from the hill towards Stamford Rd brings you to the **Singapore History Museum $**, open Tues–Sun 0900–2100, for which we have Sir Stamford Raffles to thank. Formerly the National Museum it now shares its exhibits with the Asian Civilisation Museum and the Singapore Art Museum. Exhibitions include the early history of the colony, life in a Peranakan home, a biographical display about William Farquar, the first British Resident of Singapore, the history of Chinese secret societies and an amazing collection of jade. On Wednesday nights there is a fun tour of the museum which includes dramatic representations of events and a chance to climb a spiral staircase to the roof.

Walk down Waterloo St to another ancient Singaporean institution, what was St Joseph's Institution. Built in the 19th century as a mission school, in the 1980s it was one of Singapore's most prestigious schools. Beautifully renovated as **Singapore Art Museum $** open daily 0900–1730 and Wed 0900–2100, it has no permanent exhibition but houses travelling exhibitions.

The next stop on this tour of the colonial buildings of Singapore is the **Cathedral of the Good Shepherd** in Bras Basah Rd between Queen St and Victoria St. In 1832 the Catholic faith was established in Singapore in a house which stood opposite where the church is now. The present building was begun in 1843. It is a quiet place full of 1950s floor tiles imposed on Victorian flamboyance. Close to it in Victoria St is another part of the Catholic complex, the erstwhile Convent of the Holy Jesus, now a leisure complex. Originally an orphanage and school for girls it became the place for unwanted babies to be abandoned.

THE ASIAN CIVILISATIONS MUSEUM

This is the first wing to open of this museum which will later include the Empress Place Museum. It includes a selection of ancient jade pieces which signified kindness and warmth to the ancient Chinese. Pale green jade is from China and is the oldest of the collection. Most of the jade in modern jewellery shops is bright green, much newer jade from Myanmar.

In one of the showcases are carved jade cicadas which were put into the mouths of newly deceased to keep the spirit of the deceased alive in the next world. Other pieces are *ruyi* shaped – an endless knot – worn by children for protection and longevity. In Gallery 4 there are displays about the religions of the Chinese – Confucianism, Taoism and Buddhism. Figures of the Buddha show the various Buddhist traditions, the ornately dressed Buddhas with elaborate hairstyles being Thai Buddhist figures and the plainer ones Chinese. All the figures have a serene face with very large ears. The displays include features of Chinese temple architecture, the Chinese art of writing and dress styles, and jewellery in Asian civilisations.

A SERANGOON WALK

At the top of Serangoon Rd is the newly renovated and tourist-oriented **Little India Arcade**. In between the tourist souvenir shops are real local shopkeepers selling Indian flower decorations, saris, bolts of cloth and even traditional Indian Ayurvedic medicine. Indian grocers sell economy-sized packets of spices, stone pestles and mortars, and obscure cooking ingredients, while confectionery shops sell those excessively sweet Indian desserts.

The arcade has a section aimed at tourists which includes an audiovisual presentation about local customs and some old pictures of the area. On the other side of Serangoon Rd is the relatively unreconstructed **Zhujiao Centre** with a wet-fish market underneath and clothes and haberdashery shops above. There are still a few shops up there selling real junk which are good to poke around in.

Continuing down Serangoon Rd you will see that Campbell Lane, another renovated set of shop-houses, sells more traditional goods like Indian musical instruments, furniture and brassware. Along Serangoon Rd itself the right-hand side has been left untouched but much of the left-hand side is gone with plots of waste ground waiting for building projects. The mood of the place is unchanged though.

THE DECISION TO SURRENDER

One of the main reasons the British surrendered to Japan was the acute water shortage caused by the breach in the supply pipe from Johor and the Japanese taking some of the northern reservoirs. It is ironic then that General Percival was sitting several metres underneath a large reservoir which would certainly have drowned him if it had received a direct hit.

THE BATTLE BOX

The underground fort was only three years old when it became the focus of British efforts to keep Singapore out of Japanese hands. Most of the chambers are 9 metres underground and accessed by a steep staircase at the entrance and an escape tunnel at the far end of the complex. An air compressor maintained air flow through the tunnels in the event that the bunker had to be closed. Each room and its soldiers were kept locked up, and there was rarely any movement between them. Communication was through a series of pneumatic tubes. A telephone exchange maintained contact with the outside.

Very few local people ever saw the inside of the bunker and those that did found it claustrophobic, noisy and overpoweringly hot. In 1942 the British surrendered, having destroyed as much as they could and it became the Japanese communications HQ. After the war the British took it back and after independence it became the Singapore Military Forces HQ.

No one knows when the bunker was finally abandoned but it was empty by 1976 when the Singapore Armed Forces moved out of Fort Canning Hill. It was opened again in the 1990s and a massive reconstruction programme began. Today it houses a reconstruction of 15 Feb 1942 with an animatronic Percival and taped conversations. The bunkers have been faithfully recreated and even graffiti on the walls left by Japanese soldiers have been preserved. Open Tues–Sun 1000–1800 **$$**.

On the right you will find spice-grinding shops, fortune tellers, lots of vegetarian restaurants including Komala Vilas and jewellers selling great swathes of gold necklaces, earrings and bangles. When a Hindu woman marries, her wealth is displayed by the amount of gold she is wearing. Some of these places will hire out jewellery just for the wedding.

In Dunlop St turn right to see the **Abdul Gaffoor Mosque**, originally built in wood in 1859 and rebuilt in its current form in 1910. Its cupola is made of glass. Indian Muslims living in the area use this mosque. Return to Serangoon Rd via Upper Dickson Rd, the most truly unreconstructed street in Singapore. At one end are a series of scrap merchants. Stuff lies all over the road in the process of being broken up, while saleable objects are lined up beside the fence. At night a little shrine lights up the scrap here and on Sundays this place could truly be a street in India.

Back towards Serangoon Rd along Upper Dickson St a kind of normality returns. Fast food shops, the glorious Woodlands restaurant and shops selling tapes of Indian music and saris line the street. Outside Woodlands there is usually a pan

SERANGOON AT NIGHT

This walk is best done at night when the really strange atmosphere of the street emerges, particularly on Sunday night when the migrant Tamil workers come out on the streets to talk to their friends. Include dinner in your walk and it will take about 3 hours.

wallah, a man making little arrangements of nuts and leaves which local men chew, leaving a bright red stain in the mouth. It is meant to be mildly narcotic so you might want to try it. In Cuff Rd is a spice grinder shop, where you can see the ancient machinery which produces freshly ground spices for the restaurants around here.

Back on Serangoon Rd is the **Sri Veeramakaliamman Temple**, dedicated to the Goddess Kali, the consort of Shiva. The temple has lots of statues of the goddess in her various incarnations, and beside here are her two sons, Murugan and Ganesh. Murugan is the god to whom the Thaipusam festival is dedicated. Tuesdays and Fridays are the temple's busy days when there may be music playing inside the temple and the priests take offerings from worshippers, but the temple is lively most evenings. The *gopuram* is the tower over the entrance of the temple which is covered in figures of gods and mythical creatures. Worshippers who can't make it all the way to the temple can see the *gopuram* and make their prayers from where they are.

Further down Serangoon Rd are two more temples. The **Sri Srinivasa Perumal Temple** is dedicated to Lord Vishnu and his consorts. Its wide courtyard area is used during the Thaipusam festival when devotees prepare themselves here for the walk through Singapore to the Chettiar Hindu Temple. Another colourful *gopuram* dominates the temple, built in 1966.

THE WET-FISH MARKET

Singapore can feel like London or New York, only hot and clean. Visit the wet-fish market during the day to see what lurks beneath the sanitised walkways and air-conditioning. There are vegetables you may never have seen before, pieces of animal you wouldn't want to eat, and in the deepest corners shelled creatures waiting to have their shells ripped off while they are still alive.

Behind this temple, in Race Course Rd is the very beautiful Taoist **Leong San See Temple**, which translates as Dragon Mountain temple. Dedicated to the goddess Kuan Yin, there are also statues dedicated to Buddha and Confucius, and at the back are ancestral tables bearing the name and burial place of the ancestors of the people who worship here.

Further along Race Course Rd is the **Sakaya Muni Buddha Gaya Temple**, more commonly known as the temple of a thousand lights which surround a 50 ft high

Buddha statue. This Thai influenced temple is typically garish, with two great stone lions guarding the door. To get the lights switched on make a donation to the temple. You can also get your fortune told daily 0800–1645, free. If you continue walking back towards town along Race Course Rd there are any number of good north Indian and banana leaf restaurants to choose from to round off your walk.

ARAB ST A few years ago Arab St also underwent renovations and lots of the residents were moved out to the suburbs. Restored shop-houses are at a premium and as in Chinatown prices are too high for the old community to return. But there is still a sense of the Malay community that once lived in these streets in the businesses that have survived in the unrenovated places, the mosque and the coffee shops.

The **Sultan Mosque** in North Bridge Rd is the biggest in Singapore and is the focus for most Muslim people in the country. The original mosque on this site was built with a grant from the East India Company in 1825, but it was rebuilt entirely in 1925. Open daily 0500–2030, free.

The **Istana Kampung Glam** is not open to the public at the moment but may be by the time you read this. It was built around 1840 as the residence of the Malay Sultan of Singapore who gave up control of the island to Sir Stamford Raffles. In recent years the big old house became very run-down but is about to become a visitor centre for information about Malay kampung life.

TEMPLE MANNERS

While local people are very tolerant and don't mind tourists gawping at their religious rites there are some rules to be followed. Shoes must be removed before entering the temple, make sure that your dress doesn't cause offence and avoid walking into the inner areas of worship, usually fenced off in some way. Walk around the temple in a clockwise direction. Menstruating women should not enter the temple.

OFFERINGS AT THE TEMPLE

People wishing for something from Kali or her sons usually bring some offering. Those with physical ailments may bring a silver representation of the limb or body part to the temple and offer it to the god. Some bring garlands of flowers that are sold in the street while others offer clothes to the goddess. The priests sell the offerings to go towards the cost of maintaining the temple. By the doorway is a collection of broken coconuts. People break these in a gesture symbolic of giving up their personal needs and dedicating themselves to the god.

On the corner of Jalan Sultan and Victoria St is the **Kampung Glam cemetery** where the Malay royal family are buried. The area is full of craft, batik and basketry shops and the narrow pavements along Arab St are full of gaudy things to buy.

CHINATOWN

Another area turned into bijou offices and trendy craft shops. Chinatown really has lost all its sense of an ethnic identity. Some of the old herbal remedy shops and paper burial-goods shops are still here, but it is largely given over to upmarket restaurants and 'antiques', batik and other tourist collectibles.

THAIPUSAM

In Indian legend a man called Iduban decided to show his love for the god Murugan by climbing a mountain carrying offerings of milk and honey. Murugan tested Iduban by putting many obstacles in his way. When he reached the top Iduban was offered a place in heaven beside the god. The devotees who take part in the Thaipusam festival are following Iduban's example. They walk in procession from the Sri Srinivasa Perumal temple to the Thandayuthapani temple in Tank Rd, about 5 km.

The participants are chiefly men but some women take part. They wear a heavy steel cage whose bars are embedded into their flesh. They often also pierce their bodies with steel rods and hang fruits from hooks piercing their flesh. Along the road they are given milk and honey and showered in water dyed yellow with turmeric. Most devotees carry out the ritual twice but some choose to do it every year. The devotion is not a penance – the person may be seeking help from the god with their education or health.

Ten years ago the streets of **Sago Lane** held death houses where old people were taken to end their days, and other side streets had lion dance and paper burial-goods makers out on the street working at their trade. What is left are some temples, a wet-fish market and shopping centre, and lots of tourist-oriented places. Typical of the changes made in this area is the **Tong Chai Medical Institute** in Eu Tong Sen St, once a medical centre which dispensed herbal remedies and a national monument because of its architectural style. It is now a discotheque.

DESKER RD

By day a scruffy little road with very little to attract anyone, at night Desker Rd becomes the Tamil red light area. Girls lurk in doorways and negotiate prices with the lonely migrant workers. It's strictly illegal, but tolerated as long as it stays down dark streets.

The **Sri Mariamman Temple**, another of Singapore's national monuments, is in South Bridge Rd. This is Singapore's oldest Hindu temple, built in 1827 and rebuilt in 1843. The temple was founded by an Indian who accompanied Raffles on his second trip to Singapore in 1819. From outside the temple the figures of Krishna and Rama can be seen at the bottom left and

Weld Rd Flea Market

At the junction of Weld Rd and Jalan Besar are two narrow unlit lanes where people sit on the ground with little piles of junk in front of them for sale. Some of it comes from the scrap merchants in Upper Dickson Rd and some from people's attics. Walking up here from one of the clean regulated streets, it is a shock that there should be people so poor in Singapore.

right under umbrellas. The small gold figure at the bottom of the frieze is Mariamman, the goddess of healing to whom the temple is dedicated. In October the Thimithi festival is celebrated here when penitents walk across a bed of red hot embers. Open daily 0600–1230, 1600–2130, free.

In Telok Ayer St is the **Thian Hock Keng Temple**, the temple of heavenly happiness. It is the oldest Taoist temple in Singapore, dedicated to Kuan Yin or Ma Cho Po, in her incarnation of protectress of those who travel at sea. Once situated on the waterfront it would have been the first place that thousands of Chinese immigrants came to after their dangerous sea voyage from China. The present building dates back to 1839 and incorporates Delft tiles, granite pillars from China and cast-iron railings from Glasgow.

A block north of this temple is another – the **Fuk Tak Chi**, now a museum incorporated into the trendy new Far East Square. It has been beautifully restored and retains its door guardians and other details, and contains some brief information about the life of the area in early times and the way that the temple was built.

Waterloo St If you enjoy temples than another must-see is the pedestrianised Waterloo St where two temples attract worshippers from all walks of life. The Taoist/Buddhist **Kuan Im Thong Temple** is enormously popular – so much so that you'll have to fight your way inside. The temple is dedicated to Kuan Yin, and was completely rebuilt in the 1980s. This is a working temple where busy people shake bamboo sticks out of pots to discover their future and wave joss sticks around in supplication to the goddess.

The same people call in at another temple just next door, only this time the temple is a Hindu one – the **Sri Krishnan Temple**.

West of Town Out towards Jurong on the west side of the island are several places worth a visit. At Pasir Panjang is **Haw Par Villa $$**, once the home of the Aw brothers who made their fortune with Tiger Balm Oil. The Tiger Balm Gardens, as the place was once known, was a series of stone figures set in a park showing scenes from Chinese mythology. In the 1990s the place got a massive renovation with water slides and boat rides, but the gods didn't look well on the new development and the rides have disappeared leaving the original statuary in all its technicolor bad taste. Open daily 0900–1800.

Jurong Bird Park $$, open daily 0900–1800, is an excellent afternoon's visit. It sits in 20 hectares of landscaped gardens with a massive walk through aviaries containing hundreds of species of birds. There are cages of birds as well as several hornbills, which fly free around the park and occasionally take off to the suburbs where they are an amazing sight among the high-rise flats.

There is an air-conditioned penguin house and a night birds house where you can see owls and kiwis. In the South East Asian aviary there is a daily thunderstorm. There is a panorail system around the park and daily bird shows which are very good, particularly the birds of prey show. Additional charges for the panorail and breakfast with the birds. MRT to Boon Lay, then bus No 194 or 251 to the park.

Jurong Reptile Park, next door to the bird park, is a poor second in interest value. Beside the sad crocs lurking about the muddy ponds there are reptile houses where you can see the tokay gecko and some truly gruesome snakes. Other compounds hold snake-necked turtles and iguanas, but no komodo dragons - see them at the zoo. Open daily 0900–1800 **$$$**. MRT to Boon Lay, then bus 194 or 251 to the park.

Singapore Science Centre $** also in Jurong, is aimed at Singaporean schoolchildren but is still good fun. It is a very hands-on place, with animatronics bursting out all over and lots of things to try your hand at, including computer-generated plastic surgery on your own face. Darwin is here, as is a talking gorilla, and you can fly a flight simulator or watch the Omnimax show. Open Tues–Sun 1000–1800. Omnimax or Planetarium show **$$$.

Close by at 510 Upper Jurong Rd is the **Singapore Discovery Centre $$$**, along very similar lines with an interactive robot looking frighteningly like Robin Williams in *Bicentennial Man*, virtual reality games and lots of other hi-tech fun. Open Tues–Fri 0900–1900, weekends 0900–2000. Additional charges for motion simulator and shooting gallery. Boon Lay MRT then bus No 192 or 193.

Ming Village at 32 Pandan Rd is a factory making pottery (also in Jurong). On weekdays you can wander about and watch the craftsmen and women at work making moulds, hand-throwing pots and painting the delicate blue and white porcelain. There is lots of the work for sale and a good tour explains the whole process. Inside is a perfunctory display about pewter making and some Selangor pewter for sale. Open daily 0900–1730, free. Free shuttle bus from Orchard Rd hotels at 0920 and 1045. MRT to Clementi then bus No 78.

EAST OF TOWN

Geylang is a huge complex of high-rise government housing. A lot of Malay people have gravitated to this area as the old kampungs were gradually cleared and their residents rehoused. At the heart of it is **Geylang Serai** and the **Malay Cultural Village** which was built as a focus for the Malay community and as a tourist attraction.

It is a series of Malay-style buildings housing craft shops, restaurants and a bird market. It includes the **Kampung Days Museum** with a steep entrance charge which includes a storytelling show. Close by is the Geylang Serai **wet-fish market**, by far the best one to visit in Singapore, particularly during Ramadan when it comes alive each evening after dusk.

Changi Village is another aspect of Singapore which you won't find in the city centre. It is very much like a small village with a central market and lots of small shops. There are no major attractions except the **Changi Prison Museum,** which is about to move away, and the beach - scruffy and dominated by low flying aircraft.

From Changi you can get a ferry to **Pulau Ubin**, a thoroughly unreconstructed part of Singapore where kampung houses fester quietly with chickens running about and taro plants growing beside bananas and coconuts. It is a very pleasant afternoon trip, especially if you hire a bicycle and cycle the one or two roads across the island. There are a couple of temples and several very popular seafood restaurants. Ferries leave from the jetty in Changi whenever they get enough passengers.

GREEN SINGAPORE

For a small densely populated island Singapore has a remarkable number of places which are forested or form some other natural habitat like marshland or mangrove swamp. Each patch of natural habitat is tiny but together they make up several green belts running across the island which form a sort of wildlife highway, ensuring that species can survive and do not form isolated areas with increasingly small numbers of species. Taman Negara they may not be but Singapore's green patches, manicured as many of them are, are great places to visit.

Bukit Timah Nature Reserve is the best place in Singapore. It is a tiny, 71 hectare patch of primary rainforest bounded by secondary forest on the lower slopes, which were once given over to gutta-percha plantations. There is a tarmac road to a grassy patch at the top, usually inhabited by some very cheeky macaques, but there are lots of footpaths and it is worth venturing into the trees to spot some of the things lurking beneath the vegetation.

If you are lucky you will spot a tiny, deadly poisonous coral snake or a Wagler's pit viper, or a cobra - all are fairly common. You will definitely see gutta-percha trees, betel nut trees, rattan palms, any number of different orchids, sea eagles, racket-tailed drongos and great caravans of ants.

At the bottom of the hill is an interpretive centre which gives you some clues about what to look for, but the best thing is to just get out there. Bus No 171 or 182 from Scott's Rd. Free.

LIFE IN SUNGEI BULOH

The plants are the most rewarding since they can't fly off or hide. Look out for the common bright-yellow sea hibiscus or the sea morning glory – like the Western garden flower but doing an important job in these wetlands stabilising beaches and providing a firm base for other plants to colonise.

Another fascinating tree, which is marked along the trails, is the sea poison tree, the leaves of which fishermen used to kill fish. The tree provides food for the enormous Atlas moth caterpillar which is common here. The mangroves can be seen with their aerial roots sticking out of the swamp. The mud is low in oxygen and the aerial roots take in oxygen from the air. Shellfish anchor to the roots of the mangroves and provide food for the many migrant birds which pass through here.

Sungei Buloh Nature Reserve $ is a mixture of natural mangrove swamp and reconstructed fishing ponds. Its 87 hectares are not as much fun as Bukit Timah but if you have no plans to visit wetlands in Malaysia it's an easy journey to see a very different ecosystem to the one at Bukit Timah.

A good interpretive centre, café and a quick video introduce you to the nature reserve but you have to take off over the lake and into the wetlands to see much of any interest. Open Mon–Fri 0730–1900, weekends 0700–1900. Guided walks are free. MRT to Kranji then bus No 925 to Kranji Dam carpark, a 15-minute walk to the park. On Sundays and bank holidays bus No 925 goes all the way to the park entrance.

The Botanic Gardens are 52 hectares of prime real estate which have never been built on. When it was set aside in 1860 to be the Botanic Gardens most of it was nutmeg plantations with a large area of primary rainforest. The original gardens were both a pleasure ground and an experimental agricultural station, and famously Malaysia's first rubber trees came from some planted here.

Nowadays the gardens have a new lease of life, a new area of land, and a new purpose – besides recreation and research – education. They are a great place to wander round and admire the profusion of plant life. See the beautiful jade vine which looks like a brilliant green wisteria, cannon-ball trees with their giant seed cases emerging straight from the trunks, and monkey-pot trees with seed cases that produce a perfect pot with a lid.

The **Orchid Garden $** is truly magnificent, apart from the sycophantic naming of new hybrids after visiting dignitaries. The poor plants can't get named these days until some big shot visits the country. Look out for Margaret Thatcher, Benazir Bhuto and a few other people who were once important. Visit late in the evening and wander round the jungle in the dark – great fun. Open daily 0500–midnight, free. Junction of Cluny Rd and Holland Rd.

The Night Safari is a 40 hectare site of secondary forest, turned into a kind of wildlife park except that the animals are not really roaming free but contained within large areas where the tour guides can find them. As its name suggests the place is only open at night, and visitors can wander through the park safe in the knowledge that things may seem like they can leap out and eat them but actually are safely caged up.

There is also a trolley ride around the park where guides stop the trolley when they see some interesting creatures and light them up for a few minutes. The animals are largely Asian in origin so there isn't the diversity of the Zoo, but it's the atmosphere of the place where visitors can freely wander in the dark that attracts. To walk all the trails will take an hour or so. Don't be put off by the extremely tacky entrance with its gift shop and things to amuse children. This is worth the money. Open nightly 1930–2400 **$$$**. MRT to Ang Mo Kio and then bus No 138.

Singapore Zoological Gardens $$$ have very little about them that is natural but the zoo ranks among the world's best. Two thousand animals live in 90 hectares of gardens with many of them in large enclosures separated from visitors by moats rather than fences. There are animal shows, elephant rides, baby orang-utan hugging sessions, a pets corner farm and photo opportunities with pythons. Visit the zoo if only to see the komodo dragons, a relic of the age of the dinosaurs. Open daily 0830–1800. Extra charges for breakfast and tea with the animals and tram ride. MRT to Ang Mo Kio then bus No 138.

SENTOSA

If you were blindfolded and taken on a mystery ride to anywhere in the world and then allowed to open your eyes on Sentosa you'd know it was part of Singapore. This mixture of exquisite tackiness, anally retentive cleanliness and nitpicking attention to detail could only be Singaporean. Having said that, you mustn't miss a bit of it. It's what Singapore is all about. There are several days' worth of activity on the island, especially if you have children. Singaporeans pour over to the island at weekends – they actually enjoy the place more if it's crowded.

Starting at the most westerly part of the island **Fort Siloso $** is the remains of a military base, now turned into a visitor centre where visitors are treated as new recruits and shouted at by taped sergeant majors triggered off when you pass sensors. The recreation of life at the fort isn't too tacky, you can try an assault course, there are weapons training games and the section on the Fall of Singapore is quite instructive. Open daily 0900–1900. Station 3 on the monorail.

The best place to visit on Sentosa has to be **Underwater World $$$**, an aquarium with a difference. Besides the many pools and tanks of sea creatures, including some beautiful sea dragons, there is the 'travelator' (a Singaporean word if ever there was one). You stand on a moving walkway and travel underneath a huge acrylic tank with some evil-looking denizens of the deep thrashing about. Open daily 0900–2100.

At Cable Car Plaza, the **Images of Singapore $$** exhibition is a waxworks focusing on the early days of Singapore and the festivals and cultures of its ethnic groups. Attached is the recreation in wax of the surrender by the Japanese to the British in 1945. Open daily 0900–2100. Stop 4 on the monorail.

Fantasy Island $$$ is a very large swimming complex with wave machines, rides, slides and much more. Bring a packed lunch and your own float. It's expensive. Open Sun–Thur 0900–1900, Fri–Sat 0900–2300. Extra for lockers and hire of floats. Near stop 7 on the monorail.

BIRD SINGING

At the junction of Tiong Bahru Rd and Seng Poh Rd is a café where on Sunday morning proud wild bird owners bring their charges to sing their little hearts out. People sit and eat breakfast and admire the bird song. If you watch for any length of time you will notice that the birds get shifted about from time to time and cash seems to change hands. Some kind of competition goes on with judges choosing the best singer in each species, although how they decide who wins is anyone's guess. Afterwards pop over to the wet-fish market for breakfast.

VolcanoLand $$$ is a silly singing and dancing trip through a Mayan civilisation and its concrete volcano which explodes from time to time, open 1100–1900. At **Cinemania** you can spend lots of money on video games, and at the **Butterfly Park $$** you can walk through an enclosed garden containing lots of butterflies and then visit some dead ones in the exhibition rooms. Open daily 0900–1800.

There is a good **nature walk** on the island, unfortunately added to by some plastic dragons, but there are macaques roaming around and you can see pitcher plants. There are a **campsite and two hotels** if you want to carry on having fun, and a food centre as well as all the fast food places. There is also a **night market** and in the evening a dancing fountain show which is quite impressive. You can hire **bikes** and cycle round the island or roller skate at the **skating rink**. You can even play golf on one of two **golf** courses. Access to the island is by ferry from the World Trade Center or by the more exciting cable car from Mount Faber.

Other Islands **St John's Island** is a quite undeveloped place with a few beaches good for swimming and with basic facilities. Ferries to St John's leave from the World Trade Center twice daily during the week but more frequently at weekends $$. Closer to Singapore is **Kusu Island** where there is a Chinese temple and a Malay shrine. The ferry service to St John's calls at Kusu first. Both islands get overcrowded at weekends. **Sisters island** has no ferry service but you can hire a bumboat at Clifford Pier. It is a tiny, concreted island with some shelters and barbecue pits, and coral reefs for snorkellers.

SHOPPING

Singapore is by no means cheap. Clothes, shoes and electronic goods prices compare with the UK and may well exceed those in the US. Having said that, shopping till you drop is a traditional Singaporean activity.

Orchard Rd must have more retail space than any other major shopping street in the world. Starting from the top, **Tanglin Shopping Mall** has lots of good restaurants and fast food places as well as arts and crafts, antique shops and furnishings. **Palais Renaissance** opposite the Hilton Hotel heaves with big names like DKNY, Prada, Vera Wang and Versace.

In Scott's Rd **Pacific Plaza** has Tower records and books, a Calvin Klein store and some modern furnishing shops. Opposite it **Scott's Shopping Centre** has mostly expensive European clothes shops, including Marks and Spencer and some cheaper local clothes stores. Downstairs is the Picnic Food Court.

Further up Scott's Rd is **Far East Plaz**a with the excellent local department store Metro and lots of odd places for body piercing and punky clothes shops. Back on Orchard Rd **Wisma Atria** is getting a little elderly now but has an Isetan department store and lots of small designer boutiques. Opposite it **Tangs Department Store** has a long pedigree and quite high prices.

Next door, **Lucky Plaza** has a slightly off-the-wall tone. Don't engage one of the shopowners here unless you want to buy. Check prices somewhere else first and make sure you're getting what you think you are, including batteries (are they good ones or cheap imitations), battery charger, adaptors with the right voltage, etc. Watch your purchase being packed. There are lots of camera shops and electronics shops here as well as watches, sports clothes, Chinese silks and craft items and a great food hall.

Ngee Ann City, the vast purple building, has **Takashimaya Shopping Centre** inside it. Besides the department store of the same name there are lots of upmarket restaurants and small designer stores. The basement has a good Japanese supermarket. Back on the other side of Orchard Rd are **Paragon** and **The Promenade**, another collection of designer names, while in the Paragon there is an outlet of the New York Metropolitan Museum of Art. There is another Metro department store and less well known but good local designers. The **Specialists' Shopping Centre** has John Little Department store, a very basic and inexpensive shop, while **Centrepoint** has Robinson's. Both these department stores often have good sales and are very popular with locals.

Outside Orchard Rd **Raffles City** is another huge mall with a Sogo department store and lots of jewellery shops. **Marina Square** is very tourist-oriented with prices to match but if you go in with a better price from somewhere else shops will bring their prices down. **Sim Lim Square** near Chinatown is known for computers and electronics but like Lucky Plaza it has a bit of a wide boy reputation. The **Funan Centre** is a bit more respectable and has a good food centre.

In Chinatown there are **Chinatown Point**, full of beautiful craft shops where you must bargain, and **The People's Park Complex** and centre, both good for electronics and bargaining. In Eu Tong Sen St is an excellent shop, **Yue Hwa**, which sells Chinese arts and crafts, as well as Chinese medicines and more everyday items.

In the streets around South Bridge Rd there are lots of small arts and crafts shops. A good shop to look in is the **Yong Gallery** owned and run by Yong Cheong Thye, an expert in calligraphy. The shop opposite is the **Eu Yan Seng Medical Hall,** established in 1910 and still operating.

Out at **Holland Village** where lots of expatriates live are good fixed price and not so fixed price antique and arts and crafts shops, such as Lim's, and many more. This area is full of small restaurants as well as a Body Shop, a Cold Storage supermarket, a tiny Marks and Spencer, a Metro factory outlet with some cheap if wacky clothes and inside the shopping plaza lots of dressmakers that will copy any dress that you bring them. The wet-fish market sell strange spices, and there are smaller shops on the streets worth poking around in for their beautiful Chinese pots and other unusual items.

ENTERTAINMENT

Singapore's nightlife is sedate by Bangkok standards. There are hundreds of small, well-designed independently owned bars, with live music some nights. Besides these there are the expensive discos and clubs of Orchard Rd and the big hotels with good Filipino cover bands. There are several good jazz venues and imported ballet, classical music and theatre.

KIASU

To understand what is going on in Singapore you must familiarise yourself with the Singaporean concept of Kiasu. It has no simple English translation but means something along the lines of being afraid to miss out on something. It accounts for the notices you see in buffet restaurants warning people that food left on their plates will be weighed and they will be charged for each gram or ounce that isn't eaten.

Buffet dinners offer the ultimate test of the Kiasu Singaporean. Take too little and you miss out. Take too much and you miss out again! It isn't greed that makes people take too much food but the fear that they may not be getting the full value for their money. Kiasu applies to other situations too – education, shopping, visiting Sentosa island.

In Orchard Rd **Anywhere,** 04–09 Tanglin Shopping Centre, has to be the oldest bar in town with the oldest resident band - Tania.

Hard Rock Café, 50 Cuscaden Rd, has good live music after evening meals until around 2200. A rather risqué figure, Kumar, puts on occasional comedy acts there. Closes around 0200, cover charge.

Que Pasa, 7 Emerald Hill, is a good wine bar with several levels of luxury from leather armchairs on one to less comfortable chairs but cheaper prices on another.

Venom, Pacifc Plaza Penthouse, has Eurodance, drum 'n' bass and speed garage on one level, a sushi bar on another and a chill-out area on another. A very trendy place to go. Tues–Sun 1800–0300. Happy hour Tue–Fri 1800–2100. Cover charge.

Other places to try are **Europa Music Bar,** International Building, 360 Orchard Rd, **Club Modesto's** in Orchard Parade Hotel, and **Caliente** 01–05 Scott's Walk, 25 Scott's Rd, where they play Latin American music.

In **Boat Quay** and **Clarke Quay** are lots of places open till 0100 on weekdays and a little later at weekends.

Try **Barcelona** in Robertson's Walk, Buzz 88 Circular Rd, **Cocoa Carib** in Clarke Quay or **Crazy Elephant** in Trader's Market, Clarke Quay, where hair is long and the music is rock.

SINGLISH

Singaporeans don't know if they're proud of Singlish or ashamed of it. The language of the streets of Singapore is barely recognisable to Western visitors and the words that are clear sound like baby talk – no tenses, no subject/verb agreement, lots of slang words and lots of strange aaah noises. But after a while the ears attune, and far from being a sort of pidgin language Singlish has a logic and vibrancy that fit the Singaporean.

Expressions like Kiasu from the Hokkien Chinese dialect play an important part, standing in where words are missing in standard English. Malay words have also entered the language so that Singaporeans talk about *makananing* – the Malay word for eat added to the English ending 'ing'. Singlish expressions come and go. You will hear *also can?* It means 'can I do this too?' or 'would you like this too?' or 'is this also the right bus for the zoo?'

Or what adds a question to a statement. Some fairly new Singlish expressions are *you see me no up* meaning 'you look down on me' and *this place got toilet or not?* meaning 'does this place have a toilet?' Also fascinating are the tags that get used instead of questions or for emphasis. *Lah* is a long drawn out noise which means 'I really think so', as in *No, lah no toilet, aah,* the aah adding even more emphasis. *Wah* is an expression of being impressed, perhaps at the size of something.

In 2000 a TV series remonstrated with Singaporeans for using Singlish, saying that they should be able to communicate with foreigners in standard English, so perhaps it has run its course. Whatever happens, it is a lively language full of self-deprecating humour and to be spoken to in it by a Singaporean means you have really become one of them and they trust you. Either that or they can't speak proper English.

Harry's Quayside Café in Boat Quay has been there for years and attracts middle-aged expats but is a comfortable place for a drink, while **Karma Bar** at 57 B Boat Quay is made of recycled wood from rubbish tips, and has belly dancers.

In Chinatown there are several slick places along Tanjong Pagar Rd – **Taboo Café and Bar** and the **Joy Luck Club** to name but two.

Around the City Hall area is **Chijmes** where the many trendy cafés are supplemented by even more trendy bars such as **China Jump Bar and Grill** or **Father Flanagan's Irish Pub**. Holland Village also is a good place to while away an evening.

Cinemas are all over town and the suburbs, and present most Hollywood productions as well as Bollywood offerings and Cantonese movies. Art movies can be seen at the **Picture House,** 6 Handy Rd, while more mainstream offerings are at the **Shaw Leisure Centre** in Beach Rd, **United Artists** at Bugis Junction and the **Shaw Centre** on Scott's Rd.

Singapore

For local theatre productions check out **Substation** at 45 Armenian St, tel: 337-7800, or the **Victoria Theatre** in Empress Place, tel: 336-2151. In June 2002 and every other year thereafter Singapore will have a theatre festival when local production and imports from the West End are put on. Wander round the streets of Chinatown or the suburbs and you will find makeshift stages and performances of Chinese opera. The *Straits Times* will have listings.

TOURS

There is a variety of tours available from local tour operators.

The **Flavours of New Asia tour** looks at the spices which were once grown on the island, visiting the spice garden on Fort Canning Hill and looking at Peranakan culture and its cooking style. The tour visits a wet-fish market and Serangoon Rd's spice shops, and concludes with a visit to Chinatown and the herbal shops there.

The **Heartlands of New Asia tour** goes to some kampungs in Pulau Ubin to see a typical Malay kampung home and then on to a typical suburban centre where more modern cooking styles predominate.

An evening tour, **Painted Faces**, visits a Chinese opera shop and a clan association house, where the form of Chinese opera is explained, and goes on to Clarke Quay for an opera performance.

The **Spirit of New Asia tour** takes in several temples and explains some of the religious customs of the state.

These tours can be booked with:

Holiday Tours and Travel, tel: 738-2622, 300 Orchard Rd.

RMG Tours, tel: 220-1661, 109C Amoy St.

SH Tours, tel: 734-9923, 100 Kim Seng Plaza.

Singapore Sightseeing Tours, tel: 332-3755, 3C River Valley Rd.

From Clarke Quay there are **river tours** in bumboats passing old godowns (quayside warehouses) and some historic sites on the riverside. The same companies also organise longer dinner and high tea cruises out to the harbour on ancient-looking junks. **Other tours** take visitors to Jurong, to the colonial district and on evening trishaw rides around the city. Several tours focus on **Singapore during World War II**, covering Changi prison, Sentosa and Fort Canning.

PULAU BINTAN AND PULAU BATAM

These two Indonesian islands are a few hours' boat ride from Singapore. Many Singaporeans go to one of them for the weekend for the sleazy nightlife, the beaches or just relaxation. There is a good boat service to both islands and lots of accommodation ,which makes a quick trip out of Singapore easy.

CULTURE

The concept of saving face, fairly common in south-east Asian societies, involves avoiding confrontation in social situations. What this means at a practical level is that shouting and overt displays of emotion are shunned, something that a visitor may misinterpret as indifference. Raising the voice and getting angry is seen as churlish behaviour and is often counter-productive for this reason.

When entering someone's home in Thailand, Malaysia or Singapore, observe the custom of leaving your footwear outside. The same custom of removing footwear applies to any Buddhist temple or mosque, though not to Chinese Taoist temples.

TEMPLE ETIQUETTE

As well as removing shoes before entering a Buddhist temple, visitors are also expected to dress and behave appropriately. Skimpy skirts and shorts are not acceptable and, although this is only strictly enforced at the Grand Palace in Bangkok, this dress code should observed when visiting any temple in Thailand. Women should not touch a Buddhist monk.

THAILAND In Thailand, the wish to save face is reinforced by the influence of Buddhism which values discretion and modest behaviour and shies away from aggressive confrontation. Topless bathing shocks Thais, even though it is common on Phuket and Ko Samui, and overt displays of immodesty are deprecated.

The traditional Thai form of welcome is the folding of the palms of your hand together in a prayer-like gesture to the other person. This way of greeting, called the *wai*, is traditionally extended only to people who are older or more revered than you.

Thai monarchy is highly revered and criticism of the king is not welcomed; in fact it is against the law. The national anthem is played daily at 0800 and 1800 in public places like bus and train stations, and everyone, visitors included, is expected to stand in silence. The anthem is also played in cinemas before the start of the film.

MALAYSIA In cosmopolitan Kuala Lumpur, multicultural Penang and Sarawak and Sabah, where Malays are not the majority, the influence of Islam is not as directly felt as it is on the east coast, from Kuantan northwards. Here it is difficult to purchase alcohol, there are separate queues in supermarkets for men and women, and women travelling alone, as well as women generally whose dress is not viewed as sufficiently modest, are judged unseemly by many men. Topless bathing, needless to say, is not advisable.

TROUBLESOME FILMS

The recent remake of *The King and I*, starring Jodie Foster and Chow Yun-Fat, was banned in Thailand on the grounds that it is both insulting and inaccurate. The 19th century King Mongkut employed an English governess to care for his 50-odd children and the film suggests their relationship was very close. The official view is that the relationship was very formal and everything was above board.

The 1956 version of the film with Yul Brynner was also banned, partly because it showed the king eating with common chopsticks when he should have been using a spoon. In the new film, the censors objected to a scene showing the king looking like 'a cowboy who rides on the back of an elephant as if he is in a cowboy movie.'

Hollywood is currently facing legal action from environmentalists who accuse the makers of *The Beach* (see page 208) of ruining a beautiful beach in order to create a set for the film.

CUSTOMS

THAILAND The duty-free allowance on entering Thailand is 200 cigarettes and a litre of spirits or wine. To export any antique or religious figure a licence has to be granted by the Fine Arts Department. Any reputable company selling artefacts that come under this category should be able to help organise this permit. Strictly speaking, any Buddha image would require such a licence but the regulation is not generally enforced for the mass-produced Buddhas that are sold across the country.

MALAYSIA The duty-free allowance on entering Malaysia is 200 cigarettes and a litre of alcohol.

SINGAPORE The duty-free allowance is one litre of alcohol but there is no duty-free allowance on cigarettes, and even the alcohol allowance does not apply if you are arriving from Malaysia. Oh, and don't forget that it is illegal to import chewing gum.

SINGAPORE AND CHEWING GUM

It is quite a few years now since Singapore banned chewing gum but the law is still in effect, and the whole sorry story reveals a lot about the gung ho mentality of Singaporean law-makers. Apparently, officials of the MRT, the country's light railway system, came to the conclusion that juvenile delinquents were subversively placing their gum in the doors of MRT trains and disrupting the flawless transport service. Drastic action was required and a law was passed banning the sale and importation of chewing gum. Singapore is not the only country with silly laws. Thais are forbidden to leave the house without underwear and may not drive topless.

ELECTRICITY

In all three countries 220 volts AC is standard and extends to the remotest villages.

E-MAIL AND INTERNET

The web can be accessed and e-mails sent and collected from all three countries using the growing number of small shops that set themselves up as cyber cafés and cyber shops. They can also be found at the international airports of Bangkok, Kuala Lumpur and Singapore.

Only a couple of years ago, a travel guide would need to indicate where exactly Internet access was possible but that is no longer necessary. Thailand is the most developed country in this respect and in every town and city it is easy to find shops where e-mails can be sent or received. The rate is also the cheapest of all three countries, usually 1B or 2B per minute. Malaysia doesn't have as many outlets but they are there in every big town, in both peninsular Malaysia and Sarawak and Sabah, and the number is increasing. Singapore has state of the art cyber cafés.

FESTIVALS

Festivals Calendar

Thailand

Chiang Mai Flower Festival in February.

Songkhran Festival

Thai New Year is celebrated across the country but especially in Chiang Mai where locals take great delight in soaking foreigners with water as part of the festivities.

Loi Krathong

The end of the rainy season in November is celebrated by floating small model boats (*krathongi*) down the river laden with a candle, incense and flowers.

River Kwai Bridge Festival

Starting at the end of November and continuing into December, a light and sound show at the infamous bridge at Kanchanaburi.

FESTIVALS IN MALAYSIA AND SINGAPORE

Thaipusam is an important Hindu festival, usually at the end of January or early February, and is best experienced in Singapore when a spectacular street procession marks the event.

Hari Raya Puasa marks the end of Ramadan and for the next year or so takes place in late January/early February. It is the only day of the year when Malay royal palaces are opened to the general public.

Harvest Festivals: at the end of May and early June in Sarawak and Sabah there are celebrations and family gatherings; a great time to visit a longhouse.

Deepavali is a Hindu festival in November celebrating the triumph of light over dark and marked by the lighting of small oil-lamps.

Hardly a week passes without a festival or special holiday taking place somewhere in Thailand, Malaysia or Singapore. Multicultural Malaysia, and Singapore to a lesser extent, are blessed with a profusion of religious and state holidays. The downside is that they always seem to occur when you need a bank open or an empty seat on a bus. More positively they present wonderful opportunities to catch colourful celebrations, and learn something about the rich cultural traditions that go to make up life in south-east Asia.

The Chinese New Year festivities affect Thailand, Malaysia and Singapore. It is a lunar-based festival and so the time moves forward from one year to the next. Currently it takes place in February. Chinese shops and businesses close down for days and the demand for seats on railways and flights is at an all-time high. The impact of Chinese New Year is more keenly felt in west Malaysia and Singapore than in Thailand, or along the east coast of peninsular Malaysia or in Sarawak and Sabah. Wherever there is a Chinese community, though, look out for colourful dragon dances.

Ramadan, the ninth month of the Islamic calendar, is marked by fasting between dawn and dusk. It usually takes place between February and April and makes itself felt on the east coast of peninsular Malaysia, where restaurants will be closed during the day. It is more of an inconvenience than a hindrance because food is still available in hotels and it is usually possible to find a non-Muslim Indian or Chinese place open.

In May, a public holiday in all three countries commemorates the birth, death and enlightenment of the Buddha, known as Visakha Day in Thailand and Vesak Day in Malaysia and Singapore.

MAPS

THAILAND Nelles Maps and Bartholomew Maps both publish useful country maps of Thailand. For more detail, Periplus publish a series of maps on Bangkok, Chiang Mai, Phuket and Ko Samui. The quality of free tourist maps varies a lot, depending on the location. Heavily visited areas like Bangkok, Ko Samui, Phuket and Chiang Mai are well provided for, and excellent maps showing a range of tourist-oriented facilities are readily available in tourist offices, hotels and other places. The TAT office in most other towns will have a map of some kind or other, though the quality varies.

MALAYSIA Nelles and Periplus publish good country maps of Malaysia, and Periplus also produce a series of regional maps that cover Kuala Lumpur, Melaka, Penang, Sarawak and Sabah. Tourism Malaysia offices around peninsular Malaysia have free maps of their areas, which are ok for general purposes but often lack detail. The tourist offices in Sarawak have excellent free town maps of Kuching, Sibu and Miri, and the Sabah Tourism Promotion Corporation distribute a brochure with handy maps of the state and main towns.

SINGAPORE There are good maps of Singapore published by Nelles and Periplus but for most visitors' needs the free maps available at the airport and from the tourist offices will be fine.

WHERE TO BUY GOOD MAPS

UK **Stanfords**, 12–14 Long Acre, London SW1H OQU, tel: (020) 7836-1321, web: www.stanfords.co.uk. Mail order or over the telephone. A branch is also located at Campus Travel, 52 Grosvenor Gardens, London SW1W OAG, tel: (020) 7730-1314, and at British Airways, 156 Regent St, London W1R 5TA, tel: (020) 7434-4744.

Another good source of maps is **The Travel Bookshop**, 13–15 Blenheim Crescent, London W11 2EE, tel: (020) 7229-5260, web: www.thetravelbookshop.co.uk. There is also the **National Map Centre**, 22 Caxton St, London SW1H OQU, tel: (020) 7222-2466, web: mapsworld.com.

Thailand is seven hours ahead of Greenwich Mean Time. **Malaysia and Singapore** are eight hours ahead of Greenwich Mean Time and one hour ahead of Thailand.

USA **Rand McNally**, tel: 1-800-333-0136, has shops across the country and maps can be ordered by mail. Other sources include **The Complete Traveler Bookstore**, 199 Madison Ave, New York, NY 10016, tel: (212) 685-9007, and **Traveler's Bookstore**, 22 W 52nd St, New York, NY 10019, tel: (212) 664-0995.

Public Holidays

Thailand

January 1	New Year's Day
February (day of full moon, variable)	Buddhist holiday
April 6	Chakri Day
Mid April	Songkhran (NewYear)
Early May	Royal Ploughing Day
May (day of full moon, variable)	VisakhaDay, Buddhist holiday
July (day of full moon, variable)	Buddhist holiday
August 12	Queen's Birthday
October 23	Chulalongkorn Day
December 5	King's Birthday
December 10	Constitution Day
December 31	New Year's Eve

Malaysia

January 1	New Year's Day (except in Johor, Kedah, Perlis, Kelantan and Terengganu)
Late Jan/early Feb	Chinese New Year
Late Jan/early Feb	Hari Raya Puasa (beginning of Ramadan)
March (variable)	Hari Raya Haji
Early April	Easter Friday (only in Sarawak and Sabah)
April (variable)	Muslim New Year
May 1	Labour Day
May (variable)	Vesak Day
June (first Sat)	King's Birthday
June 1 and 2	Gawai Dayak (Sarawak only)
Late June (variable)	Maal Hijrah (Mohammed's journey to Medina from Mecca)
August 31	National Day
November	Deepavali (except in Sarawak)
December 25	Christmas Day

Singapore

January 1	New Year's Day
Late Jan/early Feb	Hari Raya Puasa (beginning of Ramadan)
Late Jan/early Feb	Chinese New Year
March (variable)	Hari Raya Haji
April	Easter Friday
May 1	Labour Day
May (variable)	Vesak Day
August 9	National Day
November	Deepavali
December 25	Christmas Day

Opening Times

In Thailand, Malaysia and Singapore, large shops and department stores tend to open around 1000 until 2000 or later, seven days a week. Shop hours are more variable, either opening early in the morning and closing by 1800 or, and especially so in tourist areas, staying open until 2000 or later.

Thailand Government offices, which usually includes national museums, open Mon–Fri 0830–1630, and generally close for lunch 1300–1400. Banks open on weekdays 1000–1600. All banks and government departments are closed on national holidays. Mainstream businesses tend to follow similar hours, though they are less likely to close for lunch.

Malaysia Government offices usually open Mon–Fri 0800–1615, often closing for lunch 1300–1400, and Sat 0800–1245. Friday is different and the lunch hour is extended to 1445 to allow for a visit to the mosque.

Life is a little different in the more Islamic states of Kedah and Perlis in the northwest, and Kelantan and Terengganu on the east coast. Friday takes the place of Sunday and the working week runs from Sunday to Thursday, and Saturday morning.

Singapore Government offices are usually open Mon–Fri from 0800 to between 1600 and 1700. Saturday closing time is around 1200. Banks open Mon–Fri 0930–1500 and 0930–1130 Saturday.

POSTAL SERVICES

Efficient and reliable postal services operate in Thailand, Malaysia and Singapore. Sending home a parcel by sea is an affordable way of lightening the load of goodies picked up whilst travelling. In all three countries the cost of parcel post is determined by whether it goes by air, taking about ten days on average, or by much cheaper surface mail but taking up to two months to arrive home, and whether it is insured and for how much.

THAILAND Airmail letters cost 17B to Europe and 19B to North America. Registered and express mail services are available and there is also a way of sending home parcels that combines sea, land and air travel. Post offices sell boxes suitable for packing and tape and string is usually available free of charge. Large post offices may also have an inexpensive packing service.

MALAYSIA Airmail letters cost 90c to Europe and RM1.10 to North America. Large post offices sell boxes for sending parcels and related packaging materials.

SINGAPORE Airmail letters cost S$1 to Europe and North America. Singapore being what it is, there is a Postage Rate helpline tel: 165.

HOTEL PHONES

It pays not to make international phone calls from hotel rooms because the extra cost charged by the hotel, averaging around 25%, can be exorbitant.

TELEPHONES

The telephone country code for Thailand is 66, for Malaysia 60, and for Singapore 65. If making an international call from Thailand, dial 001 before the number. The access code for international calls from Malaysia is 007, and for Singapore 001.

THAILAND Domestic calls are made from public red phone boxes (for local calls) or blue phone boxes (local and long-distance). Local calls cost 1B for three minutes. Phone cards are available in units of 25B, 50B, 100B, 200B and 240B.

International calls can be made from private telephone offices, found in all the major tourist areas, or from a public CAT (Communications Authority of Thailand) phone office attached to the main post office in every town.

Home Direct service is available at Bangkok's main post office, and at airports and CAT phone offices in all the major tourist towns. To use the service, dial 001-999 followed by the appropriate country phone number: for the UK, tel: 44-1066; for the USA, tel: 1111 (AT&T), 12001 (MCI) or 13877 (Sprint).

For operator-assisted international calls, dial 100.

MALAYSIA Domestic calls, 10c for three minutes, can be made using coins or telephone cards, and international calls can also be made from public phones. Phone calls to Singapore are regarded as long-distance, using area code 02, rather than international. There are two phone systems, Telekom and Uniphone, and they each issue their own phone cards. Some Telekom phones, and fewer Uniphone ones, allow the user to swipe their credit cards for the payment of international calls.

Home Direct service is available from public phones, dial 102 for assistance. To use the service, dial 1-800-80 followed by the appropriate country phone number: for the UK, 0044; for the USA 0011 (AT&T), 0012 (MCI) or 0015 (Sprint).

For assistance with international calls, tel: 103.

SINGAPORE Domestic calls, costing S$0.10 for three minutes, are usually made using phone cards, although phone boxes accepting coins are still around. Local calls made inside the terminal at Changi airport are free. International calls can also be made from public phones. Phone cards come in S$2, S$5, S$10, S$20 and S$50 units and are available from 7–11 stores, some supermarkets and small stores.

TOURIST INFORMATION

THAILAND The Tourism Authority of Thailand (TAT) has offices around the country and overseas.

UK 49 Albermarle St, London WIX 3FE, tel: (020) 7499-7679, fax: (020) 76295519.
USA 1 World Trade Center, Suite 3729, New York, NY 10048, tel: (212) 432-0433, fax: (212) 912-0920; 611 North Larchmont Blvd., 1st Floor, Los Angeles, California 90017, tel: (213) 461-9814, fax: (213) 461-9834, e-mail: tatla@ix.netcom.com.
Singapore Royal Thai Embassy, 370 Orchard Rd, tel: (065) 235-7694.

MALAYSIA Tourism Malaysia is the national tourist board that covers the whole country. Although there are separate organisations handling tourism in Sarawak and Sabah, Tourism Malaysia is the only one with offices overseas.

UK 57 Trafalgar Square, London WC2N 5DU. Tel: (020) 7930-7932, fax: (020) 7930-9015, e-mail: mtpb@tourism.gov.my.

USA 595 Madison Ave, Suite 1800, New York, NY 10022, tel: (212) 754-1113, e-mail: mtpb@aol.com; 818 West 7th St, Suite 804, Los Angeles, California 90017, tel: (213) 689-9702, fax: (213) 689-1530, e-mail: malinfo@aol.com.
Thailand 9F Liberty Square, 287 Silom Rd. Tel: (02) 631-1994, fax: (02) 631-1998.

SINGAPORE The Singapore Tourism Board (STB) has offices in the city and overseas.

UK Carrington House, 1st Floor, 26–130 Regent St, London. Tel: (020) 7437-0033, fax: (020) 7734-2191.
USA 590 Fifth Avenue, 12th Floor, New York, NY 10035, tel: (212) 938-1888, fax: (212) 938-0086; 8484 Wiltshire Blvd., Suite 510 Beverly Hills, California 90211, tel: (213) 852-1901, fax: (213) 852-0129.

TOURIST AND TRAVEL INFORMATION ONLINE

Any search engine will turn up a wealth of pages on Thailand, Malaysia and Singapore, and some addresses for booking accommodation online have already been mentioned (see page 35). What follows is only a selection of some of the better sites currently available.

GENERAL

travel.excite.com/ General travel information and links to related sites.
www.asiantrail.com/ Articles, advice, lots of links to related sites.
www.stratpub.com/ Tips for inexpensive travel.
www.travel-library.com Packed with travel information and anecdotes on travel in south-east Asia.
www.asiaweek.com Catch up with the latest news affecting Asia.
www.fieldingtravel.com/blackflag Scary and not so scary stories about 'dangerous' places to travel. Reassuringly little on Thailand or Malaysia, and Singapore doesn't get a mention.

THAILAND

www.tat.or.th TAT's official site.
www.bangkokpost.com Run by Thailand's leading daily newspaper.
www.nationmultimedia.com Another leading daily newspaper.

MALAYSIA

www.tourism.gov.my Tourism Malaysia's official site.
www.sarawaktourism.com Sarawak's official tourist site.

SINGAPORE

www.travel.com.sg STB's official site.
www.happening.com.sg Local entertainment listings.

DISTANCES (approx. conversions)

1 kilometre (km) = 1000 metres (m) 1 metre = 100 centimetres (cm)

Metric	Imperial/US	Metric	Imperial/US	Metric	Imperial/US
1 cm	3/8 in.	10 m	33 ft (11 yd)	3 km	2 miles
50 cm	20 in.	20 m	66 ft (22 yd)	4 km	2½ miles
1 m	3 ft 3 in.	50 m	164 ft (54 yd)	5 km	3 miles
2 m	6 ft 6 in.	100 m	330 ft (110 yd)	10 km	6 miles
3 m	10 ft	200 m	660 ft (220 yd)	20 km	12½ miles
4 m	13 ft	250 m	820 ft (275 yd)	25 km	15½ miles
5 m	16 ft 6 in.	300 m	984 ft (330 yd)	30 km	18½ miles
6 m	19 ft 6 in.	500 m	1640 ft (550 yd)	40 km	25 miles
7 m	23 ft	750 m	½ mile	50 km	31 miles
8 m	26 ft	1 km	5/8 mile	75 km	46 miles
9 m	29 ft (10 yd)	2 km	1½ miles	100 km	62 miles

24 HOUR CLOCK
(examples)

0000 = Midnight	1200 = Noon	1800 = 6 pm
0600 = 6 am	1300 = 1 pm	2000 = 8 pm
0715 = 7.15 am	1415 = 2.15 pm	2110 = 9.10 pm
0930 = 9.30 am	1645 = 4.45 pm	2345 = 11.45 pm

TEMPERATURE

Conversion Formula: °C x 9 ÷ 5 + 32 = °F

°C	°F	°C	°F	°C	°F	°C	°F
-20	-4	-5	23	10	50	25	77
-15	5	0	32	15	59	30	86
-10	14	5	41	20	68	35	95

WEIGHT

1kg = 1000g 100 g = 3fi oz

Kg	Lb	Kg	Lb	Kg	Lb
1	2¼	5	11	25	55
2	4½	10	22	50	110
3	6½	15	33	75	165
4	9	20	45	100	220

FLUID MEASURES

1 ltr (l) = 0.88 Imp. quarts = 1.06 US quarts

Ltr	Imp. gal.	US gal.	Ltr	Imp. gal.	US gal.
5	1.1	1.3	30	6.6	7.8
10	2.2	2.6	35	7.7	9.1
15	3.3	3.9	40	8.8	10.4
20	4.4	5.2	45	9.9	11.7
25	5.5	6.5	50	11.0	13.0

MEN'S SHIRTS

NZ/UK	Eur	US
14	36	14
15	38	15
15½	39	15½
16	41	16
16½	42	16½
17	43	17

MEN'S SHOES

UK	Europe	US
6	40	7
7	41	8
8	42	9
9	43	10
10	44	11
11	45	12

MEN'S CLOTHES

NZ/UK	Eur	US
36	46	36
38	48	38
40	50	40
42	52	42
44	54	44
46	56	46

LADIES' SHOES

UK	Europe	US
3	36	4½
4	37	5½
5	38	6½
6	39	7½
7	40	8½
8	41	9½

LADIES' CLOTHES

NZ UK	France	Italy	Rest of Europe	US
10	36	38	34	8
12	38	40	36	10
14	40	42	38	12
16	42	44	40	14
18	44	46	42	16
20	46	48	44	18

AREAS

1 hectare = 2.471 acres

1 hectare = 10,000 sq meters

1 acre = 0.4 hectares

This index lists places and topics in alphabetical sequence. All references are to page numbers. **Bold** numbers refer to map pages. To find routes between cities, see pp. 16–17.

NOTES

Notes

If you enjoyed using this book, or even if you didn't, please help us improve future editions by taking part in our reader survey. Every returned form will be acknowledged, and to show our appreciation we will give you £1 off your next purchase of a Thomas Cook guidebook. Just take a few minutes to complete and return this form to us.

When did you buy this book? ______

Where did you buy it? (Please give town/city and if possible name of retailer)

______

______

When did you/do you intend to travel in Thailand, Malaysia and Singapore? ______

For how long (approx.)? ______

How many people in your party? ______

Which towns, cities and other locations did you/do you intend mainly to visit?

______

______

______

How did you/will you travel around Thailand, Malaysia and Singapore? By Rail ☐ By Car ☐ By Bus ☐ By Air ☐

______

Did you/will you:

☐ Make all your travel arrangements independently?

☐ Travel on an Airpass? ☐ Travel on a Rail Pass?

☐ If you purchased a rail or bus pass, where did you buy it? ______

☐ Use other passes or tickets, please give brief details: ______

______

Did you/do you intend to use this book:

☐ For planning your trip?

☐ During the trip itself?

☐ Both?

______

______

Did you/do you intend also to purchase any of the following travel publications for your trip?

☐ *Thomas Cook Overseas Timetable*

☐ *Thomas Cook World Timetable Independent Traveller's Edition*

☐ Other guidebooks or maps, please specify

______

______

Have you used any other Thomas Cook guidebooks in the past? If so, which?

______

______

Reader Survey

Please rate the following features within this guide for their value to you (Circle vu for 'very useful', u for 'useful', nu for 'little or no use'):

The 'Reaching Thailand, Malaysia and Singapore' section on pages 18–20	vu	u	nu
The 'Travelling betweeen Malaysia and Singapore' section on pages 21–25	vu	u	nu
The 'Travelling around Thailand, Malaysia and Singapore' section on pages 26–31	vu	u	nu
The 'Travel Basics' section on pages 32–49	vu	u	nu
The 'Travel Directory' section on pages 448–457	vu	u	nu
The recommended routes throughout the book	vu	u	nu
Information on towns and cities	vu	u	nu
The maps of towns and cities	vu	u	nu

This book will be updated annually, which allows us to amend and enhance the information we include within it, but we need our readers to tell us what they would like to see changed and improved. Please use this space to make any comments you have concerning this book.

Your age category: under 21 21–30 31–40 41–50 over 50

Your name: Mr/Mrs/Miss/Ms
(First name or initials)
(Last name)

Your full address: (Please include postal or zip code)

Your daytime telephone number:

Please detach this page and send it to: **The Editor, *Independent Traveller's Thailand, Malaysia and Singapore*, Thomas Cook Publishing, PO Box 227, Peterborough PE3 6PU, United Kingdom.**

We will be pleased to send you details of how to claim your discount upon receipt of this questionnaire.

TMS2001

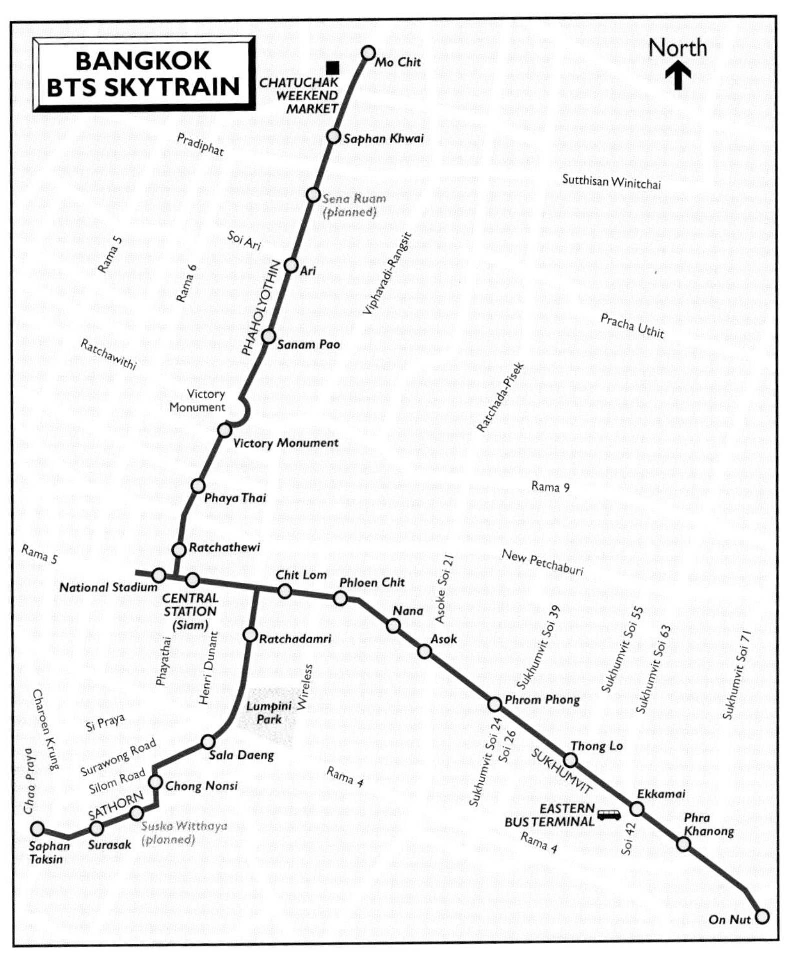
BANGKOK
BTS SKYTRAIN
North
Mo Chit
CHATUCHAK
WEEKEND
MARKET
Saphan Khwai
Pradiphat
Sutthisan Winitchai
Sena Ruam
(planned)
Soi Ari
Rama 5
Ari
Rama 6
Viphavadi-Rangsit
PHAHOLYOTHIN
Sanam Pao
Pracha Uthit
Ratchawithi
Ratchada-Pisek
Victory
Monument
Victory Monument
Phaya Thai
Rama 9
Ratchathewi
Rama 5
New Petchaburi
Asoke Soi 21
National Stadium
CENTRAL
STATION
(Siam)
Chit Lom
Phloen Chit
Nana
Asok
Ratchadamri
Sukhumvit Soi 39
Sukhumvit Soi 55
Sukhumvit Soi 63
Sukhumvit Soi 71
Phayathai
Henri Dunant
Wireless
Phrom Phong
Charoen Krung
Lumpini
Park
Si Praya
Surawong Road
Sala Daeng
Sukhumvit Soi 24
Soi 26
Thong Lo
SUKHUMVIT
Silom Road
Rama 4
Chong Nonsi
Ekkamai
Chao Praya
SATHORN
EASTERN
BUS TERMINAL
Phra
Khanong
Saphan
Taksin
Surasak
Suska Witthaya
(planned)
Rama 4
Soi 42
On Nut

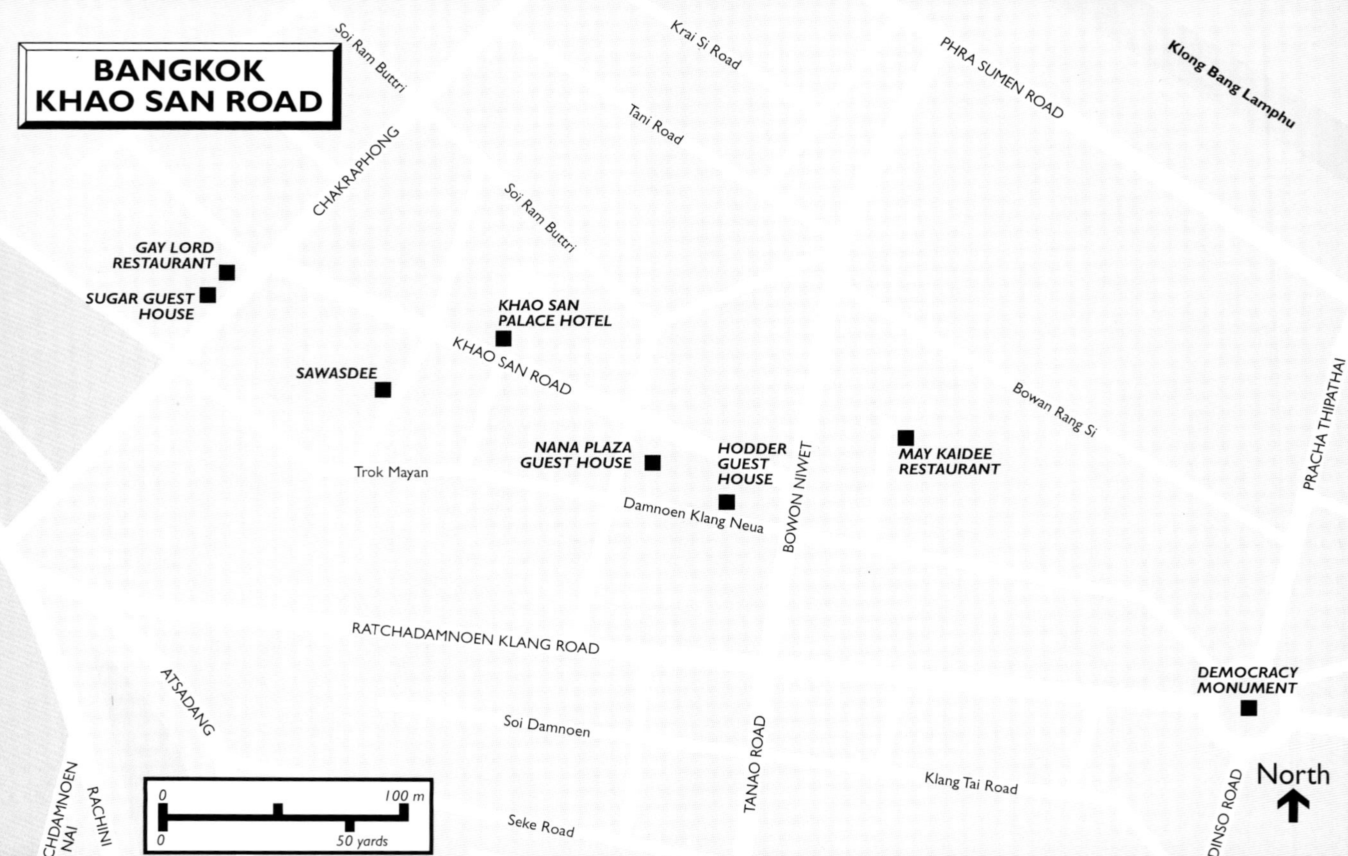
BANGKOK
KHAO SAN ROAD
Soi Ram Buttri
Krai Si Road
PHRA SUMEN ROAD
Klong Bang Lamphu
Tani Road
CHAKRAPHONG
Soi Ram Buttri
GAY LORD RESTAURANT
SUGAR GUEST HOUSE
KHAO SAN PALACE HOTEL
KHAO SAN ROAD
SAWASDEE
Bowan Rang Si
PRACHA THIPATHAI
NANA PLAZA GUEST HOUSE
HODDER GUEST HOUSE
BOWON NIWET
MAY KAIDEE RESTAURANT
Trok Mayan
Damnoen Klang Neua
RATCHADAMNOEN KLANG ROAD
DEMOCRACY MONUMENT
ATSADANG
Soi Damnoen
TANAO ROAD
Klang Tai Road
North
DINSO ROAD
CHDAMNOEN NAI
RACHINI
0
100 m
0
50 yards
Seke Road

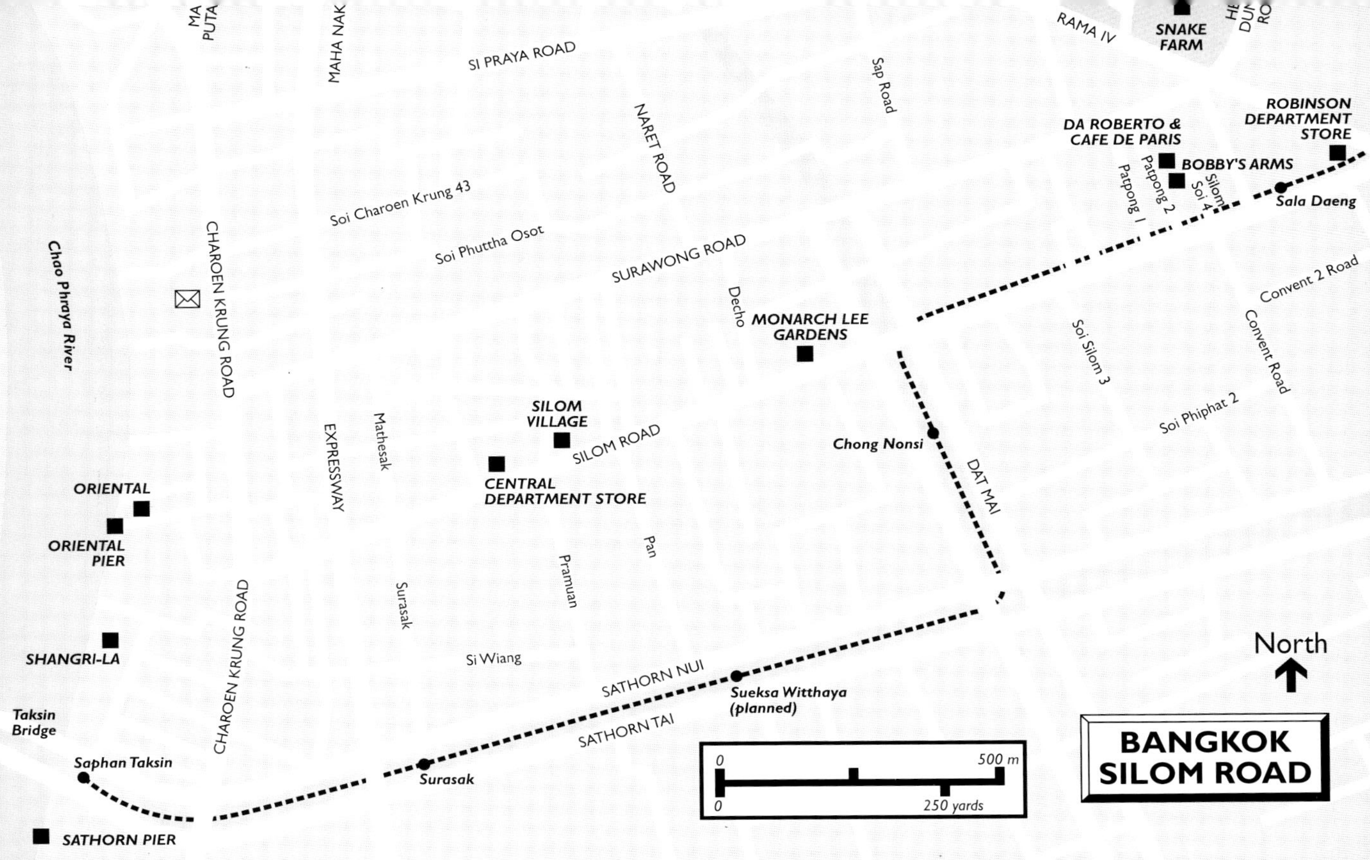

BANGKOK
SILOM ROAD
North
0
500 m
0
250 yards
ROBINSON DEPARTMENT STORE
DA ROBERTO & CAFE DE PARIS
BOBBY'S ARMS
Sala Daeng
Silom Soi 4
Patpong 2
Patpong 1
SNAKE FARM
RAMA IV
Sap Road
Convent 2 Road
Convent Road
Soi Silom 3
Soi Phiphat 2
SI PRAYA ROAD
MAHA NAK
NARET ROAD
Soi Charoen Krung 43
Soi Phuttha Osot
SURAWONG ROAD
Decho
MONARCH LEE GARDENS
Chong Nonsi
DAT MAI
Chao Phraya River
CHAROEN KRUNG ROAD
SILOM VILLAGE
SILOM ROAD
CENTRAL DEPARTMENT STORE
EXPRESSWAY
Mathesak
ORIENTAL
ORIENTAL PIER
Pan
Pramuan
Surasak
Si Wiang
SHANGRI-LA
SATHORN NUI
Sueksa Witthaya (planned)
SATHORN TAI
CHAROEN KRUNG ROAD
Taksin Bridge
Saphan Taksin
Surasak
SATHORN PIER

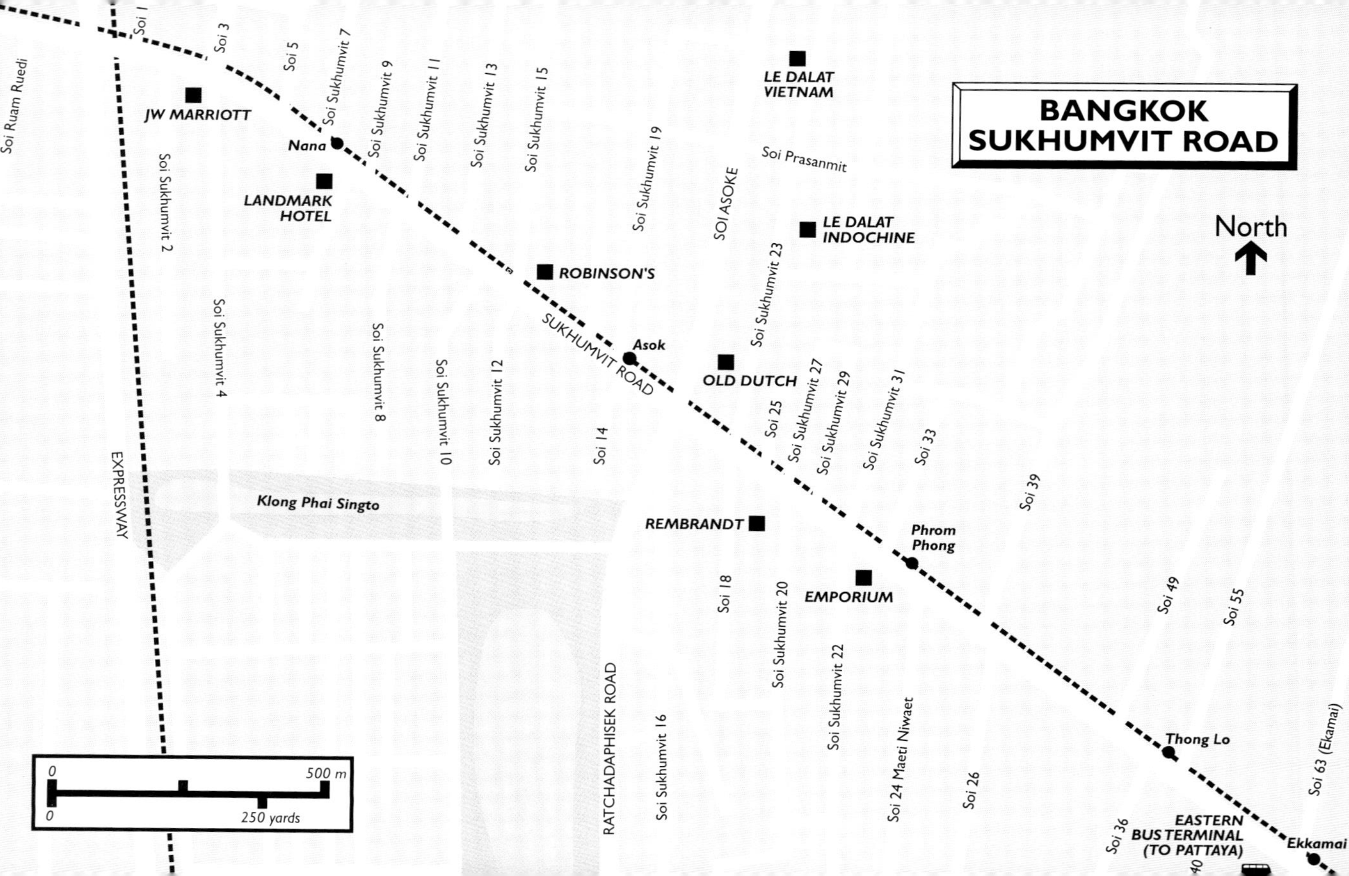
BANGKOK
SUKHUMVIT ROAD
North
JW MARRIOTT
LANDMARK HOTEL
ROBINSON'S
LE DALAT VIETNAM
LE DALAT INDOCHINE
OLD DUTCH
REMBRANDT
EMPORIUM
EASTERN BUS TERMINAL (TO PATTAYA)
Nana
Asok
Phrom Phong
Thong Lo
Ekkamai
SUKHUMVIT ROAD
EXPRESSWAY
RATCHADAPHISEK ROAD
Klong Phai Singto
SOI ASOKE
Soi Prasanmit
Soi Ruam Ruedi
Soi 1
Soi 3
Soi 5
Soi Sukhumvit 7
Soi Sukhumvit 9
Soi Sukhumvit 11
Soi Sukhumvit 13
Soi Sukhumvit 15
Soi Sukhumvit 19
Soi Sukhumvit 23
Soi 25
Soi Sukhumvit 27
Soi Sukhumvit 29
Soi Sukhumvit 31
Soi 33
Soi 39
Soi 49
Soi 55
Soi 63 (Ekamai)
Soi Sukhumvit 2
Soi Sukhumvit 4
Soi Sukhumvit 8
Soi Sukhumvit 10
Soi Sukhumvit 12
Soi 14
Soi Sukhumvit 16
Soi 18
Soi Sukhumvit 20
Soi Sukhumvit 22
Soi 24 Maeti Niwaet
Soi 26
Soi 36
40
0
500 m
0
250 yards

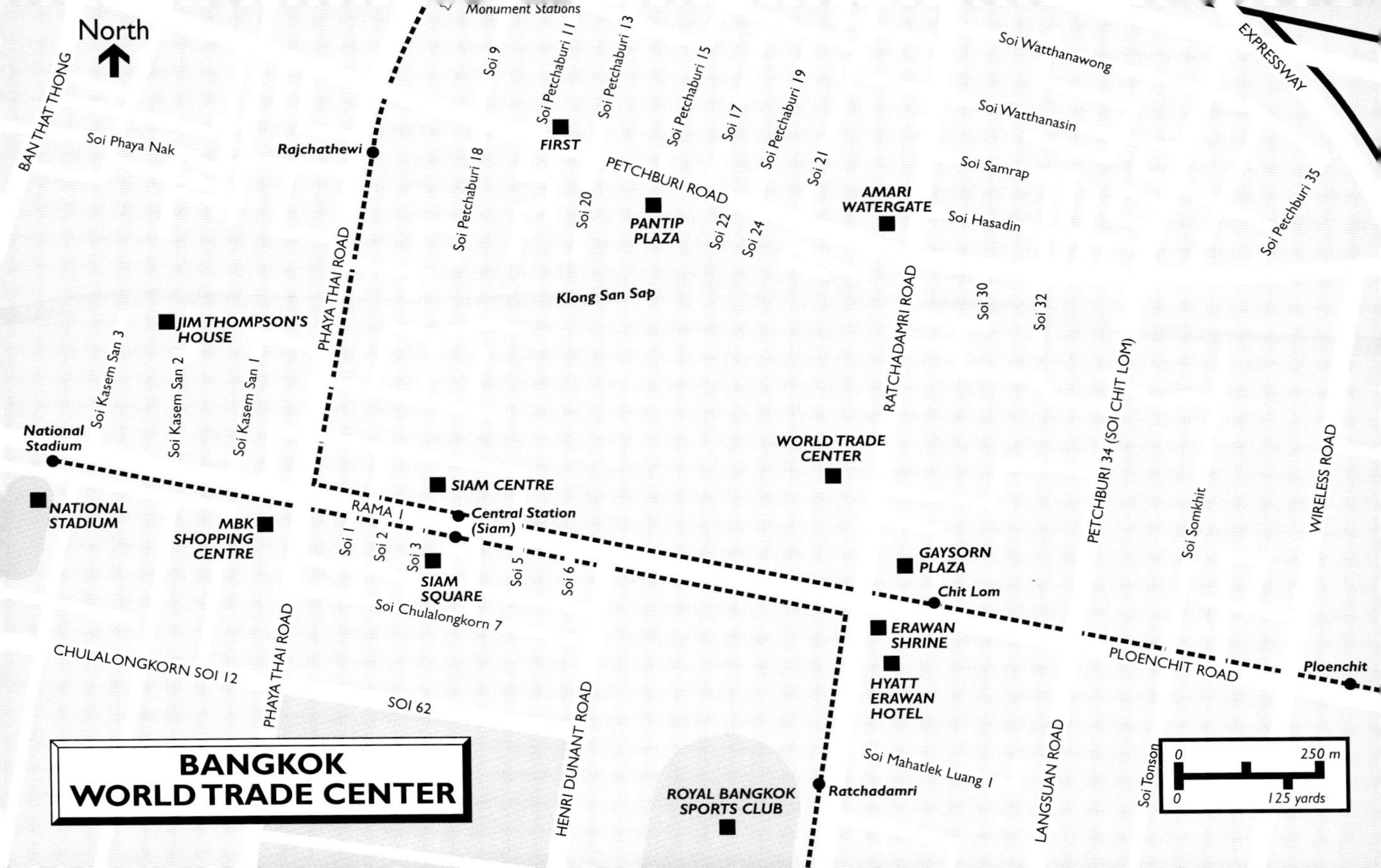
BANGKOK
WORLD TRADE CENTER
North
Monument Stations
BAN THAT THONG
Soi Phaya Nak
Rajchathewi
Soi 9
Soi Petchaburi 11
Soi Petchaburi 13
Soi Petchaburi 15
Soi 17
Soi Petchaburi 19
Soi 21
Soi Watthanawong
Soi Watthanasin
Soi Samrap
Soi Hasadin
Soi Petchburi 35
EXPRESSWAY
FIRST
PETCHBURI ROAD
Soi Petchaburi 18
Soi 20
PANTIP PLAZA
Soi 22
Soi 24
AMARI WATERGATE
Klong San Sap
RATCHADAMRI ROAD
Soi 30
Soi 32
JIM THOMPSON'S HOUSE
Soi Kasem San 3
Soi Kasem San 2
Soi Kasem San 1
PHAYA THAI ROAD
National Stadium
WORLD TRADE CENTER
SIAM CENTRE
NATIONAL STADIUM
RAMA 1
Central Station
(Siam)
MBK SHOPPING CENTRE
Soi 1
Soi 2
Soi 3
SIAM SQUARE
Soi 5
Soi 6
Soi Chulalongkorn 7
GAYSORN PLAZA
Chit Lom
ERAWAN SHRINE
HYATT ERAWAN HOTEL
PETCHBURI 34 (SOI CHIT LOM)
Soi Somkhit
WIRELESS ROAD
PLOENCHIT ROAD
Ploenchit
CHULALONGKORN SOI 12
PHAYA THAI ROAD
SOI 62
HENRI DUNANT ROAD
ROYAL BANGKOK SPORTS CLUB
Ratchadamri
Soi Mahatlek Luang 1
LANGSUAN ROAD
Soi Tonson
0
250 m
0
125 yards

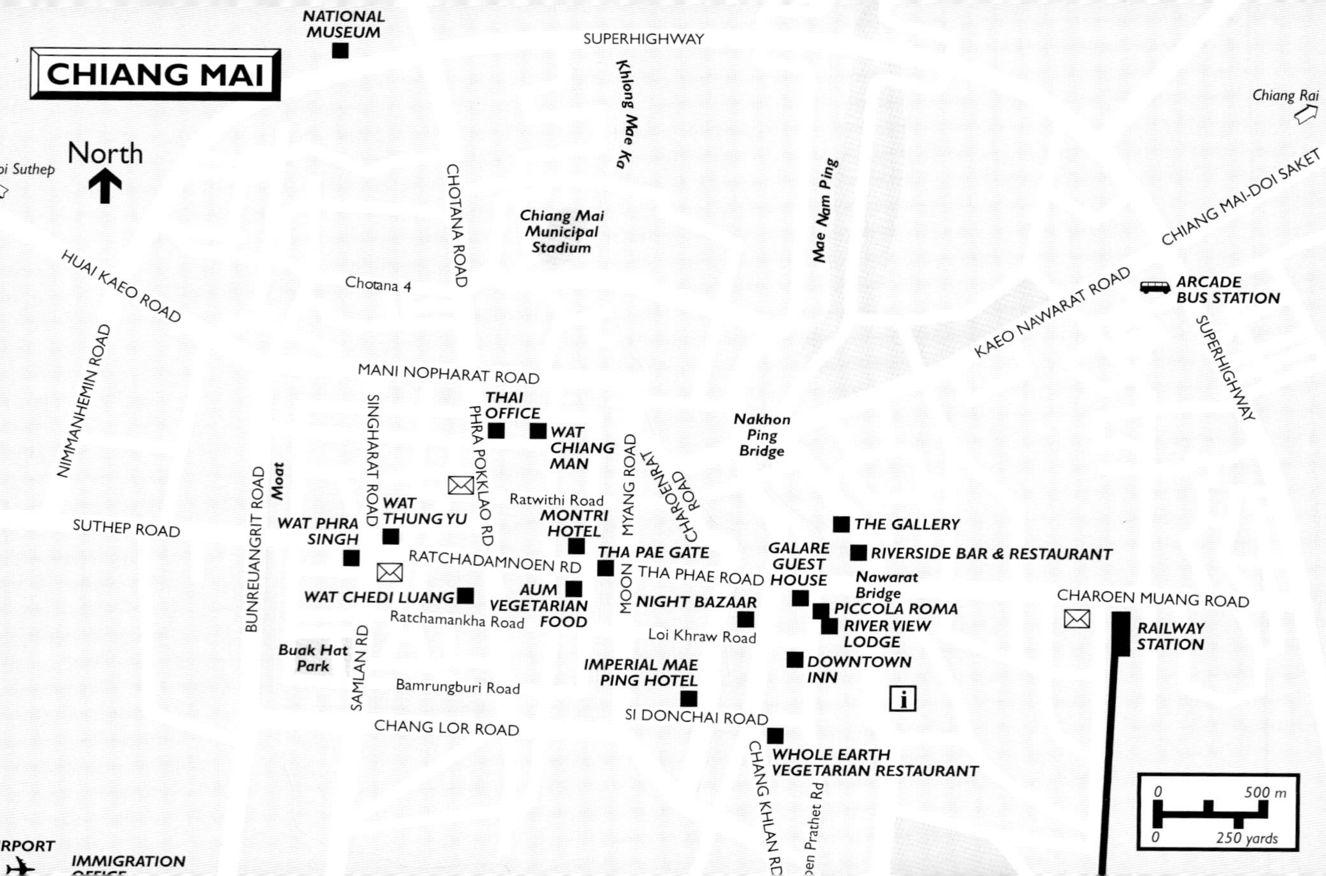

CHIANG MAI
NATIONAL MUSEUM
SUPERHIGHWAY
Khlong Mae Ka
Chiang Rai
North
Doi Suthep
CHOTANA ROAD
Chiang Mai Municipal Stadium
Mae Nam Ping
CHIANG MAI-DOI SAKET
HUAI KAEO ROAD
Chotana 4
KAEO NAWARAT ROAD
ARCADE BUS STATION
SUPERHIGHWAY
NIMMANHEMIN ROAD
MANI NOPHARAT ROAD
THAI OFFICE
SINGHARAT ROAD
PHRA POKKLAO RD
WAT CHIANG MAN
Nakhon Ping Bridge
MYANG ROAD
CHAROENRAT ROAD
BUNREUANGRIT ROAD
Moat
WAT THUNG YU
Ratwithi Road
MONTRI HOTEL
SUTHEP ROAD
WAT PHRA SINGH
THE GALLERY
RATCHADAMNOEN RD
THA PAE GATE
RIVERSIDE BAR & RESTAURANT
GALARE GUEST HOUSE
THA PHAE ROAD
MOON
Nawarat Bridge
WAT CHEDI LUANG
AUM VEGETARIAN FOOD
NIGHT BAZAAR
CHAROEN MUANG ROAD
PICCOLA ROMA
Ratchamankha Road
RIVER VIEW LODGE
RAILWAY STATION
Loi Khraw Road
Buak Hat Park
SAMLAN RD
IMPERIAL MAE PING HOTEL
DOWNTOWN INN
Bamrungburi Road
SI DONCHAI ROAD
CHANG LOR ROAD
WHOLE EARTH VEGETARIAN RESTAURANT
CHANG KHLAN RD
oen Prathet Rd
0
500 m
0
250 yards
AIRPORT
IMMIGRATION

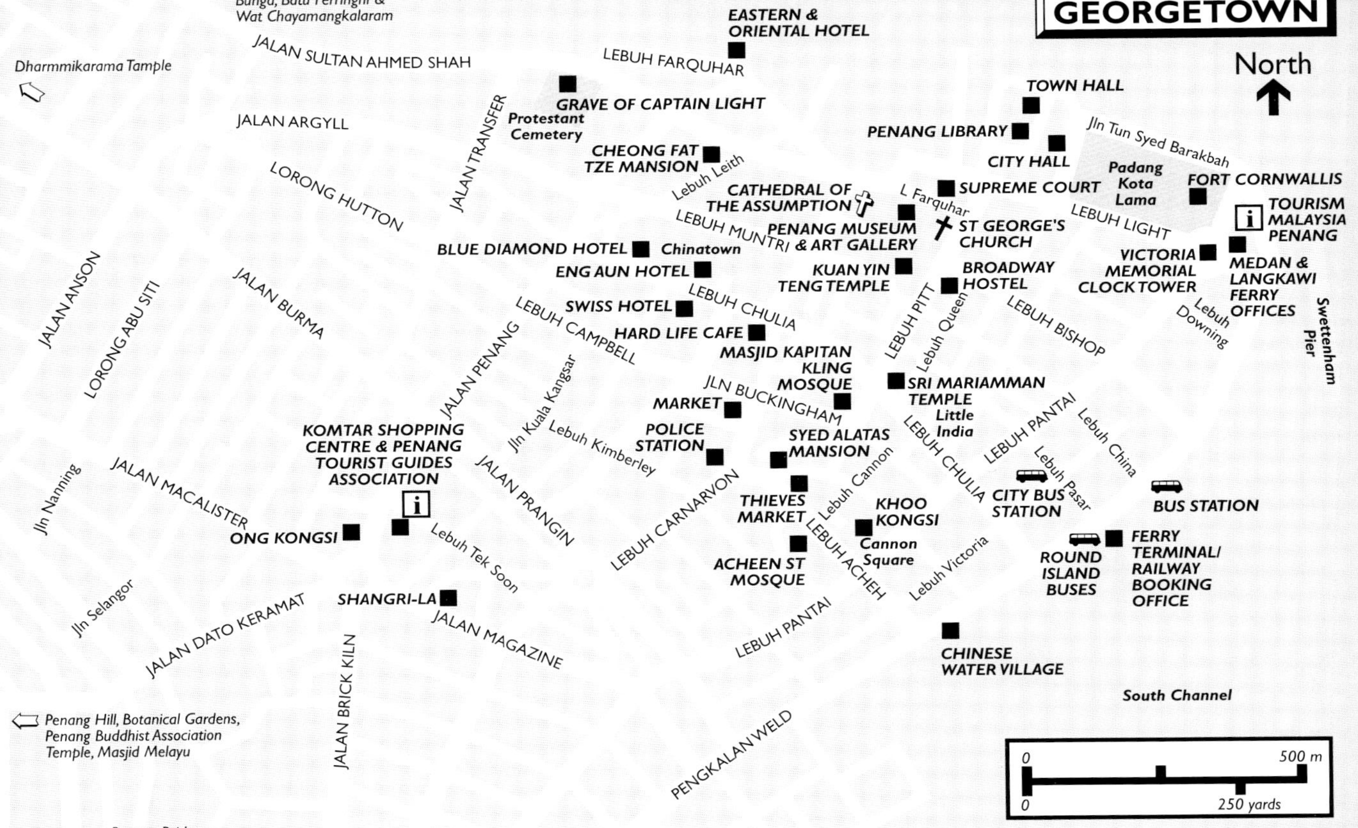
GEORGETOWN
North
Bunga, Batu Ferringhi & Wat Chayamangkalaram
Dharmmikarama Tample
EASTERN & ORIENTAL HOTEL
LEBUH FARQUHAR
JALAN SULTAN AHMED SHAH
GRAVE OF CAPTAIN LIGHT
Protestant Cemetery
JALAN ARGYLL
JALAN TRANSFER
TOWN HALL
PENANG LIBRARY
CITY HALL
Jln Tun Syed Barakbah
Padang Kota Lama
FORT CORNWALLIS
TOURISM MALAYSIA PENANG
CHEONG FAT TZE MANSION
Lebuh Leith
CATHEDRAL OF THE ASSUMPTION
L Farquhar
SUPREME COURT
LEBUH LIGHT
ST GEORGE'S CHURCH
PENANG MUSEUM & ART GALLERY
LEBUH MUNTRI
LORONG HUTTON
BLUE DIAMOND HOTEL
Chinatown
ENG AUN HOTEL
KUAN YIN TENG TEMPLE
BROADWAY HOSTEL
VICTORIA MEMORIAL CLOCK TOWER
MEDAN & LANGKAWI FERRY OFFICES
Swettenham Pier
Lebuh Downing
LEBUH BISHOP
LEBUH PITT
Lebuh Queen
LEBUH CHULIA
SWISS HOTEL
HARD LIFE CAFE
LEBUH CAMPBELL
MASJID KAPITAN KLING MOSQUE
SRI MARIAMMAN TEMPLE
Little India
JALAN ANSON
LORONG ABU SITI
JALAN BURMA
JALAN PENANG
Jln Kuala Kangsar
Lebuh Kimberley
MARKET
JLN BUCKINGHAM
POLICE STATION
SYED ALATAS MANSION
LEBUH PANTAI
Lebuh China
Lebuh Pasar
CITY BUS STATION
BUS STATION
KOMTAR SHOPPING CENTRE & PENANG TOURIST GUIDES ASSOCIATION
JALAN PRANGIN
LEBUH CARNARVON
THIEVES MARKET
Lebuh Cannon
KHOO KONGSI
Cannon Square
ROUND ISLAND BUSES
FERRY TERMINAL/ RAILWAY BOOKING OFFICE
Jln Nanning
JALAN MACALISTER
ONG KONGSI
Lebuh Tek Soon
ACHEEN ST MOSQUE
LEBUH ACHEH
Lebuh Victoria
Jln Selangor
JALAN DATO KERAMAT
SHANGRI-LA
JALAN MAGAZINE
LEBUH PANTAI
CHINESE WATER VILLAGE
South Channel
Penang Hill, Botanical Gardens, Penang Buddhist Association Temple, Masjid Melayu
JALAN BRICK KILN
PENGKALAN WELD
0
500 m
0
250 yards
Penang Bridge & Bayan Lepas Airport

Ko Pha Ngan (Hat Rin)
North
GULF OF
THAILAND
Ferry
Choeng
Mon
BIG
BUDDHA
Ban Bang Po
4169
Maenam
Bophut
4171
4169
Nathon
Ferry
Surat Thani
& Tha Thong
Hin Lat
Waterfall
Chaweng
Khao Pom
(635m)
Na Muang
Waterfall
4169
4170
Lamai
4170
Laem
Set
0
4 kms
0
2 miles
KO SAMUI

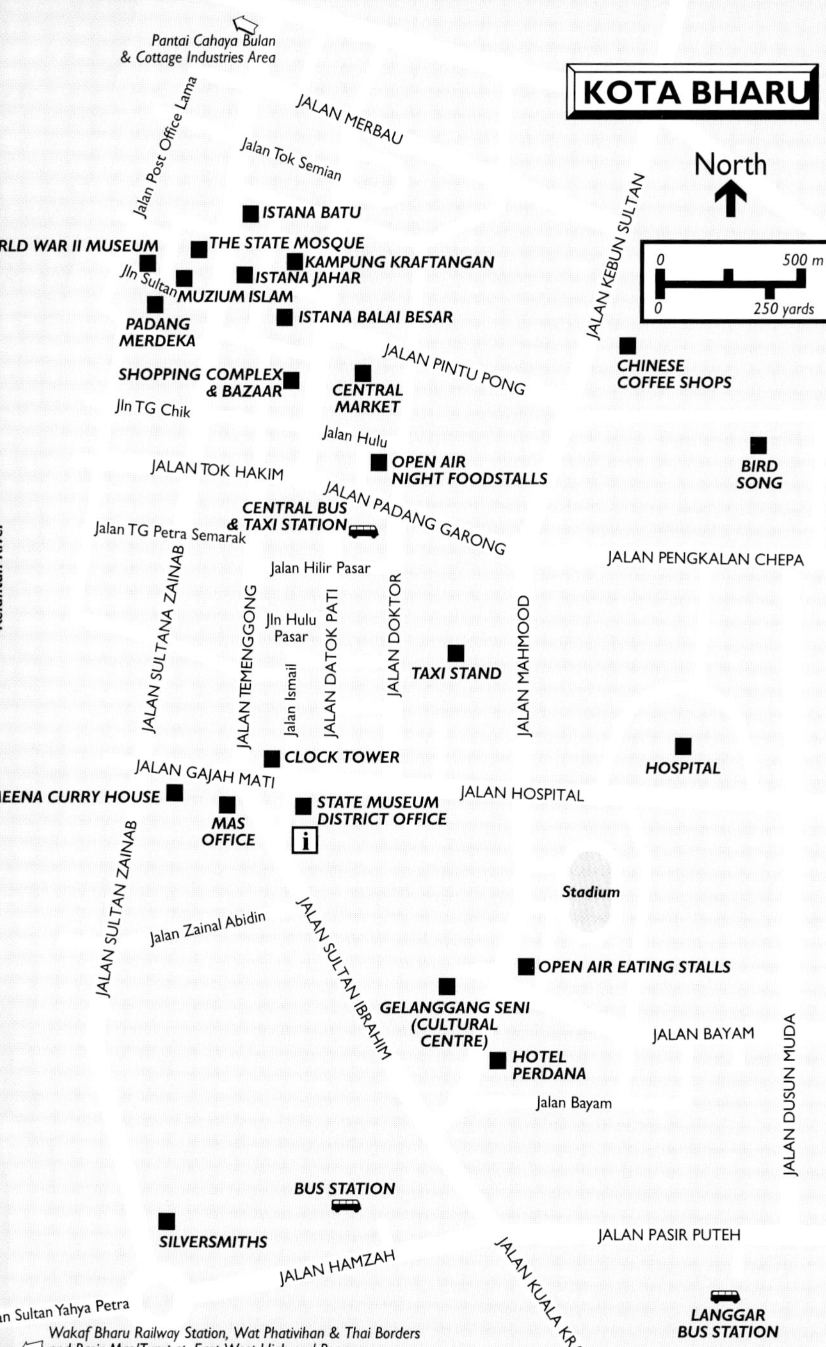

KOTA BHARU
North
0
500 m
0
250 yards
Pantai Cahaya Bulan
& Cottage Industries Area
JALAN MERBAU
Jalan Tok Semian
Jalan Post Office Lama
ISTANA BATU
RLD WAR II MUSEUM
THE STATE MOSQUE
KAMPUNG KRAFTANGAN
Jln Sultan
ISTANA JAHAR
MUZIUM ISLAM
ISTANA BALAI BESAR
PADANG
MERDEKA
JALAN KEBUN SULTAN
CHINESE
COFFEE SHOPS
JALAN PINTU PONG
SHOPPING COMPLEX
& BAZAAR
CENTRAL
MARKET
Jln TG Chik
Jalan Hulu
OPEN AIR
NIGHT FOODSTALLS
BIRD
SONG
JALAN TOK HAKIM
JALAN PADANG GARONG
CENTRAL BUS
& TAXI STATION
Jalan TG Petra Semarak
JALAN PENGKALAN CHEPA
Kelantan River
Jalan Hilir Pasar
JALAN SULTANA ZAINAB
JALAN TEMENGGONG
Jln Hulu
Pasar
Jalan Ismail
JALAN DATOK PATI
JALAN DOKTOR
TAXI STAND
JALAN MAHMOOD
CLOCK TOWER
HOSPITAL
JALAN GAJAH MATI
EENA CURRY HOUSE
JALAN HOSPITAL
MAS
OFFICE
STATE MUSEUM
DISTRICT OFFICE
i
Stadium
JALAN SULTAN ZAINAB
Jalan Zainal Abidin
JALAN SULTAN IBRAHIM
OPEN AIR EATING STALLS
GELANGGANG SENI
(CULTURAL
CENTRE)
JALAN BAYAM
HOTEL
PERDANA
Jalan Bayam
JALAN DUSUN MUDA
BUS STATION
SILVERSMITHS
JALAN PASIR PUTEH
JALAN HAMZAH
JALAN KUALA KRAI
an Sultan Yahya Petra
LANGGAR
BUS STATION
Wakaf Bharu Railway Station, Wat Phativihan & Thai Borders
and Pasir Mas/Tumpat, East West Highway/ Penang

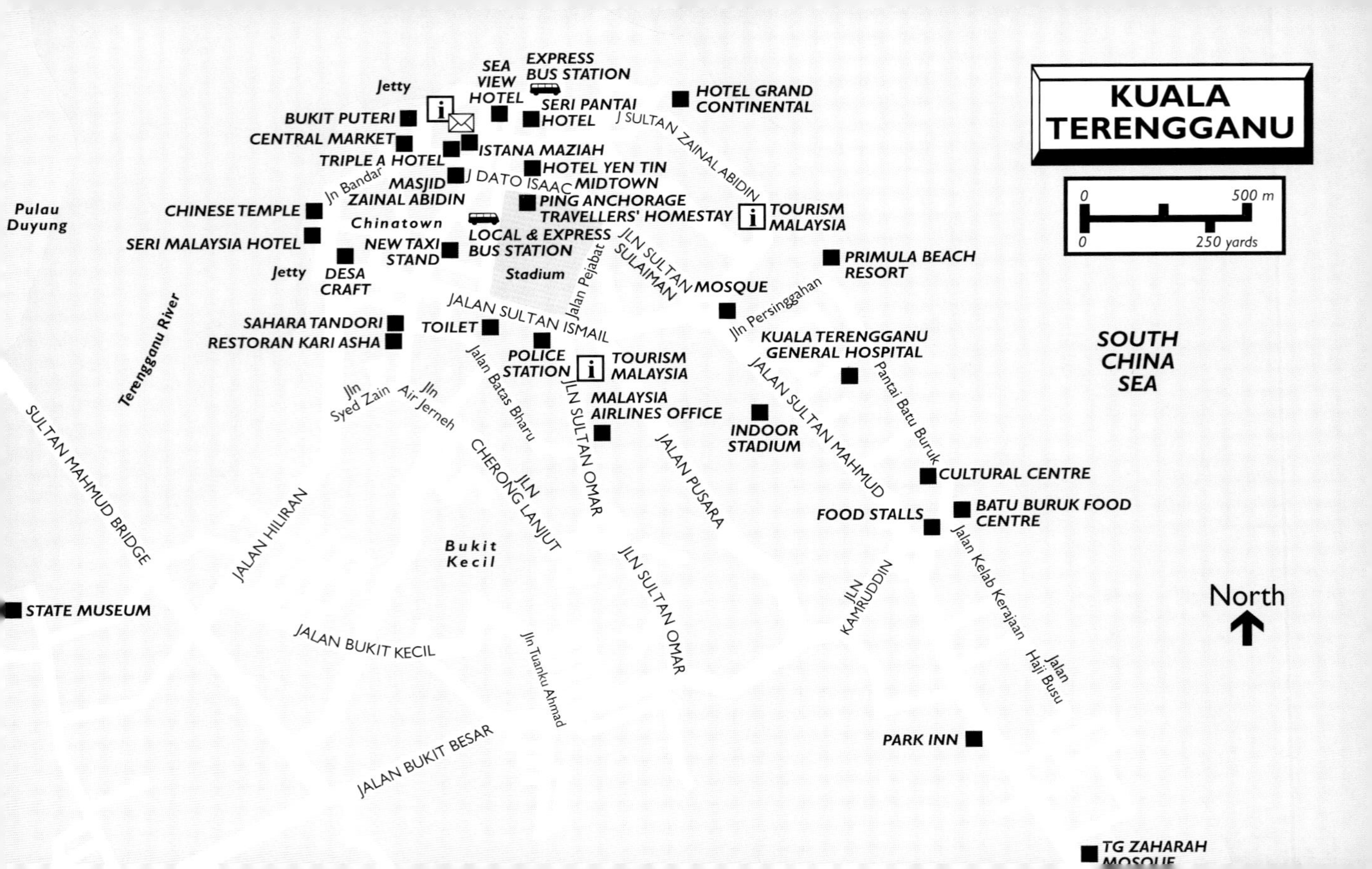

KUALA TERENGGANU

0 500 m
0 250 yards

SOUTH CHINA SEA

North

Jetty
SEA VIEW HOTEL
EXPRESS BUS STATION
SERI PANTAI HOTEL
HOTEL GRAND CONTINENTAL
BUKIT PUTERI
CENTRAL MARKET
ISTANA MAZIAH
TRIPLE A HOTEL
J SULTAN ZAINAL ABIDIN
HOTEL YEN TIN
MASJID ZAINAL ABIDIN
J DATO ISAAC
MIDTOWN
Jn Bandar
Pulau Duyung
CHINESE TEMPLE
PING ANCHORAGE TRAVELLERS' HOMESTAY
TOURISM MALAYSIA
Chinatown
SERI MALAYSIA HOTEL
LOCAL & EXPRESS BUS STATION
NEW TAXI STAND
JLN SULTAN SULAIMAN
PRIMULA BEACH RESORT
Jetty
DESA CRAFT
Stadium
Jalan Pejabat
MOSQUE
Jln Persinggahan
JALAN SULTAN ISMAIL
SAHARA TANDORI
RESTORAN KARI ASHA
TOILET
Terengganu River
POLICE STATION
TOURISM MALAYSIA
KUALA TERENGGANU GENERAL HOSPITAL
Jalan Batas Bharu
JALAN SULTAN MAHMUD
Pantai Batu Buruk
Jln Syed Zain
Jln Air Jerneh
JLN SULTAN OMAR
MALAYSIA AIRLINES OFFICE
INDOOR STADIUM
SULTAN MAHMUD BRIDGE
JLN CHERONG LANJUT
JALAN PUSARA
CULTURAL CENTRE
FOOD STALLS
BATU BURUK FOOD CENTRE
JALAN HILIRAN
Bukit Kecil
JLN SULTAN OMAR
Jalan Kelab Kerajaan
JLN KAMRUDDIN
STATE MUSEUM
JALAN BUKIT KECIL
Jln Tuanku Ahmad
Jalan Haji Busu
PARK INN
JALAN BUKIT BESAR
TG ZAHARAH MOSQUE

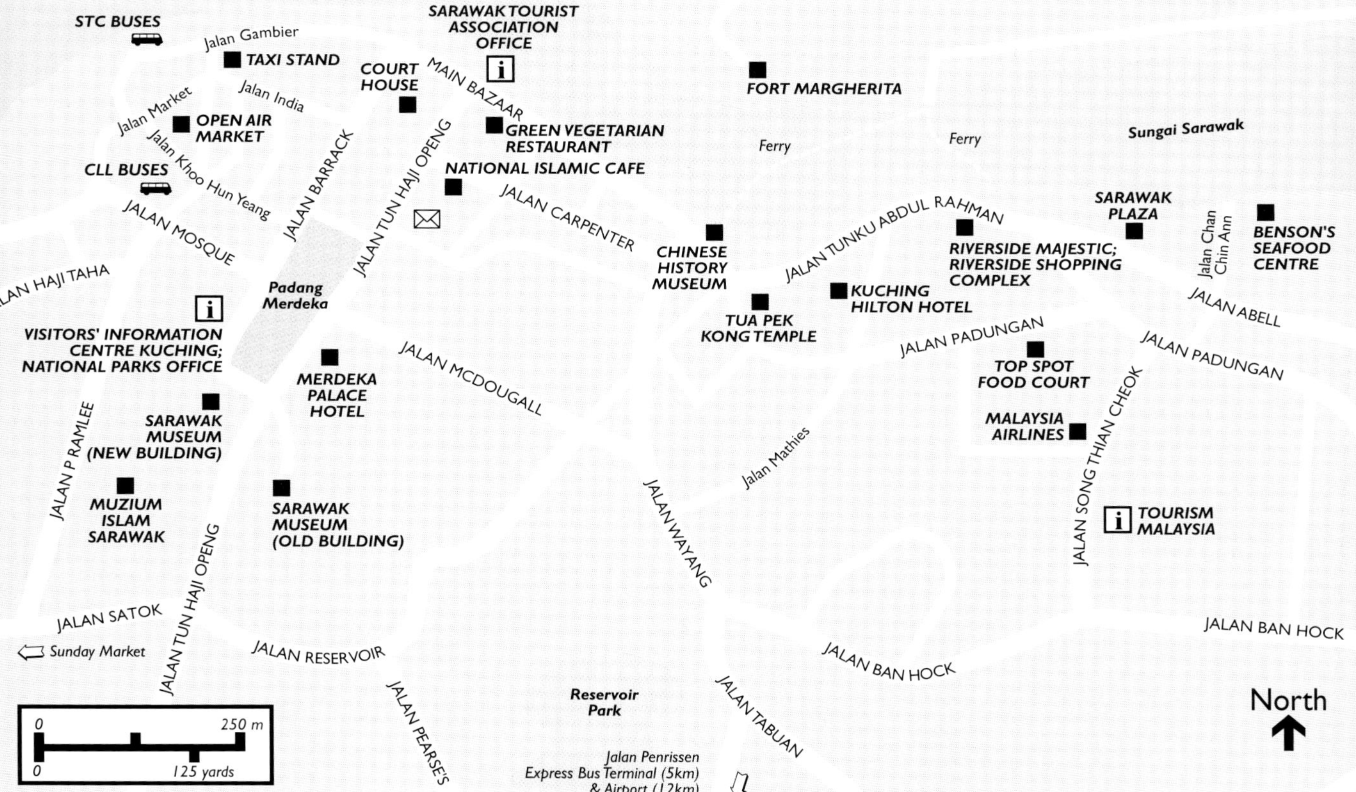
KUCHING
STC BUSES
Jalan Gambier
TAXI STAND
SARAWAK TOURIST ASSOCIATION OFFICE
COURT HOUSE
MAIN BAZAAR
FORT MARGHERITA
Sungai Sarawak
Ferry
Ferry
Jalan India
Jalan Market
OPEN AIR MARKET
Jalan Khoo Hun Yeang
GREEN VEGETARIAN RESTAURANT
NATIONAL ISLAMIC CAFE
CLL BUSES
JALAN BARRACK
JALAN TUN HAJI OPENG
JALAN CARPENTER
JALAN MOSQUE
CHINESE HISTORY MUSEUM
JALAN TUNKU ABDUL RAHMAN
RIVERSIDE MAJESTIC; RIVERSIDE SHOPPING COMPLEX
SARAWAK PLAZA
Jalan Chan Chin Ann
BENSON'S SEAFOOD CENTRE
JALAN HAJI TAHA
Padang Merdeka
VISITORS' INFORMATION CENTRE KUCHING; NATIONAL PARKS OFFICE
TUA PEK KONG TEMPLE
KUCHING HILTON HOTEL
JALAN ABELL
JALAN PADUNGAN
JALAN PADUNGAN
TOP SPOT FOOD COURT
MERDEKA PALACE HOTEL
JALAN MCDOUGALL
MALAYSIA AIRLINES
JALAN SONG THIAN CHEOK
SARAWAK MUSEUM (NEW BUILDING)
JALAN P RAMLEE
Jalan Mathies
MUZIUM ISLAM SARAWAK
SARAWAK MUSEUM (OLD BUILDING)
JALAN WAYANG
TOURISM MALAYSIA
JALAN TUN HAJI OPENG
JALAN SATOK
Sunday Market
JALAN RESERVOIR
JALAN BAN HOCK
JALAN BAN HOCK
Reservoir Park
JALAN PEARSE'S
JALAN TABUAN
North
0
250 m
0
125 yards
Jalan Penrissen
Express Bus Terminal (5km)
& Airport (12km)

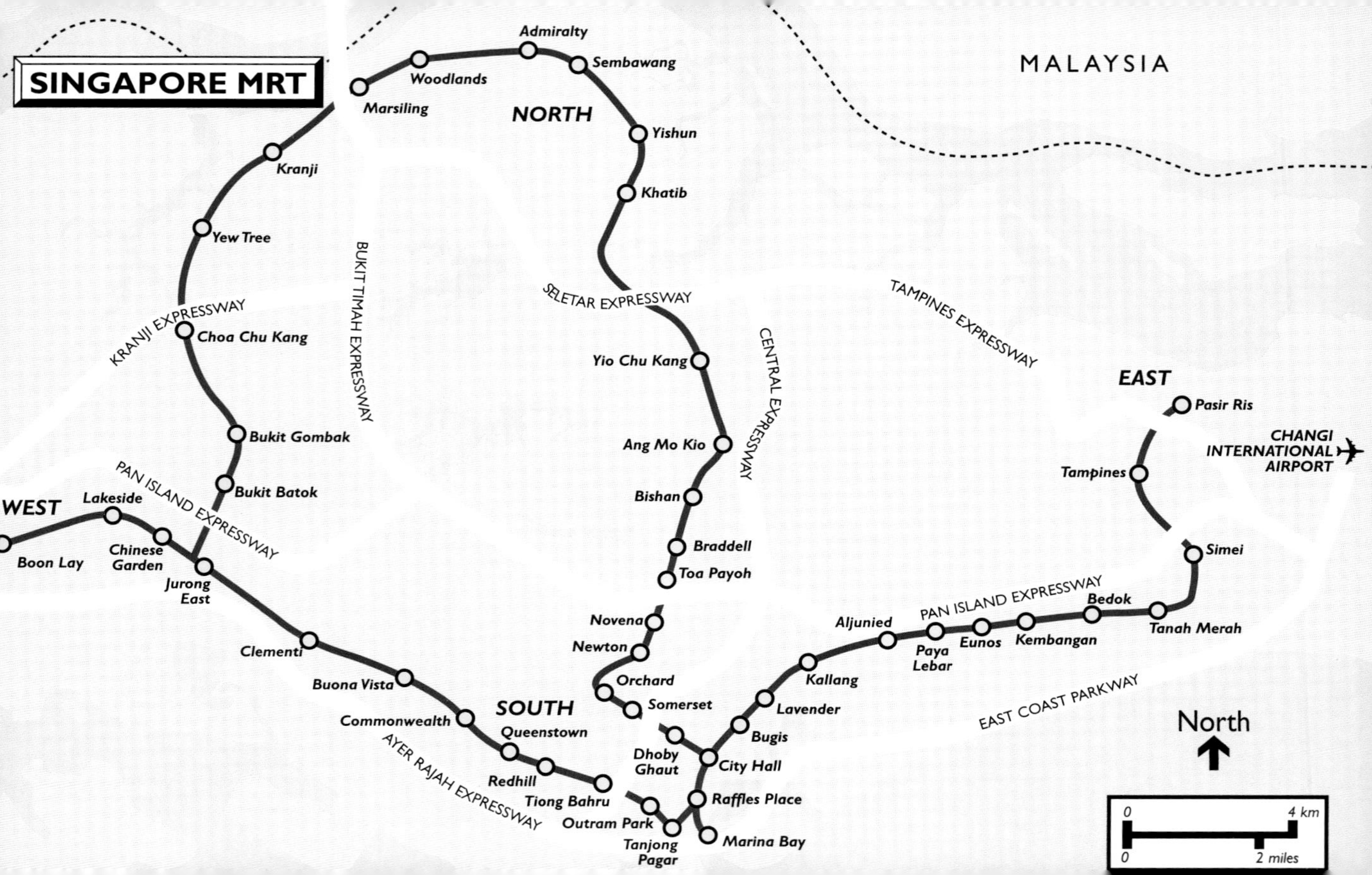
SINGAPORE MRT
MALAYSIA
NORTH
WEST
SOUTH
EAST
Marsiling
Woodlands
Admiralty
Sembawang
Yishun
Khatib
Kranji
Yew Tree
Choa Chu Kang
Bukit Gombak
Bukit Batok
Boon Lay
Lakeside
Chinese Garden
Jurong East
Clementi
Buona Vista
Commonwealth
Queenstown
Redhill
Tiong Bahru
Outram Park
Tanjong Pagar
Raffles Place
Marina Bay
City Hall
Dhoby Ghaut
Somerset
Orchard
Newton
Novena
Toa Payoh
Braddell
Bishan
Ang Mo Kio
Yio Chu Kang
Bugis
Lavender
Kallang
Aljunied
Paya Lebar
Eunos
Kembangan
Bedok
Tanah Merah
Simei
Tampines
Pasir Ris
CHANGI INTERNATIONAL AIRPORT
BUKIT TIMAH EXPRESSWAY
KRANJI EXPRESSWAY
PAN ISLAND EXPRESSWAY
SELETAR EXPRESSWAY
CENTRAL EXPRESSWAY
TAMPINES EXPRESSWAY
AYER RAJAH EXPRESSWAY
PAN ISLAND EXPRESSWAY
EAST COAST PARKWAY
North
0
4 km
0
2 miles

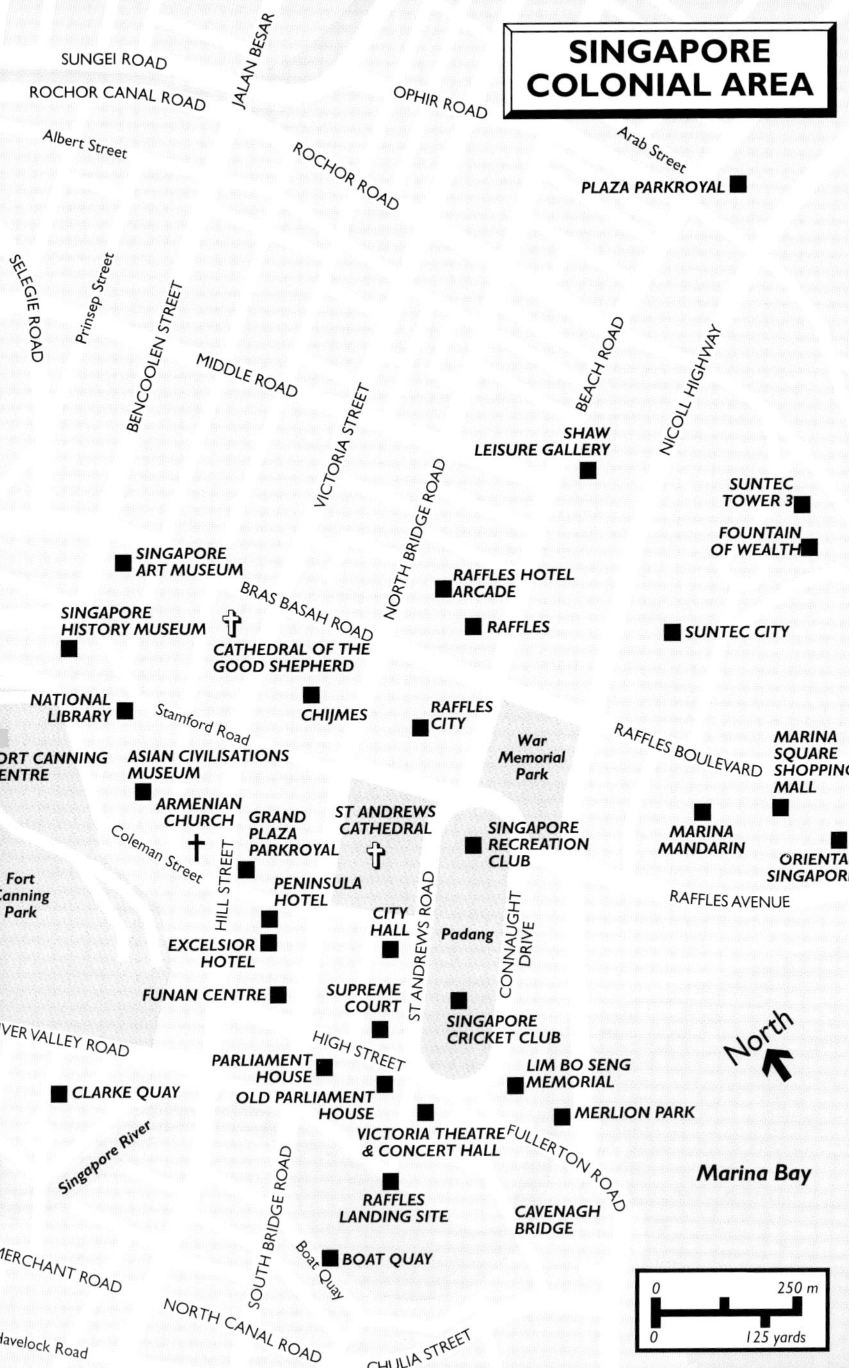

SINGAPORE COLONIAL AREA
SUNGEI ROAD
ROCHOR CANAL ROAD
JALAN BESAR
OPHIR ROAD
Albert Street
ROCHOR ROAD
Arab Street
PLAZA PARKROYAL
SELEGIE ROAD
Prinsep Street
BENCOOLEN STREET
MIDDLE ROAD
VICTORIA STREET
BEACH ROAD
NICOLL HIGHWAY
SHAW LEISURE GALLERY
NORTH BRIDGE ROAD
SUNTEC TOWER 3
FOUNTAIN OF WEALTH
SINGAPORE ART MUSEUM
RAFFLES HOTEL ARCADE
BRAS BASAH ROAD
SINGAPORE HISTORY MUSEUM
RAFFLES
SUNTEC CITY
CATHEDRAL OF THE GOOD SHEPHERD
NATIONAL LIBRARY
CHIJMES
RAFFLES CITY
Stamford Road
War Memorial Park
RAFFLES BOULEVARD
MARINA SQUARE SHOPPING MALL
ORT CANNING
:ENTRE
ASIAN CIVILISATIONS MUSEUM
ARMENIAN CHURCH
GRAND PLAZA PARKROYAL
ST ANDREWS CATHEDRAL
SINGAPORE RECREATION CLUB
MARINA MANDARIN
ORIENTAL SINGAPORE
Coleman Street
Fort
:anning
Park
HILL STREET
PENINSULA HOTEL
RAFFLES AVENUE
CITY HALL
ST ANDREWS ROAD
Padang
CONNAUGHT DRIVE
EXCELSIOR HOTEL
FUNAN CENTRE
SUPREME COURT
SINGAPORE CRICKET CLUB
North
:IVER VALLEY ROAD
HIGH STREET
PARLIAMENT HOUSE
LIM BO SENG MEMORIAL
CLARKE QUAY
OLD PARLIAMENT HOUSE
MERLION PARK
Singapore River
VICTORIA THEATRE & CONCERT HALL
FULLERTON ROAD
Marina Bay
SOUTH BRIDGE ROAD
RAFFLES LANDING SITE
CAVENAGH BRIDGE
Boat Quay
BOAT QUAY
MERCHANT ROAD
NORTH CANAL ROAD
Havelock Road
CHULIA STREET
0
250 m
0
125 yards

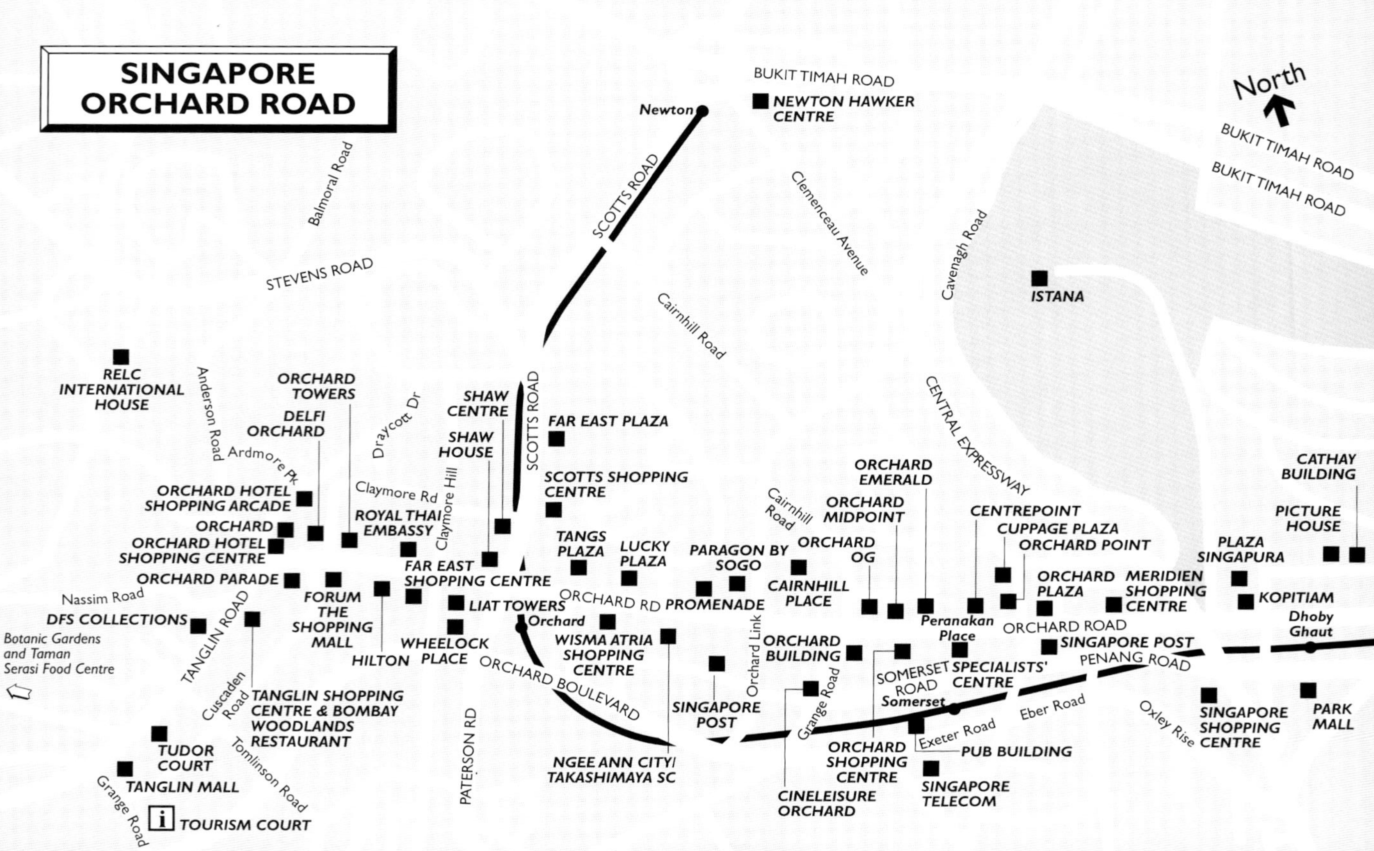
SINGAPORE
ORCHARD ROAD
North
BUKIT TIMAH ROAD
BUKIT TIMAH ROAD
BUKIT TIMAH ROAD
NEWTON HAWKER CENTRE
Newton
SCOTTS ROAD
Clemenceau Avenue
Cavenagh Road
ISTANA
Balmoral Road
STEVENS ROAD
Cairnhill Road
RELC INTERNATIONAL HOUSE
Anderson Road
ORCHARD TOWERS
DELFI ORCHARD
Draycott Dr
SHAW CENTRE
SHAW HOUSE
SCOTTS ROAD
FAR EAST PLAZA
CENTRAL EXPRESSWAY
CATHAY BUILDING
Ardmore Pk
SCOTTS SHOPPING CENTRE
ORCHARD EMERALD
ORCHARD MIDPOINT
Cairnhill Road
CENTREPOINT
CUPPAGE PLAZA
ORCHARD POINT
PICTURE HOUSE
PLAZA SINGAPURA
ORCHARD HOTEL SHOPPING ARCADE
Claymore Rd
Claymore Hill
ROYAL THAI EMBASSY
ORCHARD
ORCHARD HOTEL SHOPPING CENTRE
TANGS PLAZA
LUCKY PLAZA
PARAGON BY SOGO
ORCHARD OG
FAR EAST SHOPPING CENTRE
ORCHARD PARADE
CAIRNHILL PLACE
ORCHARD PLAZA
MERIDIEN SHOPPING CENTRE
KOPITIAM
Nassim Road
FORUM THE SHOPPING MALL
ORCHARD RD
PROMENADE
LIAT TOWERS
Orchard
Peranakan Place
ORCHARD ROAD
Dhoby Ghaut
DFS COLLECTIONS
TANGLIN ROAD
WISMA ATRIA SHOPPING CENTRE
Orchard Link
ORCHARD BUILDING
SINGAPORE POST
Botanic Gardens and Taman Serasi Food Centre
HILTON
WHEELOCK PLACE
SOMERSET ROAD
SPECIALISTS' CENTRE
PENANG ROAD
ORCHARD BOULEVARD
Somerset
Cuscaden Road
TANGLIN SHOPPING CENTRE & BOMBAY WOODLANDS RESTAURANT
SINGAPORE POST
Grange Road
Eber Road
Oxley Rise
SINGAPORE SHOPPING CENTRE
PARK MALL
PATERSON RD
Exeter Road
TUDOR COURT
Tomlinson Road
ORCHARD SHOPPING CENTRE
PUB BUILDING
NGEE ANN CITY/ TAKASHIMAYA SC
TANGLIN MALL
SINGAPORE TELECOM
Grange Road
CINELEISURE ORCHARD
i TOURISM COURT

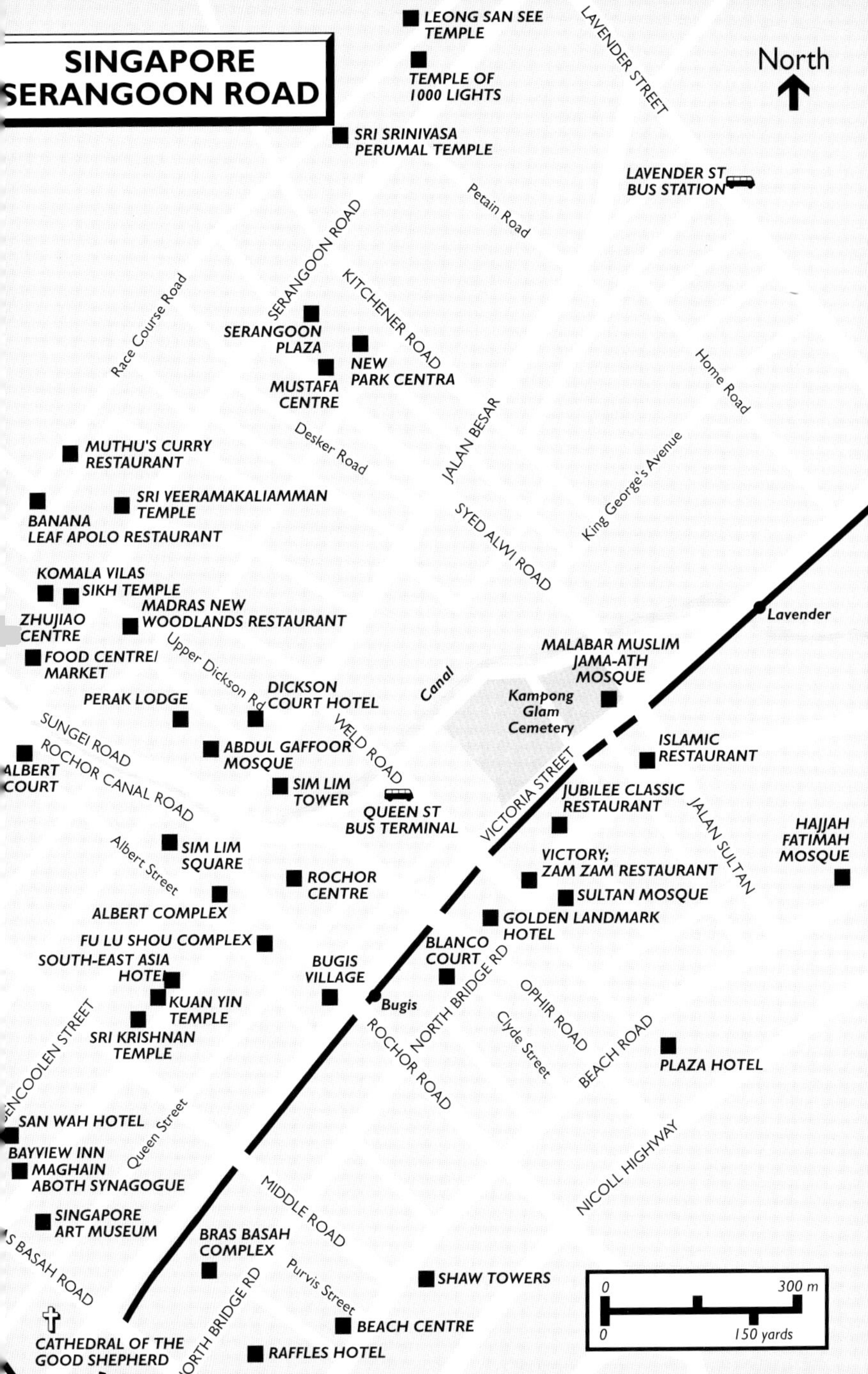
SINGAPORE
SERANGOON ROAD
North
LEONG SAN SEE TEMPLE
TEMPLE OF 1000 LIGHTS
SRI SRINIVASA PERUMAL TEMPLE
LAVENDER STREET
LAVENDER ST BUS STATION
Petain Road
SERANGOON ROAD
KITCHENER ROAD
Race Course Road
SERANGOON PLAZA
NEW PARK CENTRA
MUSTAFA CENTRE
Home Road
Desker Road
JALAN BESAR
King George's Avenue
MUTHU'S CURRY RESTAURANT
SRI VEERAMAKALIAMMAN TEMPLE
BANANA LEAF APOLO RESTAURANT
SYED ALWI ROAD
KOMALA VILAS
SIKH TEMPLE
MADRAS NEW WOODLANDS RESTAURANT
ZHUJIAO CENTRE
Lavender
FOOD CENTRE/ MARKET
Upper Dickson Rd
MALABAR MUSLIM JAMA-ATH MOSQUE
PERAK LODGE
DICKSON COURT HOTEL
Canal
Kampong Glam Cemetery
SUNGEI ROAD
ALBERT COURT
ROCHOR CANAL ROAD
ABDUL GAFFOOR MOSQUE
WELD ROAD
ISLAMIC RESTAURANT
SIM LIM TOWER
QUEEN ST BUS TERMINAL
VICTORIA STREET
JUBILEE CLASSIC RESTAURANT
JALAN SULTAN
HAJJAH FATIMAH MOSQUE
SIM LIM SQUARE
Albert Street
ROCHOR CENTRE
VICTORY; ZAM ZAM RESTAURANT
SULTAN MOSQUE
ALBERT COMPLEX
GOLDEN LANDMARK HOTEL
FU LU SHOU COMPLEX
BLANCO COURT
SOUTH-EAST ASIA HOTEL
BUGIS VILLAGE
KUAN YIN TEMPLE
Bugis
NORTH BRIDGE RD
OPHIR ROAD
SRI KRISHNAN TEMPLE
ROCHOR ROAD
Clyde Street
BEACH ROAD
PLAZA HOTEL
ENCOOLEN STREET
SAN WAH HOTEL
Queen Street
BAYVIEW INN
MAGHAIN ABOTH SYNAGOGUE
NICOLL HIGHWAY
MIDDLE ROAD
SINGAPORE ART MUSEUM
BRAS BASAH COMPLEX
S BASAH ROAD
Purvis Street
SHAW TOWERS
0
300 m
0
150 yards
NORTH BRIDGE RD
BEACH CENTRE
CATHEDRAL OF THE GOOD SHEPHERD
RAFFLES HOTEL

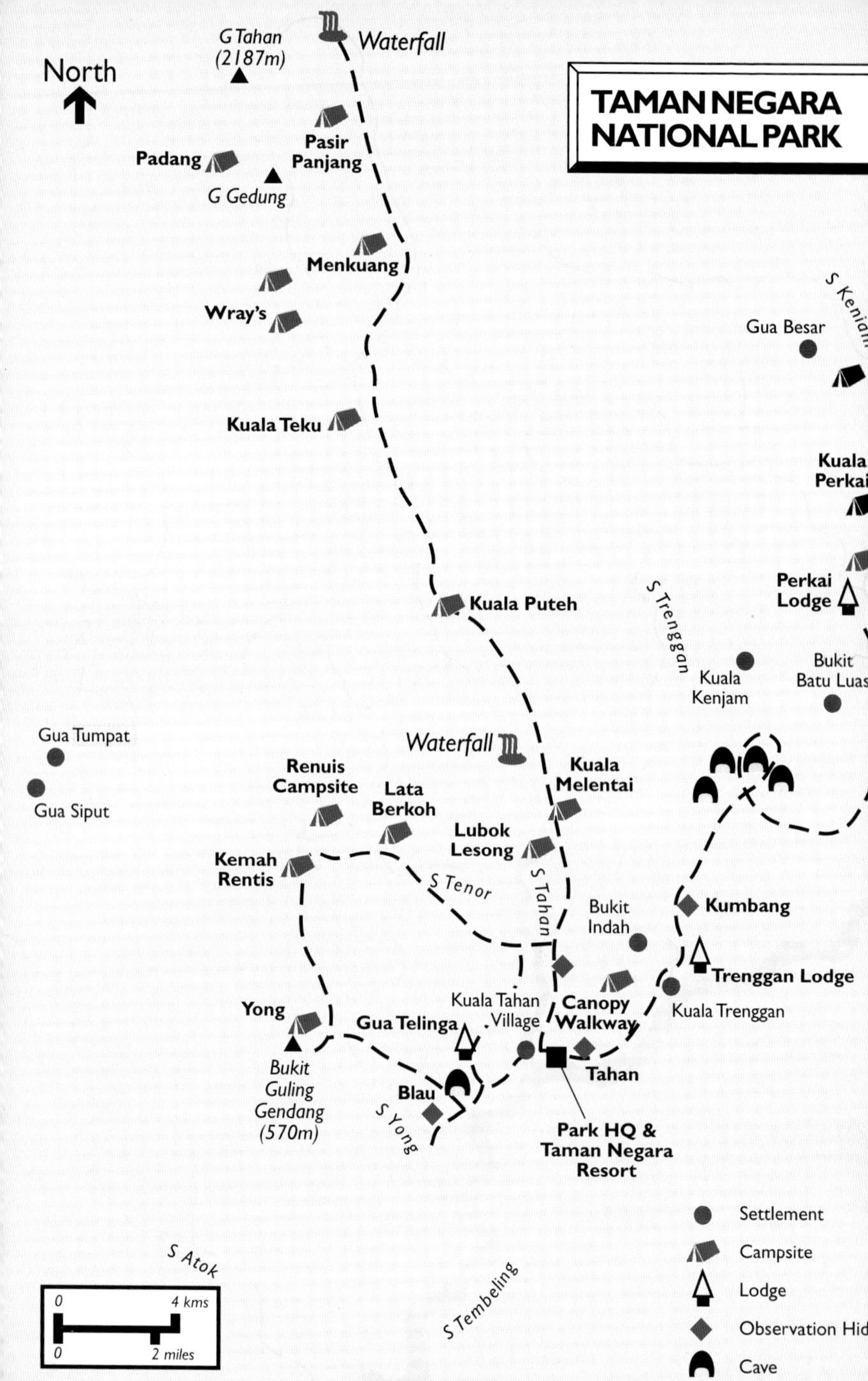
TAMAN NEGARA NATIONAL PARK
North
G Tahan (2187m)
Waterfall
Pasir Panjang
Padang
G Gedung
Menkuang
Wray's
Kuala Teku
Kuala Puteh
S Kenian
Gua Besar
Kuala Perkai
Perkai Lodge
S Trenggan
Kuala Kenjam
Bukit Batu Luas
Gua Tumpat
Gua Siput
Waterfall
Renuis Campsite
Lata Berkoh
Kuala Melentai
Lubok Lesong
Kemah Rentis
S Tenor
S Tahan
Kumbang
Bukit Indah
Trenggan Lodge
Kuala Trenggan
Canopy Walkway
Kuala Tahan Village
Yong
Gua Telinga
Bukit Guling Gendang (570m)
Blau
Tahan
S Yong
Park HQ & Taman Negara Resort
S Atok
S Tembeling
0
4 kms
0
2 miles
Settlement
Campsite
Lodge
Observation Hid
Cave